SHAKESPEARE SURVEY

73

Shakespeare and the City

SHAKESPEARE SURVEY
ADVISORY BOARD

(1) *Shakespeare and his Stage*
(2) *Shakespearian Production*
(3) *The Man and the Writer*
(4) *Interpretation*
(5) *Textual Criticism*
(6) *The Histories*
(7) *Style and Language*
(8) *The Comedies*
(9) *Hamlet*
(10) *The Roman Plays*
(11) *The Last Plays (with an index to Surveys 1–10)*
(12) *The Elizabethan Theatre*
(13) *King Lear*
(14) *Shakespeare and his Contemporaries*
(15) *The Poems and Music*
(16) *Shakespeare in the Modern World*
(17) *Shakespeare in his Own Age*
(18) *Shakespeare Then Till Now*
(19) *Macbeth*
(20) *Shakespearian and Other Tragedy*
(21) *Othello (with an index to Surveys 11–20)*
(22) *Aspects of Shakespearian Comedy*
(23) *Shakespeare's Language*
(24) *Shakespeare: Theatre Poet*
(25) *Shakespeare's Problem Plays*
(26) *Shakespeare's Jacobean Tragedies*
(27) *Shakespeare's Early Tragedies*
(28) *Shakespeare and the Ideas of his Time*
(29) *Shakespeare's Last Plays*
(30) *Henry IV to Hamlet*
(31) *Shakespeare and the Classical World (with an index to Surveys 21–30)*
(32) *The Middle Comedies*
(33) *King Lear*
(34) *Characterization in Shakespeare*
(35) *Shakespeare in the Nineteenth Century*
(36) *Shakespeare in the Twentieth Century*
(37) *Shakespeare's Earlier Comedies*
(38) *Shakespeare and History*

(39) *Shakespeare on Film and Television*
(40) *Current Approaches to Shakespeare through Language, Text and Theatre*
(41) *Shakespearian Stages and Staging (with an index to Surveys 31–40)*
(42) *Shakespeare and the Elizabethans*
(43) *The Tempest and After*
(44) *Shakespeare and Politics*
(45) *Hamlet and its Afterlife*
(46) *Shakespeare and Sexuality*
(47) *Playing Places for Shakespeare*
(48) *Shakespeare and Cultural Exchange*
(49) *Romeo and Juliet and its Afterlife*
(50) *Shakespeare and Language*
(51) *Shakespeare in the Eighteenth Century (with an index to Surveys 41–50)*
(52) *Shakespeare and the Globe*
(53) *Shakespeare and Narrative*
(54) *Shakespeare and Religions*
(55) *King Lear and its Afterlife*
(56) *Shakespeare and Comedy*
(57) *Macbeth and its Afterlife*
(58) *Writing About Shakespeare*
(59) *Editing Shakespeare*
(60) *Theatres for Shakespeare*
(61) *Shakespeare, Sound and Screen*
(62) *Close Encounters with Shakespeare's Text*
(63) *Shakespeare's English Histories and their Afterlives*
(64) *Shakespeare as Cultural Catalyst*
(65) *A Midsummer Night's Dream*
(66) *Working with Shakespeare*
(67) *Shakespeare's Collaborative Work*
(68) *Shakespeare, Origins and Originality*
(69) *Shakespeare and Rome*
(70) *Creating Shakespeare*
(71) *Re-Creating Shakespeare*
(72) *Shakespeare and War*
(73) *Shakespeare and the City*

Shakespeare Survey: A Sixty-Year Cumulative Index
Aspects of *Macbeth*
Aspects of *Othello*
Aspects of *Hamlet*
Aspects of *King Lear*
Aspects of Shakespeare's 'Problem Plays'

SHAKESPEARE SURVEY

73

Shakespeare and the City

EDITED BY

EMMA SMITH

CAMBRIDGE
UNIVERSITY PRESS

CAMBRIDGE
UNIVERSITY PRESS

University Printing House, Cambridge CB2 8BS, United Kingdom

One Liberty Plaza, 20th Floor, New York, NY 10006, USA

477 Williamstown Road, Port Melbourne, VIC 3207, Australia

314–321, 3rd Floor, Plot 3, Splendor Forum, Jasola District Centre,
New Delhi – 110025, India

79 Anson Road, #06–04/06, Singapore 079906

Cambridge University Press is part of the University of Cambridge.

It furthers the University's mission by disseminating knowledge in the pursuit of
education, learning and research at the highest international levels of excellence.

www.cambridge.org
Information on this title: www.cambridge.org/9781108830539
DOI: 10.1017/9781108908023

First published 2020

Printed in the United Kingdom by TJ International Ltd. Padstow Cornwall

A catalogue record for this publication is available from the British Library.

ISBN 978-1-108-83053-9 Hardback

EDITOR'S NOTE

Shakespeare Survey 73 has as its theme 'Shakespeare and the City', with articles on ancient, early modern and contemporary cityscapes. Volume 74 has as its theme 'Shakespeare and Education': submissions by 1 September 2020. We are actively seeking submissions for volume 75, on *Othello* (submissions by 1 September 2021); contact the editor if you would like to discuss a potential contribution. There is limited space in each volume for articles that are not on the theme; these can be submitted for consideration at any point in the year. Please send any correspondence, including submissions, as email attachments to emma.smith@hertford.ox.ac.uk. All submissions are read by me as editor and at least one member of the Advisory Board. We warmly encourage both early-career and more senior scholars to consider *Survey* as a venue for their work.

Part of *Survey*'s distinctiveness is its reviews. Review copies, including article offprints, should be addressed to the Editor at Hertford College, Oxford OX1 3BW; our reviewers inevitably have to exercise some selection about what they cover. I would like to take this opportunity to thank Stephen Purcell, Paul Prescott and Charlotte Scott for their service to *Survey*, and to welcome our new reviewers: Lois Potter and Peter Kirwan (theatre) and Jane Kingsley Smith (critical studies).

EMMA SMITH

CONTRIBUTORS

GEMMA KATE ALLRED, *University of Neuchâtel*
MICHAEL CORDNER, *University of York*
NANDINI DAS, *University of Oxford*
LARS ENGLE, *The University of Tulsa*
RUSSELL JACKSON, *University of Birmingham*
PETER KIRWAN, *University of Nottingham*
ALICE LEONARD, *University of Warwick*
MIRIAM LEUNG CHE LAU, *College of Professional and Continuing Education, The Hong Kong Polytechnic University*
CHI-FANG SOPHIA LI, *National Sun Yat-sen University, Taiwan*
NICHOLAS LUKE, *The University of Hong Kong*
HARRY R. MCCARTHY, *University of Exeter*
KAREN NEWMAN, *Brown University*
PAUL PRESCOTT, *University of Warwick*
STEPHEN PURCELL, *University of Warwick*
NEIL RHODES, *University of St Andrews*
CHARLOTTE SCOTT, *Goldsmiths College, University of London*
JAMES SHAW, *University of Oxford*
PETER J. SMITH, *Nottingham Trent University*
JENNIE M. VOTAVA, *Allegheny College*

CONTENTS

List of Illustrations   *page* ix

KAREN NEWMAN   Continental Shakespeare   1
NANDINI DAS   The Stranger at the Door: Belonging in Shakespeare's Ephesus   10
ALICE LEONARD   City Origins, Lost Identities and Print Errors in
                      The Comedy of Errors   21
HARRY R. MCCARTHY   The Circulation of Youthful Energy on the Early Modern
                      London Stage: Migration, Intertheatricality and 'Growing to
                      Common Players'   43
CHI-FANG SOPHIA LI   In Conversation with Shakespeare in Jacobean London: Social
                      Insanity and Its Taming Schools in *1&2 Honest Whore*   63
LARS ENGLE   Hearing Voices: Signal versus Urban Noise in *Coriolanus* and
                      Augustine's *Confessions*   79
MIRIAM LEUNG CHE LAU Caesar and Lear in Hong Kong: Appropriating Shakespeare to
                      Express the Inexpressible   93

NEIL RHODES   Before We Sleep: *Macbeth* and the Curtain Lecture   107
CHARLOTTE SCOTT   'The Story Shall Be Changed': Antique Fables and Agency
                      in *A Midsummer Night's Dream*   119
NICHOLAS LUKE   A Lawful Magic: New Worlds of Precedent in *Mabo* and *The
                      Winter's Tale*   129
MICHAEL CORDNER   'Cabined, Cribbed, Confined': Advice to Actors and the
                      Priorities of Shakespearian Scholarship   145
PETER J. SMITH   'What Country, Friends, Is This?': Tim Supple's *Twelfth Night*
                      Revisited   161
JENNIE M. VOTAVA   Through a Glass Darkly: Sophie Okonedo's Margaret as Racial
                      Other in *The Hollow Crown: The Wars of the Roses*   170
GEMMA KATE ALLRED   'Who's There?': Britain's Twenty-First-Century Obsession
                      with Celebrity *Hamlet* (2008–2018)   184
                      Shakespeare Performances in England, 2019
STEPHEN PURCELL   *London Productions*   203
PAUL PRESCOTT   *Productions Outside London*   223
JAMES SHAW   Professional Shakespeare Productions in the British Isles,
                      January–December 2018   240

CONTENTS

The Year's Contributions to Shakespeare Studies   252

   1 Critical Studies *reviewed by* CHARLOTTE SCOTT   252

   2 Shakespeare in Performance *reviewed by* RUSSELL JACKSON   266

   3 Editions and Textual Studies *reviewed by* PETER KIRWAN   277

Abstracts of Articles in *Shakespeare Survey 73*   289

Index   292

ILLUSTRATIONS

1. a and b. *A Catalogue of such Bookes as have Beene published, and (by authority) printed in English* (1622). Ashm.1057(14), signature D4 recto (Fig. 1a) and verso (Fig. 1b). By permission of The Bodleian Libraries, University of Oxford. *page* 4

2. First Folio, STC 22273 Fo. 1 no. 54, from the Folger Shakespeare Library, p. 99, showing the manuscript addition of 'E' to 'S.Drom.' at the top of the page. By permission of the Folger Shakespeare Library. 26

3. STC 22274 Fo. 2 no. 20, Second Folio, from the Folger Shakespeare Library, p. 86, showing Lewis Theobald's addition 'of Syracuse' to correct 'Antipholis, Erotes'. By permission of the Folger Shakespeare Library. 27

4. Arch. G. c.9. Second Folio, Bodleian Library, University of Oxford, p. 88, showing manuscript addition 'of Syracuse' next to 'Enter Antipolis Erotes'. By permission of the Bodleian Library. 28

5. Arch. G. c.9. Second Folio, Bodleian Library, University of Oxford, p. 99, showing the rather confusing list of roles. By permission of the Bodleian Library. 29

6. Smock Alley Promptbook, Third Folio, at Folger Shakespeare Library (Prompt 3d Folio Com. Err. Smock Alley), p. 91, showing a manuscript intervention which exits Antipholus of Syracuse and exchanges him for Antipholus of Ephesus, with addition of 'Anti: of E'. By permission of the Folger Shakespeare Library. 33

7. Smock Alley Promptbook, Third Folio, at Folger Shakespeare Library (Prompt 3d Folio Com. Err. Smock Alley), p. 100, showing manuscript changes which attempt to switch the two Dromios' dialogue. See the speech prefix 'S.Dro' is written over with an 'E', whilst hovering near 'E. D.' is a large manuscript 'S:'. By permission of the Folger Shakespeare Library. 35

8. Alexander Pope's *The Works of Shakespear*, 6 vols. (London, 1725), vol. 1, p. 449, showing the printing slip 'E.Dro.' for 'E.Ant.' at the line 'Thou drunken slave, I sent thee for a rope; / And told thee to what purpose, and what end.' Courtesy of the Robert D. Farber University Archives & Special Collections Department, Brandeis University. 39

9. Migrations of actors who began as boys, 1595–1609. 51

10. Migrations of actors who began as boys, 1610–1624. 52

11. Migrations of actors who began as boys, 1625–1639. 53

12. *Richard II*, 3.1, Almeida Theatre, directed by Joe Hill-Gibbins. Saskia Reeves as Bushy, Martins Imhangbe as Bagot and Leo Bill as Bolingbroke. Photograph by Marc Brenner. 204

13. *Richard II*, 1.1, Sam Wanamaker Playhouse, directed by Adjoa Andoh and Lynette Linton. Ayesha Dharker as Aumerle, Adjoa Andoh as Richard II, and Leila Farzad as Queen. Photograph by Ingrid Pollard. 208

ix

14. *Henry V*, Shakespeare's Globe, Globe Theatre, directed by Sarah Bedi and Federay Holmes. Sarah Amankwah as Henry V. Photograph by Tristram Kenton. 210

15. *A Midsummer Night's Dream*, 2.1, Bridge Theatre, directed by Nicholas Hytner. David Moorst as Puck and Gwendoline Christie as Titania. Photograph by Manuel Harlan. Manuel Harlan / Arenapal. 215

16. *A Midsummer Night's Dream*, 3.1, Regent's Park Open Air Theatre, directed by Dominic Hill. Susan Wokoma as Bottom, Amber James as Titania, and the company. Photograph by Jane Hobson. 219

17. *As You Like It*, Public Acts, Queen's Theatre Hornchurch, directed by Douglas Rintoul. Beth Hinton-Lever as Jaques, and the company. Photograph by Camilla Greenwell. 221

18. The interior of Shakespeare's Rose Theatre, York. Pre-set for *Henry V*, directed by Gemma Fairlie. Photograph by Paul Prescott. 224

19. *Timon of Athens*, The Swan Theatre, directed by Simon Godwin. Kathryn Hunter as Timon, Debbie Korley (third from right) as Alcibiades, and the company. Photograph by Simon Annand. 231

20. *As You Like It*, Royal Shakespeare Theatre, directed by Kimberley Sykes. The transition to Arden. Photograph by Topher McGrillis. 233

21. *The Taming of the Shrew*, Royal Shakespeare Theatre, directed by Justin Audibert. Joseph Arkley as Kate, Claire Price as Petruchia. Photograph by Ikin Yum. 235

22. *Measure for Measure*, Royal Shakespeare Theatre, directed by Gregory Doran. Sandy Grierson as Angelo, Lucy Phelps as Isabella. Photograph by Helen Maybanks. 237

CONTINENTAL SHAKESPEARE

KAREN NEWMAN

Shakespearians are breathing a sigh of relief: there is *Shakespeare after Theory*. In his book of that name, David Kastan quotes Adorno's famous censure of Walter Benjamin for his 'wide-eyed presentation of mere facts' and declares himself firmly on the side of Benjamin. 'Only by turning to history from theory', he claims, and by 'recognizing that a play's materializations, in the printing house and in the playhouse, *are* the play's meanings', can we read Shakespeare today.[1] In a similar vein, Zachary Lesser urges us, in his *Renaissance Drama and the Politics of Publication*, 'to stop thinking of plays simply as *texts*, and start thinking of them as *books*'.[2] He quotes D. F. McKenzie: 'every book tells a story quite apart from that recounted by its text'.[3] But this touted turn away from the linguistic turn, this swerve away from theory to book history, can only be 'theoretical', for the stories books tell are, after all, only available to us as texts, presented in a classroom or written up in a book or article – or, increasingly, posted online. Even numbers can't save us from hermeneutic obligation, for what are we to do with the facts: between 1576 and 1625, '30 percent of professional plays were reprinted within ten years'; in 1600, 'nine Stationers held Copy in nineteen Shakespearean titles'; in 1600, 'close to 31% of surviving retail titles were "literature and the arts"'; and, 'Whereas an early tragedy such as *Titus Andronicus* has only 1.3 percent prose, *Hamlet* features a full 27 percent'?[4] Even this quite useful 'new positivism' obliges us to read and interpret.

Lesser, in fact, begins his book with a textual reading, of an advertisement for *Troilus and Cressida* that

appears as an anonymous preface on a cancel sheet the publishers Bonian and Walley inserted, as Lesser puts it, 'at some point during the press run', after the title page of the first edition in 1609 of Shakespeare's play.[5] The opening pages of Lesser's book in fact remind us that often the very material evidence evoked in the appeal to 'mere facts', or 'books', is in fact a 'text' that requires reading and interpretation. Such 'texts' may in turn be evidence of another's reading – in this case, as Lesser goes on to claim, of a publisher's reading that may well have led to publication in the first place. Lesser is suitably careful and expansive in defining 'reading' to include

the publisher's understanding of a text based on its title, or its author's previous work, or its provenance – its acting company, theatre, patrons, or coterie – or its

---

[1] David Kastan, *Shakespeare after Theory* (New York, 1999), p. 13 (quoting from Adorno's *Aesthetics and Politics*) and pp. 34–5.

[2] Zachary Lesser, *Renaissance Drama and the Politics of Publication: Readings in the English Book Trade* (Cambridge, 2004), p. 10.

[3] D. F. McKenzie, '"What's past is prologue": the Bibliographical Society and history of the book', in *Making Meaning: 'Printers of the Mind' and other Essays*, ed. Peter D. McDonald and Michael F. Suarez, SJ (Amherst, 2002), pp. 259–75, esp. p. 262.

[4] Marta Straznicky, 'What is a stationer?' in *Shakespeare's Stationers: Studies in Cultural Bibliography*, ed. Marta Straznicky (Philadelphia, 2013), pp. 1–16, esp. p. 5 (quoting from Zachary Lesser and Alan B. Farmer, 'The popularity of playbooks revisited', *Shakespeare Quarterly* 56 (2005), 1–32); Alexandra Halasz, 'The stationers' Shakespeare', in *Shakespeare's Stationers*, ed. Straznicky, pp. 17–27, esp. p. 23; Douglas Bruster, 'Shakespeare the stationer', in *Shakespeare's Stationers*, ed. Straznicky, pp. 112–31, esp. p. 121.

[5] Lesser, *Renaissance Drama*, p. 1.

generic conventions, or simply based on what friends or fellow stationers may have said about the text. All these judgments, many of which may be only partly conscious, are part of the publisher's reading of the text, for they form its 'horizon of expectations'.[6]

Lesser distinguishes his work both from that of the New Bibliographers (such as A. W. Pollard, W. W. Greg and R. B. McKerrow) – who remained wedded to 'authors', 'paradigmatically Shakespeare', and the notion that 'a single, authoritative work lay behind the multiple texts of a given play' – but also from some aspects of the so-called 'New Textualism' and its various practitioners – from the conflated-text crowd who remain within the authorial paradigm by arguing that the multiple texts of *Lear* represent authorial revision, to more recent work by Joseph Loewenstein, Leah Marcus, Jeffrey Masten and Kastan himself, which focuses instead on the 'author function' and 'systems of linguistic and bibliographical codings' that books display.[7]

Lesser places his work within this more recent paradigm, sometimes now dubbed 'cultural bibliography', and his focus is on publishers so as to understand, quoting Peter Blayney, 'why *that* play was published *then*'.[8] As he goes on to argue, 'publishers tended to specialize in order to appeal to their customers'.[9] The book trade had a shaping role in producing meaning, in shaping how books were marketed and sold. Lesser considers books as 'commodities', another stubbornly ambiguous word with meanings both material and theoretical. A publisher, he argues, 'does not merely bring a commodity to market but also imagines, and helps to construct, the purchasers of that commodity and their interpretations of it'.[10] In short, as Marta Straznicky argues succinctly in her introduction to the recent collection *Shakespeare's Stationers*: '"the materiality of the text" has become integral to historicist criticism, implicating as it does the physical form of print in every act of interpretation, past and present, whether this engages with the minutiae of orthography and punctuation, ideological work performed at the level of discourse, or the formation of the Shakespearean canon'.[11]

In turning to the Continental Shakespeare of my title, I want to consider another Shakespeare advertisement, one which appeared in advance of the publication of the First Folio in 1622 and which apparently offered it for sale on the Continental book market. Bear in mind the subtitle of Lesser's book, *Readings in the English Book Trade* (emphasis added). Since the publication of Richard Helgerson's *Forms of Nationhood* (1992), scholars in early modern English literary studies, and certainly of Shakespeare, have focused increasingly on the making of the English nation, the 'writing of England', and on the early printed book in English.[12] Yet, long before Shakespeare became the national poet whom the antiquarian Maurice Morgann famously celebrated 'as the patron spirit of world empire on which the sun will never set', before the current interest in transnational Shakespeare – before, in fact, the First Folio saw print in 1623 – booksellers were marketing their intellectual property in Shakespeare internationally.[13] From W. W. Greg's *The Shakespeare First Folio*, we learn that:

The principal centre of the European book-trade at the time was the fair held every spring and autumn at Frankfort-on-the-Main, in connexion with which there was published a half-yearly advertisement known as the *Mess-Katalog*. This did not include English books, though English booksellers frequented the market to buy stocks of foreign and classical works. There was, however, an English edition published by John Bill, the King's Printer, under the title *Catalogus uniuersalis pro*

---

[6] Lesser, *Renaissance Drama*, p. 9. 'Horizon of expectations' is taken from Hans Robert Jauss, 'Literary history as a challenge to literary theory', in *New Directions in Literary History*, ed. Ralph Cohen (Baltimore, 1974), pp. 11–42.

[7] Lesser, *Renaissance Drama*, pp. 14–15. It should be pointed out that Masten in particular demonstrates the collaborative character of early modern dramatic writing and production, not an important point for Lesser's argument.

[8] Lesser, *Renaissance Drama*, p. 10, quoting Peter Blayney, 'The publication of playbooks', in *A New History of Early English Drama*, ed. John D. Cox and David Scott Kastan (New York, 1997), pp. 383–422, esp. p. 391.

[9] Lesser, *Renaissance Drama*, p. 8.

[10] Lesser, *Renaissance Drama*, p. 17.

[11] *Shakespeare's Stationers*, ed. Straznicky, p. 3.

[12] Richard Helgerson, *Forms of Nationhood: The Elizabethan Writing of England* (Chicago, 1992), p. 6.

[13] Michael Dobson, *The Making of the National Poet: Shakespeare, Adaptation and Authorship, 1660–1769* (Oxford, 1992), p. 228.

nundinis Francofurtensibus, which contained an appendix of English works. And to our surprise we find that 'A Catalogue of such Bookes as haue beene published, and (by authoritie) printed in English, since the last Vernall Mart, which was in Aprill 1622. till this present October 1622.' contains the entry: 'Playes, written by M. William Shakespeare, all in one volume, printed by Isaack Iaggard, in. fol.'[14]

'Our surprise', as Greg terms it, would seem to be prompted by two things: first, that the entry appears in 1622, before the First Folio actually appeared, in 1623;[15] and, second, that we find the entry in such an 'unexpected source', as he terms it, in a catalogue offering books for sale on the European market. Greg cites F. P. Wilson (*The Jaggards*, 1925), whose 'fortunate discovery', as Greg terms it, brought this early advertisement to light.[16] Wilson himself notes that it is 'perhaps the only contemporary advertisement of the First Folio now extant', though as recent commentators on the Folio have noted, its frontispiece, title page and front matter are, in fact, contemporary advertisements.

Both Greg and Wilson agreed that the advertisement 'does not add to our knowledge of the First Folio'.[17] Concerned with dating, they did not consider what it might mean that the First Folio was first offered for sale in a supplemental listing of *English* books to an English reprint of a *Latin* catalogue for a *German* book fair held in the city of Frankfurt. Over seventy-five years after Wilson first published his find, and almost fifty years after Greg's study of the Folio, Peter Blayney also considers this advance publicity for the Folio only in relation to dating in his 2003 catalogue for the Folger exhibition 'The First Folio of Shakespeare' (Figure 1).[18]

The mart at Frankfurt dates from at least the thirteenth century, but a market is attested there already in the eighth century; by the sixteenth, it had become a major European market where goods of all sorts were sold and exchanged – the famous French humanist printer Henri Estienne praised it in a Latin encomium as 'the sum of all the fairs of the whole world'.[19] Like many German cities, it was relatively small with some 12,000 inhabitants in 1555, and more than 20,000 by the

outbreak of the Thirty Years' War in 1618. Located in the centre of Germany, it lay on major trade routes linking the cities of northern and southern Europe, Scandinavia and the Baltic.[20] Estienne's account details the many sorts of goods traded there, but the Frankfurt fair early became a centre of the Continental book trade. From all over Europe, and also from England, came not only printers, booksellers, typefounders, paper merchants and bookbinders, but also merchants, humanists, writers, travellers, players and more. The city authorities supported the development of commerce by controlling the prices charged for food and lodging, and keeping the tolls on the movement of goods light.[21] Estienne dubbed the book fair 'the Fair of the Muses', and that part of Frankfurt in which it was sited as 'Athens'.[22] So, to rephrase Peter Blayney's question, instead of asking 'why *that* play was published *then*', we might ask instead, why *that* advertisement *there* and *then*? What might thinking about this advertisement, 'reading' it in the largest sense, mean for our understanding of the development of Shakespearian cultural capital on the Continent?

The King's Printer, John Bill, to whom Greg attributes the catalogue in which this advertisement

[14] W. W. Greg, *The Shakespeare First Folio* (Oxford, 1955), p. 3.

[15] Printing of the First Folio was underway in 1622, at the time this advertisement appeared, but seems not to have been completed until late 1623.

[16] Greg, *The Shakespeare First Folio*, p. 3, n. 3.

[17] F. P. Wilson, 'The Jaggards and the First Folio of Shakespeare', *Times Literary Supplement*, 5 November 1925, 737.

[18] Peter Blayney, *The First Folio of Shakespeare* (Washington, D. C., 1991), p. 8.

[19] James Westfall Thompson, *The Frankfort Book Fair* (Chicago, 1911; repr. New York, 1968), p. 8. On the development of the fair at Frankfurt, see John L. Flood, '"Omnium totius orbis emporiorum compendium": the Frankfurt Fair in the early modern period', in *Fairs, Markets and the Itinerant Book Trade*, ed. Robin Myers, Michael Harris and Giles Mandelbrote (New Castle, DE, and London, 2007), pp. 1–42.

[20] Flood, 'Omnium totius', p. 2.

[21] Flood, 'Omnium totius', pp. 11–12.

[22] See Thompson, *The Frankfort Book Fair*.

(a)

A CATALOGVE OF
SVCH BOOKES AS HAVE
beene publifhed, and (by authoritie) printed in
*Englifh, fince the laft Vernall Mart, which
was in Aprill 1622. till this prefent
October 1622.*

He Hiftory of the life and reigne of King *Henry* the feuenth, written by the Right Honourable *Francis* Lord Verulam Vifcount Saint Albons. The fecond Edition. Printed for *Matthew Lownes* and *William Barret*, in fol.

The Imperiall hiftory, Or a true relation of the liues and reignes of all the Roman Emperors, from the time of *Iulius Cefar*, firft founder of the Roman Empire and Monarchy, to *Ferdinand* the fecond now reigning, printed for *Mat. Lownes* in fol.

A Difcouery of Errors in *Yorkes* Catalogue of Nobilitie, publifhed 1619. with a reuiew of his fecond Edition thereof, together with the feuerall fucceffions and new creations, to this prefent yeere 1622. by *Auguftine Vincent*, Rougecrom Purfiuant of Armes, printed by *William Iaggard* in fol.

A Defenfatiue againft the poyfon of fuppofed prophecies, not hitherto confuted by the pen of any man, written by the Lord *Henry Howard* late Earle of Northampton, printed for *Matthew Lownes*, in fol.

King *Dauids* Vow, for reformation of himfelfe, his family, and his houfhold, deliuered in twelue fermons before the Prince his Highneffe, by *George Hakewill* Doctor in Diuinity, printed for *Matthew Lownes*, in 8.

The Art of Logicke, plainely taught in the Englifh tongue, by Mafter *Blundeuill*, printed for *Matthew Lownes* in 4.

A

(b)

Playes, written by M. *William Shakefpeare*, all in one volume, printed by *Ifaack Iaggard*, in fol.

The Theater of Honor and Knighthood, printed by *William Iaggard*, in fol.

1 a and b. *A Catalogue of such Bookes as have Beene published, and (by authority) printed in English* (1622). Ashm.1057(14), signature D4 recto (Fig. 1a) and verso (Fig. 1b). By permission of The Bodleian Libraries, University of Oxford.

4

appeared, was an important player in the early English book trade between London and the Continent. Bill was apprenticed to the publisher John Norton in 1592 and was admitted a freeman of the Stationers in 1601. Between 1596 and 1603, he served as agent for Sir Thomas Bodley, who was then engaged in founding and stocking the Bodleian Library. Bodley bought books out of Norton's stock amassed from his biennial importations from the fair, and by sending Bill as his agent to buy books in Paris, Venice and elsewhere in Italy, frequently in Germany, and even in Spain.[23] Bill's involvement in the Continental book trade did not end with Bodley. In 1603, the Nortons and Bill became

Copartners and Ioynt traders together in the art or trade of a Stacioner or Bookseller and in buying and bringing of bookes maps and other Stacionary wares & merchandises in and from ffrance Germany & other parts beyond the seas into England, & in selling the same again & in printinge of diuers bookes here in Englande and beyond the seas.[24]

As this document indicates, Bill's trade involved bringing stocks from the Continent to sell in England; subsequently, he also served as James I's agent, acquiring books for him from the Continent and regularly attending the Frankfurt book fair. Always on the look-out for the main chance, Bill began reprinting the half-yearly advertisement known as the *Mess-Katalog* in England, making various changes to its offerings to suit his market; later, he added an appendix of books published in England, or from his stock, for sale at the fair, a move Rees and Wakely, in their 2009 book *Publishing, Politics, & Culture*, dub a 'startling innovation'.[25] Bill not only purchased books, he and Norton also offered them for sale. We know, for example, that Bill printed a translation into French of Bacon's *Essays* in 1619 (STC 1152), no doubt for a French market in London, but also on the Continent where works by Bacon were highly sought after.[26] Bill thus had a demonstrated interest in circulating certain English materials among European readers. Bill's appendices, and changes he made to the catalogue, indicate that, in the second decade of the seventeenth century, he

was particularly engaged in publishing, printing and selling polemical books and controversialist writing relating to post-Reformation, post-Tridentine debates. As the King's Printer, Bill, with Norton, published James's *Works* and a number of folio volumes concerned with the defence of a national church and rivalries with Rome.[27] Norton was interested as well in the market for French books, for he styled himself 'imprimeur ordinaire du Roy es langues estrangeres' in books dated 1609 and 1612.[28] As Rees and Wakely show, Norton and Bill 'acted in effect as a small-scale ministry of information'.[29] Norton maintained a shop at the Frankfurt fair from 1600 on, and, from 1603, with his more junior partner, Bill.

The *Mess-Katalog* was originally the sixteenth-century initiative of an Augsburg bookseller, but it was soon taken over by the Frankfurt city council, which continued to publish an official catalogue well into the eighteenth century. The catalogue was organized consistently according to the order of precedence of university faculties:[30] theology,

---

23 Ian Philip, *The Bodleian Library in the Seventeenth and Eighteenth Centuries* (Oxford, 1983), p. 9. Bodley famously excluded English books from his Library, not, as Philip points out, because he viewed them all as 'rifferaffes' and 'baggage books', as he did plays, but because he doubted if the English vernacular was 'the right language for the communication of scholarship' (p. 32). On Bodley, Norton and Bill, see John Barnard, 'Politics, profits, and idealism: John Norton, the Stationers' Company and Sir Thomas Bodley', *Bodleian Library Records* 17.5 (2002), 385–408.

24 C3/334/73 (JB III–13), cited in Graham Rees and Maria Wakely, *Publishing, Politics and Culture: The King's Printers in the Reign of James I and VI* (Oxford, 2009), p. 15.

25 Rees and Wakely, *Publishing*, pp. 197–8. See their chapter 'John Norton, John Bill, and the Frankfurt catalogues', pp. 190–215.

26 Rees and Wakely, *Publishing*, p. 42, n. 48.

27 For a full account of the complicated legal battles surrounding patents, the print trade and the appointment of the King's Printer, see Rees and Wakely, *Publishing*.

28 David J. Shaw, 'French-language publishing in London to 1900', in *Foreign-Language Printing in London, 1500–1900*, ed. Barry Taylor (Boston Spa and London, 2002), pp. 101–22, esp. p. 120.

29 Rees and Wakely, *Publishing*, p. 194.

30 Flood, 'Omnium totius', p. 16.

law, medicine, history, philosophy, poetry and mathematics, all in Latin, followed by German books, sometimes advertised in blackletter. The catalogues ended with 'Libri peregrini idiomatis', or books in the European vernaculars, and occasionally with a section announcing future offerings. Initially, Bill reprinted the catalogue revised to suit his market, but he quickly determined also to produce one of his own that would tout his and Norton's printed books. Between 1617 and 1621, Bill's reprinted catalogues included an appendix offering his and Norton's own recent publications: James's anti-papal works and those aimed at self-canonization, patristic writing, theological texts, and Protestant polemic and controversy, which was their specialty, but they soon began to act as agents for other British associates and firms, and, finally, 'as middlemen, agents or [even] backers or partners of continental colleagues'.[31] As Rees and Wakely put it,

these were *joint-stock* businesses which means that Bill and Norton had interests [on the Continent] in a printing office or offices, and in a stock of books and other stationery wares which they presumably used in the same way that the partners used the stock in their London warehouses, i.e. as a flexible and indispensable trading resource, or indeed a form of currency.[32]

Norton died in 1612 and his cousin, Bonham Norton, took over his interests. Bill and Bonham Norton subsequently quarrelled and went to law, and in 1620, the firm sold their shares in the 'Latin stock' to the Stationers, so the appendix in which this early Shakespeare advertisement appears seems not to have been published by Bill, as Greg and Wilson believed, but on behalf of the Company itself.[33] In 1618, Bill had added to his printed catalogues a section entitled 'English Workes', an innovation taken up by the Stationers in their appendices printed between 1621 and 1628, when Bill again took over the publication of the catalogues until his death in 1630.[34] The Stationers' appendices continued to include books printed by Bill, but they also began, as might be expected, to offer a wider variety of English books under various imprints. Jaggard and Blount's First Folio was

among them, advertised not only in the 1622 catalogue, while it was still in press, but also subsequently in the 1624 catalogue, after it had finally appeared, presumably, in November 1623.

Rees and Wakely assert that 'These works of course have nothing to do with the continental trade: entries of English-language titles were simply not meant for continental audiences.'[35] But things may not be quite so simple as Rees and Wakely aver. Why might the Stationers have included the First Folio among the English books advertised in the appendix to the Frankfurt book fair catalogue? No doubt both Bill, and subsequently the Stationers, used the reprinted catalogue with its English appendix to advertise and sell books for an English market, both English printed books and books imported from the Continent. But we know that Norton and Bill were selling books at the Frankfurt fair; why might there not be, among the 'great Variety of Readers' the First Folio syndicate sought to reach through such advertisements, Continental as well as English buyers? For, as Doug Bruster puts it succinctly in his essay 'Shakespeare the stationer', 'advertised goods are typically offered for sale'.[36]

To understand the appearance of the First Folio in the 1622 and 1624 appendices, we would do well also to take into account the considerable evidence documenting the presence and popularity of travelling players from England, the so-called *Englischer Comoedianten*, in what is now sometimes termed – in parallel with Braudel's 'Mediterranean World' – the 'North Sea World'.[37] Work by Jerzy Limon and Simon Williams, and more recently by Anston Bosman, Pavel Drábek, M. A. Katritzky

[31] Rees and Wakely, *Publishing*, p. 193.

[32] Rees and Wakely, *Publishing*, p. 190.

[33] Rees and Wakely, *Publishing*, p. 41. 'The Latin stock was set up in January 1616 by a group of 112 Stationers' and was never profitable (p. 41, n. 46); on the likely reasons for the sale, see pp. 40–4.

[34] Rees and Wakely, *Publishing*, p. 204.

[35] Rees and Wakely, *Publishing*, p. 212.

[36] Bruster, 'Shakespeare the stationer', p. 118.

[37] Anston Bosman, 'Northern Renaissance drama: a media ecology', manuscript.

and George Oppitz-Trotman, among others, drawing on both contemporary documents and nineteenth-century studies and early sources, has chronicled the visits of the travelling English actors who performed in various venues, both courts and urban centres: Paris and Fontainebleau, the Low Countries and Germany, reaching Vienna, Prague and even Gdansk, from the 1580s through the first half of the seventeenth century.[38] As Bosman observes, 'in the history of cultural relations between England and Europe, especially the Netherlands and Germany, the episode of the strolling players was an unexampled success'.[39] Yet, as he shows, commentators have typically 'deplored it as vulgarization', insisted on distinguishing between the so-called 'successful' players who remained at home, and the 'failures' who travelled abroad, and lauded the 'sophisticated London play-goers' over the putative '"somewhat rude audience" on the Continent'.[40] The very use of the term 'strolling' (to walk in a leisurely way as inclination directs, to ramble, saunter, wander) by scholars serves to undermine the focus and entrepreneurship of the troupes and their endeavours.[41]

The players were not only popular – their 'material', as has been shown, had a significant impact on the development of indigenous German drama.[42] But, as Bosman observes, the burgeoning scholarship on the English Comedians has remained a 'curiosity of literary history', focused on narrow empirical questions, rather than an illustrative example of cultural interchange. From occasional court performances, to more sustained sojourns at the courts of German princes, to a 'major presence in the theatre of several German cities', the number of troupes travelling and performing on the Continent increased in the first decades of the seventeenth century and seems only to have been slowed by the advent of the Thirty Years' War. The English Comedians 'created an awareness of theatre as an activity in its own right'; their impact was so substantial that, into the eighteenth century, troupes made up entirely of *German* actors continued to draw on this international brand by calling themselves 'English Comedians'.[43] Bosman notes that the often-observed scarcity of purpose-built playhouses

in Northern Europe under-represents the dynamism and breadth of theatrical activity 'from London to Warsaw and from Copenhagen to Graz'.

From first-hand accounts of visitors to the city of Frankfurt and its book fair, and from other archival sources, we know that English troupes regularly performed at the Frankfurt fair. Fynes Moryson famously disparages the players out of England who

played at Franckford in the tyme of the Mart, having neither a Complete number of Actours, nor any good Apparell, nor any ornament of the Stage, yet the Germans not understanding a worde they sayde, both men and women, flocked wonderfully to see theire gesture and Action, rather than heare them, speaking English which they understood not, and pronowncing peeces and Patches of English playes.[44]

---

[38] Jerzy Limon, *Gentlemen of a Company: English Players in Central and Eastern Europe, 1590–1660* (Cambridge, 1985); Simon Williams, *Shakespeare on the German Stage*, 2 vols. (Cambridge, 1990), vol. 1; Anston Bosman, 'Renaissance intertheatre and the staging of nobody', *ELH* 71.3 (2004), 559–85; George Oppitz-Trotman, '*Romeo and Juliet* in German, 1603–1604', *Notes and Queries* 62.1 (2015), 96–8; and Pavel Drábek and M. A. Katritzky, 'Shakespearean players in early modern Europe', in *The Cambridge Guide to the World of Shakespeare*, ed. Bruce R. Smith, 2 vols. (Cambridge, 2016), vol. 2, pp. 1527–33. For a brief survey of the English touring companies, see Peter Holland, 'Touring Shakespeare', in *The Cambridge Companion to Shakespeare on Stage*, ed. Stanley Wells and Sarah Stanton (Cambridge, 2002), pp. 194–211.

[39] Bosman, 'Renaissance intertheatre', 559.

[40] Bosman, 'Renaissance intertheatre', 561.

[41] For an example of the pejorative impact of the modifier 'strolling' on judgements of the English players abroad, see Willi Flemming, quoted in Bosman, 'Renaissance intertheatre': 'the strolling actor lacks any connection with a cultural tradition', p. 561.

[42] See Gerhart Hoffmeister, 'The English Comedians in Germany', in *German Baroque Literature: The European Perspective*, ed. Hoffmeister (New York, 1983), pp. 142–58, esp. p. 146; Williams, *Shakespeare on the German Stage*; Albert Cohn's nineteenth-century study *Shakespeare in Germany in the Sixteenth and Seventeenth Centuries* (Wiesbaden, 1865); and a host of other studies in both English and German that cannot be detailed here.

[43] Williams, *Shakespeare on the German Stage*, p. 29.

[44] *Shakespeare's Europe: A Survey of the Condition of Europe at the End of the 16th Century: Being Unpublished Chapters of Fynes*

Moryson's judgement of the English Comedians has endured. Albert Cohn, in his study of Shakespeare in Germany, writes of the 'weak ray from the sunlight of the Shakespearian drama' falling on Germany, but he provides a multitude of examples of such intertextual exchange.[45] 'Pronouncing pieces and patches of English playes' not only attracted enthusiastic audiences,[46] it also somehow managed to provoke the publication of a German 'translated' collection, *Engelische Comedien und Tragedien*, which purported to offer up material from the English players, including a 'version' of *Titus Andronicus*.[47] That collection appeared in octavo in 1620, hardly a format destined only for princely patrons or courtly fanciers of the English Comedians, but which some hardheaded printer/publisher/entrepreneur imagined would sell. Apparently it did, as the book was reissued in 1624 and additional volumes appeared subsequently. Bosman reminds us that the anonymous German Hamlet, *Der bestrafte Brudermord*, has never received the critical scrutiny it deserves.[48] Recently Russ Leo has demonstrated *Hamlet*'s importance on the Continent in his consideration of Geeraardt Brandt's *De Veinzende Torquatus*, which 'bears unmistakable traces of an encounter with Shakespeare's best-known tragedy'.[49] In Leo's estimation, we can trace 'the emergence of a theatre inflected by Shakespeare's work and English drama at large, but mediated by itinerant companies adapting this work for international audiences'.[50]

Moryson's recognition that gesture and action can be understood onstage even when words cannot also reminds us that travelling players who depended on 'gesture and action' scoured Europe in the late sixteenth and early seventeenth centuries – Italian *commedia dell'arte* troupes, for example, toured as far away as England, the Low Countries and Spain, and in France even had their own theatre in Paris under the auspices of the French King.[51] Evidence points to a multi-lingual European theatre, in Bosman's terms, both nomadic and embodied, with ample 'action' including dance, acrobatics and other nonverbal forms.[52] In his account of the English players in Frankfurt, Moryson also observes that chief

merchants at the Frankfurt fair, both Dutch and Flemish, regretted that their brisk business kept them from attending the English players' performances. We know that both Sidney and Sir Henry Wotton, among many others, visited the city of Frankfurt and its fair. From the Nuremberg chronicler Johann Christian Siebenkees's account of an English troupe's visit to the city in 1612, we learn that they 'attracted great crowds' of young and old, men and women, city fathers and 'educated professionals'.[53] Though concerned primarily with women and the English troupes in Germany,

Moryson's Itinerary (1617), ed. Charles Hughes (New York, 1903), p. 304.

[45] Cohn, *Shakespeare in Germany*, p. ix. See also Williams, *Shakespeare on the German Stage*, pp. 33–45. For thinking about such exchange more systemically and theoretically, see Robert Henke and Eric Nicholson's introduction to their important collection *Transnational Exchange in Early Modern Theatre*, ed. Robert Henke and Eric Nicholson (Aldershot, 2008), pp. 1–15.

[46] For an excellent survey of audiences' enthusiasm for the various English troupes, with emphasis on women, see M. A. Katritzky, 'English troupes in early modern Germany: the women', in *Transnational Exchange*, ed. Henke and Nicholson (Aldershot, 2008), pp. 35–48.

[47] See Maria Shmygol, '*Titus Andronicus* in seventeenth-century Germany', as delivered at the Shakespeare Association of America, Los Angeles, 28–31 March 2018; and *Early Modern German Shakespeare*: Titus Andronicus *and* The Taming of the Shrew: Tito Andronico *and* Kunst über alle Künste *in Translation*, ed. Maria Shmygol and Lukas Erne, under contract with Arden Shakespeare.

[48] Bosman, 'Renaissance intertheatre', 570. But see Tiffany Stern, '"If I could see the puppets dallying": *Der Bestrafte Brudermord* and Hamlet's encounters with the puppets', *Shakespeare Bulletin* 31.3 (2013), 337–52.

[49] Russ Leo, '*Hamlet*'s early international lives: Geeraardt Brandt's *De Veinzende Torquatus* and the performance of political realism', *Comparative Literature* 68.2 (2016), 155–80.

[50] Leo, '*Hamlet*'s early international lives', 156.

[51] For a discussion of what Moryson might mean by 'action', see Bosman, 'Renaissance intertheatre', 567. On the travels of the *commedia dell'arte* troupes, see Robert Henke, 'Border crossing in the commedia dell'arte', in *Transnational Exchange*, ed. Henke and Nicholson, pp. 19–34.

[52] Bosman, 'Renaissance intertheatre', 570. See William West, 'How chances if they travel? Expanding Shakespeare's Globe in early modern Germany', manuscript.

[53] Cited in Katritzky, 'English troupes', p. 39.

M. A. Katritzky offers an excellent survey of evidence of the varied audiences that attended their performances and their enthusiasm for the English players.[54]

The London actor Robert Browne, who travelled with various troupes on the Continent over some thirty years, inherited a share in the Globe in 1608, which he subsequently sold to Condell and Heminges. Thomas Sackville, a clown in his troupe who, as Bosman points out, apparently performed not only in English, but in Dutch and in German, ended his career a successful merchant in Frankfurt.[55] When playing at the fair, Browne's troupe seems to have stayed regularly at a particular inn in Frankfurt, the Sanduhr, whose proprietor undertook extensive, and expensive, building renovations in order to transform it into a suitable venue for performance, not a step likely to have been taken for irregular and infrequent visits.[56] In 1620, his widow outlined these investments in her ultimately successful appeal to the city authorities, who had initially denied the players' petition for permission to perform following her husband's death. *Pace* Moryson, Henslowe, entrepreneur and purveyor of costumes and stage properties to the London theatre, apparently numbered the Continental troupes among his clients.[57] The travelling players employed not only English actors, but foreign comedians as well, and thus fostered a theatre that was multilingual and what we might today term transnational.[58] In short, many studies have shown that the English actors' presence on the Continent was regular, recurrent, various, multiple and much more than a mere curiosity.

In 1621, we know that John Bill hosted at his home debates between Anglicans and Catholic scholars, and that Edward Blount, because of his 'neerenesse of freindship' to Bill, 'was allowed to come by myself and to bring 2. or 3. of my friends'.[59] Here we should remember Lesser's account of reading quoted earlier. Publishers chose to publish, to print and to advertise, based on myriad factors – perhaps, he says, even 'based on what friends or fellow stationers may have said about the text. All these judgments, many of which may be only partly conscious, are part of the publisher's reading of the text, for they form its "horizon of expectations"'.[60] Maybe the appearance of the First Folio advertisement among sermons and Protestant polemic is neither the 'surprise' Greg saw in it, nor the irrelevance Rees and Wakely claim. John Bill, a Frankfurt fair regular, and a savvy entrepreneur, might well have believed it made good business sense to offer for sale on the Continent 'Playes, written by M. William Shakespeare, all in one volume, printed by Isaack Iaggard, in. fol.' He, and the Folio syndicate, may have had a wider 'horizon of expectations' than our own Anglocentric blinders allow.

This assemblage of facts suggests that, even before there were modern nation-states; before the First Folio arrived at the Bodleian in 1624, despite Bodley's disparagement of such 'rifferaffes'; before the First Folio made its way into the libraries of such influential figures of the Dutch Golden Age as Joost van den Vondel, Constantijn Huygens and Johan Huydekooper van Maarseveen, the mayor of Amsterdam,[61] or of the Catholic college that educated English recusants at Saint-Omer; and some years before the Folio became a part of the libraries of Louis XIV and of his cultured finance minister, Fouquet; before the playwright was mentioned in passing in a 1682 German edition of comparative poetry – Shakespeare was always already multilingual and transnational, an incipient global cultural commodity.

---

54 Katritzky, 'English troupes', p. 39.
55 Bosman, 'Renaissance intertheatre', 564.
56 See the Frankfurt Stadtarchiv, Ratssupplikationen 1619, cited in Katritzky, 'English troupes', p. 43.
57 Katritzky, 'English troupes', p. 42.
58 With regard to theatrical cultural exchange, both in early modern Europe and in response to classical models, which led to the generation of what Louise George Clubb terms 'theatregrams', see *Italian Drama in Shakespeare's Time* (New Haven, 1989), and her several articles preceding its publication. Bosman takes up this idea in a slightly different register, borrowing the term 'interlanguage' from applied linguistics, to describe these hybrid dramatic forms on the Continent as what he terms Renaissance 'intertheatre': 'Renaissance intertheatre', 565.
59 Quoted in Rees and Wakely, *Publishing*, p. 241.
60 Lesser, *Renaissance Drama*, p. 9.
61 Leo, '*Hamlet*'s early international lives', 156.

THE STRANGER AT THE DOOR: BELONGING IN SHAKESPEARE'S EPHESUS

NANDINI DAS[1]

The shadows of two familiar texts loom behind Shakespeare's *Comedy of Errors*: Plautus' *Menaechmi*, and St Paul's Epistle to the Ephesians. *The Menaechmi* introduces the action about to unfold on stage with a casual, knowing nod towards the workings of the theatre, at once wondrous and banal. Walls and boundaries dissolve. As Plautus' Prologue explains:

> atque hoc poetae faciunt in comoediis:
> omnis res gestas esse Athenis autumant,
> quo illud uobis graecum uideatur magis;
>
> [This is what writers do in comedies: they claim that everything took place in Athens, intending that it should seem more Greek to you.][2]

If Plautus was a non-Roman Italian from Umbria, as some accounts suggest, he would have been particularly well positioned to understand that, in Rome's fictional world of *comoedia palliata* ('drama in a Greek cloak'), foreignness was interchangeable. It is not difficult, in a theatre, to take one city, one person, for another. One person's 'Athenish' ('atticissat', l. 12) could easily become another's 'Sicilish' ('sicilicissitat'). But theatre pushes the limits of that interchangeability further. It is a space in which inhabiting another's position, perspective and place – for better or for worse – is entirely possible:

> haec urbs Epidamnus est dum haec agitur fabula:
> quando alia agetur aliud fiet oppidum;
> sicut familiae quoque solent mutarier:
> modo hic habitat leno, modo adulescens, modo senex,
> pauper, mendicus, rex, parasitus, hariolus.
>
> [This city is Epidamnus as long as this play is being staged. When another is staged it'll become

another town, just as households too always change. At one time a pimp lives here, at another a young man, at yet another an old one, a pauper, a beggar, a king, a hanger-on, a soothsayer.][3]

St Paul writes of the dissolution of walls and boundaries too, although his concerns are of a different order. Our readings of Paul's Epistle, when *The Comedy of Errors* is involved, hovers around descriptions of Ephesus as a city of 'curious arts' and magic (Acts 19.19), and Paul's advice on

---

[1] For the initial impetus to explore the subject of this article, I would like to thank Alan Stewart and the 'Languages of Tudor Englishness' seminar at the Shakespeare Association of America Conference (2018). Thanks also to Eoin Price for his invitation to deliver a keynote at the British Shakespeare Association Conference (2019), which inspired further work on the topic, and to Farah Karim-Cooper, Lucy Munro and Preti Taneja for their support and advice. Research for this publication was supported by the ERC-TIDE Project (www .tideproject.uk). This project has received funding from the European Research Council (ERC) under the European Union's Horizon 2020 research and innovation programme (grant agreement No. 681884).

[2] Plautus, 'The two Menaechmuses', in *Casina. The Casket Comedy. Curculio. Epidicus. The Two Menaechmuses*, ed. and trans. Wolfgang de Melo, Loeb Classical Library 61 (Cambridge, MA, 2011), pp. 428–9, ll. 7–9.
[3] Plautus, 'The two Menaechmuses', pp. 428–9, ll. 72–6.

household relationships, between husbands and wives, or masters and servants. But the Epistle to the Ephesians is also, and firstly, about a different kind of union, addressed to those whom early modern English usage would have deemed to be 'spiritual' as well as 'temporal' strangers, who were 'aliens from the commonwealth of Israel, and were strangers from the covenants of promise':

> But now in Christ Jesus, ye which once were far off, are made near by the blood of Christ.
> For he is our peace, which hath made of both one, and hath broken the stop of the partition wall, . . .
> Now therefore ye are no more strangers and foreigners: but citizens with the Saints, and of the household of God.
> And are built upon the foundation of the Apostles and Prophets, Jesus Christ himself being the chief corner stone,
> In whom all the building coupled together, groweth unto an holy Temple in the Lord.
>
> Ephesians (2.13–21)[4]

This article begins with the discourse around strangers and aliens in the 1590s, and ends with *The Comedy of Errors*, whose first recorded appearance in 1594, I would suggest, offers a specific response to the severe backlash against such figures in early modern London – from the French and the Dutch, to the Jews and blackamoors. There is an established scholarly tradition that has examined the anxiety about immigrant communities that marked this period.[5] Such anxieties were by no means limited to or characteristic of London. The influx of migrant communities had been felt in other English towns and cities, including Canterbury, Norwich, Southampton and Colchester. Yet, as the notorious May Day unrest of 1517 attested, both the outbursts of popular unrest and state repercussions were particularly visible in London, where repeated waves of accusations against strangers allegedly taking up resources that belonged to local and 'native-born' communities had a history of erupting into violence. Jacob Selwood reminds us, however, that the critical debate surrounding the implications of the same 'Evil May Day' also illuminates 'the difficulties inherent in asking quantitative questions about hostility towards strangers'. As he argues,

'Attempts to gauge xenophobia all too often fall prey to binary thinking, emphasizing the presence or absence of violence and the rationality or irrationality of fear and stereotype'.[6] There are further elements that complicate the picture. The perceived threat of non-English immigrants was often entangled with crises brought on by heightened regional and parochial mobility. Lien Luu's study of London trade and industry has shown that 'strangers' and 'foreigners', immigrants from abroad and English-born immigrants from elsewhere within the nation, were both equally attracted by London's economic promise and accused of appropriating the local population's livelihood, resources and charity.[7] At the same time, ostensibly clear-cut binaries of differentiation based on place of origin alone did not always prevail. Heavily populated urban areas like the city of London, as Andrew Pettegree and others have pointed out, also provided spaces where conflicting affiliations – such as those based on shared faith or craft, or practical conditions of living and working in close proximity – could complicate matters of identity and belonging.[8]

In the light of that existing scholarship, I want to keep the Plautine and Pauline texts hovering in our memory, because they throw a raking light across both Shakespeare's play and that backlash against strangers in early modern London. Paul's text is an implicit presence behind numerous defences of English hospitality and charity that proliferate in

---

4 All biblical passages are from the 1560 Geneva Bible.
5 See Laura Hunt Yungblut, *Strangers Settled Here Amongst Us: Policies, Perceptions and the Presence of Aliens in Elizabethan England* (London, 1996); *Immigrants in Tudor and Early Stuart England*, ed. Nigel Goose and Lien Luu (Brighton, 2005); Imtiaz Habib, *Black Lives in the English Archives, 1500–1677: Imprints of the Invisible* (Burlington, VT, 2008).
6 Jacob Selwood, *Diversity and Difference in Early Modern London* (Farnham, 2010), p. 55.
7 Lien Bich Luu, *Immigrants and the Industries of London, 1500–1700* (Aldershot, 2005), Chs. 2 and 4. Also Ian Archer, *The Pursuit of Stability: Social Relations in Elizabethan London* (Cambridge, 1991), p. 131.
8 Andrew Pettegree, *Foreign Protestant Communities in Sixteenth-Century London* (Oxford, 1986); Douglas Catterall, *Community without Borders: Scots Migrants and the Changing Face of Power in the Dutch Republic, c. 1600–1700* (Leiden, 2002).

the 1590s. It is also a critical presence, albeit largely ignored, behind the 'mortal and intestine jars' (1.1.11) with which *The Comedy of Errors* begins, as cities and their people are split by 'enmity and discord' (1.1.5), lives are threatened, and the value of individual human beings is reduced to a ransom of coins. Plautus' seemingly light-hearted comedy with its fluid, shape-shifting city full of strangers, on the other hand, could be the stuff of citizen nightmares. It resonates with the unrest that plagued English towns and cities as the influx of strangers and foreigners coincided with another simultaneous development: the increasingly felt urgency to establish mercantile and diplomatic contact with the wider world. The basic contours of that tension were reflected on the stage throughout this period. To come home, only to find a stranger installed in your place, one who wears your face and speaks with your voice, is one version of that nightmare. The other, however, is to be that outsider. It is to know, to remember, or at least to understand, what it is like to arrive in a strange place, to have the identity and name you call your own held to ransom, and to be caught up in a web of misprision and obligations which you can neither control, nor escape.

''TIS NOT OUR NATIVE COUNTRY'

Mistrust of the stranger, of course, is nothing new on the London stage. Even in the early, anonymous *Interlude of Welth and Helth* (c. 1557), 'aliaunts' like Hance Bere-pot or War, the drunken Flemish gunner, were denounced by Remedy for their ability 'with craft & subtleti [to] get/ englishme[n]s welth away', and Ill-Will the Vice spoke with a mock Spanish accent ('Me is un spanyardo compoco parlavere').[9] In Ulpian Fulwell's 1568 interlude, *Like Will to Like*, as Lloyd Kermode argues, Philip Fleming and his drunken friend (also predictably called Hance) acted as 'overt indicator[s] of social fracture and alien decay'.[10] In George Wapull's *Tide Tarrieth No Man* (1576), Paul's Cross is the favoured haunt of Greediness, and Help assures Neighbourhood, a 'straunger', that his attempt to acquire a property could not have been better timed:

For among us now, such is our countrey zeale,
That we love best with straungers to deale.
To sell a lease deare, whosoever that will,
At the french, or dutch Church let him set up his
   bill....
Therefore though thou be straunge, the matter is
   not great,
For thy money is English, which must worke the
   feate.[11]

Despite the soon-to-be-outmoded style and abstraction of personifications, these are telling views from below. To attend to them is to attend to local, popular anxiety, which permeates urban encounters (drunken or otherwise), transactions (social and commercial), trade and craft.[12] We know that such anxiety and resentment become visible increasingly in the plays performed in the city during the 1580s and 1590s, such as Robert Wilson's *Three Ladies of London* (1584), a play that has been much discussed in recent years for its representation of the stranger and the alien on the London stage.[13] As Lloyd Kermode has pointed

---

9 *An Interlude of Welth and Helth* (London, 1565), sig. D1v, sig. D3r.

10 Lloyd E. Kermode, *Aliens and Englishness in Elizabethan Drama* (Cambridge, 2009), p. 47. For other extended discussions of alien presence in early English drama, see Scott Oldenburg, *Alien Albion: Literature and Immigration in Early Modern England* (Toronto, 2014); Nina Levine, *Practicing the City: Early Modern London on Stage* (New York, 2016); Peter Matthew McCluskey, *Representations of Flemish Immigrants on the Early Modern Stage* (Oxford and New York, 2019).

11 George Wapull, *Type Taryeth No Man* (London, 1576), sig. B4v.

12 Other examples of such permeation are discussed by Emma Smith, '"So much English by the mother": gender, foreigners, and the mother tongue in William Haughton's *Englishmen for My Money*', *Medieval & Renaissance Drama in England* 13 (2001), 165–81; and John Michael Archer, 'Citizens and aliens as working subjects in Dekker's *The Shoemaker's Holiday*', in *Working Subjects in Early Modern English Drama*, ed. Michelle Dowd and Natasha Korda (Farnham, 2011), pp. 37–52.

13 See, for instance, Alan Stewart, '"Come from Turkie": Mediterranean trade in late Elizabethan London', in *Remapping the Mediterranean World in Early Modern English Writings*, ed. Goran Stanivukovic (Basingstoke, 2007), pp.

out, when Hospitality is murdered by Usury in Wilson's play, the action stands as an indictment of one kind of hospitality being rooted out by another.[14] Private, individual hospitality, closely associated with Englishness and traditional ties within the community, is depicted as a quality under threat. It is replaced by a particular form of urban, self-interested 'liberalitie' that benefits the outsider-interloper. In Wilson's play, it is represented by the character of Lady Lucre and her relationship with her unscrupulous non-English partners-in-crime, such as the Italian merchant Mercadorus. Related tensions about the stranger's position bubble under the exchange in the Maltese senate house when Barabas is summoned to the aid of the state in Marlowe's *Jew of Malta* (1589/90). Barabas rejects the option of political and military involvement in his host nation because Jews 'are no soldiers' (1.2.50).[15] 'Are strangers with your tribute to be taxed?' (1.2.59) he demands, claiming civic immunity as a resident alien. He is reminded by an attendant knight that economic involvement nevertheless carries its own obligations: 'Have strangers leave with us to get their wealth? / Then let them with us contribute' (1.2.60–1).

Yet the strangers, the ones who are 'not like us', come in multiple confusing forms, and identifying them is no easy task. In *The Three Lords and Three Ladies of London* (1590), the belated sequel to Wilson's *Three Ladies of London*, it is not difficult to figure out who will win the hands of the three ladies. It is pretty much to be expected that, within the chivalric set-piece at its centre, the eponymous three Lords of London will be victorious over their Spanish rivals, three overtly inimical 'strangers' in language, clothing and behaviour. But that the claim of the Lords of London is stronger than even that of those of their own nation – the three Lords of Lincoln – is more of a surprise. Judge Nemo's explanation that the superiority of their claim on the ladies rests on the fact that they are 'Their countrimen, in *London* bred as they' opens up a whole different layer of local and regional tensions about place and belonging.[16]

Who is one's 'countryman', after all? The proximity in legal and popular usage of the terms associated with external and internal migration ('stranger' or 'alien', and 'foreigner'), the confusing status of the rights of birth and the rights of blood (*jus soli* and *jus sanguinis*), the legally endorsed fluidity of identity signified by processes of denization and naturalization turn identity into a shifting hall of mirrors where identifying or inhabiting the stranger's place is often a matter, ultimately, of perspective.[17] Usury's 'parentes were both Jewes', but like the Lords and Ladies, he was 'borne in London' too, and pleads with his confederates in this play not to betray their 'native countrie' (F4 r). '[He]re where I am, I know the government', he declares, facing the prospect of a Spanish invasion, 'here can I live for all their threatning, if strangers prevail, I know not their lawes nor their usage'. Belonging, for him, emerges through familiarity with 'usage' – everyday practice, hostile or otherwise – which, in Usury's case, is rooted firmly in the economic structure of the city of London. Worries about the stranger becoming familiar with such 'usage' and, in the process, making himself 'at home', however, inevitably is the other side of that coin.

THE 1590S AND THE STRANGER'S CASE

The concerns that circulated in the public domain, as these plays acknowledged, focused repeatedly on a familiar cluster of issues. The disbursement of hospitality and charity was chief among them, but

---

157–77; Claire Jowitt, 'Robert Wilson's *The Three Ladies of London* and its theatrical and cultural contexts', in *The Oxford Handbook of Tudor Drama*, ed. Thomas Betteridge and Greg Walker (Oxford, 2012), pp. 309–22.

[14] Kermode, *Aliens and Englishness*, pp. 68–9.

[15] Christopher Marlowe, 'The Jew of Malta', in *Doctor Faustus and Other Plays*, ed. David Bevington and Eric Rasmussen (Oxford, 1995), p. 259.

[16] Robert Wilson, *The Three Lords and Three Ladies of London* (London, 1590), sig. N4v.

[17] Selwood, *Diversity*, and Goose and Luu, eds., *Immigrants in Tudor and Early Stuart England*, among others, have discussed these definitions and negotiations of rights extensively. See also Nandini Das, João Vicente Melo, Haig Smith and Lauren Working, *TIDE: Keywords* (2019), www.tideproject.uk/keywords-home.

it was inflected by the problems inherent in the very definition of a 'stranger', and by expectations of reciprocity from strangers that simultaneously emphasized difference, and thus resisted possibilities of reciprocity. Each of these concerns formed part of the heated public discourse around strangers and aliens in the early 1590s, when *The Comedy of Errors* was written and performed.[18] One place where it is particularly noticeable is in the fractious Parliamentary debate about the Bill on strangers' retailing of foreign merchandise in March 1593, itself the product of long-term simmering tensions in the city. The opening speech for the Bill against the strangers was made by Francis Moore of the Middle Temple, Counsel for the City of London. It set the tone of the discussion, by insisting that 'Charity must be mixt with Policy; for to give of Charity to our own Beggaring, were but Prodigality', and that the strangers' 'Priviledge of Denization is not to be allowed above the priviledge of Birth'.[19] In a later speech, Nicholas Fuller, himself the son of a successful London merchant, spoke of the 'Exclamations of the City [that] are exceeding pitiful and great against these Strangers'. 'It is no Charity to have this pity on them to our own utter undoing', he claimed, 'this is to be noted in these Strangers, they will not converse with us, they will not marry with us, they will not buy any thing of our Country-men'.[20] And in the penultimate speech of the proceedings, Sir Walter Raleigh would launch a three-pronged attack that is worth quoting at length:

Whereas it is pretended, That for Strangers it is against Charity, against Honour, against profit to expel them; in my opinion it is no matter of *Charity* to relieve them. For first, such as fly hither have forsaken their own King; ... and here they live disliking our Church. For *Honour*, It is Honour to use Strangers as we be used amongst Strangers; And it is a lightness in a Common-Wealth, yea a baseness in a Nation to give a liberty to another which we cannot receive again. In *Antwerp* where our intercourse was most, we were never suffered to have a Taylor or a Shoemaker to dwell there.... And for Profit, they are all of the House of *Almoigne*, who pay nothing, yet eat out our profits, and supplant our own Nation.... [I]t cost her Majesty sixteen thousand pound

a year the maintaining of these Countries, and yet for all this they Arm her Enemies against her. Therefore I see no reason that so much respect should be given unto them.[21]

In the end, the Bill was rejected by the House of Lords, despite being passed by the Commons. Over the next two months, through repeated letters to the city, the Elizabethan Privy Council recorded its concerns and increasing frustration with London's inability to stem public demonstrations of dissatisfaction against strangers. Apprentices' intentions to 'attempt some vyolence on the strangers' are noted on 16 April, and 'certaine libelles latelie published by some disordered and factious persons in and about the cittie of London' are mentioned in another report.[22] Its tone is worried, and understandably so, given that one such public libel threatened a purge of all strangers from the country: 'Be it known to all Flemings and Frenchmen, that it is best for them to depart out of the Realm of England, between this and the 9th of *July* next. If not, then to take that which follows: for that there shall be many a sore stripe.'[23] In the weeks that followed, the Privy Council would have further occasions to worry about 'divers lewd and malicious libells set up within the citie of London', of which the best

[18] On the dating of the play, see 'Appendix 1: date of composition', in *The Comedy of Errors*, ed. Kent Cartwright, Arden Series 3 (London, 2017).

[19] Simonds D'Ewes, *A Compleat Journal . . . of the House of Lords and House of Commons throughout the whole Reign of Queen Elizabeth* (London, 1693), p. 505. David Dean offers a useful discussion of the legal background and implications of the Bill in *Law-Making and Society in Late Elizabethan England: The Parliament of England, 1584–1601* (Cambridge, 1996), pp. 155–7.

[20] D'Ewes, *A Compleat Journal*, p. 506. The complaints about intermarriage and resistance to it, of course, form the focus of both Wilson's *Three Lords and Three Ladies*, and William Haughton's later play, *Englishmen for My Money* (London, 1598).

[21] D'Ewes, *A Compleat Journal*, pp. 508–9.

[22] *Acts of the Privy Council, 1542–1604*, ed. J. R. Dasent, 32 vols. (London, 1901), vol. 24: *1592–1593*, pp. 187, 200–1.

[23] J. Strype, *Annals of the Reformation*, 4 vols. (London, 1731), vol. 4, p. 167.

known is the verse libel that appeared on the wall of Austin Friars, the Dutch Church, in the middle of the night on 5 May.[24] This text has been much discussed due to the way in which its scattered references to 'Machiavellian Marchant' and 'paris massacre' implicated Christopher Marlowe and his plays.[25] Its equation of the guest-who-is-a-stranger with the stranger-who-is-an-enemy is predictable:

> In Chambers, twenty in one house will lurke,
> Raysing of rents, was never knowne before
>   Living farre better then at native home
> And our pore souls, are cleane thrust out of dore
>   And to the warres are sent abroade to rome,
> To fight it out for Fraunce & Belgia,
> And dy like dogges as sacrifice for you.[26]

What is perhaps less predictable is the recalcitrant trick of the eye that the text effects at the same time. 'That Egipts plagues, vext not the Egyptians more, / Th[a]n you doe us' the libel claims, 'then death shall be your lotte'.[27] But the comparison is an uncomfortable one, turning the native English subjects into the Egyptians of the Exodus, and the strangers into the chosen people of the Israelites, out to claim their rightful 'home'.

'PRINCES OF FOREIGN LANDS'

England's relationship with strangers was also under discussion elsewhere. The 'Comedy of Errors (like to Plautus his Menechmus)' is thought to have been performed when 'it was thought good not to offer any thing of Account' after 'Throngs and Tumults' disrupted the revels organized by the members of Gray's Inn on 28 December 1594, much to the annoyance of visitors from the Inner Temple.[28] At the mock enquiry held on the next night, the blame was laid squarely on 'a Sorcerer or Conjurer' who not only disrupted the embassy, but also 'foisted a Company of base and common Fellows, to make up our Disorders with a Play of Errors and Confusions' (p. 23).

The festivities of the fashionable young gentlemen of the London Inns of Court and its inset 'Play of Errors' would seem unlikely spaces for the accommodation of the debate around strangers.

The revels wove an elaborate fiction about the imaginary 'State of Purpoole' and its Prince, which gradually took shape through multiple performances from December 1594 to March 1595. It is evident from its written account, the *Gesta Grayorum* (published significantly later in 1688), that these were performances rooted in their urban environment. There is the repeated roll-call of the Prince of Purpoole's titles, which serve to beat the bounds of the city: 'Duke of the High and Nether Holborn, Marquis of St Giles's and Tottenham, Count Palatine of Bloomsbury and Clerkenwell, Great Lord of the Cantons of Islington, &c' (p. 9). Elsewhere, there is evidence that the entertainment spilled repeatedly onto London's streets and mimicked royal progresses and Lord Mayor's processions (pp. 43, 55).

It is perhaps not surprising, in the circumstances, that stranger figures were acknowledged within the performances themselves, from 'Lucy Negro, Abbess de Clerkenwell' and her 'Nunnery' (p. 12), to the silent 'Tartarian Page', reminiscent of Ippolyta the Tartarian, whom Anthony Jenkinson procured for Queen Elizabeth from his travels (p. 57).[29] A few other discordant notes within the account also reflect the larger public debates about strangers' rights. The Prince's general pardon to the nation after his coronation excludes 'All Merchant-Adventurers, that ship or lade any Wares or Merchandize, into any Port or Creek,

---

[24] *Acts of the Privy Council*, ed. Dasent, vol. 24, p. 222.
[25] See, for instance, Eric Griffin, 'Shakespeare, Marlowe, and the Stranger Crisis of the 1590s', in *Shakespeare and Immigration*, ed. Ruben Espinosa and David Ruiter (Farnham, 2014), pp. 13–36.
[26] Arthur Freeman, 'Marlowe, Kyd, and the Dutch Church libel', *ELR* 3.1 (1973), 44–52, esp. p. 50.
[27] Freeman, 'Marlowe, Kyd, and the Dutch Church libel', p. 50.
[28] *Gesta Grayorum (1688)*, ed. W. W. Greg (London, 1914), p. 22; hereafter, cited parenthetically in the text.
[29] See Duncan Salkeld, *Shakespeare among the Courtesans: Prostitution, Literature, and Drama, 1500–1650* (Farnham, 2012), pp. 133–4; Bernadette Andrea, *The Lives of Girls and Women from the Islamic World in Early Modern British Literature and Culture* (Toronto, 2017), pp. 82–98.

in any Flemish, French, or Dutch, or other Outlandish Hoy, Ship, or Bottom' (p. 18). Later, letters received by the Prince from his servants suggest a domain under assault. The letter from the 'Canton of Knights-bridge' reports 'certain Foreigners, that sieze upon all Passengers, taking from them by force their Goods, under a pretence [of] being Merchants Strangers', claiming that they have permission from the Prince to recoup their own lost merchandise (p. 48). From 'the Harbour of Bride-well' (p. 50), another innuendo-laden account reports a 'huge Armado of French Amazons' that holds 'all sorts of People … in durance; not suffering one Man to escape, till he have turned French' (p. 49).

Despite this, the overarching tone of the entertainments devised for the 1594 revels was studiedly global and cosmopolitan, shifting focus away from London – within which Purpoole had established its temporary, alternative sovereignty – to the world beyond. Its emphasis on international diplomacy and traffic reflected the ambitions of the Elizabethan state in post-Armada years. A nascent imperial vision was one part of it, and princely 'Amity' that united like-minded Christian princes against common enemies was another. They were both foregrounded strikingly in the revels of 3 January 1595, when the Grayans and the Templarians patched up their differences from the 'Night of Errors' with their emperors worshipping 'lovingly, Arm in Arm' at the altar of the Goddess of Amity (p. 25). In between, the court of Purpoole turned away from 'the Plots of Rebellion and Insurrection, that those, His Excellency's Subjects, had devised against His Highness and State' (p. 51), to celebrate embassies both local and distant. If the 'Templarians' and their Turk-defying 'emperor' featured in one instance, the pleas of the Russian Tsar 'Theodore Evanwhich' (p. 44) featured in another, setting up the Prince as the 'Bulwark of Christendom' against the 'Bigarian' and 'Negro' Tartars challenging his authority (p. 46).

By the time the final entertainment devised by Francis Davison, the *Masque of Proteus*, was performed in the presence of Elizabeth I and the court at Shrovetide, the conflation of chivalric romance with a deliberately outward-looking political vision was clearly marked out. The Prince's squire recounted the story of how the Prince wagered his own liberty, as well as the chance to control the Adamantine rocks that govern 'the wild Empire of the Ocean', by promising the sea-god Proteus that he would show him 'a Power, / Which in attractive Vertue should surpass / The wond'rous force of his Iron-drawing Rocks' (p. 63). The outcome of that wager was predictable, with Elizabeth's attendance at the performance providing the conceit on which the narrative turned. In her presence, the squire's verse could declare Proteus' prize redundant, even as the Prince offered his services to the Queen and joined her noblemen in jousting:

This Cynthia high doth rule those heavenly Tides,
  … And, Proteus, for the Seas,
Whose Empire large your praised Rock assures:
Your Gift is void, it is already here;
As Russia, China, and Negellan's Strait
Can witness bear, well may your Presence be
Impressa apt thereof; but sure, not Cause.
(*Gesta Grayorum*, ed. Greg, p. 65)

The argument that Purpoole's deferral to Elizabeth's 'attractive Vertue' is hardly an unqualified submission has been made before. Richard McCoy and Martin Butler, for instance, have both read the performance of a chivalric compromise into the masque's closing insistence that the 'Arms of Men' cannot be moved without the willing submission of 'the Hearts of Men' (*Gesta Grayorum*, ed. Greg, p. 64).[30] At the same time, however, this was the creation of young men waiting to enter the service of the state: the Gray's Inn revels were not only attended on multiple occasions by Elizabeth I and her court, its report also

---

[30] Richard McCoy, 'Lord of Liberty: Francis Davison and the cult of Elizabeth', in *The Reign of Elizabeth I: Court and Culture in the Last Decade*, ed. John Guy (Cambridge, 1995), pp. 212–28, esp. p. 220; Martin Butler, 'The legal masque: humanity and liberty at the Inns of Court', in *The Oxford Handbook of English Law and Literature, 1500–1700*, ed. Lorna Hutson (Oxford, 2017), pp. 180–97, esp. pp. 188–9.

notes gratefully how William Cecil, Lord Burghley, a former member of Gray's Inn himself, sent the organizers £10 as an unsolicited token of his favour at the start of the festivities (p. 4).

In the winter of 1594, it is possible to read their fictional representation of England's relationship with the wider world as a construct at least partially shaped and approved by the state, an imaginative response to the Parliamentary debate about the Strangers' Bill and its attendant unrest, in which the other two Inns of Court had been so closely involved.[31] 'How have We been honoured with the Presents of divers Princes, Lords, and Men of great Worth; who, confident in our Love, without Fear or Distrust, have come to visit Us', the Prince of Purpoole had exclaimed in the course of the revels; 'What Concourse of all People hath been continually at Our Court, to behold Our Magnificence!' (p. 52). His dismissal of the 'few tumultuary Disorders' and 'ill-guided Insurrections' (p. 52) of the people of his own state, conspiring to force attention away from that global recognition, was perhaps only half in jest. Now, at the revel's conclusion, that argument for the state's policy towards strangers at the level of international politics turns the feared influx of immigrants into a 'pilgrimage' received by England and its Queen:

Unto this living Saint have Princes high
Of Foreign Lands, made vowed Pilgrimage.
What Excellencies are there in this frame,
Of all things, which her Vertue doth not draw? ...
In the protection of this mighty Rock,
In Britain Land, whilst Tempests beat abroad,
The Lordly and the lowly Shepherd both,
In plenteous Peace have fed their happy Flocks.

(p. 65)

IN EPHESUS

What then, against such a backdrop, are we to make of the bustling port city at the crossroads of global traffic where the action of *The Comedy of Errors* takes place? Performed, if not commissioned specifically, for the Gray's Inn revels, this 'play of Errors and Confusions' presented by 'a Company

of base and common Fellows' provided a different rationale, I would suggest, for the entertainment of strangers. Its exploration of a stranger's rights and place is distinct both from imperial ambition and statecraft on the one hand, and from the city and 'tumultuary Disorders' of its native-born population on the other.

From its emphasis on *jus soli* in controlling the movement and rights of strangers, to the pervasive obsession with reciprocity in what Wilson's Usury might have called its 'usage', Ephesus resonates with the concerns we have seen already, but its handling repeatedly exposes the shifting sands on which those concerns are based. Take hospitality, for instance, which in Ephesus is always a matter of reciprocal transaction. Like Raleigh, who had reminded the 1593 Parliament that it is 'baseness in a Nation to give a liberty to another which we cannot receive again', Solinus's opening speech in Act 1, Scene 1, reminds Egeon that the 'rancorous outrage of your Duke / To merchants, our well-dealing countrymen /... / Excludes all pity from our threat'ning looks' (1.1.6–10). Later, Antipholus of Syracuse's generous invitation to dinner is turned down by the Merchant of Ephesus in favour of an invitation from 'certain merchants / Of whom I hope to make much benefit' (1.2.24–5). Even sexual liaisons turn into bilateral exchanges of a more material kind: 'Give me the ring of mine you had at dinner, / Or for my diamond the chain you promised', demands the Courtesan from the puzzled Syracusian Antipholus (4.3.68–9).

That last also illuminates the way in which the Ephesian conception of reciprocity is defined in material terms. The emphasis that *The Comedy of Errors* places on commodities and the circulation of things is well known. As with the doubling of characters, this is Plautine comedy with added

---

[31] Internal court politics of the pro-Essex and anti-Raleigh factions also played a role. Francis Davison and Francis Bacon, both of whom were closely involved in the production and performance of the revels, were also closely aligned with the Earl of Essex at this point. Essex himself is noted as one of the participants in the final joust (*Gesta Grayorum*, ed. Greg, p. 68).

extras. Plautus is satisfied with making one know-ing joke about *comoedia palliata* (the term often used for Roman comedy derived from Greek New Comedy) by making a *palla* ('cloak') his main instrument of confusion. Shakespeare swaps it for a chain and adds a rapidly expanding list to it for good measure. 'Mart' and 'money' occur more times here than in any other play; currency is specified ('marks', 'ducats', 'angels', 'guilders', 'sixpence'); chains, rings and purses change hands and necks and get stuffed into desks covered with Turkish tapestry; 'fraughtage' and 'stuf' is put on board ships and taken off again. That emphasis on the material props is often read as the play's ques-tioning of what constitutes personal identity, since confusion occurs when things go astray. But the problem in Ephesus is not that these material mar-kers change hands, but that their transmission is expected to be bound by a strict framework of reciprocal exchange within the community, mov-ing from person to person only along a pre-determined route. The emphasis on 'credit' is a useful shorthand for that dynamic. There is no room for rootless, creditless strangers in this economy.[32] Their appearance destabilizes Ephesian 'usage' fundamentally, and both public and domestic relationships fall apart as a result: wife becomes 'that woman' (5.1.198), husband turns into '[d]issembling villain' (4.4.101), client becomes 'wretch' (5.1.27).

Yet, within the world of the play, that emphasis on material reciprocity has no affective counter-part. 'Proceed, Solinus, to procure my fall, / And by the doom of death end woes and all', Egeon begins (1.1.1–2). His resignation offers much more than the Duke had expected, so he chooses to ignore it altogether ('Merchant of Syracusa, plead no more', 1.1.3). 'I have some marks of yours upon my pate, / Some of my mistress' marks upon my shoulders, / ... / If I should pay your worship those again, / Perchance you will not bear them patiently' (1.2.82–6), says Dromio of Ephesus. His wordplay, light-hearted as it is, illuminates the chasm that separates master and servant in Ephesus, made wider by the fact that he is addres-sing the wrong man. But the most striking

acknowledgement is Adriana's, even as she won-ders about her sister's exemplary patience:

> They can be meek that have no other cause.
> A wretched soul, bruised with adversity,
> We bid be quiet when we hear it cry.
> But were we burdened with like weight of pain,
> As much or more we should ourselves complain.
>
> (2.1.33–7)

It is within this space, where a closed legally and commercially determined framework of human transactions appears to have replaced the fluidity of all affective connection, that Antipholus of Ephesus is a model citizen, '[o]f credit infinite, highly beloved' (5.1.6) – a choice of phrase which itself is another example where potential for mate-rial reciprocity, 'credit', supersedes and determines the affective in Ephesus. When he finds himself barred from his home, his response is striking. 'What art thou that keep'st me out from the house I owe?' (3.1.42), he exclaims, eschewing the one word, 'home', which otherwise recurs pointedly and frequently throughout the play, in favour of material ownership. Only a greater dan-ger stops him from claiming his property with a crowbar. A 'vulgar comment will be made of it' (3.1.101), warns his merchant companion, Balthazar, assuming that human interest in another's business is naturally prurient. And the result of it, 'slander' (line 106) seems to be like the troublesome strangers of London: it 'may with foul intrusion enter in / And dwell upon your grave when you are dead. / For slander lives upon suc-cession, / For ever housed where once it gets possession' (3.1.104–7).

Antipholus of Ephesus's perspective, however, is not one with which we are invited to align our-selves. One of the clear changes that Shakespeare makes to his Plautine source is the switch of emphasis and focus from the 'native' brother in *The Menaechmi* (who begins the action in the play) to the 'stranger' father and twin, with

---

[32] On the way in which physical commodities became the focus of anxiety about strangers, see Stewart, '"Come from Turkie"', p. 166.

whom the action of Shakespeare's play begins, and through whose eyes we are invited to look at the workings of Ephesus for the first two acts. Verbal, affective resonances keep opening doors for these strange visitors from the moment Solinus, listening to Egeon's account, admits that he would surrender to pity 'were it not against our laws – / Which princes, would they, may not disannul – ' (1.1.-142–3). Later in the action, it is Adriana, Shakespeare's adaptation of Plautus' nameless Matrona ('Wife'), the representative of the home and of domestic life, who repeatedly generates such resonances. Fundamental human connections beyond national boundaries echo in Antipholus of Syracuse and Adriana's shared imagery of water-drops in speaking of the bonds between brother and brother, husband and wife (in 1.2.35–6 and 2.2.129–30). Elsewhere, lament about the 'defeatures' of time that inscribe themselves on the vulnerable human body, connect her to Egeon. 'Hath homely age th'alluring beauty took / From my poor cheek? /... / ... Then is he the ground / Of my defeatures' (2.1.88–97), says Adriana about Antipholus of Ephesus's neglect, while 'careful hours with time's deformèd hand, / Have written strange defeatures in my face' (5.1.299–300), says Egeon, when he thinks his son is denying acquaintance. These are the only two instances of the word being used in a play by Shakespeare. The extent to which the 'native' and 'stranger' figures are rendered interchangeable affects even the most resistant of Ephesus's citizens. 'I came from Corinth', says Antipholus of Ephesus in what seems a redundant piece of belated exposition (5.1.367). That this trajectory, coupled with his birth in Epidamnum, makes him at most a stranger-denizen who has gained residence, wealth and a wife through service and the Duke's patronage would not have been lost on the play's first audience.

At Westminster Abbey in the plague-ridden spring of 1593, the speakers arguing the cause of the strangers had repeatedly emphasized the benefits that accrued, both material and otherwise, from reciprocity. 'This Bill should be ill for London, for the Riches and Renown of the City cometh by entertaining of Strangers, and giving liberty unto them', warned Sir John Woolley; 'Antwerp and Venice could never have been so rich and famous but by entertaining of Strangers, and by that means have gained all the intercourse of the World.' And, although 'our Charity unto them must not hinder or injure our selves', Robert Cecil would say in the final speech, it 'hath brought great Honour to our Kingdom, for it is accounted the refuge of distressed Nations, for our Arms have been open unto them to cast themselves into our Bosoms'.[33] But the speech that has perhaps attracted most attention – not least because of its resemblance to Hand D's plea for the 'stranger's case' in the revisions to the roughly contemporaneous *Book of Sir Thomas More* – is a striking leap of the imagination that conflates the guest and the host, the supplicant and the benefactor. 'In the days of Queen Mary', Henry Finch asserted, 'when our Cause was as theirs is now, those Countries did allow us that liberty, which now, we seek to deny them. They are strangers now, we may be strangers hereafter. So let us do as we would be done unto' (507).[34]

It is worth pausing on this assertion for a moment, because it opens up a hall of mirrors with which Finch's early modern audience would have been deeply familiar. Paul's reminder of universal Christian brotherhood and the breaking down of walls of division was a commonplace in homilies and sermons about charity and hospitality in the period, but two other passages from the Bible were equally likely to be cited. The first is from Exodus 22.21: 'Moreover, thou shalt not do injury to a stranger, neither oppress him: for ye were strangers in the land of Egypt.' The second is from Leviticus 19.33–4: 'And if a stranger sojourn with thee in your land, ye shall not vex him. But the stranger that dwelleth with you, shall be as one

---

[33] D'Ewes, *A Compleat Journal*, pp. 506, 509.

[34] The resemblance to the speech in Thomas More was first noted in P. Maas, 'Henry Finch and Shakespeare', *Review of English Studies* 4 (1953), 142. On this and on the complex claims of Christian 'brotherhood', see also Margaret Tudeau-Clayton, *Shakespeare's Englishes: Against Englishness* (Cambridge, 2019), pp. 132–74.

of your selves, and thou shalt love him as thy self: for ye were strangers in the land of Egypt.' What both the Bible and Finch are advocating is a trick of the mind and the eye – one that suggests that a host could easily have been or become a stranger-guest, and vice versa. It is a conflation inherent in the word itself, deriving as it does from Old French '(h)oste' and Latin 'hospes', which meant both 'host' and 'guest'.

Opposition to strangers, as we have seen in the 1593 debate, extracts from this a disquieting *reductio ad absurdum* of the very idea of hospitality, when the guest takes over and becomes a host himself. 'Hospes' turns into 'hostis' – stranger, certainly, but also 'public enemy' – an imaginative leap that Raleigh makes in his Parliamentary speech when his diatribe against strangers who live in England 'disliking our Church' turns quickly into an accusation of treason ('they Arm her Enemies'). The resolution that *The Comedy of Errors* offers, as such, depends ultimately on a comically literal theatrical depiction of the Pauline message, even as it uses the Plautine acknowledgement of the theatrical space to effect it. In the Dutch Church libel of 1593, the over-crowded, fraught spaces of the city of London had produced the seemingly inevitable slide of the guest who is a stranger, into the stranger who is an enemy. In the revels of Gray's Inn in 1594, the young men behind its entertainments had attempted to provide a defence of such risky hospitality, subsuming the local concerns of the city to visions of imperial ambition and international diplomacy. What we have in Shakespeare's play, instead, is a response built around a comic reversal of that paranoia. The two figures – native and stranger – whose lives get entangled in the bustle of a port city really do turn out to be brothers united by blood. The space of the theatre makes it possible for them to exemplify overtly what scripture would have us take on faith about human connection. 'They are strangers now, we may be strangers hereafter. So let us do as we would be done unto', Henry Finch had asked the London MPs at the 1593 debate on behalf of strangers, but that is a difficult imaginative leap. There is, at the end, no need for such a leap of faith in the city of Ephesus. Instead, there is just a step, as the two Dromios 'walk in' (5.1.422) together – strangers, brothers, strange likenesses ('Me thinks you are my glass and not my brother', 5.1.420). Like the working of theatre itself, it is at once momentous, wondrous, and yet everyday.

CITY ORIGINS, LOST IDENTITIES AND PRINT ERRORS IN *THE COMEDY OF ERRORS*

ALICE LEONARD[1]

William Jaggard is today best known as the printer of Shakespeare's First Folio (1623), but he did not always have such an auspicious reputation. Jaggard was accused of poor printing by the publisher Ralph Brooke, who hired Jaggard to print *A catalogue and succession of the kings, princes, dukes* (1619).[2] Brooke claimed that the 'many escapes, and mistakings, committed by the Printer' necessitated a new edition.[3] Jaggard ridiculed this, calling Brooke's concerns 'such pettie misprisions', and insisting that 'there was no fear that the meanest Reader were like to stumble at such strawes, nor the most captious Aduersarie would go a hawking after syllables'.[4] Jaggard defended his reputation on the claim that small mistakes would not matter to the reader. Previously, he had been accused of the same shoddy workmanship by Thomas Heywood, for whom 'such strawes' were significant problems. Heywood claimed Jaggard and his men had been grossly negligent, referring to 'the misquotations, mistaking of sillables, misplacing halfe lines, coining of strange and neuer heard of words'.[5] This printerly spat suggests that mistakes emanating from the early modern print shop mattered – at least for some, if not for Jaggard – and were wholly undesirable for the author and the reader.

In *The Comedy of Errors* (1592–4), a play which Jaggard would print soon after in Shakespeare's First Folio, 'such pettie misprisions' would prove especially difficult for the reader. There is a series of small but significant printing errors which make it much easier for a reader to fall into confusion. As each subsequent edition was based on the preceding one, these same errors were perpetuated from

the First (1623) to the Second (1632), Third (1663–4) and Fourth (1685) Folios, before a large amount were corrected by Nicholas Rowe in his edition of *The works of Mr. William Shakespear; in six volumes* (1709). There is a pre-correction period of eighty-six years, during which the only available editions contained these errors and thus have impacted interpretation of the play. The most notable printing errors concern the two sets of twins. The dramatic plot is about their repeated mistaken identity, and the printing errors further complicate our ability to differentiate them. The textual and dramatic intersect; the play actively cultivates audience confusion (both on stage and off) and the text inadvertently aided this project by inserting errors in the speech prefixes and stage directions. Despite Brooke's urgency to correct

[1] My thanks go to the Folger Shakespeare Library, Washington, DC, for a short-term fellowship to conduct this research, and to Emma Depledge, Thomas Docherty and Derek Dunne for their very helpful comments. This article is dedicated to my identical twin sister.

[2] Ralph Brooke, *A catalogue and succession of the kings, princes, dukes, marquesses, earles, and viscounts of this realme of England, since the Norman Conquest, to this present yeare* (London, 1619).

[3] Brooke, 'To the Honourable and iudicious Reader', in *A catalogue and succession of the kings, princes, dukes* (London, 1622), sig. A4r.

[4] See the epistle headed 'The Printer', in Augustine Vincent, *A discouerie of errours in the first edition of the catalogue of nobility, published by Raphe Brooke, Yorke Herald, 1619. and printed heerewith word for word, according to that edition* (London, 1622), sig. 5r.

[5] Thomas Heywood's epistle 'To my approued good Friend, Mr. Nicholas Okes', appended to *An Apology for Actors* (London, 1612), sig. G4r–v.

the printer's errors and mitigate their ill effects, the correction of these textual mistakes in *Errors* is not straightforward as their dispersal through print writes them into the history of the play. Nevertheless, error is an aspect of bibliographical culture that has been overlooked in *The Comedy of Errors*. As John Jowett argues, 'error has been insufficiently treated discursively as a theoretical and practical aspect of textual transmission'.[6]

This article analyses the printing errors in the First to Fourth Folios 1–4 of *Errors*, and brings to attention seventeenth- and eighteenth-century annotations on or around them. I argue that, in their 'readerly marks',[7] the annotators of these copies demonstrate a consistent response – that readers became confused by, or else misunderstood, certain elements of the play. I then examine the editorial response to error in the eighteenth century. From 1709 onwards, named editors standardized the copy and thus prevented the reader from falling into the same kind of genuine error that readers of the Folios experienced. Consideration of this earlier reception history encourages a revision of editorial methodology, challenging the instinct to correct obvious error. Rather than ignoring or excising it, attending to error reveals a history of audience experience and participation that is quite different from the way we read present-day editions. Reading error demonstrates that the ideology of standardization creates 'correct', but also monochrome, readings, which were not the experience of the play as it was first read, nor as it was and is performed.

TEXTUAL ERRORS IN *THE COMEDY OF ERRORS*

The play centres on two sets of identical twins: the two Antipholuses and the two Dromios. After being separated from their twins in a shipwreck, Antipholus and his servant Dromio go to Ephesus to find them. The two sets of twins inhabit the same city space, which leads to a huge amount of mistaken identity. Adriana, for example, bars her husband, Antipholus of Ephesus, from his own house while she entertains his brother inside. Antipholus of Syracuse is claimed as a husband by a woman he has never seen before, is

hounded about a ring and a chain of which he has no knowledge, and his own servant seems determined not to have any idea what he is talking about. Dromio of Syracuse takes his master's gold and stows it safely at the Inn, but when Antipholus of Syracuse demands it back from the wrong Dromio, Dromio of Ephesus cannot produce it and receives a beating for theft.[8] Every single character, from the kitchen servant Nell, to Doctor Pinch the schoolmaster, to the Duke of Ephesus, is drawn into the world of mistake. A sense of madness settles on the play by the fourth act, leading the Duke to declare of his citizens: 'I think you all have drunk of Circe's cup' (5.1.271).

The huge amount of farcical mistakes is entailed by a more tragic sense of the loss of identity. Antipholus of Syracuse quests for his lost twin brother and mother:

> I to the world am like a drop of water
> That in the ocean seeks another drop,
> Who, falling there to find his fellow forth,
> Unseen, inquisitive, confounds himself.
> So I, to find a mother and a brother,
> In quest of them, unhappy, lose myself.
>
> (1.2.35–40)

Antipholus almost wilfully loses his self. Yet the extraordinary ways in which his identity will be wracked, shaken and effaced by the play surpass anything he imagines for himself. From the beginning, the identity of the twins is perilous because of their similarity. Egeon describes his sons as 'the one

---

[6] John Jowett, 'Shakespeare and the kingdom of error', in *The New Oxford Shakespeare: Critical Reference Edition*, ed. Gary Taylor, John Jowett, Terri Bourus and Gabriel Egan, 2 vols. (Oxford, 2017), vol. 1, pp. xlix–lxiv, esp. p. xlix. This is despite the fact that the most common type of readers' marks in early modern printed playbooks are 'sporadic corrections in the main body of the dramatic text', as Sonia Massai notes in *Shakespeare and the Rise of the Editor* (Cambridge, 2007), p. 14.

[7] For a justification of this term to describe the ways in which readers marked books, see Claire Bourne, 'Marking Shakespeare', *Shakespeare* 13.4 (2017), 367–86, pp. 367–8.

[8] 1.2.93 SD, *The Comedy of Errors*, in The Norton Shakespeare, ed. Stephen Greenblatt, 3rd edn (London and New York, 2016). All further references which are not Through Line Numbers (TLN) are to this edition and are given in the text.

so like the other / As could not be distinguished but by names' (1.1.51–2). Names are the *only* tool to distinguish between Antipholus of Ephesus and Antipholus of Syracuse, Dromio of Ephesus and Dromio of Syracuse, and this is how they are presented in modern editions: each twin is clearly distinguished through the standardization of their names. The problem is that Egeon's faith in the naming function is misplaced in the world of early print. While, today, clear speech prefixes are provided in modern editions, in the early printed texts these were not afforded to contemporary readers and they risked even greater loss of identity of the twins than the play intends.[9] Shakespeare mixes two sets of virtually indistinguishable twins with complex plot twists, and the audience's main task is simply to keep up. Yet the early printed text precipitates genuine, sustained confusion, distinct from the audience's temporary, comic uncertainties, which are always pleasurably corrected.

In the First Folio (F1), Antipholus of Syracuse is named 'Antipholis Erotes' or 'Antipholis Errotis' until the third act.[10] This is an error for 'Errans' or 'Erraticus', which identifies Antipholus as being in error not in the sense of being incorrect, but rather as a wanderer, as he is the twin who has travelled great distances to find his lost family.[11] F1 abbreviates 'Antipholus Errotis' (of Syracuse) to 'E.Ant.' in the speech prefix, in confusion with Antipholus of Ephesus who is also abbreviated as 'E.Anti' in Act 3, Scene 1.[12] Effectively, the only distinguishing feature is removed and both twins become 'E.Anti'. R. A. Foakes terms this a 'nice confusion': 'nice', perhaps, in the sense of coincidence, that in a play about muddled and mixed identity the twins effectively become the same person by mistake.[13] In Act 2, Scene 1, Antipholus of Ephesus is called 'Antipholis Sereptus' – 'Enter Adriana, wife to Antipholis Sereptus' – but thereafter 'Antipholus of Ephesus' (TLN 273, 617 and onwards). This is an error for 'Surreptus', referring to his being taken or stolen from his father in the shipwreck. In the speech prefixes in F1, the two Antipholuses are not usually distinguished from each other, their speech denoted only by some abbreviation of 'Antipholus'. It is not until late in the last act, when they are finally on

stage together, that they are unambiguously identified as 'S.Ant.' for Antipholus of Syracuse and 'E. Ant.' for Antipholus of Ephesus (TLN 1822, 1851).

The distinction between Ephesus/Syracuse Antipholuses that is in place by Act 3 appears earlier with the second pair of twins, the Dromios. When Dromio of Syracuse first enters, however, he is not distinguished from Dromio of Ephesus: 'Enter Antipholis Erotes, a Marchant, and Dromio' (TLN 162). In the speech prefixes, they are also fairly often left undistinguished, as 'Dromio'. Here is a brief glossary of the various names used in F1 stage directions and speech prefixes to address the Antipholus and Dromio twins:

Antipholus of Ephesus: 'Antipholis Sereptus'; 'E. Anti.'; 'E.An.'; 'Anti.'; 'E.Ant.'; 'Ant.'; 'Antipholus Ephes.'; 'Eph.Ant.'; 'Antipholus Ephes.'[14]
Antipholus of Syracuse: 'Antipholis Erotes'; 'Ant.'; 'Antipholis Errotis'; 'E.Ant.'; 'Antiph.'; 'An.'; 'Antip.'; 'Antipholus of Siracusia'; 'S.Anti.'; 'Anti.'; 'S.Ant.'[15]

---

[9] On the issues of editing Shakespeare's speech prefixes, see Leah S. Marcus, 'Editing Shakespeare in a postmodern age', in *A Concise Companion to Shakespeare and the Text*, ed. Andrew R. Murphy (Oxford, 2007), pp. 128–44; Randall McLeod, 'What's the bastard's name?' *Shakespeare's Speech-Headings*, ed. George Walton Williams (Newark, 1997), pp. 133–209; Andrew Murphy, '"Tish ill done": *Henry the Fift* and the politics of editing', in *Shakespeare and Ireland: History, Politics, Culture*, ed. Mark Thornton Burnett and Ramona Wray (Basingstoke, 1997), pp. 213–34; Margreta de Grazia and Peter Stallybrass, 'The materiality of the Shakespearean text', *Shakespeare Quarterly* 44.3 (1993), 255–83; Fredson Bowers, 'Foul papers, Compositor B, and the speech-prefixes of "All's Well That Ends Well"', *Studies in Bibliography* 32 (1979), 60–81.

[10] For a discussion of the origin of these errors, see Paul Werstine, '"Foul papers" and "prompt-books": printer's copy for Shakespeare's "Comedy of Errors"', *Studies in Bibliography* 41 (1988), 232–46.

[11] See R. A. Foakes, 'Introduction', in William Shakespeare, *The Comedy of Errors*, ed. R. A. Foakes (London, 1962), p. xii.

[12] TLN 409 and TLN 619.   [13] Foakes, 'Introduction', p. xii.

[14] TLN 273; TLN 619; TLN 641; TLN 644; TLN 662; TLN 665; TLN 995; TLN 1005; TLN 1280.

[15] TLN 162; TLN 171; TLN 394; TLN 409; TLN 421; TLN 484; TLN 542; TLN 797; TLN 815; TLN 875; TLN 1448.

Dromio of Ephesus: 'Dromio of Ephesus'; 'E.Dro.'; 'Dromio Ep.'; 'Dromio Eph.' 'E.Dr.'; 'Dro.'; 'E. Dromio of Ephesus.'; 'E.Dromio.'; 'E.D.'[16]

Dromio of Syracuse: 'Dromio'; 'Dro.'; 'Dromio Siracusia'; 'S.Dro.'; 'S.Dr.'; 'S.Dromio.'; 'Dromio. Sir.'; 'Dromio Sirac.'; 'S.Drom.'[17]

Other similar errors or confusions exist in the play. In Act 2, Scene 2, the Dromio-servant enters but, instead of being identified alongside his master, Antipholus Errotis, as a wanderer, his epithet is given as 'Siracuſia', breaking his association with Antipholus and emphasizing his existence not as a wanderer, but instead as a foreigner (TLN 401). We are presented with a puzzling arrangement whereby the master and servant are differentiated by their names rather than being drawn together, with one being 'E.Anti' and the other 'S.Dro'. Here, the specifications of the stage directions are confusing rather than just absent. They distinguish Antipholus but not Dromio: 'Enter Antipholus Ephes. Dromio from the Courtizans' (TLN 995). When Dromio speaks, his speech prefix is only given as 'Dro.', whereas when his counterpart enters in the same scene, he is identified in the heading by both the place from which he returns ('the Bay', matching 'the Courtizans') and 'Sira' for Syracuse, his place of origin.[18] At Act 5, Scene 1, the F1 stage direction states: 'Enter Antipholus and Dromio againe' and Antipholus' speech is prefixed only by 'Ant.' (TLN 1473, 1487). 'Again' could refer back to the previous act and scene, but it is not necessarily clear, especially in a play dominated by many entrances and exits which generate extra possibility for confusion.

In modern editions, the twins are always distinguished in a standardized, repetitive form, and these small, silent changes are justified in that they eradicate the possibility of textual confusion. The Folio's system of signification is more complex, relying on the reader to refer back to the character's entrance or previous scene to determine whether the character is of Ephesus or Syracuse. In F1, of the 170 speech prefixes belonging to any of the four Antipholuses or Dromios, 69 of them specify in some way which twin is being referred to – for example 'E.Dro.' or 'Syr.An.' – whereas 109

appear in some form similar to 'Dro.' or 'Ant.'. This means that 64 per cent of speech prefixes attached to the twins fail to distinguish one from another, and therefore they either rely on other means to do so or leave the reader uncertain.

The play's textual shortcomings do not just concern the twins. In both the stage directions and speech prefixes, Egeon, the father of the Antipholus brothers, is never called by his proper name. Both times he enters, he is 'Merchant of Siracusa' (TLN 2, 1599). In the speech prefixes, he is 'Marchant', 'Mer.' or 'Merch', 'Mar. Fat.' (Marchant Father) and, in the last scene, 'Fa.' or 'Fath.'.[19] Two other minor characters are not distinguished from each other and could also be mistaken for Egeon. Both of these enter as 'Merchant' (TLN 982) or 'Marchant' (TLN 4), one appearing with speech prefixes in Act 1 as 'Mer.' (TLN 163) or 'E. Mar.' (TLN 187), the second in Acts 3 and 4, with the speech prefix 'Mar.'.[20] The character most commonly known as 'Luce' and referred to as such in the speech prefixes and stage directions is called 'Dowsabell' (TLN 1099) and 'Nell' (TLN 900) by other characters. Finally, Luciana's name also appears as 'Iulia.' and 'Iuliana' (TLN 786, 787). In F1, at Act 2, Scene 1, Luciana is given the speech prefix 'Luc.', but this has to be shared with another entirely different character (TLN 278 onwards). In Act 3, Scene 1, Luce the Kitchen Maid is given the speech prefix 'Luce', but in the next scene, Juliana's abbreviated speech prefix is again given as 'Luc.' (TLN 840 onwards), rendering the speech prefixes between Luciana and Luce puzzlingly similar.

The two sets of identical twins, the Dromios and Antipholuses, are dramatic tools to encourage confusion. In the source text, Plautus' *Menaechmi*, there is only one pair of twins, which Shakespeare doubles. He also reduces distinctions between them:

---

[16] TLN 205; TLN 208; TLN 260; TLN 218; TLN 347; TLN 352; TLN 1665; TLN 1786; TLN 1909.

[17] TLN 163; TLN 179; TLN 401; TLN 408; TLN 419; TLN 1098; TLN 1195; TLN 1441; TLN 1823.

[18] TLN 1073, 995. [19] TLN 30, 35, 101, 127, 160, 1671.

[20] TLN 982, 1038, 1045, 1056, 1467, 1472, 1488, 1490, 1496, 1587, 1593, 1736.

Shakespeare's twins hold more equal roles than the *Menaechmi*, with similar-length speaking parts and equal emphasis given to each of the four characters.[21] Their similarity is effected by their greater degree of physical resemblance, making it harder for the audience to tell them apart. Shakespeare constructs the matching physicality of the Dromios, almost as if they share one body. When Luce mistakes Dromio of Syracuse for her lover, she is able to describe him down to the smallest detail. Dromio says, she 'told me what privy marks I had about me – as the mark of my shoulder, the mole in my neck, the great wart on my left arm – that I, amazed, ran from her as a witch' (3.2.146–9). Luce holds an intricate knowledge of his body because his twin carries exactly the same features. Shakespeare demonstrates that his twins are exactly the same physically, that they are the same person in all but the name of their city of origin, yet even naming confounds rather than distinguishes the twins.

Previous textual scholars have narrativized this problem. R. B. McKerrow argues: 'The names by which the characters are indicated, instead of being the same throughout, frequently depend, much as they do in a novel, on the progress of the story.'[22] For McKerrow, they are made to fit into the story, to contribute to the meaning that is constructed or read into the text. He argues that, for example, Egeon first enters as the 'Merchant of Siracusa', which is then shortened to 'Merchant'. In the next scene, a different merchant appears, and another in Act 4, Scene 1, identified as 'Mar.', 'E. Mar.' or 'Mer.' In Act 5, Scene 1, Egeon enters and recognizes his sons while this last Merchant is on stage. McKerrow claims that, as his name is in use by another character, Egeon becomes first 'Mar. Fat.' (Merchant Father) 'and later simply "Father"'.[23] But this is not quite accurate: Egeon becomes variously 'Fa.', 'Fat.', 'Fath.' or 'Father' towards the end of the scene, and there seems to be no reason for these changes.[24] McKerrow's point is that Egeon's identity changes from being a merchant to discovering his lost sons and becoming a father, yet the more complex types of inconsistency between the Antipholuses' and Dromios' names disables such straightforward conclusions. Rather than aiding understanding, as

McKerrow argues, the print errors concerning the twins' names render the play at least partially opaque. Coincidentally or not, this set of printing errors tips the reader even closer to potential confusion, but, for approximately three centuries, typographic standardization has prevented this readerly experience.

READER'S MISTAKES

There are a significant number of copies of the First to Fourth Folios in which *The Comedy of Errors* is marked by readerly confusion. Seventeenth- to early-eighteenth-century readers perhaps became frustrated with the text and attempted to correct it, or tried to sort out their own confusion by picking up their pen. Even more interestingly, their attempts to correct the text often generate more error. In her recent work on the First Folio, Emma Smith argues that, of the textual problems in the First Folio *Errors*, 'no other extant copy suggest[s] that this was a problem to early readers'.[25] Yet the Folio owned by Lucy Hutchinson, or at least her family, demonstrates that this is not the case (STC 22273 Fo. 1 no.

---

[21] As Foakes points out, Menaechmus of Epidamnum (who corresponds to Antipholus of Ephesus) is more central dramatically than his twin brother, whereas Shakespeare gives his Antipholus of Syracuse more prominence, including nearly 100 lines more dialogue than his brother. Foakes, 'Introduction', p. xxv. Plautus focuses the action of the *Menaechmi* on the twin in his home town, whilst the other twin orbits around him, whereas Shakespeare reverses this feature, focusing on the wandering, lost twin, emphasizing his being in error: Titus Maccius Plautus, *Plautus – Four Comedies*, ed. Erich Segal (Oxford, 2016).

[22] R. B. McKerrow, 'A suggestion regarding Shakespeare's manuscripts', *Review of English Studies* 11 (1935), 459–65, esp. p. 460.

[23] McKerrow, 'A suggestion', p. 461.

[24] TLN 1762, 1766, 1771, 1778, 1783, 1785, 1788, 1801, 1838.

[25] Emma Smith, *Shakespeare's First Folio: Four Centuries of an Iconic Book* (Oxford, 2016), p. 241. On Shakespeare and the history of reading, see: Jean-Christophe Mayer, *Shakespeare's Early Readers: A Cultural History from 1590 to 1800* (Cambridge, 2018); Jean-Christophe Mayer, 'Annotating and transcribing for the theatre: Shakespeare's early modern reader–revisers at work', in *Shakespeare and Textual Studies*, ed. Margaret Jane Kidnie and Sonia Massai (Cambridge, 2015), pp. 163–76; and Bourne, 'Marking Shakespeare'.

2 First Folio, STC 22273 Fo. 1 no. 54, from the Folger Shakespeare Library, p. 99 showing the manuscript addition of 'E' to 'S.Drom.' at the top of the page. By permission of the Folger Shakespeare Library.

54, West 112). The annotator in this copy uses 'E' or 'S' to specify the twins, adding 'E' next to the unspecified 'Dro.' on p. 93, or writing two 'S:'s above 'Enter Antipholus and Dromio againe', to clarify that these are both 'of Syracuse' (p. 96). Yet the accuracy of the corrections seems difficult to maintain. On p. 99, the reader adds an 'E' to 'S.Drom.' (Figure 2). Dromio's speech is a continuation from the previous column and it is in fact still 'S.Drom.' who is speaking. The reader may have thought this was stichomythia, which the Dromios elsewhere employ, and it was now Dromio of Ephesus's turn to speak. The reader's error is not corrected, and instead stands as a small, almost unnoticeable mark of slippery, faulty interpretation. Their concern to correct the text does not just focus on the twins but also on the first and second Merchant, and Luciana, easily mistaken with the other character 'Luce'.[26] On p. 91, for example, the reader crossed out the misleading 'Iuliana', which should refer to Luciana. They added 'Luciana' above, as well as a large capital 'L' to the first speech prefix. Attention to copies not just of F1 but of F2–4 reveals other readers attending to

these same textual problems, illuminating patterns of confusion.

Lewis Theobald made annotations throughout his second Folio copy, some of which are signed 'L. T.' (STC 22274 Fo. 2 no. 20). He struggled to distinguish the twins and took up his pen to try to order the text. On p. 86, the stage direction announces 'Enter Antipholis, Erotes' while the subsequent speech prefixes just use 'Ant.'. Theobald clarifies the stage direction by adding 'of Siracuse' (Figure 3). Another eighteenth-century reader also found 'Erotes' confusing and successfully corrected it. A Second Folio (1632) in the Bodleian Library (Arch G c 9) contains annotations by two hands.[27] The

[26] On other types of 'corrections' in Shakespeare, see Anthony James West, 'Correcting the First Folio's table of contents', *Papers of the Bibliographical Society of America* 108.2 (2014), 238–42.
[27] For discussion of this copy, see Noriko Sumimoto, 'Updating Folios: readers' reconfigurations and customisations of Shakespeare', *Early Modern Literary Studies* special issue 21 (2013) at https://extra.shu.ac.uk/emls/si-21/07-Sumimoto_Updating%20Folios.htm.

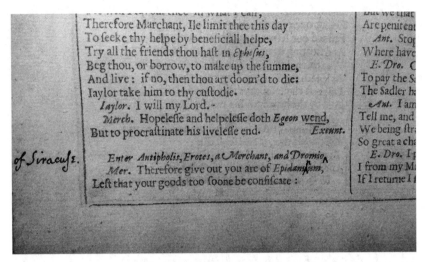

3 STC 22274 Fo. 2 no. 20, Second Folio, from the Folger Shakespeare Library, p. 86, showing Lewis Theobald's addition 'of Syracuse' to correct 'Antipholis, Erotes'. By permission of the Folger Shakespeare Library.

marginal notes are believed to belong to John Prater, who owned the book at least from 1698 to 1709. The copy also belonged to Edmund Malone (1741–1812), but it is not known when the book changed ownership. Prater's marginal notes throughout the copy are concerned chiefly with stage directions. The only correction in the play concerns the ambiguity between the Antipholi. On p. 88, the stage direction instructs: 'Enter Antipolis Erotes' and, like Theobald, Prater has carefully written next to it 'of Syracuse' (2.1, TLN 162) (Figure 4). Both Folios represent separate readers struggling with the insufficiencies and mistakes of the text, which present enough of a difficulty for them to record the same written correction.

In the Bodleian copy, the emendations and corrections are only conceived of as additions; there are no erasures. The final page of the play (p. 99) has a pasted-in rectangle of paper over the tailpiece giving a list of characters, and similar pastings can be found at the end of other plays (Figure 5). These additions distinguish the characters, a particularly useful inclusion for a reader of *Errors*, demonstrating a desire to straighten out the confusion of the twinned twins. As the Antipholuses appear in the play under two different names, a reader-reviser

might have chosen to designate them according to the single, more common designation of 'Ephesus' or 'Syracuse'. Yet this inclusive annotator gives them as: 'Antipholis Sereptis of Syracuse' and 'Antipholis Erotas of Ephesus', using two descriptors in an attempt to integrate both printed names, exemplifying careful if long-winded textual fidelity. Nevertheless, where this character list succeeds in identifying and separating the twins, it moves into opacity by doubling other characters. The same hand and ink lists Doctor Pinch twice, only one line apart – first as 'Pinch A Scoolmaster' then 'Dr Pinch a Scool Mast: & a Conjurer'. Similarly, the Abbess Emilia is first given as 'Aemilia Wife to Aegeon an Abbiss at Ephesus', and two lines later as 'Emelia an Abbess'. The Jailer, who silently holds custody of Egeon in the opening scene, appears first as 'Jayler. headsman', then, in a line opposite, 'Jalor Officers & other Attend^{ts}'. These repetitions make the number of characters unclear. They are curious because their proximity to each other must surely have been obvious to the annotator, yet they were included, despite undermining the aim to order the characters.

In a Fourth Folio (Arch. G. c.13) held in the Bodleian Library, an eighteenth-century hand has made a large amount of emendations: crossing out,

Since that my beautie cannot pleafe his eie,
Ile weepe (what's left) away and weeping die.
Luc. How manie fond fooles ferve mad Iealoufie?

Exeunt.

Enter Antipolis Erotes. of Syracuse

Ant. The gold I gave to *Dromio* is laid up
Safe at the *Centaur*, and the heedfull flave
Is wandred forth in care to feeke me out
By computation and mine hofts report.
I could not fpeake with *Dromio*, fince at firft
I fent him from the Mart: fee here he comes.

Enter Dromio Siracufan.

How now fir, is your merrie humor alter'd?
As you love ftrokes, fo jeft with me againe:
You know no *Centaur*? you receiv'd no gold?
Your miftris fent to have me home to dinner?
My houfe was at the *Phœnix*? Waft thou mad,
That thus fo madlie thou didft anfwere me?
  S. Dro. What anfwer fir? when fpake I fuch a word?
  E. Ant. Even now, even here, not halfe an houre fince.
  S. Dro. I did not fee you fince you fent me hence
Home to the *Centaur* with the gold you gave me?
  Ant. Villaine, thou didft denie the golds receit,
And toldft me of a Miftris, and a dinner.
For which I hope thou feltft I was difpleas'd.
  S. Dro. I am glad to fee you in this merrie veine,
What meanes this jeft, I pray you Mafter tell me?
  Ant. Yea, do'ft thou jeere and flowt me in the teeth?
Thinkft I jeft? hold, take thou that, and that. *Beats Dro.*
  S. Dr. Hold fir, for Gods fake, now your jeft is earneft,

4 Arch. G. c.9. Second Folio, Bodleian Library, University of Oxford, p. 88, showing manuscript addition 'of Syracuse' next to 'Enter Antipolis Erotes'. By permission of the Bodleian Library.

replacing words, suggesting alterations, making marginal notes, inserting asterisks, dividing scenes, adding settings, giving stage directions in square brackets, circling text for omission and adding occasional longer explanations in the bottom margin.[28] Clarification of the twins was clearly important to the reader, as, on p. 82, there are extensive additions to clarify the 'Ant.' speech prefixes by adding 'S' seven times over. On p. 77, the reader has emended 'Enter Antipholus, Erotes', by crossing out 'Erotes' and interlining 'of Syracuse' above. Similarly, on p. 79, where the direction given is 'Enter

Antipholus Erotes', 'Erotes' is crossed out and 'of Syracuse' is written just to the right. The speech prefixes, however, are left unregularized and so, thirteen lines later, the printed 'E. Ant' no longer corresponds to the stage direction. Following the corrections which remove 'Sereptus' and 'Erotes', 'E.Ant.' can now only refer to Antipholus of

[28] William Shakespeare, *Mr. William Shakespear's comedies, histories, and tragedies published according to the true original copies* (London, 1685).

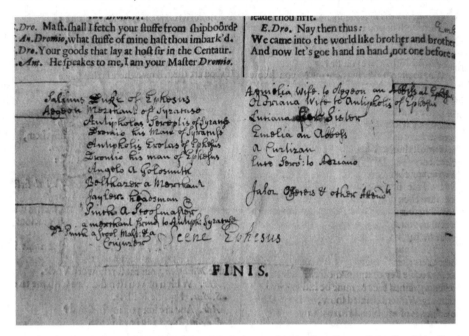

5 Arch. G. c.9. Second Folio, Bodleian Library, University of Oxford, p. 99, showing the rather confusing list of roles. By permission of the Bodleian Library.

Ephesus – the wrong twin. On p. 78, at the beginning of Act 2, to the stage direction '*Enter* Adriana, *wife* to Antipholis Sereptus, *with* Luciana, *her Sister*' has been added: 'The House of Antipholis of Ephesus'. The failure to emend 'Sereptus' to 'Ephesus' distances Adriana from her husband through their designators of place, rather than being brought closer to him, disturbing swift readerly comprehension. While these interventions seek to clarify the text, emendation risks, and potentially even increases, misunderstanding.

THEATRICAL ERROR

The evidence left in these copies of the First to Fourth Folios suggests various readers' confusion and their attempted correction in response. While readerly marks are fleeting and not every moment of the struggle to follow the text is recorded, the interventions follow a pattern, with the same problems being addressed.[29] Smith argues, however, that the inconsistent and confusing speech prefixes 'only [emerge] as an ambiguity when using the Folio as a performance text'.[30] This is based on the assumption that texts designed for or coming from the theatre must demonstrate a higher level of accuracy as a working text, whereas, implicitly, texts created for reading can tolerate a higher level of mistake. As R. B. McKerrow argues, 'a copy intended for use in the theatre would surely, of necessity, be accurate and unambiguous in the matter of the character-names'.[31] Not only do the First to Fourth Folios surveyed above suggest that the textual errors were

---

[29] Bourne argues, for attention to readers' marks in Shakespeare, that they 'can teach us about the idiosyncrasies of some (sometimes identifiable) early modern readers and, when studied across large corpora, help crystallize the range of possible ways that early play-readers in general could and did interact with printed books by Shakespeare and his contemporaries': 'Marking Shakespeare', p. 368.

[30] Smith, *Shakespeare's First Folio*, p. 241.

[31] McKerrow, 'A suggestion', p. 464. This idea has been highly influential, and W. W. Greg follows McKerrow's reasoning in arguing that a manuscript prepared for the prompter will have unambiguous character designations: W. W. Greg, *The Shakespeare First Folio* (Oxford, 1955), p. 114.

a problem for non-performance reading, inspection of F1–4 performance copies fall short of the expected textual rectitude for a reliable guide to performance.

The first example comes from the 'Nursery' promptbooks. These are rare examples from Restoration-era theatre.[32] *A Midsummer Night's Dream* and *The Comedy of Errors* were separated from F1 and bound individually to make them into manageable theatrical scripts, both held in Edinburgh University Library (EUL JY 439 and 438). The names written into the Nursery *Errors* are identifiable as members of one of the two theatre companies licensed by Charles II on his restoration to the monarchy.[33] Evans suggests that the text may have been used by an offshoot of the King's Company, the Nursery Company of younger players, or possibly for touring, in Norwich and elsewhere.[34] In this copy, the many annotations throughout the play enforce the distinctions between the Antipholus brothers that only become fully apparent in the final act. In the stage directions, one of the Antipholuses is linked with 'Seracuse' or some abbreviation of it, and the other with 'Ephesus'. The speech prefixes 'S' or 'E' are appended to every instance of the Antipholuses to distinguish them, while the Dromios are mainly neglected and left ambiguous. The received critical argument is that the text must clearly specify which twin is which in order for the prompter to give correct instruction for the stage, yet the three theatrical texts of the Folio *Errors* which survive from the later seventeenth century all display an inability to correct error.

In the Nursery copy, an annotator is shown to be in complete confusion about which twin is which, but nevertheless demonstrates a desire to separate them. At the opening stage direction of Act 1, Scene 2, an annotator (whom Evans describes as 'Hand 1') has deleted 'Erotes', adds 'Seracuse' above, and placed 'Se' after 'Dromio'.[35] This clears up the imprecise stage direction by specifying, as present-day editors do, 'Ephesus' or 'Seracuse' to either Dromio or Antipholus. Yet, throughout the rest of Act 1, Scene 2, the same hand added an 'E:' to all the speech prefixes of Antipholus, presumably for 'Erotes', reinstating the confusion they had just

clarified. Realizing that 'E:' was ambiguous and would be confused with 'Ephesus', Hand 1 deleted 'E:' and added 'S', presumably for 'Syracuse'. This occurs at lines 9, 19, 30, 33, 53, 58, 68, 72, 77, 87, 91, 95.[36] In the opening stage direction of Act 2, Scene 2, Hand 1 substitutes 'Errotis.' with 'Seracus:'. Again, Hand 1 has added 'E:' to the prefixes of all the speeches of Antipholus (of Syracuse) speeches, then, again realizing the mistake, they either wrote 'S' over 'E:', or deleted 'E:' and wrote 'S' next to it. This textual change is significant and occurs twenty-two times.[37]

At the opening stage direction of Act 3, Scene 1, Hand 1 places 'Sera' above 'Ephesus', which again is incorrect.[38] At some point, the mistake is realized and 'Sera' is crossed out. From line 25, Hand 1 adds 'E:' to the speech prefix 'Anti.', referring to Ephesus, adopting a different means of distinguishing the twins – one which is used today, where 'E' refers to Ephesus and 'S' to Syracuse.[39] The opening stage direction of Act 3, Scene 2, demonstrates that the annotator was thoroughly lost in the play.

---

[32] See *Shakespearean Prompt-books of the Seventeenth Century*, ed. G. Blakemore Evans, 8 vols. (Charlottesville, 1964). vol. 3; online edition available, see: http://bsuva.org/bsuva/promptbook/ShaComP.html.

[33] Smith, *Shakespeare's First Folio*, p. 241. Smith argues that 'Mr Biggs (who played Antipholus of Ephesus) and Mr Disney (his Syracusan twin), Mrs Cooke, who played Luciana, and Mr and Mrs Coysh (Dromio of Ephesus and Adriana) were all members of Thomas Killigrew's King's Company performing at Drury Lane in London in the 1660s and 1670s.'

[34] *Shakespearean Prompt-books of the Seventeenth Century*, ed. Evans, vol. 3.1, p. 3.

[35] *Shakespearean Prompt-books of the Seventeenth Century*, ed. Evans, vol. 3.2, p. 89. For a digitization, see: http://bsuva.org/bsuva/promptbook/images/ce12open.jpg. For all images, see: http://bsuva.org/bsuva/promptbook/images.

[36] See Evans, http://bsuva.org/bsuva/promptbook/images/ce-p88a.jpg.

[37] At lines 1, 14, 17, 22, 41, 43, 46, 51, 54, 58, 60, 62, 65, 149, 157, 162, 165, 168, 183, 198, 200, 214. See http://bsuva.org/bsuva/promptbook/images/ce-p88b.jpg.

[38] See *Shakespearean Prompt-books of the Seventeenth Century*, ed. Evans, vol. 3: http://bsuva.org/bsuva/promptbook/images/ce-p90.jpg.

[39] This occurs another twelve times. See lines 27, 40, 42, 54, 57, 59, 63, 69, 73, 80, 84, 123.

'Siracusia' is deleted and Hand 1 adds 'Ephe:' above, but then crosses this through and writes in 'Sera:'. Similarly, in the stage direction at 4.1.13, Hand 1 makes a deletion which has to be restored, crossing out 'Ephes.' and writing 'Serac.' above – then, realizing the error, deletes 'Serac.'.[40]

At this point in the penultimate act, the annotator has spent most of the play in confusion over the Antipholus twins, and a large portion of the annotations consists in trying, and failing, to distinguish them.[41] Hand 1 continues to attempt to separate them out by adding 'S:' or 'E:' not just on a scattering of lines, assuming another reader would make a straightforward deduction, but at every instance where this character speaks. The frequency of this type of mark seems inconsistent with the fact that this annotator ended up in such confusion, where the efforts to divide the twins eventuate in the state that they were meant to guard against.

The annotations in this promptbook represent a process of learning and understanding as a confused annotator makes their way through the text, trying and failing to straighten it out, correcting things that are not wrong and introducing further obfuscation. It shows a reader uncertain about their own emendations, re-reading them and making another round of corrections. Whereas Smith claims that the theatrical text requires a clear ordering for performance, Paul Werstine cites this text as evidence to the contrary, arguing that, of the three theatrical texts of the Folio *Errors* which survive from the later seventeenth century, 'in one way or another, all three theatrical texts compound such confusions'.[42] It may be that the Nursery copy is an incomplete attempt at making sense of the play theatrically. As Tiffany Stern reminds us, we should 'distrust the unity and completion of the playscript', emphasizing the 'patchiness' of early modern plays.[43] Nevertheless, the record we are left with shows that being in error, or at least uncertainty, was one of the defining experiences of encountering the play.

The Douai Manuscript (MS 787) is another theatrically based text of *Errors* from the seventeenth century which carries significant annotation and emendation, and has a troubled relation with error correction. Around 1694–5, six Shakespearian plays were copied separately before being bound together around 1697–9.[44] These plays originate from one of the English Roman Catholic foundations at Douai, Northern France, and are believed to be transcribed from the Second Folio, or from manuscripts copied from it.[45] It is thought that the purpose of the plays was to use 'dramatic exercises' to test the students. Evans argues that there are 'numerous readings in which the Douai transcripts anticipate the emendations proposed by the later eighteenth- and nineteenth-century editors of

40 See *Shakespearean Prompt-books of the Seventeenth Century*, ed. Evans, vol. 3, http://bsuva.org/bsuva/promptbook/images/ce-p92.jpg.

41 See also 3.2.54, where Hand 1 prefixes the F speech-head 'Ant.' with 'S:' – also at lines 56, 58, 60, 66, 71, 75, 79, 84, 90, 95, 103, 107, 110, 114, 118, 122, 125, 128, 133, 136, 142, 152, 161, 170, 174, 176, 181, 184 (http://bsuva.org/bsuva/promptbook/images/ce-p92.jpg); 4.1.15, where Hand 1 prefixes the F speech-head 'Ant.' with 'E:' – also at lines 34, 41, 43, 48, 54, 57, 62, 64, 66, 74, 80, 93, 96, 100; 4.3.15, where Hand 1 prefixes the F speech-head 'Ant.' with 'S:' – also at lines 21, 29, 34, 42, 48, 50, 63, 66, 80, http://bsuva.org/bsuva/promptbook/images/ce-p94.jpg; 4.4.1 where Hand 1 prefixes the F speech-head 'An.' with 'E:'; also at lines 11, 13, 15, 17, 24, 27, 43, 47, 56, 61, 63, 71, 73, 75, 77, 79' 85, 90, 98, 104, 112, 127, 129, http://bsuva.org/bsuva/promptbook/images/ce-p95.jpg; and 5.1 23 where Hand 1 prefixes F speech-head 'Ant.' with 'S:', also at lines 25, 29, http://bsuva.org/bsuva/promptbook/images/ce-p96.jpg.

42 Paul Werstine, *Early Modern Playhouse Manuscripts* (Cambridge, 2013), p. 117.

43 Tiffany Stern, *Documents of Performance in Early Modern England* (Cambridge, 2009), pp. 4, 1.

44 See G. Blakemore Evans, 'The Douai Manuscript – six Shakespearean transcripts (1694–95)', *Philological Quarterly* 41 (1962), 158–72; and Ann-Mari Hedbäck, 'The Douai Manuscript reexamined', *Papers of the Bibliographical Society of America* 73.1 (1979), 1–18.

45 *Catalogue général des manuscrits des bibliothèques publiques*, vol. 6: *Manuscrits de la Bibliothèque de Douai*, ed. C. Dehaisnes (Paris, 1978), of the Douai Public Library states: 'Provient sans doute de l'un des couvents anglais de Douai' (pp. 477–8). Accordingly, Evans claims 'There cannot be any serious doubt, I believe, that the Douai transcripts were originally prepared for some kind of theatrical production, most probably of an amateur nature': Evans, 'The Douai Manuscript', p. 164.

Shakespeare'.[46] He points out forty-eight emendations that anticipate changes by later editors, such as Rowe, Capell, Pope, Malone and others, yet he does not mention a set of emendations, similar to those found in the Nursery copy, which pull in the opposite direction.

In the fifth act of *The Comedy of Errors*, the Douai Manuscript uses the following speech prefixes: 'M' for the Merchant of Ephesus; 'A:E' for Antipholis Erotes, i.e., Antipholus of Siracusia; 'D:E' for Dromio of Ephesus; 'D:S' for Dromio of Siracusia; 'A:S' for Antipholus Sereptus, i.e., Antipholus of Ephesus; and 'M:S' for Merchant of Siracusia, i.e., Egeon. The main source of confusion of the twins' speech prefixes in the Folio comes from the introduction of 'Erotes' and 'Sereptus'. When transcribing the play, the scribe chose to increase the usage of these alternative designators and applied them unevenly to the twins: to the Antipholuses but not the Dromios. This has the effect of removing the point of place around which the characters can be organized, as each couple of an Antipholus and Dromio who come from the same place and understand each other fully are distinguished by different referents, 'Erotes' or 'Siracusia'. The scribe uses 'S' to designate the Syracusan Dromio, Egeon and the Ephesian Antipholuses; they use 'E' for the Ephesian Dromio and the Syracusan Antipholis. As Werstine argues, this 'theatrical text introduces complication that exceeds anything to be found in the F version', refuting the idea that a performance text requires greater rectitude and clarity.[47] In its inflation of identity confusion, the Douai Manuscript demonstrates a way of reading with error, of coping with confusion even in performance, and resists the modern simplification of the twins into either Ephesus or Syracuse by permitting the multiple speech prefixes to remain. It shows a pre-existing alternative to the eighteenth-century ideals of error eradication: of greater toleration towards inconsistency and ambiguity.

Despite these textual states, which would surely hamper performance, critics have tended to emphasize the ways in which layers of annotation and emendation of a copy are linked to the preparation of a play for performance. Arthur Marotti and Laura Estill argue of the Douai Manuscript that 'Many of the changes made to the plays in these manuscripts would have been helpful for performance.'[48] The additions of several stage directions, such as 'gives him mony' (1.2.8), may well have been helpful, but the unmentioned increase of ambiguous speech prefixes would not. Marotti, Estill and others perceive the manuscripts as encoding performance, and in many ways it seems correct to interpret the textual additions as instructions for either an intended or actual performance.[49] Yet Charles Shattuck warns of the perils of trusting promptbooks to lead us to a reliable record of performance. They 'chatter and exclaim about what we hardly need to know'; 'They tell lies, they are misleading and incomplete.'[50] In the Nursery and Douai texts, the annotations reveal less about the stage than about the revisers' misunderstanding. The available evidence shows error being wrestled with, compounded or simply ignored by prompters, scribes or annotators. Critics have tended to explain error straightforwardly, an impulse which fails to capture the messy reality and incorrigibility of *Errors*, and its afterlife.

The 'Smock Alley' promptbook shows the annotator/prompter getting confused in distinguishing the twins, specifically in remembering their separate characteristics. This is a copy of Shakespeare's Third Folio (1663–4) that was annotated for performances at Dublin's Smock Alley Theatre in the 1670s and

---

[46] Evans, 'The Douai Manuscript', p. 165.

[47] Werstine, *Early Modern Playhouse Manuscripts*, p. 118.

[48] Arthur Marotti and Laura Estill, 'Manuscript circulation', in *The Oxford Handbook of Shakespeare*, ed. Arthur F. Kinney (Oxford, 2012), pp. 53–70, esp. p. 64.

[49] Mayer invests the Douai text with a similar type of meaning – they 'allow us to catch a glimpse of how late seventeenth-century readers and amateur performers escaped from the constraints of print by moving back to a manuscript medium, which enabled them to give free rein to their creativity and shape Shakespeare's texts to their personal idea of how they should be performed': Mayer, 'Annotating and transcribing for the theatre', p. 171.

[50] Charles Shattuck, *The Shakespeare Promptbooks: A Descriptive Catalogue* (Urbana, 1965), p. 3.

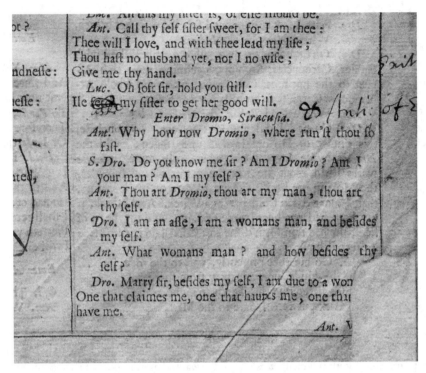

6 Smock Alley Promptbook, Third Folio, at Folger Shakespeare Library (Prompt 3d Folio Com. Err. Smock Alley), p. 91, showing a manuscript intervention which exits Antipholus of Syracuse and exchanges him for Antipholus of Ephesus, with addition of 'Anti: of E'. By permission of the Folger Shakespeare Library.

1680s, held in the Folger Shakespeare Library (Prompt 3d Folio Com. Err. Smock Alley).[51] The annotator experiments with changing around the roles of the twins, enabled by the printed speech prefixes, the majority of which are imprecisely either 'Ant.' or 'Dro.' This first occurs in Act 3, Scene 2, where Luciana is in conversation with Antipholus of Syracuse. An annotator hovers an 'exit' next to Antipholus of Syracuse's speech. Presumably, Luciana exits at this point too, but this is left unspecified. In the Folios, Antipholus of Syracuse remains on stage for the rest of the scene, conversing with Dromio and Angelo, but in the Smock Alley promptbook Antipholus of Syracuse exits at line 70, exchanged for Antipholus of Ephesus (Figure 6). Antipholus of Ephesus and Dromio of Ephesus carry on the dialogue describing Luce the kitchen maid through to line 151. The scene sets up Antipholus asking questions about Luce, which

prompts Dromio's farcically exaggerated description of her. Antipholus asks 'What claim lays she to thee?', 'What is she?', 'What complexion is she of?' (3.2.84, 89, 102), but, given that Antipholus of Ephesus is Luce's master, it seems strange for him to be asking such uninformed questions.

The annotator exits Antipholus of Ephesus and re-enters Antipholus of Syracuse, who takes up the address to Dromio to 'Go hie thee presently, post to the rode' (TLN 937), restoring the Folio speech prefixes in the scene. Dromio's couplet to Antipholus, 'As from a Bear a man would run for

---

[51] Evans describes the Smock Alley promptbook to be 'of uncertain date but almost certainly before 1700': Evans, 'Introduction "The Comedy of Errors" First Folio', in *Shakespearean Prompt-books of the Seventeenth Century*, ed. Evans, vol. 3: http://bsuva.org/bsuva/promptbook/ShaComP.html.

life, | So flie I from her that would be my wife' (TLN 945), makes little sense to Antipholus of Syracuse who was not party to the previous conversation and would not understand that the 'Bear' refers to Luce, or why Dromio is fleeing. From his entrance at line 70, Dromio remains on stage throughout the Antipholuses' entrances and exits, but it is not specified what Dromio is supposed to make of them: is he to remain on stage in suspended animation? Or should these be separate scenes? If so, it would make two very short scenes: the first of seventy-one lines, with the main point being to discuss the 'claim' Luce has over Dromio, followed by another even shorter scene of forty lines which would lack a sense of purpose altogether. The aim of the prompter seems to be to increase the confusion by adding another exchange between Dromio of Syracuse and Antipholus of Ephesus who mistake each other for the other's twin. Evans describes these alterations as 'apparently quite senseless, rearrangements', where a different kind of confusion thus ensues as the dialogue fails to match up with the characters.[52]

The annotator's second change concerns the final scene, the only scene in the printed Folios where the twins are unequivocally distinguished according to both the plotline and the speech prefixes. In Act 5, Scene 2, Dromio of Syracuse says: 'There is a fat friend at your Masters house | That kitchin'd me for you to day at dinner: | She now shall be my sister, not my wife' (TLN 1906-8). The first two lines of Dromio of Syracuse's speech are reassigned to Dromio of Ephesus, while the third line remains with Dromio of Syracuse. The speech prefix 'S. Dro' is written over with an 'E', whilst hovering near the 'E. D.' is a large manuscript 'S:' (Figure 7). But the content is not interchangeable: Dromio of Syracuse declares that Nell, the kitchen maid whom they have both known sexually, 'shall be my sister, not my wife', which does not work if these lines are spoken by Dromio of Ephesus because Nell is to be his wife and not his sister. Reading and altering the play is a treacherous activity, which risks falling into different types of error. The minor confusions on which the play thrives can easily turn into major ones. Evans comments that 'this redistribution of the

dialogue makes nonsense, and I can only suppose that here (as in III.ii) Hand I has fallen victim to his own comedy of errors'.[53] Evans's reference to the reflexivity of error links the mistaken identity in the plot with textual error in printing, and we see its consequence as readerly mistake in this text. This 'comedy of errors' can in fact be identified as a pattern of reader response. The repeated interaction between textual and readerly error raises questions about editorial intervention: correcting error moves us much further away from the play as it was first experienced.

'THAT VAST CROP OF ERRORS'[54]

The eighteenth century saw the 'great editing tradition of Shakespeare's plays', with works published by Rowe (1709), Pope (1723-5, 1728), Theobald (1733), Hanmer (1743-4), Warburton (1747), Johnson (1765), Capell (1767-8), Johnson-Steevens (1773, 1778), Johnson-Steevens-Reed (1785) and Malone (1790).[55] These editors invented the idea that error was a problem in Shakespeare, arguing it was the most important issue in the text. The textual confusion and printing errors found in *Errors* were exactly the kind of accumulated mistakes that required urgent action. Rowe's primary reason to produce his new edition was 'to redeem him [Shakespeare] from the injuries of former impressions'.[56] He feared that a reader 'may still find

---

[52] Evans, 'Smock Alley "The Comedy of Errors" Third Folio Introduction', in *Shakespearean Prompt-books of the Seventeenth Century*, ed. Evans, vol. 8: http://bsuva.org/bsuva/prompt book/Sha8CEP.html#.

[53] Evans, 'Smock Alley "The Comedy of Errors" Third Folio Introduction'.

[54] Lewis Theobald, *Shakespeare Restored, or, A specimen of the Many Errors, as well Committed, as Unamended, by Mr. Pope* (London, 1726), p. i.

[55] Although Massai has recently challenged the idea of Nicholas Rowe's edition as a 'crucial watershed' by examining the editorial practices of 'annotating readers' pre-1709, the distinction is meaningful in terms of the turn towards error in Shakespeare's text by Rowe and subsequent editors, the like of which had not before been seen. See Massai, *Shakespeare and the Rise of the Editor*, p. 2.

[56] Nicholas Rowe, 'Dedication', in *The works of Mr. William Shakespear*, vol. 1 (London, 1709).

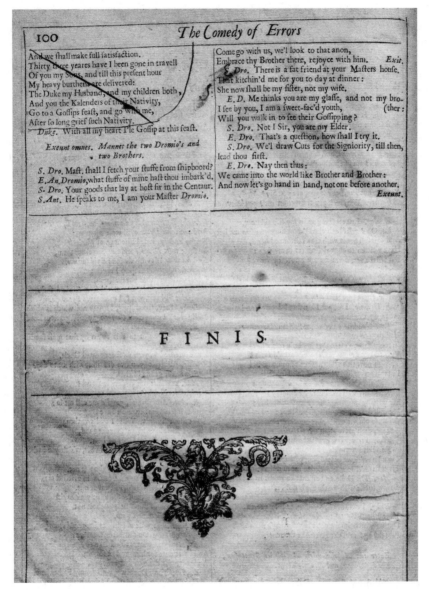

7 Smock Alley Promptbook, Third Folio, at Folger Shakespeare Library (Prompt 3d Folio Com. Err. Smock Alley), p. 100, showing manuscript changes which attempt to switch the two Dromios' dialogue. See the speech prefix 'S.Dro' is written over with an 'E', whilst hovering near 'E. D.' is a large manuscript 'S:'. By permission of the Folger Shakespeare Library.

some faults, but I hope they are mostly literal, and the errors of the press'.[57] His main intervention, as he describes it, was the correction of the errors in Shakespeare's text to reveal or return to 'the true reading'. Rowe's intervention in 1709 initiated the slow but steady standardization of the texts that proceeded through the centuries, and forms an important

---

[57] Rowe, 'Dedication'.

part of the editorial task today. Margreta de Grazia describes the history of Shakespearian textual criticism thus: 'Over the centuries and in the hands of a long succession of editors, editions of Shakespeare have come to conform to the standards of correctness regulating the printed word.'[58] One of the most fundamental tasks for an editor of Shakespeare today is the correction of error; John Jowett describes it as 'the most defining act of editing, the act that separates editing a text from copying a text'.[59] While the more complicated question of what to correct and how has varied considerably over the centuries, the impulse to correct as a legitimate editorial action became formalized during the eighteenth century, and is recognizable today.

Alexander Pope, the next editor of Shakespeare's drama following Rowe, perceived that error opposed beauty as well as rectitude, inspired by his idiosyncratic notions of taste. In his 1725 edition, he claimed that Shakespeare affords 'the most numerous, as well as most conspicuous instances, both of beauties and faults'.[60] His errors and the excellencies are constantly balanced: 'I cannot however mention some of the principal and characteristic excellencies, for which (notwithstanding his defects) he is justly and universally elevated' (p. ii). Whereas Rowe deflected the charge of error elsewhere, Pope is forthcoming in ascribing errors to Shakespeare: 'As to a wrong choice of the subject, a wrong conduct of the incidents, false thoughts, forced expressions etc. if these are not to be ascribed to the foresaid accidental reasons, they must be charged upon the Poet himself, and there is no help for it' (p. ix). Here, Pope's conception of error spreads from printing concerns to literary matters. Despite holding Shakespeare to account, he also lays the charge of error at the feet of the 'first publishers of his works', as well as 'the ignorance of the players, both as his actors, and as his editors' (p. xiv). He describes 'the excessive carelessness of the press: every page is so scandalously false spelled, and almost all the learned or unusual words so intolerably mangled', whereas 'had Shakespeare published his works himself ... we should not only be certain which are genuine but should find in those that are, the errors lessened by some

thousands' (p. xx). The claim of having identified grievous error, made by both Rowe and Pope, forms the justification for their own editions. Pope claims that he had returned Shakespeare to an imaginary state by making his errors 'vanish' (p. xxi), but in fact he relegates them to the bottom of the page.

Both Pope and Rowe ring-fence what they perceive as the rectitude of the text for Shakespeare, and attribute any other textual qualities they find wanting to external influence. Pope asks, 'how many faults may have been unjustly laid to his account from arbitrary additions, expunctions, transpositions of scenes and lines, confusion of characters and persons, wrong application of speeches, corruptions of innumerable passages by the ignorance and wrong corrections of 'em again by the impertinence of his first editors?' (p. xxi). By 1726, Lewis Theobald developed the rhetoric of error correction by taking direct aim at Pope's edition, rather than just the 'first editors'. In *Shakespeare Restored*, Theobald delivers a devastating critique of Pope's edition almost immediately upon its publication, setting out to expose 'the Many Errors, as well Committed, as Unamended, by Mr. Pope', and promising 'to restore the True Reading of Shakespeare'.[61] He declares that 'we have scarce any book in the English tongue more fertile of errors than the plays of Shakespeare' (p. i). He perceived his role as an editor to be 'rooting out that vast crop of errors, which has almost choked up his beauties' (p. i). Theobald's text is a dissection of many parts of various plays that pose some difficulty of understanding, which he alters with explanation. He identifies errors as: variants through collation with some but not all editions; 'false pointing', being what he sees as errors of punctuation; requiring 'conjectural emendation', where he alters the text

---

[58] Margreta De Grazia, *Shakespeare Verbatim: The Reproduction of Authenticity and the 1790 Apparatus* (Oxford, 1991), p. 18.
[59] Jowett, 'Shakespeare and the kingdom of error', p. xlix.
[60] Alexander Pope, 'Preface', in *The Works of Shakespear* (London, 1725), p. i.
[61] Theobald, title page, *Shakespeare Restored*.

in order to improve it. He defined the job of the editor as: 'wherever he finds the Reading suspected, manifestly corrupted, deficient in sense and unintelligible, he ought to exert every power and faculty of the mind to supply such a defect' (p. v). Theobald demonstrates the centrality of error to the beginnings of the editorial tradition of Shakespearian drama, and defines an attitude towards textual correction that still dominates today.

It was Rowe who first corrected the two confusing stage directions referring to 'Antipholus Erotes' printed in F1–4 (1.2.0, 2.2.0).[62] He removed 'Erotes' and added 'of Syracuse', which was followed from then on, with the exceptions of George Lyman Kittredge's 1936 edition, and the *Riverside Shakespeare*, where 'of Syracuse' is given in square brackets, after 'Erotes'.[63] Elsewhere, Rowe renders more precise the F1–4 stage direction that fails to distinguish which Dromio is which, specifying 'Dro.Eph.' (4.1.13). This correction is imitated by Capell, Johnson and Steevens, and Malone.[64] Rowe was the first to insert a *Dramatis Personae* list, which attempted to sort the confusion of names, introducing 'Antipholis *of* Ephesus' and 'Antipholis *of* Syracuse'.[65] Yet he did not produce the fully standardized play we would recognize today. He does not correct the F1–4 reference to 'Antipholis Sereptus' in the opening stage direction at Act 2, Scene 1. Instead, he removes this reference to Antipholus altogether, making the stage direction less clear. It is the next editor, Alexander Pope, who reinstates the reference and corrects it to 'Antipholis of Ephesus'.[66] At 2.2.14, where Antipholus of Syracuse is referred to as 'E. Ant.', in confusion with Antipholus of Ephesus, Rowe mediates the ambiguity by removing 'E.', leaving just 'Ant.'. This is followed through twelve editions by Pope, Theobald and up to Samuel Johnson, until Capell specified which Antipholus was which with the change to 'A.S.' for Antipholus of Syracuse.

Despite Rowe's reputation for standardization as the first editor of Shakespeare, recently challenged by Massai, it is Capell who regularizes all the speech prefixes from the beginning, using 'A.S' or 'D.S',

leaving no 'Ant.' or 'Dro.' unspecified, unlike Rowe. Finally, Malone, in his 1790, edition consistently presents them in a way that is more familiar to us, as 'S.Dro' or 'E.Ant.'. While Rowe instigated a process of standardization, for some printing ambiguities there was a joint effort to eradicate them. At 5.1.9, the F1 stage direction states: 'Enter Antipholus and Dromio againe'. Rowe makes this more precise, with: 'Enter Antipholis and Dromio of Syracuse', but it is Capell who is the first to distinguish them separately, as they are always today: '*Enter* Antiphilus Syracusan, *and* Dromio Syracusan'.[67] While Massai resists the dominance of 1709 as a crucial highpoint of editing, *The Comedy of Errors* demonstrates that editorial correction and standardization were in fact ongoing processes across the eighteenth century.[68]

Since then, no modern edition lets the various textual errors and ambiguities stand. The *Riverside Shakespeare* (1997) corrects the text but uses square brackets for 'Erotes' and 'Sereptus' to retain some F1 variants.[69] The ongoing and complex confusions created by the absent or misleading speech prefixes referring to the two sets of twins are

---

[62] At 2.2.0, this is spelled 'Antipholus Errotis' in F1 and 'Erotes' in F2–4.

[63] *The Complete Works of Shakespeare*, ed. George Lyman Kittredge (Boston, MA, 1936). The *New Oxford Shakespeare*, ed. Taylor et al., has 'Enter Antipholus erratus [of Syracuse]', which neither is faithful to F1 nor renders the text correct, but introduces a new descriptor to emphasize Antipholus' wandering state.

[64] Edward Capell, 'Dromio Ephesian', in *Mr William Shakespeare: his comedies, histories, and tragedies* (London, 1768), vol. 2, p. 35; Samuel Johnson and George Steevens, 'Dromio of Ephesus', in *The Plays of William Shakespeare: With the Corrections and Illustrations of Various Commentators* (London, 1773), vol. 2, p. 188; and Edmond Malone, 'Dromio of Ephesus', in *The plays and poems of William Shakespeare* (London, 1790), p. 172.

[65] Rowe, *The works of Mr. William Shakespear*, p. 272.

[66] Pope, *The Works of Shakespear*, p. 189.

[67] Rowe, *The works of Mr. William Shakespear*, p. 309; Capell, *Mr William Shakespeare*, p. 50.

[68] Massai, *Shakespeare and the Rise of the Editor*, pp. 1–10.

[69] William Shakespeare, 'The Comedy of Errors', in *The Riverside Shakespeare*, 2nd edn, ed. G. Blakemore Evans and J. J. M. Tobin (Boston, MA, 1997), pp. 111–37.

silently emended. Even the *Variorum Shakespeare* (2011) does not record emendations to the speech prefixes – neither the places where F1–4 leave 'An.' or 'Dro.' repeatedly unspecified, nor where the speech prefixes are actively misleading, as in the 'E. Ant' example which refers to the wrong twin.[70] Similarly, the *Oxford Shakespeare* individual edition (2002) does not mark this emendation, despite Charles Whitworth's claim that disputable speech prefixes are put in square brackets; they are not used here.[71] The edition distinguishes the two Merchants in the play as either First or Second, and also from Egeon the Merchant, which F1–4 lump together as 'Merchant' in some form. It always separates Luce the kitchen maid from Luciana, Adriana's sister, by giving their names in full, as their speech prefixes (both 'Luc.') are confusing in F1-4. The edition gives every speech prefix in full, specifying each twin as either 'of Syracuse' or 'of Ephesus'.

Whitworth demotes what are deemed to be incorrect variants to the notes, including the appellations 'Erotes' and 'Sereptus', and makes a passing reference to the twins' ambiguous speech prefixes: '*Ant.* F (*so thoughout play, with few exceptions*)'.[72] Similarly, referring to Dromio's expanded speech prefixes, which represent editorial intervention, the notes give: '*Dro.* F (*so throughout play*)'.[73] Whitworth's parenthetical comments mislead the reader into imagining that the speech prefixes are regular, and that the 'few exceptions' are of little note. In the *New Oxford Shakespeare* (2016), all speech prefixes are given in full, for example 'Dromio of Ephesus', removing the variety of abbreviation and lack of specificity regarding which twin is which.[74] In modern editions, the names of the characters are made to work much harder to guide the reader. The body of evidence from readers' marks in copies of the early printed editions demonstrates that, rather than being accidental or insignificant, the printing errors that originate with F1 have a direct impact on the experience and understanding of the play. Uniquely for *The Comedy of Errors*, the editorial response has obscured a history of reading where

printing error precipitates the type of confusion the play itself creates.

INERADICABLE ERROR

Although the ability to experience, correct or interact with these errors diminished after the standardization of them, their slippery ineradicability remains into the eighteenth century and within an editorial tradition which waged war against them. While Pope's 1725 edition claimed to make Shakespeare's errors 'vanish', he makes the same historic mistake as the Folios.[75] In Act 4, Scene 1, Dromio of Syracuse discusses his proposed departure with Antipholus of Ephesus, who does not understand and instead calls him 'Thou drunken slave' (TLN 1085). Instead of 'E. Ant.' accusing Dromio of being a drunken slave, Pope's edition gives this line to Dromio of Ephesus, and consequently both Dromios are momentarily on stage talking to each other, an encounter which must be deferred until the last scene (Figure 8). Dromio of Syracuse responds to the imposter Dromio of Ephesus, before the correct speech prefix is applied and 'E.Dro' is replaced with 'E.Ant' two lines later.[76] This textual slip is perhaps less confusing than the original errors found in the Folios, and can be apprehended by a reader more quickly as a mistake. Nevertheless, it demonstrates the difficulty of disbarring this type of error, even after a major shift in editorial practice.

There is evidence that the early modern conception of error in printed playbooks and its

---

[70] William Shakespeare, 'The Comedy of Errors', ed. Standish Henning, *A New Variorum Edition of Shakespeare* (New York, 2011).

[71] Charles Whitworth, 'Editorial procedures', in *The Comedy of Errors*, ed. Charles Whitworth (Oxford, 2002), p. 82.

[72] Whitworth, *The Comedy of Errors*, p. 97.

[73] Whitworth, *The Comedy of Errors*, p. 98.

[74] William Shakespeare, 'The Comedy of Errors', ed. Sarah Neville, in *The New Oxford Shakespeare*, ed. Gary Taylor et al. (Oxford, 2016), p. 727.

[75] Pope, 'Preface', p. xxi.

[76] Pope, *The Works of Shakespear*, p. 449.

The Comedy of ERRORS.   449

SCENE II.

Enter Dromio Sira. *from the bay.*

S. Dro. Mafter, there is a bark of *Epidamnum,*
That ftays but till her owner comes aboard;
Then, Sir, fhe bears away. Our fraughtage, Sir,
I have convey'd aboard; and I have bought
The *Oyl,* the *Balfamum,* and *Aqua-vitæ.*
The fhip is in her trim; the merry wind
Blows fair from land; they ftay for nought at all,
But for their owner, mafter, and your felf.
   E. Ant. How now! a mad man! why, thou peevifh fheep,
What fhip of *Epidamuum* ftays for me?
   S. Dro. A fhip you fent me to, to hire waftage.
   E. Dro. Thou drunken flave, I fent thee for a rope;
And told thee to what purpofe, and what end.
   S. Dro. You fent me for a rope's-end as foon:
You fent me to the bay, Sir, for a bark.
   E. Ant. I will debate this matter at more leifure,
And teach your ears to lift me with more heed.
To *Adriana,* villain, hie thee ftrait,
Give her this key, and tell her in the defk
That's cover'd o'er with *Turkifh* tapeftry
There is a purfe of ducats, let her fend it:
Tell her I am arrefted in the ftreet,
And that fhall bail me; hie thee, flave; be gone:
On officer, to prifon 'till it come.   *[Exeunt.*
   S. Dro. To *Adriana!* that is where we din'd,
Where *Dowfabel* did claim me for her husband;
She is too big I hope for me to compafs.
Thither I muft, altho' againft my will,
For fervants muft their mafters minds fulfil.   *[Exit.*
   V oi. I.   M m m   SCENE

8 Alexander Pope's *The Works of Shakespear,* 6 vols. (London, 1725), vol. 1, p. 449, showing the printing slip 'E.Dro.' for 'E.Ant.' at the line 'Thou drunken slave, I sent thee for a rope; / And told thee to what purpose, and what end.' Courtesy of the Robert D. Farber University Archives & Special Collections Department, Brandeis University.

interaction with the theatre were far more complex than any strategy the eighteenth-century culture of correction could offer. In Thomas Dekker's *Satiromastix* (1602), an address to the reader offers a highly self-conscious picture of the interaction between comedy, the theatrical and readerly audience, and textual error. The address 'Ad Lectorem' reads: 'IN steed of the Trumpets sounding thrice, before the Play begin: it shall not be amisse (for him that will read) first to beholde this short Comedy of Errors, and where the greatest enter, to giue them in stead of a hisse, a gentle correction.'[77] There follows a list of seven mistakes. The erratum is designated as a 'Comedy of Errors', referencing the play that preceded it by five or six years. The theatrical references make it even more likely that Dekker was referring to Shakespeare's play. Here, the textual errors of one dramatic work are made to relate to the conceptual errors of another, where the comedy of errors of mistaken identity becomes the comic or chaotic textual confusions of this play's printing. Each of the textual errors listed has the potential to create the kind of confusion found in *The Comedy of Errors*, with the textual slippage from 'Ile strate thence poore' to 'Ile starue their poore' having the same potential to mislead the audience.

Despite being addressed 'Ad Lectorem', Dekker's conceit conflates the reader and theatregoer. Where one would 'hisse' at a particularly bad onstage character, one should here give them a 'gentle correction' with a pen. The erratum suggests the equivalence of the two forms of page and stage by tying the paratextual to the performative. It is explicit about the response required from the reader – not only to correct the text, as is common in other early modern errata, but to participate in the comedy of errors, to watch, judge and respond as if they were in a theatre as well as reading a book. It makes the public acknowledgement of textual error part of the satirical comedy of the play itself. In its imagining of readers, it creates a space for faulty readers who participate in the correction of the printed text and the humour of the performance text (whilst the erratum acknowledges incorrect printers). Readers are expected to show a more commanding involvement in the text, just as reader-revisers of the various Folios of *The Comedy of Errors* practise such interventions, with varying degrees of success and playful consequence.

Dekker presents error not as a thing to be discreetly excised, but as theatrically valuable and comically important to both types of audiences. These errors are not hidden at the back of the text but take the place of the prologue of trumpets 'sounding thrice, before the Play begin'. He conflates the 'greatest' of presumably bad characters with textual errors to which the audience are imagined responding. The address thus undermines the desirability of correction: the audience's hisses at the 'greatest' sound very much like fun, where the bad characters are booed while the best are cheered. Correction is superficially the purpose of the erratum, but correcting the text's errors is potentially the equivalent to removing the best of the villains, the Barabases and Iagos, where their badness signifies their error. The resistance to correction is contained within the instructions to correct, where what is identified as incorrect is also productive of comedy. The reference to textual error as a 'comedy of errors' recontextualizes *Errors* as not only a play about controlled mistaken identity, but also an uncontrolled mixing of textual and performative error to be noted and even enjoyed by readers and theatre-goers alike. Nevertheless, these early printing errors and ambiguities are relatively invisible in modern editions. The annotations of readers responding to them surveyed here remind us of this history of reading textual error and the continuing 'comedy of error' which frequently ensues.

Recent scholarship in the history of reading has paid little attention to these misinterpretations, focusing instead on stories of readers' personal interactions with their books. The annotations of John Dee represent an exceptional reader interacting with an intellectual community, and Lady Anne Clifford's marginalia create spaces of female ownership and education.[78] Conversely,

---

77 Thomas Dekker, 'Ad Lectorum', in *Satiro-mastix, or The untrussing of the Humorous Poet* (London, 1602), sig. A4v.

78 See William H. Sherman, *John Dee: The Politics of Reading and Writing in the English Renaissance* (Amherst, 1995); Stephen Orgel, 'Marginal maternity: reading Lady Anne Clifford's *A Mirror for Magistrates*', in *Printing and Parenting*

annotations in the printed First to Fourth Folios and performance texts created from them show that the dominant way to read *The Comedy of Errors* in the seventeenth and early eighteenth century was not to comment, commonplace or cross-reference, but to attempt to correct the printing errors that affected comprehension of the plot. The corrections, and especially their failures, in *Errors* suggest stymied or restricted reading: unexceptional, repetitive, lax. These mundane forms of interaction do not deliver the kinds of reading we hope to see inside a Shakespeare First Folio, but instead represent the messy reality of reading *Errors*.

CONCLUSION

The printing errors characterize the play as it first emerged and was engaged with by its earliest readers, challenging the ideologies of rectitude that have developed across drama, reading and editing. Current editorial practice, however, takes a different approach to the value of error. Whitworth argues: 'Some of the confusions in the text are of the sort usually attributed to unperfected authorial copy: descriptive or narrative stage directions, imprecise distinctions between characters, uncertain or alternate names for characters, missing or imprecise entrances and exits, and so on. All of these require editorial emendation.'[79] He labels these features as 'mistakes', assuming they have little meaning and that they need removing. Michael Warren, on the other hand, carefully raises the possibility of leaving errors uncorrected in Shakespeare: 'What if, denying the editorial impulse to detect and manage error, one were to assume that the text is correct?'[80] To leave the errors uncorrected in an edition would not provide the reader with the text they expect, and would lead them to fall into confusion much more easily and often. Yet to remove them misses the potential playfulness of error and its comedy, strongly advocated by Dekker.[81] The Rowean impulse to correct that is germane to modern editorial policy is in tension with the history of reading *Errors* in early printed editions and manuscripts which retain this comic, performative, residual interaction with

error. To assume the First to Fourth Folios are correct is, then, to *experience* error rather than understand it, since understanding is something that the playtext and performance text both resist.

What is lost by correcting *Errors* is a historical effect of error, of confusion not easily remedied, and the memory of this experience by previous readers and performers. Attending to individual readers' falling into error replicates what often happens in performance, where a director embraces the play of sibling similarity by having one actor play each pair of twins. In 1983, James Cellan-Jones directed the play for BBC Television, with Michael Kitchen performing both Antipholuses, and Roger Daltry both Dromios. At the Globe in 1999, Kathryn Hunter also chose to use a single actor to double the twin parts. As Lois Potter states, this doubling 'gave the audience almost the same sense of bewilderment as the characters themselves, and Hunter may have felt that, at the Globe, this was a more desirable response than a sense of superiority'.[82] It is often assumed that the play's humour depends on

---

in *Early Modern England*, ed. Douglas A. Brooks (Aldershot, 2005), pp. 267–90; Katherine Acheson, 'The occupation of the margins: writing, space, and early modern women', in *Early Modern English Marginalia*, ed. Katherine Acheson (London, 2018), pp. 70–89.

79 Charles Whitworth, 'Rectifying Shakespeare's errors: romance and farce in bardeditry', in *The Comedy of Errors: Critical Essays*, ed. Robert Miola (New York, 1997), pp.227–60, esp. p. 242.

80 Michael Warren, 'The perception of error: the editing and the performance of the opening of "Coriolanus"', in *Textual Performances: The Modern Reproduction of Shakespeare's Drama*, ed. Lukas Erne and Margaret Jane Kidnie (Cambridge, 2004), pp. 127–42, esp. p. 130.

81 That Shakespeare's confusions have been easily written away has been noted by Patricia Parker. She argues against the dismissal of error or inconsistency by editors, exemplified in the opening scene where Egeon tells the story of the shipwreck that separates the twins and the parents: Parker, 'Elder and younger: the opening scene of "The Comedy of Errors"', *Shakespeare Quarterly* 34.3 (1983), 325–7, p. 325.

82 Lois Potter, 'Roman actors and Egyptian transvestites', *Shakespeare Quarterly* 50.4 (1999), 508–17, pp. 516–17.

spectators' awareness of which identical twin is which, but this was not always the case. William Drummond in 1618, recounting Ben Jonson's explanation for his never writing a play featuring twins, states: 'He had ane intention to have made a play like Plautus Amphitrio, but left it of, for that he could never find two so like others that he could persuade the spectators they were one.'[83] For Jonson, the entire conceit of the play is the audience's mistaking the twins, rather than being 'superior' to the onstage error, as is often assumed to be the experience of *The Comedy of Errors*. Genuine audience confusion is the historical condition of reading the play, both in the theatre and in the book. To take

seriously the idea of reading the First to Fourth Folios and approach them as 'correct' opens our experience to a pre-standardized textual world of flawed readers and playful mistakenness. The annotations and corrections early readers left behind serve to remind us that these small errors, which modern editors mostly conceive as accidental and only worthy of silent correction, *did* trouble readers and should be included more loudly in the texts we read today.

---

[83] Ben Jonson, *Ben Jonson's Conversations with William Drummond of Hawthornden*, ed. R. F. Patterson (London, 1923), p. 37.

THE CIRCULATION OF YOUTHFUL ENERGY ON THE EARLY MODERN LONDON STAGE: MIGRATION, INTERTHEATRICALITY AND 'GROWING TO COMMON PLAYERS'

HARRY R. McCARTHY

Globe Theatre, London, early 1630s. As three boy actors, fresh from that afternoon's performance, remove their costumes amidst the usual squabbles over who stole whose limelight, a fourth, younger boy slips into the room. Claiming to have been sent from a short-lived all-boy company to offer the Globe his services, he gives a disastrous audition speech. Nevertheless, in these troubled financial times, the company is, for now, stuck with him – until, that is, the opportunity presents itself to showcase the boy on stage in the hope of palming him off on another new boys' company. The performance, unexpectedly, is a triumph, and the sale of the boy to the company's new rivals is called off. The Globe troupe, it is agreed, need to keep the boy for themselves.

The scenario I describe is, fairly obviously, not taken directly from early modern theatre history, but from Nicholas Wright's 2000 play *Cressida*.[1] Nevertheless, it is a version of the truth: as the boy reveals in his opening scene, his name is Stephen Hammerton, initially apprenticed by his parents to a draper and bought out of his indenture by theatrical impresarios Christopher Babham and William Blagrave to join a company of boys being trained as players at the newly built Salisbury Court playhouse. The point of the enterprise, Hammerton tells the King's Men's John Shank, was that, 'one day, if we were good enough, we'd be your pupils'.[2] Such a venture was indeed launched in 1629, and the real Hammerton (fl. 1629–47) was among the boys to be brought up 'in the quality of playing with intent to be a supply

of able actors to your Majesty's servants of the Blackfriars when there should be occasion'.[3] Against a backdrop of theatrical upheaval and infighting over exactly who had the right to Hammerton's apprenticeship indenture, the boy probably performed with the company – known as the 'Children of the Revels' or the 'King's Revels' – during its opening season in 1630–1, and perhaps on tour a few months earlier. A surviving petition by those who held shares in the boy's indenture, however, demonstrates that, by 12 November 1632, Hammerton was performing for the King's Men. It was with this troupe that Hammerton would earn his theatrical name: he played the significant role of Oriana in a revival of John Fletcher's *The Wild Goose Chase* in 1632. After 1637, we find him playing leading male roles in Thomas Killigrew's *The Parson's Wedding*, John Suckling's *The Goblins*, and James Shirley's *The Doubtful Heir*. James Wright's nostalgic *Historia Histrionica*, printed in 1699, recalls that, in a revival of Beaumont and Fletcher's *The Maid's Tragedy*, '*Amyntor* was Play'd by *Stephen Hammerton*, (who was at first a most noted and

---

[1] Nicholas Wright, *Cressida*, dir. Nicholas Hytner (Almeida Theatre, London, 2000). Script published by Nick Hern Books, 2000.

[2] Wright, *Cressida*, 1.2, p. 19.

[3] Cited in G. E. Bentley, 'The Salisbury Court theater and its boy players', *Huntington Library Quarterly* 40.2 (1977), 129–49, esp. p. 137, pp. 139–40.

beautiful Woman Actor, but afterwards he acted with equal Grace and Applause, a Young Lover's Part)'.[4]

Hammerton's story is rather different from those we are accustomed to hearing when it comes to early modern boy actors. It has long been acknowledged that boys such as Hammerton, though initially trained as female impersonators in the adult acting troupes, would typically 'graduate' to playing adult men, and perhaps also take on sharers' duties. Far less often noted, however, is the possibility that, in the continually shifting theatrical landscape of early modern London, boys moved from one company to another. Though the circumstances of Hammerton's transfer as depicted in Cressida are not entirely accurate, the real boy did begin in one acting 'tradition', only to transfer to another often thought of as markedly distinct. Moreover, Hammerton was not the first to have done so, and was certainly not alone: thanks to G. E. Bentley, Mark Eccles and David Kathman, among others, it is possible to trace the movements of thirty other boy players who, from as early as 1596 to as late as 1639, made at least one transition from acting company to acting company. The ongoing circulation in which the youngest members of the theatrical community were demonstrably imbricated is the subject of this article. Given the fact that boy players, unlike their adult counterparts, formed, in part or whole, the personnel of every single acting company operating in London, their movements between companies constitute a promising point of connection between supposedly distinct acting companies and repertoires. The aim of this article is therefore twofold: to provide, for the first time, a comprehensive, biographical overview of boy actor migration across forty years of English theatre history; and to model the kinds of imaginative (though necessarily speculative) inter-company and cross-repertorial play that knowledge of such movements and migrations can initiate.

A partial attempt to amend what Andy Kesson has recently diagnosed as 'a scholarly climate that appears unwilling to think between boy and adult theater'[5] – despite Roslyn L. Knutson's important questioning of the divide between boy and adult acting companies' repertories and audiences in 2001[6] – this article's focus on migrating boy actors proposes that innovation could be achieved through the refreshing presence of new company members, whose physical arrival established potent points of connection between troupes and their repertories. As Stephen Greenblatt reminds us, 'Shakespeare's theater was not isolated by its wooden walls ... : rather the Elizabethan and Jacobean theater was itself a *social event* in reciprocal contact with other social events'.[7] What Greenblatt refers to as a 'circulation of social energy' might playfully be reconceived here as a 'circulation of *youthful* energy' to which the acting companies and repertories of early modern London were demonstrably open. In addition to finding a wealth of inspiration in the formal and stylistic elements of individual plays performed by other companies, that is, acting companies and their playwrights may have found a kind of 'source' in the actors who circulated through the theatrical landscape.

Boy actors, I suggest, were a prominent feature of what Richard Andrews has described as the 'amorphous stock of material which lent itself to dramatization' between companies and repertories,[8] infiltrating even the performances of plays in which they themselves did not appear. In this, they constitute a lively facet of the intertheatrical 'reverberant constellation of speeches,

[4] James Wright, *Historia Histrionica* (London, 1699), sig. B2v. The revival probably took place after 1636, when star actor Joseph Taylor was still performing the role: see Martin Wiggins with Catherine Richardson, *British Drama 1533–1642: A Catalogue*, 9 vols. (Oxford, 2015), vol. VI: *1609–1616*, p. 184.

[5] Andy Kesson, 'Playhouses, plays, and theater history: rethinking the 1580s', *Shakespeare Studies* 45 (2017), 19–40, pp. 34–5.

[6] Roslyn Lander Knutson, *Playing Companies and Commerce in Shakespeare's Time* (Cambridge, 2001), pp. 18–20, p. 58.

[7] Stephen Greenblatt, *Shakespearean Negotiations: The Circulation of Social Energy in Renaissance England* (Berkeley, 1988), pp. 45–6.

[8] Richard Andrews, 'Resources in common: Shakespeare and Flaminio Scala' in *Transnational Mobilities in Early Modern Theater*, ed. Robert Henke and Eric Nicholson (Aldershot, 2014), pp. 37–52, p. 38.

gestures, and interactions' which, William N. West has evocatively argued, characterized the early modern theatrical environment.[9] Jeremy Lopez has similarly advocated a scholarly method that 'attempts to imagine the way early modern acting companies, and their playwrights, might have used actors' bodies as formal devices not distinct from dramaturgical elements such as verse style, subject matter, and staging habits' to 'help put early modern plays into vivid and as yet unfamiliar dialogue with one another'.[10] This article picks up on Lopez's assertion of the importance of an actor's physical presence for forging links between repertories and individual plays, taking the mobile bodies of a number of boy actors as an unacknowledged source of interdramatic dialogue.

MAPPING MIGRATION

A century ago, Charles William Wallace observed that, in 'the whole course of theatrical and dramatic history of the Elizabethan–Jacobean period … [,] no feature … can be treated as quite isolated'.[11] Particularly striking in this regard is Wallace's assertion that 'the boys of the children-companies … ultimately dominated the stage. Their members … are found as leaders thereafter in every company but one, and for more than fifty years their influence was a factor in the theatre'.[12] Wallace does not substantiate this claim with names and details of the actors to whom he refers; such substantiation is, however, possible. What follows provides a biographical outline of thirty-two actors who began their careers as boys and subsequently moved – either as adults or while still in minority – through the early modern theatre industry. Actors are listed alphabetically, with intercompany moves listed in abbreviated form. Additional information relating to plays in which each actor performed is provided where available. To offer a clearer sense of the wide-reaching and inter-repertorial overlaps of the actors' careers, Table 1 is followed by a series of diagrams outlining the performers' dispersal across London's theatrical landscape.[13]

Table 1 Migrating Boy Actors: Biographical Summaries[14]

Hugh Attwell (c. 1592–1621)
Movements: CQR before 1608; LEM by c. 1611.
Known roles: 1679 Folio cast list for Beaumont and Fletcher's *The Coxcomb* (1609); Sir Amorous La Foole in Jonson's *Epicene* (1610).[15]
William Barksted (c. 1590–<1638)
Movements: CKR before 1608 (?); CQR in 1609; LEM in c. 1611.

(continued)

---

9 William N. West, 'Intertheatricality', in *Early Modern Theatricality*, ed. Henry S. Turner (Oxford, 2013), pp. 151–72, esp. p. 152.
10 Jeremy Lopez, 'Imagining the actor's body on the early modern stage', *Medieval and Renaissance Drama in England* 20 (2007), 187–203, p. 187.
11 Wallace, *The Children of the Chapel at Blackfriars, 1597–1602* (Lincoln, NE, 1908), p. xii.
12 Wallace, *The Children of the Chapel*, p. 14.
13 For ease of reading, I have arranged the companies in proximity to the geographical location in which they principally performed according to the interactive map on the Shakespearean London Theatres website. Companies, such as the King's Men and Lady Elizabeth's Men, who performed in more than one location at certain points in their history are restricted to one location, again to facilitate easy reading. Companies which went under more than one name during the period outlined in the diagrams are listed under all names from that period. I list the Children of the Queen's Revels as one company despite its two phases at the Blackfriars and Whitefriars, given the considerable overlaps in repertory and company personnel. The interactive map can be found at http://shalt.dmu.ac.uk/locations.html.
14 In each biographical entry, dates are provided for all performances using the 'best guess' given in Martin Wiggins and Catherine Richardson's *British Drama: A Catalogue*, 9 vols. (Oxford, 2012–). Plays are listed in chronological order.
15 Mark Eccles, 'Elizabethan actors I: A–D', *Notes & Queries* 38.1 (1991), 38–49, p. 39; Andrew Gurr, 'Attwell, Hugh (c. 1597–1621)', *Oxford Dictionary of National Biography* (hereafter *ODNB*), last modified 23 September 2004: https://doi.org/10.1093/ref:odnb/880; Lucy Munro, *Children of the Queen's Revels: A Jacobean Theatre Repertory* (Cambridge, 2005), p. 179. It is admittedly uncertain whether the cast list for *The Coxcomb* records a Queen's Revels or Lady Elizabeth's Men performance. Along with several of the actors listed here, Attwell would have appeared in both. See Munro, *Children of the Queen's Revels*, p. 185.

Table 1 (cont.)

Known roles: Morose in *Epicene*; 1679 Folio cast list for *The Coxcomb*.[16]

Richard Baxter (fl. 1605–48)

Movements: QAM from *c.* 1605; KM by 1628.

Known roles: Cast list for Ford's *The Lover's Melancholy* (1628); named in marginal annotations to Beaumont and Fletcher's *The Mad Lover* (revived *c.* 1630); Titus, Officer and Servant in Massinger's *Believe as You List* (1631).[17]

Christopher Beeston (*c.* 1576–1638)

Movements: LCM by *c.* 1597 (apprenticed to Augustine Phillips?); WM from 1602; later manager of PCM, LEM (also seems to have acted with the company), QHM, BB.

Known roles: Attendant, Captain and Soldier in the plot of *The Second Part of the Seven Deadly Sins* (*c.* 1597); 1616 Folio cast list for Jonson's *Every Man in His Humour* (1598).[18]

Robert Benfield (*c.* 1583–1649)

Movements: CQR by *c.* 1608; LEM from 1613; KM from *c.* 1616.

Known roles: 1679 Beaumont and Fletcher Folio cast lists for *The Coxcomb*, *The Honest Man's Fortune* (1613), *The Mad Lover* (1616), *The Knight of Malta* (1618), *The Custom of the Country* (1619), *The Humorous Lieutenant* (1619), *Women Pleased* (1620), *The False One* (1620), *The Little French Lawyer* (1620), *The Pilgrim* (1621), *The Island Princess* (1621), *The Spanish Curate* (1622), *The Prophetess* (1622), *The Double Marriage* (1622), *The Maid in the Mill* (1623), *The Lovers' Progress* (1623) and *A Wife for a Month* (1624); Junius Rusticus in Massinger's *The Roman Actor* (1626); cast list for *The Lover's Melancholy*; King in Carlell's *The Deserving Favourite* (1629); Ladislaus in Massinger's *The Picture* (1629); Doctor Makewell in Clavell's *The Soddered Citizen* (1630); Antharis in Wilson's *The Swisser* (1631); De Gard in Fletcher's *The Wild Goose Chase* (possibly 1621 original and when revived in 1632).[19]

Theophilus Bird (*c.* 1608–63)

Movements: PM by 1623; QHM by 1625; BB in 1636–7; KM from 1638.

Known roles: Paulina in Massinger's *The Renegado* (1625); Toota in Heywood's *The Fair Maid of the West* (1630); Massinissa in Nabbes's *Hannibal and Scipio* (1635).[20]

(continued)

Table 1 (cont.)

John Blayney (fl. 1609–25)

Movements: CQR by 1609; QAM by 1616; QHM by 1625.

Known roles: 1616 Folio cast list for *Epicene*.[21]

Nicholas Burt (b. 1614)

Movements: KM before 1631 (apprenticed to John Shank); QHM from 1631.

Known roles: Clariana in Shirley's *Love's Cruelty* (1631).[22]

William Cartwright, Jr (1608–86)

Movements: PM before 1625 (?); QHM after 1625.[23]

(continued)

16 G. E. Bentley, *The Jacobean and Caroline Stage* (hereafter *JCS*), 7 vols. (Oxford, 1941–68), vol. 2, pp. 357–8; Mary Bly, *Queer Virgins and Virgin Queans on the Early Modern Stage* (Oxford, 2000), pp. 122–5; Giorgio Melchiori, 'Barksted [Backsted, Baxter], William (fl. 1607–1630)', *ODNB*, last modified 23 September 2004: https://doi.org/10.1093/ref:odnb/1427; Munro, *Children of the Queen's Revels*, p. 179.

17 Bentley, *JCS*, vol. 2, pp. 360–2; Edwin Nungezer, *A Dictionary of Actors and of Other Persons Associated with the Public Representation of Plays in England before 1642* (New Haven, 1929), p. 32.

18 Bentley, *JCS*, vol. 2, pp. 363–70; Nicola Boyle, 'The documentary history and repertory of the Lady Elizabeth's Men' (unpublished Ph.D. diss., De Montfort University, 2017), pp. 30–2; Eva Griffith, 'Christopher Beeston: his property and properties', in *The Oxford Handbook of Early Modern Theatre*, ed. Richard Dutton (Oxford, 2009), pp. 607–22; Andrew Gurr, 'Beeston [Hutchinson], Christopher (1579/80–1638)', *ODNB*, last modified 23 September 2004: https://doi.org/10.1093/ref:odnb/66593; David Kathman, '*The Seven Deadly Sins* and theatrical apprenticeship', *Early Theatre* 14.1 (2011), 121–39, p. 123.

19 Eccles, 'Elizabethan actors I', p. 40; Munro, *Children of the Queen's Revels*, p. 179.

20 John Astington, 'Bird, Theophilus (bap. 1608, d. 1663)', *ODNB*, last modified 23 September 2004: https://doi.org/10.1093/ref:odnb/67756; Bentley, *JCS*, vol. 2, pp. 377–9; David Kathman, 'How old were Shakespeare's boy actors?' *Shakespeare Survey 58* (Cambridge, 2005), 220–46, p. 236.

21 Bentley, *JCS*, vol. 2, pp. 381–2; Munro, *Children of the Queen's Revels*, p. 179.

22 Bentley, *JCS*, vol. 2, p. 397; Kathman, 'How old', pp. 241–3.

23 Bentley, *JCS*, vol. 2, pp. 404–5; Andrew Gurr, 'Cartwright, William (1606–1686)', *ODNB*, last modified 23 September 2004: https://doi.org/10.1093/ref:odnb/4824.

Table 1 (cont.)

Giles Cary (fl. 1609–13)

Movements: CQR from *c.* 1609; LEM from 1611.

Known roles: Boy in Jonson's *Entertainment at Britain's Burse* (1609); 1616 Folio cast list for *Epicene*; 1679 Beaumont and Fletcher Folio cast list for *The Coxcomb*.[24]

Hugh Clark (fl. 1626–53)

Movements: QHM from *c.* 1626; KM from *c.* 1636 to 1637.

Known roles: Gratiana in Shirley's *The Wedding* (1626); Bess Bridges in *The Fair Maid of the West*; Syphax and Nuntius in *Hannibal and Scipio*; Hubert in Davenport's *King John and Matilda* (revival).[25]

William Ecclestone (fl. 1610–24)

Movements: CQR before 1610 (?); KM from 1610; LEM in 1612–13; KM by 1614.

Known roles: Kastril in Jonson's *The Alchemist* (1610); 1616 Folio cast list for Jonson's *Catiline's Conspiracy* (1611); 1679 Beaumont and Fletcher Folio cast lists for *The Honest Man's Fortune*, *Bonduca* (1614), *The Mad Lover*, *The Loyal Subject* (1618), *The Custom of the Country*, *The Humorous Lieutenant*, *The Laws of Candy* (1620), *Women Pleased*, *The Little French Lawyer*, *The Island Princess*, *The Spanish Curate* and *The Sea Voyage* (1622); named as a principal player in the 1623 Shakespeare Folio.[26]

Ezekiel Fenn (b. *c.* 1620)

Movements: QHM by 1635; BB from 1636 to 1637.

Known roles: Sophonisba in *Hannibal and Scipio*; Winifred in Dekker, Ford and Rowley's *The Witch of Edmonton* (revived before 1637); prologue speaker of an unnamed play (in which Fenn performed his first male role) before 1639 (prologue published in Glapthorne's *Poëms*).[27]

Nathan Field (1587 – *c.* 1620)

Movements: CQR from 1600; LEM from 1613; KM from 1616.

Known roles: 1616 Jonson Folio cast lists for *Cynthia's Revels* (1600), *Poetaster* (1601) and *Epicene*; Bussy in Chapman's *Bussy d'Ambois* (1604); Key Keeper in the *Entertainment at Britain's Burse* (1609); leading role (Cokes?) in Jonson's *Bartholomew Fair* (1614); Voltore in Jonson's *Volpone* (revival); Face in *The Alchemist* (revival); 1679 Beaumont and Fletcher Folio cast lists for *The Coxcomb*, *The Honest Man's Fortune* (which he co-wrote), *The Mad Lover*, *The Queen of Corinth*

(continued)

Table 1 (cont.)

(which he co-wrote) (1617), *The Knight of Malta* (likewise) and *The Loyal Subject*; named as a principal player in the 1623 Shakespeare Folio.[28]

Stephen Hammerton (fl. 1629–47)

Movements: 2KR from 1629; KM by 1632.

Known roles: Oriana in *The Wild Goose Chase* (1632 revival); leading role (Orsabrin?) in Suckling's *The Goblins* (1637); King Ferdinand in Shirley's *The Doubtful Heir* (1638); Ward in Killigrew's *The Parson's Wedding* (1641); Amintor in Beaumont and Fletcher's *The Maid's Tragedy* (revival after 1636).[29]

James Jones (fl. 1608–24)

Movements: KM from 1608 (apprenticed to Robert Armin); LEM by 1611 (apprenticed to William Perry).[30]

Thomas Jordan (*c.* 1617–85)

Movements: 2KR from 1629; QHM by 1636–7.

(continued)

---

[24] Munro, *Children of the Queen's Revels*, p. 180.

[25] Bentley, *JCS*, vol. 2, pp. 406–7.

[26] Bentley, *JCS*, vol. 2, pp. 429–31; Mark Eccles, 'Elizabethan actors II: E–J', *Notes & Queries* 38.4 (1991), 454–61, p. 454; Eva Griffith, 'Ecclestone, William (d. *c.* 1624)', *ODNB*, last modified 23 September 2004: https://doi.org/10.1093/ref: odnb/8441.

[27] *The Cambridge Guide to Theatre*, 2nd edn, ed. Martin Banham (Cambridge, 1995), p. 366; Bentley, *JCS*, vol. 2, pp. 433–4; Henry Glapthorne, *Poëms* (London, 1639), sig. E1v–E2r; Kathman, 'How old', p. 236.

[28] Bentley, *JCS*, vol. 2, pp. 434–6; Munro, *Children of the Queen's Revels*, p. 181; Margaret Ellen Williams, 'Field, Nathan (bap. 1587, d. 1619/1620)', *ODNB*, last modified 23 September 2004: https://doi.org/10.1093/ref:odnb/9391.

[29] Bentley, *JCS*, vol. 2, pp. 460–1; 'Bentley, 'The Salisbury Court theater and its boy players', pp. 139–40; Martin Butler, 'Exeunt fighting: poets, players, and impresarios at the Caroline hall theaters', in *Localizing Caroline Drama: Politics and Economics of the Early Modern English Stage, 1625–1642*, ed. Adam Zucker and Alan B. Farmer (Basingstoke, 2006), pp. 97–128, esp. p. 102, p. 105; Andrew Gurr, *The Shakespeare Company, 1594–1642* (Cambridge, 2004), p. 229.

[30] David Kathman, 'Grocers, goldsmiths, and drapers: freemen and apprentices in the Elizabethan theater', *Shakespeare Quarterly* 55.1 (2004), 1–49, esp. pp. 12–13.

Table 1 (cont.)

Known roles: Lepida in Rawlins's *The Tragedy of Messallina* (1635).[31]

Samuel Mannery (fl. 1631–49)

Movements: 2PCM by 1631; BB by 1639.

Known roles: Bawd in Marmion's *Holland's Leaguer* (1631).[32]

William Ostler (fl. 1601–14)

Movements: CQR by 1601; KM by 1610.

Known roles: 1616 Jonson Folio cast lists for *Poetaster*, *The Alchemist* and *Catiline's Conspiracy*; Shopkeeper in the Entertainment at Britain's Burse; 1679 Beaumont and Fletcher Folio cast lists for *The Captain* (1612), *Bonduca* and *Valentinian* (1614); Antonio in Webster's *The Duchess of Malfi* (1613); named as a principal player in the 1623 Shakespeare Folio.[33]

John Page (1614–41)

Movements: QHM by 1626; BB from 1636 to 1637.

Known roles: Jane in *The Wedding*; Lelius in *Hannibal and Scipio*.[34]

Salomon Pavy (c. 1588–1602)

Movements: 2CP before 1600 (apprenticed to Edward Pearce); CQR 1600–2.

Known roles: Salomon, a schoolboy in Percy's *The Faery Pastoral* (1599) (?); First Child (and Criticus?) in *Cynthia's Revels*; 1616 Jonson Folio cast list for *Poetaster* (as Horace?).[35]

William Penn (fl. 1609–36)

Movements: CQR by 1609; PCM by 1616; KM by 1625.

Known roles: 1616 Folio cast list for *Epicene*; Sir Abraham Ninny in Field's *A Woman is a Weathercock* (1609) (?); Julio Baptista in *The Picture*; cast list for *The Lover's Melancholy*; Clephis in *The Swisser*; Nantolet in 1632 revival of *The Wild Goose Chase*.[36]

Richard Perkins (c. 1579–1650)

Movements: AM from 1596 (apprenticed to Edward Alleyn); EPM in 1597; AM from later in 1597; WM from 1602; KM by 1623; QHM from 1625.

Known roles: Flamineo in Webster's *The White Devil* (1612); Sir John Belfare in *The Wedding*; Fitzwater in *King John and Matilda*; Captain Goodlack in *The Fair Maid of the West*; Hanno in *Hannibal and Scipio*; took over Alleyn's roles when AM plays were revived by QHM, including Barabas in Marlowe's *The Jew of Malta*.[37]

(continued)

Table 1 (cont.)

Thomas Pollard (1597 – c. 1650)

Movements: PHM/PM before 1616 (apprenticed to John Shank) (?); KM from c. 1616.

Known roles: 1679 Beaumont and Fletcher Folio cast lists for *The Queen of Corinth*, *The Humorous Lieutenant*, *The Laws of Candy*, *The Island Princess*, *The Maid in the Mill*, *The Spanish Curate* and *The Lovers' Progress*; Silvio in a revival of *The Duchess of Malfi* (c. 1619–23); Aelius, Lamias and Stephanos in *The Roman Actor*; Ubaldo in *The Picture*; Brainsick in *The Soddered Citizen*; Timentes in *The Swisser*; cast list for *The Lover's Melancholy*; Berecinthius in *Believe as You List*; Pinac in the 1632 revival of *The Wild Goose Chase* (and possibly the 1621 original).[38]

(continued)

[31] Bentley, *JCS*, vol. 2, pp. 487–90; Lynn Hulse, 'Jordan, Thomas (c. 1614–1685)', *ODNB*, last modified 8 January 2008: https://doi.org/10.1093/ref:odnb/15122; Lucy Munro, 'Infant poets and child players: the literary performance of childhood in Caroline England', in *The Child in British Literature: Literary Constructions of Childhood, Medieval to Contemporary*, ed. Adrienne E. Gavin (London, 2012), pp. 54–68, esp. pp. 55–62.

[32] Bentley, *JCS*, vol. 2, p. 506; Kathman, 'How old', pp. 223–4.

[33] Bentley, *JCS*, vol. 2, p. 610; Herbert Berry, 'Ostler, William (d. 1614)', *ODNB*, last modified 3 January 2008: https://doi.org/10.1093/ref:odnb/20908; Munro, *Children of the Queen's Revels*, p. 182.

[34] Bentley, *JCS*, vol. 2, p. 518; Kathman, 'How old', p. 237.

[35] W. Reavely Gair, *The Children of Paul's: The Story of a Theatre Company, 1553–1608* (Cambridge, 1982), p. 64, p. 184; Munro, *Children of the Queen's Revels*, p. 183; Matthew Steggle, 'Pavy, Salomon (bap. 1588, d. 1602)', *ODNB*, last modified 22 September 2005: https://doi.org/10.1093/ref:odnb/93076.

[36] Bentley, *JCS*, vol. 2, pp. 523–4; Munro, *Children of the Queen's Revels*, p. 183. The initials 'W. P'. appear after an entrance for Sir Abraham on sig. D2r of the 1612 quarto of *Weathercock*. Wiggins and Richardson take the initials to refer to Penn (*British Drama: A Catalogue*, vol. 6, p. 28).

[37] John H. Astington, 'Perkins [Parkins], Richard (c. 1579–1650)', *ODNB*, last modified 23 September 2004: https://doi.org/10.1093/ref:odnb/67767; David Mateer, 'Edward Alleyn, Richard Perkins and the rivalry between the Swan and the Rose Playhouses', *Review of English Studies* 60.243 (2009), 61–77, pp. 63–9.

[38] Bentley, *JCS*, vol. 2, p. 566; Kathman, 'Grocers, goldsmiths, and drapers', p. 37; Kathman, 'How old', pp. 227–8.

Table 1 (cont.)

Emmanuel Reade (1592–<1620)

Movements: CQR by 1610; LEM by 1613; QAM by 1617.

Known roles: 1679 Beaumont and Fletcher Folio cast lists for *The Coxcomb* and *The Honest Man's Fortune*.[39]

Timothy Reade (fl. 1626–47)

Movements: QHM by 1626; 2KR/2KRa from *c.* 1631; QHM by 1637.

Known roles: Cardona in *The Wedding*; Buzzard in Brome's *The English Moor* (1637).[40]

John Rice (fl. 1603 (?) – 1630)

Movements: KM by 1607 (perhaps as early as 1603) (apprenticed to John Heminges?); LEM in 1611; KM from 1612.

Known roles: Delivered a speech in a Merchant Taylors entertainment on 16 July 1607; Corinea of Cornwall in a city pageant honouring Prince Henry on 31 May 1610; Marquess of Pescara in *The Duchess of Malfi*; 1679 Beaumont and Fletcher Folio cast list for *The False One*; named as a principal player in the 1623 Shakespeare Folio.[41]

Richard Robinson (*c.* 1595–1648)

Movements: may have begun with CQR (if he was the son of James Robinson, one of the managers of that company); KM by 1611 (apprenticed to Richard Burbage?).

Known roles: Lady in Middleton's *The Lady's Tragedy* (1611); 1616 Jonson Folio cast list for *Catiline's Conspiracy*; 1679 Beaumont and Fletcher Folio cast lists for *Bonduca*, *The Double Marriage* and *A Wife for a Month*; Wittipol in Jonson's *The Devil is an Ass* (1616); Cardinal in *The Duchess of Malfi* (*c.* 1619–23 revival); Aesopus in *The Roman Actor*; Orsino and Hermit in *The Deserving Favourite*; La-Castre in *The Wild Goose Chase* (probably 1621 original and 1632 revival); named as a principal player in the 1623 Shakespeare Folio.[42]

Joseph Taylor (*c.* 1586–1652)

Movements: may have begun with CQR before 1609; PCM by 1610; KM in 1619.

Known roles: 1679 Beaumont and Fletcher Folio cast lists for *The Coxcomb*, *The Honest Man's Fortune*, *The Custom of the Country*, *The Humorous Lieutenant*, *The Laws of Candy*, *Women Pleased*, *The Little French Lawyer*, *The Prophetess*, *The False One*, *The Pilgrim*, *The Spanish Curate*, *The Sea Voyage*, *The Lovers' Progress* and

(continued)

Table 1 (cont.)

A Wife for a Month; roles previously played by Burbage and/or Field in revivals of *Hamlet* (Hamlet), *Othello* (Iago), Beaumont and Fletcher's *Philaster* (Philaster), Beaumont and Fletcher's *A King and No King* (Arbaces), *The Duchess of Malfi* (Ferdinand), *The Maid's Tragedy* (Amintor), *Epicene* (Truewit), *The Alchemist* (Face) and Fletcher and Massinger's (and Chapman/Field/Jonson's?) *The Bloody Brother* (1617) (Rollo); Mosca in a revival of *Volpone*; cast list for *The Lover's Melancholy*; Paris in *The Roman Actor*; Mathias in *The Picture*; Duke in *The Deserving Favourite*; Mirabel in *The Wild Goose Chase* (probably 1621 original and 1632 revival); Arioldus in *The Swisser*; named as a principal player in the 1623 Shakespeare Folio.[43]

William Trigg (fl. 1625–42)

Movements: KM from 1625 (apprenticed to John Heminges); BB from 1637.

Known roles: Julia in *The Roman Actor*; cast list for *The Lover's Melancholy*; Modestina in *The Soddered Citizen*; Selina in *The Swisser*; Rosalura in 1632 revival of *The Wild Goose Chase*.[44]

Alvery Trussell (fl. 1601)

Movements: 2CP before 1600 (apprenticed to Thomas Giles); CQR from 1600.[45]

(continued)

[39] Bentley, *JCS*, vol. 2, p. 539; Munro, *Children of the Queen's Revels*, p. 183.

[40] Bentley, *JCS*, vol. 2, pp. 540–1; Kathman, 'How old', p. 237.

[41] Bentley, *JCS*, vol. 2, pp. 546–7; Mark Eccles, 'Elizabethan actors III: K–R', *Notes & Queries* 39.3 (1992), 293–303, p. 303; David Kathman, 'John Rice and the boys of the Jacobean King's Men', *Shakespeare Survey* 68 (Cambridge, 2015), 247–66, p. 250.

[42] Bentley, *JCS*, vol. 2, pp. 550–3; Lucy Munro, 'Robinson, Richard (*c.* 1595–1648)', *ODNB*, last modified 4 January 2007: https://doi.org/10.1093/ref:odnb/75572.

[43] Bentley, *JCS*, vol. 2, pp. 590–8; Mark Eccles, 'Elizabethan actors IV: S to end', *Notes & Queries* 40.2 (1993), 165–76, pp. 173–4; Andrew Gurr, 'Taylor, Joseph (bap. 1586?, d. 1652)', *ODNB*, last modified 23 September 2004: https://doi.org/10.1093/ref:odnb/27065; Munro, *Children of the Queen's Revels*, p. 183.

[44] Bentley, *JCS*, vol. 2, pp. 604–6; Gurr, *The Shakespeare Company*, p. 244; Kathman, 'How old', pp. 226–7.

[45] Gair, *Children of Paul's*, p. 184; Munro, *Children of the Queen's Revels*, p. 183.

Table 1 (cont.)

John Underwood (c. 1588–1624)
Movements: CQR from 1600; KM by 1610.
Known roles: 1616 Jonson Folio cast lists for *Cynthia's Revels* and *Poetaster*; Bonario in *Volpone* (presumably a revival); Dapper in *The Alchemist*; 1679 Beaumont and Fletcher Folio cast lists for *Valentinian*, *Bonduca*, *The Queen of Corinth*, *The Knight of Malta*, *The Loyal Subject*, *The Custom of the Country*, *The Humorous Lieutenant*, *The Laws of Candy*, *The False One*, *Women Pleased*, *The Little French Lawyer*, *The Pilgrim*, *The Island Princess*, *The Sea Voyage*, *The Double Marriage*, *The Lovers' Progress*, *The Maid in the Mill* and *A Wife for a Month*; Delio in *The Duchess of Malfi* (possibly original 1613 production and *c.* 1619–23 revival).[46]

Abbreviations: 2CP = Second Children of Paul's (founded 1599); 2KR = Second King's Revels (boy company); 2KRa = Second King's Revels (restructured mixed company); 2PCM = Second Prince Charles's Men; AM = Admiral's Men; BB = Beeston's Boys; CKR = Children of the King's Revels; CQR = Children of the Queen's Revels; EPM = Earl of Pembroke's Men; KM = King's Men; LCM = Lord Chamberlain's Men (later KM); LEM = Lady Elizabeth's Men; PCM = Prince Charles's Men; PHM = Prince Henry's Men (later PM); PM = Palsgrave's Men; QAM = Queen Anna's Men (later Revels Company, or RC); QHM = Queen Henrietta Maria's Men; WM = Worcester's Men (later QAM)

The complexity suggested by these diagrams provides a staunch rejoinder to more separatist models of the early modern theatre and its actors, such as the case advanced by David Edgecombe that, 'In many ways', the theatrical industry of the sixteenth and seventeenth centuries 'could be considered a closed system. Rarely did actors from one company cross over to another troupe.'[47] The fact that it remains possible, in the face of markedly scant evidence, to detect a trend of transferral among numerous boys' and adult companies from at least 1596 (when Richard Perkins temporarily moved from the Admiral's Men to Pembroke's Men) to the end of the 1630s (when company closures and reorganization appear to have accelerated the dispersal of boy players) is telling. From the twists and turns of the narrative of almost fifty transitions made by thirty-two actors over the course of forty-three years, it is possible to discern a number of consistent trends: newly formed companies seizing upon the opportunity of having those trained as boys among their ranks; pre-established companies renewing their personnel with the youthful energy of members of other troupes; boys being trained as actors – be it in an all-boy troupe or one which combines adult men and boys – and graduating, either within their own company or another, to the status of leading man or sharer, or both; and, relatedly, the transition of a young actor from one company to another coinciding with his transition from female to male roles, perhaps signifying an acknowledgement of his versatility and/or a gap in company personnel that he is thought particularly ripe to fill. In each case, the divisions between company operations, particularly the operations of the somewhat unhelpfully monikered 'boy' and 'adult' companies, start to dissolve. In line with Alfred Harbage's distinction between 'rival traditions', one might be compelled to discern a potential disparity in the skill of the players who comprised the two types of troupe, particularly in periods such as 1599–1600 and 1629–37 when boy companies were only just beginning to resurface.[48] However, the fact that boys may have been moving from the Queen's Revels company to the King's Men as early as 1603–4 (see Figure 9) suggests that such a discrepancy quickly ceased to be perceived (if perceived it ever was) by early modern theatre personnel.

'BY THEIR NAMES': BOY ACTOR IDENTITIES AND 'GROWING TO COMMON PLAYERS'

What, then, did acting companies do with the 'material' that came to them in the form of newly

---

[46] Bentley, *JCS*, vol. 2, pp. 610–11; Kathman, 'John Rice', pp. 256–7; Munro, *Children of the Queen's Revels*, p. 184.

[47] David Edgecombe, *Theatrical Training During the Age of Shakespeare* (New York, 1995), p. 30.

[48] Alfred Harbage, *Shakespeare and the Rival Traditions* (London, 1952), esp. pp. 29–47.

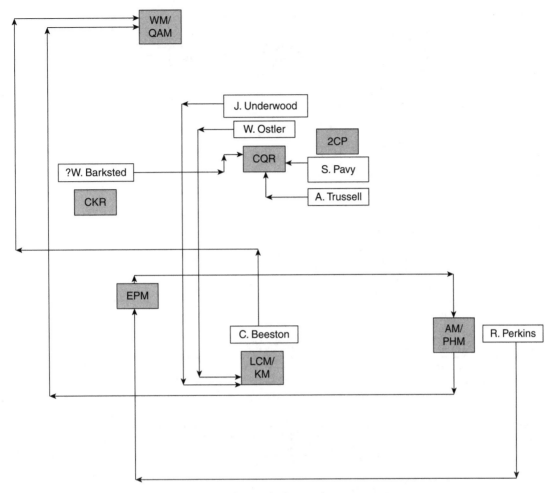

9 Migrations of actors who began as boys, 1595–1609.

recruited, often famed, boy players? How might knowledge of such processes of inter-company exchange illuminate our reading of early modern drama? It will not escape notice that these original boy actors did not always remain boys as they moved. But it is often as boys – in actuality or memorialization – that they are referenced and remembered by playwrights and acting companies. The evidence that boys might have been known to spectators as individuals as well as one of a generic stock of actors is slight, but not altogether non-existent. In a much-quoted passage from Thomas Heywood's *Apology for Actors*, printed when boy actor migration was in full

flourish, the author defends the practice of employing boys to play women (presumably in both the adult and child companies) by unequivocally assuming audience knowledge of the actor beneath the character: 'But to see our youths attired in the habit of women, who know not what their intents be? who cannot distinguish them by their names, assuredly knowing, they are but to represent such a Lady, at such a time appoynted?'[49] Heywood's claims have

---

[49] Thomas Heywood, *An Apology for Actors* (London, 1612), sig. C3v.

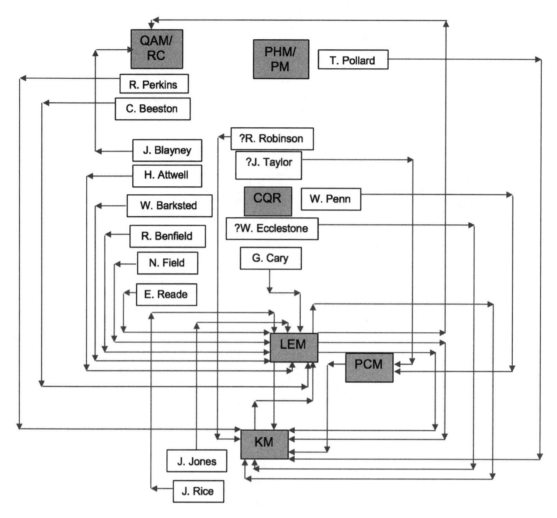

10 Migrations of actors who began as boys, 1610–1624.

often been impressed into service in pro-theatrical discussions of what Michael Shapiro influentially termed the audience's 'dual consciousness' of the boy under the dress;[50] far less commonly noted is the fact that Heywood seems to expect that the spectators will know the actors *by their names*. Such recognition is occasionally encouraged within the plays themselves: as early as 1600, Jonson took pains in *Cynthia's Revels* to advertise the fact that, among the new company for which he was writing, was the boy Salomon Pavy. In the induction, one of the three squabbling children refers to another, the First Child, as 'Sall', giving him leave to speak the play's coveted prologue.[51] Pavy seems also to have been name-checked as 'Salomon, a schoolboy' in William Percy's *The Faery Pastoral*, which was certainly

[50] Michael Shapiro, *Children of the Revels: The Boy Companies of Shakespeare's Time and their Plays* (New York, 1977), pp. 103–5.

[51] Jonson, *The Fountaine of Selfe-loue, or Cynthias Reuels* (London, 1601), sig. A4v.

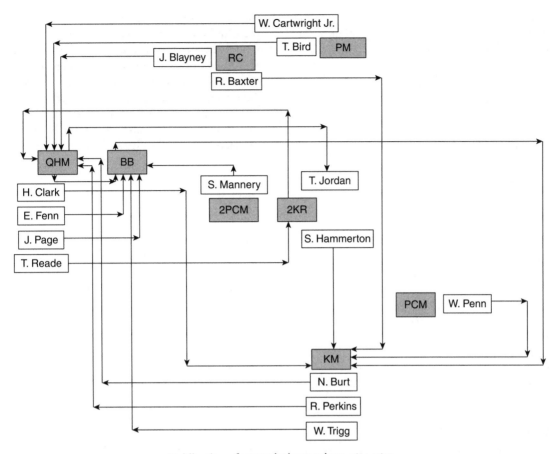

11 Migrations of actors who began as boys, 1625–1639.

designed for performance by his previous company, the Children of Paul's, before Pavy transitioned to the Revels outfit.[52] Jonson's assertion of Pavy's identity in the opening scene of what was probably the opening performance at the Blackfriars theatre therefore draws, however briefly, a connection between the two children's troupes through the named presence of the boy actor, encouraging spectators to recognize Pavy as a member of *this* troupe as opposed to the one where they quite probably last saw him performing.

If the archetypal spectator did indeed know at least some of the boy actors 'by their names', we might reasonably expect them to have followed their transitional careers, perhaps with a similar interest to those for whom, today, professional football's 'transfer

window' garners considerable interest and excitement. One such spectator is Shakespeare's Hamlet. The dangers of reading the Danish prince as an arbiter of seventeenth-century theatrical taste notwithstanding, a speech unique to the 1623 folio version of *Hamlet* sheds light on Shakespeare's and the King's Men's attunement to boy actor migration. All three versions of the play see Hamlet engage with the notion of boy company players (probably fictional avatars for the Children of the Queen's Revels) who, within the world of the fiction as well as the world outside, pose a threat to the 'tragedians of the city'. In the folio rendering of this scene, Hamlet seems as

---

[52] See Steggle, 'Pavy, Salomon'.

concerned with the future of the boys as with the detrimental effect they may be having on the activities of his favourite troupe:

> What are they Children? Who maintains 'em?
> How are they escoted? Will they pursue the
>   Quality no
> longer than they can sing? Will they not say
>   afterwards
> if they should grow themselves to common Players (as
>   it is like most if their meanes are not better) their
>   Writers
> do them wrong, to make them exclaim against
>   their
> own Succession?
>
> (TLN 1392–8)

Particularly interesting for our purposes is Hamlet's entertaining the possibility that the boys 'should grow themselves to common players'. As James P. Bednarz writes in his discussion of the passage's possible role in the 'War of the Theatres' of 1600–1, 'Hamlet's warning that these same children would perceive the "wrong" that "their writers" had done them if they themselves became "common players" is prophetic' since, as indicated in Table 1 and Figures 9, 10 and 11, three Revels boys – Nathan Field, William Ostler and John Underwood – eventually joined the King's Men.[53]

These transfers were clearly ingrained in the memories of theatre professionals, including the heirs to James Burbage's theatrical empire who, in 1635, defending their property rights against a group of young actors, recalled of the Blackfriars that

Our father . . . made it into a playhouse . . . ; which after it was leased out to one Evans, that first set up the boys commonly called the Queen's Majesty's Children of the Chapel. In process of time the boys growing up to be men, which were Underwood, Field, Ostler, and were taken to strengthen the King's service; and . . . it was considered that house would be as fit for ourselves, and so purchased the lease remaining from Evans with our money, and placed men players, which were Heminges, Condell, Shakespeare, &c.[54]

Clearly, the three Blackfriars boys becoming 'common players' was considered sufficiently important to merit mention over two decades after it had

happened. Though the move itself was significant to the defendants, however, the time at which it occurred appears not to have been: Ostler and Field are known not to have joined the company until 1609–10 and 1616, respectively. With Underwood, we are on less certain ground (he does not appear in cast lists between *Poetaster* in 1601 and *The Alchemist* in 1610),[55] though Kathman has recently advanced the plausible theory that he may have been called upon to 'strengthen the King's service' as early as 1603–4, when, it seems, the company was in need of talented young players.[56] Whenever the boys joined, the fact remains that, even in 1635 when all of them were long dead, their presence in the company was deemed as important as that of John Heminges, Henry Condell and William Shakespeare, as well as the very theatres in which they all worked together.

If Underwood's move to the company was indeed earlier than the Sharers' Papers imply, the dating of the revised 'common players' passage becomes all the more interesting. Knutson plausibly suggests that the accusations levelled against the boy company correspond to the seditious and politically sensitive material so abundant in Queen's Revels plays performed in 1605–8.[57] Reading the *Hamlet* passage as an admonishment on the part of the King's Men to the boys who were, in these years,

---

[53] James P. Bednarz, *Shakespeare and the Poets' War* (New York, 2001), p. 242.

[54] The lawsuit is fully transcribed in *Dramatic Records: The Lord Chamberlain's Office*, ed. Allardyce Nicoll and Eleanore Boswell, Malone Society Collections 2.3 (Oxford, 1931), pp. 321–416.

[55] Ben Jonson, *The VVorkes of Beniamin Ionson* (London, 1616), sig. Z3v, sig. Kkk3v.

[56] Kathman, 'John Rice', pp. 256–7. Admittedly, as Holger Schott Syme points out in his reconsideration of the Jacobean King's Men, the evidence for Underwood's transfer around this date is 'fairly slim', and 'There are no other known instances of a player from one of the children's companies entering an apprenticeship with a sharer in one of the adult companies.' See Syme, 'The Jacobean King's Men: a reconsideration', *Review of English Studies* 70.294 (2019), 231–51, p. 245.

[57] Knutson, *Playing Companies*, p. 104 and p. 126.

increasingly overstepping the mark, Knutson argues for a Shakespeare with an eye firmly trained on the activities of boys outside his own company. If Shakespeare was at this time attuned to this facet of boys' performance, it is entirely reasonable to suggest that he may have been attuned to their physical potential to influence his own company's dramaturgy, too, particularly if Kathman's estimation of Underwood's transfer to the company in 1603–4 is correct. Indeed, Hamlet's allusion to boys becoming 'common players' could, in this light, be taken as a reference to the evolution of Underwood from Blackfriars boy to strengthener of the 'King's service', perhaps brought home all the more by Underwood's presence on stage, as the ageing boy actor now grown 'by the altitude of a chopine' (Hamlet, 2.2.429–30). That Shakespeare may have been revising Hamlet in 1606–8, when boys had already begun to move from one company to another (and, in the case of Underwood, may even already have moved to his), suggests that he was becoming increasingly aware of the potential of boy players to act, quite literally, as a shared resource throughout the early modern theatre industry.

READING REPUTATIONS AND RESPONSES

Underwood may not have been on stage in Hamlet, but Nathan Field probably was when, in 1614, his newly merged company, the Lady Elizabeth's Men, performed Jonson's Bartholomew Fair. Though the role Field took in the debut performance of the play is uncertain, it is likely that he played the leading role of Bartholomew Cokes.[58] On the surface, this role does not appear to square readily with the witty trickster roles Field is recorded as having played later in his career with the King's Men – Voltore in a revival of Jonson's Volpone, and Face in a revival of The Alchemist; however, I discuss below that the part does facilitate overlaps with physically demanding roles Field seems to have played as a boy.

Before discussing Cokes's particularly boyish physicality, it is worth beginning with the famous moment in which the part is brought into captivating collision with Field's extradramatic identity during Littlewit's motion, enacted by Leatherhead's troupe of 'Pretty youths' or 'Players minors' (puppets).[59] The imminent onstage performance quickly garners the attention of the overexcited Cokes, who, failing to grasp that the promised performance of Hero and Leander will not feature real actors, naïvely asks Leatherhead, 'Which is your Burbage now? ... Your best actor: your Field?', only to be presented with the puppet 'that acts young Leander' (L.iv; emphasis added). As Kenneth Gross argues, puppet shows on the early modern stage 'point us toward the inner dramatic life of their particular plays', 'remind[ing] us of the insistent presence of the actor's body'.[60] With Field as Cokes, this moment is a particularly acute instance of the effect Gross describes, further heightened by Littlewit's bemused response of 'Good, i'faith! You are even with me, sir', for which a literal, comic gloss would be 'You, Nathan Field, are standing right in front of me' (L.iv).[61]

Admittedly, the representation of Field as a puppet is a rather complex form of flattery. Edel Lamb is correct, I think, to suggest that reducing Field to a doll-like status harkens back to moments in the repertory of Field's boy company that position the actors – the real 'players minors' – as vulnerable, available objects.[62] Leatherhead's

---

[58] I am grateful to Holger Schott Syme for sharing with me his calculations of number of words spoken by each character in the play. Though Cokes has less than 10 per cent of the play's word share, this nevertheless makes him one of Bartholomew Fair's most verbally dominant characters. For other suggestions in favour of Field taking the role, see Nora Johnson, The Actor as Playwright in Early Modern Drama (Cambridge, 2003), p. 62; Alexander Leggatt, 'Introduction', in Bartholomew Fair, ed. G. R. Hibbard (London, 2007), pp. vii–xxvii, esp. p. xxvi; and Keith Sturgess, Jacobean Private Theatre (London, 1987), p. 177.

[59] Ben Jonson, The VVorkes of Beniamin Ionson. The Second Volume (London, 1641), sig. L.iv.

[60] Kenneth Gross, 'Puppets dallying: thoughts on Shakespearean theatricality', Comparative Drama 41.3 (2007), 273–96, p. 276.

[61] Johnson, Actor as Playwright, p. 62.

[62] Edel Lamb, Performing Childhood in the Early Modern Theatre: The Children's Playing Companies (1599–1613) (Basingstoke, 2008), pp. 135–8.

description of the Field-puppet as 'extreamly belov'd of the womenkind' (L1v) and Cokes's suggestive '*handling*' of the players-in-miniature also gestures towards the type of sexual availability often assumed by scholars – particularly in the case of the children's companies with which Field began – to have characterized the figure of the boy player. I would also not dispute Nora Johnson's observation that presenting Field and his fellows as 'wooden blocks who perform debased versions of *Hero and Leander* for audiences too stupid to understand Marlowe' vexes the complimentary identification of him as the company's 'best actor'.[63] There is, however, a further dimension to the moment that has often been overlooked by scholars – the particularly physical nature of the reference to Field. Presenting the Field/Leander puppet to Cokes, Leatherhead elaborates that the 'womenkind' who love the actor so 'extreamly', and 'the green gamesters, that come here', 'doe so affect his *action*' (L1v). Beyond, or perhaps as well as, nodding to Field's own sexual past and present, the moment may also engage on a deeply metatheatrical level with his historically proven capacity to portray virtuosic roles – including, it seems, those of lovers.[64] As I have written elsewhere, the repertory of the boy company of which Field was doubtless the star is characterized by virile, charismatic youths under frequent threat of emasculation, just as the adult Field appears playfully to be threatened here.[65] Moreover, the plays performed by Field's boy company – among them *Cynthia's Revels* and *Poetaster* – are, like the puppet, acutely marked by 'action': indeed, Truman, in Wright's *Historia Histrionica*, remembers Field first and foremost as one of the 'Chappel Boys', whose company were 'at that time famous for good Action'.[66]

A glimpse of this 'action' surfaces in another Queen's Revels play in which Field demonstrably performed: Francis Beaumont's *Knight of the Burning Pestle* (1607). Towards the beginning of the play, the perennially disruptive Citizen's Wife draws the actor playing Humphrey aside and, knowingly or not, brings the fictional world of the play and the actor's real-world origins into collision: 'Sirrah, didst thou ever see a prettier

child? how it behaves it selfe, I warrant yee, and speakes, and lookes, and pearts up the head? I pray you brother, with your favor, were you never none of M. Monkesters schollars?'[67] It is difficult to resist the temptation to assign the role of Humphrey to Field given the actor's known history as a pupil of Richard Mulcaster at St Paul's

---

[63] Johnson, *Actor as Playwright*, p. 58.

[64] Jonson would adopt a similar strategy in his treatment of Richard Robinson in *The Devil is an Ass* (1616). In that play, the scheming Merecraft and Ingine plot to dupe the acolyte and would-be cuckold Fitzdottrel by dressing up a boy as a Spanish lady. Seeking a 'witty boy' able to live up to 'the true height' of such a performance, the pair do not take long to turn to the professional stage for inspiration, with Ingine suggesting '*Dicke Robinson* / A very pretty fellow', before extolling Robinson's virtues as a female impersonator (Jonson, *The VVorkes of Beniamin Jonson. The Second Volume*, sig. R3r). Roberta Barker has recently argued, along similar lines to those followed here, that this metatheatrical reference indicates that Robinson, who had been a prominent boy player with the King's Men since at least 1612, 'may have been associated in the public imagination with the roles of noble, dignified "Spanish ladies": that is, with the very kinds of parts spoofed by Wittipol's feminine masquerade in *The Devil is an Ass*'. See Barker, 'Dick Robinson and the Spanish ladies, or, the English Farsanta unmask'd', unpublished paper presented at 'Early Modern Theater as Transnational and Transhistorical Nexus: Performance/Text/Acting/Embodiment', 30 May 2017, University of Cologne, Germany.

[65] See Harry R. McCarthy, 'Men in the making: youth, the repertory, and the "Children" of the Queen's Revels, 1609-13', *English Literary History* 85.3 (2018), 599–629, pp. 607–22. For a plausible argument in favour of Field having taken such roles, including those of Freevill in Marston's *The Dutch Courtesan* (1604), Lysander in Chapman's *The Widow's Tears* (1605) and Young Loveless in Beaumont and Fletcher's *The Scornful Lady* (1610), see Steve Orman, 'Nathan Field's theatre of excess: youth culture and bodily excess on the early modern stage' (unpublished Ph.D. dissertation, Canterbury Christ Church University, 2014), pp. 238–9. Field's own, real-life capacities as a lover appear to have invited public speculation to the end of his life and career: in 1619, he appears to have been the target of rumours that he had cuckolded the Earl of Argyll and fathered a child by his wife (see Munro, *Children of the Queen's Revels*, p. 51).

[66] Wright, *Historia Histrionica*, sig. C4v.

[67] Francis Beaumont, *The Knight of the Burning Pestle* (London, 1613), sig. B4r.

grammar school prior to 1600.[68] Mulcaster's investment in the physical aspects of pedagogy and the value of performance were well known: in this light, the Wife's attention to how the actor 'behaves it selfe … and speakes, and lookes, and pearts up the head' thus reads as more than an in-joke relating to the author's familiarity with the actor's origins (as Hilton Kelliher has uncovered, the two appear to have been together briefly at Cambridge in 1604).[69] It is, after all, Humphrey's moving, disciplined body – his *action* – that garners the Wife's attention and prompts her to draw connections between role, actor and the actor's earlier physically demanding training at the hands of Mulcaster.

The role of Cokes places a similar emphasis on the moving, performing body of the actor to that of Humphrey in *Knight*. Field's famous 'action', that is, seems to have transferred with him to the Lady Elizabeth's Men when he joined that company. Though a simpleton on the page, the role of Cokes is bursting with exuberant physicality. Before spectators are even afforded a glimpse of him, his long-suffering tutor, Wasp, alludes to the young man's physically uncontainable nature: 'Gentlemen, you doe not know him: hee is another manner of peece then you think for! but nineteen yeere old, and yet hee is taller then either of you, by the head, God blesse him.'[70] When the play's action moves to the fair, Cokes amply demonstrates this sprawling physicality through a number of frantic interactions. The diminutive Wasp's increasingly frustrated attempts to contain the young man, for example, bring about a humorous and agile exchange:

WASP

…
> *He gets him up on pick-packe.*

By this light, I'le carry you away o' my backe, and you will not come.

COKES

Stay *Numpes*, stay, set mee downe: I ha' lost my purse, *Numps*, O my purse! one o' my fine purses is gone.

(E3v)

It is not only onto Wasp's back that Cokes comically leaps: throughout his travel through the fair,

a kind of restless energy is discernible, and characters repeatedly point spectatorly attention towards it – the tricksy Quarlous, for instance, suggests that at the conclusion of the play Cokes will be 'spectacle enough' (E4v). Cokes's interactions at the market stalls, in particular, seem to prompt comic busyness:

COKES

[*To Leatherhead*] Those six horses, friend I'le have –

WASP

How!

COKES

And the three Jewes trumps; and halfe a dozen o'Birds, and that Drum, (I have one Drumme already) and your Smiths; I like that device o'your smiths, very pretty well, and foure Halberts—and (le'me see) that fine painted great Lady, and her three women for state, I'le have.

…

A set of these Violines, I would buy too, for a delicate young noise I have i'the countrey, that are every one a size lesse then another, just like your fiddles. I would faine have a fine young Masque at my marriage, now I thinke on't: but I doe want such a number o'things. And *Numps* will not helpe me now, and I dare not speake to him.

TRASH

Will your worship buy any ginger-bread, very good bread, comfortable bread?

COKES

Ginger-bread! yes, let's see.
> *He runnes to her shop.*

(F3v–F4r)

---

[68] A surviving complaint lodged against the founders of the Children of the Chapel in 1600 recalls that Field, 'a scholar of a grammar school in London kept by one Mr Mulcaster', was among the boys 'impressed' into performing at the Blackfriars playhouse. Cited in Glynne Wickham, Herbert Berry, and William Ingram, *English Professional Theatre, 1530–1660* (Cambridge, 2000), p. 265.

[69] See Hilton Kelliher, 'Francis Beaumont and Nathan Field: new records of their early years', *English Manuscript Studies 8* (2000), 1–42, pp. 26–7.

[70] Jonson, *The VVorkes of Beniamin Ionson. The Second Volume*, sig. C1r.

The breathless syntax as Cokes moves through the traders' wares and runs from one stall to the other seem to invite precisely the kind of physical exuberance Wasp describes himself as striving to keep under control. Watching his young charge as '[h]e runn's [sic] to the Ballad man' Nightingale, Wasp remarks: 'Why so! hee's flowne to another lime-bush, there he will flutter as long more; till hee ha' ne'r a feather left. Is there a vexation like this, Gentlemen?' (G1v).[71]

The encounter with Nightingale appears to facilitate a yet more visible opportunity for virtuosic display when the ballad-singer promises to deliver a ballad '[t]o the tune of *Paggington's Pound*' (G1v). As the notes to John Creaser's Cambridge edition of the play point out, the tune to 'Packington's Pound', sometimes attributed to the lutenist Francis Cutting, 'is a form of galliard, *les cinq pas* or cinquepace, a dance in triple metre performed in five thrusting steps, with a leap between the last two, sometimes fast and lilting and sometimes more flowing and stylised'.[72] It is difficult to resist the temptation to imagine the frantic Cokes dancing along to the tune – whose performance he frequently interrupts – not least since he excitedly describes the tune as 'mine own country dance!' It is worth pointing out that galliards feature in the plays of Field's boy company. In John Marston, William Barksted and Lewis Machin's *The Insatiate Countess* (Children of the Queen's Revels, 1610), for instance, during a masque the character of Rogero '*dances a Lavalto, or a Galliard, & in the midst of it, falleth into the Bride's lap, but straight leapes up, and danceth it out*'.[73] In his 2014 Ph.D. thesis on Field's career as a boy actor and playwright, Steve Orman plausibly assigns the role to him.[74]

By the time spectators encounter the Field puppet as *Bartholomew Fair* reaches its conclusion, then, they have had ample opportunity, via the role of Cokes, to attend to the attractive action Leatherhead describes. As well as pointing up the ridiculous nature of Cokes, the puppet's stage counterpoint, or harkening back to Field's pliable, and sexually available, position as a boy actor, this densely metatheatrical moment also reinforces his status and skill, forcibly bringing his physical

performing body, and the extradramatic persona it represents, centre stage. Inviting the audience to recall Field's past performances, the moment constitutes a particularly potent form of what Marvin Carlson has influentially termed 'haunting', in which 'The recycled body of an actor, already a complex bearer of semiotic messages, will almost inevitably in a new role evoke the ghost or ghosts of previous roles ...', a phenomenon that often colors and indeed may dominate the reception process'.[75] Manipulating the boy company repertory and perceived sexual availability of young players embodied by Field and his subsequent celebrity, Jonson allows the actor's skill and reputation, fostered in an earlier acting company, to bleed into the highly metatheatrical

---

[71] Frantic movement, and speed in particular, seem also to have featured in Field's offstage persona. A jest that appears in the first printing of John Taylor's *Wit and Mirth* (London, 1628) describes: 'Master *Field* the Player riding up *Fleetstreet*, a great pace, a Gentleman called him, and asked him what play was playd that day: he (being angry to be upon so frivolous a demand) answered, that he might see what play was to bée playd upon every *Poste*, I cry you mercy (said the Gentleman) I tooke you for a *Poste*, you road so fast' (sig. B5v). A subsequent iteration of the jest in 'Poor Robin's' *Jests* (London, 1667) replaces Field with Richard Burbage (sig. C7v), while Robert Burton's *Versatile Ingenium* (London, 1679) and the second edition of Humphrey Crouch's *England's Jests* (London, 1687) simply name the figure as 'A Player' (sig. G8v; sig. E5r). It is significant, I think, that Field appears to be the first to have conjured the image of the fast-riding player.

[72] Ben Jonson, *Bartholomew Fair*, ed. John Creaser, in *The Cambridge Edition of the Works of Ben Jonson*, ed. David Bevington, Martin Butler and Ian Donaldson, 7 vols. (Cambridge, 2012), vol. 4, 3.5.49n.

[73] Marston *et al.*, *The Insatiate Countesse* (London, 1613), sig. C2v.

[74] Orman, 'Nathan Field's theatre of excess', p. 238. Admittedly, the quarto printing of the text is remarkably confused as to who speaks which line or carries out which action in the masque scene. In his edition of the play (Manchester, 1984), Melchiori assigns the dance, and several of Rogero's other lines, to Guido. It is not impossible that Field took this role, either, though both characters are required to dance earlier in the scene.

[75] Carlson, *The Haunted Stage: Theatre as Memory Machine* (Ann Arbor, 2001), p. 8.

tissue of his play. The play thus lends credence to the suggestion that the portability evidenced by boy actors' inter-company movements could also manifest at an intertheatrical level, highlighting how Field's earlier career, within a different acting company, remained integral to the ongoing creation of his actorly reputation. Namechecking Field with reference to a 'player minor' when he himself is on stage thus straddles multiple performance moments and traditions, all of which are mediated by the now-mature body of the actor.

Celebrity actors such as Field, then, demonstrate the portability and memorability of boy actors' skills – many of them physical – across companies and repertories. His case is not, however, an isolated one: similar attention gathers around the performing body of Stephen Hammerton, with whom this article began. In remembering Hammerton's 'beautiful' portrayals of women and his 'young lover' roles, of which Amintor in a revival of *The Maid's Tragedy* is the only given example, *Historia Histrionica*'s Truman may be referring exclusively to Hammerton's work for the King's Men – his second acting company – for whom he played female and, later, male roles after his transfer in 1632. Yet it is my contention that the King's Men would not have taken Hammerton on – against a backdrop of confusing litigation – without some idea of his stage potential: their history of recruiting seasoned performers such as Field, Ostler and Underwood suggests a preference for actors who had considerable stage experience behind them. Though the roles Hammerton took in his brief time with the boys' company before joining the King's Men are unknown, I suggest that what knowledge we do possess of his later work places us in a reasonable position to read backwards onto his theatrical origins, initiating the inter-repertorial readings I am proposing. Hammerton's imagined presence in these plays, I argue, forges numerous connections between the two phases of his career, and the two companies with which he performed, bringing plot devices, isolated moments of stagecraft, and the appealing body and skill of the actor into productive and exciting collision.

Several metatheatrical references from the King's Men's later repertory capitalize on audience familiarity with Hammerton and his transitory acting career. His later appeal to King's Men audiences is suggested in the epilogue to *The Doubtful Heir*. Inviting responses from the audience at the play's conclusion, the comic Captain asks, '*How did King Stephen do, and tother Prince?*' – a question which seems to prompt so many responses that he is forced to continue, '*Enough, enough, I apprehend.*'[76] 'Stephen's' centrality to audience appreciation of the play once he had transitioned to male roles is further emphasized in *The Goblins*, in whose epilogue an appeal is made to '*The Women _____ Oh if Stephen should be kil'd, / Or misse the Lady, how the plot is spil'd?*'.[77] Likewise, the epilogue to *The Parson's Wedding* asserts that, if the audience does not indulge the play's romantic conclusion, '*Stephen misses the Wench*', which, '*they say, ... alone is enough to spoil the Play*', in addition to suggesting that Hammerton's stage persona and real-life appeal are inextricably intertwined: '*Stephen is as handsome, when the Play is done, as Mr. Wild was in the Scene.*'[78] This cluster of moments at the plays' conclusions suggests that Hammerton was a considerable draw to King's Men audiences, who were encouraged to respond to his performances. At the same time, I argue, such moments, and the plays in which they appear, harken back to earlier moments in Hammerton's career.

Killigrew's amusing parallel between 'Stephen' and 'Mr. Wild' aligns Hammerton with the role of Wild in *The Parson's Wedding* – a role which is insistently figured in terms of its visual appeal. So great is this appeal, in fact, that, within the space of a short scene, the Captain refers to Wild's handsomeness and beguilingly 'sound parts', which are subsequently put to use in gulling one of the female characters.[79] Later in the play, the audience is provided with impressive scope to judge this for

---

[76] James Shirley, *The Doubtful Heir* (London, 1652), sig. F6r.

[77] John Suckling, *The Goblins* (London, 1646), sig. D8v.

[78] Thomas Killigrew, *Comedies and Tragedies* (London, 1664), sig. V1v.

[79] Killigrew, *Comedies and Tragedies*, sig. M1v.

themselves: in the comic climax, Wild and his confederate, Careless, trick Pleasant and the young Widow into marriage by sneaking into their bedchamber 'in their Shirts, with drawers under', declaring themselves 'naked'.[80] While it is important not to overemphasize the characters' state of undress, the fact that the play's central wooing takes place against the partial exposure of the male body is striking in the case of an actor who was memorialized as visually impressive. That these qualities are central to the plays' plots and, by extension, commercial success is further illustrated by the threat of young Stephen 'missing' the 'lady' or 'wench' by the drama's conclusion.

Though, unlike *The Parson's Wedding* and *The Doubtful Heir* (where the reference to 'King Stephen' places Hammerton in the role of the charismatic young lover, King Ferdinand), the epilogue to *The Goblins* does not provide direct evidence of the role Hammerton took in that play, aligning him with a character who must escape death and win the one he loves provides two candidates: the central, daring wooers Orsabrin and Samorat. From the play's outset, these two men, who refer to themselves as '[n]oble youth[s]',[81] repeatedly find themselves in near-death situations which are ultimately resolved by their triumph in obtaining Reginella and Sabrina. Of the two characters, Orsabrin is doubtless the more striking, not least from a visual perspective, if the Jailor's description of how '[h]is haire curles naturally' and conclusion that he is 'a handsome youth' are to be believed.[82] Though both he and Samorat eventually win their 'wenches', it is Orsabrin's success the final scene centralizes, and his triumphant words close the play in a distinct prefiguration of the celebration of 'Stephen's' success in the epilogue:

> A Life! a Friend! a Brother! and a Mistres!
> Oh! what a day was here:
> Gently my Joyes distill,
> Least you should breake the Vessell you should fill.[83]

The plots of the plays in which Hammerton appeared had been hanging upon the success of the

central lover in obtaining the object of their affection before this point, however: *The Muses' Looking Glass* and *Amyntas* both bear resemblances to this later King's Men cluster in a number of ways, and Hammerton can be implicated in all of them.[84] With their markedly high concentration of female roles, both plays would have provided Hammerton with ample opportunity to stretch his acting wings while also (inadvertently?) catching the eye of the boys' troupe's competitors. *The Muses' Looking Glass*'s vain Philotima, for instance, provides a comic, exaggerated rendering of femininity whose concerns over her prosthetic gender construction speak forcefully to the tradition of taking cross-dressed boys for women. If the onstage spectators' comparison of her to 'the Idoll of *Cheap-Side*' are anything to go by, Mediocrity, too is clearly something to behold.[85] More favourably, *Amyntas* unquestionably provides scope for considerably deeper characterization than its predecessor through several female characters that, again, are repeatedly represented as beauteous. This play, too, would therefore have showcased Hammerton as an appealing prospect to the adult company who would later capitalize on his visual appeal and charismatic prowess through characters such as Killigrew's 'handsome' Wild. Of these, the central role of the lovelorn Amaryllis is by far the most impressive, and, like her striking counterparts in *The Muses' Looking Glass*, is characterized by her beauty: she and her twin brother, Amyntas, are described as a 'matchlesse paire of beauteous infants', while Amaryllis herself calls attention to her 'poore face that wer't so oft beli'de / For faire and beauteous, by my flattering

---

[80] Killigrew, *Comedies and Tragedies*, sig. R4v, sig. S3r.
[81] Suckling, *The Goblins*, sig. A4r.
[82] Suckling, *The Goblins*, sig. B4v.
[83] Suckling, *The Goblins*, sig. D8r.
[84] On the likelihood of these plays having been performed shortly after the Salisbury Court's opening, see Butler, 'Exeunt fighting', p. 103, p. 105; Lucy Munro, 'Actors, plays and performances in the indoor playhouses, 1625–42: boy players, leading men and the Caroline ensemble', *Yearbook of English Studies* 44 (2014), 51–68, pp. 54–5.
[85] Thomas Randolph, *The Muses' Looking-Glasse* (London, 1643), sig. E8v.

glasse'.[86] Repeated reference to such qualities arguably looks proleptically towards the reputation for beauteous roles that would continue to haunt Hammerton even after he had long stopped acting.

What is more, specific moments of stagecraft enacted by this role recur in Hammerton's King's Men career. The role of Oriana in *The Wild Goose Chase* would be second nature to an actor with experience of playing Amaryllis. Like that character, Oriana is concerned throughout the play with obtaining the man she loves – Mirabel, the 'Wild Goose' of the play's title. Like Amaryllis, the young woman is frequently characterized by her looks: upon meeting her, De Gard notes that she is 'grown a handsome woman', and her later attempt to dupe Mirabel by disguising herself as a merchant's daughter prompts exclamations of wonder at '[h]ow handsomly her shape shews!'[87] Oriana can also be connected to the beautiful Amaryllis through what she is required to do on stage. In one of several contrivances to catch Mirabel and secure their marriage engagement, Oriana feigns rapid physical deterioration, entering '*on a bed*' and convincingly adopting the guise of one on the point of death.[88] Such histrionics were also being performed at Salisbury Court a year or so earlier: in *Amyntas*, having been spurned by her lover, Damon, Amaryllis stabs herself and writes with her own blood. In the following scene, Dorylas discovers her having fainted, and she continually protests that she is dying, only to be revived and eventually go on to win back her lover (just as Oriana does).[89] Likewise, Orsabrin's narrow scrapes with death in *The Goblins*, such as when he '[e]nter[s] ... *bleeding*' following a confused scuffle in the dark with Samorat, bears striking resemblance to the pathetically bleeding Amaryllis.[90]

The plays additionally provide repeated opportunities for Hammerton to demonstrate the emotional depth fostered by *Amyntas*, reprising Amaryllis's considerable amount of weeping in recurrent appearances as Oriana in *The Wild Goose Chase* and King Ferdinand in *The Doubtful Heir*.[91] These roles thus recall elements of the earlier King's Men – and the even earlier King's Revels – repertories that centralize the leading actor: near-death experiences,

bleeding and the successful snaring of the object of desire, be they male or female. In addition, Hammerton's physicality is brought to the fore in his adult male roles, recalling erotic attention to the cross-dressed roles he played with the boys' and adult companies. As the conventionally wooed becomes the wooer, the erotic attraction of the boy actor about which so much ink has been spilled is turned on its head. The body of the actor – which, Rebecca Schneider reminds us, constitutes an archive in and of itself[92] – provides the means by which this happens, transporting the audience in the unfolding performance between temporally disparate theatrical moments, companies and performance practices. Reading Hammerton's later wench-catching reputation in the light of the earlier lovelorn – though ultimately successful – Amaryllis in *Amyntas*, via the intermediary figure of *The Wild Goose Chase*'s Oriana, initiates, in short, cross-repertorial dialogues that the recurring presence of the actor makes possible and exciting.

***

How far might we push this? Did actors need to be present on stage for their amassed, inter-company influence to be felt? To return to Field, it would appear that the actor's youthful energy could continue to infect performances even in his absence. The year 1604 had seen Field originate the title role of George Chapman's *Bussy D'Ambois*.[93] His centrality to the performance history of this play, and the ongoing association of the character with its originating actor, is suggested long after this debut, in

[86] Randolph, *Poems with The Muses Looking-Glasse and Amyntas* (London, 1638), sig. P4v, sig. V1r.

[87] Beaumont and Fletcher, *Comedies and Tragedies. Never Printed Before, and Now Published by the Authours Originall Copies* (London, 1647), sig. B1v, sig. O2v.

[88] Beaumont and Fletcher, *Comedies and Tragedies*, sig. N1r–v.

[89] Randolph, *Poems*, sig. Z3r–v.

[90] Suckling, *The Goblins*, sig. B2v.

[91] Beaumont and Fletcher, *Comedies and Tragedies*, sig. E2v; Shirley, *The Doubtful Heir*, sig. C4v.

[92] Rebecca Schneider, 'Performance remains', *Performance Research* 6.2 (2001), 100–8, p. 103.

[93] Munro, *Children of the Queen's Revels*, p. 136.

a prologue, printed in the revised 1641 quarto, which reflects a performance given after Field's death:

> *Field* is gone
> Whose Action first did give it name, and one
> Who came the nearest to him, is denide
> By his gray beard to shew the height and pride
> Of *D'Ambois* youth and braverie; yet to hold
> Our title still a foot, and not grow cold
> By giving it o're, a third man with his best
> Of care and paines defends our interest;
> As *Richard* he was lik'd, nor doe wee feare,
> In personating *D'Ambois*, hee'le appeare
> To faint, or goe lesse, so your free consent
> As heretofore give him encouragement.[94]

The prologue calls upon the audience's collective memory to engage with a performance of 'youth and braverie' by the young Field and actively to speculate on the insufficiency of an older, 'gray beard[ed]' actor to emulate it. Calling attention to the vital role Field's 'Action' played in 'first [giving the play] name', it further suggests that the memory of such a performance can endure long after the actor has 'gone' and the play transferred to a different, adult, acting company.[95] It thereby represents yet another 'haunting' of the play, albeit one by an actor who does not even need to be present in order to affect the performance and the audience's response to it. The continual movement of Field's youthful energy through the theatrical institution, it would appear, was sustained long after the actor ceased to move across its stages.

The intertheatrical mesh of references to the omnipresent status of popular skilled performers such as Field and Hammerton, combined with Shakespeare's prescient comment that such boys might, as adults, become 'common players', suggests that, in recruiting new boys from old companies, the early modern theatre built an archive of past boy performances. This article has established the recovery of such an archive as a new line of enquiry in the ongoing project of bringing once-disparate companies, repertories, plays, playwrights and players into previously uninitiated dialogue with one another. Increasing our knowledge of a theatrical culture which – by the seventeenth century, at least – could expect and respond to the migrating tendencies of its boy actors, that is, has the potential to provide new materials for building bridges across the scholarly chasm between 'rival traditions'. Might it be time, then, to return to individual company repertories or discrete moments in theatre history – the composition of Shakespeare's final plays for the King's Men following the arrival of John Underwood and William Ostler; the post-1613 repertory of the Lady Elizabeth's Men following the influx of Queen's Revels boys; the imitative dramaturgies of the Salisbury Court and Blackfriars playhouses in the early 1630s – with a sharper eye on company composition and actor biography? What patterns across casting and role requirement might be traced if we are more willing to insert specific performers between the lines of scrappy cast lists and company licences? The prompts for and possible answers to such questions lie in a more sustained investigation than has been possible here. The fact that such questions can be asked at all, however, lays testament to the investigative possibilities brought about when we remember that early modern actors' bodies and reputations – which, theatre history has long reminded us, animated the individual plays to which they were so central – moved outside and between individual playhouses, as well.

---

[94] George Chapman, *Bussy d'Ambois* (London, 1641), sig. A2r–v.

[95] It would appear that *Bussy d'Ambois* was so associated with Field and his acting career that it became part of the King's Men repertory after he joined that company (see Munro, *Children of the Queen's Revels*, p. 136).

IN CONVERSATION WITH SHAKESPEARE IN JACOBEAN LONDON: SOCIAL INSANITY AND ITS TAMING SCHOOLS IN *1&2 HONEST WHORE*

CHI-FANG SOPHIA LI[1]

In 1604, the Fortune Playhouse staged Dekker and Middleton's first Italian production, *The Patient Man and the Honest Whore* (hereafter *1 Honest Whore*), located in Milan.[2] In a new decade that is considered 'sick' and 'mad',[3] the creation of the play's two morally oxymoronic protagonists – 'patient madman' Candido and 'honest whore' Bellafront – is meant to unsettle the received notions of madness and prostitution. 'Madness' being the play's leitmotif, the main plot puts on stage the mad passion of two star-crossed lovers (Hippolito and Infelice) tying their knots in the Bethlem Monastery, and the equally mad passion of Bellafront pursuing her (supposed) love Hippolito. Paralleling the theme of romantic madness, the subplot presents the madness of Candido's miraculous patience as he endures the extreme double provocations of Milan's mad roaring boys and of his mad shrewish wife Viola. With the new subject matter of moral singularity introduced to the Jacobean stage in 1604, the play enjoyed an immediate accolade. Hard upon its success, its sequel – solely by Dekker – was performed within a year.[4] Extending the theme of madness, *2 Honest Whore* highlights the madness of the age by dramatizing the roaring boys' mad provocations and Candido's mad patience. It also gives the audience new material in the three deranged marriages of Hippolito and Infelice, Bellafront and Matheo, and Candido and his second shrewish wife. Not only does *2 Honest Whore* prick mad romanticism in Part I, but it also lays bare the affliction of marital infidelity. While Part I ends in Bethlem (an oxymoronic crossroads of redemption and insanity), Part II ends in Bridewell (an oxymoronic home for punishment and reform). In the wake of 1604, when

Elizabethan optimism and moral values – typified in Dekker's *The Shoemakers Holiday* (1599) – started to fade, Dekker's *Honest Whore* plays pronounce a deep cultural anxiety about the social change.

Despite both productions' conspicuous success and their continued revivals by Queen Henrietta's Men in the 1630s,[5] over the last 400 years, little critical attention has been paid to Dekker's

[1] A preliminary version of this article was read at the 2015 Literary London Conference. This thoroughly revised piece would not have been completed without the sponsorship of the Ministry of Science and Technology of Taiwan, which funded my research trips to Oxford and London, as well as to the Istituto Nazionale di Studi sul Rinascimento and the Kunsthistorisches Institut in Florence. My deepest debt is to Professor Julian Gardner (Professor Emeritus, University of Warwick), who alerted me to the wealth of Italian scholarship on the Anglo-Italian historical context.
[2] *Henslowe's Diary*, ed. R. A. Foakes (Cambridge, 2002), p. 209, f. 110.
[3] Synonyms of 'sick' and 'mad' brim over Dekker's and Middleton's satiric pamphlets published during 1603–4, the most noted one being Dekker, *The Wonderfull Yeare* (London, 1603; STC (2nd edn) 6535), to which Middleton replied with *Plato's Cap: Cast at this Year 1604* (London, 1604).

Quotations of *1 Honest Whore* and Dekker and Middleton's collaborative pamphlets are from *Thomas Middleton: The Collected Works*, ed. Gary Taylor and John Lavagnino (Oxford, 2007). References to Dekker's plays are from *The Dramatic Works of Thomas Dekker*, ed. Fredson Bowers, 4 vols. (Cambridge, 1955), vol. 2.
[4] M. T. Jones-Davies, *Un Peintre de la vie londonienne: Thomas Dekker*, 2 vols. (Paris, 1958), vol. 2, pp. 369–71.
[5] *1 Honest Whore*, which was revived in 1615, 1616 and 1635, was more successful than *2 Honest Whore*, which was revived in 1630.

intention of staging the madness of his Italian romances. For instance, early critical observations by William Hazlitt and Algernon Charles Swinburne are partial to Dekker's sentimentalism.[6] Cyrus Hoy's four-volume critical edition of Dekker not coming into being until 1980, pre-1980 research on *1&2 Honest Whore* is predominantly about the analysis of the plays' thematic structure and comic devices.[7] In 1966, while Peter Ure sees *1 Honest Whore* as an oxymoronic collaboration between sympathetic Dekker and cynical Middleton, in 1993 Viviana Comensoli establishes for the plays the *commedia dell'arte* tradition.[8] Even though Joost Daalder has rightly nullified the legitimacy of a Foucauldian reading of insanity,[9] it is not until the late 1990s that John Twyning starts to take a strong historical interest in the social dispossession of London's Bethlem and Bridewell,[10] which elicits more research on the myth and mystery surrounding the two civic institutions and the place of women in early modern London.[11] In the 2000s, Ken Jackson goes further to supply an in-depth investigation of Bethlem and Bridewell by engaging the discussion of *1&2 Honest Whore* with the literary representations of madness in the works of Shakespeare, Jonson and Marston, which make great play of classical literary conventions.[12] Moreover, Sarah Scott takes a different line of enquiry by situating her commentary on *1 Honest Whore* in a pathological context of medical humanities.[13]

Despite these increasingly interdisciplinary approaches, what remain unsaid are the nature of the plays' Italianness and the ways in which Dekker conceptualizes different cultural notions of madness under the dialogic framework of Shakespeare. That is, madness being an important theme, what has not been thoroughly investigated is the extent to which *1&2 Honest Whore* as a whole are indebted to Shakespeare's plays (mostly Italian) that exhibit individualized symptoms of madness.

It has been noticed that *2 Honest Whore* is indebted to Shakespeare's *Measure for Measure*, which, in the eyes of Dekker and Middleton, shares similar social problems to their own 'mad', 'sicke' world' (*1HW*, 12.147; *2HW*, 1.1.4).[14] Dekker's Duke of Milan, Count Hippolito and pander Bots bear some

dramaturgical resemblance to Shakespeare's Duke Vincentio, Angelo and Lucio. Dekker's Orlando Friscobaldo also has some moral affinity with Shakespeare's Vincentio as both attempt to restore moral order.[15] But could Dekker have appropriated Shakespeare's topoi *only* in Part II, given that both

---

[6] See William Hazlitt, *Lectures on the Dramatic Literature of the Age of Elizabeth* (New York, 1845), p. 69; A. C. Swinburne, *The Age of Shakespeare* (London, 1908), p. 78.

[7] See Michael Manheim, 'The thematic structure of Dekker's *2 Honest Whore*', *SEL* 5.2 (1965), 363–81; and Larry S. Champion, 'From melodrama to comedy: a study of the dramatic perspective in Dekker's *The Honest Whore, Parts I & II*', *Studies in Philology* 62.2 (1972), 192–209.

[8] See Peter Ure, 'Patient madman and honest whore: the Dekker–Middleton oxymoron', *Essays and Studies* 19 (1966), 18–40; Viviana Comensoli, 'Merchants and madcaps: Dekker's *Honest Whore* plays and the *commedia dell'arte*', in *Shakespeare's Italy: Functions of Italian Locations in Renaissance Drama*, ed. Michele Marrapodi (Manchester, 1993), pp. 125–39.

[9] Joost Daalder, 'Madness in Parts 1 and 2 of *The Honest Whore*: a case for close reading', *AUMLA: Journal of the Australasian Universities Language and Literature Association* 86 (1996), 63–79.

[10] John Twyning, *London Dispossessed: Literature and Social Space in the Early Modern City* (London, 1998).

[11] Jean E. Howard, 'Civic institutions and precarious masculinity in Dekker's *The Honest Whore*', *Early Modern Culture: An Electronic Seminar* 1 (2000); Barbara Kreps, 'The paradox of women: the legal position of early modern wives and Thomas Dekker's *The Honest Whore*', *ELH* 69.1 (2002), 83–102.

[12] Ken Jackson, 'Bethlem and Bridewell in *The Honest Whore* Plays', *SEL* 43.2 (2003), 395–413; *Separate Theaters: Bethlem ('Bedlam') Hospital and the Shakespearean Stage* (Newark, 2005).

[13] Sarah Scott, '"Sell[ing] your selues away": pathologizing and gendering the socio-economic in *The Honest Whore, Part I*', *Research Opportunities in Medieval and Renaissance Drama* 45 (2006), 1–22.

[14] See F. G. Fleay, *A Biographical Chronicle of the English Drama, 1559–1642*, 2 vols. (London, 1891), vol. 1, p. 132; Manheim, 'Thematic structure', pp. 364, 365; Ure, 'Patient madman', pp. 36–7; Cyrus Hoy, *Introductions, Notes, and Commentaries to Texts in 'The Dramatic Works of Thomas Dekker'*, 4 vols. (Cambridge, 1980), vol. 2, pp. 71–4; Larry S. Champion, *Thomas Dekker and the Traditions of English Drama* (New York, 1985; repr. 1987), p. 52; Lois Potter, 'A stage where every man play a part?' *Shakespeare Quarterly* 50.1 (1999), 74–86, p. 79.

[15] Hoy, *Introductions*, vol. 2, pp. 71–4.

parts were conceived as a whole?[16] In this article, I'm going to show that Shakespeare's plays do supply Dekker with a repertoire of mad characters who suit the dialogic purposes of Dekker's satiric creations of *1&2 Honest Whore*. Romeo, Benvolio, Tybalt, Hamlet, Ophelia, Duke Vincentio, Isabella, Angelo, Lucentio's father Vincentio and 'madman' Petruccio all strategically fill the new cultural space on Dekker's Italianized stage of theatre realism.[17] But, as I attempt to establish the link between Dekker and Shakespeare, I also want to ask: what is Dekker's dialogic agenda behind such intense theatrical appropriation? How does Dekker interpret Shakespeare's mad characters, whose heat of passion is synonymous with mad Italian roaringness? In the first decade of the 1600s, can *1&2 Honest Whore* constitute a cultural criticism of Shakespeare's penchant for Italian material and on Shakespeare's silence about England's social angst?

I am going to demonstrate that, as a critical reader of Shakespeare, Dekker is particularly interested in Shakespeare's plays that showcase different symptoms of madness. While *1 Honest Whore* draws the dramaturgical lexicon of madness from *The Taming of the Shrew*, *Romeo and Juliet* and *Hamlet*, *2 Honest Whore* develops it and cites Shakespeare's themes of double standard, moral hypocrisy and prostitution from *Measure for Measure* to dramatize the roaringness of Italian lunacy. In *Romeo*, mad Romeo's impatience, the friar's remedy, the clandestine marriage held in the monastery, and Verona's street provocations detonated by the Italian gallants' 'mad blood' (3.1.4) constitute the cultural stimuli with which Dekker conceptualizes his own Milanese stories of Hippolito and the 'mad' roaring boys who pester Candido. In *Hamlet*, the madness of Hamlet and Ophelia elicits Dekker to pen the madness of Hippolito and Bellafront, whose journey to Bethlem professes a moral purpose. In the *Shrew*, Petruccio's performative madness, for Dekker, is a fertile semantic field. Petruccio's mad impatience, 'mad attire' (3.2.43–71, 3.2.117), mad sartorial play and 'mad marriage' (3.3.55), where he exercises his mad taming provocations in his 'taming-school' (4.2.55), elicit Dekker to dramatize one female Petruccio

(Viola) and a 'mad' Kate (Viola's successor) to wreak havoc in Candido's household. 'Madness' being a liberally used notion feasting Shakespeare's romantic imagination, Dekker naturalizes such madness into what he sees as the insane social realism to be unpacked in Britain's own taming schools of Bethlem and Bridewell. While the moral solutions in Shakespeare's plays look problematic, the moral remedies in *1&2 Honest Whore* are intended to restore our faith in human goodness, embodied in Dekker's extreme moral examples of Candido and Orlando Friscobaldo, whose deeds and names call forth high moral ideals. In an age rife with new social problems, *1&2 Honest Whore* are Dekker's pioneering Italian plays that critique Shakespeare's silence about Jacobean Britain's social dispossession.

WRITING ROMANTIC LOVE

The main plot of *1 Honest Whore* is not so much about the problems of prostitution as about two interwoven romances of mad love in which 'mad' Hippolito (*1HW*, 1.9) is both '[m]adman' Romeo (*Romeo*, 2.1.7) and 'mad' Hamlet (*Hamlet*, 2.2.93). The first romance is set in the Court of Milan, which tells of two star-crossed lovers – Hippolito and Infelice – whose mutual commitment provokes parental objection similar to that faced by Romeo and Juliet. Had it not been for the ancient rivalry between the two feuding families, Hippolito, an enemy's child ('Did not mine enemy's blood boil in his veins', *1HW*, 3.28), would have become the Duke's son-in-law. *1 Honest Whore* opens the scene with the funeral procession of Infelice's coffin, in which Infelice is drugged to look dead, by her father's command. While Infelice is sent to Bergamo to recover from grief, 'mad' Hippolito contemplates alone with

---

16 I agree with Joost Daalder that when Dekker wrote *1 Honest Whore*, he had in mind the second part, *2 Honest Whore*, because Infelice's name – 'the unhappy one' in Italian – anticipates a sequel.

17 Duke Vincentio pretends to see Isabella 'mad' (*Measure*, 5.1.60).

a 'skull' (10.38–91) on Infelice's death, just like mad Hamlet soliloquizing Ophelia's mortality with the skulls (*Hamlet*, 5.1.75 SD).[18] Infelice's funeral (1.1), as we recollect, recalls both Ophelia's funeral procession (*Hamlet*, 5.1) and Juliet's death in the family vault (*Romeo*, 5.3).

Dekker's Doctor Benedict (the Duke's physician) is Shakespeare's Friar Laurence incarnate, but Benedict is a more meddlesome character. To counter the Duke's fear of the lovers' future reunion, Benedict suggests that Hippolito be poisoned. However, his ignoble proposal is rejected. Out of self-inflicted shame, Benedict leaks out Infelice's whereabouts to Hippolito and arranges for the couple to meet '[a]t Bethlem Monastery' (13.101), which recalls Romeo and Juliet's secret rendezvous at Friar Laurence's monastery. Seeing Infelice at Bethlem, Hippolito is delirious with joy because such madness is safely harboured in real lunacy:

> The place well fits –
> It is the *school* where those that lose their wits
> Practise again to get them. I am sick
> Of that disease; all love is lunatic.
>
> (13.102–5, emphasis added)

Dekker has apparently absorbed Shakespeare's romanticism of love, typified in Theseus's speech in *A Midsummer Night's Dream*:

> Lovers and madmen have such seething brains,
> Such shaping fantasies, that apprehend
> More than cool reason ever comprehends.
> The lunatic, the lover, and the poet
> Are of imagination all compact
>
> (5.1.4–8)

However, Dekker's intention is to direct the audience to see real insanity unfold in Bethlem, Britain's taming 'school' that accommodates untold stories of mad realism on Dekker's stage.

At Dekker's Bethlem Monastery, there is one Friar Anselmo, the 'knitter' (14.100) of Hippolito and Infelice's clandestine wedding, who performs the same moral duty as Shakespeare's Friar Laurence. The naming of Dekker's Friar Anselmo is not random: it is taken from one of the guests' names –

'County Anselme' (*Romeo*, 1.2.65) – on the list of the 'ancient feast of Capulet's' (1.2.84). However, while *Romeo* ends in death, *1 Honest Whore* ends in marriage. Before Friar Anselmo successfully marries the lovers, their elopement has reached the Duke's ears. Mad and angry, the Duke vows to catch the besotted 'lunatics' (*1HW*, 14.119) on the spot, whilst at the same time he also intends to visit on-site the 'madmen' (15.102). At Bethlem, Hippolito and Infelice are 'disguised in the habits of friars' (15.342 SD), only to be exposed by Bellafront, an honest, reformed whore whose life converges with theirs because her frenzied love for Hippolito finds no outlet. She therefore banishes herself to Bethlem.

How does Bellafront get to know Count Hippolito, who, in the second romance of the main plot, is shaped like Shakespeare's mad Hamlet? Their paths cross at a brothel when 'mad' Hippolito (1.9) – believing Infelice dead – is taken there by a friend called Matheo. However, Hippolito is above prostitution and his contempt for it convinces Bellafront that he can cleanse her soul. Eager to redeem her corrupt past, she enters Hippolito's chamber as a page boy to confess her love, only to be bluntly told off when Hippolito, Hamlet-like, is contemplating with a skull and Infelice's picture (10.38–91). In this scene, Dekker draws from the plot of mad Hamlet questioning the oxymoronic 'honest' 'beauty' (*Hamlet*, 3.1.109, 110) of Ophelia (whom he believes a 'whore' and tells she should get her away to 'a nunnery', 3.1.123) to script the scene for Hippolito rejecting Bellafront the honest whore. Claiming that 'beauty' and 'honesty' can never reconcile, Hamlet says to Ophelia: 'the power of beauty will sooner transform honesty from what it is to a bawd than the force of honesty can translate beauty into his likeness. This was sometime a paradox, but now the time gives it proof' (3.1.113–17). Hamlet's lines anticipate Dekker's invention of the 'honest whore'. Hamlet's subsequent prolonged scorn of

---

[18] Dekker alludes to Hamlet's madness in *Westward Ho* (1605), in which Master Tenterhook says, 'let these husbands play mad *Hamlet*, and crie revenge; come, and weele do so' (5.4.50–1).

the bawdy trade vented on Ophelia (*Hamlet* 3.1.119–21, 123–32, 137–43, 145–52) also seems to have provided a speech model for the amplified diatribe on prostitution aired through the lips of Dekker's Hamlet-like Hippolito (*1HW*, 6.371–403). As Hamlet's madness drives Ophelia insane, which forces her to drown herself (*Hamlet*, 4.7.136), Hippolito calls Bellafront a '[m]adwoman' (7.500), an abusive term that shames her to 'fly / From this undoing city' (10.202–3) to Bethlem. It is in Bethlem that Bellafront's 'bare life' contrasts Hippolito and Infelice's mad aristocratic romance.[19]

Hearing Bellafront's exposé of Hippolito's elopement to Bethlem, the Duke of Milan challenges Hippolito to 'draw' and questions the couple's friar-like 'holy habits' that are the 'cloaks for villainy' (15.383–4), which is a line that obliquely refers to Lucio's criticism of Duke Vincentio's disguise (*Measure*, 5.1.348–52). However, Friar Anselmo stops their duel, advising them 'To turn the ancient hates of your two houses / To fresh green friendship' (15.408–9). Such is the voice that echoes the prologue of *Romeo*. In the finale of *1 Honest Whore*, Dekker's Duke of Milan not only marries Hippolito and Infelice but also attempts to right the wrongs that have 'led' Bellafront's 'spirits into a lunacy' by 'marry[ing] her' with her first client Matheo (15.-453–4) amongst the Bethlem inmates. The moral decision of Dekker's Duke of Milan resembles that of Shakespeare's Duke Vincentio, who tries to restore moral order by contracting three marriages between Lucio and Kate Keepdown, Angelo and Marianna, and himself with Isabella.

In *2 Honest Whore*, Dekker extends the conversation with Shakespeare by putting on stage Shakespeare's themes of moral hypocrisy and double standards extracted from *Measure for Measure*. Part II's romantic plot darkens as Dekker makes married Hippolito a fickle Romeo and an Angelo-like, sexually crazed hypocrite who attempts to seduce married Bellafront to sin. The play opens the scene with Hippolito's gallants gossiping about his virility with Infelice, but the focus quickly shifts to Hippolito's intended infidelity at his own house

where Bellafront comes to plea for her newly wed husband Matheo, who's given the death penalty for manslaughter (1.1.116–39). This scene implicitly recalls Shakespeare's Isabella begging Angelo at his home for her brother Claudio, who is sentenced to death because of his premarital conduct with Julietta. As Shakespeare's Angelo asks Isabella to '[c]ome again tomorrow' (*Measure*, 2.2.148), Dekker's Hippolito says to Bellafront, 'To morrow let me see you' (1.1.149). In the same way that Angelo decides to spare Isabella's brother Claudio after hearing Isabella's speech, Hippolito agrees to discharge Matheo upon hearing Bellafront's petition. Both pardons are granted with a condition: Shakespeare's Angelo obliges Isabella to '[g]ive up' her 'body' 'to such sweet uncleanness' (*Measure*, 2.4.54), whereas Dekker's Hippolito intends to make Bellafront a kept woman (2.1.140–70) if Matheo the 'madcap' (2.1.223) agrees. (The irony is that chastity for the nun is an uncompromising bodily matter, whereas for the honest whore it is a hardline spiritual principle.) As Angelo feels contrite whilst alone ('What's this? What's this? Is this her fault or mine? / The tempter or the tempted, who sins most, ha?', *Measure*, 2.2.168–9), Hippolito mutters to himself, '[t]he face I would not looke on! sure then 'twas rare, / When in despight of griefe, 'tis still thus faire' (1.1.161–2).

Conceiving *1&2 Honest Whore* as one complete production, Dekker consistently translates the provocative Italian roaringness typified in *Romeo* into the characterizations of his own Italian gallants, especially Matheo, who is a composite creation drawn from Shakespeare's Benvolio and 'fiery Tybalt' (*Romeo*, 1.1.106). As Shakespeare's Benvolio advises 'mad' (1.2.53) Romeo to 'forget' (1.1.222) the pain of love that makes him 'despair' (1.1.219), Dekker's Matheo in Part I asks his friend Hippolito to disremember Infelice, whose death drives him 'mad' (*1HW*, 1.9). While Benvolio accompanies sad Romeo to see Rosalind at the Capulets' 'ancient feast' (1.2.84), where Tybalt

---

[19] My notion of 'bare life' is indebted to Giorgio Agamben in *Homo Sacer: Sovereign Power and Bare Life* (Stanford, 1998).

asks for a 'rapier' (1.5.54) to kill the Montagues, Matteo takes love-stricken Hippolito to see 'a wench' (*1HW*, 1.134) at the brothel, where he 'draws his sword' (9.72 SD) when gallant Fluello 'spurn[s]' his 'punk' (9.72–3). In Part II, Matteo in Dekker's Shakespearian re-imaginings is not merely a feisty rogue who kills 'Old Iacomo' (*2HW*, 1.1.125). He is a corrupt version of Shakespeare's easily provoked Tybalt, who kills Mercutio in 3.1. Benvolio asks Mercutio, 'Why, what is Tybalt?' (2.3.17), to which Mercutio replies: 'More than Prince of Cats [Catso, a rogue]. O, he's the courageous captain of compliments. He fights as you sing pricksong ... the very butcher of a silk button. A duellist, a duellist; a gentleman of the very first house of the first and second cause. Ah, the immortal *passado*, the *punto reverso*, the *hai*'(2.3.18–24). But Mercutio's compliment is imbued with sneer. He curses Tybalt's affected, diseased roaringness:

The pox of such antic, lisping, affecting phantasims, these new turners of accents! 'By Jesu, a very good blade, a very tall man, a very good whore.' Why is not this a lamentable thing, grandsire, that we should be thus afflicted with these strange flies, these fashionmongers, these 'pardon-me's', who stand so much on the new form that they cannot sit at ease on the old bench? O, their bones, their bones!   (2.3.26–33)

Mercutio's view of Tybalt as a duelist, fashion-monger and lecher provides a template for Dekker's construction of Matteo, whose aspiration for living like an aristocrat is akin to Mercutio's depiction. We know in Part II that, upon Matteo's return from prison, he tells Bellafront that he wants to 'flye hye' and spouts the insult 'Catzo Catzo' (*2HW*, 2.1.10). Refusing to perform the duties of a husband, Matteo consorts with 'mad rogues' and 'roaring boyes' (*2HW*, 2.1.18–19). Having pawned his cloak and rapier, Matteo unleashes his high-flown fantasy of 'wants': 'Must haue money', 'Cloake', 'Rapier, and things' and 'cash and pictures' (3.2.27–31). Seeing Matteo 'grieue at want' (3.2.101), roaring boy Ludovico Sforza bestows on him 'a suite of Sattin' and 'all things else to fit a Gentleman' (3.2.139–40), which

he feels unabashed to 'weare' to 'keep the fashion' (4.1.8, 15). The glittering accessories delude Matteo into believing that he could enjoy his grandeur: '*La, fa, sol, la, fa, la*, rustle in Silkes and Satins: there's musique in this, and a Taffety Petticoate, it makes both flie hie, – *Catzo*' (4.1.26–8).

At Matteo's home, where Bellafront's emotional captivity is staged, Dekker presents various moral trials to test Bellafront's uncompromising virtues when she faces a seducer whom she once loved. Dekker's arrangement is to present a moral contrast – whore versus nun – to Shakespeare's Isabella. As ineffectual Matteo is dogged by debts, which makes him 'flea' [flay] (3.2.38) and pawn Bellafront's gown, emotionally abused Bellafront remains unmoved when Hippolito's diamond, letter and gold are laid before her. Although Hippolito takes advantage of her emotional vulnerability to tempt her in the name of sexual liberty (4.1.260–89), Bellafront turns down such male temptation. Bellafront's uncompromising long speech against Hippolito's coercion (*2HW*, 4.1.301–30, 332–42, 347–62, 366–95) is tailored to highlight Isabella's situation, in which she answers Duke Vincentio's deviousness with silence in *Measure*. Bellafront is an extreme moral creation of Dekker, who exhibits her moral strength.

In the finales of *2 Honest Whore* and *Measure*, both dukes scapegoat the prostitutes to resurrect moral order. As Shakespeare's Duke Vincentio plucks down the city's 'houses of resort in the suburbs' (*Measure*, 1.2.93–4), Dekker's Duke of Milan 'purge[s]' the city with 'Phisicke', 'Med'cine' (4.2.89) and 'new laws' to hunt 'harlots' who flow like fish (*2HW*, 4.2.112–13) in each street. However, regardless of Bellafront's innocence, she is sent to Bridewell (5.1.10). Social outcast Bellafront is saved by no-one but her own father, Orlando Friscobaldo, the invention of Dekker alone, who in timely fashion rights her wrongs with his healing presence, a point which I will return to and develop.

WRITING DOUBLE PROVOCATIONS

The main plots of the *Whore* plays typify Dekker's Shakespearian indebtedness. In the subplots where linen draper Candido endures double provocations from home, Dekker exhibits a different critical response to the riotous Italian roaringness in *Romeo* and Petruccio's uproarious madness in the *Shrew* to express his deep anxiety about the mad humours of the age. For Dekker, such outlandish Italian roaringness in Shakespeare is coherently embodied in the seminal wording – 'to move' (to provoke) – that surfaces in the texts of both *Romeo* and the *Shrew*. In Dekker's view, Shakespeare's roaring gallants who 'distur[b]' 'our streets' (*Romeo*, 1.1.88) are Tybalt and Samson (the Capulets), as well as Mercutio and Benvolio (the Montagues), whose 'mad blood' (3.1.4) – that is, heat of passion – dictates their provocative humours. We already considered Tybalt and Mercutio. And feisty Samson boasts to Gregory in 1.1 that he will 'strike quickly' (3.1.5) if 'A dog of the house of Montague *moves*' him (3.1.7, emphasis added). Gregory warns him, 'To move is to stir, and to be valiant is to stand' (1.1.8). But Samson's reply is charged with aggressiveness: 'A dog of that house shall *move* me to stand. I will take the wall of any man or maid of Montagues' (1.1.10–12). Quarrelsome Samson then bites his thumb to provoke the Montagues, which connects the tense tempo of 1.1 with 3.1 where Benvolio cautions Mercutio that on 'hot days' (3.1.2) they must 'retire' (3.1.1), otherwise they both 'shall not scape a brawl' (3.1.3) when their 'mad blood is stirring' (3.1.4). But bellicose Mercutio retorts: 'thou art as hot a jack in thy mood as any in Italy, and as soon moved to be moody, and as soon moody to be moved' (3.1.11–3). 'Benvolio' on Mercutio's lips is a contentious gallant, who will 'quarrel with a man' (3.1.17) who has 'a hair more' or 'less' than 'his beard' (3.1.17–18). He'll also challenge someone 'for cracking nuts' (3.1.19) and 'for coughing in the street' (3.1.24–5). I will show shortly that Dekker's nit-picking roaring boy Castruccio behaves like hair-splitting Benvolio and, whatever Castruccio does in his provocations, Candido will answer with patience.

'To move' is a crucial performative lexicon that appears again eleven times in the *Shrew*, where Dekker finds the foremost template for

Shakespeare's outlandish roaring boy, Petruccio, whose strategic actions of taming are structured around the nuanced verb 'to move'. For Petruccio, 'to move' is to complete his 'mad' 'politic [...] reign' (3.3.55, 4.1.174). Most significantly, it is a verb that effects the comic madness that feasts Shakespeare's 'festive comedy'.[20] In 1.2, Petruccio, having left Verona for Padua, where he intends to 'wive and thrive as best' he 'may' (1.2.55), he tells servant Grumio that 'rough' Kate 'moves' him 'not' (1.2.71–2). Although she's as mad as the 'swelling Adriatic seas' (1.2.73), she won't 'remove' 'affection's edge' in him (1.2.6.71–2). In 2.1, when proposing to Kate, he frames her up in his verbal trap, through which he declares he's 'moved' by the 'prettiest Kate in Christendom' (2.1.187), whom he'll 'woo' for 'wife' (2.1.194). But Kate finds him a nuisance, wanting to '[r]e-move' him as a 'movable' (2.1.195–6), only to invite more intimate verbal and physical sparring of erotic taunts that finally ensnares and moves her. From 2.1 on, Petruccio's strategic 'move' acts jointly with his 'mad' humours, which provoke Kate to call him 'one half-lunatic', 'madcap ruffian' and 'swearing Jack' (2.1.282–3).[21] Having won Baptista's bid, which Baptista 'venture[s] madly' (2.1.323), Petruccio, the 'mad-brain rudesby' (3.2.10) on Katherine's lips, is entitled to wear his outlandish 'mad attire' (3.2.124) to 'move' Kate's 'impatient humour' (3.2.29). Not only is Kate 'madly mated' (3.3.116) in this 'mad and merry' (3.3.98) wedding feast where Petruccio is '*fantastically dressed*' (3.2.85 SD), but her 'mad and headstrong humour' is 'curb[ed]' (4.1.195) by the mad sartorial play performed by her 'mad master', who afterwards, in his own 'taming-school' (4.2.55), tames her by denying her food, cap and gown. Facing Petruccio's extreme domestic provocations in this 'mad marriage' (3.3.55), Kate is well advised by Tranio to cultivate 'patience', a moral remedy (3.2.21).

---

[20] C. L. Barber sees the *Shrew* as a 'festive comedy' in *Shakespeare's Festive Comedy: A Study of Dramatic Form and Its Relation to Social Custom* (Princeton, NJ, 1959).

[21] 'Madman' is a catchphrase in the *Shrew*.

Shakespeare's portraiture of these reckless Italian gallants gives Dekker a strong impression of the Italian roaringness of uncontrollable passion. From it, Dekker integrates Shakespeare's lexicons of performativity – 'to move' and 'madness' – to create the uproarious humours of his own Milanese roaring boys and Candido's two shrewish wives, whose mad provocations challenge the fundamental moral values of Candido – an antitype to Kate – whose 'patience', a moral solution, makes him *stand* as an 'immovable' 'patient man' (*1HW*, 4.8–10). In *1 Honest Whore*, the word 'move' appears sixteen times and 'mad/madness' appears forty-two times, as Dekker intends to highlight the extreme provocations to project a topsy-turvy world.

Dekker's roaring boys who frequent Candido's shop with provocative intents behave as badly as Shakespeare's gallants in *Romeo*. In *1 Honest Whore*, Candido's reputed patience is much talked about in Milan, which provokes every impatient gallant to deflate his fame. In Scene 4, Castruccio is the first one that wants to devise 'a trick' to 'sting him' (4.22–3). His sidekick Pioratto replies, 'Thou stir him? Thou move him? ... thou mayest sooner raise a spleen in an angel than rough humour in him' (4.26–30), which implicitly echoes Shakespeare's line 'To move is to stir'. Castruccio thus wagers 100 ducats to 'move ... him' (4.57). In Scene 5, three ill-intentioned roaring gallants 'find fault' with Candido's 'best' 'lawn' of Milan (5.20–1) 'without a cause' (5.50), like Shakespeare's nit-picking Benvolio finding fault with his own ill humours. Not only complaining that Candido's cambrics are 'too dear' (5.64), Castruccio also asks for a pennyworth of lawn cut from the 'middle' (5.90). Candido answers his request with well-controlled '[p]atience' (5.103). As Castruccio is unable to win, Fluello attempts another 'trick' (5.149). When Candido requites their provocations with courtesy wine served in 'the best' 'silver and gilt beaker' 'in the house' (5.186), Fluello 'bear[s] away the beaker' (5.176). Candido isn't 'moved' (5.181). When Candido's servingman George brings the constable, the roaring boys

curse Candido, who replies, 'Nay, swear not gallants, / Your oaths may move your souls, but not move me' (5.217–18).

At home, Candido endures the domestic provocations of shrewish Viola, whose humours get out of control. Seeing 'no tempest can move' (2.76) Candido, the 'man in print' (2.75), Viola yearns 'to make him horn-mad' (2.103). She solicits her brother Fustigo – an impoverished roaring boy coming to Candido's shop for money 'in some *fantastic* sea-suit' (2.1 SD, emphasis added), which recalls the '*fantastically dressed*' Petruccio (*Shrew*, 3.2.85 SD) – to play the lover, who in turn is promised to be 'put' 'into better fashion' (*1HW*, 2.50–1) and get free cambrics to furnish his 'punk' (7.50). However, Viola's trick fails, and Candido takes Fustigo to be 'a fool' (7.60) and 'madman' (7.69), which are two important signifiers that project the image of Petruccio the 'fool' (*Shrew*, 2.1.212) and 'madman'.

As Viola fails to 'vex' Candido (7.210), she plays the role of the female Petruccio to exercise a series of female rages to provoke Candido. She first denies Candido's access to his 'gown' needed for investiture 'at the senate-house' (7.189), just like Shakespeare's peremptory Petruccio refusing to allow Kate to wear the new 'gown' to return to her 'father's house' (*Shrew*, 4.3.181). When George suggests that Candido 'break open chest' (7.216–17) to get the gown, Candido disagrees because to do so would 'show impatience', which is 'against' his 'blood' (7.219–20). Candido then asks George to fetch him 'the saddest coloured carpet' (7.223), cut a hole in the middle and put it on him like a poncho, which recalls the scene of Petruccio marring Kate's new gown (4.3.60–166). As Kate wears her 'marred', 'mean habiliments' (*Shrew*, 4.3.114, 168) to return home in 'the meanest habit' (4.3.172), Candido wears the 'patient carpet' of 'the saddest colou[r]' 'without a frown' (7.223, 256–7).

As Petruccio the male tamer always wins, Viola the female Petruccio also relishes her triumph. Her next trick stages the plot of Lucentio and Tranio's master-and-servant exchange of clothes that generates the confusion of mistaken identities (*Shrew*, 1.1.208–46), which is called 'a good comedy of errors' (*1HW*, 12.25) by Dekker.[22] Viola asks servingman George to 'put on' Candido's 'best apparel, gown, / Chain, cap, ruff, everything' and 'be like' Candido (7.273–4). While presumptuous George sees such transgressive cross-dressing as 'a good comedy of errors', which delights Viola, who gloats over her trick of 'the maddest fashion' that makes Candido a 'patient madman' (12.63), Candido plays along with their game but queries the danger of such sartorial transgression: 'this chain and welted gown, / Bare to this coat? Then the world's upside down' (12.68–9). Candido's worry is not without a cause. As soon as Candido finishes his line, two 'arrant knaves' (12.117) enter Candido's shop to find fault with prentice-like Candido. One of them '*strikes him*' (12.97 SD). George summons all the prentices to 'beat and disarm' the rogues (12.99 SD), but Candido asks George to let them go. Viola finds his mad reaction unfathomable and takes in two officers to dispatch 'mad' Candido to Bethlem. Candido's imprisonment evokes Shakespeare's 'right Vincentio' (4.4.12) – Lucentio's father – who is mistaken as a 'madman' (5.1.51), 'lunatic' (5.1.65) and 'mad ass' (5.1.77) nearly sent to 'prison' (5.1.88) by Tranio the servant.

However, sending Candido to Bethlem doesn't make Viola a successful tamer. Her mad intent is reported to the Duke of Milan in the finale, where she is seen as a 'madwoman' (15.494), who longs to turn Candido 'more mad than ever was Orlando [Furioso]' (15.496–7). At Bethlem, where the Duke encounters different spectacles of madness – mad lovers, real lunatics, mad Candido and mad Viola, who begs the Duke's 'pardon' for her mad 'offence' (14.60) – staged in one place, Candido's moral singularity clears him of the charge. Hearing Candido insist that 'patience', 'the sap of bliss', should be no 'madness' but 'the soul of peace', the 'near'st kin to heaven' that 'makes men look like gods', the Duke invites Candido, the civic exemplum, to 'teach' his 'court to shine' (15.515–51).[23] As we can see, as *1 Honest Whore* is consumed with symptoms of

Shakespearian madness, it is also tinged with Dekker's revisionist irony.

In the subplot of *2 Honest Whore*, Dekker deepens the double provocations of the roaring boys and the shrew to stage the imminent social pressure menacing Candido. Dekker's purpose is to spotlight on stage the unbridled social madness encroaching on good citizenship. In the sequel, the Milanese courtiers don't believe that Candido's patience can gain currency in their venal world. When invited to Candido's second wedding feast (as Viola has died), they insult the citizens' flat-caps (1.3), just like the Capulets taunting the Montagues. But, whenever Candido is challenged, he always resorts to traditional morality (1.3.41–7), which is experiencing a sea change in a proto-capitalist society where the pursuit of wealth is dissolving good character. Candido's shop, to say the least, is synecdochically a site that has to accommodate constant social bedevilments. And outside Candido's house at Matheo's, where Candido is tricked into buying the purloined goods (4.3.66–7) and drinking to a whore (4.3.85–6), good citizen Candido is embroiled in criminal offences.

After Viola's death, Candido's domestic life continues to be disrupted by the second shrewish wife as, in Dekker's view, women on top have become a mad normality. Candido's new bride is a 'mad' Kate, who beats the servant only because she is given the wrong wine (*2HW*, 1.3.81 SD). When Candido wants to ease the situation with a toast, she walks out (1.3.92 SD). Seeing Candido's masculinity so abused, Ludovico (disguised as an apprentice) offers advice (2.2.19–21), which Candido is reluctant to follow. As

---

22 Dekker is aware of the plot of mistaken identity in Shakespeare's *Errors*, but George and Candido's cross-dressing is indebted to the master-and-servant cross-dressing plot in the *Shrew*.

23 Candido's final speech on 'patience' is modelled on Portia's speech on 'mercy' in *The Merchant of Venice* (4.1.181–202). See Harold Reinoehl Walley and John Harold Wilson, *Early Seventeenth-century Plays, 1600–1642* (New York, 1930), p. 106.

Candido's wife continues to ignore him, he, feeling like 'an asse', loudly exclaims, 'Wife, Ile tame you' (2.2.74)![24] On stage, husband and wife fight to wear 'the breeches' (2.2.77–98). When she threatens 'Ile not strike in iest' (2.2.99), Candido welcomes the challenge: 'Strike' (2.2.104). To everybody's surprise, she *kneeles* (2.2.105 SD), just as Shakespeare's Kate suggests in the submission speech: 'they [women] should kneel for peace' (*Shrew*, 5.2.167). Like Kate, Candido's bride not only 'disdaine[s] / The wife that is her husbands Soueraigne' but also compromises on female sovereignty: 'You win the breeches, but I win the day' (*2HW*, 2.2.108–15; *Shrew*, 5.2.141–84). With Shakespeare's *Shrew* in mind, Dekker ends Candido's domestic bedevilments by making the couple renounce the right to control.

1604: SHAKESPEARE'S SILENCE

As I have shown, most of Dekker's Italian characters in *1&2 Honest Whore* – Hippolito, Doctor Benedict, Matheo, Candido's shrews, Fustigo, roaring boys and courtiers – drawn from Shakespeare's prototypes, have become the sources of moral chaos in his Italian romances. Even Dekker's fictional Ludovico Sforza – an antitype to the historical Ludovico Sforza (il Moro), the fourth Duke of Milan (1452–1508), as documented in Francesco Guicciardini's *La historia d'Italia* (1561)[25] – is dwindled to be a yob. These characters project Dekker's Italophobic sentiments about foreign influences to contrast Shakespeare's Italophile sensibilities about cultural aspirations. Indeed, Shakespearian romanticism in the eyes of Dekker is essentially a social nightmare. Why, then, does Dekker appropriate Shakespeare's Italian imaginings to create a mad world in which Renaissance Milan is reduced to a rogue state and her problematic people are collectively shut in Bethlem and Bridewell, Britain's two taming schools?

Using Shakespeare's materials, especially in a year when *Measure* was performed almost concurrently with the publications of Dekker's (and Middleton's) satiric pamphlets that depict the social madness of a 'London that yee see howerly',[26] Dekker intends to debunk Shakespeare's rosy imaginations of Italy to redirect the audience's attention to England's home issues, which Shakespeare has never written about. I want briefly to provide a context of the plague-stricken year of 1603/4 – to read against Shakespeare's silence about social change – for which Dekker and Middleton supply a 'thick description' of pathologized discourses of a sick London whose 'madness', a new lexicon, is invested with social realism.[27]

In 1603, when the plague silenced London's raucous theatres and deferred King James I's royal entry into London, prayers, sermons and pamphlets published in that 'annus mirabilis' were meant to console the perturbed souls who couldn't make sense of such a 'strange out-landish' 'Change' (*The Wonderfull Yeare*, B2v). As the figures in London's mortality bills prompted an upsurge of almanacs and prognostications, Dekker's and Middleton's satiric pamphlets also register the 'horor of a change' (B2v). Amongst the pamphlets that best capture the acute social angst of 1603 is *The Wonderfull Yeare*. It envisions a new kingdom – a 'sicke Country' (C3r) – falling into an 'ague' and 'feauer' (C1r). Its imminent-distress narrative graphically captures Britain's acute conditions: 'the great impostume of the realme was drawne Euen to a head'; 'corruption' 'did make it swell with hop'd sedition'; 'ruine, bloud, and death' 'share our kingdome, and deuide our breath' (B3r). The 'plague', 'Burning feauers, Boyles, Blaines, and Carbuncles', and 'Death' 'pitcht his tents ... in the sinfully-polluted Suburbes' (D1r). 'Phlebotomies, Lozenges, Electuaries, with their Diacatholicons, Diacodions, Amulets, and Antidotes' work no better than 'a pot of Pindar's

---

[24] *1&2 Honest Whore*, which critique Shakespeare's *Shrew*, predate John Fletcher's *The Tamer Tamed* (c. 1611–12).

[25] The Italian text was translated into English by Sir Geoffrey Fenton in 1579: STC (2nd edn) 12458. Both texts were available to Dekker.

[26] Thomas Heywood, *The Four Prentices of London* (London, 1615), sig. A4v: STC (2nd edn) 13321. The play was performed c. 1592.

[27] The term 'thick description' is taken from *Western Drama Through the Ages*, ed. Kimball King, 2 vols. (Westport, CT, 2007), vol 1, p. 43.

ale' (D3r). 'In such a panting time and gasping yeare' (B3vr), 'the loude grones of rauing sicke men' and 'the strugling panges of soules departing' become the loud 'Allarum' (C3v) of this 'dangerous sore Citie' (D2r) shot by 'arrowes of pestilence' (D2v). Groans echoed through the trunk of the quills complain about fickle life and sudden death, false hope and real despair. Such is a sick world of social madness. Such is a London that Shakespeare sees hourly but remains reticent about.

In *News from Gravesend* (1604), which was written in the 'queasy times' (l. 442), Dekker and Middleton invoke the 'aid' of '[p]hysic' (l. 444) because the contagious winds of pestilent miasma and 'poisonous fumes' (l. 528) have penetrated into 'our arteries' (l. 546). Pestilence is construed as God's 'vengeance' (l. 626). '[P]rinces' errors', 'faults of peers', 'courtier's pride, lust, and excess', 'churchman's painted holiness', 'lawyer's grinding of the poor', 'scholar's envy', 'farmer's curse' (ll. 639–49) and Britain's complacency constitute the corporate sins of a nation awaiting a cure. In the '"Railing"' (l. 254) of *The Ant and the Nightingale* (1604), Middleton, through an ant's voice, also attributes the national afflictions to the moral failings of prodigal landlords and 'fantastical sponge[s]' (l. 576), because they have victimized ploughmen, soldiers and scholars, the three fundamental estates of the nation (ll. 953–1047, 1145–69). The voice of such collective suffering resonates with the 'sore discourse' (l. 212) of Dekker and Middleton's *The Meeting of Gallants at an Ordinary* (1604), where tales told in jest would best be served as 'anchovies to relish your drink well' (l. 314). But these tales in earnest identify various representations of 'drunken madness' (ll. 353–4) as a new cause of death. Such pathologized 'madness' becomes the new 'comedy of errors' (l. 541) – again, a term that mocks Shakespeare's romanticism – whereby various 'shipwreck[ed]' (l. 525) drunkards are ditched into the infected corpses waiting to be burnt (ll. 362–540). Equally pathetic scenes 'played upon the stage both of the city and the suburbs' (ll. 543–4) include masters dispatching 'porters' to 'carry their servants out in sacks' to 'poor men's houses' (ll. 545–57), and

'ravenous' sextons living upon 'dead carcasses' (ll. 558–76). Where ghoulish mirth registers an anaesthetized mode of life, laughter becomes an uncharitable commodity of the tavern, evoking a kind of 'sore' 'violence' (l. 608) that destabilizes the traditional belief in *ars moriendi*.

Middleton goes further in *The Black Book* (1604), examining with a magnifying glass the black villainies of 'this cunning age' (l. 12). Through the narration of Lucifer the night-walker, Middleton uncovers an invisible sick economy of London in which the squalid details of whore-mongering, cozenage, panderism and exploitation are troped in the objects of revelation of Lucifer's tour. Grotesque scenes spotlit inside the pernicious brothel-houses are the bawd's 'fat-sag chin hanging down like a cow's udder' (l. 132), 'floor' 'strewed with busk-points, silk garters, and shoestrings' (l. 149), a whoremonger 'more' outrageous than 'Cerberus' (ll. 169–70), and 'knaves div[ing] into the deeds and writings of lands left to young gull-finches' (ll. 318–19). Inside the nefarious room of another 'ragged' and 'tattered' brothel, Lucifer finds it a 'pitiful' sight under King James's royal carpet (ll. 409–13). Why? As Lucifer marches into an ordinary (l. 509), gamblers who 'rage, curse and swear like' 'Emperors of Darkness' are members of the twelve livery companies (ll. 531–2). As he 'walked in Pauls to see fashions', he chances upon 'villainous meetings, pernicious plots, black humours and a million of mischiefs' 'bred in that cathedral womb' (ll. 557–9). Shrouding Britain's moral outlook are black villainies that make Lucifer 'sick in soul' (l. 594).

Moreover, in his *Plato's Cap: Cast at this Year 1604*, which responds to Dekker's *The Wonderfull Yeare*, Middleton predicts dishonesty will become the reigning virtue. Using the language of 'comic prognostication' (ll. 24–5), Middleton vents his moral ridicule: when the sun enters into Taurus (Lent), butchers sell 'beef', so the 'red herring' must 'hang himself' (ll. 81–8); into Gemini, maids should 'beware of having twins (ll. 96–9); into Leo, coiners counterfeit money (ll. 123–8); into Virgo, 'maidenheads will be cheaper than mackerels' (l. 132); into Libra, the grocer 'turn[s] the scales with a false finger' (l. 140); into Scorpio, all must 'beware of brokers, usurers and pettifoggers', the 'scorpions of the kingdom' (ll. 146–7); into Aquarius, 'brewers' will 'put too much Thames in their beer' (ll. 175–6). As 'this dangerous and perilous conjunction portends many sudden and furious tempests' in 1604 (ll. 261–2), 'palsy' is believed to be the 'shrewd disease this year' (l. 326). Britain would be paralysed (ll. 326–35) by 'consumptions', which have made her 'so consumed in their members', 'so consumed in conscience' and 'so consumed by inchastity' (ll. 341–6). Dekker's and Middleton's serious warnings forebode an acute sense of moral crisis that echoes a mad world, demonstrated not only in *1&2 Honest Whore*, but also in Middleton's *Michaelmas Term* (1604), *A Trick to Catch the Old One* (1605) and *A Mad World, My Masters* (1605).

During 1603–4, publications almost always scrutinize the moral causes of the nation's epidemic crises, through which the new representations of the seven deadly sins reflect the pathological psychology of the crowds and their imitative habits spreading fast like the plague. Nevertheless, in a decade in which the plague intermittently returned (1604, 1606, 1607–9), Shakespeare's silence – compared to Dekker's and Middleton's 'sore discourse' – marks a provocative (in)difference.[28] While Dekker and Middleton are keen to capture the crude reality, Shakespeare is tacit about it. While Dekker and Middleton are more alert to national misfortunes and collective moral crises, Shakespeare is more interested in problems of personal insanity. Hamlet's madness (1600–1), Angelo's sick mind (1603–4), Othello's mad jealousy (1603–4), Lear's insanity (1605–6), Macbeth's crazed obsession (1606) and Timon's envy (1606), for Dekker and Middleton, all look too individualized to relate to England's boiling social pressure.

Measure for Measure, in particular, for Dekker (and Middleton) is a provocative 'problem play'[29] full of moral oxymorons. Duke Vincentio's devious self-regard is well justified; Angelo's immoral intent is rewarded by forsaken Mariana's self-offering; Isabella's chastity is more a bodily matter than a selfless sacrifice. Sex is paradoxically a problem and solution, whereas marriage is a quick fix for all. While bawds, lechers and drunkards run loose, the causes of prostitution and criminal offences are underrepresented. *Measure* lacks effective moral solutions. Therefore, Dekker's extreme creations of the oxymoronic moral examples in *1&2 Honest Whore* are meant to answer Shakespeare's oxymoronic moral examples of Vincentio, Angelo and Isabella. To harness the critical agenda that responds to Shakespeare, Dekker sets up polarized views of the world in his plays. That is, the comparative deeds of whore versus nun, father versus duke, and citizen versus gallant are set in parallel. Dramatic arrangements such as marriage versus romance, national plight versus individual tragedies, moral remedies versus quick-fix solutions, good-willed guise versus devious disguise, patience versus calculation, charity versus leniency are overwritten with Dekker's critical awareness of Shakespeare's silence.

DEKKER'S MORAL PROPOSAL

Most importantly, in the *Whore* plays, Dekker puts forward an urgent moral proposal by staging Bellafront's goodness, Candido's patience and Orlando Friscobaldo's healing presence of moral action and love. Their persistence in practising goodness – a moral rarity and madness – is intended to defend benevolence that is precariously at stake. We have already considered Bellafront and Candido. I want to round off this article by looking at Dekker's foremost moral pillar, Orlando Friscobaldo, an ingenious invention that not only contrasts Shakespeare's Duke Vincentio with the authoritarian parents, but sets a high moral benchmark in an age replete with growing unease.

The uniqueness of Orlando Friscobaldo is not so much that he is Bellafront's 'guardian angel'[30] as

---

[28] Perhaps for this reason, Middleton returns to revise *Measure for Measure*. See Gary Taylor and John Jowett, *Shakespeare Reshaped, 1606–1623* (Oxford, 1993).

[29] F. S. Boas, *Shakspere and his Predecessors* (London, 1896), pp. 344–408.

[30] George Saintsbury, *A History of Elizabethan Literature* (London, 1887), p. 205.

that he is a creation that integrates the chivalric repute of Ludovico Ariosto's *Orlando furioso* (1516, 1532) and the financial bounty of a prominent banking family, the Frescobaldi of medieval Florence.[31] Ariosto's mad Orlando is known for his chivalric deeds and frenzied love for Angelica. As Sir John Harington's translation (1591) and Robert Greene's dramatization (1594) of Ariosto's *Orlando* tell us, Orlando is one of the twelve paladins of Charlemagne.[32] When Charlemagne's Paris is under siege by the Saracens, Orlando is supposed to defend it. However, he is enamoured of the beautiful Angelica, the Princess of Cathay, who causes great rivalry between Christian and pagan knights. Orlando's chivalric quest for Angelica in the adventures is motivated by crazed love that, when unrequited, makes him fall 'starke mad, with sorrow taken' ('The Argument', Canto XXIII). As Orlando witnesses Angelica and Medoro's names engraved on a tree, he's swollen with a 'raging pang' (XXIII, 88). After three sleepless nights, Orlando 'rents his clothes', 'runs about starke naked', sheds all armour, and wanders naked alone in the forest, raging like a savage beast (XXIII, 106–8). His madness elicits pity from other Christian knights, among whom English knight Astolfo is in quest for a cure. Orlando, his sanity restored, continues to champion the Christian cause. I will demonstrate shortly that, from Ariosto's Orlando, Dekker translates his reputed madness and quest for Angelica into Orlando Friscobaldo's fatherly love and quest for a lost daughter, Bellafront, to fulfil a moral obligation.

The surname 'Friscobaldo' is extracted from Dekker's cultural knowledge of the Frescobaldi of Florence, who, like the Riccardi of Lucca, were active in their money-lending business in medieval England when King Edward I (1272–1307) and King Edward II (1307–27) needed money to wage war against France and Scotland. As an important money provider to the English Crown,[33] the Frescobaldi – starting from founder Berto and his two sons Bettino and Amerigo (heads of the company) – in return enjoyed certain economic privileges, including receiving revenues from the customs and wool duties.[34] The English Crown also entitled them to own (not hereditary) manors, castles, lands and woods.[35] During the sixteenth century, Thomas Cromwell and Henry VIII continued to benefit from the Frescobaldis' timely loans resulting from the banking family's achievements in their English branch directed by Bettino's and Amerigo's descendants.[36] The friendship between Thomas Cromwell and Francesco Frescobaldi is well known,[37] and was widely circulated in Matteo Bandello's Italian *novelle*. Bandello writes that, when the two met in Florence, Thomas was begging for alms because of the battle of Garigliano (1503). Without the extreme generosity of Francesco, who housed and financed Thomas (then a stranger), the latter's safe return to England wouldn't have been possible. After reaching a prestigious position at Henry VIII's court, Thomas was able to repay Francesco's goodwill when Francesco's wheel of fortune in Florence was turned. The Frescobaldis' good name lived

---

[31] Regarding the Frescobaldi, I owe this point to Professor Julian Gardner (Professor Emeritus of the University of Warwick), who advised me to consult *Il Dizionario biografico degli italiani* (Rome, 1960; hereafter cited as *DBI*), particularly the 'Frescobaldi' in vol. 50, pp. 465–508.

[32] Ariosto's Italian *Orlando furioso* having been published in 1532, Sir John Harington translated it into English heroic verse in 1591: STC (2nd edn) 746. Three years later, English playwright Robert Greene dramatizes the story in *The historie of Orlando Furioso* (London, 1594): STC (2nd edn) 12265. Both translations were known to Elizabethan playwrights.

[33] See W. E. Rhodes, 'The Italian bankers in England and their loans to Edward I and Edward II', in *Historical Essays by Members of the Owen College, Manchester*, ed. T. F. Toot and James Tait (London, 1902), pp. 137–68.

[34] See especially 'Berto', 'Bettino' and 'Amerigo' under the 'Frescobaldi' entry in the *DBI*.

[35] See 'Frescobaldi, Amerigo', in the *DBI*, vol. 50, pp. 465–7.

[36] The Frescobaldi were honoured with the title of 'Royal Merchants' ('regi mercanti' in Italian). See A. Sapori, *La compagnia dei Frescobaldi in Inghilterra* (Florence, 1947), p. 30. For modern history critic R. Goldthwaite, they are 'the ubiquitous agents of exchange' in England. See R. Goldthwaite, 'Italian bankers in medieval England', *Journal of European Economic History* 2 (1973), 763–71, p. 765.

[37] See 'Frescobaldi, Francesco' in the *DBI*, vol. 50, pp. 477–8.

on: Bandello's story is translated into English by John Foxe in *The Book of Martyrs* (*Actes and monuments*, 1596).[38] Francesco is subsequently dramatized as 'Master Friskiball' in a comedy entitled *The True Chronicle Historie of the whole life and death of Thomas Lord Cromwell* (1602), which is attributed to W. S.[39] Francesco's brother Leonardo Frescobaldi also maintained a reciprocal relationship – both official and private – with Henry VIII, who granted him a special guardianship and a ten-year right to trade with England.[40] So, for Dekker, what 'the Frescobaldi' epitomizes is a moral reputation for helping and providing. Based on the chivalric actions of Ariosto's Orlando and the good name of the Frescobaldi, Dekker's Orlando Friscobaldo will surely come to the rescue: he will enter Bellafront's tormented life to take moral action and to give largesse to honour his given name.

In *2 Honest Whore*, Dekker's Orlando introduces himself as 'old mad Orlando' (1.2.35) as he enters the stage. Why is he calling himself 'mad'? Because his persistence in practising his extraordinary moral philosophy makes him 'mad' like no other. From the outset of the play, Dekker makes firm the moral singularity of his 'mad Orlando' as a moral contrast to Shakespeare's devious Vincentio. When Hippolito asks his old acquaintance Orlando Friscobaldo what makes him young and happy (1.2.48), Orlando replies that his freedom from wants makes him worthy of happiness:

He that makes gold his wife, but not his whore.
He that at noone-day walkes by a prison doore,
He that 'ith Sunne is neither beame nor moate,
He that's not mad after a Petticoate,
He for whom poore mens curses dig no graue,
He that is neither Lords nor Lawyers slaue,
He that makes This his Sea, and That his Shore,
He that in's Coffin is richer then before,
He that counts Youth his Sword, and Age his staffe,
He whose right hand carues his owne Epitaph,
He that vpon his death-bead is a Swan,
And Dead, no Crow, he is a happy man.

(1.2.54–65)

His philosophy of life sets him apart from courtiers obsessed with venery and luxury. And in the face of the temporality of secular possessions and attachments, Dekker's mad Orlando is one who can enjoy his inner peace and good name: 'I am not couetous, am not in debt, sit neither at the Dukes side, nor lie at his feete … no man I wrong, no man I feare … I take heed how farre I walke, because I know yonders my home. I would not die like a rich man … but like a good man, to leaue *Orlando* behind me' (1.2.68–73).

In 1.2, when told of Bellafront's circumstances due to Matheo's act of manslaughter, Orlando, knowing well that 'pouerty dwells next doore to despaire' (1.2.169), sets out on a father's quest for a daughter whom he hasn't seen for seventeen years. Disguised as Orlando's old servant, called Pacheco, he enters Bellafront's life just in time, upon Matheo's return from prison. Orlando/Pacheco is no ordinary wage-seeking servant: he is a money provider who has 'gold' (2.1.87) and will secretly watch Matheo to protect Bellafront. He tells the couple that his household service is out of his love for the old master (2.1.214–17), so he seeks no financial gain. In 2.1, he offers Matheo 'twenty pound[s]' (2.1.90) in the hope that Matheo can abstain from 'letchery' and 'Couetousnes' (2.1.77–84), the cause of Bellafront's sufferance.

Orlando's moral character is an intangible asset that Bellafront inherits, and Dekker wants to mark her moral singularity in the same scene. When Hippolito sends Bellafront gifts (2.1.150) and 'gold' (2.1.233), Bellafront stoutly rejects the seeming 'almes' from 'a Lord' (2.1.234–5): 'He thinks a siluer net can catch the poore, / Here's baite to choake a Nun, and turne her whore' (2.1.236–7). Seeing Bellafront's incorruptible soul, Orlando finds Bellafront his 'Girle still' (2.1.250). Her moral lustre contrasts with Hippolito's dark lust

---

[38] See 'Frescobaldi, Francesco' in the *DBI*, vol. 50, pp. 476–7. See also John Foxe, *Actes and monuments of these later and perilous dayes* (London, 1596), vol. 2, p. 1082; M. Bandello, *Le novella*, ed. G. Brognoligo (Bari, 1911), vol. 3, pp. 233–41.

[39] As the STC speculates, W. S. could be William Shakespeare or William Smith. See STC (2nd edn) 21532, sigs. C2v, C3r, E4r and E4v.

[40] See 'Frescobaldi, Leonardo' in the *DBI*, vol. 50, p. 497.

(2.1.254–8) as she is a 'Starre' brighter than 'the moon' (2.1.252).

Knowing Hippolito's adulterous intent, Orlando takes action to prevent it. In 3.1, Orlando/Pacheco calls upon Infelice with Hippolito's gifts bestowed upon Bellafront. However, compassionate Orlando is reluctant to denounce Hippolito before Infelice, 'the unhappy one'. He discreetly conceals the truth in the metaphor of an inherited land, which is to be enclosed by a Lord who 'would faine be a Ranger'. On behalf of Bellafront, Orlando/Pacheco beseeches Infelice 'the Huntresse' to let that lord 'runne a course' in his 'owne Parke' (3.1.41–4). With Hippolito's gifts laid before her, Infelice, upon Orlando's departure, interrogates Hippolito with the clock-going-false conceit in their domestic drama of emotional tension (3.1.86–225). As Orlando returns the gifts, he acts as moral compass for Hippolito, who nearly wrecks his marriage.

Upon returning home, Orlando/Pacheco continues his moral duty to provide when he discovers that Matheo has squandered his 'twenty pounds' (3.2.49–50). Seeing ruined Matheo stripping Bellafront's gown, Orlando/Pacheco cannot bear to see him strip away her last shred of dignity. He gives 6 ducats to Matheo's broker, and another 2 ducats to Bellafront (3.2.154). As Orlando bestows charity, he also condemns Matheo's depravity: 'Sell his wiues cloathes from her backe?' 'He Riots all abroad, wants all at home; he Dices, whores, swaggers, sweares, cheates, borrowes, pawnes … i'the end he'll delude all my hopes' (3.2.157–61).

Unlike Shakespeare's Duke Vincentio, Dekker's Orlando is an uncompromising moral force who requires no disguise to challenge, face-to-face, his antitype. In 4.1, where Orlando – 'like himself' (4.1.28 SD) – sees Matheo dote upon the new satin suit, he reproaches his recklessness. Hearing Matheo insist that Bellafront 'be maintained' 'like a Queane' (4.1.82, 85), Orlando castigates Matheo the 'Thiefe', 'Murtherer', 'Cheater', 'Whoremonger', 'Pothunter', 'Borrower' and 'Begger' (4.1.91–2). Matheo in return calls Orlando 'old Asse', 'Dog', 'Churle', 'Chuffe', 'Vsurer', 'Villain', 'Moth' and 'mangy Mule' (4.1.94–5). The collision of good and

evil provokes Bellafront to explain the cause of her fall. She asks Orlando why for so many years she was left 'frozen to death' (4.1.125–6). It was never her intention to 'sell' her 'body to base men' (4.1.130) because she was very 'poore' and wanted 'bread to eat' (4.1.142). However, Orlando pretends not to believe her. His anger, vented upon Matheo's 'satin' (which should be baked and stewed, 4.1.145–7) and Bellafront's past, is actually aimed at nihilism. On stage, it is Orlando's moral conviction that contrasts with Matheo's nihilistic wants.

At Bellafront's house, Orlando's/Pacheco's presence constitutes an important moral space, which is meant to absorb Bellafront's emotional stress. Upon hearing Matheo ask poverty-stricken Bellafront to bring him 'some meate', Orlando protests against Matheo's lack of conscience: 'Doe but touch one haire of her, and Ile so quilt your cap with old Iron … Does she looke like a roasted Rabbet, that you must haue the head for the braines' (4.1.190–3)? As their confrontation persists, Orlando reproaches Matheo for the complete 'Shipwracke' (4.1.195–230). For Bellafront, who has no-one to turn to, Orlando/Pacheco offers a safe harbour.

In 4.3, where Orlando makes a brief appearance, he/Pacheco also demonstrates moral courage to rescue Candido, who is trapped in Matheo's villainy. Seeing the roaring boys corrupting Candido's goodness (4.319–29), Orlando/Pacheco quietly brings in the constable when asked to bring in the lawns (4.3.116–35). With Orlando's/Pacheco's moral intervention, all are sent to Bridewell.

In the finale, where Dekker keeps reminding the audience of the charitable purpose of the 'ancient' establishment of Bridewell (5.2.2), Orlando performs one final chivalric deed to right the wrongs for Bellafront, who scapegoats the sins of Milan's civic selfishness. When Matheo and Bellafront are brought forward to the Duke, Bellafront begs his 'mercy' to spare 'desperate' Matheo (5.2.55–7). Yet recalcitrant Matheo incriminates Bellafront as his culprit: 'she set the robbery, I perform'd it; she spur'd me on, I gallop'd away' (5.2.122–3). Such an outrage appals the Duke: 'What fury prompts thee on to kill thy wife?' (5.2.143). Matheo answers with mad delusions: 'it's my humour, Sir, 'tis a foolish Bag-pipe that I make my selfe merry with: why should I eate hempe-seed at the Hangmans thirteen-pence half-penny Ordinary, and haue this whore [Bellafront] laugh at me as I swing, as I totter' (5.2.144–7). At this point, Matheo, Infelice and Hippolito put forward their three-way allegations of collective bullying, exacerbating Bellafront's pain. Matheo alleges that she is Hippolito's 'Whore' (5.2.154); Infelice accuses her of stealing her husband and 'gold' and 'Iewels' (5.2.169–72); Hippolito denies that he would 'tempt her to lust' (5.2.177). Seeing such mad evilness engulfing her innocence, Orlando 'recouers himselfe' (5.2.178 SD) to provide a testimony of Bellafront's guiltlessness (5.2.179–90). When the Duke asks Orlando for a verdict on Matheo's offences, Orlando probes the depth of Bellafront's soul: 'Has he not beaten thee, kickt thee, trod on thee …? has hee not pawned thee to thy Petticoate, sold thee to thy smock … ?', 'yet woodst haue me saue him' (5.2.463–7). Just as compassionate Orlando never disowns his daughter, good Bellafront will never forsake her husband. She says to Orlando: 'Oh yes, good sir, women shall learne of me, / To loue their husbands in greatest misery, / Then shew him pitty, or your wracke my self' (5.2.467–9). Seeing Bellafront's rare virtue, Orlando furnishes Matheo with his 'house', 'meate', 'wine' and 'money' (5.2.479–82) to fulfil his uncompromising principles of charity. In the finale, where Bellafront and Orlando's deeply religious moral decision redeems Matheo, it is their unfaltering moral conviction that triumphs over the mad iniquity of Milan.

In *The Taming of the Shrew*, Shakespeare's Tranio (as Lucentio), having watched Petruccio torture Kate, says to Bianca, 'Faith, he [Petruccio] is gone unto the taming-school' (4.2.55). Bianca wonders, 'The taming-school – what, is there such a place?'

Tranio/Lucentio answers, 'Ay, mistress, and Petruccio is the master' (4.2.56–7). Shakespeare's creation of a raucous madhouse is to entertain, but Dekker seizes the tail-end of the *Shrew* to create a mad world where his own Milanese tales scapegoat the sins of Britain, whose own taming schools are laden with boiling social pressure. Through honest whore Bellafront, patient madman Candido and old mad Orlando, whose paths are crossed by many nobilities and inmates whose lives converge with theirs, we see the ways in which Dekker interrogates the nature of madness to trace the causes of individual and collective misfortunes. At Bethlem, we see the inmates' hereditary deformity and tragedies unfold. At Bridewell, we hear the intense stories of fraudulent and abused prostitutes, whose names embody the oxymoronic truth of moral pretence and corporate venery. 'Dorothea Target', 'a bride' (5.2.266), is both 'God's gift' and every lecher's target. 'Penelope Whore-hound', 'like a Cittizens wife' (5.2.313 SD), pretends to be as steadfast as Odysseus' wife to be sought after by every whore-hound. 'Cathyryna Bountiful', 'burnt', 'whipt', 'carted', 'duck'd', 'search'd' countless times (5.2.374–6), continues to feign virginity to live a 'bare life'. If the Shakespearian madness of romanticism is a theatrical expression of poetic aspiration, the Dekkerian madness of social realism projects a phenomenal social nightmare of the new age. If Shakespearian romanticism advances an ardent pursuit of romantic passion, Dekkerian optimistic realism is dedicated to bolstering traditional moral order in Jacobean London. From Dekker's morally ambitious plays, we see the ways in which Dekkerian optimistic realism revises Shakespearian romanticism. Such optimistic realism under Dekker's compassionate quill is no oxymoron, but an honest looking-glass, which showcases the roaring madness of Italy as the cultural other to mirror London's own moral predicaments.

HEARING VOICES: SIGNAL VERSUS URBAN NOISE IN *CORIOLANUS* AND AUGUSTINE'S *CONFESSIONS*

LARS ENGLE

Sound studies is a relatively new area of academic writing. The issue of separating signal or true voice from a noisy environment might be thought a distinctive problem of modernity. Certainly, the need to screen out noise figures prominently in modern fiction. Saul Bellow, in *Humboldt's Gift*, has his stand-in character Charlie Citrine say this about what went wrong for Von Humboldt Fleisher, himself a stand-in for the dead poet Delmore Schwartz. Citrine explains to his companion Renata Koffritz how true poets screen out noise to hear an inner voice, something Humboldt couldn't do:

'Where are the poets' power and interest? They originate in dream states. These come because the poet is what he is in himself, because a voice sounds in his soul which has a power equal to the power of societies, states, and regimes. You don't make yourself interesting through madness, eccentricity, or anything of the sort but because you have the power to cancel the world's distraction, activity, noise and become fit to hear the essence of things.'[1]

Citrine's position – in a novel full of the comic energies of a noisy world – strikes a hierarchical, old-fashioned, even Platonizing claim for the possibility of a transcendent inner life in which one attends to the soul's true voice. This article explores how signal, voice, sound and noise, terms of art in contemporary sound studies, bear on Shakespeare's *Coriolanus* and Augustine's *Confessions*.

In a vatic passage often cited by contemporary practitioners of sound studies, Michel Serres hints that the greatest human creations, 'masterworks'

rather than mere 'works', incorporate not only order but also disorder, not only melody but also noise: 'The work is made of forms, the masterpiece is the formed fount of forms; the work is made of time, the masterpiece is the source of time; the work is in tune, the masterwork shakes with noises. Whoever doesn't hear this noise has never written sonatas. The masterwork unceasingly makes noise and sound.' Serres makes an implicit metaphysical argument that noise must necessarily be present as an element or background or defining other of formal order:

We must keep the word noise, the only positive word that we have to describe a state that we always describe negatively, with terms like disorder ... There is chaos, there is a circumstance, and that is all the foundation there is. There is the white noise, then a noise in the white noise, and that is all the song there is. There is the permanent flow, then a fluctuation in this flow and that is the river of time.

Serres continues by politicizing this appreciation of noise in a populist way:

There is the Roman crowd, a turbulent, agitated, strong, magnificent throng, there are the mob and the multitude, there is the population, what chain of small circumstances made it move along throughout its history? The mob is always the bearer of the possible, this flow is always the bearer of different times, chaos is always there to serve as a foundation,

---

[1] Saul Bellow, *Humboldt's Gift* [1975] (New York, 1984), p. 312.

the noise is always there to invent new music and new harmonies.[2]

However they feel about noise and order, whether or not they see the Roman plebeians as a magnificent throng, modern egalitarians like me tend to follow the democratizing tendencies of this oracular passage in evaluating the actions of arrogant aristocrats like Coriolanus who see the members of the Roman crowd as 'things created / To ... be still and wonder / When one but of my ordinance stood up / To speak of peace or war' (3.2.10–14).[3] Nor do most critics see any of the many voices that sound in *Coriolanus* reaching into the protagonist's soul to speak to him of what Saul Bellow's Citrine calls 'the essence of things'. In what follows, however, I set aside discomfort at Coriolanus' autocratic convictions to focus on his tragic attempt to follow an authentic inner voice.

To accomplish this, I compare Caius Martius in a sustained way to someone who announces at every turn that he seeks to attend to a voice that speaks of the essence of things: St Augustine. *Coriolanus* and Augustine's *Confessions* map the life-trajectories, amid Roman noise, of very different men: the Augustine who becomes the sainted Bishop of Hippo, and the Martius who becomes Coriolanus. Different as they are, their lives have many similarities. Martius plays an important part in the transformation of Rome from a monarchy to a republic, which he then almost destroys because it cannot satisfy or live up to his convictions about how to live. Augustine plays a large role in the transformation of the Roman empire from a pagan polity to a Christian idea, from the supreme city of Western man to the City of God, and, at the end of his life, witnesses Rome's political destruction. Both men resist, separate from, then acquiesce to, their formidable mothers, Volumnia and Monnica. Both seek, then flee, then return to the necessities of Roman political life. Both die engulfed by an alien crowd, attempting to reiterate the truth of an inner voice: Augustine in continual prayer as the Vandals approach Hippo, Coriolanus reasserting his Roman self as he invites a crowd of furious Volscians to cut him down. In this article, I argue that, in both *Confessions* and *Coriolanus*, the protagonist's central struggle can be described as an effort to separate signal from noise in the urban soundscapes of their worlds.

We have all become used to deconstruction's reversal of the value binary of speech and writing, and to its arguments for the centrality of absence rather than presence. As Bruce Smith points out in *The Acoustic World of Early Modern England: Attending to the O Factor*, sound studies as a field reverses that reversal: 'Listening is accepting presence – and not being apologetic about it.'[4] Acoustemology is a kind of phenomenology, stressing embodied experience over rational abstraction. It can be allied with attention to orature as well as literature, and to general suspicion about the Cartesian exaltation of rational mind over body. Indeed, it reclaims reading from absence by showing that it is an embodied process. Augustine's well-known anecdote about Ambrose's unusual silent reading suggests that revocalization of writing – making the author's absent voice present in one's physical being and auditory surround – dominated ancient reading practice. Various psychological experiments described by Charles Fernyhough suggest that this may still happen – that we still subvocalize.[5] Thus reading, even silent reading, overlaps with sound studies and always has.

So sound studies as a field resists certain philosophic consequences of the literacy/print revolution, itself both a product and an agent of the primacy of urban sensibilities and their preoccupation with screening out noise. But it also owes a good deal to recent techno-philosophizing arising from the electronic transmission of information

[2] Michel Serres, 'Noise', trans. Lawrence R. Schehr, *SubStance* 12.3 (1983), 50 (emphasis added). Hereafter cited parenthetically in the text.

[3] William Shakespeare, *Coriolanus*, ed. Peter Holland, Arden Third Series (London, 2013). Hereafter cited parenthetically in the text.

[4] Bruce Smith, *The Acoustic World of Early Modern England: Attending to the O Factor* (Chicago, 1999), p. 10. Hereafter cited parenthetically in the text.

[5] Charles Fernyhough, *The Voices Within: The History and Science of How We Talk to Ourselves* (New York, 2016), pp. 75–9.

and the mechanical, then electronic, then digital reproduction, preservation and analysis of sound. One of the paths that leads to sound studies begins in a particular technical measure in information transmission: the signal/noise ratio. Another related path begins with the feedback loop, which in its malign form turns recirculated signal to very loud noise, but in its complex constructive form as progressive recursion has proved foundational for artificial intelligence. The signal/noise ratio was described scientifically with respect to telegraphy in the late 1920s, but became widely discussed – and thus available for metaphoric use in the human sciences – with the work of Claude Shannon in the late 1940s, notably his mathematical definition of information. Shannon's work coincided with Norbert Weiner's descriptions of feedback in control systems, and with the beginnings of digital/analogue distinctions, to herald the rise of cybernetics and information science.[6] Since, in the late 1940s, Shannon, Weiner, John von Neumann and Alan Turing were all developing ideas and mechanisms generated during their World War II work on cryptography, radar and automated fire control, systems theory was born in urgent conflict out of the necessity of incorporating meaningful feedback as information necessary for command and control.

War justifies the forcible integration and subordination of many voices into one important purpose. Given that I am headed towards a comparison between *Coriolanus* and *Confessions*, it should be added that salvation also justifies the forcible integration and subordination of many voices into one important purpose: that is what the Church Fathers tried to do with their sacred books. A good deal of noise needs to be screened out, or converted to signal, to lead to victory in either endeavour.

Following this path in subjective experience, one might conceptually divide the ineluctable modality of the audible, for any hearer at any moment, into signal and noise. Insofar as this division accompanies choices about what to attend to, signal and noise might seem parallel to the division of the visual field for any viewer at any moment into figure and ground. As Michel Serres puts it

somewhat hyperbolically, 'Noise is not a phenomenon, all phenomena separate from it, *figures on a ground*, as a light in the fog, as any message, cry, call, signal must each separate from the hubbub that fills the silence, just to be, to be perceived, sensed, known, exchanged' (Serres, p. 50, emphasis added). But the figure/ground parallel Serres draws is not exact. For one thing, visual focus isolates figures and effectively blurs or even blocks ground. Attentive hearing (say of a conversation partner in a crowded restaurant, or of the violist in a string quartet, or of a series of bumps in the night) does not in fact screen out other sounds. I focus visually on the computer screen, not looking at my watch, and my watch effectively disappears. Thinking about my watch does not allow me to see it: I have to move my eyes off the screen to do that. But, at the same time, I am aware that either the furnace fan, or possibly the exhaust fan in the bathroom, is humming. I can hear TV voices – MSNBC, I think – from the room down the hall where my wife is working. The light crackles slightly, and the keyboard makes its distinctive semi-percussive rattle, so different from the typewriters of my youth. Occasional car sounds from outdoors. A helicopter? 'My urban soundscape', sound studies has encouraged us to call this. In terms of me as an intended recipient, all of this is noise, none of it signal (well, maybe the keyboard sounds, if writing involves subvocalized inner speech, are a kind of rhythm section accompanying a halting signal I'm composing, partly for myself, partly for you, O Reader). At the same time, I can situate myself meaningfully in respect to these noises, and some of it – the voices from the TV – could in some general way be said to signal to me. Five or ten minutes ago, my cellphone buzzed with an amber alert, for instance.

All this raises questions about whether auditory attention and visual attention work in the same way. In both sensory domains, paying attention involves evaluative choice: this or that is worth

---

[6] See N. Katherine Hayles, *How We Became Posthuman* (Chicago, 1999), pp. 64–5 and 84–112.

focusing on, this or that is not worth listening to. But, partly because of urban sonic overload, our auditory equipment, or our brain, does not 'focus' on sound in the same way. Most of us don't even try to echo-locate most of the time, though we imagine we perhaps could if we worked on auditory focus.[7] As Smith notes, different cultures map the soundscape differently: 'If the range of sounds that human beings everywhere make and apprehend can be visualized as a circle, cultures vary in how they use that compass of sounds to get their bearings in the world' (p. 291). Jungle dwellers echo-locate, where city dwellers do not.

In ordinary language, 'noise' is sound I do not value; 'signal' is intentional communication I interpret or could interpret or should interpret. 'Sound' seems neutral in this regard. 'Voice' requires intentionality, or (in boundary cases such as the 'voice' of a violin) being the instrument of intentionality – a voice is thus potentially a signal, but may also need to be wilfully ignored as noise. Urban soundscapes not only feature lots of noise, but also lots of voices that need to be ignored as if they were noise, as one pursues one's particular purposes.

This tentative distinction between visual and auditory attention rests on differences between the apparently similar binaries 'figure/ground' and 'signal/noise'. Ground complements figure: without ground there can be no figure. In many cases, ground and figure are reversible. Noise threatens signal; in the transmission circuits from which the binary derives, too much noise would mean no signal, as in a malign feedback loop. Something like this might conceivably happen with figure and ground, I suppose. A howl of feedback is too much signal self-interfering and self-reinforcing to produce signal-overwhelming noise. Too powerful a figure might overwhelm ground in a similar way. 'Dark with excessive bright thy skirts appear', as Milton's angels sing to the invisible Father.[8]

We might postulate a category of 'strong hearers', whose auditory focus on a particular signal (a particularly valued voice, perhaps), or aversion to a particular kind of noise, gives them a much better-defined sorting mechanism for the field of the audible than most of us enjoy. I shall suggest Coriolanus is such a strong hearer. A more typical, even paradigmatic, strong hearer is St Augustine in *Confessions*. Paradigmatic strong hearers are empowered by the belief that there is a single consistent all-important signal or voice to hear. Early in his narrative of struggle towards conversion, Augustine, remembering his chaotic feelings after the death of his beloved friend, meditates on finding a friend in the God he addresses, a God whose full atemporal being exempts his lovers from pain and loss inevitable amid the Heraclitean changefulness of the contingent world. Augustine begins the passage in the present tense to indicate that he is describing a long-term truth rather than narrating a particular event or phase of feeling:

Things rise and sink, and begin to be by rising, then progress toward being all they can, and when they have become all they can, they grow old and perish, though some things perish even without growing old. So when they rise and begin to be, the sooner they reach full being the sooner they rush on toward non-being. Such is the limit of their being, set by you, since they are parts of a universe whose parts are not simultaneously all in being. The entirety of things acts by the passage and replacement of the parts that make it up – just as we speak by the passage of meaningful sounds, which would not form a sentence if one word, its syllables sounded, did not yield to the next word. . . . But there is no resting in things that will not stay. . . .

Be not giddy, my soul, nor block your heart's hearing with a clangor of giddiness.[9]

So the mature Augustine urges himself to treat the world's changefulness as signal-blocking noise, 'clangor of giddiness', while acknowledging that, for human hearers, the intelligibility of signals resides in the hearer's capacity to put together distinct sounds into grammatical structures that unfold

[7] Compare Smith's discussion of auditory and visual experience, pp. 9–10.

[8] *Paradise Lost*, 3.380.

[9] St Augustine, *Confessions*, trans. Garry Wills (New York, 2002), pp. 71–2 (Book 4, Ch. 4). Page references included parenthetically henceforth.

in time. A masterful reader and writer and speaker, Augustine not only understands the temporal unfolding of meaning, but also infers from it the existence of an atemporal wholeness never realized in any temporal moment.

Augustine's relation to signal and noise helps me to tease out my own vexed respect for *Coriolanus*, for its protagonist, and for its almost invariably harsh soundscape. The play's recent Arden 3 editor, Peter Holland, brings the soundscape to our attention while recording a similarly mixed set of responses to play and protagonist: 'Like its hero, *Coriolanus* can, by turns or simultaneously, be exhilarating, troubling, noisy, unnerving, bold, and astonishing' (p. 2). As we will see, *Coriolanus* is rich not only in discussions of voice but also in soundscape-setting folio stage-directions. The nouns 'voice' and 'voices' appear in the play an unusual forty-eight times; the Harvard Concordance puts *Troilus* second with thirteen. *Coriolanus* also has the highest incidence of the word 'noise', though only by one.[10] As these observations suggest, the play is preoccupied with the meaning and value of sounds. Caius Martius, like Augustine, yearns for pure signal and sets himself against giddy clamour. Kenneth Gross remarks, in a fine consideration of noise in the play:

For Coriolanus, the clamor of battle is something that no merely political order, no cult or social hypocrisy, can possess for itself. . . . it is a noise . . . that sharpens rather than dulls Coriolanus's ear for the tricks of Roman political debate. The war, in fact, gives to Coriolanus a wilder, a more capacious sense of hearing than that possessed by anyone else in the play.[11]

Coriolanus' taste for battle-noise parallels, as Gross suggests, his distaste for urban political noise, the noise of human disagreement, disunity and negotiation. Augustine characterizes the partiality and disunity of temporal experience as 'noise' while remembering his lost work *On Beauty and Decorum*, which tried to categorize and bring order to aspects of the physical world. The 'you' in the passage is (of course) God:

This was my plight at the age of twenty-six or twenty-seven, when I wrote that book, hugging to me my own conceptions of the physical world, which filled my ears with their outer noise while I was trying to hear your inner music, my sweet truth. By dealing with beauty and decorum, I was trying to lift myself up and listen to you, gladdened by the glad call of my spouse, but I could not – the noise of my errors pulled me outside myself, while the weight of my pride sank me below myself, where you could not grant me 'news of real happiness and joy'.

(4,5, p. 78)

'The noise of my errors pulled me outside myself' well describes Coriolanus' reluctant and awkward participation in Roman public celebration. As Gross suggests, for Coriolanus clarity of meaning and purpose comes in noisy violent action, not vocal politics: 'Before him / He carries noise, and behind him he leaves tears' (2.1.153–4), Volumnia comments, in a phrase (like so many in *Coriolanus*) that reaches beyond its immediate celebratory or derogatory intent to foreshadow the protagonist's future fortunes. Locating her son in a moment between noise and tears, she inadvertently suggests that tears, not words, may be the appropriate response in others to his self-articulation. Certainly, the merchandising inventory of his scars Volumnia and Menenius undertake prior to Coriolanus' triumphant re-entry to Rome does not, in his mind, appropriately describe his or their meaning. Wound-counting is part and parcel of the triumphal apparatus he tries to abbreviate as out of tune with his inner meaning: 'No more of this, it does offend my heart. / Pray now, no more' (2.1.163–4). His wife Virgilia, weeping noiselessly, is more on track, though Coriolanus

---

[10] It is a measure of the play's concentration of purpose that this sort of thing can be said of many words: Peter Holland in his introduction points out that *Coriolanus* has much the highest use of not only 'voice' and 'voices' (p. 77), but also 'Rome' and 'Romans' (p. 93), and 'wounds' (p. 47). I point out in a past consideration of the play that it uses the word 'noble' to an extent unparalleled elsewhere in Shakespeare: see Engle, *Shakespearean Pragmatism* (Chicago, 1993), p. 254, n. 25. Robert N. Watson has analysed the play's unique concentration of various prefixes associated with the necessity of social exchange in 'Coriolanus and the common part', *Shakespeare Survey 69* (2016), 181–97.

[11] Kenneth Gross, *Shakespeare's Noise* (Chicago, 2001), p. 146. Hereafter cited parenthetically in the text.

finds a way to separate his being-in-battle from her response as well:

> My gracious silence, hail.
> Wouldst thou have laughed had I come coffined
>   home,
> That weep'st to see me triumph? Ah, my dear,
> Such eyes the widows in Corioli wear
> And mothers that lack sons.
>
> (2.1.170–4)

Noise in itself, and loud battle-speech, are for Martius a true voice to be harkened to. He comments happily before the double battle outside Corioles, 'Then we shall hear their 'larum, and they ours' (1.4.10). As Titus Lartius makes clear in his premature (and, in its mention of Cato, anachronistic) obituary, after Martius enters Corioles alone and is shut in, some of this 'alarum' is produced by Martius himself:

> Thou wast a soldier
> Even to Cato's wish, not fierce and terrible
> Only in strokes, but with thy grim looks and
> The thunder-like percussion of thy sounds
> Thou mad'st thine enemies shake, as if the world
> Were feverous and did tremble.
>
> (1.4.60–5)

In a rare moment of persuasive public speech, Martius, covered with the blood of those he killed in Corioles, exhorts Cominius' troops to follow him against Aufidius' Antiates. He both invokes the idea of sin and exalts the moral clarity of battle. In so doing, he apparently embraces a logic of public evaluation of action that he violently repudiates when applied to himself – he is, as it were, translating his own battle-selfhood into terms that might reach ordinary soldiers. But Martius, as a strong hearer, edits his own speech carefully to avoid being misheard as a pleader for approval. The 'if–then' structure he uses avoids any speech-acts of request that register interdependency. And his speech divides around a soundscape:

> If any such be here
> (As it were sin to doubt) that love this painting
> Wherein you see me smeared, if any fear
> Lesser his person than an ill report,

> If any think brave death outweighs bad life
> And that his country's dearer than himself,
> Let him alone, or so many so minded
> Wave thus [*waving his sword*] to express his
>   disposition,
> And follow Martius.
>
>   *They all shout and wave their swords, take
>   him up in their arms, and cast up their caps.*
> O me alone! Make you a sword of me?
>
> (1.6.66–76)

As close as Martius comes to a reconciliation with Roman noise, this moment also marks his awareness that he can be instrumental, made into a sword, for a shared purpose. Clad in the blood of Coriolans – the 'painting wherein you see me smeared' – fresh from his solo victory against an entire city, he momentarily can be both 'alone' and a Roman leader.

Augustine's famous moment of self-discovery also is a moment of hearing. His recommitment to the call that speaks to his inmost self comes from what might have been a bit of 'outer noise', but what he takes to be 'your inner music':

I was carrying on so, crying acrid tears of 'heart's contrition', when I heard from a nearby house the voice of a boy – or perhaps a girl, I could not tell – chanting in repeated singsong: Lift! Look! My features relaxed immediately while I studied as hard as I could whether children use such a chant in any of their games. But I could not remember ever having heard it. No longer crying, I leaped up, not doubting that it was by divine prompting that I should open the book and read what first I hit on.... . I grabbed, opened, read: 'Give up indulgence and drunkenness, give up lust and obscenity, give up strife and rivalries, and clothe yourself in Jesus Christ the Lord, leaving no further allowance for fleshly desires.' The very instant I finished that sentence, light was flooding my heart with assurance. [Wills translates 'Tolle! Lege!' as 'Lift! Look!' rather than the more familiar 'Take! Read!']

(8,5, pp. 181–2)

And part of Augustine's new 'assurance', represented at this point in familiar visual terms as light flooding what had been darkness, is silence overtaking or reducing what had been distracting noise. The silence emerges in Augustine's remarkable description of his shared mystical experience with his mother Monnica, not long after his conversion and shortly before her unexpected death. They look out of a window on the port of Ostia, discussing 'what kind of life the saints will live in eternity' (9,4, p. 200). As happens in *Confessions*, a spiritual high point is marked by the present tense:

Ascending higher, within ourselves, to speech and questioning and admiring such works, we encounter our own minds, and go beyond them to the outskirts of that region where 'you give eternal pasture to Israel', feeding it on truth. There, living is the same as wisdom, through which all things were made, all in the past, all in the future, and which was not itself made but is as it always was and always will be, for eternity knows not past or future. And while we speak of this, and yearn toward it, we barely touch it in a quick shudder of the heart. Then we sighed our way back down.

(9,4, p. 201)

The passage from atemporal shared mystical yearning conversation to temporal memory is marked by the transition from present tense to narrative past: 'we barely touch it ... Then we sighed our way back down.' As Augustine and Monnica discuss what has just happened – or almost happened – to them, they represent the condition of its possibility as the world's noise self-silencing to get out of the way of pure signal:

Of our experience we asked this question: If fleshly importuning were to fall silent, silent all shapes of earth, sea, air; silent the celestial poles; silent the soul, moving (oblivious of self) beyond the self; silent, as well, all dreams and internal visions, all words and other signs, silent everything that passes away, all those things that say, if one listens, We did not make ourselves, he made us who never passes away; if, after saying this, they too were silent, leaving us alert to hear the One who made them; and if He should speak, no longer through them but by himself, for us to hear his word, not as that is relayed by human tongue or angel's voice, not in cloudy thunder or 'dim reflection', but if we hearken to him we love in other things without those other things (as even now 'we strain upward', and, in a mind's blink, touch the ageless wisdom that outlasts all things), and if this were to continue ... would that not be what is meant by the words 'Enter the joy of your God'?

(9,4, p. 201)

So 'the joy of your God' is hearing pure divine voice, perfect eternal signal, without any intervening noise, where even the sacred mediating voices of angels or words of scripture are silenced. One can, of course, read this epiphany with different emphases. Catherine Conybeare comments that 'talking together is somehow at the center of the moment of stillness ... [g]iven this, the next paragraph reads like a revision: it dwells on silence, not sound'.[12]

I am tempted, given my extended comparison, to paraphrase Augustine's fantasy of an unmediated, noise-free condition of complete reception of the divine signal as 'My gracious silence, hail.' At any rate, unlike Conybeare, I see Augustine's paragraph about silence as entirely integral to his mystical near-epiphany.

Despite the apparent assimilation of personal action to noisy public good suggested by the seemingly delighted question 'Make you a sword of me?', Martius hates to have his battle-behaviour talked about by others when battle is over. In fact, though he certainly 'fear[s] / Lesser his person than an ill report' (1.6.68–9), for Martius any report seems to be 'an ill report'. For him, the voices of battle, the noises of pain and death and anger, are sacred and not suitable for purposes beyond themselves. He articulates this view in rebuffing spontaneous expressions of awe at what he has just done on the battlefield by two of the very few Romans he values as friends, Titus Lartius and Cominius:

LARTIUS [*to Cominius*] O general,
    Here is the steed, we the caparison.
    Hadst thou beheld –
MARTIUS Pray now, no more. My mother,
    Who has a charter to extol her blood,
    When she does praise me, grieves me.

(1.9.11–15)

---

[12] Catherine Conybeare, '*Quotquot haec legerint meminerint*: all who read this will remember', *Modern Language Notes* 127.5 (December 2012), S30. Conybeare, writing for a *Modern Language Notes* issue commemorating Eugene Vance, ends with the comment that '[i]n this inner conversation Gene has also helped me to realize anew how much more satisfactory is conversation than the monologic process of writing' (S33).

Martius attempts to edit praise out of his sounds-cape. He reluctantly exempts his mother's voice from those he tries to silence, but in so doing he reveals how burdensome her 'charter to extol' is to him. And his dislike stems in part from his acute awareness that praise serves as the currency that converts battle action into civic credit – it will situate him inevitably in the urban marketplace he hates.

We might postulate of strong hearers an unusual sensitivity to what is said about them. Augustine comments of his own unregenerate post-conversion egotism that 'I am annoyed when another praises in me what I am not proud of ... I can accept no praise if the praiser does not share my self-image, since he is either praising what I am not proud of at all, or praising too much what I take little pride in' (p. 249). This non-acceptance of praise looms even larger in *Coriolanus*. Later in the scene just quoted, and as part of the same rising agitation at the redescription of his actions, Martius objects strongly, and indeed rudely (in calling Cominius' offer 'a bribe'), to any hint that his behaviour in battle aims at an afterlife in reward or praise:

COMINIUS Of all the horses –
    Whereof we have ta'en good, and good store – of all
    The treasure in this field achieved and city,
    We render you the tenth, to be ta'en forth,
    Before the common distribution,
    At your only choice.

MARTIUS I thank you, general,
    But cannot make my heart consent to take
    A bribe to pay my sword.

                              (1.9.31–8)

Having thwarted this gesture, he becomes passionately agitated when the response to his demurral turns into a misplaced military soundscape:

                I do refuse it,
    And stand upon my common part with those
    That have beheld the doing.
        A long flourish
        *They all cry, 'Martius, Martius', cast up their caps
        and lances.*
        Cominius and Lartius stand bare.

    May these instruments which you profane
    Never sound more. When drums and trumpets
        shall
    I' th' field prove flatterers, let courts and cities be
    Made all of false-faced soothing.

                              (1.9.38–42)

Martius flares up at two linked profanations: first, sounds that he wishes to confine to the sacred world of action, and, second, his own voiced refusal of spoils, have been 'profaned' by being turned into political speech. Thus, Martius shows the characteristic noise-intolerance of a strong hearer, filtering the sacred from the profane like Augustine, but, unlike Augustine at Ostia, he cannot find anyone at all who will hear the same inner truths he does.

Volumnia may resemble Monnica in pursuing a son relentlessly to a destined commitment, empowered by her own total commitment to a distinctive set of values, but unlike Monnica she never seeks transcendence in conversation with him. Moreover, Monnica, unlike Volumnia, dies before her son. After her death, Augustine moves back to Africa and, after a period of monastic reflection, undertakes a very public life in the church. We are reminded in the post-conversion chapters of *Confessions* that Augustine's progress towards an individual conversation with God never takes him out of thousands of conversations with human beings. As Peter Brown puts it, 'Having read the life of this very inward-looking man, we suddenly realize, to our surprise, that he was almost never alone.' Moreover, as Brown comments in explaining the troubling nature of the four post-conversion books (10–13) of *Confessions*, the silence around his own saved soul that Augustine has hoped for does not emerge: 'for Augustine, conversion was no longer enough ... The "harbour" of the convert was still troubled by storms.'[13] In the final books of *Confessions*, Augustine develops a refrain that amounts to a prayer to God to strengthen Augustine as

---

[13] Peter Brown, *Augustine of Hippo: A Biography*, new edn (Berkeley, 2000), pp. 174, 171.

a listener to the privileged voice that must, with effort, be picked out and attended to among many necessary but noisy conversations. He recalls his conversion as a triumph of voice over noise: '"I heard your voice behind me calling me back", though I heard it only faintly through a clamor of those who know no peace.' The last two books offer a meditative reading of the early chapters of Genesis, hearing God's signal: Augustine repeats variations on the phrase 'your voice resonant in my inner hearing' over and over (thrice on p. 290, twice on p. 293), and then uses it in his predictive summary of the questioning reflection on Genesis that will follow: 'I would continue to converse before you, my God, with those who grant as true what your truth resonates in my inner hearing. As for those who deny it, let them deafen themselves with their own barking. Still I will try to calm them' (12,3, p. 296). That is, despite a heart that hears the resonant voice of God, Augustine still needs to talk with others – even others who will not grant his truths. He remains, after all, a bishop, not a monk. Consequently, the soundscape of *Confessions* contains plenty of noise all the way through. As a result of this immersion in the world's giddy clamour, even a paradigmatic strong hearer needs reassurance. When Augustine, after much interrogation of the words of the creation myth, comes to the comment that on the sixth day 'God saw that it was eminently good', he returns to the idea of inner hearing, but here to register his sense of temporal paradox in the words of Moses:

So I asked: Lord, surely your Scripture is true, since it comes from you, who are not only truthful but the truth. Then why do you tell me that you made things on successive days (I have counted how many), and then saw they were good? In answer to me – for you are my God, speaking forcefully into your follower's inner hearing, breaking through my dullness with your ringing clarity – you said: Surely you know, man, that what is said in Scripture is said by me. Yet it is said to those who exist in time, while time does not affect my own Word, which exists as my equal in eternity.

(13,13, pp. 347–8)

Augustine seeks to deny what God's reply to him rather strongly suggests: that scriptural virtues exist in the interpretation of the time. Augustine denies this because, as a strong hearer, he believes he can filter out uncertainty and receive a pure signal, bearer of an unmistakable and timeless truth, even as he admits that temporality and interpretive uncertainty are necessary features of mortal understanding, and as he remains in conversation before God with other human beings.

From this example, we could hypothesize that the strongest hearers are, in Bakhtinian terms, able to listen through the noise of heteroglossia – the phenomenal world's variety of voices, dialects and noises – to hear the supreme monological voice: the Logos. In Derridean terms, Augustine here models the acoustics of logocentrism. But in terms of sound studies, we could say (with appreciative readers of *Confessions*) that, while Augustine undoubtedly hierarchizes experience and believes in the primacy of the Logos, as a hearer he recognizes that heteroglossia and general natural noisiness are necessary features of the experiential world and must be duly heard. The solitary transcendence of the desert prophets needs to be remembered, but cannot be entirely replicated, amid the urban urgencies of multiple conversations. Augustine recognizes his own necessary participation in dialogic exchange. Learning what is noise and what is voice is a necessary process of becoming. The silence in which only the voice of God speaks can be found only in the afterlife, not life.

We have already seen Lartius and Cominius refuse to allow Martius to escape the urban political soundscape that follows Roman heroic action, thus violating Martius' own sense of why he does the things he does. In the consulship crisis, Cominius, Menenius and Volumnia all conspire to push Coriolanus towards the marketplace – first, to perform a very incomplete version of the scar-mongering customary in consular election, then to apologize to the plebeians for his angry speech when they revoke their voices for his consulship. Coriolanus balks at the second self-abasement, indicating that this would be going back on what, to paraphrase Augustine, has resonated in his heart in communion with the gods:

MENENIUS Repent what you have spoke.

CORIOLANUS

    Fore them? I cannot do it to the gods,
    Must I then do't to them?

                      (3.2.20–2)

This seems a moment to step back and reflect. But, unlike Augustine, Coriolanus has almost no contemplative leisure to cultivate this communion – nor is it a communion based on quiet listening, but rather one grounded in violent action. It is presumably this absence, given that he in fact invokes the gods at several key moments of decision, that leads Kenneth Gross to remark that Coriolanus 'never seeks valorization or blessing from any transcendental source' (p. 134). Unlike Gross, I would consider the speech I have just quoted (and 'You bless me, gods' (4.5.137), discussed below) as implicitly a self-valorizing reference to the divine, characteristically refusing to negotiate with noisy people on the assumption that he has already heard what the divine has to tell him. One assumes that Coriolanus' god speaks to him in battle rather than in public negotiation. Gross goes on to remark insightfully that Coriolanus 'seeks his voice in a world where all other voices have become poison or coercion, a promise of curse, where even his mother's praises limit rather than enlarge the self' (p. 135). Volumnia repeatedly pushes him towards compromise and gains his reluctant agreement. Another lengthy quotation, beginning with his submission to her, shows how his meditations on his own voice and his own truth turn towards soundscapes and towards the production of sound. Once again, Martius contrasts the implicitly sacred space of the battlefield with the debased civic space in which quid pro quo exchanges occur, and once again the 'licence' Volumnia has as mother to profit by her child emerges as an element in his capitulation:

CORIOLANUS To th' market-place!
    You have put me now to such a part which never
    I shall discharge to th' life.

COMINIUS Come, come, we'll prompt you.

VOLUMNIA   I prithee now, sweet son, as thou hast said
    My praises made thee first a soldier, so,

    To have my praise for this, perform a part
    Thou hast not done before.

                   (3.2.105–11)

Most readers of the play doubtless notice that Coriolanus constructs his own nobility in opposition not only to plebeian fickleness and aristocratic irresolution, but also to the economic interdependence that locates itself in marketplaces. Comparison to Augustine's self-construction as a hearer and speaker alerts us to the distinctively vocal and sonic terms in which Coriolanus resists this debasement:

CORIOLANUS Well, I must do't.
    Away my disposition and possess me
    Some harlot's spirit! My throat of war be turned,
    Which choired with my drum, into a pipe
    Small as an eunuch or the virgin voice
    That babies lull asleep! . . . A beggar's tongue
    Make motion through my lips and my armed knees
    Who bowed but in my stirrup bend like his
    That hath received an alms! – I will not do't,
    Lest I surcease to honour mine own truth
    And by my body's action teach my mind
    A most inherent baseness.

                 (3.2.111–23)

Again, one might emphasize the way this passage stresses the economic. It forces the would-be self-valuer into the urban marketplace of negotiated value, making him repeat the speech-act of requesting a favour that he found so intolerable when he took his scars out into the public sphere to be appreciated.[14] For my purpose in this article, I highlight the emphasis on the sonic and the embodied, suggesting that integrity requires singing one's native song (in Coriolanus' case, his war-cry) and making one's body and one's sounds – one's personal expressive equipment – honour one's inner truth. In this, Coriolanus resembles the Augustine who heeds 'your voice resonant in my inner hearing', except that in

---

[14] For extended argument along these lines, with citations of others making the same sort of claim, see Engle, *Shakespearean Pragmatism*, pp. 164–95. Similar arguments appear cogently in Watson, 'Common part', 190–1.

Coriolanus' case the resonant voice in question is in large part his own voice 'which choired with my drum' in sacred battle-service, his own history of past action and speech, and adult awareness that his actions can only be of value to him if they are not tainted by a political soundscape that translates action into promiscuous noisy public evaluative talk.

Coriolanus thus has a logocentric disposition without any well-articulated transcendent Logos, and one that has formed itself in resistance to the idea of an evangelizing community of shared believers. Thus, his actions might seem those of a man blindly persisting in a category error, and he is often so described.[15] But such descriptions slight Coriolanus' efforts to forge or find such a community, and they underrate the extent to which he should be seen, like Augustine, as striving to find himself while also shaping one of the world's great institutions – in Coriolanus' case, what Menenius prophetically terms 'The Roman state, whose course will on / The way it takes' (1.1.64–5). At times, Coriolanus plausibly attempts 'to honor [his] own truth' as that of any Roman soldier: 'I have done as you have done, that's what I can, / Induced as you have been, that's for my country' (1.9.16–17). At times, he represents his own truth as that of his class, the nobility: 'us, the honoured number, / Who lack not virtue, no, nor power, but that / Which they have given to beggars' (3.1.74–6). He is aware that he is partly constituted by a complex love–hate rivalry with Aufidius: 'were I anything but what I am, / I would wish me only he' (1.1.226–7). He's also aware that, given the near-impossibility of generalizing or communalizing his distinctive sense of self, he may live better serving the state idiosyncratically than attempting to rule it.

VOLUMNIA I have lived,
  To see inherited my very wishes,
  And the buildings of my fancy. Only
  There's one thing wanting, which I doubt not but
  Our Rome will cast on thee.

CORIOLANUS Know, good mother,
  I had rather be their servant in my way,
  Than sway with them in theirs.
                              (2.1.192–8)

Coriolanus shows the same awareness that he is better suited to service than to mastery when he comes unrecognized to Aufidius' door, remembering his humiliation in sonic terms as being 'suffered . . . by th' voice of slaves to be / Whooped out of Rome' (4.5.76–80). He offers Aufidius his throat to cut, saying 'I . . . cannot live but to thy shame, unless / It be to do thee service' (4.5.102–3). Aufidius' response again marks how the play flirts analogically with the Logos: 'If Jupiter / Should from yond cloud speak divine things / And say, "Tis true", I'd not believe them more / Than thee, all-noble Martius' (4.5.105–8). Here Coriolanus' personal integrity, the truth in his voice, stands in for divine revelation to a person who otherwise incarnates worldly Machiavellian scepticism.[16] When Aufidius embraces Coriolanus and accepts his service, Coriolanus says 'You bless me, gods' (4.5.137). And when Volumnia pleads with him for Rome, she too acknowledges a quasi-

---

[15] See Stanley Fish, 'How to do things with Austin and Searle', *Modern Language Notes* 91.5 (1976), 995–9, where the category error is illustrated by the 'unhappy' speech act 'I banish you', and, as Fish says, 'The truth is that there is no world elsewhere, at least not in the sense Coriolanus intends' (p. 999); more broadly, the feminist psychoanalytic account of the play by Janet Adelman sees in Coriolanus a category error about masculinity and familial interdependence, epitomized by the impossible aspiration to behave 'As if a man were author to himself / And knew no other kin' (5.3.36–7); see Adelman, *Suffocating Mothers: Fantasies of Maternal Origin in Shakespeare's Plays,* Hamlet *to* The Tempest (New York, 1992), pp. 150–4. See also Holland, pp. 137–9, on the Ralph Fiennes movie's focus on Coriolanus as baffled sociopathic isolate, and pp. 47–9 for Holland's admiration for Cynthia Marshall's claim that Coriolanus' lack of interiority provokes audiences into frustrated projections of motive. Kenneth Gross sums up this critical position well: 'To many critics, his attitude suggests a mad resistance to the facts of living in the world' (p. 142).

[16] A similarly incongruous invocation of the divine occurs earlier when the tribune Brutus deplores the unified public clamour that greets Coriolanus' triumphal entry into Rome after the victory at Corioles:

        Such a pother,
  As if that whatsoever god who leads him
  Were slyly crept into his human powers
  And gave him graceful posture.
                              (2.1.212–15)

Augustinian god-orientation in her son, expressed sonically:

> Speak to me, son.
> Thou has affected the fine strains of honour,
> To imitate the graces of the gods,
> To tear with thunder the wide cheeks o'th' air.
>
> (5.3.148–51)

To summarize and draw to an end: locating voices in *Coriolanus* brings us to the key moral and political question that led Augustine to renounce his ambitions for a Roman governorship to become a Christian bishop: in evaluating a soundscape of voices, should one listen for the truest voice, for the loudest voice or for the most voices? Shakespeare rarely imagines a character like Augustine who commits himself to hearing the voice of God yet also engages in conversation with others so minded. But he does, in *Coriolanus* more than elsewhere, consider what it means to hear an all-important inner voice and be impelled by familial and political commitment to betray it:

> ([*He*] *holds her by the hand, silent.*)
> O mother, mother!
> What have you done? Behold, the heavens do ope,
> The gods look down and this unnatural scene
> They laugh at.
>
> (5.3.182–5)

In the silence, while Coriolanus holds his mother's hand, something quasi-Augustinian – but very sad – happens. Coriolanus hears the pure signal through the noisy conflict of familial and political obligation, and it is divine laughter at his failure to attend to the divine voice within.

While Coriolanus stands out an extraordinary person – one who can fight a whole city and win, one who cannot be dispraised but in a kind of praise – his inability to follow the dictates of what, as a strong hearer, he receives as the best inner signal may not be unusual. Much later literature shows this to be a kind of failure common in those who seek extraordinary lives. In the passage quoted from Saul Bellow's *Humboldt's Gift*, Charlie Citrine sums up Von Humboldt Fleisher's failure as an inability to hear the true inner voice amid the world's storm of noise, but Citrine himself spends the entire novel attempting to hear such a voice with very limited success. In a beautiful moralized soundscape in *Middlemarch*, George Eliot turns Bellow's idea inside out as she comments on the ordinary erotic disappointment Dorothea Brooke experiences in the months after her marriage to Casaubon: 'If we had a keen vision and feeling of all ordinary human life, it would be like hearing the grass grow and the squirrel's heart beat, and we should die of that roar which lies on the other side of silence.'[17]

Coriolanus' failure has been to accept ordinary human life as obliging him to give way to a mother's threatened curse. He has been extraordinary when he can heed his inner voice, that of 'whatsoever god who leads him' (2.1.213), as Brutus puts it, half in scepticism and half in dismayed wonder. Coriolanus won his name acting alone and like a different kind of being, a solitary city-destroyer:

> Alone he entered
> The mortal gate of th' city, which he painted
> With shunless destiny, aidless came off
> And with a sudden reinforcement struck
> Corioles like a planet.
>
> (2.2.108–12)

The 'sovereignty in nature' (4.7.35) Aufidius attributes to him, Coriolanus reclaims in the final scene, implicitly retracting the conversion into a debased urban bargainer that his capitulations to his mother have forced him to become.

The Volscian crowd, shouting 'Tear him to pieces! Do it presently! He killed my son! My daughter! He killed my cousin Marcus! He killed my father!' (5.6.121–3), reminds us of how Coriolanus' greatness, his solitary incarnation of the inner voice of war, creates ordinary

---

[17] George Eliot, *Middlemarch* (London, 1994), p. 162.

unhappiness in others. As he himself notes to the weeping Virgilia, 'Such eyes the widows in Corioli wear' (2.1.173). Critics often remark on how *Coriolanus* differs from other tragedies in that only the hero dies: Shakespeare inserts 'my cousin Marcus' in this final scene to remind us that ordinary people, even people with names like that of the hero, bound in familial relations like his, have died as well, and died because of him. Thus, the unhappiness of ordinary human life returns to overwhelm an extraordinary in a roar of civic noise that lies on the other side of the silence in which Martius held his mother's hand.

More generally, however, Coriolanus' tragedy, and Augustine's very qualified divine comedy, both reflect the asymmetry between figure/ground and signal/noise discussed at the outset of this article. The attentive mind, striving for the true signal, cannot in life shut out the noises that are part of the soundscape. This applies with special force when the mind is urban, enmeshed in the knot of collective purposes involved in city-founding and city-sustaining. The experience of listening is ineluctably various, and even strong hearers must accept noise with their signal. With noise comes acknowledgement that, as Augustine discerns in communion with Monnica, only in death can one obtain the silence in which truly perfect strong hearing could happen. Coriolanus dies amid the shouts of others, but he also dies invoking the divine, reasserting his own deference to those he serves, and eloquently rejecting a false description of himself by another who, as Augustine puts it, 'does not share [his] self-image':

CORIOLANUS Hear'st thou, Mars?
AUFIDIUS Name not the god, thou boy of tears.
CORIOLANUS Ha?
AUFIDIUS No more.
CORIOLANUS Measureless liar, thou has made my heart
Too great for what contains it. 'Boy'? O slave!
– Pardon me, lords, 'tis the first time that ever
I was forced to scold . . .
Cut me to pieces, Volsces; men and lads
Stain all your edges on me. 'Boy'! False hound!
If you have writ your annals true, 'tis there
That, like an eagle in a dovecote, I

Fluttered your Volscians in Corioles.
Alone I did it. 'Boy'!

(5.6.98–115)

The Volscian Lord who calls for 'judicious hearing' of Coriolanus is drowned out by the noise of the angry crowd: 'Kill, kill, kill, kill, kill him!' (5.6.124, 128). When their imperative has been fulfilled, and judicious hearing of a live Coriolanus has been rendered safely impossible, Aufidius steps off Martius' corpse and recomposes the soundscape: 'My rage is gone / And I am struck with sorrow . . . / Beat thou the drum that it speak mournfully' (5.6.145–8). Those sounds of measured homage mark our relief from the effort judiciously to hear, or overhear, a strong self-hearer – one whose conversation with the divine signal within, even more than Augustine's, treats anything we might say about him as noise.

Moreover, if we consider the multiple legacies passed from Rome to early modern Europe, the self-sacrificing self-regarding commitment to militant male selfhood of Republican Rome counts as important – probably less important than the Augustinian commitment to the inner voice of God that, in Luther and Calvin, caused such massive disruption, but not at all unimportant. Montaigne, that insightfully proto-modern interrogator of questionable attitudes, nonetheless deeply admired Cato the Younger, and refused to regard Cato's self-disembowelment to avoid being taken by Julius Caesar as mere stoicism:

When I see him die, tearing and mangling his entrails, I cannot simply content my selfe to beleeve, that at that time, he had his soule wholy exempted from all trouble, or free from vexation . . . I verily believe, he felt a kind of pleasure and sensualitie in so noble an action . . . a manlike voluptuousnesse, at which time it beheld the worthinesse, and considered the generosity and haughtiness of his enterprise . . . not urged or set-on by any hope of glorie, as the popular and effeminate judgements have judged.[18]

---

[18] *The Essays of Montaigne: The John Florio Translation* (New York, 1933), II, 11, 'Of crueltie', p. 374.

Some of Shakespeare's anachronisms are thematic. Coriolanus was indeed a Roman 'even to Cato's wish' (1.4.61), and I think we need, like Montaigne reflecting on the younger Cato, to recognize Coriolanus' death in Epicurean rather than Stoic terms, and certainly not as merely the final term in a long series of stupid category errors about the nature of social life. Coriolanus dies voluptuously while hearing and honouring his own true voice, heedless of 'the popular and effeminate judgments' of urban others – us included.

CAESAR AND LEAR IN HONG KONG: APPROPRIATING SHAKESPEARE TO EXPRESS THE INEXPRESSIBLE

MIRIAM LEUNG CHE LAU

HONG KONG SHAKESPEARE: A MISSING PIECE IN THE MAP OF ASIAN SHAKESPEARE

Several Shakespearian scholars have categorized the twenty-first century as a significant moment for Asian Shakespeare. Poonam Trivedi argues that the twenty-first century is the moment of Asia's resurgence,[1] whereas Alexa Huang advocates the concept of 'Asian Shakespeare 2.0', which she proclaims is more an attitude than a method.[2] She further explains that 'Neither Asia nor Shakespeare has unified identities in any meaningful sense or even consolidated economic interests. Rather, they are defined by remarkable internal divisions and incongruities' (p. 1). Dennis Kennedy illustrates that Asian Shakespeare speaks in many voices, accents and contradictory performance styles.[3] He also suggests that Asian Shakespeare usages are parallel to European and American usages, and sometimes even in advance of them.[4] To call for increasing exchanges among Asian Shakespearians, the Asian Shakespeare Association held an inaugural Asian Shakespeare Conference in Taipei in 2014, which I attended.[5] Asian Shakespeare is worth investigating, as its roots travel back as far as the nineteenth century. Trivedi lists the first performances of Shakespeare's plays by Asians in Asian languages: 1852 in India, 1885 in Japan, 1913 in China, 1949 in Taiwan.[6] However, if Huang claims that Asia and Shakespeare do not have unified identities but are instead marked by internal incongruities, then where is Hong Kong's position on the map of Asian Shakespeare?[7] It is puzzling why Hong Kong Shakespeare is absent from the discussion of Asian Shakespeare. The popular English burlesque *Shylock, or The Merchant of Venice Preserved* (by Thomas Talfourd) was staged in 1867 for British expatriates, and was later revived by the Hong Kong Amateur Dramatic Club in 1871.[8] Even Shanghai, known to be the 'most modern place in China' and the 'cradle of the civilized drama movement', only had its first Shakespeare performance, *The Merchant of Venice*, held by students of St John's University, in 1902, which is thirty-five years later than the performance of *Shylock* in Hong Kong.[9]

---

[1] Poonam Trivedi, 'Re-playing Shakespeare in Asia: an introduction', in *Re-playing Shakespeare in Asia*, ed. Poonam Trivedi and Minami Ryuta (New York, 2010), p. 2.

[2] Alexa Huang, 'Asian Shakespeare 2.0', *Asian Theatre Journal* 28.1 (2011), 1–6; p. 1.

[3] Dennis Kennedy, 'Foreword: the future is fusion', in *Shakespeare in Culture*, ed. Bi-qi Beatrice Lei and Ching-Hsi Perng (Taipei, 2012), pp. 1–14; esp. p. 12.

[4] Kennedy, 'Foreword: the future is fusion', p. 11.

[5] Asian Shakespeare Association: http://asianshakespeare.org.

[6] Trivedi, 'Re-playing Shakespeare in Asia', p. 2.

[7] Huang, 'Asian Shakespeare 2.0', p. 1.

[8] Shormishtha Panja, Suematsu Michiko, Alexa Huang and Yong Li Lan, 'Intercultural theatre and Shakespeare productions in Asia', in *Routledge Handbook of Asian Theatre*, ed. Siyuan Liu (Routledge, 2016), pp. 504–25, esp. p. 515.

[9] Lee Chee-keng and Yong Li-lan, 'Ideology and student performances in China', in *Shakespeare on the University Stage*, ed. Andrew James Hartley (Cambridge, 2015), pp. 90–109, esp. pp. 107–8.

Beatrice Lei suggests that Shakespeare's presence in Asia is often attributed to British colonization and Anglo-American cultural imperialism.[10] But this is not completely true in the context of Hong Kong, where British colonialism is not so much rejected as embraced. This distinctive psychological condition is noted by Tu Wei-ming: 'For the majority of Hong Kong residents, being Chinese as a British subject is . . . arguably superior to being Chinese as a citizen of the People's Republic of China'.[11] Shakespeare is not merely confined to the entertainment for expatriates in Hong Kong. During the colonial era, three Shakespeare Festivals were organized by Hong Kongers from the 1950s to the 1980s.[12] This means the Hong Kong Shakespeare Festival preceded the Shakespeare Festival in China by more than thirty years. While the Inaugural Shakespeare Festival was only held in Beijing and Shanghai in 1986, with twenty-eight productions in total, the First Shakespeare Festival was held in Hong Kong on 23 April 1954 by a Chinese drama group of the Sino-British Club, featuring a Cantonese Shakespeare play-reading of *Romeo and Juliet*.[13] In the Second and Third Shakespeare Festivals, held in 1964 and 1984 respectively, Shakespeare's plays were staged in a mixture of Cantonese and English. For example, to celebrate Shakespeare's 400th birthday in the Second Shakespeare Festival in 1964, *The Merchant of Venice* and *Twelfth Night* were, respectively, staged in Cantonese and English. The Third Shakespeare Festival in 1984 increased its repertoire to five performances. Besides again presenting *The Merchant of Venice* and *Twelfth Night*, parts of *Othello*, *Julius Caesar* and *Romeo and Juliet* were also staged, involving a total of eight drama groups and 18,600 participants.[14] Shakespeare drama was a 'part of the repertoire of the Hong Kong Amateur Dramatic Club that was active in the 1860s and 1870s'.[15] The performance of Shakespeare by the club not only entertained British expatriates, but also brought a 'touch of British culture to Hong Kong residents'. Furthermore, the Hong Kong Repertory Theatre, established in 1977, regularly featured Shakespeare, with eleven plays performed in the twenty years up to the hand-over to China in 1997. Daniel S. P. Yang, its first artistic director, altogether directed six Shakespearian plays for the theatre company, including *The Merchant of Venice* in 1984, *Much Ado About Nothing* in 1990, and *King Lear* in 1993.[16] Yang categorizes the Shakespearian productions of the Hong Kong Repertory Theatre into three stages – namely, early experimentations in the 1970s, more polished productions in the 1980s, and ambitious productions mounted by highly experienced theatre professionals, including himself, in the 1990s.[17] In spite of its vitality and its long history, it is rather disappointing to see Hong Kong Shakespeare still treated as an orphaned child in the discourse of Asian Shakespeare. One of the few

---

[10] Beatrice Bi-qi Lei, 'Paradox of Chinese nationalism: *Two Gentlemen of Verona* in silent film', *Shakespeare in Culture* (2012), 251.

[11] Tu Wei-ming, 'Cultural China: the periphery as the centre', in *The Living Tree: The Changing Meaning of Being Chinese Today*, ed. Tu Wei-ming (Stanford, 1994), pp. 1–34, esp. p. 11.

[12] Dorothy Wong, 'Shakespeare in a Hong Kong frame', in *Shakespeare Global/Local: The Hong Kong Imaginary in Transcultural Production*, ed. Kwok-kan Tam, Andrew Parkin and Terry Siu-Han Yip (Frankfurt am Main, 2002), pp. 63–74, esp. p. 68.

[13] Wong, 'Shakespeare in a Hong Kong frame', p. 64, p. 68.

[14] Wong, 'Shakespeare in a Hong Kong frame', p. 68.

[15] Panja *et al.*, 'Intercultural theatre and Shakespeare productions in Asia', p. 516.

[16] Daniel S. P. Yang, 'Shakespeare at the Hong Kong Repertory Theatre', in *Shakespeare Global/Local*, ed. Tam *et al.*, pp. 76–83, pp. 80, 82.

[17] According to Daniel Yang, the early experimentations of the Hong Kong Repertory Theatre in the 1970s included Richard Ho's *Hamlet: Sword of Vengeance* (1977 and 1978), Chow Yung-ping's *Macbeth* (1979) and Glen Watford's *Romeo and Juliet* (1980). In addition, the more polished productions in the 1980s comprised Daniel Yang's *The Taming of the Shrew* (1982) and *The Merchant of Venice* (1984), Ying Ruo-cheng's *Measure for Measure* (1986), Joanna Chan's *Othello* (1986) and Cai Qin's *Twelfth Night* (1988). Finally, the ambitious productions in the 1990s were made up of Daniel Yang's *Much Ado About Nothing* (1990), *King Lear* (1993) and *A Midsummer Night's Dream* (1997): Yang, 'Shakespeare at the Hong Kong Repertory Theatre', pp. 76–83.

publications in this area is *Shakespeare Global/Local: The Hong Kong Imaginary in Transcultural Production*, a book written by Hong Kong scholars from 1997 to 1998, shortly after the handover of Hong Kong. Kwok-kan Tam, one of the editors of the book, argues that Shakespeare has transcended British heritage and has become part of the Hong Kong Chinese tradition.[18] But Huang claims that Tam's statement is only partly true, as she believes that Shakespeare 'transcends his British heritage' because 'Britain never colonised Hong Kong the way it did with India.'[19] Quoting Mao Ze-dong's description of Hong Kong as a 'semi-colony', Huang argues that this unique historical backdrop informs Hong Kong's performance culture in the late nineteenth and early twentieth centuries.[20] Another key researcher in Hong Kong Shakespeare is Adele Lee, whose research on 'Teaching Shakespeare in Hong Kong' is part of the British Council's 'Shakespeare: A Worldwide Classroom' project.[21] Through workshops and online materials, she has worked with teachers, school curriculum designers and students in Hong Kong to explore in what ways the study of Shakespeare benefits students, how he is commonly taught, and what role Shakespeare plays in a new liberal arts education in Hong Kong.[22] Rex Gibson argues that the study of Shakespeare should be neither ahistorical nor apolitical, with the focus limited to character, plot and major themes, but should take into account the social, political and cultural factors that have shaped Shakespeare.[23] In line with Gibson's assertion, Lee attempts to find out how the role and reception of Shakespeare have changed in the light of cultural, economic and political changes prompted by 1997.[24] However, she mainly focuses on the learning activities in Hong Kong classrooms, but not on any Hong Kong productions of Shakespeare. My article attempts to further her lines of study by offering a cultural and political reading of theatrical productions of Shakespeare's plays in post-1997 Hong Kong. It is indeed difficult to fit Hong Kong comfortably into the common strands of postcolonial studies, as the Hong Kong narrative neither follows Frantz Fanon's discourse of describing colonialism as destructive and harmful to the

mental health of the natives who were subjugated into colonies,[25] nor complies with the studies of Ian Buruma and Avishai Margalit who argue that Occidentalism is summoned to describe the hatred borne by the Orients towards the West.[26] On the contrary, Howard Choy, a Hong Kong-bred academic, rightly proclaims that, to many locals, the 'postcolonial (re)turn is actually more a recolonization than a decolonization of the capitalist Cantonese city by the mainland Mandarin master'.[27] He further quotes Michel Foucault's saying, 'one should totally and absolutely suspect anything that claims to be a return ... there is in fact no such thing as a return' (p. 52).

The post-1997 Hong Kong adaptation of Shakespearian plays, with specific reference to sociopolitical issues, is a topic that Asian Shakespeare scholarship has singularly failed to address. Hong Kong Shakespeare is often subsumed under the discourse of Chinese Shakespeare, against which I argue that Hong Kong Shakespeare is distinctive, should be viewed as a separate entity, and follows a narrative

---

[18] Kwok-kan Tam, 'Preface', in *Shakespeare Global/Local*, ed. Tam *et al.*, p. ix.

[19] Panja *et al.*, 'Intercultural theatre and Shakespeare productions in Asia', p. 517.

[20] Panja *et al.*, 'Intercultural theatre and Shakespeare productions in Asia', p. 517.

[21] Adele Lee, 'Teaching Shakespeare in Hong Kong': http://blogs.gre.ac.uk/shakespeareinhongkong/2013/02/26/teaching-shakespeare-in-hong-kong.

[22] Adele Lee, 'Shakespeare and the educational reforms in Hong Kong': http://blogs.gre.ac.uk/shakespeareinhongkong/2013/02/26/shakespeare-and-the-educational-reforms-in-hongkong.

[23] Rex Gibson, 'Teaching Shakespeare in schools', in *Teaching English*, ed. Susan Brindley (Routledge, 1994), pp. 140–53.

[24] Lee, 'Shakespeare and the educational reforms in Hong Kong'.

[25] Frantz Fanon, *The Wretched of the Earth* (London, 1965), p. 250.

[26] Ian Buruma and Avishai Margalit, *Occidentalism: The West in the Eyes of Its Enemies* (London, 2005), p. 404.

[27] Howard Yuen-fung Choy, 'Schizophrenic Hong Kong: postcolonial identity crisis in the *Infernal Affairs* trilogy', *Transtext(e)s Transcultures* 3 (2007), 52–66, p. 53.

of its own. Otto Heim, a professor at the University of Hong Kong, has researched extensively in postcolonial writing, specifically in theatre and poetry.[28] Heim distinguishes the function of Hong Kong Shakespeare from that of mainland Shakespeare, as he asserts that Hong Kong Shakespeare '[serves] to underline the identification of Western culture with Britishness and eventually to nurture the colony's aspirations to metropolitan status'.[29] In contrast, mainland Shakespeare has traditionally been used to signify China's relationship with the West, in terms of rivalry and recognition, thus Shakespeare in China serves as a 'touchstone for the expression of Chinese cultural identity and political ideology'.[30] While Alexa Huang categorizes Hong Kong as one of the multiple ideological positions embodied by China, my endeavour is to distinguish their respective positions. James Brandon has categorized Asian Shakespeare into three main subsets – canonical Shakespeare, localized Shakespeare and postmodern Shakespeare.[31] Canonical Shakespeare is defined as 'high culture' Shakespeare that is transplanted from England, whereas localized Shakespeare hides foreign origins so that the audience is unaware that a 'foreign' play is being staged. On the other hand, postmodern or intercultural Shakespeare is exhibited when, simultaneously, Shakespeare's text is acknowledged, and the performance is also rooted in local culture and theatrical practices. However, Shakespearian scholars have reservations about how far these classifications can be generalized.[32] For instance, given the complexities of different countries in Asia, some critics disagree with the one-size-fits-all nature of Brandon's categories. Others argue that Brandon draws a close analogy between Chinese and Japanese Shakespeare, but, due to political frictions between the two countries, it is faulty to push the analogy too far.[33] In addition, the implicit teleology of Brandon's thesis is contested by scholars, as they question how Asian Shakespeare can evolve from a localizing phase, to a canonical phase, and finally to a postmodern phase.[34]

Recognizing the inadequacies of Brandon's categories, I propose that post-1997 Hong Kong Shakespeare corresponds to the political climate in the neocolonial period, the variously sinicizing, aestheticizing and explicitly socio-political productions of this time all commenting on aspects of Hong Kong's uneasy cultural and political circumstances. My article focuses on discussing two post-1997 Shakespearian adaptations staged by a Hong Kong theatre director, Hardy Tsoi, who has founded two theatre companies in Hong Kong: Prospects Theatre and Hong Kong Theatre Works. Tsoi's theatre companies are uniquely located in a former village school in Cha Kwo Ling, Kowloon. Situated near Tin Hau Temple, Sze Shan School was a primary school built by the villagers of Cha Kwo Ling in the 1960s of the colonial era. The Black Box Theatre is located on the ground floor, which is also the place where Tsoi conducts rehearsals with his actors. As suggested by Bernice Chan Kwok-wai, manager of the International Association of Theatre Critics (Hong Kong), it is very difficult for any theatre company in Hong Kong to survive solely on income from the box office, thus they have to depend on various forms of government funding.[35] Likewise, Hong Kong Theatre Works have had a venue partnership with the Leisure and Cultural Services Department at the North District Town Hall since 2012. Because of this

---

[28] School of English, The University of Hong Kong, 'Profile of Dr Otto Heim': http://www.english.hku.hk/staff/heim.htm.

[29] Otto Heim, 'Introduction: Chinese and Hong Kong Shakespeares', in *Teaching Shakespeare to ESL Students: The Study of Language Arts in Four Major Plays*, ed. Miriam Leung-che Lau and Anna Wing-bo Tso (Singapore, 2017), pp. xix-xxii, p. xix.

[30] Heim, 'Introduction: Chinese and Hong Kong Shakespeares', p. xix.

[31] James R. Brandon, 'Some Shakespeare(s) in some Asia(s)', *Asian Studies Review* 20.3 (1997), 1–26, esp. p. 3, p. 12, p. 18.

[32] John Gillies, Ryuta Minami, Ruru Li and Poonam Trivedi, 'Shakespeare on the stages of Asia', in *The Cambridge Companion to Shakespeare on Stage* (Cambridge, 2002), pp. 259–83, p. 281, n. 1.

[33] Gillies *et al.*, 'Shakespeare on the stages of Asia', p. 266.

[34] Gillies *et al.*, 'Shakespeare on the stages of Asia', p. 280.

[35] Bernice Chan, telephone interview, 7 January 2016.

venue partnership, the plays produced by Hong Kong Theatre Works target audiences of secondary school students and inhabitants in Hong Kong's North District, as the North District is far away from major performance venues in the city.

From 2010, Tsoi embarked on what he called a 'Shakespeare cycle' in his artistic productions.[36] He had twice directed Richard Ho's *Hamlet: Sword of Vengeance* in 2010 and 2012, and his own version of *Hamlet* set in Hong Kong in 2012. Furthermore, Tsoi had directed *Twelfth Night* and *Romantic Shakespeare* in 2011, *Julius Caesar* (2012) and *Shamshuipo Lear* (2015). His Shakespearian productions differ from those of other Hong Kong directors in that they often emphasize social and educational purposes. Tsoi had three principles in staging theatre works: caring for mankind, reflection of society, and embodiment of the spirit of the times. Through theatrical works, he aims to represent the value of mankind and to arouse social awareness.[37] In the past, Prospects Theatre had staged plays that centred on societal themes, such as *Simply Charles* (2017), which aroused people's concern regarding patients with dementia, and *Brandon and Louise* (2018), which addressed issues around environmental protection.[38] His most recent play in 2019, *Bertolt Brecht and Zhou Enlai: Two Lives, One Sky*, compares Brecht with Zhou, the first premier of the People's Republic of China, in their attempt to change society and to build an ideal world.[39] Of the seven Shakespearian plays that Tsoi has directed in post-1997 Hong Kong, I have chosen to discuss *Julius Caesar* (2012) and *Shamshuipo Lear* (2015) in particular, due to their clear engagement with Hong Kong's socio-political situation in the neocolonial era.

MIME IN *JULIUS CAESAR* (2012): VOICES OF THE OPPRESSED

Tsoi has a history of rewriting Shakespeare for social and political purposes. In 2012, he directed *Julius Caesar* for Hong Kong Theatre Works, and it was funded by the Hong Kong government. *Julius Caesar* is not regarded as a popular play among Hong Kong theatre directors and, excluding Tsoi's production, it had only been staged twice since 1997. He nonetheless chose to stage the play as a means of using the past to satirize the present, and to express his concerns about Hong Kong society. Tsoi staged *Julius Caesar* in 2012, which was an important electoral year in Hong Kong, as the elections for both the Chief Executive and the Legislative Council took place. Tsoi asserts, 'There is a certain amount of significance in my choice of staging *Julius Caesar* in the Year of Election in Hong Kong.'[40] He notes similarities between Roman and Hong Kong societies, such as parallels between the hierarchy of the Roman senators and that of the Hong Kong Legislative Council, and the ways in which Roman and Hong Kong citizens were exploited and pacified by their respective governments to serve the political interests of the stakeholders. After Caesar is assassinated, Antony compels Brutus to step down by drawing support from the crowd. Antony also announces to the Roman citizens that Caesar has granted each of them 75 drachmas in his will, a gesture that Tsoi finds curiously comparable to the Hong Kong government's granting of HKD $6,000 to every Hong Kong citizen in 2011, serving to pacify

---

36 Bernice Chan, Heung-sing Lee and Hardy Tsoi, 'Shakespeare's famous characters: an inspiration of men facing hopeless situations', post-performance talk on *Shamshuipo Lear*, Hong Kong, 12 September 2015.

37 Su Zi, 'Hardy Tsoi: I am a Hong Konger', *AM730*, 11 September 2015.

38 Prospects Theatre, 'Our Story', www.facebook.com/pg/ ProspectsTheatre/about/?ref=page_internal.

39 The comparison between Brecht and Zhou is based on the fact that they were both born in 1898 and grew up in the 1920s. Respectively involved in theatre and politics, they had similar ideals regarding changing the world. Prospects Theatre, 'A Few Facts about Bertolt Brecht and Zhou Enlai', www.facebook.com/ProspectsTheatre/photos/p .2290792084302078/2290792084302078/?type=1&theater.

40 Hong Kong Theatre Works, *Programme for Julius Caesar* (Hong Kong, 2012), p. 6.

dissatisfaction with the government.[41] From this perspective, Tsoi's *Julius Caesar* fits into the social and political realms of Hong Kong Shakespeare.

From Acts 1 to 3, Tsoi's *Julius Caesar* is situated in Rome and it follows the source text quite faithfully. The actors are dressed as Romans – for example, men wear short-sleeved tunics – and the action takes place in a setting similar to the Colosseum in Rome, made of ancient pillars. Nevertheless, Acts 4 and 5 of Shakespeare's text are entirely removed from Tsoi's production. He transposes the play from Rome to Hong Kong in a ten-minute mime that portrays the lives of Hong Kong citizens. The actors in the mime are dressed in black, and their actions are accompanied by slow music. The mime partly depicts the daily routine of lower classes in Hong Kong, in which an elderly woman pushes heavy cardboard boxes, a homeless man sleeps on the floor, and a street hawker is being chased away by government officials in black suits. The mime in *Julius Caesar* relates to the opening scene in the source text, which depicts the lives of commoners gathering in the streets and their interactions with the tribunes. This reminds us of Sanders's remark that an appropriation stands alone in its own right, but still engages in dialogue with Shakespeare's source text.[42] Ironically titled 'la dolce vita' – meaning 'the good life' in Italian[43] – Tsoi's mime illustrates three social problems in Hong Kong: the hegemony of property developers, the wide disparity between rich and poor, and the difficulties in seeking employment.[44] Under the silhouette of Hong Kong's high rises, actors playing property agents post onto Roman pillars advertisements that read 'Open Day of Roman Garden'. This symbolizes Tsoi's critique of the collusion between large property developers and the government, which results in property price inflation beyond the purchasing power of most Hong Kongers.

Shakespeare's *Julius Caesar* primarily centres on the lives of the ruling class and their struggle for power, while the commoners in Rome only constitute minor roles in the play. Calpurnia, wife of Caesar, exclaims, 'When beggars die there are no comets seen; / The heavens themselves blaze forth the death of princes' (2.2.30–1). Calpurnia's remark reinforces the idea that the poor and the powerless are of no significance at all, whether living or dead. Contrastingly, Tsoi's *Julius Caesar* elevates the commoners' role to the 'fifth main character', where the first part of his production depicts the lives of the aristocracy in Rome, and the second part illustrates the lives of commoners in Hong Kong.[45] The non-Shakespearian part of the play added by the director highlights poverty and other social problems in Hong Kong, as I have outlined in the above. This parallels the social unrest in *Julius Caesar*, showing how the commoners in both Hong Kong and Rome are mistreated and exploited by the government. By superimposing Hong Kong's social and political realities onto Shakespeare's play via the mime, Tsoi's appropriation carries his play decisively away from the source text and makes it a new cultural product, fitting into Sanders's categorization of an appropriation.[46]

In the source text, Brutus recounts that Caesar's ghost has repeatedly appeared to him in dreams that foreshadow his own death; the ghost appears on stage the night before the defeat at Philippi (4.2.326–37). In Tsoi's *Julius Caesar*, rather than appearing as an image of nemesis only to Brutus, Caesar's ghost appears at the end of the mime, where he quietly observes the lives of ordinary Hong Kongers and the

---

41 'Scheme 6000' was implemented by the Hong Kong government in 2011, resulting from Hong Kong people's dissatisfaction with the government's initial proposal to inject the equivalent sum of money into their mandatory provident funds for retirement: Joseph Li, 'Road to Universal Retirement Protection', *China Daily*, 7 July 2011: www.chinadaily.com.cn/hkedition/2011-07/07/content12850917.htm.

42 Julie Sanders, *Adaptation and Appropriation* (London, 2006), p. 26, p. 60.

43 Tsoi borrows the phrase 'la dolce vita' from the Italian film of the same title (dir. Federico Fellini, 1960): Hong Kong Theatre Works, *Programme for Julius Caesar*, p. 6.

44 Hong Kong Theatre Works, *Programme for Julius Caesar*, p. 6.

45 Tsoi asserts that there are five main characters in his production. In order of importance they are Caesar, Brutus, Cassius, Antony and the commoners. Hong Kong Theatre Works, *Programme for Julius Caesar*, p. 6.

46 Sanders, *Adaptation and Appropriation*, p. 26.

playback of significant socio-political events in Hong Kong after the 1997 handover. By having a Roman leader overlooking contemporary Hong Kong, Tsoi suggests that the catastrophe of politics in the Roman Republic echoes or prefigures that of Hong Kong. He argues that the senator Cicero makes the most profound remark of the play: 'Indeed it is a strange-disposèd time; / But men may construe things after their fashion, / Clean from the purpose of the things themselves' (1.3.33–5).[47] The absurdity of neocolonial Hong Kong is reflected by Tsoi's critique of China's domineering economic and political influences. First, Tsoi depicts Hong Kong in the mime as distinct from China. The actors dressed in black clothing hold candles to commemorate the Tiananmen Square Massacre in Beijing in 1989, with an image of the Statue of Liberty in the background. As Hong Kong is the only city in China where commemorating the Tiananmen Square Massacre is legal, the action in the mime signifies that freedoms of speech and demonstration are widely embraced by Hong Kongers. Unfortunately, since the city's handover to China, freedoms previously enjoyed have gradually diminished. This is symbolically represented in the mime's opening, where the old Hong Kong Legislative Council building from the colonial era collapses into a pile of rubble. The Legislative Council is a place in Hong Kong where elected legislators meet to enact, amend and repeal laws. It also symbolizes the rule of law that Hong Kong upholds, and the common law system that Hong Kong practises, which is different from the civil law system in China with socialist roots. Therefore, the collapse of the Legislative Council building represents the loss of freedoms of speech and demonstration in Hong Kong. Moreover, a strong sense of irony is evident when a group of actors march to protest against the government, which takes place simultaneously with the fireworks to celebrate 1 July, marking Hong Kong's handover to China on 1 July 1997.[48] But the protest is abruptly disrupted when two mainland Chinese tourists appear in the spotlight. Carrying lots of shopping bags, one of them shouts loudly in Mandarin, 'I love Hong Kong! I love shopping! Everything is so cheap!' The line in Mandarin breaks the silence of the protesters, who are now walking gradually behind the tourists and heading towards back stage. This is symbolic of the voices of the oppressed Hong Kongers, which remain largely ignored by the Hong Kong government. Ackbar Abbas suggests that the 1997 handover does not signify Hong Kong's liberation from colonial rule – it instead indicates the city's transition to another form of governance.[49] This marks the double colonization of Hong Kong. While the Hong Kong government welcomes economic gains derived from mainland Chinese tourism, it fails to convey Hong Kongers' quest for democracy and universal suffrage effectively to China for fear of antagonizing the neo-colonizer. Abbas further argues that, as a result of efficient colonial management, the decadence of energy, referring to energy channelled in a one-dimensional development in a closed field, is projected exclusively into economic interests, such that there is 'almost no outlet for political idealism'.[50] For instance, it is observed that a significant proportion of Hong Kongers are more concerned with speculation on the property or stock markets than about who wins the elections at the Legislative Council. While mainland Chinese tourists are dressed in colourful outfits and appear in the spotlight, the silenced protesters' black clothing almost reduces them to the appearance of the backstage crew. The contrast of colours, and of the loudness of fireworks celebrating 1 July with the silence of the anti-government march, signify that Hong Kongers' quest for a spiritual home is thwarted by the intangible control of the authority.

---

[47] Hong Kong Theatre Works, *Programme for Julius Caesar*, p. 5.

[48] Since the large-scale protest in 2003 against the enactment of Article 23 in the Basic Law of Hong Kong, which would circumscribe freedom of speech upon effective legislation, there have been anti-government protests held on 1 July in Hong Kong every year: Jianne Soriano, 'July 1 March', *South China Morning Post*: www.scmp.com/topics/july-1-march.

[49] Ackbar Abbas, *Hong Kong: Culture and the Politics of Disappearance* (Minneapolis, 1997), p. 2.

[50] Abbas, *Hong Kong*, p. 5.

ABSENCE OF *KING LEAR* IN *SHAMSHUIPO LEAR* (2015)

Shamshuipo Lear was co-written by Hardy Tsoi and Michael Fung, which resulted in a Shakespearian appropriation that is firmly rooted in the social reality of Hong Kong. The play is staged before a realistic backdrop, as there are sofas, chairs and beds on the stage. This corresponds to the living conditions of the homeless people in Hong Kong, where they primarily gather in Shamshuipo. Shamshuipo, literally meaning 'deep water bank', was once the 'site of British army barracks built on reclaimed land in the 1920s'.[51] It is now the poorest district in Hong Kong, which is primarily inhabited by new immigrants from China and ethnic minorities. At first glance, *Shamshuipo Lear* appears to belong to Brandon's category of localized Shakespeare, since it is situated in Hong Kong and the characters consist of Hong Kongers, which coincides with Brandon's definition of localized Shakespeare as stories transposed into local settings.[52] By signalling in its title that it is set in Shamshuipo, *Shamshuipo Lear* signifies for the first time in the theatre history of Hong Kong that a local context is brought to bear on *King Lear*.

The inclusion of a Hong Kong context distinguishes Tsoi's appropriation from the canonical *King Lear* productions staged by Vicki Ooi and Daniel Yang in Hong Kong during the British colonial era, in which authenticity to Shakespeare's source text was a primary concern,[53] thus reflecting the colonized people's mentality of mimicking the colonizer's literary works.[54] However, Tsoi's appropriation comments much more on Hong Kong's social reality than on the source text, to the point that Shakespeare's source text disappears in the midst of his commentary on poverty and political instability in Hong Kong. Michael Fung had conducted in-depth research about the problem of homelessness in Hong Kong in order to equip himself with background knowledge when writing

the play.[55] For instance, he had interviewed Wong Hung, a Hong Kong social-work professor on the problem of homelessness. Similarly, Tsoi spoke of the inter-relationship between *Julius Caesar* and *Shamshuipo Lear* in an interview.[56] He affirmed that *Shamshuipo Lear* is a continuation of *Julius Caesar*'s mime, where he depicts the poor, thus showing his recurrent concern with problems of poverty and wealth inequality in Hong Kong. For example, there are scenes in *Julius Caesar*'s mime where an elderly woman pushes a trolley of used cardboard boxes, and a homeless man sleeps on a cardboard box. There is also a direct reference to Shamshuipo in *Julius Caesar*. The characters in the mime buy and sell used materials in the Dawn Market, an actual locality in Shamshuipo where the poor make a living by selling used materials early in the morning, just before government officers chase them away.[57]

Interestingly, Michael Fung honestly told me that he had not read Shakespeare's *King Lear* while preparing this script, though he knows the story well.[58] Tsoi, who co-wrote and directed *Shamshuipo Lear*, admits that he was the one who

---

[51] Mike Ingham, *Hong Kong: A Cultural and Literary History* (Oxford, 2007), p. 189.

[52] Brandon, 'Some Shakespeare(s)', p. 12.

[53] Vicki Ooi's Seals Theatre Company staged the first Hong Kong production of *King Lear* in 1981, where Ooi employed Jane Lai's faithful translation of the play (Daniel S. P. Yang, '*King Lear* in Beijing and Hong Kong', *Asian Theatre Journal* 28.1 (2011), 184–98, p. 190). Daniel Yang, who was the first artistic director of the Hong Kong Repertory Theatre, directed *King Lear* in 1993. He argued that his translation of the play was extremely faithful to Shakespeare's text, and the production's scale was 'not far from a typical main house production at Stratford-upon-Avon': Yang, 'Shakespeare at the Hong Kong Repertory Theatre', pp. 82–3.

[54] Homi Bhabha, *The Location of Culture* (Abingdon, 2004), p. 85.

[55] Michael Fung, personal interview, 16 August 2015.

[56] 'Interview with the cast of *Shamshuipo Lear*', narr. Kin-hao Chan and Oi-ling Liu, Our Radio (Hong Kong, 7 September 2015).

[57] 'Dawn Markets in Hong Kong: Stand On His Own Feet', https://onlinejour.wordpress.com, accessed 8 April 2017.

[58] Fung, personal interview.

had later added the lines of Shakespeare into the appropriation.[59] There are two reasons why Tsoi chose to appropriate *King Lear*. He appropriated Shakespeare's text *not* because of the reasons asserted by Hutcheon – to pay homage to, or to contest the aesthetic or political values of, the adapted text.[60] This shows the limitation of Hutcheon's adaptation theories outside of the Western cultural context. Knowing that Hong Kongers are generally not very familiar with Shakespeare, especially beyond educated audiences in academic circles, Tsoi appropriated *King Lear* in a manner whereby knowledge of the source text does not matter to the understanding of *Shamshuipo Lear*. He simply appropriated particular motifs and concerns of *King Lear* to enable his audience to understand Hong Kong's social problems. On a personal level, he appropriated Shakespeare's text to commemorate a friend, who lost his family business and later drank himself to death. His deceased friend thus served as a tragic prototype for the Uncle Lee character in *Shamshuipo Lear*.[61] This corresponds to Alexa Huang's argument that the notion of the 'universality of Shakespeare' has become 'retrograde', and that 'Asian interpretations for the stage [present] the creativity of imaginative directors willing to create new hybrids of dramatic spectacle by combining the personal with the fictional'.[62]

Subsequently, on a societal level, Tsoi appropriated Shakespeare to critique the socio-political problems of Hong Kong, a tactic he believed was 'more effective than writing a new play about the city'.[63] Tsoi considered appropriating *King Lear* as 'more effective' in terms of marketing appeal. As the homeless in Hong Kong belong to a minority group, the subject matter of the play was not very appealing to the mostly affluent middle-class audience, who were traditionally more concerned with escapism and cultural capital. As there are fewer than 2,000 homeless people in the population of over 7 million in Hong Kong, the government does not consider the number to be significant and refuses to help this group of people.[64] By drawing parallels between King Lear and a homeless elderly man, Uncle Lee, Tsoi markets

Shamshuipo Lear as an appropriation of Shakespeare, which might help to increase the play's popularity, since Shakespeare is the most often staged Western playwright in Hong Kong. Tsoi and Fung have rather intentionally named three homeless characters as Uncle *Lee*, Wen *Yee*-tak and *Wong* Tong. The combination of the Chinese characters taken from each of their names is 'Lee', 'Yee' and 'Wong', which amounted to the Chinese translation of 'King Lear'.[65]

With several newly added characters and scenes, *Shamshuipo Lear* positions itself as an appropriation of Shakespeare's *King Lear*. Yet it was not a full-scale appropriation, as Tsoi merely extracted a few motifs from the source text and transplanted them onto a new text: if anything, it is a play almost about the absence of *King Lear*. Bernice Chan Kwok-wai, manager of the International Association of Theatre Critics (Hong Kong), calls it a 'mix and match play', since the 'characters in Tsoi's appropriation experience despondent situations *like* the characters in Shakespeare's source text'.[66] She implies that *Shamshuipo Lear*'s characters are not identical to *King Lear*'s characters, and I argue that the differences between the two plays are larger than their similarities. This coincides with Sanders's assertion that appropriation signifies a 'more decisive journey away from the informing source into a wholly new cultural product and domain',[67] where Tsoi has transformed the tragedy of Lear into a satire about the predicaments of Hong Kongers. *Shamshuipo Lear*, through its very title, asks us to think about its characters and events

---

[59] Hardy Tsoi, personal interview, 5 November 2015.
[60] Linda Hutcheon, *A Theory of Adaptation* (New York, 2006), p. 20.
[61] Tsoi, personal interview.
[62] Alexa Huang, 'Shakespeare, performance, and autobiographical interventions', *Shakespeare Bulletin* 24.2 (2006), 31–47.
[63] Tsoi, personal interview.
[64] Prospects Theatre, *Programme for* Shamshuipo Lear (Hong Kong, 2015), p. 3.
[65] Fung, personal interview.
[66] Chan *et al.*, 'Shakespeare's famous characters'.
[67] Sanders, *Adaptation and Appropriation*, p. 26.

in the light of Shakespeare's tragedy, while refrain-
ing from offering a re-enactment of that tragedy.

Tsoi's new story about the survival of
Hong Kong people is superimposed onto the
source text to the extent that most of the main
plots and subplots in *King Lear* are lost, such as the
parallel parent–child relationships of Lear and his
daughters, and Gloucester and his sons. In
Shamshuipo Lear, the main plot is Uncle Lee's
estranged relationship with his son, Jack. The two
subplots are, respectively, the stories of other
homeless characters, and Jack's relationship with
his girlfriend-*cum*-social worker for the homeless,
Kimmy / Miss Chan. There are *merely* four
instances in *Shamshuipo Lear* whereby Tsoi employs
Shakespeare's elements. First, a homeless elderly
man, Uncle Lee, imagines himself as King Lear.
In the opening scene titled 'Mingling of good and
evil in the street', Uncle Lee wears a paper crown,
and a toy trumpet is hung around his neck. He
walks unsteadily with a wine bottle in one of his
hands. When Wong Tong, a homeless neighbour,
greets him, 'Uncle Lee, good morning!', Uncle
Lee replies:

No! I am King Lear! You have to call me king; I will
announce a plan that has not been officially decreed . . .
Come, give me a map, I will divide my territories, as I am
determined to cast away all the troubles of my worries
from my old and feeble body. I will pass my lands to the
young people, ha ha ha . . .[68]

Nevertheless, Uncle Lee's social status is drastically different from that of Lear. While Lear is a real
king who distributes his inheritance among his
daughters and sons-in-law, Uncle Lee is only an
imaginary king living in the slums of Shamshuipo,
and he does not even have sufficient financial means
to provide for himself. By depicting Uncle Lee as
a drunkard and slightly detached from reality, Tsoi
perhaps hints that Lear in the source text is also mad
when he surrenders all his territories to his daughters. Lear's division of his kingdom reflects his 'imagined expansion of his own territory – he would
have three homes instead of one'.[69] Unfortunately,
his imagination is distorted, and in reality he has no
home at all. It is ironic for Uncle Lee, a homeless

character in *Shamshuipo Lear*, to want to distribute
his 'home' to other characters. This metaphorically
alludes to the homelessness of Hong Kong people
during the neocolonial era, which I shall explain in
the next section.

HOMELESSNESS AS A METAPHOR IN SHAMSHUIPO LEAR

As Adele Lee points out in the 'Shakespeare in
Hong Kong' podcast, Hong Kong people have
clung on to the British cultural heritage for fear of
the loss of freedom after 1997. Hence, Shakespeare
is something that Hong Kong directors hold on to
as a protest against China, the neo-colonizer.[70] For
financial and pragmatic reasons, Tsoi asserts, 'No
Hong Kong director will openly stage a play that
directly criticises the Hong Kong government.'[71]
Uncle Lee in *Shamshuipo Lear* indirectly appropriates Lear's lines to criticize the Hong Kong government, which I interpret as a feature of socio-
politicized Shakespeare. In Scene 6 of the play,
a legislator leads a team to post notices of eviction,
and workers encircle the area occupied by the
homeless with tape and metal barricades. At this
point, Uncle Lee appropriates Lear's lines (*Lear*,
3.4.28–36) to accuse the government of indifference towards Hong Kong's problem of poverty.

UNCLE LEE: We who are utterly poor, with only rags for
clothes, suffering from this merciless storm, we have
no roof above our heads, and facing hunger, just how
can we survive? Sigh, *you* who only indulge in enjoyment, and don't care about the difficulties of ordinary
citizens! *You* should experience hunger and coldness,
and then *you* can learn how to become a human being!

---

[68] Michael Fung and Hardy Tsoi, *Script of Shamshuipo Lear*
(Hong Kong, 2015), p. 4. All translations of *Shamshuipo
Lear* from Chinese to English are done by myself.

[69] Chih-chiao Joseph Yang, 'A search for home: displacement
in *King Lear*', *Tamkang Review* 43.1 (2012), 67–80, p. 71.

[70] Lee interviewed by Grant, in Neva Grant, 'Shakespeare in
Hong Kong', Shakespeare Unlimited (Folger Shakespeare
Library: Shakespeare Unlimited podcast series), 1 July 2015,
episode 27.

[71] Tsoi, personal interview.

LEGISLATOR: Old man, I am Legislator Fong, is there anything we can . . .

UNCLE LEE: I stand here, only as your slave, a pitiful, weak, powerless old man. But I still need to reproach you, you despicable accomplices, who join my two evil daughters to oppose me, a white-haired old man. Ah! How wicked![72]

In the source text, the word 'thyself' in Lear's exclamation of 'Expose thyself to feel what wretches feel' (*Lear*, 3.4.34) refers to those who personify 'pomp' in Lear's preceding line, such as aristocrats, members of royal families, and wealthy people. However, the word 'you' in Uncle Lee's uttering of '*You* should experience hunger and coldness, and then *you* can learn how to become a human being' specifically addresses the legislator who supervises the demolition of the shelter area that the homeless are residing in. Through borrowing Shakespeare's lines, Tsoi wishes to arouse the audience's concern for marginalized groups in society, as he believes that 'theatre contains a kind of social responsibility'.[73] This makes his style of staging Shakespeare worth noting. It is unlike the dominant feature of Hong Kong theatre during the British colonial period, when theatre's social function was minimized and its entertainment function was maximized.[74] It is also different from the early Shakespearian productions performed in English for expatriates in Hong Kong, where the British colonizers simply imported Shakespeare to make themselves feel at home.[75]

I further propose that *Shamshuipo Lear* comments on the metaphorical homelessness of Hong Kongers during the neocolonial era. Not all the characters in the production are literally homeless; for example, Jack and his girlfriend Kimmy have material homes to return to. But in Scene 12, titled 'Discussing the Future', the young couple discuss Hong Kong's social problems and Jack tries to persuade Kimmy to emigrate to Australia. Tsoi suggests that people from almost all classes of Hong Kong society are dissatisfied with the present-day circumstances: the homeless complaining about the government's indifference towards poverty, and educated young people feeling powerless in the midst of socio-political frictions:

JACK: If we settle daddy's accounts, go to Sydney with me.

CHAN: It isn't so simple, Jack! I like you very much too . . . But, Hong Kong is the city that I was born and raised in . . .

JACK: It's better if you follow me to Australia. The place is larger, and there's also no pollution.

CHAN: But Hong Kong is my home!

JACK: But this home isn't going well! The politics are messed up . . .

CHAN: There's wide disparity between the rich and poor.

JACK: Exactly! Though you have a university degree, it's difficult to get a job, and the pay's little!

CHAN: And you can't even afford to buy a flat!

JACK: So that's why . . .

CHAN: [*interrupting Jack*] I know you have very good living standards there, but I am not envious of you! You're right; Hong Kong isn't doing well in many aspects: it's difficult for young people to move upwards, we feel powerless in politics, people lose mutual trust, and the society is full of friction and negativity. Some say that times have chosen us, and we need to fight back . . . But I have another role. I am to become a social worker. During my internship here, I saw that this place is full of love, trust, friendship . . . The most powerful weapon that kills the poor is alienation. The government doesn't help the homeless, political parties even chase them away, and exploit them further . . .

JACK: [*speechless*] . . .

CHAN: You were raised in Sydney, and may not have feelings for Hong Kong. But I am different![76]

In *Reflections on Exile and Other Essays*, Edward Said describes the mentality of exiles, where they are 'cut off from their roots, their land, their past'.[77] He also distinguishes nationalisms from exiles, for he asserts that 'Nationalisms are about groups, but in a very acute sense exile is a solitude experienced

---

[72] Fung and Tsoi, *Script of Shamshuipo Lear*, p. 17.

[73] Zi, 'Hardy Tsoi: I am a Hong Konger'.

[74] Zi, 'Hardy Tsoi: I am a Hong Konger'.

[75] Grant, 'Shakespeare in Hong Kong'.

[76] Fung and Tsoi, *Script of Shamshuipo Lear*, pp. 38–9.

[77] Edward Said, *Reflections on Exile and Other Essays* (Cambridge, MA, 2000), p. 177.

outside the group'.[78] While Said describes an exile as being away from home, I argue that it is possible to become an exile even though one is situated in one's material home. Though Jack and Kimmy have material homes in Hong Kong, they both feel insecure about their spiritual homes. A spiritual home is far more complex in its construction than a material home – the latter simply meaning having a roof to live under. A spiritual home, however, encompasses more subjective elements, such as whether one's personal values are aligned with societal values and the government's rule, whether one can envision a long-term relationship with one's home, or whether one feels happy and settled at home. The above conversation between Jack and Kimmy represents the insecurities felt by Hong Kong's young generation, who are faced with difficulties in social mobility, powerlessness in politics, and a society full of friction and negativity. The estrangement of Hong Kongers is intensified in neocolonial Hong Kong. The depiction of home as blurry and disappearing is a characteristic of Hong Kong's newly created plays.[79] In Tsoi's own words, his production has a 'mix and match flavour', and he admits that *Shamshuipo Lear* masquerades as a Shakespearian play.[80] With reference to socio-politicized Shakespeare, Tsoi gives a Chinese title to each of his eighteen scenes in *Shamshuipo Lear*, and the titles are shown to the audience on the screen at the beginning of each scene. The scene titles provide a condensed description of the action that is going to take place, which corresponds to Brecht's epic theatre, as the spectators are turned into observers instead of being completely involved in a stage situation in dramatic theatre.[81] As actors in the epic theatre detach themselves from the characters portrayed, the spectators are forced to look at the play's situation from an analytical perspective. By employing Brecht's strategy, Tsoi wants his audience to examine Hong Kong's social problems critically, and he does not intend his production purely to serve the purpose of entertainment.

The figure of Lear not only is marginalized in Tsoi's production, but also serves as a transient phase in the construction of Uncle Lee's identity. From the moment Uncle Lee regains sanity at the end of the play, he rejects his earlier appropriation of Shakespeare's protagonist and never quotes another line. Thus, he breaks free from the fictionalized circumstances of Lear's world in Shakespeare's text. Just before the coda, the last lines of *Shamshuipo Lear* uttered by Uncle Lee are: 'Can you all hear the bells? New Year has come . . . A new year starts all over again . . . now I know who I really am, let us embrace a new beginning!'[82] Tsoi's play ends with the main protagonist's rediscovery of his identity, which is a crucial element in Hong Kong's newly created plays. For instance, the affirmation of local values, language and people in the newly created plays is suggestive of the construction of Hong Kong identity, as summarized by Chan.[83]

Apart from Uncle Lee's occasional appropriation of Lear's lines, *Shamshuipo Lear* also exemplifies the indirect absorption of Shakespeare's scenes. This echoes Robert Miola's argument that appropriations can represent a continuum of relations ranging from 'direct contact to indirect absorption'.[84] In the last scene of the play, the homeless neighbours hold a farewell party-*cum*-rehearsal of a Buddhist funeral for Uncle Lee. Aunt Lan, as a protector of Uncle Lee resembling Kent in Shakespeare's text, hopes that Uncle Lee will be awakened from his past and be reborn through the symbolic funeral rites. Tsoi explains that this scene parallels the near-death experience of Gloucester, where Edgar leads his blinded father to jump from a 'cliff' at Dover to cure his sorrow and encourage him to

[78] Said, *Reflections on Exile and Other Essays*, p. 177.
[79] Shelby Kar-yan Chan, *Identity and Theatre Translation in Hong Kong* (Berlin, 2015), p. 206
[80] Prospects Theatre, *Programme for* Shamshuipo Lear, p. 4.
[81] *Brecht on Theatre: The Development of an Aesthetic*, ed. and trans. John Willett (London, 1964), p. 37.
[82] Fung and Tsoi, *Script of Shamshuipo Lear*, p. 45.
[83] Chan, *Identity and Theatre Translation in Hong Kong*, p. 178.
[84] Robert Miola, *Shakespeare and Classical Tragedy: The Influence of Seneca* (Oxford, 1992), p. 7.

carry on living.[85] In *Shamshuipo Lear*, Uncle Lee's neighbours think that the remedy for curing Uncle Lee's despair is to encourage him to face death through a rehearsed funeral. Aunt Lan and Wen Yee-tak also parallel Edgar's role, as they employ traditional customs to pay 'last respects' to Uncle Lee. Aunt Lan passes him a bowl of soba noodles, and Wen tells Uncle Lee, 'After you have eaten it, bad luck will go away, and may all your wishes come true!'[86] Finally, Ah Sing, who is a South Asian, dresses in traditional Indian costume and dances around Uncle Lee. Wen tells Uncle Lee, 'Time is short! Drink the Meng Po Tea quickly, and be on your way! Look! The King of Hell has already sent the underworld judge to take you away!'[87]

The last scene of *Shamshuipo Lear* witnesses a creative fusion of Shakespeare with the transposed customs of distinctive cultures. Both an appropriation of Lear's lines and a transplantation of Shakespeare's scene are evident. There is also a flexible transference of identity in which Uncle Lee sometimes resembles Lear by speaking his lines, and at times Gloucester by undergoing a near-death experience. Furthermore, there is a conglomeration of the Japanese custom of eating soba noodles as a symbol of good luck on New Year's Eve, the Chinese superstition about drinking Meng Po Tea in the underworld, and the Indian custom of dance as performed by Ah Sing. This kind of hybridity is distinctive in Hong Kong Shakespeare. It corresponds to Bhabha's assertion that cultural hybridity results in 'something different, something new and unrecognisable, a new area of negotiation of meaning and representation'.[88] Tsoi's production seems to suggest that there is no fixedness in anything, be it identity or home. I interpret the hybridity and the flexible transference of identity in *Shamshuipo Lear* as symbolic of the fluid identity of Hong Kong people, in line with Gilbert Fong's observation that, through its postcolonial drama, Hong Kong carves its own 'flexible hybrid identity between its two colonisers'.[89]

The fluid identity of Hong Kongers is exemplified by the insertion of Sam Hui's song 'Where Can My Home Be?' in the coda of the play. Sam

Hui, known as the 'godfather of Cantonese pop',[90] represents the heyday of Hong Kong's popular culture from the 1970s to the 1990s. This period also corresponded to Hong Kong's phase of economic affluence.[91] According to Liu Ching-chih, a Hong Kong professor of music, the lyrics of Canto-pop in this period, such as those sung by Hui, often reflected Hong Kongers' 'energy, confidence, hope and strong identity with the city'.[92] In the epilogue of *Shamshuipo Lear*, Aunt Lan sings the following lines from 'Where Can My Home Be?':

> Footsteps trodden everywhere, having witnessed
>   the prosperity of foreign countries,
> The utopia of peach blossoms is like a dream; still
>   I cannot find my home.
> To live stably is like an illusion, clouds looming
>   from afar,
> When will the mist disappear one day, children and
>   grandchildren laughing under the sunset,

---

85 Tsoi, personal interview.

86 Fung and Tsoi, *Script of Shamshuipo Lear*, p. 42.

87 Fung and Tsoi, *Script of Shamshuipo Lear*, p. 43. Traditional Chinese belief states that, before the deceased reincarnate, they will be forced to drink the Meng Po Tea, or the Oblivion Tea, so that they will forget everything that happened to them in their former lives. See Hua-long Xu, ed., *A Comprehensive Dictionary of China's Ghost Culture* (Nanning, 1994), p. 731.

88 Jonathan Rutherford, 'The third space: interview with Homi Bhabha', in *Identity: Community, Culture, Difference* (London, 1990), p. 211.

89 Cited in Chapman Chen, 'Postcolonial Hong Kong drama translation', in *Beyond Borders: Translations Moving Languages, Literatures and Cultures* (Berlin, 2011), p. 42.

90 Adam Wright, 'In pictures: Canto-pop superstar Sam Hui turns 70', *South China Morning Post*, 21 October 2016: www.scmp.com/culture/music/article/2038717/pictures-canto-pop-superstar-sam-huis-40-years-limelight.

91 Kevin Kwong, 'Hong Kong localism, and nostalgia, behind revival of interest in Canto-pop', *South China Morning Post*, 6 July 2016: www.scmp.com/culture/music/article/1985636/hong-kong-localism-and-nostalgia-behind-revival-interest-canto-pop.

92 Professor Liu Ching-chih, cited in Kwong, 'Hong Kong localism, and nostalgia, behind revival of interest in Canto-pop'.

Ah . . . Ten thousand lights shining through the
high-rises ah . . .
Where can my home be![93]

Recorded in one of Hui's songs in the album
'Songs of Summer in 1979', the lyrics of 'Where
Can My Home Be?' emphasize Hong Kongers'
homelessness at a time when the future of
Hong Kong was uncertain, for it was only in 1984
that the signing of the Sino-British Joint Declaration
confirmed that Hong Kong's sovereignty would be
returned to China in 1997. The frustrations of
Hong Kongers regarding the city's future are illustrated in the line 'To live stably is like an illusion,
clouds looming from afar', in the song.
Furthermore, Aunt Lan's singing in the epilogue
of *Shamshuipo Lear* accompanies the departure
of the homeless characters, as they begin to pack their
luggage and subsequently leave their temporary
homes in Shamshuipo. The departure of the homeless characters in *Shamshuipo Lear* symbolically suggests that there is no sense of homecoming for
Hong Kongers, corresponding to their disillusion-
ment in the search for a stable home, as exhibited in
the song. As argued by Chan, Hong Kong people
are proud of their multiple identities and their
adaptability to Chinese–Western cultures. For
them, home is here and there, and seems to be
everywhere and nowhere.[94] To escape from the
plight of 1977, many Hong Kongers had emigrated
to Western countries, echoing Hui's lyrics as their
'footsteps [had] trodden everywhere', and they had
'witnessed the prosperity of foreign countries'.
Though enjoying freedom and democracy in the
West, many complained of the difficulty in securing
decent jobs, leading to a reflux of emigrants back to
Hong Kong in the 1990s. During the neocolonial
period, the trend of emigration from Hong Kong
has revived, especially in recent years when
Hong Kong's freedom has been increasingly eroded
by the mainland.[95] Many Hong Kongers find that
Hong Kong does not feel like their home anymore.
Both Hong Kongers and the homeless characters in
Shamshuipo Lear undergo a continuous process in
search of their ideal homes. When Uncle Lee walks

towards centre stage, he discards his paper crown,
symbolizing that he is no longer King Lear, the
illusion that he previously held on to. This reflects
that Hong Kongers' identities have always been
floating, or 'out of place', as Said suggested of the
exile's mentality.[96] Uncle Lee's appropriation and
rejection of Shakespeare's protagonist is circumstantial, just as Hong Kongers do not pledge complete
loyalty to the ex-colonizer's cultural symbols.

CONCLUSION

Hardy Tsoi's *Shamshuipo Lear* is more a new story
about Hong Kongers' survival in the neocolonial
period than it is about Shakespeare's *King Lear*. The
stories of Hong Kong's homeless and non-homeless
characters superimpose upon the source text,
reflecting the city's social problems, such as the
wide disparity between rich and poor, the housing
shortage, and the government's ignoring of people's
voices. Tsoi has inserted many Hong Kong contexts
that override the source text's supremacy. For
instance, he adds characters that are absent from
King Lear, such as Jack and Kimmy, to illustrate
Hong Kong people's homelessness in the neocolonial context. His adaptation of *Shamshuipo Lear* thus
serves more as a critique of Hong Kong society than
as a tribute to Shakespeare. Moreover, Tsoi highlights the distinctive element of hybridity in
Hong Kong Shakespeare, which is displayed by
the flexible transference of identity from both Lear
and Gloucester to Uncle Lee. This again reflects the
fluidity of Hong Kong identity, or that
Hong Kongers are actually forced to be fluid due
to the changing times that are beyond their control.
Just like employees who behave differently under
a new boss, Hong Kongers have also responded in
disparate ways when faced with different colonizers.

---

[93] Fung and Tsoi, *Script of Shamshuipo Lear*, p. 46.
[94] Chan, *Identity and Theatre Translation in Hong Kong*, p. 205.
[95] Shih Wing-ching, 'Hong Kong's Gini-coefficient will still deteriorate', *AM730*, 13 June 2017.
[96] Said, *Reflections on Exile and Other Essays*, p. 558.

BEFORE WE SLEEP: *MACBETH* AND THE CURTAIN LECTURE

NEIL RHODES

Macbeth has been described as Shakespeare's most topical play, engaging with recent events such as the Gunpowder Plot and reflecting upon issues close to King James himself, the official patron of Shakespeare's playing company.[1] This is to give the play a very public dimension, highlighting its historical and political concerns, and suiting it too to the large arena theatre in which it was first performed. Yet there are many aspects of *Macbeth* that work in a quite opposite way. Acted in daylight, it is nevertheless a play dominated by darkness and by the liminal territory between day and night. Though it was staged in the broad, open playing space of the Globe, some of its most memorable scenes take place in intensely private locations. Most crucially – and this is central to my concern in this article – while the play charts the swift and murderous route to the throne of an ambitious individual, and the aftermath of this bid for power, it is a play which has at its dark heart an extraordinary intimacy between husband and wife. To say that the Macbeths are Shakespeare's closest couple is not in itself an original observation, but it is one that is usually made, as it were, in passing.[2] What I want to show here are some of the formal and linguistic means by which Shakespeare makes this intimacy central to our experience of the play, embedding the private and domestic world within its public and political superstructure.[3]

***

We can begin with the matter of location. The F1 stage directions are not particularly helpful in establishing a specific sense of place, but it is clear that

many of the play's most memorable scenes are set in private spaces within the Macbeths' castle. A. R. Braunmuller, in what is still the best edition of *Macbeth*, spells these out: in 1.5, we first see the couple together 'in some private room of their castle at Inverness'; for the soliloquy 'If it were done when 'tis done' in 1.7, 'Macbeth has withdrawn from the off-stage ceremonial dinner ... to some more private place'; of 2.2, where the Macbeths confer immediately after the murder, Braunmuller notes that 'The setting is somewhere in Macbeth's castle

---

1 See Stephen Greenblatt in *The Norton Shakespeare*, ed. Stephen Greenblatt, Walter Cohen, Jean E. Howard, Katharine Eisaman Maus and Andrew Gurr (New York, 1997), p. 2555; also James Shapiro, *1606: William Shakespeare and the Year of Lear* (London, 2015), esp. p. 150, pp. 212–18, 242–4; Arthur F. Kinney, *Lies Like Truth: Shakespeare, Macbeth, and the Cultural Moment* (Detroit, 2001). This kind of issue is the principal focus of articles in the first part of *Shakespeare Survey 57* (Cambridge, 2004), '*Macbeth* and its Afterlife', though Carol Chillington Rutter, 'Remind me: how many children had Lady Macbeth?', pp. 38–53, revisits a topic which is closer to the subject of my own concerns.

2 See Ian McKellen and others cited in *Macbeth*, ed. Sandra Clark and Pamela Mason (London, 2015), p. 1; Jonathan Bate refers to the Macbeths as a married couple 'working together as partners', and to the 'moments of exceptional tenderness' between them, in William Shakespeare, *Complete Works*, ed. Jonathan Bate and Eric Rasmussen (Basingstoke, 2007), p. 1861.

3 On the 'mutual imprinting of domestic and political spheres' in relation to the domestic tragedy genre, especially *Arden of Faversham*, see Lena Cowen Orlin, 'Domestic tragedy: private life on the public stage', in *A New Companion to Renaissance Drama*, ed. Arthur F. Kinney and Thomas Warren Hopper (Oxford, 2017), pp. 388–402, p. 394.

that is private'; of 3.2, where they share their anxieties about Banquo, he suggests that 'The location is some private area of Macbeth's castle where intimate conversation (8ff.) is possible'; 5.1, the sleepwalking scene, 'occurs in Lady Macbeth's private rooms'.[4] These are not Shakespeare's stage directions, but they are reliable guides as to how these scenes should be imagined or staged. Soliloquy is, of course, a characteristic feature of tragedy, but *Macbeth* is unusual in its focus on private conversations *à deux*, when the couple need to be in a place where they cannot be overheard.

What this means is that the play is constantly moving between public areas of various kinds and private domestic space; at various points, we seem to be not so much in a castle as in a house. This may be a reflection of what W. G. Hoskins termed the 'Great Rebuilding' of the late sixteenth and early seventeenth centuries, but this is not to suggest that there would have been more private spaces in an ordinary domestic dwelling than in a castle.[5] More significantly, for the purposes of the present article, it is the play's focus on marital intimacy that brings with it an accommodation to a more middling kind of household environment and a corresponding shift in social register. Emma Whipday has recently written about the representation of the late sixteenth-century home as a castle.[6] For *Macbeth*, we might turn this around and say that here the castle is represented as a home. Image and idiom determine our sense of location. Our first impression of the Macbeths' castle is the very opposite of the hell-gate of the porter scene. When Duncan and his entourage arrive there, Banquo describes it as a nest and nursery, a place where 'The temple-haunting martlet [house-martin] ... / Hath made his pendent bed and procreant cradle' (1.6.4–8).[7] Lady Macbeth is there to welcome them and it is in her role as hostess that she reacts to the news of Duncan's murder with the cry, 'Woe, alas – / What, in our house?' (2.3.86–7). This has been seen both as banal (as in MacDuff's implicit rebuke, 'Too cruel, anywhere', 2.3.87) and as an inspired piece of subterfuge, but it certainly sounds like the shock of the middle-class housewife at finding her domestic arrangements thrown into confusion.

That is for public display, but the terms of endearment which she and her husband exchange in private, and which help to create such a strong sense of their intimacy, also have a middle-class ring to them, suggesting a slight lowering of social register. He greets her as 'My dearest love' (1.5.57); 'My husband?' she says later (2.2.13), and tells him 'Get on your nightgown' (2.2.68). Before the banquet in 3.2, he calls her 'dear wife' (37); he responds to her encouragement with 'so shall I, love, / And so I pray be you' (30–1), and then tells her: 'Be innocent of the knowledge, dearest chuck, / Till thou applaud the deed' (3.2.46–7). The puritan preacher William Gouge, who was based in the theatre district of Blackfriars, warned his readers against the use of endearments in public in case a stranger should 'espie any matrimoniall familiaritie betwixt you'. He vetoed not just pet names such as '*Ducke, Chicke* [and] *Pigsnie*', but even '*Sweet-heart, Loue, Ioy* [and] *Deare*'.[8] Shakespeare's audience would have been alert to the 'matrimonial familiarity' of the exchanges between the Macbeths, as well as the middle-class register of the term 'chuck' (Gouge's '*Chicke*').[9] This intimacy is embodied by gesture. Rowe's 1709 addition of

---

[4] William Shakespeare, *Macbeth*, ed. A. R. Braunmuller (Cambridge, 1997), pp. 122, 131, 142, 169, 217.

[5] W. G. Hoskins, 'The rebuilding of rural England, 1570–1640', *Past and Present* 4 (1953), 44–59.

[6] Emma Whipday, *Shakespeare's Domestic Tragedies: Violence in the Early Modern Home* (Cambridge, 2019), pp. 8–13. Whipday's discussion of *Macbeth* focuses on 'neighbourhood' and 'boundary-crossing', pp. 156–202; the 'Great Rebuilding' is discussed in relation to *Othello*, pp. 113–28.

[7] The subjects of fertility, infertility and the childless marriage are adjacent to my own concerns, but not ones that I wish to pursue here; see, especially, Sarah Wintle and René Weis, '*Macbeth* and the barren sceptre', *Essays in Criticism* 41.2 (1991), 128–46.

[8] William Gouge, *Of Domesticall Dvties. Eight Treatises* (London, 1622), p. 283, sig. T6r.

[9] See *Macbeth*, ed. Braunmuller, p. 243. 'Chick' is used twice in *Othello* as a term of endearment between husband and wife (3.4.49; 4.2.25); cf. also the expressions of the 'home-spun Lover', such as 'Dearest Duckling' and 'Chick' in Richard Brathwait, *Ar't Asleepe Husband? A Boulster Lecture* (London, 1640), pp. 31, 118, sigs. C8r, I3v.

the stage direction 'Embracing him' at the point where Lady Macbeth greets her returning husband is echoed and underwritten by her final, fractured utterances in the sleep-walking scene: 'Come, come, come, come, give me your hand' (5.1.64).[10]

The sense that tragic grandeur is reconfigured in the language of ordinary life, that there is a kind of downsizing in the play, is something that was recognized (though not necessarily appreciated) early on in the reception of *Macbeth*. Samuel Johnson addressed the subject of the 'new or noble sentiment delivered in low and vulgar language' in 1751, claiming that 'Every man, however profound or abstracted, perceives himself irresistibly alienated by low terms.' He illustrates the point by quoting Lady Macbeth's self-urging soliloquy in 1.5:

> Come, thick night,
> And pall thee in the dunnest smoke of hell,
> That my keen knife see not the wound it makes,
> Nor heaven peep through the blanket of the dark
> To cry, 'Hold, Hold!'
>
> (1.5.49–53)

Johnson argues that the solemnity of the 'smoke of hell' is spoiled by a term that comes from the stable ('dunnest'), and then complains about 'knife', which is 'the name of an instrument used by butchers and by cooks in the meanest employments'.[11] He is even more scathing about the expression 'peep through the blanket of the dark', though 'peep' is a word used quite often by Shakespeare and suggests here both the starlit sky and (possibly) the image of a frightened child holding a blanket to her face.[12]

Johnson's strictures are rather weakened by the fact that he attributes the speech to Macbeth rather than to his wife; otherwise, he might grudgingly have admitted the aptness of a woman using terminology drawn from the kitchen and the bedchamber. In another respect, however, that gendered reading is undone – and this helps to explain Johnson's mistake – by the fact that this kind of language is interchangeable between the couple. It is echoed by Macbeth immediately after the murder in the elegy on sleep, which lists the ordinary domestic comforts that their blood-soaked path to the throne will deny them:

> Methought I heard a voice cry 'Sleep no more,
> Macbeth does murder sleep' – the innocent sleep,
> Sleep that knits up the ravelled sleave of care,
> The death of each day's life, sore labour's bath,
> Balm of hurt minds, great nature's second course,
> Chief nourisher in life's feast
>
> (2.2.33–8)

Macbeth evokes the daily grind of work and its relaxing aftermath: 'bath' means a soothing liquid, so it is quite similar to the modern term, and it is followed by the main course of the evening meal. Even more striking (and even less aristocratic) is the image of darning the frayed sleeve of a woollen coat, suggesting the dutiful housewife at the same time as it points forward to the unravelling of everything that Macbeth and his partner had hoped for. This is all very much more specific than the generalized apostrophes to sleep in Ovid and Seneca, which are probably the closest analogues to the passage.[13] Here, Shakespeare's couple

[10] Nicholas Rowe, 'Macbeth', in *The works of Mr. William Shakespear; in six volumes. Adorn'd with cuts* (London, 1709), vol. 5, p. 2311 (1.5.53).

[11] Samuel Johnson in *The Rambler* 168, 26 October 1751, pp. 68–71. The issue was revisited more objectively in D. S. Bland, 'Shakespeare and the "ordinary" word', *Shakespeare Survey 4* (Cambridge, 1951), 49–55, and F. P. Wilson, 'Shakespeare and the diction of common life', in *Shakespearian and Other Studies*, ed. Helen Gardner (Oxford, 1969), pp. 100–29.

[12] For a modernist reworking of the image as '[t]he old star-eaten blanket of the sky', see 'The Embankment', in *The Collected Writings of T. E. Hulme*, ed. Karen Csenger (Oxford, 1994), p. 3. Clark and Wright found a similar 'homeliness of expression' in Drayton: 'In heauens black night-gowne couered from our sight' (*Mortimeriados* (1596), sig. C2r); and they also compare 'The sullen night in mistie rugge is wrapp'd' in the same poem (sig. F1v) – see Shakespeare, *Select Plays: Macbeth*, ed. W. G. Clark and W. A. Wright (Oxford, 1869), p. 94.

[13] Ovid, *Metamorphoses*, vol. 2, trans. Frank Justus Miller, rev. G. P. Goold, Loeb Classical Library 43 (Cambridge, MA, 1916), XI.623–9; Seneca, 'Hercules furens', in *Tragedies*, vol. 1, trans. John G. Fitch, Loeb Classical Library 62 (Cambridge, MA, 2002), line 1068f.; see *Macbeth*, ed. Clark and Wright, p. 107.

speak in the shared language of the home. Both these speeches show how the interior world of *Macbeth* is filled with what George Herbert called 'household-stuffe', and both take us into the most private space of all, in either castle or domestic dwelling – not so much the bedchamber, as the bed itself.[14]

***

The bed is the item of household furniture that is always present in *Macbeth*, but (probably) never actually there. The tester bed, popularly known as the 'four-poster bed', was something that increasing numbers of the middling sort expected to be able to acquire for their homes in the last decades of the sixteenth century.[15] It was a large and elaborate structure, with four posts supporting a canopy from which curtains hung, drawn when the couple retired to shut out the light and create a completely private space. There are many scenes in early modern drama that call for a bed to appear on stage, but there is no reason to assume that this is the case with *Macbeth*.[16] F1 is the earliest text of the play that we have, and the only hint of the bedchamber provided by the stage directions there is the reference to the 'taper' carried by Lady Macbeth at 5.1.17. Yet the vestigial presence of the bed was built into the stage itself, as its posts and canopy echoed the pillars and 'heavens' of the large arena theatre.[17] In a domestic setting, this echo would have confirmed the sense of the home as a little commonwealth, presided over by the patriarch and his wife. It is a context where the rather well-worn term 'status symbol' has a quite precise application. In the theatre, the stage architecture reminds us that such beds would come to be called 'state beds'.[18] This cross-over between the public and the private is reflected principally in the language of the play, but it remains connected to its staged environment. The bedtime experiences of intimacy and sleep (and sleeplessness) permeate the poetry of *Macbeth*, but are always framed by greater matters. The play situates the private world of the curtained bed within the grander context of affairs of state, replicated on the stage itself as the pillars of state shift in the

audience's imagination between a diagram of the wider world and the structure of the standing bed, nested within.[19]

A medieval Scottish castle is, of course, at some centuries' remove from the period 1570–1640,

---

[14] George Herbert, 'Affliction (I)', in *The English Poems of George Herbert*, ed. Helen Wilcox (Cambridge, 2007), p. 162.

[15] See Tara Hamling and Catherine Richardson, *A Day at Home in Early Modern England: Material Culture and Domestic Life, 1500–1700* (New Haven, CT, 2017), p. 239. Hamling and Richardson also note that in the second half of the sixteenth century there was a substantial increase in dedicated bedchambers, located on the upper floors, in the homes of the middling sort (p. 30). For a closely documented account of the significance of beds and other household goods in relation to early modern tragedy, see Catherine Richardson, *Domestic Life and Domestic Tragedy in Early Modern England* (Manchester, 2006), pp. 64–95.

[16] For a detailed survey of the subject, see Leslie Thomson, 'Beds on the early modern stage', *Early Theatre* 19.2 (2016), 31–57.

[17] The curtained 'discovery space' at the back of the area marked out on stage by the pillars and the canopied 'heavens' would supply a further visual reminder of the tester bed. Thomson has questioned the existence of a 'discovery space' ('Beds, 34–5), but there are many scenes in early modern drama that would seem to require such a facility, and it remains an accepted feature of the make-up of the early English public theatre; see Andrew Gurr, *The Shakespearean Stage*, 4th edn (Cambridge, 2009), pp. 180, 183–4. (It should perhaps also be noted here that the 'canopy' was more often used to refer to the gathered hanging at the bolster-end of the bed than to the roof above it.)

[18] This is the term preferred by Sasha Roberts, '"Let me the curtains draw:" the dramatic and symbolic properties of the bed in Shakespearean tragedy', in *Staged Properties in Early Modern English Drama*, ed. Jonathan Gil Harris and Natasha Korda (Cambridge, 2002), pp. 153–74, pp. 154–5, though the *OED* gives a rather later first citation date. The network of associations would include the large movable stage property known as the 'state'; see Gurr, *Shakespearean Stage*, pp. 183–7.

[19] I draw here upon metaphors used by Gaston Bachelard in *The Poetics of Space* (New York, 1958), pp. 111–24. A systematic use of Bachelard's work would require a different kind of approach from the one followed here, but it remains an exceptionally valuable resource for thinking about the relationship between imagined domestic space and the language of the poetic text. In *Macbeth*, Shakespeare uses the metaphor of the nest with brutal effect in the murder of MacDuff's family (4.2.9–11; 4.3.219–20).

designated by Hoskins as the timeframe of the Great Rebuilding, as well as being the period of the early modern English theatre. But, as with other examples of anachronism in Shakespeare, the locations in *Macbeth* imply an accommodation to the lived experience of his audience, particularly that of the middling sort. In creating a sense of intimacy between husband and wife, *Macbeth* draws upon the development of private space in the Elizabethan and Jacobean home, as well as upon a middle-class language of endearment. The nature and extent of that private space remains the subject of debate, and Hoskins's original thesis has been extensively qualified in recent years, but that is not really the issue here.[20] Although the language of the play evokes the atmosphere of the bed-chamber, it is the more clearly defined space of the curtained bed itself that I want to focus upon. 'It was the place where two contemporary definitions of "intimate" met for early modern house-holders', write Tara Hamling and Catherine Richardson: '"inmost, most inward, deep-seated" and familiar, "close personal relations." In other words, the bed was a space of personal exploration and of the most intimate interaction between the married couple.'[21]

This is the locus of what Macbeth calls '[t]he curtained sleep' (2.1.51) immediately after the murder, imagining in that moment what will for-ever be denied to him, but it is also the locus of the 'curtain lecture'. John Ray defined the expression in his proverb collection of 1678 as follows: 'A *Curtain*-lecture. Such an one as a wife reads her husband when she chides him in bed.'[22] The ear-liest recorded reference to it appears in the Wolverhampton preacher Richard Lee's *The Spirituall Spring* (1625): 'Get a good conscience that will cast vp thy accounts euery night, and reade thee a curtaine lecture for thy negligence.'[23] But this looks very much like the figurative employment of a term that was already in use in a different context, though one that had not yet found its way into print. The speech form itself was certainly recognized well before Lee, or indeed *Macbeth*. It is described towards the end of Edmund Tilney's fictional discussion of the duties

of marriage, *The Flower of Friendship*, first printed in 1568. Here, the lady Julia, in whose house the debate is taking place, offers the view that, in matters of great importance, 'verie circumspect, and warie must the woman be in reprehending of hir husband', and stipulates that:

The best tyme is, when anger, and malincholy raigneth not, and in any case, let no person be in place, to heare hir. For it is a wise mans griefe, to beare the open reproofe of his wife. The best place, is, as I sayde, when they are both in bed . . . where she maye lawfully poure out into his bosome all the thoughts, and secrets of hir loving hart.[24]

This is a humanist marriage treatise in the manner of Erasmus or Vives, both of whom appear as characters in the work. Erasmus himself had sug-gested in the colloquy *Coniugium* (*Marriage*) (1523) that the wife sometimes had a duty to reprehend: 'in a serious matter, when something important's at stake – it's right for a wife to reprove her husband'.[25] The essential point was that the reproof should take place in secret, where it could not be

---

[20] The most important work of revision has been by Lena Cowen Orlin in *Locating Privacy in Tudor London* (Oxford, 2007).

[21] Hamling and Richardson, *Day at Home*, p. 239. Although they do not cite Bachelard, their book provides the material underpinning for an understanding of the poetics of space in the early modern English domestic dwelling.

[22] John Ray, *A Collection of English Proverbs* (Cambridge, 1678), p. 69, sig. F3r.

[23] Richard Lee, *The Spirituall Spring. A Sermon Preached at Pavls* (London, 1625), p. 15, sig. C4r. The *OED* gives Thomas Adams (1633) as its first citation. There are classical antece-dents; see Juvenal, *Satires*, 6.36–8, which suggests that a man might prefer boys to women because a boy, as his seven-teenth-century English translator puts it, 'reads no curtain-Lecture': *Mores Hominum: The Manners of Men, Described in sixteen Satyrs by Juvenal*, trans. Robert Stapylton (London 1660), p. 154, sig. U2v.

[24] Edmund Tilney, *The Flower of Friendship: A Renaissance Dialogue Contesting Marriage*, ed. Valerie Wayne (Ithaca, 1992), p. 140.

[25] Erasmus, *Colloquies*, trans. and ed. Craig R. Thompson, *Collected Works of Erasmus* 39 (Toronto, 1997), p. 313. On the wife's duty to issue a reprimand, see Ralph A. Houlbrooke, *The English Family, 1450–1700* (London, 1984), p. 102.

heard by family or servants, and that meant the privacy of the curtained bed.[26]

The curtain lecture was also known as the 'bolster lecture' (or 'canopy lecture') and the 'curtain sermon', and these alternative terms spell out the two different directions in which the form developed, both of which have application to *Macbeth*. What was presented quite solemnly by Tilney's lady Julia as proper wifely conduct took on a rather more light-hearted and satirical character in Thomas Heywood's *A Curtaine Lecture* (1637) – the only work of the period to adopt the term as a book title – and Richard Brathwait's *Ar't Asleepe Husband? A Boulster Lecture* (1640). The first six chapters of Heywood's book are morally serious, but, after the conventional survey of marital duties, he changes tack: 'I come now to shew you what manner of Lectures wives use to read unto their husbands.'[27] Beginning with country wives who 'when they are willing to sleepe, whisper many private lectures in their [husbands'] eares', Heywood continues through different social groupings, ending with '*A Curtaine Lecture read by a Queene to her Husband*'.[28] This part of the book is essentially a story collection. Like Heywood, Brathwait uses fabliau-type material, with the curtain lecture or 'bolster lecture' as a framing device. But he also turns the form inside-out, since it is the man who does the lecturing, offering a vast compendium of stories about women gathered under different headings, in order, he says in his verse prologue, to '*silence a* Canopy Lecture'.[29] All this is despite a frontispiece engraving which shows a wife haranguing her husband in bed as he pretends to sleep. The two works are roughly in the same genre, but, while the first part of Heywood's book has some continuity with Tilney, writing seventy years earlier, Brathwait's moves more in the direction of sexual badinage.

The term 'curtain sermon' points in a rather different direction. It first appears in a story from the 'Saxon Monarchs' section of John Speed's *History of Great Britaine* (1611), in which a newly married husband seeks to prevent his wife from being seduced by King Edgar by having her dress 'in the meanest attires' with 'the nightly curtaines

drawne about our new-Nuptiall bed, and the dayly cloudes to hide thy splendent Sunne from his sharpe, and too too piercing sight'. But this plan does not have its intended effect, as the lady Elfrida 'began seriously to thinke vpon this Curtaine Sermon, whose text she distasted', and decides to pursue a quite opposite course.[30] John Donne says in a sermon delivered in 1622 that 'We have used to speak proverbially of a Curtain Sermon, as of a shrewd thing', which makes it clear that the expression had already been in use, both in its principal sense and figuratively, for quite a long time.[31] And the term also appears in Jeremiah Dyke's *Good Conscience* (1624), where the reader

---

[26] On the need for secrecy see, for example, Robert Cleaver: 'Let there be therfore reasonings secretly betweene themselues, of such matters as might breede a skarre', in *A Godlie Forme of Hovseholde Government* (London, 1598), p. 90, sig. F5v; William Whateley: 'the third & most necessary part of wisedom is to giue a reproofe in secret', *A Bride-bush, or A Wedding Sermon* (London, 1617), p. 26, sig. D3v. Erasmus's character Eulalia in *Coniugium* emphasizes that any reprimand should be 'in private' (Erasmus, *Colloquies*, p. 313), without specifying the bed; but Robert Snawsel, reworking the colloquy in the early seventeenth century, writes that the reproof should be given 'either in bed, or in some conuenient place': *A Looking Glasse for Maried Folkes* (London, 1610), sig. B4r.

[27] Thomas Heywood, *A Curtaine Lecture* (London, 1637), p. 145, sig. H1r. On Heywood and Brathwait, see LaRue Love Sloan, '"I'll watch him tame, and talk him out of patience": The curtain lecture and Shakespeare's *Othello*', in *Oral Traditions and Gender in Early Modern Literary Texts*, ed. Mary Ellen Lamb and Karen Bamford (Aldershot, 2008), pp. 85–99; and Kathleen Kalpin Smith, *Gender, Speech, and Audience Reception in Early Modern England* (London, 2017), pp. 19–57, which discusses the form in relation to *Othello* and *The Winter's Tale*.

[28] Heywood, *Curtaine Lecture*, pp. 146, 241, sigs. H1v, M1r.

[29] Brathwait, *Ar't Asleepe Husband?*, sig. A2r. Brathwait's book is attacked in 'Mary Tattle-well', in *The Womens Sharpe Revenge* (London, 1640) alongside other misogynistic tracts which 'are called *Lectures*, as the *Juniper Lecture*, the *Crab-tree Lecture*, & the *Worm-wood Lecture*': p. 5, sig. B3r.

[30] John Speed, *The History of Great Britaine* (London, 1611), p. 371, sig. Sss2r.

[31] John Donne, 'A sermon preached at Lincoln's-Inn Ascension-day, 1622', in *The Oxford Edition of the Sermons of John Donne: Sermons Preached at Lincoln's Inn, 1620–23*, ed. Katrin Ettenhuber, 12 vols. (Oxford, 2015), vol. 5, p. 124.

is advised that, while preachers may often be ignored, 'God hath giuen men a Preacher in their own bosome, and this Preacher will make many a Curtayne Sermon, wil take men to taske vpon their pillow.'[32] It cannot be claimed that these various terms are used very consistently (and they are not even consistent in defining the form as female speech), but what they do is to map out the territory of the curtain lecture as it moves between sexual discord, more general marital issues, and night-time spiritual anxieties, within the private space of the curtained bed.

This is also the territory of *Macbeth*. After receiving her husband's letter about his encounter with the witches, Lady Macbeth expresses her desire to get him home, and in private:

> Hie thee hither,
> That I may pour my spirits in thine ear
> And chastise with the valour of my tongue
> All that impedes thee from the golden round
>
> (1.5.24–7)

This combines the secretive persuasions of those wives who 'whisper many private lectures in their [husbands'] eares' with the stridency of a female tongue-lashing, and both are characteristic of the curtain lecture.[33] When she does confront him and tries to stiffen his resolve, she does so in terms of sexual reproof, which is also entirely typical of the curtain lecture. What is less typical is that the reproof does not take the form of accusations of adultery – a staple of the genre, as the stories in Heywood and Brathwait attest – but of lack of virility. And this seems entirely appropriate in a play where so much depends upon the intimacy of its two central protagonists. Lady Macbeth's fear is not of another woman, but that her husband, to use the words of Calvin's English translator, may 'proove a milkesop, or a white-livered souldier', too cowardly to do the deed: that he is one of those 'Masculine milke-sops that dare doe nothing, and we the Feminine undertakers, that dare to enterprise all things', as the author of *The Womens Sharpe Revenge* puts it in what may even be an echo of *Macbeth*.[34] Lady Macbeth's version of this is her concern that he is 'too full o'th' milk of human

kindness' (1.5.16), which she turns into an accusation that challenges his masculinity:

> Was the hope drunk
> Wherein you dressed yourself? Hath it slept since?
> And wakes it now to look so green and pale
> At what it did so freely? From this time
> Such I account thy love. Art thou afeard
> To be the same in thine own act and valour
> As thou art in desire?
>
> (1.7.35–41)

The husband's drunkenness was another common theme of the curtain lecture. Here, in an accusation facetiously echoed in the porter scene – that drink 'provokes the desire but it takes away the performance' (2.3.28–9) – Lady Macbeth translates her husband's slackening of desire to go ahead with the murder into a slackening of desire for herself. Her reference to the 'act' fuses the killing of Duncan with the sexual act, implying that if Macbeth is incapable of the one, he is incapable of the other. Stephen Greenblatt has called this 'sexual taunting' and 'sexual terrorism'.[35] If the latter expression is viable, it is so because Lady Macbeth relocates the

---

[32] Jeremiah Dyke, *Good Conscience: or a Treatise Shewing the Nature, Meanes, Marks, Benefit, and Necessitie thereof* (London, 1624), p. 71, sig. F4r.

[33] Edmund Hickeringill writes that 'Souldiers wives are more properly seated in their husband's *Kitchin*, then his *Tent*', and though he claims to be immune to the 'dreadfull Catechisme of a *Curtain* Lecture', he advises prospective husbands to get a charm against 'th' Curtain-whisper in the ear': *Jamaica Viewed . . . With several other collateral observations and reflexions upon the island* (London, 1661), pp. 67–9, sigs. F2r–F3r.

[34] Jean Calvin, *Two and Twentie lectures vpon the fiue first chapters of Ieremiah* [trans. Clement Cotton] (London, 1620), p. 41, sig. D5r; 'Mary Tattle-well', in *The Womens Sharpe Revenge*, p. 56, sig. D4v. 'Milksop' was perhaps the most popular seventeenth-century term of abuse in this context and would repay further investigation. If this is an echo of *Macbeth*, it is certainly unconscious, since the author then claims that women have never been guilty of 'trayterous conspiracy against their King and Country' like the actors in the Gunpowder Plot.

[35] *The Norton Shakespeare*, ed. Greenblatt *et al.*, pp. 2557–8. The term 'terrorism' is replaced by a second reference to 'taunting' in subsequent editions.

assassination of Duncan to the context of the marital bed.

The strong erotic undercurrent in the language of *Macbeth* highlights the sexual charge between the couple that powers their murderous ambitions – something that is frequently recognized in productions of the play. This extends to failures of will, as above, and to the detumescent aftermath. There are hints of this even before we see the couple together. Tony Tanner comments – on the Captain's description of the battle in 1.2, 'Doubtful it stood, / As two spent swimmers that do cling together / And choke their art' (1.2.7–9) – that 'spent swimmers clinging together suggests exhausted lovers rather more than exhausted warriors', but also 'a barren, self-destructive sexuality (to be succinctly expressed by Lady Macbeth later in the play when she says bleakly: "Nought's had, all's spent, / Where our desire is got without content" – II, ii, 4–5)'.[36] It is echoed in the dream that Aufidius recounts in *Coriolanus*:

> We have been down together in my sleep,
> Unbuckling helms, fisting each other's throat –
> And waked half dead with nothing.
>
> (4.5.125–7)

And this erotic undercurrent takes other disturbing forms in *Macbeth* itself. After the disrupted banquet, where Lady Macbeth reverts to her sexual taunting, calling Macbeth 'unmanned' (3.4.72), though now in public, the scene closes with Macbeth's words:

> Come, we'll to sleep. My strange and self-abuse
> Is the initiate fear that wants hard use.
> We are yet but young in deed.
>
> (3.4.141–3)

'Self-abuse' is not recorded in the sense of 'masturbation' until 1718 (*OED* 3), but it is still difficult to avoid hearing a sexual element in these lines. Macbeth invites togetherness, but we know they will not sleep; the respite that remains is the 'hard use' of sexual intercourse (and both 'abuse' and 'use' certainly did have sexual associations at this time).[37] Macbeth is vowing to commit more murders, but the lines have a more immediate application. Like Lady Macbeth's reference to the 'act' at 1.5.40, Macbeth's 'deed' fuses killing and copulation.

'Come, we'll to sleep' takes us to the threshold of the bedchamber and thus to the bed itself, the locus of the curtain lecture. Lady Macbeth's intention to 'chastise [her husband] with the valour of my tongue' (1.5.26) is realized in the challenges to his virility which form part of a latent language of sexuality in the play more broadly. But the curtain lecture does not only have a sexual dimension. Another typical theme is the wife's urging her husband to be more ambitious, which is, of course, the occasion for Lady Macbeth's aspersions on her husband's virility in the first place. We might call this the motivational curtain lecture. One example appears in the English translation of Famiano Strada's history of the wars in the Low Countries of 1650, which reports the efforts of Jeanne d'Albret to stir her more reluctant husband into action. This lady, 'impatiently longing for a Crown, rung in her husbands ears, *That he must not suffer this onely opportunity of recovering the Kingdome of Navarre, to slip out of his hands*' (the passage continues as reported speech). But since her husband is unmoved, she turns to his more adventurous brother: 'But this furious *Tullia*, was married to a milder *Tarquin*; so as the Duke of *Bourbon* being cold, for all this fiery curtain-Lecture: his brother the prince of *Condé*, a *Tarquin* that well-matched the Lady *Alibret*, is said to have undertaken the Advance of the Conspiracie.'[38] Another

---

[36] Tony Tanner, *Prefaces to Shakespeare* (Cambridge, MA, 2010), p. 570.

[37] In fact, *Macbeth* provides first citation for 'self-abuse' as 'self-deception' (*OED* 1a) which means that this sense was not already established. 'Abuse', however, is recorded in a sexual sense from 1556, and specifically in connection with witchcraft; see Gordon Williams, *A Dictionary of Sexual Language and Imagery in Shakespearean and Stuart Literature*, 3 vols. (London, 1994), vol. 1, p. 3 (there is a second example from a witch trial transcript of 1613); for the sexual sense of 'use', see Williams, vol. 3, pp. 1462–3.

[38] Famiano Strada, *De Bello Belgico: The History of the Low-Countrey Warres*, trans. Robert Stapleton (London, 1650),

illustration of the motivational curtain lecture comes from Richard Brathwait again, this time from his romance *Panthalia*, where he recounts how the wife of Bellonius rouses him to action:

especially in this private Curtain-Lecture which she with much vehemency read unto him ... This perswasive Lecture delivered by a tongue that had a commanding influence over him, became so prevalent with *Bellonius*, as it quickly raised and roused him from a secure sleep: enlivening his thoughts with actions of an higher temper. Ambition now begun strongly to work upon him.[39]

There are a number of incidental parallels here: Macbeth is described as 'Bellona's bridegroom', i.e. Bellonius, at 1.2.54; he imagines himself as Tarquin at 2.1.55, though – as Lady Macbeth suggests – too mild to do the act; and William Painter's story of Tullia has recently been identified as a source for the play.[40] But the essential parallel lies in the speech form itself through which a wife rouses ambition in her husband. This is decisive with regard to the murder: the one contemporary witness to a performance of the play that we have, Simon Forman, records in his diary that 'Mackebeth contrived to kill Dunkin, & thorowe the persuasion of his wife did that night Murder the kinge in his own Castell, being his guest.'[41]

What I am arguing, then, is that both the form and setting of the curtain lecture provided Shakespeare's audience with a way of imagining things which are at the very heart of this play, but which are difficult to convey in a large arena theatre in daylight. The Macbeths are not literally talking in bed, but in an era when the concept of a private room within the average domestic dwelling did not really exist, the tester bed with its curtains drawn to create a room within a room was the most powerful image of a space in which two people could speak together in private, exchanging 'reasonings secretly betweene themselves', as Robert Cleaver put it in a much more innocent context.[42] So it provides a model for some of the most crucial scenes in *Macbeth*, both in terms of the spectacle of intimate conversation between husband and wife and, as we have just seen, in the form of the wife's speech itself.

But the term 'curtain lecture' was also used in another way, and one which has a powerful resonance in the play. Because it is a speech delivered in the prelude to sleep, the liminally conscious state when the mind is most receptive to suggestion and most fearful, it was used by seventeenth-century preachers when they wanted to make appeals to conscience. This is the sense in which the term was first recorded, and which is represented by the alternative expression 'curtain sermon', as we saw earlier. This kind of curtain lecture is experienced not by a couple, but by the individual alone, and it is invoked by a number of writers later in the seventeenth century. 'Doth not conscience carry thee to thy closet ... Doth it not carry thee into the secret chamber, and read thee a curtain lecture? O conscience do thy duty', writes Joseph Alleine;[43] in his book on dreams, Philip Goodwin comments on Psalms 16.7: 'Even in the seasons of the night, the most retired motions of *David's* mind, the most hidden thoughts of his heart, did read him, as *one* calls it, a *Curtein Lecture*'; Edward Buckler uses the term as the equivalent of a *memento mori* in his *Midnights Meditations of Death*; in his account of how Sir Anthony Monk plotted King Charles's restoration in 1659, John Price

---

p. 57, sig. I1r. (Jeanne d'Albret, Queen of Navarre, was leader of the French Huguenots, and the passage deals with the events of 1568–9 in the third religious war.)

39 Richard Brathwait, *Panthalia: or the Royal Romance* (London, 1659), pp. 106–7, sigs. H5v–H6r.

40 John-Mark Philo, 'Shakespeare's *Macbeth* and Livy's legendary Rome', *Review of English Studies* 67 (2016), 250–74. The Tarquin in this story is the father of Lucrece's rapist, as Painter points out.

41 Simon Forman, 'Booke of Plaies', in *William Shakespeare: A Study of Facts and Problems*, ed. E. K. Chambers, 2 vols. (Oxford, 1930), vol. 2, p. 337.

42 See Cleaver, *A Godlie Forme of Hovseholde Government*, p. 90, sig. F5v.

43 On the closet as private space, see Alan Stewart, 'The early modern closet discovered', *Representations* 50 (1995), 76–100. Stewart focuses on the male couple, though the closet would also (and primarily) have been a space in which the individual could be alone.

speculates 'that he had been in the Night, quickned with a Curtain-Lecture of Damnation'.[44] Macbeth's speech 'If it were done when 'tis done ... ' (1.7.1–28), which intervenes between the scenes of private conversation with his wife, is the most famous soliloquy in the play, but it is also a curtain lecture on the prospect of damnation read to him by conscience. In the comic version of the curtain lecture, the husband is kept awake by the 'Curtaine clamours' of his wife, or, as Brathwait puts it, 'the too forward discourses of such, who distemper their Husbands quiet with their Conventuall Lectures, and that at uncanonicall hours'.[45] Here, the religious terminology ('Conventuall' ... 'uncanonicall') is merely ironic. In its tragic vein, the midnight torments of the individual, male or female, which prevent them from sleeping, are the workings of the guilty soul. The curtain lecture becomes a window onto eternal perdition.[46]

***

Reading Macbeth through the prism of the curtain lecture focuses our attention on the characteristic speech forms of the play, one of which is the proverb or saying. Sayings are typically described as 'homely', so are very much part of the play's 'household stuffe'. Even the Erasmian 'adage' is referred to in this way, as the ballad writer Martin Parker illustrates in his verses on the 'homely adage / ... The proofe of a pudding is all in the eating.'[47] So it is not surprising that proverbs were seen as a feature of female discourse. Marriage conduct books counselled women to have a store of proverbial wisdom on hand to use as a set of instructions for daily living. 'Necessaryly [sic] it is that she knowe these common sentences & learne them by harte', writes Thomas Becon in the most widely read of the Reformation-era manuals, offering examples such as 'Stretche out thyne arme no farther than thy sleaue wyll reatche' – a 'sentence' that Lady Macbeth is determined to invert.[48] It seems appropriate, then, that the most explicit definition of the curtain lecture in the seventeenth century comes from a collection of proverbs, as we noticed earlier.[49] Proverbs have a vital role in Macbeth, as A. R. Braunmuller has pointed out, helping to blend the homely with the eloquent, and the most famous instance of this – at least, the one that actually draws attention to its proverbial status – is the 'adage' which Lady Macbeth uses to seal the end of her speech in the curtain-lecture mode ('Was the hope drunk ... '):

> Wouldst thou have that
> Which thou esteem'st the ornament of life,
> And live a coward in thine own esteem,
> Letting 'I dare not' wait upon 'I would',
> Like the poor cat i'th'adage?

(1.7.41–5)[50]

---

44 Joseph Alleine, *An Alarme to Unconverted Sinners* (London, 1672), p. 57, sig. E5r; Philip Goodwin, *The Mystery of Dreames, historically discoursed* (London, 1658), sig. B2v; Edward Buckler, *Midnights Meditations of Death* (London, 1646), sig. F2v; John Price, *The Mystery and Method of his Majesty's Happy Restauration, Laid Open to Publick View* (London, 1680), p. 20, sig. C2v.

45 Heywood, *Curtaine Lecture*, sig. A3v; Brathwait, *Ar't Asleepe Husband?*, p. 14, sig. B7v.

46 The frontispiece to Heywood's *Curtaine Lecture* captures something of the comic and tragic versions of the form. We see the wife lecturing her husband in bed, but also the hour-glass and a burnt-out candle (the latter being an image with particular resonance for *Macbeth*).

47 M.P., *Tryall brings Truth to Light* (London, 1634), [broadsheet].

48 Heinrich Bullinger, *The Golde[n] Boke of Christen Matrimonye*, trans. Theodore Basille [Thomas Becon] (London, 1543), sig. L4v. (Bullinger's book was translated by both Coverdale – which is the earlier version – and Becon.)

49 See Ray, *A Collection of English Proverbs*. The point is reinforced by Donne's reference to the term 'curtain sermon' being used 'proverbially'.

50 On 'the eloquent, the homely, the proverbial' in the play, see *Macbeth*, ed. Braunmuller, pp. 46f.; for an overview of proverbial expression in Shakespeare, including *Macbeth*, see Martin Orkin, 'The poor cat's adage and other Shakespearean proverbs in Elizabethan grammar-school education', in *A Reader in the Language of Shakespearean Drama*, ed. Vivian Salmon and Edwina Burness (Amsterdam, 1987), pp. 489–98; Neil Rhodes, 'Shakespeare's sayings', in *Shakespeare and Elizabethan Popular Culture*, ed. Stuart Gillespie and Neil Rhodes (London, 2006), pp. 155–73.

The adage in question is 'The Cat would eat fish but she will not wet her feet' and it unwittingly looks forward to the sea of blood that Macbeth will have to wade through after succumbing to his wife's pretensions. It anticipates the callous resignation of 'I am in blood / Stepped in so far that, should I wade no more, / Returning were as tedious as go o'er' (3.4.135–7), which itself echoes the proverbial 'Having wet his foot he cares not how deep he wades' and 'Over shoes over boots'.[51] It is a striking example of the way in which the homely and the eloquent are woven together in the textual fabric of the play.

It also shows how the language of *Macbeth* works through reverberation.[52] Proverbial expression and its derivatives resonate through the play, working on the reader just as Lady Macbeth intends it to work on the mind of her husband. Although many writers emphasize the public and demotic aspect of sayings – they are common property, after all – they were also understood to have hidden depths. Erasmus introduced his *Apophthegmata* (in Nicholas Udall's translation) with the claim that 'as thei bee learned w^t pleasure & delite, and dooe lightly synke and settle in ye mynde, so dooe thei contein more good knowelage and learnyng in ye deepe botome or secrete privetee, then thei shew at the first view'.[53] Tapping into the 'secrete privetee' of sayings maximizes their persuasive power and may affect the reader (or hearer) in a deeply personal way. This is what John Heywood implies when he says in the preface to his *Dialogue of Proverbes*: 'This write I not to teach, but to touche.'[54] The suggestion of emotional (touching the heart) as well as physical intimacy here, alongside Erasmus's emphasis on the wellsprings of meaning in the pithy saying, gives us a sense of how this speech form might have a particular application in private dialogue between wife and husband. These observations also help to define the reverberative power of Shakespeare's use of proverb, or saying, or adage, in *Macbeth*.

To illustrate this, we can go to a specific text. Because proverbial language is common property, it might seem futile to look for any one source for its deployment in a work of literature. But in the case of *Macbeth* there is one possibility that may help us to illuminate how the proverbial underlies and draws together some of the principal themes of the play. When Udall was working on Erasmus's *Apophthegmata*, Richard Taverner was busy translating selections from the *Adagia*. His first selection appeared in 1539 and was clearly successful, since he produced an expanded version in 1545, adding English equivalents for Erasmus's Latin proverbs, which was reprinted in 1550, 1552 and 1569. One page-spread in particular seems to have a special relevance for *Macbeth*.[55] The proverb with the obvious connection to Shakespeare's play is 'The thynge that is done can not be undone', echoed by Lady Macbeth in the sleep-walking scene: 'what's done cannot be undone' (5.1.65). The proverb links Lady Macbeth's utterance back to 'If it were done when 'tis done' (1.7.1), while the previous injunction in Taverner 'to do the thynge spedyly' prompts the second half of the sentence in Shakespeare. And these proverbs on 'doing' appear alongside the reflection on the transience of life, 'Man is but a bubble.'

---

[51] Morris Palmer Tilley, *A Dictionary of the Proverbs in England in the Sixteenth and Seventeenth Centuries* (Ann Arbor, 1950), C144; R. W. Dent, *Shakespeare's Proverbial Language: An Index* (Berkeley, 1981), F 565.1; Tilley, *Dictionary*, S379.

[52] I borrow the term from Bachelard, *The Poetics of Space*, p. 2; but see also Russ McDonald on the 'auditory pattern [of] . . . repetition' in *Shakespeare's Late Style* (Cambridge, 2006), p. 47.

[53] Erasmus, *Apophthegmes, that is to saie, prompte, quicke, wittie and sentencious saiynges*, trans. Nicholas Udall (London, 1542), sigs. ✱✱ 6v–✱✱7r. Although Erasmus is commenting here on *apophthegmata*, this was precisely his view of *adagia*, which was why he worked on them throughout his career.

[54] John Heywood, *A Dialogue of Proverbs*, ed. Rudolph E. Habenicht (Berkeley, 1963), p. 97.

[55] Desiderius Erasmus, *Proverbes or Adagies gathered out of the Chiliades of Erasmus*, trans. Richard Taverner (London, 1545), sigs. E2v–E3r.

It is the witches who are the bubbles of the earth (1.3.77–8), rather than Macbeth himself, but Taverner's addition of the English version of *Homo bulla*, 'To day a man to morow none', captures the mood of Macbeth's 'Tomorrow, and tomorrow, and tomorrow' (5.5.18), with its reflection that 'Life's but a walking shadow' (23), while harking back to his wife's accusations that he is no man (1.7.49–51).[56] Furthermore, Lady Macbeth's own 'adage' about the timid cat is the only one to appear twice in Taverner's collection: 'The catte wold fishe eate, but she wol not her feete wette.'[57] So it does look rather as though Taverner's book provided Shakespeare with a proverbial matrix for some of the central lines of thought in *Macbeth*.

Lady Macbeth's 'what's done cannot be undone' is part of a series of speech fragments which represent her final words in the play: 'To bed, to bed. There's knocking at the gate. Come, come, come, come, give me your hand. What's done cannot be undone. To bed, to bed, to bed' (5.1.63–5). Uttered in the liminal state of consciousness between sleeping and waking, these lines return us to the domain of the curtain lecture. If Macbeth's 'If it were done when 'tis done' is a midnight curtain lecture read to him by conscience, in this recension of the form we see conscience working through the kind of anguished repetition described by Jeremiah Dyke in his account of the 'Curtayne Sermon': the guilty person may try to suppress the prickings of conscience, he writes, 'yet they haue a repeater in their bosome, that will be at priuate repetitions with them in spight of them'.[58] This is exactly what happens here, as the dismissive resolution of '[t]hings without all remedy / Should be without regard. What's done is done' (3.2.13–14) finally fractures under the accumulated weight of blood-guiltiness. The sleep-walking speeches are the most intense and most compressed instances of the play's use of reverberation, recalling thoughts and moments that Lady Macbeth has

tried so hard to suppress: the indelible stain, the irreversibility of the deed, the terrifying sound of impending retribution – the knocking at the gate – which, recalled in the bedchamber, feels like an invasion of private space. And these thoughts mingle with the only thing she has left to hold on to, the intimacy with her husband, as she echoes his words to her when we last see them together: 'Come, we'll to sleep' (3.4.141). It seems entirely appropriate that Lady Macbeth should go to her death with words that summon up the private place which is so often at the centre of the play, but always out of reach: 'Come, come, come, come, give me your hand . . . To bed, to bed, to bed.'

The curtain lecture draws together many of the features that have long been recognized as part of the special ambience of *Macbeth* and helps us to understand why a play which is ostensibly about assassination, war and affairs of state should impact upon its audience in such a personal way. The focus on a husband and wife working together in partnership, the privacy of the locations where they speak, the play's atmosphere of enveloping darkness, and a characteristic poetic idiom which can translate a castle into a home where heaven might 'peep through the blanket of the dark', all help to create the conditions of the curtain lecture in the mind of the audience. The form itself is enacted in the combative sexual accusations of wife to husband, and then in the night thoughts of conscience – first in Macbeth's rehearsal of the prospect of damnation, and finally as the 'Repeater' which hammers in the mind of his dying wife. No other play of Shakespeare's blends horror and homeliness in the way that *Macbeth* does, bleakly evoking the comforts of love which are ultimately made worthless by the irreparable spiritual damage that its central couple have visited upon themselves. This is also a play that works on our own deepest anxieties as it explores the liminal imaginative space that lingers, for minutes or for hours, before we sleep.

---

[56] Erasmus, *Proverbes*, sig. E3r.
[57] Erasmus, *Proverbes*, sigs. F7r, H3r.
[58] Dyke, *Good Conscience*, pp. 71–2, sigs. F4r–v.

'THE STORY SHALL BE CHANGED': ANTIQUE FABLES AND AGENCY IN *A MIDSUMMER NIGHT'S DREAM*

CHARLOTTE SCOTT

Shakespeare's *A Midsummer Night's Dream* is full of stories: Titania's narrative of the votaress's baby, the mechanicals' play, the allusions to Ovid and Virgil, and the resolution in which the young couples imagine their entire experience has been a fiction, a shared hallucination – perhaps one of Puck's offensive shadows – evince the power of *fabula* to shape narrative and translate thought into action. The play's focus on the critical contours of narrative – *fabula*, text and story – supports an apparent fascination with the cultural relationships between language and imagination as they are represented by the construction and recognition of narrative experience.[1] The 'continuous discussion about meaning' that sustains narrative analysis becomes the central motif through which story is asserted in *Dream*.[2] The *fabula*, or fable, a term used in narrative theory to denote the ways in which things are presented, maintains the anamorphic perspective in which, according to Hermia, 'everything seems double' (4.1.189).[3] The 'parted eye' (4.1.188) of Hermia's cognition reflects her story as both experienced and imagined, 'undistinguishable' (4.1.186), and 'Melted as the snow' (4.1.165) as Demetrius would have it, so that the 'dream' becomes the dominant motif through which events are both experienced and denied.[4] The language in which both Hermia and Demetrius represent their time in the wood supports the ethereal qualities of their stories: interspersed with reflections on their own memories, consciousness and temporal awareness, the young lovers establish themselves as unreliable narrators even as the audience stands by as witness. Such narrative

reflexivity, which calls into question how the story is presented, even as it attempts to represent it, highlights the play's self-conscious fascination with the relationship between imagination and hypotheses. Yet the idea of story – the 'visualizable contours of an absent fictional world', as Rawdon Wilson defines it – takes on many forms in *Dream* and extends its formative role well beyond the layered fabric of intertextuality.[5]

Perhaps more than any other play by Shakespeare, *A Midsummer Night's Dream* has inspired a critical focus on the play's untold stories, as well as its allusions, and the 'airy nothing' (5.1.16) of the lunatic, the lover and the poet have come to symbolize the affective landscape of the play and the ambitions of the creative

---

[1] Mieke Bal, *Narratology: Introduction to the Theory of Narrative* (Toronto, 2017), pp. 8–10.

[2] Bal, *Narratology*, p. 10.

[3] Bal, *Narratology*, p. 55. The term 'fable' as used by Theseus refers to fictitious – and hence, according to the *OED*, 'ridiculous' – stories. Here, the term 'fable' is distinct from 'history' or 'story' in that it specifically refers to mythological or legendary events.

[4] Unlike the word 'story', the word 'dream' does not presuppose a logical connection between events or images, and is specifically allied with the illusory or supernatural.

[5] Rawdon Wilson, *Shakespearean Narrative* (Newark and London, 1995), p. 100. Barbara A. Mowat observes the multilayered allusions within the play, including Plutarch, Chaucer, Ovid and Reginald Scot, whose *Discoverie of Witchcraft* provides Shakespeare with a sceptical critique of the role of story in facilitating fantasy in 'A local habitation and a name: Shakespeare's text as construct', *Style* 23.3 (1989), 335–51.

imagination.[6] Where Peter Holland observed the many shadows of the allusive Theseus in the play, Anthony Nuttall understands the formative role that myth plays in repressing, as well as telling, stories.[7] For both Holland and Nuttall, the play produces a series of multidimensional narratives through the prehistories of the onomastic roles of many of the characters, including Theseus, Egeus and Hippolyta.[8] Within these terms, Nuttall attends to what he calls the 'background terror' of the play's allusions and the deliberate role that exclusion plays in shaping the action of the comedy: what we begin to observe, so Nuttall suggests, is what does not happen, rather than what does, and this, in turn, creates 'a half-memory' 'at the edge of consciousness'.[9] It is precisely this half-memory that Holland perceives as a shadow, 'a man on the stair', who can be noticed as well as ignored.[10] The play seems to challenge its audience to take a position on how we engage with such shadows, and, in doing so, define our relationship not only to the play world, but to comedy itself. One of the most formative stories for the narrative action, the medieval legend of Tristan and Iseult, in which a magic love potion is used to forge a strategic bond but unwittingly drunk to tragic consequences, is rerouted here, like the tale of Pyramus and Thisbe, towards comedy, where love can be celebrated as magic, rather than condemned. The half-memories, shadows, man on the stair or uncanny allusion become metaphors for the imaginative role that story plays in *Dream*.

But the role of story, as a reflexive model of change, dominates the play's action not only through the ways in which events are shaped and controlled by the imaginative magic of the fairy world, but in the terms through which the characters in the play call on the story as a powerful motif of transformation, in which both the past and the present are still in contention. Story is the dominant design through which this potential for change can be invoked. As Hannah Arendt suggested, in *The Human Condition*, stories become a form of action in relation to both remembrance and work, which, as Paul Ricoeur explains, serve as 'witness to the difference between time as duration and time as passage'.[11] Where Shakespeare's use of the term 'history' is frequently embedded in temporal relations between the past and the present, his use of the word 'story' is more concerned with the relationship between truth and fiction. On many occasions, however, both meanings collide, so that the value of the story is in relation to the past, and the power of history is its fiction. Shakespeare's Scrivener in *Richard III* notoriously calls the veracity of written record into question in the middle of this most famous history play, when he produces the trumped-up dossier for Hastings's execution: the 'indictment of the good Lord Hastings' (3.6.1) is 'the palpable device' (3.6.11) of a 'sequel [which] hangs together' (3.6.4). Calling attention to the illogical (and unjust) temporality of events in which Hastings lives 'Untainted, unexamined, free, at liberty' (3.6.9) while his indictment is prepared, the Scrivener reflects on the injustice of a world in which we know but cannot know:

> Here's a good world the while! Who is so gross
> That cannot see this palpable device?
> Yet who so bold but says he sees it not?
> Bad is the world, and all will come to naught,
> When such ill dealing must be seen in thought.
> (3.6.10–14)[12]

---

[6] Joan Rees's *Shakespeare and the Story: Aspects of Creation* is especially invested in locating narrative patterns in Shakespeare's work as an analytical structure through which she can observe the creative process (London, 1978).

[7] Peter Holland, 'Theseus' shadows in A Midsummer Night's Dream', *Shakespeare Survey 47* (Cambridge, 1994), 139–52; A. D. Nuttall, 'A Midsummer Night's Dream: comedy as *apotrope* of myth', *Shakespeare Survey 53* (Cambridge, 2000), 49–59.

[8] Barbara Mowat also writes on the role of Chaucer in the play's portrayal of Theseus, as she addresses some of the many threads that contribute to Shakespeare's characterization: 'A local habitation and a name'.

[9] Nuttall, 'Comedy as *apotrope* of myth', 52–4.

[10] Holland, 'Theseus' shadows', 140.

[11] Paul Ricouer, 'Action, story and history: on re-reading *The Human Condition*', *Salmagundi* 60 (1983), 60–72, p. 65. See Hannah Arendt, *The Human Condition* (Chicago, 1958).

[12] Janette Dillon writes very well on this scene in *Shakespeare and the Staging of English History* (Oxford, 2012), p. 18.

Producing a theatrical focus on the textual uncanny, the written, legal, record, 'set in a fair hand' but containing false information, unsettles the very documents of history that the play appears to dramatize.[13] What matters to the Scrivener is not the record itself but the ways in which we can respond to it. Such formal records defy critique and refuse revision; most significantly, when thought is the only recourse for response, action is denied. Story, on the other hand, can be distinguished through its potential, in iteration, for action. Hamlet's play, Lavinia's Ovid, Mamillius's tale – all appear at moments to illuminate the unforeseen. There are, of course, a great many different types of stories in Shakespeare's drama: allusions, intertexts, memories, exemplars, images, narratives, chronicles, tapestries, dreams, letters and books, for example, all support descriptive, consecutive events, and, as Barbara Hardy has shown, are as much dependent on the listener or viewer as they are on the teller.[14] The power of stories, in all their various manifestations, lies in the imaginative opportunities that they promote for the exorcising and the exercising of change.

It is this vivid potential of story that I want to explore. Here, I will focus on the invocation of story as one of infinite possibility in which change is inscribed in the very process of relating narrative precedent, as well as alerting the audience to a shift in action.[15] The story in this way becomes a powerful motif of possibility in this period since it stands on the threshold, like Iago at the door of truth, between two meanings: (1) its originary meaning of history or factual record; and (2) its developing sense of fictional account or imaginative narrative.[16] Othello is a resonant point of reference here since the stories of Othello's life that so bewitched Desdemona, to which she inclined her ear, ravenous for more tales, are, to Iago, nothing more than 'fantastical lies' (2.1.224).[17] In a play so preoccupied by the circumstantial relationships between truth and fiction, between perception and event, the story becomes, for Othello, at least, 'the cause, … the cause' (5.2.1) of his destruction.[18]

In A Midsummer Night's Dream, however, the story emerges as a pre-history against which the play's characters must exert or absolve their identities. When Hermia and Lysander are discussing the impossible situation they are in, with Hermia condemned by her father to marry someone she doesn't love or else die, and just before they decide to escape into 'the wood, a league without the town' (1.1.165), Lysander reflects on the pre-histories of love: 'Ay me, for aught that I could ever read, / Could ever hear by tale or history, / The course of true love never did run smooth' (1.1.132–4). Locating his sorrow in the context of stories, Lysander appears to comfort himself in the authenticity of his emotion because example elicits empathy. The distinction between tale and history is not clear-cut, since both terms refer to accounts or sequences of events believed to be based on fact. What seems more important to Lysander is that he is referring to the modes of transmission, hearing or reading, through which such stories have been translocated. Appealing to his sensory reception of story, Lysander's character

[13] Natalie Zemon Davis, Fiction in the Archives: Pardon Tales and their Tellers in Sixteenth-Century France (Stanford, 1987), is one of the best books on the subject of the relationship between history and story in this period. See also David Scott Kastan, Shakespeare and the Shapes of Time (London, 1982).

[14] Barbara Hardy, Shakespeare's Storytellers (London, 1997); Stanley Cavell, Disowning Knowledge in Six Plays of Shakespeare (Cambridge, 1987), esp. pp. 193–221; John Astington, Stage and Picture in the English Renaissance: The Mirror up to Nature (Cambridge, 2017); Keir Elam, Shakespeare's Pictures: Visual Objects in the Drama (London, 2017). John Kerrigan's Shakespeare's Originality (Oxford, 2018) also explores the relationships between 'origins' and 'sources', and the contexts in which one text produces the conditions for the development of another.

[15] Wilson, Shakespearean Narrative, p. 9.

[16] Nuttall, 'Comedy as apotrope of myth', pp. 49–59; Subha Mukherji, 'Trying, knowing and believing: epistemic plots and the poetics of doubt', in Fictions of Knowledge: Fact, Evidence, Doubt, ed. Yota Batsaki, Subha Mukherji and Jan-Melissa Schramm (Basingstoke, 2012), pp. 84–109.

[17] Laurie Maguire, Othello: Language and Writing (London, 2014), esp. pp. 19–76.

[18] See also John Money, 'Othello's "It is the cause … ": an analysis', Shakespeare Survey 6 (Cambridge, 1953), 94–105. Wilson notes that 'Iago narrativizes Desdemona's adultery out of many formally disconnected pieces, including questions, exclamations, broken repetitions (and other indirect echoes of Othello's own private discourse)': Shakespearean Narrative, p. 99.

is animated by the hypothetical authority of legible love affairs. This is the interconnected discourse of story and remembrance through which the past is kept active in its appropriation by the present. Lysander, like the lovers in his narrative recall, inhabits a shared experience that is both familiar and different – or, in Arendt's terms, suggestive of the distinction between time as duration and time as passage. What follows is a pithy exchange between Hermia and Lysander in which they both remember and rehearse the kinds of obstacles lovers have to face in order to render their love 'true': impediments such as status, age, friends, death, sickness or parents have made love 'momentany as a sound, / Swift as a shadow, short as any dream, / Brief as the lightning in the collied night' (1.1.143–5). This mutual recognition of the 'customary cross' (1.1.153) that lovers must bear affirms that their love is 'true', since 'It stands as an edict in destiny' (1.1.151). Calling on the language of trials, customs and destinies, Hermia establishes the significance and stature of their love through its relation to both narrative and circumstance. In this way, as George Puttenham explains, story takes on the function of 'example', 'which is but the representation of old memories, and like successes happened in times past'.[19] Puttenham emphasizes example as the apotheosis of persuasion, which, as Lorna Hutson has recently suggested, is amplified by narrative circumstance. Circumstances are, she suggests, 'topical aids to the composition of persuasive arguments'.[20] In this way, Hermia and Lysander produce recalled love stories as evidence of hypothetical realities to which their own story may adhere.

The authority that the play world seeks in its own status as fiction resides in the precarious position between art and nature that story inhabits. The relationship between art and life was, of course, one which preoccupied every Renaissance writer, not just Shakespeare. Philip Sidney had famously attempted to move this conversation on from the anxieties of the anti-theatricalists who perceived narrative art – and drama, especially – as too persuasive in its affective capacities. Sidney's audibly pleasing claim that 'neither philosopher nor historiographer could at the first have entered into the gates of popular judgements, if they had not taken

a great passport of Poetry', suggests that poetry – as the persuasive language of imagination – animates debate, event and action.[21] The pedagogic relationship between fact and fiction, written deep into the history of plot, chronicle and narrative, produces the most compelling arguments for the importance of art and the sustainability of stories. Despite Sidney's dismissal of history as dry and limited, he recognizes that all forms of writing take their cues from the environments in which they emerge. Using a potent metaphor, he explains: 'There is no art delivered to mankind that hath not the works of Nature for his principal object, without which they could not consist, and on which they so depend, as they become actors and players, as it were of what Nature will have set forth.'[22] In this way, stories are written, read, told, performed and remembered as an uncanny version of the manifest world. Arthur Golding suggests something similar when he prefaces his translation of Ovid with the hint that

Now when thou readst of God or man, in stone, in beast, or tree
It is a myrrour for thy self thyne owne estate too see.
For under feyned names of Goddes it was the Poets guyse,
The vice and faultes of all estates too taunt in covert wyse.[23]

The pleasure and significance of stories is that they bind communities together through shared associations, moral empathy and a coherent structure. What makes narrative especially appealing in this context is that it appears to bridge the gap, just as Sidney suggested, between the phenomenal and

---

[19] George Puttenham, *The Arte of English Poesy* (London, 1589), p. 31, sig. F4r.
[20] Lorna Hutson, *Circumstantial Shakespeare* (Oxford, 2015), p. 2.
[21] Sir Philip Sidney, *Selected Writings: Astrophil and Stella, The Defence of Poesy and Miscellaneous Poems*, ed. Richard Dutton (Manchester, 1987), p. 104.
[22] Sidney, *Selected Writings*, p. 106.
[23] *Shakespeare's Ovid: being Arthur Golding's Translation of the Metamorphoses*, ed. W. H. Rouse (London, 1904) (reprint of the 1st edn of 1567), 'The Preface Too The Reader', p. 16, lines. 81–4.

imaginary worlds. Stories are both sympathetic and disruptive: they offer structures of relief, but also of potential change. Within these terms, the relationship between fact and fiction becomes infinitely more accessible and defensible. The history of all our lives is both the collective structures of shared memories and the individual impulses of perception. Hermia and Lysander insert themselves into this history, in which they are both the conventional figures of true love and the unique agents of its consequences. What dominates this exchange between the lovers is the idea that story – whether fact or fiction – is the driving impulse for the resolution of their destinies and the value system against which their feelings can be measured. Ironically, of course, Lysander writes himself into history with the observation that 'The course of true love never did run smooth' (1.1.134), pre-empting the trials of his own experiences but also the deviations from that paradigm. The 'crossed' lovers (1.1.150), the 'edict' of 'destiny' (1.1.151) and the 'jaws of darkness' that threaten to 'devour' (1.1.148) the dream of love references the other great stories of this play, 'The most lamentable comedy and most cruel death of Pyramus and Thisbe', and, of course, *Romeo and Juliet*. The compositional relationships between *Romeo and Juliet* and *A Midsummer Night's Dream* has long been the subject of speculation, and editors have tended to accept that *Romeo and Juliet* is the later work because it represents a slightly more sophisticated, and therefore experienced, dramatist at work.[24] It is perfectly possible that Shakespeare wrote both plays within a very short time of each other and that he may have written *Romeo and Juliet* first, so that *Dream* references the success of his own work. What is clear, however, is that Shakespeare is fascinated by 'Love's stories written in love's richest book' (2.2.128) and the place those stories have in the dialogue between the experienced and the imaginary.

Structurally, we can quickly observe the importance of Shakespeare's fictional worlds in *Dream*. Having established that the lovers will escape into the wood, we encounter the mechanicals, who will also retire into the wood to rehearse their play,

where we then meet the fairy world for the first time. Following the winding paths of romance, we move deeper into the wood and away from the 'sharp Athenian law' (1.1.162). Our first encounter with Puck celebrates him as a teller of stories: not only within the narrative of the play – filling us in, for example, on the argument between Titania and Oberon – but also as the 'knavish sprite' (2.1.33) who tells his own history.[25] Recalling his impish pastimes in toying with the mortal world, Puck remembers a moment when:

> The wisest aunt telling the saddest tale
> Sometime for three-foot stool mistaketh me;
> Then slip I from her bum. Down topples she,
> And 'tailor' cries, and falls into a cough,
> And then the whole choir hold their hips, and laugh,
> And waxen in their mirth, and sneeze, and swear
> A merrier hour was never wasted there. –
>
> (2.1.51–7)

Puck's story – his history, a narrative sequence of events – hangs on another story, that of the sagacious aunt telling a serious tale to her 'choir', during which time she mistakes Puck for a stool, sits on him, and then collapses to the ground, bringing intense amusement to the assembled company. The real pleasure of this moment, according to Puck's retelling of events, is the disruption of the serious tale by the amusing accident. Producing a model of storytelling based on recall, improvisation and narrative reflexivity, Puck demonstrates that transformation is inscribed in the processes of transmission. The aunt's story is interrupted and changed; and sadness is replaced by the merriest

---

[24] Despite the now dated context of his essay, Samuel B. Hemingway positions the plays very close to each other, with *Dream* the slightly later play, suggesting that 'Dream is the natural reaction of Shakespeare's mind from Romeo and Juliet': 'The relation of *A Midsummer Night's Dream* to *Romeo and Juliet*', *Modern Language Notes* 26.3 (1911), 78–80, p. 79.

[25] See also Laura Levine, 'Balanchine and Titania: love and the elision of history in A Midsummer Night's Dream', *Shakespeare Survey* 65 (Cambridge, 2012), pp. 110–20, for an exploration of the presentation of the history of the Indian child.

of moments. This, for Shakespeare, is the greatest power that the story can present: the ability to change, re-route, interrupt, transform the moment, the event, and even the ending. What makes this possible is not the exclusively fictional nature of the story – this is yet to be its defining motif – but precisely the opposite: that the story holds within its power the real and the imaginary; the factual and the possible; the predictable and the accidental.

Sidney's great justification of poetry was, of course, that it could makes things 'anew': unlike the limiting structures of reality, poetry's transformative power lies in the fact that it is not driven by 'what is, hath been, or shall be', but by the 'divine consideration of may be and should be'.[26] Where poetry, 'lifted up with the vigour of his own [the poet's] invention' (p. 107) can lay claim to the imagination as its governing impulse, the story is rooted in record, dependent upon a sequence of events believed to have been true. It is the spectre of truth, the pre-history of fact, or the presence of a past that makes story such a powerful medium for the exploration of change and the pursuit of feeling. If, as Lorna Hutson suggests, circumstances are the events through which stories gather their narratives, then the story as it is told within the play, and the stories that are referenced by the play, become enmeshed in a powerful dynamic between assertion and disruption, with one always having the potential to overrule the legitimacy of the other. This dynamic is perhaps at its most obvious in *A Midsummer Night's Dream* because of the play's structural and spatial interest in the relationship between fantasy and reality, and the authority of the imagination. The main action of the play takes place within the framing structure of the Athenian adults and the marriage between Hippolyta and Theseus. Within this narrative, however, critics have frequently observed the shadows of myth, which haunt the cheerful presentation of the play's opening marriage ceremony. Antony Nuttall, Peter Holland and Richard Wilson, among others, have recognized that the allusions to Theseus and Hippolyta record the story of a Greek myth in which scores of Amazonian

women are massacred, their queen taken prisoner and forced into marriage; her son, Hippolytus, is then killed, having rejected the incestuous advances of his step-mother. In Nuttall's and Holland's respective readings of the play, the presence of these myths serves to highlight the stories that Shakespeare represses – the stories he excludes, which remain as powerful markers of what has not been told: what Nuttall calls 'background terror'. Wilson, on the other hand, perceives that the play proceeds though a positive rejection of possible stories: 'Seneca's *Hercules*, Euripides' *Bacchae* ... are all evaded during the action'.[27] For Nuttall, especially, calling the character Theseus but changing his story provides one of the many layers of darkness that the play produces.[28] In this way, myth serves a potentially apotropaic function, averting evil or the potential consequences of evil by being the story *not* told. If Shakespeare is banishing those stories by not telling them, then the story itself becomes a fundamental place of re-invention. What becomes especially potent in this narrative of change, however, is the story's residual function as reality: you can only change the story, the plays suggest, if you accept it as having once been true.

Moving the action into the wood, the province of the fairies, the rehearsal ground for the mechanicals' play, and an escape from Athens, *Dream* appears to acknowledge the centrality of fiction in the potential resolutions of the play's narrative. The story within the story becomes the central locus of action through which the play then references further stories – Pyramus and Thisbe, Dido and Aeneas, Cupid's history, and the thwarted lovers who are attempting to escape their destinies. The

---

[26] Sidney, *Selected Writings*, p. 109.

[27] Richard Wilson, 'The kindly ones: the death of the author in Shakespearean Athens', in *A Midsummer Night's Dream*, *'New Casebooks'*, ed. Richard Dutton (Basingstoke, 1996), pp. 198–222, p. 205.

[28] Laura Aydelotte pursues a similar argument through the character of Oberon, and his pre-history in Berner's translation of *Huon de Bordeaux*, as well as Greene's 1594 play *The Scottish Historie of James the Fourth*, in her article '"A local habitation and a name": the origins of Shakespeare's Oberon', *Shakespeare Survey 65* (Cambridge, 2012), 1–11.

transitional space of the wood, as it becomes so powerfully associated with Ovid, the play-within-the play and 'fairy favours' (2.1.12), presents a structural space for the exploration of fiction within the framing narrative of theatrical time. Within this context Shakespeare develops a technique of 'narrative hints', or reflexivity, through which allusions, and specifically Ovidian allusions, 'suggest different possible outcomes to the events and actions that we have seen'.[29] The story, as it is networked by allusion, becomes a radical site of possibility where the potential for change becomes the *leitmotif* through which the plot progresses. Like Puck, the fairy world is presented to us through stories or recalled events that contextualize and characterize the fairies' behaviour: we learn of Oberon's jealousies, Titania's friendship with a votaress, where they met and the history of the 'little changeling boy' (2.1.120). Theseus, too, we learn, has a history, largely defined by his ravishing of women, including Aegles, Ariadne, Antiopa and Perigouna. Presenting this past through a set of shared memories, the King and Queen of the fairies offer a mythological world of mermaids, cupids and potions where everything adheres to a symbiotic relationship between cause and effect. As Wilson explains, 'Narrative explores alternatives. One kind of alternative is a causally linked past. In this sense, narrative clearly performs hypothesis-making work: in narrative imaginative accounts are unfolded to explain the present shape of things.'[30] We gather, for example, that the flower, love-in-idleness, or the wild pansy, prized within the play for its hypnotic effects, accrued such power because Cupid's arrow fell to the ground, accidently piercing the white flower and giving it its now purple streaks. Such stories, as the play presents them, deliver a pleasing correlation between fantasy and reality, the imaginative and phenomenal worlds that can observe the streaked pansy and understand 'the present shape of things'. This happy synthesis between fiction and reality, imagination and experience, is rehearsed in different registers throughout the play: the lovers, the mechanicals and the fairies all depend on and

inspire a dynamic between experience and imagination that authorizes their presence within the play.

Yet the idea of the story is at its most powerful in the play as an agent of change – as a marker of 'different possible outcomes', and 'the truth', as Keats would later have it, 'of Imagination'.[31] The story must adapt to survive, and that process of evolution is marked by its continual re-invention through allusion and action.[32] When Demetrius, desperate to get away from the devoted Helena, attempts to escape the wood and flee, she declares:

> Run when you will. The story shall be changed:
> Apollo flies, and Daphne holds the chase.
> The dove pursues the griffin, the mild hind
> Makes speed to catch the tiger: bootless speed,
> When cowardice pursues, and valour flies
>
> (2.1.230–4)

Helena takes possession of this moment by changing the story; not only the mythological story of Daphne's flight from Apollo, but the power dynamics apparently decreed by the history of romantic love, which define women as weak and cowardly. By reversing the story, here construed as precedent, Helena suggests that she can also change how it ends – that the future is not determined by precedent, but by deviation.[33] Central to this paradigm is the dramatic potential of bringing forth a narrative of expectation in order to render it unfulfilled – only by raising expectations and then rerouting them does the play find its most

---

29 Colin Burrow, *Shakespeare and Classical Antiquity* (Oxford, 2013), p. 123. See also Kerrigan, who refers to '[a]n extrapolation of possible outcomes' in relation to *Much Ado about Nothing: Originality*, p. vii.

30 Wilson, *Shakespearean Narrative*, p. 32.

31 Kerrigan, *Originality*, p. vii; John Keats, 'To Benjamin Bailey, 22 November 1817', in *Selected Letters of John Keats*, ed. Grant F. Scott (Cambridge, MA, 2002), p. 54.

32 Jack Zipes discusses the fairytale as a meme, which must adapt in order to survive: *The Irresistible Fairy Tale: The Cultural and Social History of a Genre* (Princeton, 2012), pp. 48–9.

33 Titus Andronicus records a different attitude to story, when he thinks on the woods in which Lavinia was raped and, remembering Ovid, declares: 'O, had we never, never hunted there! – / Patterned by that the poet here describes, / By nature made for murders and for rapes' (4.1.55–7).

sustaining register of pleasure. Beyond the allusion to Apollo's pursuit of Daphne, however, lies a landscape of sexual inequality and assault where women are hunted and possessed because they are unable to defend themselves against the desires and strengths of the amorous gods. The terms through which Helena imagines changing the story are also the terms through which she would acquire agency within the play. In Ovid's story, pursuit is predicated on the beloved as both prey and enemy:

> Stay Nymph: the Lambes so flee ye Wolves, the
> Stags ye Lions so:
> With flittring fethers sielie Doves so from the
> Gossehauke flie,
> And every creature from his foe. Love is the cause
> that I
> Do followe thee[34]

'Love' is made visible to us through the power that one species has over another, and fulfilment, within these terms, is tantamount to death. Daphne's flight from the rapacious sun god centres on his unremitting desire for her and her unrelenting fear of him:

> So farde *Apollo* and the Mayde: hope made *Apollo*
> swift,
> And feare did make the Mayden fleete devising
> how to shift.
> Howebeit he that did pursue of both the swifter
> went,
> As furthred by the feathred wings that *Cupid* had
> him lent:
> So that he would not let hir rest, but preased at hir
> heele
> So neere that through hir scattred haire shee might
> his breathing feele.
> But when she sawe hir breath was gone and
> strength began to fayle,
> The colour faded in hir cheekes, and ginning for to
> quayle . . .[35]

Helena's fantasy of changing the story goes deeper than getting her man – it speaks to the play's wider interest in the sexual politics of power. Ovid's description of the terrified Daphne appears to amplify her erotic appeal as Apollo closes in on her; as he breathes through her 'scattred haire', she weakens before us, losing both breath and colour.

The sublimation of the self that 'love' promotes is written deep into the language of the hunt so lucidly rehearsed by Helena.[36] The fantasy that the hind could catch the tiger, or the dove the griffin, retains the inequality of desire that regulates power as love. Helena's alternative story is not one of equality but one of ascendancy: changing the story, in this case, would also rewrite history. Helena's great moment here is that she uses a brief history of female oppression to suggest its potential for change: despite the incongruity of the images, the play bears it out – the hind catches the tiger, and the imagination, despite Theseus's denigration, renders hypothesis meaningful. Against the 'background terror' of male assault, the fantasy of change lurks in the stories of the female imagination.

Changing the story becomes the dominant motif through which the play can fully develop its narrative reflexivity – not only from tragedy to comedy, but in the heuristic potential of the story as explanation and opportunity. Having found their green plot on which to rehearse, the mechanicals approach the translocation of words to story as reflective dramaturgs. As they consider the narrative and performance of 'The most lamentable comedy and most cruel death of Pyramus and Thisbe', the mechanicals focus on the challenges of telling their story. The first thing they do, of course, is change it: as Starveling says, 'we must leave the killing out' (3.1.13). Recognizing that there 'are things in this comedy of Pyramus and Thisbe that will never please' (3.1.8–9), the amateur actors devise various ways in which to interfere in the audience's experience of the story, as well as their representation of it. Focusing on the affective problems of realism and naturalism, the characters lay bare the gendered sensibilities of storytelling. Considering the potential emotional consequences of their story, the character-actors focus on how best to redress the negative effects

---

[34] *Shakespeare's Ovid*, ed. Rouse, p. 33, lines 611–14.

[35] *Shakespeare's Ovid*, ed. Rouse, p. 34, lines 659–66.

[36] For an engaging account of the complexity and development of this language of pursuit, see Catherine Bates, *Masculinity and the Hunt: Wyatt to Spenser* (Oxford, 2013).

of the persuasive imagination. Inserting formal narrative techniques in the shape of explanatory prologues, the play references its own status as story in search – like Pirandello's six characters – of realization: it is, we might say, an unrealized story, dramatically speaking.[37] Through the terms of performance, the mechanicals change the story to expose the processes through which imagination is translated into words, and the means by which characters edit the relationship between cause and effect. Editing the potential effects of realism, the amateur actors interfere with the proper function of imagination as persuasion, and mitigate the impact of example. Discussing Snug's performance as the Lion, Bottom declares: 'Nay, you must name his name, and half his face must be seen through the lion's neck, and he himself must speak through, saying thus or to the same defect: "ladies", or "fair ladies, I would wish you" or "I would request you" or "I would entreat you not to fear, not to tremble"' (3.1.33–8). The comedy works here on several levels – firstly, of course, we laugh because the mechanicals fail to understand or observe theatre as a temporary and collective illusion; and, secondly, because they perceive the representative power of Snug as a lion to be so convincing that he needs to identify himself as an actor, show his face through the costume and directly address the audience's imagined fears, thereby thoroughly distancing himself from the presentation of the wild animal. We know that Shakespeare is fascinated by the mechanics of theatre and the potential that such meta-theatrics afford, but the real pleasure of this scene lies in the visible processes by which the actors interfere in the precedent of the play to tell a different story. Much like the province of the fairytale and Helena's remit in changing her story, the adaptation of this *fabula* becomes a place of power for the actors, precisely because it allows them to construct something other than themselves, and to which they belong. Re-telling the story in this way supports the play's search for authority in the imaginative intersections between teller and listener. Highlighting the role of the storyteller as one of mediator, improviser and translator, the focus on the imagination presents a surrogate space for the exploration of alternatives. In Doreen Maitre's formulation, the imagination functions as 'the ability to bring to mind that which is absent from current perception' and, by doing so, comprehend reality better through the 'superimposition on it of some component of a possible non-actual world'.[38] The vibrant reflexivity of the play's double vision on the actual and non-actual worlds of story ceaselessly seeks to define the role of the storyteller and the agency of narrative.

The profound opportunities for change that the story promotes run deep throughout the play – the young couples' attempts to alter their destinies, the transformative powers of the love juice and the interventions of the fairies; Bottom's acquisition of an ass's head, and Demetrius's change of heart. When Snout exclaims, 'O Bottom, thou art changed' (3.1.109), we see the hypothetical agency of the imaginative process actualize within the context of the play-world. Bottom's unwitting mutation into an ass not only promotes transformation as the objective of art but recalls Apuleius's *The Golden Ass*, a set of interlocking stories focusing on trials and suffering, alteration and endurance. Unlike Shakespeare's play-worlds, however, where mutability is a recurring process, Apuleius's transformations, like Ovid's *Metamorphoses*, tend to occur only once. Despite the mythical appetite for change, it is almost always a fixed process, whereas, for Shakespeare, the story offers a dynamic and mobile opportunity for change, supported by the imagination, as something that can happen repeatedly. Bottom's dream allows him to turn and turn again, just as his intervention in the story of Pyramus and Thisbe allows him to be actor, audience, storyteller and character in quick succession. There is no fixed point of fulfilment in the play – no apotheosis through which revelation or comprehension can ever be fully realized and therefore fixed,

---

[37] In Pirandello's play, *Six Characters in Search of an Author*, the Son states: 'I'm a character that, dramatically speaking, remains unrealized': Luigi Pirandello, *Pirandello's Major Plays*, trans. Eric Bentley (Evanston, IL, 1991), p. 86.
[38] Doreen Maitre, *Literature and Possible Worlds* (London, 1983), pp. 13, 22.

but a series of possible stories through which transformation, like change, is always possible and infinitely contingent. The play's deep impulse to change is in part reflective of comedy, and the genre that was to become associated most powerfully with rituals of transformation. In *A Midsummer Night's Dream*, however, Shakespeare seems especially concerned with the role of the story as apparatus for change because it provides a narrative structure against which the characters and the plot can trial our expectations. To know which story we are in allows us the possibility of changing that story, even, as Helena suggests, when it is against all precedent.

As the play draws to its close, the mechanicals present their version of 'Pyramus and Thisbe' to a sceptical audience of grand Athenians. As we watch the amateur production and listen to its in-house audience critique the crude representation, tortured performances and unsophisticated attempts at oratory, we are gloriously reminded of the spectre of the story that might have been. Here, the lovers leave the stage in triumph and in ceremony, each person apparently happy in love. The play began by imagining a different narrative where lovers were separated, divided or dead, and yet this story was changed, brilliantly and magically averted in the wood, a league without the town – but the first, untold, story remains a potent reminder of an alternative narrative; in the end, of course, the mechanicals didn't 'leave the killing out', and their lamentable comedy ends as a tragedy, which, according to Theseus, needs 'no excuse' (5.1.350) and 'no epilogue' (5.1.349), 'for when the players are all dead there need none to be blamed' (5.1.350–1). But, of course, the players are not all dead, and up pops Bottom for one more explanation. The story, it seems, is always reinventing itself as a heuristic model of opportunity. The great wonder of this play – its magic, allusion and illusion – is a powerful paean to the art of storytelling and the ways in which the greatest art is in knowing when to change the story, or be changed by it.

A LAWFUL MAGIC: NEW WORLDS OF PRECEDENT IN *MABO* AND *THE WINTER'S TALE*

NICHOLAS LUKE

On 2 June 1992, the day before the landmark *Mabo (No. 2)* decision was handed down by the High Court of Australia, the past was straightforward: on 7 February 1788, when Governor Arthur Phillip 'caused his second Commission as Governor to be read and published', British sovereignty was asserted over 'all the country inland (from the eastern coastline) westward as far as longitude 135 east', and absolute ownership of the land was vested in the Crown.[1]

On 3 June 1992, however, the past became considerably more complex: while British sovereignty had certainly been asserted in 1788, it was now only *thought* that absolute ownership of the land had vested in the Crown. It was so thought for some 200 years, until the High Court decided that, whereas radical title (i.e. sovereignty or jurisdiction) had vested in the Crown, absolute beneficial title had not. In brief, the Crown had not acquired 'ownership' of the land in 1788, but a radical title subject to the 'burden' of Indigenous native title.[2] No doubt this would have surprised everyone involved in the history that followed: both the settlers who, with increasing brutality, drove the Indigenous occupants off the land, and the Indigenous occupants so brutally driven. It certainly would have surprised the colonial governments, which, as Justice Dawson notes, 'did not consider that any recognizable form of native title existed', and acted upon that assumption for two centuries.[3] No-one, it turned out, was doing what they thought they were doing.

In this article, I explore how the seemingly unrelated texts of *Mabo* and *The Winter's Tale*

address the question of how to escape tragic precedent. In their (very different) reactions against past injustice, these texts both retroactively – even anachronistically – rethink the past. However, they also struggle with the conditions, difficulties and limitations of historical redemption. No clean break with the past is possible. Rather, both texts fold, twist upon, and occasionally explode out of a tension between continuity and discontinuity, repetition and redemption. They reveal, perhaps pessimistically, that the radically new never arrives unpolluted by the tragic past. But they also reveal the redemptive possibilities of a repetition with a difference, which may unsettle precedent even as it repeats it. 'Redemption', so understood, is not something that is ever achieved, but something that 'preserves itself in a small crack in the continuum of catastrophe'.[4] It is something that we must rediscover and reactivate by, to quote Walter Benjamin, 'brush[ing] history against the grain'.[5] I therefore look to how these texts attempt, in strained, shame-filled and creative ways, to find cracks in tragic repetition.

---

[1] *Mabo and Others* v. *Queensland (No. 2)* HCA 23 (1992), 175 CLR 1, Justices Deane and Gaudron, decision, [3].

[2] *Mabo*, Justice Brennan, decision, [62].

[3] *Mabo*, Justice Dawson, decision, [36].

[4] Walter Benjamin, 'Zentralpark', quoted in Richard Wolin, *Walter Benjamin: An Aesthetic of Redemption* (Berkeley, 1994), p. 130.

[5] Walter Benjamin, *Selected Writings*, 4 vols. (Cambridge, MA, 2003), vol. 4, p. 392.

First, however, some context regarding *Mabo* is required. In finding that Eddie Mabo and four other plaintiffs from Murray Island, in the Torres Strait, had a legally enforceable title over their traditional lands, the court overturned two established principles: first, that Australia had been settled as a *terra nullius* (empty and unoccupied territory); and, second, that the Crown was the absolute owner of all land in the colony (now the nation). The court thereby established a new form of 'native title', grounded in the 'traditional laws and customs of an indigenous people'.[6] At the time, the decision seemed to make the continuum of history explode. A quarter-century later, however, this seems like wishful thinking. While the decision remains among the High Court's most significant, any notion that it might set things right between Indigenous and non-Indigenous Australians has long since faded. If *Mabo* marked a moment of acute national attention on Australia's oppression and dispossession of its Indigenous inhabitants – described by Justices Deane and Gaudron in their joint-judgment as 'leav[ing] a national legacy of unutterable shame'[7] – that attention has slowly faded. The question of Indigenous ownership is now largely treated as something done and dusted, settled by the regressive bureaucratic claims processes of the Native Title Act (1993).[8]

Australia's attempt to 'move on' from our inconvenient history into the supposedly reconciled (and postcolonial) future is undercut, however, by a persistent repetition of the tragic past. The first and most basic fact of the *Mabo* judgment is that, when Australia was settled 'on 7 February 1788, the English common law ... automatically' became the law of the land.[9] The common law is envisaged as a sort of relentless automaton that applies not only 'automatically', but also ubiquitously, within its territory. *Mabo* may recognize that the doctrine of *terra nullius* is a 'fiction', as Justice Brennan describes it,[10] but it remains, in Peter Fitzpatrick's words, an 'operative and potent fiction'.[11] Indeed, it is the founding fiction of Australian law: 'Although "contemporary law" would not accept the theory, the common

law riding on it was, somehow and nonetheless, successfully introduced.'[12] According to the judgment, the law took over the continental body – the virus inhabited the host – and that can never be undone: the 'acquisition of sovereignty ... cannot be challenged in an Australian municipal court'.[13] That legal takeover is the unmistakable context for the case: its ultimate tragic law. Or, as the Indigenous legal scholar Irene Watson puts it, *Mabo* is 'a decision which assists the laundering of its own colonial history, but the stains remain embedded in the fabric of Australian sovereign laws, yet to be removed'.[14] As in the restorations of Shakespeare's romances, the supposedly redeemed future is irrevocably marked by the tragic past and its oppressive sovereign power. There remains 'a persistent colonial imposition that cannot be shaken off'.[15]

If earlier commentators focused on the radical and even heartwarming restoration of what seemed to have passed away (traditional laws and customs), the decision's more recent critics have questioned just how radical a transformation took place. As they rightly note, it is a form of delusion – of comforting inattention – to think that the tragic past has been 'shaken off' and the time set right. But perhaps there is another type of false comfort: the dream that the colonial past *could* have been 'shaken off' if only a more pure or profound judicial decision had been delivered. *Mabo*'s critics highlight the decision's central difficulty – that, although

---

[6] *Mabo*, Justice Brennan, [66].

[7] *Mabo*, Justices Deane and Gaudron, [50].

[8] See Irene Watson, 'Buried alive', *Law and Critique* 13.3 (2002), 253–69.

[9] *Mabo*, Justices Deane and Gaudron, [6].

[10] *Mabo*, Justice Brennan, [42].

[11] Peter Fitzpatrick, '"No higher duty": Mabo and the failure of legal foundation', *Law and Critique* 13.3 (2002), 233–52, p. 245.

[12] Fitzpatrick, '"No higher duty"', 248.

[13] *Mabo*, Justice Brennan, [87].

[14] Watson, 'Buried alive', p. 260.

[15] Stewart Motha, 'Reconciliation as domination', in *Law and the Politics of Reconciliation*, ed. Scott Veitch (Aldershot, 2007), pp. 69–91, esp. p. 70.

the fiction of *terra nullius* is overturned, the Court cannot question the sovereignty that resulted from that fiction – and how this undercuts the Court's quest for absolution.[16] Indeed, Veitch *et al.* suggest that, 'by refusing to engage with the acquisition of sovereignty, the original act of dispossession and its legitimacy based in racist doctrines [both] remains intact as the founding act . . . [and] is legitimated in the present'.[17] While these commentators raise important questions of bad faith, they also beg a different question: how *could* the court question the acquisition of sovereignty? They imply that the acquisition of sovereignty is not unchallengeable after all, but they provide no legal basis on which it could be challenged. In a logical sense, a legal sense and, ultimately, a tragic sense, however, it is unchallengeable: 'settlement' happened, the common law happened, and the court now deciding the case is the product of that sovereignty – indeed, is its highest court.

In the end, what the critics want of *Mabo* is something more than a legal decision can give: justice, reconciliation – perhaps ultimately a system of dual sovereignty. I do not deny *Mabo*'s failure to provide these things, or that they are desperately needed; I simply claim that the commentators are looking in the wrong place. Legal judgments involve pragmatic compromises rather than wholesale alterations of the nation's legal system, and they speak, in the end, from the position of the extant law. '[O]ur law', as Justice Brennan notes, 'is the prisoner of its history'.[18] The *Mabo* decision could hardly redeem this history. It was not a participatory forum but a legal pronouncement, made from the position of power, of sovereignty. Indigenous Australians did not speak in it, except in a ventriloquized form through the judges. 'Native title' may be grounded in 'traditional laws', but Indigenous law and its spiritual underpinnings remain largely unexpressed, almost ghostly, in the decision. The hope that *Mabo* still offers is a more limited one. Amidst the decision's equivocations, impasses and compromises, there is a redemptive kernel that should be recovered and reactivated: a singular instance of the interruption and unsettling of the legal imagination.

It is in the tension between settlement and unsettlement, radical change and conservative restoration, that *Mabo* and *The Winter's Tale* come together. In both these texts, seemingly revolutionary and redemptive moments appear to congeal back into the very same forms of oppressive sovereignty that (tragically) necessitated redemption in the first place. Reading them together can, I argue, help us to uncongeal our imaginative responses to the texts themselves and, indeed, to the very idea of historical redemption. It can help prevent us from falling into the old binaries: triumphalist celebration on the one hand (Leontes is redeemed, Hermione recovered, the kingdom saved), or defeatist disillusion on the other (patriarchal power is restored, Hermione silent, like the Indigenous in *Mabo*). It reveals how forms of oppressive sovereignty may be simultaneously intractable *and* open to unsettlement.

It may be less obvious, but precedent is also altered in *The Winter's Tale* through a sort of temporal folding. The 'precedent' here, however, is the rules of genre. In tragedy, certain things are permissible and possible – in other words, precedented – and others are not. Shakespeare is famously not content to rest in a settled genre, and yet even Shakespeare's tragedies cannot escape what we might call 'tragic law'. Although *Hamlet* bends the (broad and evolving) genre of 'revenge tragedy' in unprecedented ways, it nonetheless ends with Hamlet killing his father's killer and then falling silent on a corpse-ridden stage. Moreover, the general law of tragedy is manifest *within* the play, as a sort of local law that regulates what is possible. There is a strange moment before their duel, in which Laertes accepts Hamlet's apology and peace-offering in 'nature' (5.2.190) but 'stands aloof' in 'honour' (192–3), which offers no 'precedent' that allows him to save face: Laertes will allow 'no reconcilement / Till by some elder

---

[16] See Motha, 'Reconciliation as domination', pp. 69–91.

[17] Scott Veitch, Emilios Christodoulidis and Lindsay Farmer, *Jurisprudence: Themes and Concepts* (London, 2012), p. 172.

[18] *Mabo*, Justice Brennan, [29].

masters of known honour / I have a voice and precedent of peace / To keep my name ungored' (5.2.193–6).[19] While Hamlet and Laertes may exchange forgiveness and offer some intimation of a new 'precedent', it comes too late to end the overarching cycle of violence. They are already fatally poisoned. In the most basic terms, then, tragic law operates to *repeat the horrors of the past*. In the romances, Shakespeare at once incorporates, and transforms, such tragic law.

SOVEREIGN FICTIONS

The Winter's Tale and *Mabo* are both responses to tragedy, and the tragedies they respond to both result from destructive sovereign fictions that overwrite others. One way of understanding these fictions is as expectations about the future. As Reinhart Koselleck has shown, a society's 'horizon of expectation' is a key aspect of its present make-up and attitude.[20] Expectation gives the 'not-yet' a present reality: it emits 'impulses' that have concrete effects and produce 'new possibilities at the cost of passing reality'.[21] When these expectations are held by a sovereign power, the cost to 'passing reality' can be truly catastrophic.

According to Koselleck, the development of the idea of History as a 'collective singular' in the eighteenth century permitted 'the attribution to history of the latent power of human events and suffering ... in whose name one could believe oneself to be acting'.[22] Men and women became handmaidens of History. By the nineteenth century, the 'horizon of expectation' was one of ever-increasing improvement, and this had a very real bearing on colonized peoples: 'Looking from civilized Europe to a barbaric America' (or Australia) was 'a glance backward', at a time when 'world history ... was increasingly interpreted in terms of progress'.[23] The colonial understanding of Indigenous Australians as relics of the past, doomed by the unstoppable march of progress, led to their temporal negation: belonging to the past, they had no place in the imagined future. As Ann Curthoys and Jessie Mitchell point out: 'After the introduction of responsible government in 1856, there was

minimal government policy of any kind, in an expectation that Aboriginal people would disappear altogether, and indeed, population decline had been catastrophic.'[24] The expectation that Indigenous Australians would pass from history emitted an impulse to strip them of their present reality: at first to strip them of their sovereignty and land, and, later, of their children (the Stolen Generations).

The *Mabo* judgment makes clear that such racist models of progress and evolution directly 'underpin[ned] the application of English law to the Colony'.[25] As Brennan notes, during the eighteenth century, the 'enlarged concept of terra nullius' began to cover territories that were occupied, but occupied inadequately or '*barbarously*' from a European perspective.[26] The categorization of Indigenous people as 'backwards peoples', so 'primitive in their social organization' that they were 'without laws',[27] 'provided the common law of England with the justification for denying them their traditional rights and interests in land'.[28]

Leontes, too, is guided by a mythic 'horizon of expectation'. Critics have long noted that the discussion between Hermione and Polixenes that precedes Leontes's sudden suspicion establishes an opposition between the kings' static boyhood idyll (their expectation was 'to be boy eternal' (1.2.66)) and the 'Temptations' (1.2.79) (and dynastic issues) born of women. As Hermione

---

[19] See Nicholas Luke, *Shakespearean Arrivals: The Birth of Character* (Cambridge, 2018), pp. 136–7.
[20] Reinhart Koselleck, *Futures Past: On the Semantics of Historical Time*, trans. Keith Tribe (New York, 2004), p. 260.
[21] Koselleck, *Futures Past*, p. 263.
[22] Koselleck, *Futures Past*, p. 35.
[23] Koselleck, *Futures Past*, p. 238.
[24] Ann Curthoys and Jessie Mitchell, '"Bring this paper to the good governor": Aboriginal petitioning in Britain's Australian colonies', in *Native Claims: Indigenous Law against Empire: 1500–1920*, ed. Saliha Belmessous (Oxford, 2012), pp. 182–203, esp. p. 194.
[25] *Mabo*, Justice Brennan, [36].
[26] *Mabo*, Justice Brennan, [36].
[27] *Mabo*, Justice Brennan, [36].
[28] *Mabo*, Justice Brennan, [38].

observes, this suggests that the men's wives 'are devils' (1.2.84) ... or at least descendants of Eve: women are 'false' and will 'say anything' (1.2.133). A cloudy mythic horizon is thus evoked in the opening scenes: an expectation that this woman will, like the first, lead her man into the mire of sin. Men and women, here, are handmaidens not of the progressive future but of the ever-repeating mythic past. Indeed, Leontes's expectation is expressed in the serpentine imagery of a (theatrical) fall: 'Thy mother plays, and I / Play too; but so disgraced a part, whose issue / Will hiss me to my grave' (1.2.188–90). Once this mythic expectation takes hold of his imagination, Hermione cannot *do* anything to dissuade the sovereign power. She is overwritten by Othello-like fantasies of invasive corruption in which she becomes a property to be (dis)possessed: her 'gates opened' (1.2.198), she is imaginatively 'sluiced' (195), her 'pond' violated (196).

Hermione's first issue, Mamillius, embodies the future that is annulled by Leontes's sovereign fiction. The young prince is introduced as the ultimate sovereign fantasy: the brilliant male heir, 'of the greatest promise', who carries all 'hopes' for the future and offers an 'unspeakable comfort' that 'makes old hearts fresh' (1.1.34–9). He seemingly possesses just the sort of heart-warming comfort that Paulina's elaborate theatre must stage at the play's end. Of course, the very need for Paulina's crafty restoration shows that Mamillius's dynastic promise is not possible in this play. Even in his brief scenes, Mamillius does not enact renewal so much as act out Leontes's obsessions. He is an odd, disturbing figure, veering between a baby-like victim and a preternaturally aware surveyor of ladies' faces who both echoes and foreshadows his father's obsessions about the falsity of (women's) appearances.

Mamillius's focus on his attending lady's 'black brows' (2.1.9) recalls both his father's comments about his hardening 'brows' (1.2.121) and Leontes's assessment that 'women ... will say anything' and may be as 'false / As o'er-dyed blacks' (1.2.132–4). The face-shifting phantasmagoria begins with Leontes suspiciously watching his wife: 'This

entertainment / May a free face put on' (1.2.113–14). It then turns to his 'boy's face' (1.2.156), in which Leontes sees his own youthful reflection from 'Twenty-three years' ago (1.2.157). The son's face peels off to reveal the sexually vulnerable, 'unbreeched' (1.2.157) father at the moment before his corruption (or emasculation). As Leontes's sovereign fantasy swells, Mamillius is consumed: 'we are / Almost as like as eggs' (1.2.129), Leontes tells us. When Mamillius comes to pass a critic's eye over female beauty practices – flaunting a knowledge he 'learned ... out of women's faces' (2.1.13) – it is thus hard not to hear Leontes. As Simon Palfrey writes, the son's words, 'stiltingly spoken as if ventriloquized through some elder spirit', lead us back to the lurking father, who will, of course, shortly silence his 'precocious double'.[29]

The result of Leontes's suspicious gaze is that he follows his tragic forebearer, Othello, in overwriting his wife with his own perverse visions. After he begins to suspect his wife of infidelity with Polixenes, Leontes feels that 'Affection ... stabs the centre' of his being. And there, inside Leontes, it folds and twins itself with 'nothing':

> Affection, thy intention stabs the centre.
> Thou dost make possible things not so held,
> Communicat'st with dreams – how can this be? –
> With what's unreal thou coactive art,
> And fellow'st nothing. Then 'tis very credent
> Thou mayst co-join with something, and thou
>   dost –
> And that beyond commission; and I find it –
> And that to the infection of my brains
>
> (1.2.140–7)

There is an almost mad coupling between something and nothing, affection and dreams, in this famously difficult speech: an unholy union that births a deformed fantasy of Hermione's guilt. What is even more remarkable is that Leontes *knows* that it is fantasy. He knows that the 'unreal' ('dreams') is 'infect[ing]' him. Nevertheless, he is

---

[29] Simon Palfrey, *Late Shakespeare: A New World of Words* (Oxford, 1997), pp. 105–6.

powerless to resist. Knowledge here – as with the knowledge that Australia wasn't 'really' *terra nullius* – spectacularly fails to forestall desire and fantasy. We come to the core of what St Paul sees as the tragic law: 'For that which I do I allow not: for what I would, that do I not; but what I hate, that do I' (Romans 7.15). Indeed, in a fantastical leap of logic, the fact that he can see affection's capacity to 'fellow'st nothing' convinces Leontes not only that it can also 'co-join with something', but that it *is* doing so. In a rhetorical click of the fingers, two negatives make a positive, forming the new tragic reality: Leontes's very pregnant wife is having an affair with his childhood friend Polixenes. She is pregnant with Polixenes's child!

Leontes here conforms to Sarah Beckwith's (Stanley Cavell-inspired) idea that Shakespeare's tragic 'protagonists ... define a world from their single perspective – and lose it and everyone they love'.[30] We might think of *terra nullius* in this light too: as the ultimate avoidance of the other, the continent-wide wiping out of the other's existence. The result is, as Hermione declares, a legal travesty:

> if I shall be condemned
> Upon surmises, all proofs sleeping else
> But what your jealousies awake, I tell you
> 'Tis rigour, and not law.
>
> (3.2.110–13)

The mythic view of history stones the imagination and voids the lives of others. As Watson writes: 'Imperial Britain imposed *terra nullius*, of territory/land, law and people, and covered every part of my Nunga being with their myth of emptiness.'[31] The sovereign's fiction obliterates all dialogue, relation or meaningful action. Indeed, it voids the past itself. The way Hermione has lived until this point, or the actual laws, customs and spiritual practices of Indigenous Australians, simply do not matter to the sovereign. Sovereignty seems inseparable from a compulsive phantasmagoria: 'Your actions are my "dreams"' (3.2.81).

We might link this unhearing repetition to Benjamin's argument that 'the essence of mythic happenings is recurrence'.[32] For Benjamin, 'the phantasmagoria of modernity [is] governed by

a hellish-mythological compulsion to repeat'.[33] Leontes repeats the timeworn role of cuckold and Othello's tragic fall. Australia, the last 'discovered' continent, repeats the same pattern of civilized settlement and native extermination seen in the Americas. Moreover, the notion of *terra nullius* is repeated down the centuries. By 1971, in *Milirrpum* v. *Nabalco* (the only previous Australian case to address the possibility of native title rights), the doctrine is so ingrained that, although Justice Blackburn notes that the Indigenous people in question had developed 'a subtle and elaborate system' of social order that amounted to 'a government of laws, and not of men', legally, these facts amounted to nothing.[34] Even when another law is seen to be operative factually, it is not legally *recognized*, and tragic precedent is repeated.

We begin to see why redemption, for Benjamin, is an arrest of repetition: revolutions are not 'the locomotive of world history [but] ... an attempt ... to activate the emergency brake'.[35] Examining *Mabo* and *The Winter's Tale* together highlights ways of reading and remembering that (momentarily) break through sovereign fantasies that impose mythic repetition on others. Key to the redemptive kernel of both texts is the (generic) *strangeness* of this interruption. These grotesque sovereign fictions are only recognized as such through the violent shock of a recognition scene, which leads to a strange blurring of competing pasts, laws and futures. As Ken Gelder and Jane Jacobs have stressed, the *Mabo* decision helped produce an 'uncanny Australia' in which 'one's place is always already another's place and the issue of possession is never complete, never entirely settled'.[36] '[U]nsettlement', they argue, is

---

[30] Sarah Beckwith, *Shakespeare and the Grammar of Forgiveness* (Ithaca and London, 2011), p. 2.

[31] Watson, 'Buried alive', p. 257.

[32] Benjamin, *Selected Writings*, vol. 4, p. 404.

[33] Wolin, *Walter Benjamin*, p. li.

[34] *Milirrpum* v. *Nabalco* (1971), 17 FLR 141, [267].

[35] Benjamin, *Selected Writings*, vol. 4, p. 402.

[36] Ken Gelder and Jane M. Jacobs, *Uncanny Australia: Sacredness and Identity in a Postcolonial Nation* (Melbourne, 1998), p. 138.

potentially a 'productive feature of the postcolonial landscape'.[37] Following their lead, I argue that the hope offered by these texts is not a settled utopian vision but a sometimes violent, often perplexing, blurring of temporality and causation that unsettles 'what was' and thereby opens a new horizon of 'what may be'.

UNSETTLEMENT

For Gelder and Jacobs, Indigenous claims for sacredness (and thereby ownership) have an estranging effect on modern Australia, capable of 'turn[ing] what seems like "home" into something . . . less familiar and less settled'.[38] Their argument shares something with Benjamin's vision of redemptive criticism, which works to make mythic repetition truly phantasmagoric, truly unreal, and thereby puncture its façade of inevitability. By producing an 'estrangement or shock-effect on objects . . . Benjamin hoped to divest them of their familiarity and thereby stir the reader from a state of passivity into an active and critical posture'.[39]

This process of estrangement relies – precariously – on radical contingency. The interruption rests upon a storm, a shipwreck, a bear hunt, leading to pastoral clowning. It rests upon a native title claim by an outlier group: from an isolated island, unencroached upon by modern development, with an unusually individual-centric method of dealing with property (the judges often stress that the Meriam people are 'devoted gardeners'[40]). Contingency on its own is not sufficient, however, for the outlier, the anomaly, must – artfully and creatively – come to take on a decisive importance. In Benjamin's terms, something of the past must be 'appropriat[ed]' – 'blast[ed]' out of its 'specific era' – 'as it flashes up in a moment of danger'.[41] The peripheral must be *made* central.

But why take this leap? Why decide matters from the perspective of the unknown periphery rather than established precedent? Here difficult notions of affect and emotion come into play. The key, for Gelder and Jacobs, is a sudden and reorienting sense of responsibility for suffering and injustice. This sense of responsibility is not straightforwardly

present but emerges through the shock of the uncanny: our home is suddenly rendered 'unfamiliar' as we realize that 'what is "ours" is also potentially, or even always already, "theirs"'.[42] '[U]nsettlement . . . reminds us that (whether we like it or not) "all of us" are implicated . . . in this modern predicament'.[43] Responsibility may ultimately be rational and juridical but, in both *Mabo* and *The Winter's Tale*, it arises from an emotional shock, a visceral feeling of shame.

Leontes's journey towards a more adequate mode of remembrance certainly begins with a disorienting blow. In the trial scene, Leontes attempts to declare 'a state of exception', in which suspicion counts as proof and the rulings of the oracle may be ignored. In this, as James Kuzner notes, the King of Sicilia seemingly 'believes, with James I, that "Rex est lex loquens" ("the King is the law speaking")'.[44] Unlike the long-enduring doctrine of *terra nullius*, however, Leontes's legal fiction immediately implodes. Not only do Leontes's commands 'solicit [. . . his] subjects to transgress',[45] the (failed) declaration of exception redounds on his head swiftly and brutally. Mamillius dies and then Hermione falls:

PAULINA
This news is mortal to the Queen. Look down
And see what death is doing.

(3.2.147–8)

What death is 'doing', to Leontes, is puncturing his fantasy: 'I have too much believed mine own suspicion' (3.2.150). It overturns his horizon of expectation and turns the trial scene on its head. It puts Leontes – the king, the law – on trial. Shame

---

[37] Gelder and Jacobs, *Uncanny Australia*, p. xvi.

[38] Gelder and Jacobs, *Uncanny Australia*, p. xiv.

[39] Wolin, *Walter Benjamin*, pp. 124–5.

[40] *Mabo*, Justice Brennan, [33].

[41] Benjamin, *Selected Writings*, vol. 4, pp. 391, 396.

[42] Gelder and Jacobs, *Uncanny Australia*, p. 23.

[43] Gelder and Jacobs, *Uncanny Australia*, p. xvi.

[44] James Kuzner, *Shakespeare as a Way of Life: Skeptical Practice and the Politics of Weakness* (New York, 2016), p. 91.

[45] Kuzner, *Shakespeare as a Way of Life*, p. 91.

prompts a sudden imaginative re-orientation of sovereignty so that *Leontes* is now the one who must confess. As Paulina tells him: 'Therefore betake thee / To nothing but despair' (3.2.208–9). And Leontes consents: 'Come, and lead me / To these sorrows' (3.2.241–2).

Shame is also crucial to the unsettling core of *Mabo*. It is what causes the law to face the law with the eyes of justice and put itself on trial. But this shame in the old law (that the fiction of *terra nullius* ever existed) is coupled with a sense of legal embarrassment. In *Mabo*, the existing precedent could not be massaged or reframed with a straight face, and this produces a certain anxiety about a rupture being required in a system that is supposed to operate through slow incremental development. It is as if there is something illicit happening, something legal but not quite the law: 'those that think it is unlawful business / I am about, let them depart' (5.3.96–7). Indeed, at the end of their judgment, Justices Deane and Gaudron acknowledge that they 'have used language and expressed conclusions which some may think to be unusually emotive for a judgment in this Court'.[46] Their explanation is that they use 'unrestrained language' because 'the full facts of [Indigenous] dispossession' are required in order to judge the case.[47] But one wonders why the need for 'facts' necessitates 'unusually emotive' language. It suggests, perhaps, that the Justices are trying to see the past sympathetically – to see it feelingly.

Legally, it wasn't a question of facts at all. Justice Dawson's dissenting judgment agrees on the essential facts. It was, rather, a question of the law's (affective and creative) relationship to 'justice'. For Dawson, the question was not one of responsibility, but of sovereign power: it is 'irrelevant' how sovereignty was acquired, what matters is that it *was* acquired and 'declared' the law.[48] 'Whatever the justification for the acquisition of territory by this means ... there can be no doubt that it was, and remains, legally effective'.[49] For Justices Deane and Gaudron, in stark contrast, true remembrance alters the present. They write: 'If this were any ordinary case, the Court would not be justified in reopening the validity of

fundamental propositions which have been endorsed by long-established authority.'[50] But this is not an ordinary case. Why? Because, as Deane and Gaudron continue, the 'practical effect' of the legal principles in question – *terra nullius* and the Crown's ownership of the land – 'constitute[s] the darkest aspect of the history of this nation'.[51] Because 'The nation as a whole must remain diminished unless and until there is an acknowledgment of, and retreat from, those past injustices.'[52] Because the treatment of this country's 'Aboriginal peoples ... leave[s] a national legacy of unutterable shame'.[53] Here we see, as with Leontes, the power of shame to unsettle 'long-established authority'.

Shame, so understood, is not simply a psychological state or private emotion, it is a shock of responsibility: a sudden awareness of one's role in past injustice, an acknowledgment of one's failure to acknowledge. In shame, Leontes sees himself as if through another's eyes: sees his failure to see Hermione, sees himself as he might have been – if he had seen. The role of shame is also apparent in Justice Brennan's measured seminal judgment (though his sense of responsibility is more equivocal):

According to the [previous] cases, the common law itself took from indigenous inhabitants any right to occupy their traditional land ... and made the indigenous inhabitants intruders in their own homes ... Judged by any civilized standard, such a law is unjust and its claim to be part of the common law to be applied in contemporary Australia must be questioned.[54]

There is something strange happening here: something similar to the way that Leontes flipped from prosecutor (and judge) to the accused (and penitent). The law is sitting in judgment of the law. It

---

[46] *Mabo*, Justices Deane and Gaudron, [78].

[47] *Mabo*, Justices Deane and Gaudron, [78].

[48] *Mabo*, Justice Dawson, [35]. [49] *Mabo*, Justice Dawson, [2].

[50] *Mabo*, Justices Deane and Gaudron, [56].

[51] *Mabo*, Justices Deane and Gaudron, [56].

[52] *Mabo*, Justices Deane and Gaudron, [56].

[53] *Mabo*, Justices Deane and Gaudron, [50].

[54] *Mabo*, Justice Brennan, [28].

faces itself across the gulf of time, not only as the law but something other as well: as 'civilized standards' or justice. Above all, Brennan judges that the law is 'unjust' because it *missed* something: the claim of another upon it, a claim it had no right to refuse. Through its shame in itself, the law is exposed, opened to the outside, to things it cannot quite define. And this is not merely a dissolution, but an opportunity for a new creation in which the nature and limitations of the Crown are reconfigured.

That creativity is not unbounded: the Court cannot 'adopt rules that accord with contemporary notions of justice and human rights if their adoption would fracture the skeleton of [legal] principle'.[55] The clear implication of Brennan's statement, however, is that the Court *is* free to adopt new rules if they do not fracture this skeleton. The law may creatively step outside of the existing law – to 'justice' – as long as this convulsion doesn't break its own bones. Brennan continues: 'no case can command unquestioning adherence if the rule it expresses seriously offends the values of justice and human rights (especially equality before the law) which are aspirations of the contemporary Australian legal system'.[56] The law here begins to bend under the strain of various indeterminate questions. What principles are 'skeletal'? What are the legal bases of these 'values' and 'aspirations'? Do these ill-defined 'aspirations' operate prospectively or retrospectively? The law here is far from a clear system of rules. It is, to be frank, all quite vague, quite flimsy. But, then again, the law must be flimsy at the point of its rupture, at the moment when part of it ceases to be law, when the past is bent over and the old principle breaks away.

There are two competing forms of violence (and opacity) at play here, which reveal the decision's tension between continuity and radical change. The first is the violence that *does* cut away something (non-skeletal) of the law. We might call this a 'revolutionary violence' that ruptures existing authority. This violence drew the fire of the decision's positivist or conservative critics. But Brennan's words also imply that some 'essential

doctrine[s]' may need to be retained *even if* they seriously offend 'justice and human rights'. Indeed, the High Court ruled that native title had been *lawfully* extinguished across much of the country by Crown grants of land that were inconsistent with Indigenous ownership.[57] This type of 'structural violence' has drawn the fire of the decision's more progressive critics. It stems from the common law's fictional foundation and its violence is ongoing.

What the revolutionary side of *Mabo* represents is a rare moment when the history of the oppressed intrudes into and re-orients the law. The law's repressed truth is recognized (however incompletely, belatedly and inadequately) for the first time by the law: that Australia's Indigenous inhabitants were systematically excluded, rendered legally invisible, in order for Australia to come into existence; that the law was founded on what it failed to acknowledge. In other words, the common law was (and remains) sutured to the Australian continent through the very act (not omission) of refusing (not failing) to acknowledge those who already possessed the land. The oppression of Indigenous Australians was not exceptional but foundational for Australian law. As Brennan remarks: 'Their dispossession underwrote the development of the nation.'[58] Simply to follow the existing law, as Dawson does in black letter fashion, is thus to follow injustice and void Indigenous Australians, for the law *itself* was based on the fantastical lie that there was nobody here before it.

The sense of obscurity or indiscernibility in the decision arises because something outside the existing language and parameters for decision-making forces itself into the law. In *Milirrpum*, Justice Blackburn held that communal native title was alien to the rights of private property that could be recognized by the common law. In *Mabo*, the High Court is therefore trying to name something

---

55 *Mabo*, Justice Brennan, [29].
56 *Mabo*, Justice Brennan, [29].
57 *Mabo*, Justice Brennan, [55].
58 *Mabo*, Justice Brennan, [82].

(a type of ownership or relation) that was unknown to the law – to declare it into existence; hence, Brennan's vague terms and Deane and Gaudron's emotive language. Ultimately, the result of their declaration was that the law was retroactively restructured:

If the land were desert and uninhabited, truly a terra nullius, the Crown would take an absolute beneficial title ... But if the land were occupied by the indigenous inhabitants and their rights and interests in the land are recognized by the common law, the radical title which is acquired with the acquisition of sovereignty cannot itself be taken to confer an absolute beneficial title to the occupied land.[59]

The 'if' in Brennan's second sentence – 'if ... their rights and interests in the land are recognized by the common law' – is the location of the bend in time, for, quite obviously, these rights and interests were *not* recognized by the common law over the preceding centuries. Even as Brennan composed this sentence, they were not recognized. No court had recognized them. No claim for them had been successful. So when the Court concludes that 'the common law of this country recognizes a form of native title which ... reflects the entitlement of the indigenous inhabitants, in accordance with their laws or customs, to their traditional lands',[60] it is making a performative statement. It is calling into being a past that never was but that *should* have been. The unfulfilled promise of the past is not merely an unreachable messianic horizon; it is activated in the judgment. That is the importance of *Mabo*: despite its manifest inadequacy and subsequent erosion, it is the point at which the repressed past interrupted, even invaded, the continuum of Australia's legal history. The common law is being (re-)created in the Court's statement. Old laws are dying and new ones are being born; new ones that are, in fact, the re-activation of ancient ones. Sovereignty is being imaginatively re-orientated: burdened with what it had refused to know.

In *The Winter's Tale*, too, precedent is altered through a violent but artful movement to the obscure borders of the law. We see this artfulness in the 'dazzling piece of *avant-garde* work' that Nevill Coghill described as the 'dramaturgical hinge' of the play.[61] The hinge scene's violent and absurd unsettlement is witnessed by its famous, fantastic stage direction. Poor Antigonus has just followed his orders to dispose of Leontes's supposedly illegitimate daughter, and then: 'This is the chase. / I am gone for ever! *Exit, pursued by a bear*' (3.3.56–7). Thus, the unwilling agent of the old, tragic law meets his tragi-comic end. The play devours Antigonus for Leontes's crime, and leaves us (and the baby Perdita) in the hands of clowns. Violent unsettlement and loss of life are at once foregrounded as the condition of generic and communal renewal – the tearing open whereby Perdita is implanted on the non-existent coast of Bohemia – and are dismissed as laughable.

Nothing stays in its place in this scene, in which the sea 'chafes' and 'rages' and 'takes up the shore' (3.3.86–7). The storm's chaos is, most basically, a marker of the new: by drawing our eyes to the edge of the representational structure, Shakespeare signals an intrusion from beyond the existing frame.[62] The structures of authority bend, and the obscurity of the not-law, the uncounted, rushes in, like Deane and Gaudron's emotive language, from the situation's void. On the obscure shore of Bohemia, 'things dying' make way for 'things new-born' (3.3.111). The claustrophobic, tragic situation of Leontes's Sicilia is ruptured by an uncontrollable but creative excess that renders genre and topography topsy-turvy. 'The bear begins this shift': the 'obvious theatricality' of its 'mixture of the terrifying and the ludicrous "forbids any simple response" and leads the audience "out of mere passive participation in an ongoing story to an active disorientation which leaves

---

59 *Mabo*, Justice Brennan, [51].
60 *Mabo*, Chief Justice Mason and Justice McHugh, [2].
61 Nevill Coghill, 'Six points of stage-craft', in William Shakespeare, *The Winter's Tale: A Casebook*, ed. Kenneth Muir (London, 1968), pp. 198–213, esp. pp. 204–5.
62 I make a similar point about *Othello*'s 'high-wrought flood' (2.1.2): Luke, *Shakespearean Arrivals*, p. 82.

[them] no choice but to question [their] own responses'".[63] As with Benjamin's (Brecht-inspired) estrangement techniques, the unsettling of genre prompts the audience to take a more active, critical role.

Above all, the scene's 'active disorientation' enables the holding together of opposites. Shakespearian romance, as John Pitcher puts it, 'lets us have it both ways'.[64] '[A] wronged queen ... is able to die and not die'.[65] Paulina's concluding ceremony is both magical and lawful; it is absurdly unbelievable but animates our belief. We hear 'of a world ransomed, or one destroyed' (5.2.15). These generic unsettlements begin with the hinge scene, which holds together tragedy and comedy at the mid-point of the play. They then flower in Bohemia's pastoral uncanny: a field of ghostly doublings, superimpositions, displacements and substitutions. Polixenes doubles Leontes, at once haunting pastoral Bohemia with the same fear of women and tyrannical vision that infect Sicilia, and introducing a crucial distance. Perdita and Florizel both jointly embody – and dismember – Mamillius's promise. And Perdita is at once 'both "Shepherdesse" and "Queene" whilst, paradoxically, being identical to neither'.[66]

With Perdita, the play's "promise" is thus displaced, deposited into an alien soil, diffused from its initial life-forms. As Palfrey writes, 'the extinction of one type of "promise" here implants the need for others. And, therefore and therein, a new type of romance.'[67] If something is 'reborn' from Mamillius's transplanted promise, it is neither a singular heir nor a sovereign will but something far more strange: a 'posthumous capability' through which his tale 'Of sprites and goblins' (2.1.28) is grafted onto Bohemia, where Hermione's ghost 'shrieks' (3.3.35) to Antigonus and 'the daemonic bear and the fairy-child, the "Changeling" Perdita, add to the sense that the stopped tale is afoot'.[68] The promise of Shakespeare's romance is not already there, as a promising heir may be, but is born through the deterritorialization of the existing order of authority, precedent and timely (dynastic) succession. Romance, so understood, is not a form of redemptive closure but an interruption of repetition – of the tragic form, the sovereign ruler, the myth of womanly deceit – that diffuses narrative authority and potential.

If Perdita now embodies the chance for Leontes's (and Sicilia's) redemption, the chance nonetheless requires time – indeed, a sort of temporal folding. Personified as the Chorus, 'Time' declares that the play's culminating dramatic event is about the past as much as the present. Leontes must wait in 'saint-like sorrow' (5.1.2) for sixteen years, sequestered in his shame. In Sicilia, life is suspended, while in Bohemia time is shooting to fruition. The coming together of these two times is the miracle of the fifth act. 'Shame is a chrysalis, after all', as Ewan Fernie remarks.[69] Indeed, Time directly announces the breach opened in tragic law: 'Impute it not a crime ... that I slide / O'er sixteen years ... since it is in my power / To o'erthrow law, and in one self-born hour / To plant and o'erwhelm custom' (4.1.4–9).

Upon the opening of time's chrysalis – when his daughter Perdita returns, like Proserpina, bearing the hope of regeneration – Leontes declares: 'Welcome hither, / As is the spring to th'earth!' (5.1.150–1). The ice is melting but, for redemption to spread its wings, Leontes must take his chance. He must accept a resurrection that is 'monstrous to our human reason' (5.1.41). In short, *he*, the sovereign, must accept an intrusion from outside the law – an 'unlawful business' – which unsettles existing history and authority. Paulina shows the

---

[63] Christopher J. Cobb, *The Staging of Romance in Late Shakespeare: Text and Theatrical Technique* (Newark, 2007), p. 160; the quotations included in Cobb's text are taken from William Matchett, 'Some dramatic techniques in "The Winter's Tale"', *Shakespeare Survey 22* (Cambridge, 1969), 93–107.

[64] William Shakespeare, *The Winter's Tale*, ed. John Pitcher (London, 2010), p. 6.

[65] *The Winter's Tale*, ed. Pitcher, p. 1.

[66] Palfrey, *Late Shakespeare*, p. 225.

[67] Palfrey, *Late Shakespeare*, p. 110.

[68] Palfrey, *Late Shakespeare*, pp. 108–11.

[69] Ewan Fernie, *Shame in Shakespeare* (London, 2002), p. 245.

penitent Leontes a strikingly lifelike statue of his deceased wife:

> I am ashamed. Does not the stone rebuke me
> For being more stone than it? O royal piece!
> There's magic in thy majesty, which has
> My evils conjured to remembrance
>
> (5.3.37–40)

Paulina's 'magic', her art, is a work of justice. That justice relies on the artful 'conjur[ing]' of a certain type of remembrance: personal, affective and attentive to a wronged other. Her art both prompts, and draws its power from, the 'unutterable shame' that accompanies genuine self-knowledge. '[R]esurrection', as Beckwith writes, 'both requires and releases remorseful remembrance'.[70] To truly remember Hermione, Leontes must remember his own wrongs: 'Whilst I remember / Her and her virtues I cannot forget / My blemishes in them' (5.1.6–8). This is a rare magic indeed. For how often do kings admit crimes? How often does the law rebuke the law? This only happens in moments of grace. 'It is required', Paulina tells Leontes, 'You do awake your faith' (5.3.94–5):

PAULINA   Music; awake her; strike!
Music
(*To Hermione*) 'Tis time. Descend. Be stone no more.
Approach.
Strike all that look upon with marvel. Come,
I'll fill your grave up. Stir. . . .
Hermione slowly descends
Start not. Her actions shall be holy as
You hear my spell is lawful. . . .
Nay, present your hand.
. . .

LEONTES   O, she's warm!
If this be magic, let it be an art
Lawful as eating.

(5.3.98–111)

The sovereign, here, is he who is subjected to the moment of exception (a not uncommon occurrence in Shakespeare). The exception is not a sovereign state or political structure, but a break in structure, something impossible: a lawful spell. The break is aesthetic, theatrical, sorrowful, perhaps even loving. And Leontes's wonderful response is a decision to welcome the break, the magic, the unsettlement, the outside-of-the-law, into the situation, as something as necessary as eating. It is not a Schmittian state of exception, declared *against* an other, but an exceptional aesthetic event that *recognizes* another. She moves. He touches her hand. It is warm. It is simple. It is magical.

Magic works like that in Shakespeare's late plays: it ruptures and transforms the present, but it also ruptures and transforms the past. Something 'dead' is resurrected. Something 'dark' is acknowledged. Or, as Slavoj Žižek (channelling Benjamin) suggests: 'the past itself is not simply "what there was", it contains hidden, non-realised potentials, and the authentic future is the repetition/retrieval of *this* past, not of the past as it was'.[71] Shakespeare's romance magic resurrects the past in order to grasp something that was not seen the first time around: the past that, tragically, never was. To see another, for one thing: 'Do not shun her / Until you see her die again, for then / You kill her double' (5.3.105–7). Hermione herself was not seen by Leontes, only her paddling hand, only his own fantastical suspicion. Now, finally, he sees her and she becomes present before him. Such is the power of 'sovereign shame' (to quote the Quarto-text of *King Lear*, 17.43) to act as 'a bridge to the other',[72] and thereby to open a genuine future.

This is a moment of grace, no doubt, but the miracle doesn't just happen. It is made to happen. Its grace is rendered by art, a (wo)man-made grace. Paulina's art is neither natural nor divine, but is elaborately constructed. And, as a human art, it is not without difficulty, or even incredulity. The miracle is, in theatrical terms, that something so outlandish, so 'unrealistic', even absurd, should be so moving. A statute coming to life! Or a wife

---

70 Beckwith, *Grammar of Forgiveness*, p. 137.
71 Slavoj Žižek, *In Defense of Lost Causes* (London, 2008), p. 141.
72 Fernie, *Shame in Shakespeare*, p. 244.

hiding for sixteen years under the King's nose! Leontes's acceptance of this absurdity reflects Christopher Cobb's point that the ultimate success of Shakespearian romance depends on moving the spectator's 'sense of what is possible'.[73] That movement is what opens a new law of grace. As Hermione finally speaks: 'You gods, look down, / And from your sacred vials pour your graces / Upon my daughter's head' (5.3.122–4). Hermione has lain dormant, 'preserv[ing] [her]self to see the issue' (5.3.128–9). Not expired, not extinguished, but silent, unheralded, waiting for the moment of recognition. She is not what she was. She has known loss and waited long in the shadows. Nonetheless, she steps out now, into the autumnal sunshine of the late afternoon, in time to see the reconfiguration of the law in which 'Every wink of an eye some new grace will be born' (5.2.109–10).

To stop turning away from another may be far from a moral triumph, but it is the first step away from a moral tragedy. In *Mabo*, too, something from the past – or, indeed, something that was shamefully *not* recognized in the past – was implanted in new ground. If this is not quite a statue coming to life, it is still re-animating. It begins to un-stone the legal imagination. '[T]raditional laws and customs'[74] that seemed to be dead legal artefacts buried in the common law's prehistoric sands now have legal life and presence *in* the common law. But if the law now 'recognizes' Indigenous laws and customs, they are not the same as they were. Their implantation in the common law radically alters their nature. They are given renewed legal force only through the common law's (retroactive) recognition, not through their own sovereignty. They are translated into something they never were: legal rights that are 'held under the Crown'.[75] And this translation is both the tragedy and triumph of *Mabo*. The triumph is that the sovereign is subjected to this title, burdened by something previously unknown. The tragedy is that these rights are also subjected to the Crown, which has largely unburdened itself by extinguishing native title across much of the country.

INADEQUATE REDEMPTIONS AND FUTURE COMMUNITIES

Extinguishment. The word carries the burden of so much tragedy and suffering in *Mabo*. If, in one sense, the past can be changed by remembrance, in another, the change comes too late. The losses suffered due to the delay in recognition (from 1788 to 1992) are so catastrophic that no adequate restitution is possible. The apocalyptic 'tide of history … washed away' so much Indigenous ownership before it was recognized; so much 'cannot be revived'.[76] Brennan's euphemistic 'tide' conveys both the judgment's helplessness in the face of this devastating loss and its continuing complicity. The suggestion that it was (abstracted) 'history' – not the law – that did this damage is an evasion of responsibility. The Europeans are still the handmaidens of history; the Indigenous, still its victims. We see this evasiveness in what initially appears to be Brennan's commonsense:

Aboriginal rights and interests were not stripped away by operation of the common law on first settlement by British colonists, but by the exercise of a sovereign authority over land exercised recurrently by Governments. To treat the dispossession of the Australian Aborigines as the working out of the Crown's acquisition of ownership of all land on first settlement is contrary to history. Aborigines were dispossessed of their land parcel by parcel, to make way for expanding colonial settlement.[77]

Brennan is trying to 'dispel the misconception that it is the common law rather than the action of governments which made many of the indigenous people of this country trespassers on their own land'.[78] And his comments seem quite sensible, until one remembers one thing: the common law helped to *make these Crown actions legal*. Brennan himself recognizes that, under the common law, extinguishment of native title by the Crown was legal. So, if the common law did not (im)personally

---

73 Cobb, *Staging of Romance*, p. 23.
74 *Mabo*, Justice Brennan, [66].
75 *Mabo*, Justice Dawson, [15].
76 *Mabo*, Justice Brennan, [66].
77 *Mabo*, Justice Brennan, [82].
78 *Mabo*, Justice Brennan, [82].

and automatically strip Indigenous Australians of their land on first settlement, it nonetheless automatically applied to the whole of the colony. So applied, it made the Indigenous people subject to the Crown and its *lawful* expropriation of their land. Once the common law applied (before most Indigenous people even knew about the colonizers), they were no longer sovereign owners of their land. The legal dispossession of their sovereignty cleared the way for the physical dispossession that followed. There is thus something absurd in Brennan's machinations, as if he is waving his hands in the air saying 'it's not the Law's fault! It's the Crown!' – when the Crown and the law walked hand in hand over the land of the dispossessed. The law here is closing up, re-settling. It is avoiding both its own responsibility and the fact that the Indigenous people and laws that survived the 'tide of history' survived *in spite* of the law – not because of it.

If the original sin of sovereignty is a phantasmagoria that obliterates others, there are strong signs that the redemptions on offer in *Mabo* and *The Winter's Tale* also rely on deceptive fictions. Paulina convinces Leontes that Hermione is nothing – extinguished – and relies on a stage-managed illusion to instil her lessons in his heart. Moreover, the illusion re-invigorates, or redeems, the same tyrannous, patriarchal monarchy that first caused the tragedy. Hence Stephen Orgel's suggestion that we shouldn't get too carried away with the satisfactions the play offers: 'The tragic loss that Perdita represents is not the loss of her company . . . but the loss of an heir . . . That is what is found, the essential thing. . . . What is restored, finally, in this quintessentially Jacobean drama, is royal authority.'[79]

Something similar could be said of *Mabo*: a limited, somewhat guilty, legal fiction is meant to set right the catastrophe of legal dispossession. Not only does the belated granting of recognition only occur after – perhaps only because – native title has been safely extinguished across most of the country, but also there remains something phantasmagoric about the restoration itself. According to the evidentiary requirements for proving native title, 'the native must conform to the characteristics

of one that would have been found in pre-colonial time'.[80] But, of course, the colonial time has wiped away the conditions for such a 'native', a point Watson expresses with devastating irony: 'native title applicants are required to prove the extent to which their nativeness has survived genocide. If nativeness is not proven it is considered extinguished. If it is proven it is open to extinguishment. Native title is extinguishment.'[81] If we accept native title as it stands, we overlook the bizarre fact that ongoing extinguishment results from a now derided fantasy that nonetheless remains legally effective. We overlook the scandalous legal requirement of *continuous* connection to the land (to establish native title), when connection is precisely what was forcibly interrupted. And we thereby fail both to recognize the haunting Indigenous presence that remains even in 'extinguishment', and to allow other modes of displaced, transplanted or diffused connection to take root and flourish.

We must recognize these evasions and limitations. We must not get too carried away with the rhetoric of redemption. Yet both *Mabo* and *The Winter's Tale* show that, if we do not get carried away, at least for a moment, we do not truly see the other or our own implication in the history of oppression. Royal authority may be restored in Sicilia but the monarchy itself falls to its knees and is wondrously carried away. The whole scene is designed to carry us away. In *Mabo*, too, the judges are carried away with their 'unusually emotive' language even as they remain within the law's skeleton. Brennan is more cautious, but he too implies that the law must be transported beyond itself – to contemporary notions of justice and human rights – if it is to right its wrongs. The law, in *Mabo*, *gets carried away even as it remains in force*. We reach a point of irresolvable tension: a radical alteration of

[79] William Shakespeare, *The Winter's Tale*, ed. Stephen Orgel (Oxford, 1996), p. 79.
[80] Motha, 'Reconciliation as domination', p. 76.
[81] Watson, 'Buried alive', p. 263.

precedent that simultaneously replicates the law's oppressive colonial foundations.

And perhaps this is what redemption looks like in an unredeemed world: always fleeting and fragmentary, always under threat from the oppressive forces of mythic repetition, always sliding back. For Theodor Adorno, the 'messianic light' of redemption only occurs in the 'rifts and crevices' of the present world – a world which must be 'estrange[d]' by actively thinking 'from the standpoint of redemption'.[82] Such estrangement is both the 'simplest of all things' and 'also the utterly impossible thing, because it presupposes a standpoint removed, even by a hair's breadth, from the scope of existence, whereas we well know that any possible knowledge ... is also marked ... by the same distortion and indigence it seeks to escape'.[83] The tremendous convulsions of *Mabo* and *The Winter's Tale* testify to the extreme difficulty – and inherent violence – of attaining even a hair's-breadth remove from the impoverishing fantasies they seek to escape.

Despite their ongoing distortions, however, this sliver of distance is the most precious of things. For, through its razor-thin translucence, the tragic reality begins to appear in a distorted light. The shapes of official history warp, and what were long considered pillars of the law are now apprehended as monstrous, fantastical figures gliding through a nightmare. A crack opens in long-established authority, through which other pasts and potentially other futures may be glimpsed. To think redemptively and creatively about the past, then, requires holding together the opposites of repetition and transformation. It requires an openness to contingent miracles and inadequate restorations. And it requires a willingness to be unsettled, to be disappointed, to be torn in two directions, to be at once disillusioned and enchanted, to feel that uncanny sense of homelessness, to have heard it all before but to hear it for the first time. Ultimately, we need more such disappointing redemptions, not fewer.

Taken in these terms, the silences that haunt *The Winter's Tale*'s end are not merely markers of failure, but also of the necessarily unfinished and unsettled nature of redemption. There is the permanent silence of Antigonus and Mamillius, who cannot be revived. And there is the silence of Hermione, who speaks, but not to Leontes. Her silence is pregnant with unanswered questions: what was she doing all that time? How did she appear to die? Can she love Leontes again? Can she forgive him? Does she want to? Hermione harboured no hidden desire at the outset of the play, but her silence now establishes an unmistakable gulf between matrimonial minds: her thoughts are unknown to Leontes. The moment of reconciliation, then, is not one of knowledge or oneness but a 'ceremony of separation' in which, to quote Stanley Cavell, Leontes finally acknowledges 'a life [and a knowledge] beyond his'.[84] Leontes's final command, which concludes the play, is less a royal decree than the opening of an unassured future:

> Good Paulina,
> Lead us from hence, where we may leisurely
> Each one demand and answer to his part
> Performed in this wide gap of time since first
> We were dissevered. Hastily lead away.
>
> (5.3.152–6)

The 'dissever[ing]' of perspective, so common in the late plays, indicates that the sovereignty that is restored is no longer one-dimensional but formed of various 'part[s]'. The future is not a sovereign possession but the communal construction of a multiply 'dissevered' past. *Mabo*'s promise, too, is not something settled or achieved. Rather, by loosening Australia's founding myths, *Mabo* opened us to the spectre of another law moving in and through the common law. To quote the Indigenous leader Galarrwuy Yunupingu:

a simple white man's paper cannot extinguish a traditional law, the culture, the language, the painting on the rocks, the painting on the barks, the painting on the bodies.... The Aboriginal Law still stands where it

---

[82] Adorno, *Minima moralia*, quoted in Wolin, *Walter Benjamin*, p. 91.

[83] Wolin, *Walter Benjamin*, p. 92.

[84] Stanley Cavell, *Disowning Knowledge in Seven Plays of Shakespeare* (Cambridge, 2003), p. 220.

cannot be seen. It's in the river, it's in the billabong, it is in the rock, it is in the caves, it is in the sea, the law still remains. It remains intact as it was for the last 60,000 years or maybe more.[85]

Yunupingu may express a cosmology quite alien to the Western sensibility but, as Moira Gatens and Genevieve Lloyd note, 'to those whom it sought to erase, the doctrine of *terra nullius* was no more or less a fiction, part of an elaborate and alien imaginary'.[86] The unspeakable promise of *Mabo* rests upon the disorienting idea that two cosmologies, two legal systems, two histories, two expectations for the future, may co-exist at once.

Redemption, in this sense, *must* be fragmentary, heterogeneous and unsettled. For what necessitated redemption was the attempt to settle: to legislate matters according to the expectations of a single sovereign and thereby obliterate others. 'Your actions are my dreams.' What happens at the close of *The Winter's Tale* is not salvation, but the beginning of what *should* have happened in the beginning: a mutual conversation, and hence the *possibility* of reconciliation. We again see the uncanny blurring of Shakespearian romance. Reconciliation is both absolutely achieved (Hermione takes Leontes's hand and our emotional energies flow forth) and absolutely deferred (she does not speak to him). The play does not perform, but gestures to, this new community: they will go away and talk about these things.

Perhaps this is also true for *Mabo*: that its ultimate success or failure lies outside of itself. The sense of participation and mutuality that is, of necessity, absent from the law's judgment, awaits a broader audience: a community that may or may not come. If we want more than the judgment can give – be it the structural reforms contained in the 'Uluru statement from the heart' or even a truly dispersed sovereignty[87] – it is we who must take up its redemptive potential and transplant it in new ground. That would, of course, be politics. But it would also be aesthetics: an un-stoning of the imagination, a feeling sight, a hand outstretched. Like Leontes, we stand in the face of our tragic history. Will we, too, acknowledge our darkness? Will we be transformed in shame's chrysalis? For that, in Shakespeare's late plays, is the true lawful magic: that a stony heart may melt and an audience burst into life and action. Music. Awake. Strike. 'Tis time. Be stone no more.

---

[85] 'Cape York Land Council 1997', quoted in Moira Gatens and Genevieve Lloyd, *Collective Imaginings: Spinoza, Past and Present* (London and New York, 1999), p. 149.
[86] Gatens and Lloyd, *Collective Imaginings*, p. 149.
[87] See 'Uluru statement from the heart': www.referendumcouncil.org.au/sites/default/files/2017-05/Uluru_Statement_From_The_Heart_0.PDF.

'CABINED, CRIBBED, CONFINED': ADVICE TO ACTORS AND THE PRIORITIES OF SHAKESPEARIAN SCHOLARSHIP

MICHAEL CORDNER

Shakespeare took blank verse and ran with it.

(Ian McKellen)[1]

The actor Leigh Lawson played the Theseus/Oberon double in *A Midsummer Night's Dream* for the Royal Shakespeare Company in 1990.[2] He has notated the thoughts spinning in his mind as he spoke the play's opening lines during the first public performance:

"Now, fair Hippolyta, our nuptial hour"
No comma no full stop so breath slightly upwards inflection carry the energy through

"Draws on a pace [sic],"
Snatch top-up breath carry through

"Four happy days bring in"
Same breath vocal energy carry through

"Another moon – but O, methinks, how slow"
Carry through the same breath

"This old moon wanes."
Throw ball, change chairs[3]

He is policing his performance by recalling rehearsal-room instructions on how to breathe, and phrase, the verse. The scrutiny he underwent there was intense. It included being handed, after each day's rehearsal, 'a list of our mistakes in the text, every word, full stop, and comma'. He welcomed this watchful 'care and tuition' and celebrated how RSC actors received 'more support than a boxer's bollocks'.[4]

An experienced actor, Lawson was a relative novice in Shakespeare. Shortly before, he had received a high-pressure initiation from Peter Hall, when the latter directed him as Antonio in *The Merchant of Venice*. As a result, Lawson started work on the *Dream* with a true believer's determination 'to learn my Shakespeare with my "ends of lines" as taught by Peter Hall': 'Basically, at this stage, it involves clicking fingers to help mentally mark the end of a line. If marked by a comma, a breath may be taken. A pause only at a full stop.'[5] He was relieved that his current director, Adrian Noble, had similar priorities: the 'technique he subscribes to for speaking the verse, though not as strictly adhered to as Peter Hall's, is basically the same, thank God'. Lawson had imbibed from Hall the conviction that attentive observation of line structure was 'the way the poet from Stratford wanted his lines spoken', and he applauded Noble's credo that 'People come to the RSC to hear Shakespeare spoken the way it should be spoken, and it's our job to do that.'[6]

[1] Ian McKellen, 'Introduction', in Ian McKellen, *William Shakespeare's Richard III: A Screenplay Written by Ian McKellen & Richard Loncraine, Annotated and Introduced by Ian McKellen* (London, 1996), p. 32. This article originated as a platform paper at the International Shakespeare Conference at Stratford-upon-Avon in 2016, which has since been substantially revised.
[2] Draft versions of this article were read by Tom Cantrell, Oliver Ford Davies, Peter Holland, Oliver Jones, Perry Mills, Felicity Riddy, Richard Rowland and Penelope Wilton. It has been greatly improved by their feedback. Remaining faults are entirely my responsibility.
[3] Leigh Lawson, *The Dream: An Actor's Story* (London, 2008), pp. 78–9.
[4] Lawson, *The Dream*, pp. 58–9. [5] Lawson, *The Dream*, p. 46.
[6] Lawson, *The Dream*, p. 53.

Lawson was especially grateful to the company voice coach Lyn Darley, who combined 'sympathy to the actors' problems' – in handling the alien, if exciting, medium of blank verse – with 'knowledge of the text'.[7] This pairing of qualities moved 'her role way beyond that of a voice coach'. Darnley introduced him, in a series of 'one-to-one classes', to games geared to reinforce the sanctity of Shakespearian line-division, including 'throwing a ball to each other to mark the ends of lines while doing a speech from the play'. This exercise could also be used 'to place the points to take a breath, or run on through a phrase'. In another, two chairs were placed side by side, 'and as I recite a speech I move from one to the other sitting at each punctuation mark'. Though this sounds simple, he reported, 'the mental concentration makes my brain ache'. His '*Throw ball, change chairs*' notation illustrates how recollecting these games shaped his painstaking negotiation of his way forwards at that first performance. Despite this, he was surprised to find that the lines were proving 'a bugger to learn'. It does not occur to him that the burden of remembering the tutors' instructions as well as the lines themselves might partly explain this.

Seven years later, a BBC documentary on the RSC observed another distinguished actor, Antony Sher, who was currently rehearsing Rostand's Cyrano, being led through the chair exercise by the company's first Head of Voice, Cicely Berry. The objective this time was to assist Sher to discover the moments in one of Cyrano's long orations when a new mood, subject, point of emphasis or style of address invites a change in vocal registration. Among those watching the programme was the actress Eileen Atkins, who found the experience thoroughly depressing: 'he did a speech where she made him keep changing chairs. It would be like "To be (moves) or not to be (moves); that is the question." I thought "You're an intelligent man, Tony Sher. Why can't you look at the speech, know you need variation, work out where it is, and just think it through?"'[8] Atkins added: 'to me, that's homework!' From her perspective, a gifted man was being infantilized by institutional process, and

ceding to his instructor responsibilities he should have shouldered himself.

There is a generational divide in play here. Eileen Atkins came to prominence as an actress in the late 1950s / early 1960s. She earned her spurs in a professional world where no theatre possessed the kind of support departments the major national companies now consider indispensable. Jerome Willis, returning to the Stratford-upon-Avon company in 2002, fifty years after his first appearance there, celebrated the transformation: 'My first impression . . . was how well-supported the actors are. There is regular movement work, looking specifically at the play and more generally at mobility and expressiveness, plus a large team of vocal and dialect coaches.'[9] Sher could accordingly rely on the availability of experts like Berry. But, in Atkins's view, he had become inappropriately dependent on them and risked undermining his own professional autonomy.

The potential advantages of such in-house resources are readily apparent. But the Lawson and Sher anecdotes highlight the accompanying dangers. The issues at stake in them are distinct, but related. Atkins judges that Sher's professional qualifications for undertaking such a taxing role should include the ability to work through the text, detecting these potential points of change for himself, as a preparation for fuller explorations (and hoped-for revelations) in rehearsal. Instead, he appears to need Berry's coaching, in order to equip himself for this basic task. (There is likely to be a staged element to the session the documentary records, designed as it is to demonstrate a workshop method; but the fact remains that Sher was happy to be filmed being tutored in this way by Berry.)

7 Lawson, *The Dream*, pp. 58–9. Lyn Darnley has sketched her own overview of the development of voice training in the RSC in 'Theatre-voice pedagogy within the Royal Shakespeare Company: a historical perspective', *Voice and Speech Review* 13 (2019), 5–30.

8 Carole Zucker, *In the Company of Actors: Reflections on the Craft of Acting* (London, 1999), pp. 9–10.

9 Jerome Willis, 'A tale of two tempests', *The Guardian*, 31 August 2002.

Similarly, Lawson, although he was about to play leading roles, cast himself as a humble apprentice and strove to obey, to the letter (or, rather, the punctuation-point), his tutors' hyper-detailed instructions. He never queried these directions' legitimacy, nor asked whether this puppet-mastering was the best way to prepare himself to meet performance's likely vicissitudes. His delivery of Theseus's opening lines is throughout dictated by others' voices and others' expertise. It is as if a distinguished professional pianist were to perform a virtuosic Schumann or Prokofiev sonata in a concert, with her thoughts and fingers anxiously clinging to her first lessons in keyboard technique. This RSC trainee leading actor never attains adult command of his craft, because he has subjected himself so rigorously to external monitoring by those whose authority he presumes to be superior to his own.

Both stories start from an actor's diffidence in the face of formally demanding text. The Sher/Berry encounter is devoted to what might be regarded as essential work. Cyrano's extended rodomontades need the kind of variety in execution this exercise aims to enable. Atkins is simply surprised that Sher does not regard this kind of preliminary exploration as initially his responsibility, and appears to lack the craft skills to do it effectively on his own. Lawson is awed by the undertaking ahead of him and, assuming there is one true way in which Shakespeare 'should be spoken', places implicit faith in those he deems the guardians of that truth. The outside observer, however, is likely to ask the questions Lawson does not pose. What justifies these tutors' certainty that a specific line can be legitimately breathed in only one way, and that the ends of lines should invariably be marked in performance? What is the authority of the revered punctuation in which they place such total trust? And what are the long-term effects on an actor of being subject to such stringent regimes of instruction and invigilation?

In the four decades between Atkins's début and the filming of Sher's exercise, such practices, and the departmental infrastructures which deliver them, have become habitual in both the RSC and the National Theatre, and the employment of similar experts, contracted on an ad hoc basis, is now normal in professional productions of the early modern repertoire elsewhere. This is an institutional development which has yet to find its historian. But it is of pressing interest to anyone concerned with the study of the translation of pre-1642 scripts into contemporary performance. It also, as I hope to demonstrate, issues an implicit challenge to the default procedures of Shakespearian scholarship.

It is not only in rehearsal rooms that such experts have made their presence felt over the past half-century. A new sub-genre of advice manuals, focused on performing Shakespeare's plays, has developed in the same period. Their authors draw on their own experience as actors, directors or voice coaches. The mantra justifying the need for their services is that the majority of performers' work nowadays involves naturalistic writing, which arguably leaves them ill equipped to meet early modern playwriting's formal challenges. Accordingly, when confronted by an early modern script, many performers share Lawson's sense of nervous inadequacy. From this arises the call for expert guidance on how to handle this repertoire's special requirements. The pedagogical urge to produce clear, easily inculcated headlines, however, betrays many of these authors into espousing over-simplifications.[10]

In *Acting Shakespeare's Language*, for instance, the director and acting teacher Andy Hind offers, as a foundational principle, the proposition that 'Every human utterance is an explanation, a question, an order.'[11] Some of the examples, however, that Hinds chooses to demonstrate the

---

[10] The first wave of such writing generated critical responses in two scholarly monographs: Sarah Werner, *Shakespeare and Feminist Performance: Ideology on Stage* (London, 2001), and Abigail Rokison, *Shakespearean Verse Speaking: Text and Theatre Practice* (Cambridge, 2009). But publication in this field continues to proliferate, and the examples analysed here postdate those studies.

[11] Andy Hinds, *Acting Shakespeare's Language* (London, 2015), p. 3.

truth of his assertion expose its limitations. To illustrate his third category, for example, he cites Antony's words, over Caesar's corpse: 'Oh, pardon me, thou bleeding piece of earth / That I am meek and gentle with these butchers' (3.1.257–8). He wishes to discourage an actor from assuming that Antony is simply 'lamenting to himself', and to enable him to conceive of the lines as performing an action. But then this assertion follows: 'They constitute an order; an order purposefully directed towards the remains of Caesar. He is ordering the corpse to pardon him.'[12] The idea of ordering a corpse to do something is paradoxical in itself. But construing as a command a couplet which begins with a request for pardon suggests that the urge to fit every utterance into a trio of pre-set categories has taken priority over an ability to listen to what the language is actually doing. Antony's words might be read as a plea, a petition, a prayer, an invocation and, doubtless, other possibilities, but not as a forceful utterance which anticipates obedience. Reducing all Shakespearian speech acts to a choice of one of only three options misrepresents the dialogue's expressive diversity. An actor who relied on these categories in rehearsal or performance would be condemned to using an unnecessarily circumscribed expressive palette.

A different set of issues arises with Kelly Hunter's book *Cracking Shakespeare*. Hunter has played a number of Shakespearian leads, including for the RSC, with distinction. She has also carried out distinctive, though controversial, work with autistic children, based on the premise that 'drama – particularly Shakespeare – can break through the communicative blocks of autism'.[13] She begins each session with what she calls a '*Heartbreak Hello*', in which the group beats out 'the rhythm of a heartbeat whilst saying "Hello"'.[14] She claims to derive her inspiration for this from the Shakespearian 'iambic beat', since an 'iambus takes the form of a heartbeat, making it arguably the first rhythm we hear in the womb'.[15]

The *Oxford English Dictionary* defines iambus as a 'metrical foot consisting of a short followed by a long syllable; in accentual verse, of an unaccented followed by an accented syllable'.[16] The

assumption of a kinship between this metrical pattern and the heartbeat's rhythm has developed within the actor-training tradition of which Hunter is an inheritor, and is treated by it as a given, not something which requires proof. To this, one response is provided by Paul Menzer: 'doesn't the trochaic beat more closely resemble the human heartbeat than iambic?'[17] But the heart/metre analogy is too useful to these instructors for such scepticism to unsettle it, however briefly.

Hunter urges her readers to 'consider your own heartbeat, a fundamental task because as an actor you must bring your own heart and feelings to your character'.[18] So, from the heartbeat as a physiological function, Hunter segues to the metaphor of the heart as the source of human emotions. She reminds us that the 'rhythm and rapidity of your heartbeat is constantly changing according to circumstance and emotion', and claims that it equips us with 'an emotional barometer, registering your own authentic visceral existence'. In exactly the same way, she asserts, Shakespeare deploys iambic pentameter, both in its default regularities of patterning, and in its frequent oscillations and reversals of expectation, in order to notate '*the rhythm of your character's feelings*' (emphasis in original). In this reading, all those lines that begin with a trochaic first foot represent 'tiny heart attacks', revealing the emotional disturbance afflicting their speakers.[19] Shakespeare requires

---

[12] Hinds, *Acting Shakespeare's Language*, p. 11.
[13] For a radical interrogation of the questionable assumptions underpinning Hunter's work with autistic children, see Sonya Freeman Loftis, 'Autistic culture, Shakespeare therapy and the Hunter Heartbeat Method', *Shakespeare Survey 72* (Cambridge, 2019), 256–67.
[14] Kelly Hunter, 'Shakespeare and autism', *Teaching Shakespeare* 3 (2013), 9.
[15] Hunter, 'Shakespeare and autism', 9.
[16] 'iambus, n.', *OED Online*, Oxford University Press, December 2019, www.oed.com/view/Entry/90686.
[17] Paul Menzer, 'Lines', in *Early Modern Theatricality*, ed. Henry S. Turner (Oxford, 2013), pp. 127–8.
[18] Kelly Hunter, *Cracking Shakespeare: A Hands-on Guide for Actors and Directors + Video* (London, 2015), p. 4.
[19] Hunter, *Cracking Shakespeare*, pp. 4, 7.

each actor to become a 'detective of emotion'; but he has made the clues easy to decode.[20] The implicit message is: there is no need to panic, because what may look like an alien form of stage dialogue is, in fact, perfectly designed to facilitate your performance. But, as with Hinds, that reassurance depends on dubious presuppositions.

The rhetorical deployment of the imputed resemblance between the iambic pulse and the heartbeat's rhythm breeds what are, in effect, metaphorical elaborations, rather than a coherently demonstrated set of logical moves. Even if a degree of similarity could be staked out between the two phenomena, that is not the same as assuming that they function identically, or that fluctuations in the maintenance of an even metrical pattern inevitably have the same degree of significance for the character who speaks the relevant lines as marked: recurrent instabilities in a heartbeat's pattern and tempo may signify for the body whose continued existence is sustained by that heart's operations.

Hunter's reliance on this analogy's presumed force means that, for her, Shakespearian verse becomes a kind of X-ray of a speaker's state of feelings, which testifies to the truth of the latter even before the character herself consciously perceives what she is experiencing. If aptly mapped, these data will afford the performer vivid insight into how the character instinctively responds, second by second. The route to emotional authenticity, therefore, is via an alert observation of metrical nuancing. What this account presumes to be twenty-first-century actors' default priorities – the wish to ground a performance in a character's innermost impulses and sensations – are therefore comprehensively catered for by the early modern text.

All of this rests on an assumption that the predominant goal of Shakespearian dialogue is the revelation of his characters' interior emotional landscapes. That Shakespeare does often create verse which points to internal pressures not directly articulated by the paraphrasable meaning of the words spoken is an entirely arguable proposition. But the belief that this is his invariable mode of operation is trickier to sustain. Similarly

questionable is Hunter's implicit limitation of his metrical resourcefulness to the deployment of trochees as the equivalent of 'tiny heart attacks', each of which allegedly reveals the imminence for the character who employs it of 'potential heartbreak or ecstatic happiness'.[21] Shakespeare's arsenal of metrical variations and irregularities is far more richly stocked than this suggests. Hunter's highlighting of only one of the ways in which the iambic beat can be varied miscues the actor about the range of effects Shakespeare's experimentation constantly generates from this invaluable resource.[22] In addition, he uses trochees – especially at the start of lines – with marked frequency. If these are all 'tiny heart attacks', we must fear for the patient's mental, if not physical, health.[23]

Shakespeare was trained by an educational curriculum which foregrounded the study of language as a precisely honed instrument of human interaction and negotiation, and, ultimately, of governance and power.[24] Grammar school boys learned

---

20 Hunter, *Cracking Shakespeare*, p. 4.

21 Hunter, *Cracking Shakespeare*, p. 128.

22 This spotlighting of trochaic inversions, to the exclusion of all the other metrical variations common in early modern dramatic verse, is recurrent in the genre of 'how to' manuals on which the present article focuses. But it is only fair to add that a similar limitation of vision occurs, on occasion, in studies by literary scholars – as, for instance, in Michael Alexander, *Reading Shakespeare* (Basingstoke, 2013), p. 46. For a more surely grounded, concise introduction to the flexibilities of Shakespeare's practice, see Ros King, *Shakespeare: A Beginner's Guide* (Oxford, 2011), pp. 135–42.

23 For an argument that such trochaic reversals are 'common and acceptable at the beginning of an iambic pentameter line, and the sentence stress does not jar if the second syllable of the trochee … is of almost but not quite equal stress with the first', see G. S. Fraser, *Metre, Rhyme and Free Verse* (London, 1970), p. 8. See also, to similar effect, Derek Attridge, *Poetic Rhythm: An Introduction* (Cambridge, 1995), pp. 115–16. Whether or not one accepts these writers' propositions, the issues are certainly far more nuanced than Hunter's bold generalizations admit.

24 The literature on this is substantial. For a recent, authoritative overview, see Peter Mack, 'Learning and transforming conventional wisdom: reading and rhetoric in the Elizabethan grammar school', *Renaissance Studies* 32 (2018), 427–45.

how to fashion language to achieve targeted ends. The tools they were equipped with included the deft deployment of emphasis and patterning to woo consent, to win respect, to move others' emotions to their own advantage, and to counter difficult opposition. Shakespeare's plays document his fascination with the processes of persuasion, in domestic bargaining and in political confrontation, as also with the deceitful manoeuvres by which the unscrupulous, gifted in verbal manipulation, can work their will, undetected, upon their chosen victims. So, how safe is the assumption that inversions of stress patterns are invariably to be read as trustworthy monitors of the private, often otherwise undeclared, perturbations or excitements engulfing the character who speaks the verse?

In *Troilus and Cressida*, 1.3, Ulysses addresses his fellow Greek leaders, in an attempt to seize the initiative and revitalize their conduct of the war. His major speech on the subject starts with three lines, in which line 1 starts with a spondee, and line 3 with a trochee, while, in line 2, the first stronger stresses are delayed until the third and fourth syllables:

> **Troy, yet** upon his basis, had been down,
> And the **great Hec**tor's sword had lacked a master
> **But** for these instances . . .
>
> (1.3.74–6, emphasis added)

Hunter's method encourages the actor to seek reasons of internal disturbance for these metrical phenomena – and, doubtless, Ulysses finds his peers' inaction galling. But he is also a skilled politician, crafting what he says to achieve a hoped-for outcome. The oratory gifted to him by Shakespeare reflects this, as it deploys emphases which work in counterpoint to the iambic beat, in order to underline rhetorically, to those he holds responsible for it, the preposterousness of this history of wasted military opportunities. Whether or not Ulysses feels indignant is of secondary concern, since the rhetorician's art is to deploy for tactical purposes what Hunter takes to be spontaneous revelations of personal turbulence. A method which, like Hunter's, prioritizes the personal to this extent risks rendering the plays effectively apolitical and narrows the

questions players influenced by it are likely to ask. At a late point in her book, Hunter defines rhetoric as 'a multifarious means of persuading others you are right'.[25] If she had only absorbed the potential implications of that for those who perform Shakespeare's plays, her book might have been much richer and more effective. As it currently stands, however, reading *Cracking Shakespeare* makes me recall John Whiting's praise for the young Ian Holm, in the course of his ascent to playing leading roles for the RSC: 'It is satisfying to see a young actor who obviously knows exactly what he is doing. An actor with a head as well as that vastly overestimated thing in the theatre, a heart.'[26]

Two other points about Hunter's book are relevant here. Firstly, she shares with Hinds a desire to enunciate principles of general applicability – and with similarly doubtful results. Thus, in her account, all lines ending on a weak eleventh syllable provide the performer with 'the opportunity to explore a moment of doubt'.[27] Similarly, monosyllabic lines 'usually offer a particular plain prosaic quality of thought in direct opposition to lines of fewer words made of more syllables (**polysyllabic**), which are often more poetic or descriptive' (bold as in original).[28] In polysyllabic passages, you can sense 'how much imaginative power your character is using at that moment', with the implied corollary that the imaginative pressure is not so intense, or largely in abeyance, in monosyllabic ones. A 'densely alliterative' passage indicates that the ideas in it are 'quickly borne out of you, as if your mind is on fire', whereas, 'if the alliteration is more even spaced, or indeed absent, you can afford to speak more slowly, as if the thoughts were chipped from ice and taking longer to be formed'.[29] Every list of words should be handled on a rising inflection, as 'if climbing steps towards the top of a mountain'.[30] Every soliloquy should be

---

[25] Hunter, *Cracking Shakespeare*, p. 128.
[26] John Whiting, *John Whiting on Theatre* (London, 1966), p. 83.
[27] Hunter, *Cracking Shakespeare*, p. 15.
[28] Hunter, *Cracking Shakespeare*, p. 10.
[29] Hunter, *Cracking Shakespeare*, p. 22.
[30] Hunter, *Cracking Shakespeare*, p. 79.

launched 'as if you are about to explode with the frustration of not being able to express yourself'.[31] The appearance of brackets in the dialogue invites you to use the words enclosed in them 'to laugh your way *through* the line' (emphasis in original).[32] And so on, and on.

In each of these cases, even where the proposition advanced might have a degree of cogency in some specific instances, it cannot claim the overarching application Hunter's rhetoric assigns to it. Equally, consult a different advice book, and you are likely to find each of these *ex cathedra* pronouncements contradicted by another writer. Prunella Scales and Timothy West have, for instance, this rule of thumb to offer on how to handle lists:

When you have 'lists' of words or phrases, separated by commas, be aware that to lift the inflection on each creates an expectation of further words or phrases in the list, i.e. it will sound literary and prepared. If you want to sound spontaneous, as though the character is thinking up each addition as he speaks, repeat the inflection you would use on the first word if it stood alone.[33]

Multiple stand-offs between Hunter and competing authors could easily be provided.

An overriding urge to generate definitive statements is at work here. Hunter launches her explorations with a declaration that her aim is to 'demystify the "rules" of verse speaking, teaching them clearly and frankly, demonstrating how they always relate to human experience and can be used by the actor or director to bring a character to life'.[34] Though she modestly shrouds 'rules' there in quotation marks, she is, in fact, as committed to legislating emphatically on her chosen subject as Hind was, with his three kinds of 'human utterance', or the RSC coaches, with their relentless enforcement of favoured norms, about how to phrase Theseus's verse, on their docilely obedient student Leigh Lawson.

George T. Wright has brilliantly documented Shakespeare's dexterity in using the same metrical effects to radically different ends in contrasting passages of dialogue.[35] That sustained, and constantly exploratory, technical inventiveness means that pedagogical generalizations which insist that one resource – trochees, for instance, or passages of

dense alliteration – will always, and in all dramatic circumstances, yield one kind of effect are doomed from the start. Writing like this misleads those it seeks to instruct and will ultimately inhibit their ability to react alertly, and questioningly, to the specific challenges and opportunities afforded by the writing's (potentially provocative) idiosyncrasies in the sequence currently being rehearsed.

In addition, Hunter fails another key test. She proves to be a fallible paraphraser. She strongly recommends the practice, but then exemplifies it problematically. She chooses for this purpose the Caliban passage which begins 'His spirits hear me, / And yet I needs must curse' (2.2.3–4). Her paraphrase for that sentence is 'I can be heard but I will swear', which omits all reference to the forces he fears – Prospero's 'spirits' – which are the subject of the first clause in the original, substitutes 'swear' for the much stronger, and differently nuanced, 'curse' (an important verb for this character), and dissipates completely the compulsive force of '*needs must* curse' into the bland '*will* swear'.[36] Similar losses occur throughout her paraphrase of the following lines. Thus, 'For every trifle are they set upon me' (2.2.8) becomes 'they hurt me for every tiny thing I do'. This mislays completely the presence of Prospero's authorizing power in the sufferings meted out to Caliban – something which Shakespeare's line, like the speech as a whole, firmly insists upon.

From my own experience in rehearsal rooms (both professional and non-professional), I would enthusiastically echo Hunter's faith in the potential value of paraphrase on the apt occasion. But, to be productive and supportive, it has to be more intimately responsive than this to the exact implications of particular lines. Performance based on a generalized, and inaccurate, sense of what obsesses, riles, frightens,

---

[31] Hunter, *Cracking Shakespeare*, p. 95.

[32] Hunter, *Cracking Shakespeare*, p. 116.

[33] Prunella Scales and Timothy West, *So You Want To Be an Actor?*, revised edn (London, 2016), p. 57.

[34] Hunter, *Cracking Shakespeare*, pp. xi–xii.

[35] George T. Wright, *Shakespeare's Metrical Art* (Berkeley, 1988).

[36] Hunter, *Cracking Shakespeare*, pp. 44–5.

enrages, torments, perplexes Caliban will forfeit specific definition, together with creative alertness to how Caliban's perception of his own subjugation, and his relationships with others (on stage and off), might be fluctuating and mutating line by line, pulse by pulse, moment by moment. Hunter claims that her teaching will enable actors 'to capture the dynamic movement of thought from mind to mouth, as if you are speaking your thoughts for the very first time', but then exemplifies a style of paraphrase which winnows away the individuality of the language whose performance potency she promises to unlock.[37]

Similar problems affect Giles Block's recent book on performing Shakespeare. Block has had a variegated career, in which Shakespeare's plays provide a central leitmotif, as both actor and director. His final transmigration has been as 'Master of the Word' at Shakespeare's Globe, charged with being 'a pair of ears solely focused on the liveliness and accuracy of the actors' speaking'.[38] His long association with the Globe, and the scrutineering role he has sustained there, add especial interest to his views. In 2011, the theatre bestowed the Sam Wanamaker Award on its Master of Movement Glynn MacDonald and on Block, for 'sharing their particular and pioneering approaches to their craft with hundreds of actors, directors, students and teachers every year'.[39] Through Globe Education's agency in particular, Block's influence was already widespread, and his 2013 Speaking the Speech aimed to extend it yet further.

Block chooses a moment from Julius Caesar to demonstrate and validate his approach – the passage where Lucilius, captured by Antony's men, initially pretends to be Brutus, only to be confronted with Antony himself.[40] He is fascinated by one 'six-line speech of Lucilius's':

ANTONY. Where is he?
LUCILIUS. Safe, Antony, Brutus is safe enough.
    I dare assure thee that no enemy
    Shall ever take alive the noble Brutus.
    The gods defend him from so great a shame.
    When you do find him, or alive or dead,
    He will be found like Brutus, like himself.

                      (5.4.19–25)

The first line of Lucilius' speech opens with two strong stresses ("**Safe An**tony"). Thereafter, with the exception of the third line's additional unstressed syllable at its end, it works to a regular iambic pentameter pattern. Block invokes a familiar analogy: the speech's 'rhythm is ... like the beating of our own hearts': 'So the very lines, with these heartbeats threaded through them, sound alive and vibrant. When we hear someone speaking in this rhythm, subliminally we are reminded of our common humanity. The lines sound human.'[41] Accepting the heartbeat/iambic parallel, for Block, serves to establish that iambic lines will always sound 'alive and vibrant'. What, all iambic lines? Regardless of their quality, inventiveness or craftsmanship? Even those laboriously stitched together by the most pedestrian of poetasters? The proposition invites challenge. The same applies to the accompanying claim that hearing iambic rhythms reminds us 'of our common humanity'. I cannot imagine what evidence could be mustered to prove such a claim accurate; but none is offered here. We have to make do with trusting in what Block affirms, because he affirms it.

He then asserts that 'If we want to describe our own heartbeat, we would probably say it was regular, consistent, reliable', and, by another extraordinary leap, derives an ambitious conclusion from that premise: 'Our heartbeat is dependable. So another message that is carried subliminally to the audience by the iambic rhythm is a sense of dependability. We listen to such a speaker and we feel that they mean what they say.'[42] He follows this with an encapsulating headline in bold: '**Shakespeare's blank verse is "the sound of sincerity"**'. The same questionable impulse as with my two previous examples – i.e., to enunciate propositions which brook no exceptions – also operates in Block's book.

---

[37] Hunter, Cracking Shakespeare, p. xii.
[38] Mark Rylance, 'Foreword', in Giles Block, Speaking the Speech: An Actor's Guide to Shakespeare (London, 2013), p. xi.
[39] www.london-se1.co.uk/news/view/5349.
[40] Block, Speaking the Speech, p. 7.
[41] Block, Speaking the Speech, p. 8.
[42] Block, Speaking the Speech, p. 9.

However, he tucks into the end of the paragraph that follows his headline about verse as **'the sound of sincerity'** this sentence: 'All the more terrible then are those characters, like Iago in *Othello*, whose lines of verse sound so sincere, yet whose intentions are anything but.' Which raises the question: if sincerity in this medium can be so expertly simulated, what then are the consequences of that fact for the claim that iambic pentameter convinces us, because of its heartbeat rhythm, that its speakers 'mean what they say'? But Block swiftly passes on, without confronting the fundamental difficulty he has just raised for our acceptance of his core proposition.

He isolates Lucilius' third line and notes that in it 'the first stress is on the *'ev'* of "ever"'. He asserts that the recurrent Shakespearian pattern, as he promulgates it, is for a line's first stress to warrant extra weight, which, he argues, is logical here, because this adverb 'is an "extreme" word, since it "admits of no other possibility"'. (With characteristic rhetorical overkill, it later becomes 'this magical, little, yet so powerful word').[43] From this, he moves to a parallel proposition – or, rather, assertion – that a matching extra emphasis is also required for the final stress in a line. What about the middle words of the line? He claims that they merely 'complete the phrase', so 'probably need no more special stress than that they are said with clarity'.[44]

However, the words whose importance he thus downgrades articulate, for the first time, the central concern of Lucilius' speech – that Brutus' reputation for nobility demands that he must/will never let himself be taken alive by his enemies. So how can they then be regarded as merely completing the phrase? Block is moving to enforce what he treats as an absolute law, one he constantly reiterates throughout his book – that the primary emphases in Shakespearian iambic pentameter fall on a line's first and final stressed syllables. I know of no historical warranty for this proposition, nor does Block seek to provide any. In the process, he overrides the actor's need to prioritize the flow of information, and to seek to ensure clear communication of each new development in the dialogue.[45] That, however, requires attending carefully to exactly what is

being said, phrase by phrase – a process which Block's advice that the major stresses will routinely fall at two repeated points in every line obviates. This is advice which takes much of the creative decision-making out of acting.

Block twice paraphrases the passage and, on both occasions, misexplains 'take alive' – as, initially, 'defeat' and, then, 'overcome'.[46] Both of these glosses work to mask what is actually at stake here for Lucilius: a Brutus who, *having already been defeated in battle, then allowed himself to be taken alive* would no longer be the epitome of Roman nobility this loyal soldier devotedly serves. So, as Lucilius sees it, suicide is likely, in the present military exigency, to become the only valid choice for such a man. But thraldom to an overarching position makes Block an unreliable interpreter of textual detail. In effect, he needs to misrepresent the verb's true meaning in order to make his central assertion appear sustainable.

He puzzles over the 'two-line thought' with which the speech ends. It would be 'possible', he concedes, to deliver it 'all on one breath'. But that would be to 'undervalue the thought', 'because if Lucilius said these two lines on one breath he would sound less caring'.[47] He moralizes: 'To convey to others how *much* we care we have to look

---

43 Block, *Speaking the Speech*, p. 25.
44 Block, *Speaking the Speech*, p. 10.
45 The relevant principle is neatly encapsulated in an exchange from Roger Gellert, *Quaint Honour: A Play in Three Acts* (London, 1958), pp. 53–4. A sixth-former is rehearsing a younger boy for a school production of *Richard III*. He objects to the latter's choice of stress in one speech: 'Grandam, one night, as we did sit at supper, / My uncle Rivers talk'd how I did *grow* / More than my brother – '. The schoolboy director explains: 'We've already *been* talking about how you grow more than your brother, so that's not the new point you want to make. We all know that Mummy and Granny have been talking about it. What York says is: "That's funny, because *Uncle Rivers* was talking about that the other night, and *Uncle Glocester* said something quite different." The Uncles are the new factor; they're what you've got to underline. Right?' The intelligent wish to focus the flow of new information here means, *pace* Block, removing the stress from the final syllable in the second line (on 'grow').
46 Block, *Speaking the Speech*, pp. 24-25.
47 Block, *Speaking the Speech*, p. 21.

after our words with care.' As a general acting principle, this is fair enough. But why should handling the words we speak on stage with apt care entail using only certain prescribed, tightly limited and repetitive spans of breath? This makes a performer's ability to communicate feeling with conviction entirely a function of his/her loyalty to an arbitrarily restricted choice of phrasal lengths, and decrees that a delivery of Lucilius' couplet on a single breath will always seem less 'caring' than one which includes a pause to breathe. I find this logic impenetrable.

Block concedes that his readers might wish to experiment with breathing the two lines as a single unit, but is confident what the result is likely to be: 'well, it would be possible, but you would probably feel that you were getting a little short of breath by the end of the second line'.[48] Who is this imagined 'you' Block is instructing? Certainly not a professional actor with a reasonable level of technical competence, if s/he is unable to breathe twenty syllables without becoming breathless. His insistence that Shakespearian verse resembles 'normal' speech generates this *reductio ad absurdum*, whereby performance's possibilities are bounded by the abilities of a speaker whose breath supply gives out so quickly.

It is worth pausing to remark how extraordinary this move is. It isolates Block from a core emphasis in contemporary actor-training – the aim to equip performers 'to be able to use their breathing systems creatively in order to meet the challenges of both characterization and performance'.[49] In other words, the player needs to develop resources sufficient to match the requirements of even the most demanding writing, rather than assuming that dialogue will be thoughtfully tailored to his/her likely technical limitations. As one conservatoire acting coach put it, 'Until the breath supports effectively, the artist can never be free',[50] while the director Declan Donnellan, in a comment especially apt to the subject in hand, has observed that 'When actors do not take in enough breath, they savage their text and butcher longer thoughts.'[51]

Block's presuppositions on this topic also look ahistorical. Early modern medicine, following classical precedent, prescribed vocal exercise as an indispensable aid in strengthening 'the body against a wide variety of disease', and treated as axiomatic the 'idea that lungs and thorax can be strengthened and expanded by use', with advantageous consequences for the individual's health.[52] Eloquent and moving vocal delivery was also a central objective of early modern school pedagogy, and a pupil's success in achieving that was underpinned by the importance of physical exercise – in the words of the schoolmaster Richard Mulcaster, 'a vehement, & a voluntarie stirring of ones body, which altereth the breathing, whose ende is to maintaine health, and to bring the bodie to a verie good habit'.[53] In any case, why assume that the actor's voice should never be under palpable strain? A recent interpretation of an extraordinary poem by George Herbert observes 'how insistently it forces the vocal performer almost to gasp for breath'.[54] What would rule out a dramatist occasionally aiming for a comparable effect in a dramatic situation which might logically demand such near-collapse from a character *in extremis*? Where, then, does the belief originate that the actor Shakespeare envisages always needs tidily to confine him-/herself to breathing-units of not more than ten syllables at a time?

---

[48] Block, *Speaking the Speech*, p. 22.
[49] David Carey, 'Transformation and the actor: the responsive breath', in *Breath in Action: The Art of Breath in Vocal and Holistic Practice*, ed. Jane Boston and Rena Cook (London and Philadelphia, 2009), pp. 185–98, p. 187.
[50] Jane Boston, 'Breathing the verse: an examination of breath in contemporary actor training', in *Breath in Action*, ed. Boston and Cook, pp. 199–214, p. 201.
[51] Declan Donnellan, *The Actor and the Target* (London, 2002), p. 156.
[52] Gretchen Finney, 'Vocal exercise in the sixteenth century related to theories of physiology and disease', *Bulletin of the History of Medicine* 42.5 (1968), 422–49, pp. 424 and 427.
[53] Richard Mulcaster, *Positions wherin those primitive circumstances be examined, which are necessarie for the training up of children, either for skill in their booke, or health in their bodie* (London, 1581), p. 53, sig. G3r.
[54] Clarissa Chenovik, 'Reading, sighing, and tuning in George Herbert's *Temple*, *Huntington Library Quarterly* 82.1 (2019), 155–74, p. 172.

Speaking the Speech provides no answer to that question. For Block, it is simply self-evident that each line-ending is designed for a catch-up breath, and that the passage from one line to another is to be marked by an additional pressure on the final stressed syllable of one line and the first stressed syllable of the next. We must, in effect, take his word for it. He thus imprisons the restless inventiveness of Shakespeare's experiments with the patterns blank verse can be made to yield within constraints which are entirely of his own decreeing. It is only logical that someone with this set of mind should relish marking up, in prescriptive detail, what he has decided are the required breathing-patterns for specific passages in his book (see, for instance, pp. 61–2) and he is famous for the 'coloured scripts' he busily circulates to the same effect in rehearsals.[55] We have come full circle back to those daily lists Leigh Lawson received throughout the RSC *Dream* rehearsals, which so untiringly enforced a self-validating regime of metrical correctness.

Block dates the birth of his method to a 1989 rehearsal in which he assisted Peter Hall. During it, Hall spoke of 'the importance of Shakespeare's line endings'.[56] From that moment of epiphany, Block has extrapolated a teaching practice which reflects, at numerous points, Hall's priorities, but also obeys imperatives Block has himself generated from the Hall model.[57] In expounding his creed, he otherwise invokes almost no authority beyond the one that another contributor to this sub-genre cites as the key qualification possessed by writers like Block: 'many years' experience with actors and with Shakespeare'.[58] This is clearly a significant resource to draw upon. Yet it remains concerning that, on the rare occasions when Block quotes others' expertise, the latter's testimony contradicts his most fundamental convictions.

We saw how crucial for him the belief is that a ten-syllable breathing length is the natural one for humans, and that pressing beyond that limit is likely to tax a player's voice uncomfortably and so make a character seem less 'caring', less authentic, in his/her possession of the emotions s/he expresses. He quotes two articles as shaping his thinking about 'the way we breathe'.[59] One of them starts from the established fact that humans possess remarkable power to modulate 'lung volume level' in order to vary the length of utterances,[60] while the other takes for granted humans' 'greatly enhanced breathing control as compared with that of non-human primates', which its authors describe as 'an important component of human speech'.[61] So both articles Block invokes in his support deny a central presupposition of his approach.

Citing these articles, however perfunctorily, is an unusual move for him. More normally, he lays out firm conclusions and seeks no external support or validation. As a result, he gives the impression of operating in a hermetically sealed environment, isolated from interacting with the thinking of others with relevant experience and expertise, whether from the world of theatre or of scholarship. This means that he fails to acknowledge, or engage with, work and testimony which would either complicate or deny the positions he espouses.

Scholars have mapped, for instance, the remarkable diversity of the variations on basic iambic

---

[55] Block, *Speaking the Speech*, p. xi.

[56] Block, *Speaking the Speech*, p. 2.

[57] I have analysed the problematic nature of Peter Hall's own writing on how to perform Shakespeare in Michael Cordner, '(Mis)advising Shakespeare's players', *Shakespeare Survey 66* (Cambridge, 2013), 110–28. Hall's own doctrines ultimately derive, in a somewhat intricate manner, from the teaching of the Cambridge academic George Rylands. I have examined his work and inheritance in Michael Cordner, 'George Rylands and Cambridge University Shakespeare', in *Shakespeare on the University Stage*, ed. Andrew Hartley (Cambridge, 2015), pp. 43–59.

[58] Donna Soto-Morettini, *Mastering the Shakespeare Audition: A Quick Guide to Performance Success* (London, 2016), p. ix.

[59] Block, *Speaking the Speech*, p. 342.

[60] Alison L. Winkworth, Pamela J. Davis, Roger D. Adams and Elizabeth Ellis, 'Breathing patterns during spontaneous speech', *Journal of Speech and Hearing Research* 38.1 (1995), 124–44.

[61] Ann MacLarnon and Gwen Hewitt, 'Increased breathing control: another factor in the evolution of human language', *Evolutionary Anthropology* 13.5 (2004), 181–97, p. 182.

pentameter patterning that Shakespeare deploys throughout his career. They have also demonstrated how the characteristic patterns of metrical stress he favours alter between different periods of that career, as does also the subtlety of the varied effects he derives from the same metrical manoeuvre in distinct dramatic contexts.[62] Russ McDonald has charted the extreme experimentalism of Shakespeare's late style, whereby 'Blank verse, usually a guarantor of order and regularity, is now aggressively irregular, encompassing long lines, chopped lines, unruly lines, enjambed lines, light or weak endings, frequent stops or shifts of direction, and other threats to lineal integrity.'[63] George T. Wright has mapped the ways in which that experimentalism often makes it difficult in performance 'to follow the meter line by line': 'It is hard enough for a textual editor to arrange the words in lines; for a listener in the theater to do so accurately or long is almost impossible.'[64] On that topic, one might also cite the testimony of perhaps the most intelligently self-analytical of great twentieth-century English Shakespearian actors, Michael Redgrave: 'I must confess that I would find it very hard to write out from memory the whole of the part of Prospero [a role Redgrave had played to critical acclaim] and find that I had shaped it, line for line, clearly.'[65] Wright, McDonald and Redgrave all assume that this loosening of blank verse patterning is not inadvertent, but deliberate, and creates a radically innovative vocal aesthetic, with massive consequences for the play's interpreters, whether on stage or in the study. All of this erodes confidence in any advice which insists that, in every Shakespeare play, a special emphasis should invariably be placed on the first and final stressed syllables in a verse line.

There is no imperative that requires Block to agree with any or all of these viewpoints. But simply ignoring their testimony, as if it were of no weight, has to be problematic. Block's 'one size fits all' insistence that the same repetitive method of articulation applies unvaryingly to the language of Posthumus and of Polixenes as to that of Julia and Adriana comes to look like another instance of these books' default tendency to enforce headline generalizations, which constrain Shakespeare's restless adventurousness within neat formulae which can be readily taught.

Hunter prefaces her book with a series of questions which she reports students often ask her, one of which is 'When do I breathe?'.[66] Her reply is: 'the structure of the verse tells you where to breathe'.[67] There is an odd circularity to this exchange. The question itself presupposes that actors should look to an expert like Hunter for guidance on their choice of breathing-patterns in handling early modern verse, and that a conclusively authoritative answer can be hoped for from the latter, which will soothe a performer's doubts and fears. The trainee actors are accordingly operating within a culturally determined set of expectations which lead them to assume that the issue is naturally to be posed in these terms. In effect, this way of asking the question rules out the possibility that basic decisions about how to phrase verse dialogue are best trusted to the agency of the individual interpreter, and that different actors can legitimately, persuasively and powerfully solve them in different ways, reflecting the local nuancing of the interpretation they are devising. To a player of Eileen Atkins's generation, as we have seen, such presuppositions make little or no sense. But a pedagogical transformation has, in the interim, created a cadre of specialists, whose professional status is based on their claim to possess the knowledge to answer that enquiry with crisply defined legislative responses.

[62] See, for example, among many others, Marina Tarlinskaja, 'Evolution of Shakespeare's metrical style', *Poetics* 12.6 (1983), 576–87.

[63] Russ McDonald, '"You speak a language that I understand not": listening to the last plays', in *The Cambridge Companion to Shakespeare's Last Plays*, ed. Catherine Alexander (Cambridge, 2009), pp. 91–112, p. 92.

[64] George T. Wright, *Hearing the Measures: Shakespearean and Other Inflections* (Madison, WI, 2001), p. 238.

[65] Michael Redgrave, *Mask or Face: Reflections in an Actor's Mirror* (London, 1958), p. 86.

[66] Hunter, *Cracking Shakespeare*, p. xi.

[67] Hunter, *Cracking Shakespeare*, p. 4.

Meeting the demands she has set for herself often ensnares Hunter in difficulties. Take, for instance, this statement of hers: 'The technical term for a punctuation mark in the middle of a line that signals a change of thought is a **caesura**' (emphasis in the original).[68] Contrast the *OED*'s definition of a 'caesura': 'In English prosody: a pause or breathing-place about the middle of a metrical line, generally indicated by a pause in the sense.'[69] There is no mention of a 'punctuation mark' here. Hunter's mis-understanding is a characteristic one, because her instinct is to seek to locate a visible sign in the printed text which will give the actor an anchor to stabilise their work. On the basis of this miscalculation, she erects a further debatable conclusion, which she claims applies to every line divided by a caesura (as she defines that term): '**Just as a change in the iambic dictates an upset in the emotions, the half-lines within the verse-structure dictate an upset in your thought patterns; it gives you more to act**' (bold as in original).[70] Another unsustainable totalizing claim has been generated. This one is especially odd, because Hunter is perfectly capable of acknowledging elsewhere that punctuation differs, in unpredictable ways, between editions.[71] Despite that, however, in passages like this, it is suddenly accorded an absolute authority she has already conceded it cannot possess. The wish that the text will lay down the law authoritatively runs very deep here and lures Hunter into overt self-contradiction.

Though their handling of the text is constantly debatable in the ways I have demonstrated, there is something strangely bookish about the approach of these performance coaches, proud though they are to proclaim their plentiful experience in professional theatre. Their practice seems designed to deny the thought that written or printed scripts 'massively underdetermine their performances', that a 'gap between "text" and performance' is 'a *desired*, *intended* and logically *required* ontological fact' (emphasis in original), and that the interpretative work which generates performance consequences from scripts happens 'within the interstices of notation'.[72]

The quotations in the preceding sentence are cited in a musicological essay on the intricate relationship between score and performance which I have found provocative in thinking about the process from script to performance in theatre. One concern that the 'quest for historically authentic performances' in classical music has raised is that it might place / has placed 'the musicologist in the combined role of legislator and law enforcement officer', with inhibiting and deleterious consequences for the resulting performances.[73] A parallel worry is raised by the pedagogical literature I have been interrogating. Attempting to generate rules, and prohibitions, about allegedly correct and incorrect, legal and illicit, delivery from the imputed significance of punctuation and lineation looks to me similarly dangerous in its likely deadening consequences for the players whose practice it seeks to influence. Here one of the greatest twentieth-century English actors, Sir Ralph Richardson, has a key distinction to propose between playing a musical score and performing in a play: 'In music, the punctuation is absolutely strict, the bars and the rests are absolutely defined. But our punctuation cannot be quite strict, because we have to relate it to the audience. In other words, we are continually changing the score.'[74] Block and Hunter, when at their most legislative, risk denying that crucial freedom to the performers they seek to instruct.

Contributing to a fascinating debate about the future of oral history, Raphael Samuel argued that 'serious distortion arises when the spoken word is boxed into the categories of written prose'. He continued: 'The imposition of grammatical forms, when it is attempted, creates its own rhythms and

---

[68] Hunter, *Cracking Shakespeare*, p. 4.

[69] 'caesura, n.', *OED Online*, Oxford University Press, December 2019, www.oed.com/view/Entry/26025.

[70] Hunter, *Cracking Shakespeare*, p. 44.

[71] See, for instance, Hunter, *Cracking Shakespeare*, pp. xii–xiii.

[72] The quotations (by three different musicologists) in this sentence derive from: Nicholas Cook, 'Between process and product: music and/as performance', *Music Theory Online* 7.2 (2001), [11].

[73] Cook, 'Between process and product', [4].

[74] Kenneth Tynan, *Profiles*, ed. Kathleen Tynan and Ernie Eblan (London, 1989), p. 290.

cadences, and they have little in common with those of the human tongue.'[75] Alessandro Portelli took up the same theme:

writing reduces language to segmentary traits only – letters, syllables, words, phrases. But language is composed of another set of traits, which cannot be reduced within a single segment, but are also bearers of meaning. For instance, it has been shown that the tonal range, volume range, and rhythm of popular speech carry many class connotations which are not reproducible in writing (unless it be, inadequately and partially, in the form of musical notation).[76]

He also pointed out: 'The same statement may have quite contradictory meanings, according to the speaker's intonation, which cannot be detected in the transcript but can only be described, approximately.' He made a parallel observation about pauses: 'The exact length and position of the pause has an important function in the understanding of the meaning of speech: regular grammatical pauses tend to organise what is said around a basically expository and referential pattern, whereas pauses of irregular length and position accentuate the emotional content.' Anne Karpf, participating in the same discussion, instanced her own experience with the recorded testimony of a woman talking 'about her Chilean husband who "disappeared"'.[77] In transcript, what she said read 'somewhat generically'. It was only when Karpf subsequently listened to the original recording that the woman's words were 'transformed through the voice into ... an anguished, highly *embodied* attempt to make sense of senseless acts' (emphasis in original). With that came a further revelation: 'you also became aware of a certain ambiguity: that the torture she refers to is that which was inflicted upon her husband but is also, in some sense, that which has been inflicted upon her'. As Karpf records, it was only this experience that allowed her to understand 'properly that her voice was expressing this double agony'.

Here the interplay is between words actually spoken and the (inevitably fallible) attempt to convey them through transcription. With a script, the movement is in the opposite direction; but the glory of performance at its height is that it can render as complex an experience of human emotion and experience as Karpf encountered in listening to the voice of Mercedes Rojas.[78] To achieve that, however, performers have to employ, with maximal flair and resourcefulness, a host of resources that notation on the page lacks the signs to convey: tone, timbre, volume, pitch, inflection, relative tempi, length and nature of pauses (from the slightest hesitations to significant silences), agogic elongations of syllabic duration – and apt choices of phrasal lengths. Hemming all this in through insistence on strict fidelity to a narrow set of alleged rules is ultimately an act of creative self-mutilation.

Shakespeare was shaped by an educational culture which placed at its centre the cultivation of 'the voice and gesture appropriate to persuasive speech' and inculcated 'a form of embodied, non-linguistic expression traced in Roman oratory and performed in Renaissance school halls'.[79] It was supremely alert to the varieties of ways in which the voice could be modulated, and re-calibrated, to convey contrasting responses and endeavours. A 1588 rhetorical handbook, for instance, noted that, to express 'anguish and griefe of mind without compassion; demanded a hollow voyce fetcht from

[75] Raphael Samuel, 'Perils of the transcript', *Oral History* 1.2 (1972), 19–22, p. 19.

[76] Alessandro Portelli, 'The peculiarities of oral history', *History Workshop* 12 (1981), 96–107, p. 98.

[77] Anne Karpf, 'The human voice and the texture of experience', *Oral History* 42.2 (2014), 50–5, p. 52.

[78] This is not to imply that the delivery of Shakespearian verse ought to emulate the rhythms and tonal colouration of the speaking voices of interviewees for oral history investigations. Stage speech always simplifies and codifies the patterns of real-life conversation. But it does need to be animated and varied in enunciation, rhythm, tempo and inflection, as well as responsive to the intricacy of the experiences communicated and the situations enacted. To do that, it has to employ vocal resources that no written or printed text can adequately represent.

[79] John Wesley, 'Rhetorical delivery for Renaissance English: voice, gesture, emotion, and the sixteenth-century vernacular turn', *Renaissance Quarterly* 68.4 (2015), 1265–96, pp. 1265–6.

the bottome of the throate, groaning', whereas anger was 'shrill, sharpe, quick, short'.[80]

The pedagogical scrutiny of each pupil's achievements could be relentless and demanding, but the system did open up space for individual improvisation. It remembered that 'Aristotle and Cicero are explicit that delivery cannot be reduced to a set of written rules', and therefore accepted that 'Delivery, because of its dependence on performance, demands a lacuna in the written form.'[81] Persuasion, in any case, was a socially specific process and always needed to be adjusted to changing, potentially volatile, circumstances. Consequently, seeking to preset minutely the length and patterning, for example, of particular phrasings could only be counter-productive. This unintentionally provided the perfect training ground for students who might later become actors, and who would, therefore, have to face the daily oscillations of audience response to which the performer, as Ralph Richardson instructs us, needs always to be alert and responsive.

However fallible their practice may be, writers such as Block and Hunter do address live concerns I have myself confronted in the rehearsal room. Verse is no longer the default medium of drama, and performers often question its logics and benefits at a very fundamental level. At such moments, I have occasionally been asked by professional actors what Shakespearian scholarship can offer which might help them. The trigger has always been their desire to hear better, and react more vividly to, the crafting of the writing in the scene before us. Technically alert actors can easily detect that the verse of, say, *Julius Caesar* is, in key aspects, radically unlike the verse of *Measure for Measure*, though the two plays were written within a few years of each other. Why so, they ask? What are the implications of those striking differences for the performances they might give, and the productions they are working to create?

It is not just a question that Shakespeare's plays raise. The director Simon Usher throws down the gauntlet in a couple of sentences: 'Know the difference, from an actor's point of view, between Shakespeare and Middleton, or Webster and Marston. Each makes a different and unique demand on an actor.'[82] There is, however, very little scholarly work that seeks to address that crucial issue substantively. I have directed productions of Middleton's *A Mad World, My Masters* and Marston's *The Dutch Courtesan* within a couple of years of each other.[83] Two city comedies, and also both of them trickster plays, both featuring a courtesan as a pivotal figure, and written for performance by boys' companies, one hard on the heels of the other – but, stylistically, so radically diverse. The manner in which characters verbally engage with each other, play off each other, interrogate, offend, deceive, woo and seduce one another proved so distinct that it came to seem almost as if we were working with two competing models of human interaction. Pursuing the analytical implications of that experience for these two plays, and for those who perform them, is work for another article and another day. But, in the rehearsal room, we had to do our best to listen attentively to the cues each script offers and seek to generate fully realized productions responsive to the contrasting distinctiveness of the writing the two playwrights had bequeathed to us.

Actors' attentiveness to such matters has led a couple of them to ask me why editions of early modern plays can be luxuriantly detailed about, say, their bibliographical histories and critical traditions, but remain completely silent about the specific properties of the verse in the play upon which they have expended so much dedicated effort. These actors are grateful for all the care that has been taken to unpack linguistic intricacies and unfamiliar idioms, and to contextualize cultural preconceptions, implicit in the action, which they might not otherwise have comprehended.

---

[80] Abraham Fraunce, *The Arcadian Rhetorike*, ed. Ethel Seaton (Oxford, 1950), p. 116 and p. 113.

[81] Wesley, 'Rhetorical delivery', pp. 1283 and 1282.

[82] Simon Usher, *Directing: A Miscellany* (London, 2014), p. 10.

[83] Films of the two productions, along with my productions of Shirley's *Hyde Park*, Vanbrugh's *The Provoked Wife* and Dryden's *Amphitryon*, plus other related material, can be viewed at www.earlymoderntheatre.co.uk.

But, since their own work begins in seeking to make the given words rise to new life from the page, they would welcome help with that too.

Vocalizing the verse of, say, *Coriolanus* poses a different set of problems – but also opportunities – from vocalizing the verse of *The Comedy of Errors*. Musicologists take it as a given that it is part of their subject's mission to offer concrete observations on how the demands Wagner, for instance, places on the singing voice change between *Rienzi* and *Parsifal*. Shakespeare was equally, though in a different way, an artist of the voice, working in a culture which trained some at least of his spectators in a sophisticated connoisseurship of vocal prowess, versatility and persuasiveness. From one perspective, Hunter and Block have moved to fill a space that Shakespearian scholarship has largely left vacant. The fact that, in the event, their practice is so accident-prone challenges others to attempt to do better.

'WHAT COUNTRY, FRIENDS, IS THIS?': TIM SUPPLE'S *TWELFTH NIGHT* REVISITED

PETER J. SMITH

Trevor Nunn's 1996 film version of *Twelfth Night* is the play's best-known and most popular cinematic incarnation.[1] It was warmly received by journalists and academics alike: Mick La Salle writes, 'Nunn conceives the play in ... wistful terms. There's an ever-present sense of loss, of time passing, of beautiful moments that can't be held and dreams that can't be realized', while Peter Holland shares this sense of contented sorrow, pronouncing that the film 'is nearly as satisfyingly unsatisfying as the play could demand, more than adequately alive to the text's awareness of the fragility and vulnerability of the possibilities of happiness'.[2] Philippa Sheppard probably overstates her case when she writes, 'In his subtle and intelligent screen adaptation of *Twelfth Night*, English director Trevor Nunn has improved on Shakespeare's original', but her conclusion is more measured: 'Trevor Nunn's *Twelfth Night* is evidence that it is possible to make Shakespeare's plays truly filmic without losing what is Shakespearean about them.'[3]

In a documentary to accompany his 2003 Channel 4 television version of *Twelfth Night*, Tim Supple is similarly anachronistically adamant about the suitability of the film medium to the works of Shakespeare: 'The truth is that this film would not have been made if Shakespeare was around because he'd have made it himself.'[4] Supple's version offers a striking contrast to that of Nunn. Indeed, one might assume that, in his parodying of Nunn's film at various points, Supple was explicitly 'writing back' to the earlier version. However, in an email to me of 4 June 2018, Supple writes: 'to be very honest I can't remember if I saw

[Nunn's] film before I started work on [my] film or during or after!'[5] This he reiterates in a subsequent email (17 June 2018): 'there is categorically zero intended reference'.[6] But, in spite of Supple's insistence on a lack of deliberate allusion, he is fully prepared to allow a critical engagement with the films as a contrasting pair: 'it is entirely valid to read them together, and for a critical eye to see one as arising from some oppositional thinking to the other on broad and subliminal, cultural and artistic terms' (TS2).

Although made only seven years later, Supple's version feels distant from Nunn's film – historically,

1 For an analysis of Nunn's film and especially its maritime imagery, see Peter J. Smith, 'Goodbye wave: Trevor Nunn's *Twelfth Night* – a maritime valediction', *Shakespeare* 14.4 (2019), 390–8.

2 Mick La Salle, 'Film benders genders but not Shakespeare: Nunn's wistful version of *Twelfth Night*', *San Francisco Chronicle*, 8 November 1996; Peter Holland, 'The Dark pleasures of Trevor Nunn's *Twelfth Night*', *Shakespeare: A Magazine for Teachers and Enthusiasts* 1.3 (1997): www.shakespearemag.com/spring97/12night.asp.

3 Philippa Sheppard, *Devouring Time: Nostalgia in Contemporary Shakespearean Screen Adaptations* (Montreal, 2017), pp. 303 and 319.

4 '21st century bard: the making of *Twelfth Night*', *Twelfth Night*, dir. Tim Supple, with Chiwetel Ejiofor, Michael Maloney, Parminder Nagra. Projector Productions, 2003.

5 Email to the author, 4 June 2018. All subsequent references to this email will be referenced in the text as 'TS1'. I am extremely grateful to Tim Supple for his assistance with the writing of this article, as well as his thoughtful correspondence.

6 Email to the author, 17 June 2018. All subsequent references to this email will be referenced in the text as 'TS2'.

culturally and generically. If Nunn's is an elegiac Edwardian comedy that ends happily as the lovers, in the company of Olivia's full household, celebrate their double wedding by dancing in the gallery of an aristocratic mansion, Supple's is a contemporary mixture of thriller and fantasy that ends with Olivia's tears and an uncertain melancholy. Whereas Nunn had Andrew and Cesario duel in the manner of a knock-about comedy, with their swords getting stuck in apple baskets and Andrew being firmly kneed in the crotch, Supple's version of the scene has Andrew and Cesario slashing dangerously at each other's faces with carving knives whilst Toby and Fabian savagely goad them on – as Supple's co-screenplay writer, Andrew Bannerman, puts it, 'the duel does have to have an edge of danger about it'.[7] Whereas Nunn prefixes the box-tree scene with Malvolio comically checking his toupée against his reflection in the garden fountain and haughtily correcting the sundial according to his pocket watch, while the conspirators huddle behind a hedge, Supple prefixes his with Fabian and Maria rigging up a closed-circuit television camera and microphone: Nunn traditionally uses eavesdropping, Supple mordantly uses surveillance. Whereas Nunn's Andrew enters with a grazed head and Toby with a tiny cut over one eye, Supple has Andrew's and Toby's shirts covered in blood from gaping head wounds. Whereas Nunn incarcerates Malvolio in a coal house which is filthy and cold, Supple has his Malvolio hooded in a wine cellar, his hands bound to wine racks and cut by the smashed glass resulting from his enraged struggle. Whereas Nunn has Antonio arrested by elegantly uniformed, cutlass-wielding cavalry, Supple has his apprehended violently by two plain-clothes, secret-service men, one of whom holds a hand-gun menacingly to Antonio's temple in the style of a Tarantino hit-man. As we hear of the death of Olivia's brother, there is a sudden flash of an Inspector Morse-style Jaguar car buckled from a road accident, and as Sebastian tells Antonio of his parentage – 'My father was that Sebastian of Messaline whom I know you have heard of' (2.1.15–16) – we cut to a flash of a much-decorated military general, who looks not unlike Augusto Pinochet, followed rapidly by a black-and-white news photo of the same man lying on the street with blood pouring from his head, the victim of a political assassination. 'Violence', observes Alfredo Michel Modenessi, is 'the keynote to Supple's reading of *Twelfth Night*'.[8] But what Modenessi suggests is Supple's gloss on the play, Supple himself urges is part of its essence: '*Twelfth Night* is a very violent play and all the more so for the repression and restraint of that violence ... the violence of frustrated desire, the extreme condition of not getting what, or doing, or living as, you really want and moreover having to repress that thing you really want within the restraints of your social condition' (TS2).

When Supple directed *Twelfth Night* on stage at the Young Vic in 1998, the critical consensus seemed to be that the style of the piece was earnest, even grave. Michael Billington noted the production's 'refusal to bang home the comedy'.[9] David Benedict described how Sandy McDade, who played Maria, 'ditches the usual bawdy Elizabethan-style Joan Sims [in favour of a] quick and lean [persona]', while Andy Williams's Aguecheek is 'Far from the traditional dandy'.[10] Robert Smallwood criticized the production as underselling the play's comic dimensions: 'The mood ... was monotonously gloomy. There is, of course, a certain melancholy wistfulness about *Twelfth Night*, but there is hope too, even joy, and these were lost in the general dourness.'[11] Similarly, for Maurice Hindle, Supple's Channel 4 film is marred by 'an inappropriate seriousness',

---

[7] '21st century bard'.

[8] Alfredo Michel Modenessi, '"This uncivil and unjust extent against thy peace": Tim Supple's *Twelfth Night, or, what violence will*', *Shakespeare Survey 61* (Cambridge, 2008), 91–103, p. 97.

[9] Michael Billington, 'Twelfth Night', *The Guardian*, 4 June 1998.

[10] David Benedict, 'Theatre: Dusty Heat and Magic', *The Independent*, 15 June 1998.

[11] Robert Smallwood, 'Shakespeare performances in England, 1998', *Shakespeare Survey 52* (Cambridge, 1999), 229–53, p. 235.

and, he goes on, 'to perform *Twelfth Night* as earn-estly as this is to do it too much violence'.[12] Clearly, Supple has very different ideas about *Twelfth Night* from those of Nunn (and, we might add, Smallwood and Hindle), since both his stage and film versions dwell on the play's 'darker pur-pose' (*King Lear*, 1.1.36). While the objections of Smallwood and Hindle raise interesting questions about the process of reviewing, since each is jud-ging the stage or film versions according to his own reading of Shakespeare's play, rather than evaluat-ing the production or movie in terms of its own success or failure, the fact that they both identify Supple's attitude towards Shakespeare's play as cheerless or sombre suggests that Supple's agenda is more sceptical, or possibly more urgent, than that of Nunn. In fact, Supple's film raises awkward political questions about racism, multiculturalism and social class, and its contemporary setting pre-cludes the comfort of historical distance which Nunn's Edwardian *mise en scène* ensured. As Supple puts it, the point 'of the film was to translate everything into convincing contemporary form' (TS2).

Instead of the English Heritage feel of Nunn's cinematic locations, Supple thrusts us into a night-time *coup d'état*. The film's titles roll as the sound of a slamming car door, the smashing of glass and the muffled shouts of an invasive guerrilla manoeuvre are heard. Sebastian (played by Ronny Jhutti) is seen shaking awake his twin sister, Viola (Parminder Nagra). He is holding a hand-gun and gestures for her to keep quiet. As she gets up, he peeps outside from behind a shutter to see a group of soldiers dragging their mother away. She looks back pitifully over her shoulder but she is heavily outnumbered and Sebastian is unable to help her. As she leaves the frame, a soldier throws a burning match onto a puddle of petrol and torches the house. Sebastian and Viola crouch on the window-sill of the room and disappear into a star-lit sky. This sequence is intercut with an extreme close-up of Orsino (Chiwetel Ejiofor) luxuriating in the heartfelt intensity of a soprano's private perfor-mance (Claire Wild). The contrast between the life-threatening situation of the twins, on the one

hand, and the Duke wallowing in his own frustra-tion, on the other, could not be more pointed.

We then cut to the hold of a transport ship as Sebastian, Viola and their relatives are stowed away as illegal immigrants. A tense Antonio (Andrew Kazamia) enters and receives payment for their transport and leaves them locked in the hold. The sounds of a gathering storm, wind and waves, menace over the churning engine in the back-ground and, to the groans of the ship disintegrat-ing, the screen whites out. As Supple remarked, 'We didn't film the shipwreck; we wanted to give the idea of contemporary catastrophe.'[13] Not only did this have an obvious financial advantage (as producer Rachel Gesua points out in the accom-panying documentary), but it provides an original take on the traditional opening of the tempest.[14] Moreover, in replacing the threatening elements of the storm and the drowning sequence of Nunn's version with the huddled vulnerability of a pathetic group of newly dispossessed asylum-seekers, Supple has emphasized an immediately pressing man-made threat of political usurpation. The potency of the natural elements upon which Nunn's opening sequence meditates is here replaced by the destructiveness of a corrupt social system. This is intensified when we see the rescued Viola on board a trawler offer the Sea Captain (Vic Tablian) several of her bangles: 'there's gold' (1.2.16). Her beautiful sari, now tattered and wet, as well as her jewellery, suggest she was once poli-tically and financially powerful. In this, we see Supple's stated priority: to make a film 'that fully updated [Shakespeare's play] and that would be most alive and most vivid'.[15]

Remarkably, a film made in 2003 has anticipated the migrant crises of today (which have risen to catastrophic levels in the aftermath of the Syria conflict), the rise of the populist Right, Brexit and the emergence of political isolationism typified

---

[12] Maurice Hindle, *Studying Shakespeare on Film* (Basingstoke, 2007), p. 241.
[13] '21st century bard'.
[14] The film was shot in four weeks on a budget of £870,000.
[15] '21st century bard'.

by Trump's 'America first' policy. When asked about this, Supple responded, 'Shakespeare constantly gives exile a firm, harsh political context and started as he meant to go on in *Comedy of Errors. The Tempest, Twelfth Night, As You Like It* – all these exiles are men and women forced by revolution or war to flee.' Of central concern to our understanding of Supple's *Twelfth Night*, however, is his elaboration, '*Twelfth Night* is ... acutely about England ... Viola is a refugee to England' (TS2).

The importance of making the work up to date was emphasized by Bannerman, who eschewed the valedictory tone of Nunn's film (though without mentioning it, explicitly), remarking, 'You couldn't do it with a whole load of people prancing about in a pretty park with box trees and doublet and hose; it just wasn't going to work like that.... I felt that we could actually translate it into contemporary terms.'[16] While Smallwood and Hindle regard this updating as a 'violence' upon the play, Paul Edmondson defends it: 'This uncompromisingly modern and multi-cultural interpretation is full of clever interpretative choices, which are sufficiently integrated to avoid becoming mere conceits.'[17] Stephanie Merritt concurs with this, calling the device of casting the twins as fleeing asylum-seekers 'a modernising touch which doesn't feel at all forced'.[18] Modenessi reads the violence of Supple's version as a symptom of unresolved cultural and racial tensions: 'Conflict and violence abound in Illyria, and a good part of this may reflect on the stark ethnic and social contrasts therein.'[19] As we will see, the ending of Supple's film is less assured by the mixed marriages of the two couples than is the conclusion of Nunn's version with its homogeneously 'white' weddings.[20]

Clearly, there is some critical disagreement over whether Supple's reading is in harmony with the play, but the one thing all the critics agree upon is the film's pronounced multiculturalism. In fact, this was a deliberate objective of Rachel Gesua: 'We'd all known from the very beginning that we wanted it to be a multi-cultural, multi-racial cast that reflected the Britain that we all live in today and would make it more accessible to people who think of Shakespeare as something for white,

middle-class, middle-aged audiences.'[21] In the light of this stated intention, the choice of Supple to direct was obvious. Supple has a track-record of working on projects that reflect contemporary multicultural concerns. In 1999, he adapted and directed Salman Rushdie's *Haroun and the Sea of Stories* for the National Theatre, as well as *Midnight's Children* for the RSC in 2002 (which starred Zubin Varla who also plays Feste in *Twelfth Night*). His 2000 production of *Romeo and Juliet* at the National (which featured Chiwetel Ejiofor as Romeo, who is the film's Orsino) was set 'in an apartheid state; this Verona was segregated on racial grounds with the Montagues cast as black actors and the Capulets as white'.[22] Charles Spencer opined that this device was trivial – 'It's been glibly colour-coded so that the Capulets are a white family, the Montagues are black, and Mercutio and Friar Laurence are Irish' – but my own review maintained that this casting raised important social questions: 'the racial divide only served to intensify an already volatile Verona and while the device could so easily have been a lazy shorthand for the clans' internecine politics, Supple ensured that it was merely an additional source of friction rather than its only cause'.[23]

---

[16] '21st century bard'.

[17] Paul Edmondson, *Twelfth Night*, The Shakespeare Handbooks (Basingstoke, 2005), p. 63.

[18] Stephanie Merritt, *The Observer*, 4 May 2003.

[19] Modenessi, 'Supple's *Twelfth Night*', p. 99.

[20] 'About multi-cultural casting ... this is constantly evolving for me and has subsequently (since India 2005) developed into what I would call international casting or casting beyond culture.... If we are gazing through the lens of the RSC, and more recently Globe, traditions; only through the habits of British theatre; only through the experiences of single cultures then our understanding will be limited also.... For me, mixing it up is the core project ... mixing it up for me, the artists and the audiences. What we lose is context, what we gain is depth and breadth and richness' (TS1).

[21] '21st century bard'.

[22] Peter J. Smith, 'Review of *Romeo and Juliet*, directed by Tim Supple', *Cahiers Elisabéthains* 59 (2001), 96–8, p. 96.

[23] Charles Spencer, 'Romeo and Juliet', *The Daily Telegraph*, 5 October 2000; Smith, 'Review of *Romeo and Juliet*, directed by Tim Supple', p. 97.

Supple contributed to the RSC's Complete Works Festival. His 'Indian' *Dream* (as it became known) used a company from across the Indian subcontinent and was performed in no fewer than seven languages (Tamil, Malayalam, Sinhalese, Hindi, Bengali, Marathi and English). When it played in the Swan in June 2006, the theatre was transformed 'into something between a temple, a playground and a circus ring', and produced what Michael Dobson considered to be 'an intelligent, original and cogent reading of the play'.[24] For Elinor Parsons, the production's significance was specifically in its blending of different cultures and customs: 'The project took over two years to evolve. It pushed at the boundaries of conventional actor/audience relationships, integrating English theatrical culture with Indian and Sri Lankan performance traditions.'[25]

Supple's proven strength in multicultural work means that this aspect of his *Twelfth Night* is no mere accessory, but essential to the film's vision. As Bannerman put it:

This is where I think the production company have done so well with this production. It is the most multi-cultural *Twelfth Night* that I have ever seen and I think that that does bring a very particular flavour to a play which is, in a sense, all about identity and expression. . . . Sebastian and Viola are shown in the way that they assimilate themselves to the society that they come to and also the values that they themselves bring to that society and I think that's an interesting point for our multi-cultural society today.[26]

Identity and expression, for Bannerman, are seen to go hand in hand. As the twins are reunited, they address each other in their native Hindi, and their mother tongue both separates them from Orsino and Olivia as well as binding the two of them together. Both in the East End café, where Antonio and Sebastian meet, as well as in the shots of Brick Lane's exotic market stalls, there is a pronounced sense of cultural and linguistic hybridity. Kendra Preston Leonard registers the play's far-fetched narrative features as being similar to those of contemporary Asian cinema: 'The play itself . . . has many qualities that dovetail well with the Bollywood film genre, including the use of melodramatic story lines mixing tragedy with comedy, the separation and reunion of siblings, love triangles or forbidden romances, and convenient coincidences'.[27]

Fittingly for one of Shakespeare's most musical plays, the film's score is an amalgam of various musical traditions. Of Nitin Sawhney's percussive music, Supple comments:

I think music in this film provides an inner temperament. The fusion of traditional Indian and Western and African musics – it's a culture that characters in *Twelfth Night* share. Music is very important to the emotion of contemporary existence. What the music in the film does is link the collision of cultures; the music interlaces itself with what the characters do and say to provide the emotional inner score.[28]

What Supple identifies as 'the collision of cultures' can be seen in the co-existence of the soprano's

---

[24] Michael Dobson, 'Shakespeare performances in England, 2006', *Shakespeare Survey 60* (Cambridge, 2007), 284–319, pp. 301 and 302. Jonathan Bate's reaction to the production, if a little overawed, is, nonetheless, not unique: 'On leaving *Dream* that warm June night, I stood on Waterside with a group of seasoned Stratford playgoers. For some moments, we were unable to speak. I then said: "That is the most magical night I have ever spent in a theatre." Everyone agreed. Several people present had seen Peter Brook's 1970 production, habitually cited as the greatest show in RSC history. They all said that this was its equal, probably its better': 'Introducing the Complete Works Festival', *Cahiers Elisabéthains: Special Issue*, ed. Peter J. Smith and Janice Valls-Russell (2007), 3–6, p. 4.

[25] Elinor Parsons, 'Review of *A Midsummer Night's Dream*, directed by Tim Supple', *Cahiers Elisabéthains: Special Issue*, ed. Peter J. Smith and Janice Valls-Russell (2007), 38–9, p. 38.

[26] '21st century bard'.

[27] Kendra Preston Leonard, 'The sounds of India in Supple's *Twelfth Night*', in *Bollywood Shakespeares*, ed. Craig Dionne and Parmita Kapadia (New York and Basingstoke, 2014), pp. 147–64, p. 148. It seems nothing could have been further from Supple's own imagination: 'I had not a jot of thinking about Bollywood, I knew very little about Bollywood then and what I did know I had little interest in. I can honestly say that there was zero reference to Bollywood movies in the whole process!' (TS2).

[28] '21st century bard'.

classical voice, Feste's folk-song rendering on acoustic guitar of 'O Mistress Mine', as well as the electronic techno of 'Hold Thy Peace' with Toby's thrash electric guitar sound and Andrew's febrile percussion. At one point, Olivia is animated by a vision of her brother's ghost playing a jaunty piano melody. But what Supple calls 'fusion' is the basis of the film's predominantly Bhangra style of accompaniment, so that, as much aurally as visually, this world of the film is thoroughly mixed, while English and Asian influences are most conspicuous.

Of course, the Anglo-Indian experience is the topic of such postcolonial texts as *Midnight's Children* and *Haroun*, both of which, as we have already seen, Supple has adapted. Rushdie's novels are possibly the most conspicuous examples of 'magical realism', and when Billington reviewed Supple's stage version of *Twelfth Night*, he noted that 'Supple succeeds in creating an Illyria filled with madness and magic realism.'[29] Supple's film version also demonstrates a postmodern self-consciousness that is typical of Rushdie's fiction: a willingness to deploy self-conscious narrative strategies, to complicate the linearity of plot and radically to challenge the univocality of canonical authority (in Rushdie's case, notoriously, The Koran; in Supple's, Shakespeare). Perhaps most pointedly postmodern is the film's hyperreality. Gavin Finney, the film's cinematographer, talks about the virtues of the hand-held camera used to shoot the market scenes: 'Tim did want a gritty, hyperreal, pushed look.'[30] This technique produces a reality-TV style and intensifies what Susanne Greenhalgh and Robert Shaughnessy identify as the film's proclivity to 'introduce a contradictory set of markers, apparently specific and intensely topical but actually serving to cast adrift any concrete sense of time and place'.[31] Supple suggests that this is a quality for which he deliberately strove: 'a heightened kind of beauty or intensity that would not pretend that you really were in that place' and, again, 'You mustn't pin him [Shakespeare] down in too literal a space.'[32] More recently, Supple has reconsidered the location of his film's setting in a way that stresses both

its mythical elusiveness and its English topicality: 'Shakespeare invents a place with a name that obviously calls to mind both illusion and delirium and this is immediately not anywhere. At the same time it feels exactly like England. Bang on' (TS2).

As defined by Andrew Bennett and Nicholas Royle, the hyperreal is that 'in which reality is fabricated by technology'.[33] Along with the hand-held camera, the other obvious technological device that the film employs in order to achieve this sense of hyperreality is bluescreen. As we have noted above, when the twins bail out of their burning house, they fade into a star-filled sky which resembles something out of a Disney fairy tale (compare Rushdie again). The reunion of the twins, and Orsino comforting the weeping Olivia, take place against a similar sky while, throughout, Orsino's court is pictured against a magnificent dawn panorama complete with diffuse sun and gentle surf. Supple describes how 'bluescreening was a practical way of expanding the vision of the film – a kind of poetry so that there would be a heightened kind of feeling to the skies that you saw'.[34]

In contrast to Orsino's open-plan and sparsely furnished salon, with its enormous rectilinear opening onto magnificent swathes of sky, Olivia's house is a place of dark corners. As in Nunn's film, there is a Miss Havisham-like dread of brightness. As Tom Pye, the production designer of Supple's version put it, 'If Orsino's is a place of light, Olivia's is a place of total darkness.'[35] In Olivia's house, there are three principal interior spaces: the chapel, the basement and the porter's lodge. The latter,

---

[29] Michael Billington, *The Guardian*, 4 June 1998.

[30] '21st century bard'.

[31] Susanne Greenhalgh and Robert Shaughnessy, 'Our Shakespeares: British television and the strains of multiculturalism', in *Screening Shakespeare in the Twenty-First Century*, ed. Mark Thornton Burnett and Ramona Wray (Edinburgh, 2006), 90–112, p. 103.

[32] '21st century bard'.

[33] Andrew Bennett and Nicholas Royle, *An Introduction to Literature, Criticism and Theory* [1995], 4th edn (Abingdon and New York, 2009), p. 284.

[34] '21st century bard'. [35] '21st century bard'.

Fabian's den, is festooned with photos of the former boxer's triumphs and girlie calendars, and functions as the place whence he (Fabian is played by Vincenzo Nicoli as a Mafioso heavy) allows entry to the gated garden via an intercom buzzer system. The office also provides the haven in which huddle the box-tree conspirators to monitor, via a TV screen from a safe distance, the posturing of Malvolio – an innovation which is typically Supplesque in replacing the comic immediacy of the eavesdropping scene with the more sinister mode of electronic bugging.[36]

The below-stairs world of cakes and ale is – again, typical of the film's melancholy worldview – the storage space for the possessions and reminders of Olivia's deceased brother. We see Toby (David Troughton) slumped drunkenly over a photo album of the family on the occasion of a birthday or celebratory get-together. There are skis, cricket bats, a set of golf clubs and a fencing mask, as well as a record collection and other memorabilia. The dart board fixed to the wall is a low-life parody of Orsino's archery target. The intention seems to be to banish these painful memories to the basement in order to lessen Olivia's pain. The locked wine cellar, a wire-meshed enclosure, itself part of the basement, will become Malvolio's mad cell. In the closing sequence, as Malvolio is released and Olivia (Claire Price) pronounces that he 'hath been most notoriously abused' (5.1.375), she looks around her and clocks the higgledy-piggledy possessions of her brother along with photographs of him, and, throwing Malvolio's letter behind her, rushes out in tears. As Supple observes of the setting: 'They're rich people, playing and drinking in the mess of their past lives.'[37]

The third interior setting – the chapel – demonstrates most graphically Supple's directorial inventiveness, as well as, paradoxically, his faithfulness to Shakespeare's *Twelfth Night*. Supple remarks, apropos the Elizabethan period, how the play 'is about England at the time politically and in one sense it tells the story of the great clash that was taking place between Catholicism and Protestantism'.[38] This religious rupture, seemingly anachronistic in the film's modern setting, is described in terms no less divisive, albeit more secular:

the specifics of Shakespeare's moment translate into something that reverberates through time and across cultures. . . . The great schism in the heart of the play is the wider conflict between [Olivia's] past loyalties (of which Toby has become the moth-riddled Falstaffian standard-bearer and Aguecheek is the laughable champion) and the new Puritanism of which Malvolio is the unpalatable self-proclaimed spokesman. The Catholic/Protestant 1000-year civil war is internalised into the core of the play and becomes character, psychology and narrative.   (TS2)

To this end, Olivia's mourning rituals take place in a recognizably Catholic chapel. We see her receive Holy Communion from Ewart James Walters's frocked Priest, and the candle-lit altar before which she kneels is draped with rosaries and relics of her brother – photos and trinkets – like those which cluster around the shrines of saints in contemporary Spanish and Italian churches. As Toby staggers in to bring the news of the arrival of 'A gentleman' (1.5.114), his apostate contempt for this religion, which is incarcerating his niece in her own grief, is nicely signalled by his unashamed and lengthy fart – 'A plague o' these pickle herring!' (1.5.116–17). But his *delirium tremens* causes him to double-take at the altar, and the memory of his nephew and Catholic ritual merge in a feverish panic: the camera jump-cuts between his horrified expression and the festooned altar as Toby collapses. The comical mishearing of Olivia's 'lethargy' for 'lechery' (1.5.121) is too trite for such a moment of spiritual crisis and is cut. In this way, Supple accounts for Toby's sudden and unexpected religious exclamations: 'Let him be the devil an he will, I care not. Give me faith, say I' (1.5.123–4). In the light of this eschatological frenzy, the insistence on the 'gate' ('There's one at the gate', 1.5.121) takes on a sinister connotation as a hell's mouth, and adumbrates the devilish transformation which Cesario undergoes in the yearning rhetoric of Olivia: 'A fiend like thee might bear my soul to hell' (3.4.212).

---

[36] The fact that the conspirators are not physically close to Malvolio makes 'her very c's, her u's, and her t's' (2.5.85) unworkable, and it is cut.

[37] '21st century bard'.   [38] '21st century bard'.

The world of Catholic ritual is a darkly oppressive one, with Olivia kneeling obediently in front of the presiding priest and watched hawkishly by Michael Maloney's Malvolio. Miraculously, at one moment Olivia looks up to see the ghost of her smiling brother at the piano, playing a childish jingle, and, as she smiles at her remembrance of him, the elaborate chandelier over her shoulder mystically burns more brightly as if to symbolize her fraternal adoration. In spite of her perverse determination to sequester herself in darkness, we remember that Cesario describes her as 'Most *radiant*, exquisite, and unmatchable beauty' (1.5.163, emphasis added). Just as her inner light, veiled in the rigmarole of Catholic mourning, is hinted at in this way, so her sexual promise is also alluded to by the presence in the chapel of several Titianesque canvases displaying the naked forms of supine women. The camera tracks down one of the painted bodies as Olivia dwells on the 'five-fold blazon' (1.5.283) of Cesario, and we cut ingeniously to Viola, laying on her bed wearing only Cesario's loosely buttoned shirt. She approaches the mirror and unbuttons it to contemplate her own breasts: 'Fortune forbid my outside have not charmed her ... I am the man' (2.2.18–25). The scene of intimate self-revelation balances that in which we saw Viola (like Imogen Stubbs's Viola in Nunn's film) bandage her breasts in affectation of a masculine torso. As in Nunn's film, questions around identity and appearance are underlined: the publicity of disguise contrasting neatly with the privacy of revelation. The sensuousness of the nudes in Olivia's chapel anticipates the use of Orsino's Petrarchanism as he compares his adoration of Olivia to an intense religious experience:

> You uncivil lady,
> To whose ingrate and unauspicious altars
> My soul the faithfull'st off'rings hath breathed out
> That e'er devotion tendered
>
> (5.1.110–13)

As in the poetry of John Donne, there is little to choose between religious passion and sexual ecstasy.

In spite of its tonal distance from Nunn's film, as well as Supple's assertions about 'zero intended reference' (TS2), there are several intertextual references (regardless of the degree of deliberation, accident or otherwise). While Orsino fantasizes about Olivia in Nunn's film, laying in the bath, Cesario sponges his back and steals glimpses at his naked form under the water. Supple's version is more explicit, and Orsino calls Cesario to him while he lolls in a sunken bath, which demands that Cesario sit on the floor behind him while she sensuously anoints and massages his shoulders. As he remarks upon Cesario's 'happy years' (1.4.30) which give 'him' the appearance of a woman, Orsino steps up out of the bath and stands naked in front of Cesario/Viola. Her face is a fleeting mixture of embarrassment, astonishment and arousal before she recovers her composure and passes him a towel.

Elsewhere, the two of them listen to Feste's singing 'Come Away Death' (2.4.50–65). Here, the person of the fool is taken by a compact disc player, which leaves Cesario and Orsino alone to discuss the nature of desire. The absence of the fool echoes the related scene in Nunn's movie in which master and servant smoke and play cards over the instrumental version of Feste's song. In Supple's version, at Viola's 'I am all the daughters of my father's house, / And all the brothers too; and yet I know not' (2.4.120–1), Orsino remains in his seat while a ghostly image of him rises to kiss her – the fact that such 'trick' photography is used so sparingly makes it all the more effective. Clearly, like Olivia seeing her brother's ghost at the piano, this is a moment in which phantasm blends with fantasy.

While Supple picks up these reflective moments from Nunn's autumnal version, the films' endings are quite different. Nunn's party atmosphere celebrates the twins' double weddings while Malvolio et al. are banished from the country house. Supple's ending is much less confident. As the twins are reunited, Olivia registers the irrevocable fact that she is married to the 'wrong' one. Still traumatized by the photos of her brother and the savagery of the treatment meted out to Malvolio, she bursts into tears. What is usually a triumph of diplomacy as Orsino pronounces his intention to enjoy Olivia's party invitation is here very much an attempt to make the best of a bad job and comfort Olivia in her weeping. As the film closes, we see Olivia and Orsino embrace and the twins also embrace, but the unusually conspicuously married couples are not positioned as such. While the seated Viola and Orsino kiss, behind them Olivia merely strokes Sebastian's cheek. The film ends with the couples close but not yet commingled, and there is the suggestion that there is much further to go. As Supple reflects, 'The fact that Shakespeare's marriages in *Twelfth Night* are between two who are from "here" and two who are "others" and the fact that Olivia has discovered her Cesario is not who she thought he was and Orsino is re-focussing his intense passions ... I wonder how this can possibly be assured!' (TS2).

How might we read the ending of Supple's version? Might its dissonance be a marker of the instability of marriage as a binding institution in the contemporary world? Are Olivia's tears the index of the religious upheavals that Supple has attributed to the period of the play's composition, or do they register the emotional trauma of something much more modern, such as the claustrophobia of an apparently emancipated feminism which remains subjected to the residual cultural weight of patriarchal control (particularly through the institution of marriage)? And what of the film's attitude to multiracial Britain? Does it encourage inter-racial relationships which constructively wrench authority from the homogeneous white establishment? The casting of a black actor as the Duke suggests that it

does but, if so, why does the Asian–white couple never embrace? Leonard reads this modesty in the light of Bollywood's expectations: there is 'little or no sexual contact between romantic partners until after their marriage has been formalized', but Shakespeare, as Stanley Wells has so convincingly argued, seems generally less worried by explicitly erotic encounters than does Bollywood.[39] Supple himself suggests that the complexity of his film's ending is essentially Shakespearian, rather than taking its cue from the presence of multicultural partners: 'I feel that the endings are never about easy, definite wrap-ups, however good that might feel for audiences. Uncertainty, ambivalence, unease, complexity of feeling – that's what he's getting at and that's what life feels like for most of us' (TS2).

Perhaps the safest way to conclude is with the rather pedestrian observation that Supple's is a very different film from that of Nunn. Supple's own description of the two films is that they are 'respectfully antagonistic and competitive, that they lay out diametrically opposed views of the play and perhaps of priorities in playing Shakespeare' (TS2). What is certain is that, whereas Nunn's settles in romantic confidence, Supple's leaves these social and political questions hanging in mid-air. The fact that the endings of these film versions (which are separated by a mere seven years) are so diverse illustrates as much about the kaleidoscopically shifting tones of Shakespeare's play as it does about the pressing nature of contemporary cultural concerns.

---

[39] Leonard, 'The sounds of India in Supple's *Twelfth Night*', p. 148. See both Stanley Wells, *Looking for Sex in Shakespeare* (Cambridge, 2004), and his *Shakespeare, Sex and Love* (Oxford, 2010).

THROUGH A GLASS DARKLY: SOPHIE OKONEDO'S MARGARET AS RACIAL OTHER IN *THE HOLLOW CROWN: THE WARS OF THE ROSES*

JENNIE M. VOTAVA

The presence of a Black actress, Sophie Okonedo, as Queen Margaret in the second season of the BBC's *The Hollow Crown* brings to mainstream television a practice that is decades old in theatrical productions of Shakespeare. That is the practice of colourblind casting: choosing the best actor to play a given part, regardless of race or ethnicity. But how blind can or should an audience be to race? This question becomes all the more compelling when a Black actor is cast as a historically 'white' character, and especially when, as in the case of Margaret of Anjou, that character's ethnic otherness has long been a central issue in her theatrical representation. In this article, I position Okonedo's Margaret and the larger conversation about non-traditional casting in the context of feminist and historicist criticism concerned with the character's status as a French woman in plays about English masculinity, as well as the more recently burgeoning field of race studies in Shakespeare. Often cut in contemporary productions of *Richard III*, Queen Margaret functions there as a powerful spokesperson for marginalized feminine historical agency. Throughout the less frequently performed *Henry VI* plays, she appears as an often demonized gendered and ethnic other. By adding the visual semiotics of a marginalized race to its televisual representation of Margaret of Anjou, *The Hollow Crown* demonstrates both the pitfalls and the potentials of non-traditional casting, and at times transcends the British concerns of these plays to produce a more global and diachronic view of the 'imagined communities' they question and call into being.

What the word 'race' means in Shakespearian performance is an ever-moving target. The phrase Okonedo uses to describe her own national and ethnic identity, 'Jewish Nigerian Brit', encapsulates the insufficiency of the modern, black and white binary to describe the differences among individuals of European, African and mixed ancestry at this moment in the early twenty-first century.[1] Born over five centuries earlier, the historical Margaret of Anjou was the daughter of two Northern European nobles of what today would be considered French and German descent. She became, by marriage at the age of 15, Queen Consort of England. In Shakespeare's lexicon, as a Frenchwoman, Margaret did indeed belong to a different 'race', as defined by national origin rather than by skin colour, hair texture and facial features. In this period, as Arthur Little notes, '"race" ... works less as a stable identity category than as a semiotic field, one as infinitely varying as the cultural discourses constituting what we have come to identify as the early modern era or the Renaissance'.[2]

[1] Alyssa Klein, 'Sophie Okonedo looks absolutely boss as Queen Margaret in "The Hollow Crown: The Wars of the Roses"', *Okayafrica*, 18 November 2016: www.okayafrica.com/sophie-okonedo-queen-margaret-the-hollow-crown-the-war-of-the-roses.

[2] Arthur L. Little, Jr, *Shakespeare Jungle Fever: National-Imperial Re-Visions of Race, Rape, and Sacrifice* (Stanford, 2000), p. 1.

Then and now, the semiotics of race inevitably intersect with the somewhat differently unstable semiotics of gender. When originally performed in the early 1590s, most likely by an adolescent English boy, the complexities of Queen Margaret's gendered and ethnic representation made her potential identification with England's own Queen a site of tension that the *Henry VI* plays actively evade.[3] Nonetheless, in their various foreign female characters, these plays probably provoked what Leah Marcus describes as 'dark fantasies' around Elizabeth I's youthful potential for marriage to a French Catholic, as well as her ongoing 'self-portrayal as both a man and a woman'.[4] Over four centuries later, a 2003 condensed adaptation of the *Henry VI* plays, Edward Hall's *Rose Rage* for the Chicago Shakespeare Theater, deployed a mostly male cast, including numerous actors of colour. This production, according to Francesca Royster, consciously and deftly refused 'blindness' to both gender and race. Scott Parkinson's Margaret spoke with a French accent and was 'strikingly paler than any of the other actors' – features that marked Margaret's 'difference'. Along with the actor's male gender and his doubled role as Margaret and a white-smocked 'butcher' in Hall's interpolated chorus, these choices forced the audience of *Rose Rage* to interrogate both whiteness and femininity as performed roles.[5]

The BBC's *The Hollow Crown,* which aired in two seasons divided by the four-year gap between 2012 and 2016, was, in contrast, created for the medium of television. Productions by four different directors across both seasons for the most part deployed a style of cinematic realism, with the stated goal of making Shakespeare *less* strange and hence more accessible to a mainstream audience.[6] This goal required that an actor of colour as Margaret *not* disrupt the programme's illusion of an authentically medieval setting. In practice, however, several public commentators perceived Okonedo's casting as a deviation from the norm. Most notorious was the following tweet by UK Independence Party Councillor Christopher Wood: 'So the @BBC has given up on any kind

of historical accuracy. How can Margaret of Anjou be played by Sophie Okonedo?'[7] Beneath this question, Wood posted two side-by-side images. One was a medieval illustration depicting a pale-skinned, red-haired Margaret. The other was a production still of Okonedo in medieval battle gear.[8] On the opposite end of the political spectrum came a headline from okayafrica.com: 'Sophie Okonedo looks absolutely boss as Queen Margaret in "The Hollow Crown: The Wars of the Roses"'. As a display of African pride, the blog presented the same image of Okonedo that so outraged Councillor Wood.[9]

These divergent responses to Okonedo's Margaret attest to a fundamental problem with colourblind casting. As Ayanna Thompson asks, 'If the onus of being "blind" to race is completely upon the audience, then how can a director or an

---

[3] Leah Marcus, *Puzzling Shakespeare: Local Reading and its Discontents* (Berkeley, 1988), pp. 66–96. See also Barbara Hodgdon, *The End Crowns All: Closure and Contradiction in Shakespeare's History* (Princeton, 1991), pp. 56–9; Nina Levine, *Women's Matters: Politics, Gender, and Nation in Shakespeare's Early History Plays* (Newark, 1998), pp. 68–96; Patricia-Ann Lee, 'Reflections of power: Margaret of Anjou and the dark side of queenship', *Renaissance Quarterly* 39.2 (1986), 183–217, pp. 211–17.

[4] Marcus, *Puzzling Shakespeare*, pp. 62, 72–4, 88.

[5] Francesca T. Royster, 'The Chicago Shakespeare Theater's *Rose Rage*: whiteness, terror, and the fleshwork of theatre in a post-colorblind age', in *Colorblind Shakespeare: New Perspectives on Race and Performance*, ed. Ayanna Thompson (New York, 2006), pp. 221–39, esp. pp. 230, 233, 229.

[6] Peter Kirwan, 'The Hollow Crown: an introductory essay', www.dramaonlinelibrary.com/context-and-criticism/the-hollow-crown-an-introductory-essay-iid-173357/ba-9781474208659-3000012; 'The making of a king, *Henry V*', dir. Thea Sharrock, *The Hollow Crown: The Complete Series*. Universal Pictures Home Entertainment, 2013.

[7] @CllrChrisWood, 21 April 2016, screenshot in Bethan McKernan, 'Ukip councillor attempts to blast BBC for "historical inaccuracy", gets destroyed by actual historian', *Indy100*, 16 May 2016: https://www.indy100.com/article/ukip-councillor-attempts-to-blast-bbc-for-historical-inaccuracy-gets-destroyed-by-actual-historian-ZyZAasU2fb.

[8] McKernan, 'Ukip councillor attempts to blast BBC for "historical inaccuracy"'.

[9] Klein, 'Sophie Okonedo looks absolutely boss'.

actor be sure that this will occur?'[10] Even if colour-blindness is possible, it may not be desirable. Playwright August Wilson has famously denounced colourblind casting as 'an aberrant idea that has never had any validity other than as a tool of the Cultural Imperialist'.[11] He has also directly censured Black actors who play Shakespeare's monarchs for letting their bodies 'be used in "the celebration of a culture which has oppressed [Black people]"'.[12] In the wake of Wilson's commentary, Royster insists, we cannot 'be satisfied with the mere substitution of white bodies by black (or other racial identities) without a nuanced attention to history and the economics of cultural production'.[13]

I argue here that Okonedo's role in the second season of the BBC's *The Hollow Crown* is an exemplary case of non-traditional Shakespearian casting that professes to be 'colourblind', but is at its best when it demonstrates a consciousness of colour. Attending to how the intersectional categories of race and gender are constructed in a mass-marketed TV mini-series of some of Shakespeare's most rarely performed plays is crucial to both understanding and shaping these plays' continued influence in our increasingly global, digitalized age – in which this single production has the potential to reach viewers around the world for many years to come.

'WHO WE ARE AS A SOCIETY'

From their initial performances up through the present day, Shakespeare's English history plays have not only reflected contemporary, rather than historical, ideas about Englishness, but also actively fashioned the ever-shifting landscape of political identity. In their original contexts, these plays helped formulate the distinction among English, Irish, Welsh and Scottish peoples, the invention of Great Britain as a unified state, and the gender-based division between the public and private spheres.[14] Shakespearian drama also contributed to the emergence of a novel, racializing understanding of the somatic differences among populations.[15] As Royster, Little, Mary Floyd-

Wilson and Sujata Iyengar have argued, we see in these plays the 'gradual and at times contradictory' process of constructing a 'white English identity still in flux', absorbing 'those "others" who might support the English cause ... and casting out those who threaten the stability of the nation'.[16] The continuous violence of the *Henry VI* plays in particular, despite the external guise of 'loyalist drama', betrays the extreme social and political anxieties of an Elizabethan government facing the constant threat of Catholic terror[17] – a threat transposed in Hall's *Rose Rage* into the realm of twenty-first-century America's post-September 11 anxieties.[18]

As a production of the BBC, *The Hollow Crown* presents itself most immediately to a British audience. However, because of its medium, it also

---

[10] Ayanna Thompson, 'Practicing a theory/theorizing a practice: an introduction to Shakespearean colorblind casting', in *Colorblind Shakespeare*, ed. Thompson, pp. 1–26, esp. p. 10.

[11] August Wilson, 'The ground on which I stand', *Callaloo* 20.3 (1997), 493–503, p. 498.

[12] Angela C. Pao, 'Recasting race: casting practices and racial formations', *Theatre Survey* 41.2 (2000), 1–22, p. 3.

[13] Royster, 'The Chicago Shakespeare Theater's *Rose Rage*', p. 222.

[14] Jean E. Howard and Phyllis Rackin, *Engendering a Nation: A Feminist Account of Shakespeare's English Histories* (New York, 1997), pp. 10, 14. See also Richard Helgerson, *Forms of Nationhood: The Elizabethan Writing of England* (Chicago, 1992) and Claire McEachern, *The Poetics of English Nationhood: 1590–1612* (Cambridge, 1996).

[15] Kim F. Hall, *Things of Darkness: Economies of Race and Gender in Early Modern England* (Ithaca, 1995); Dympna Callaghan, *Shakespeare Without Women: Representing Gender and Race on the Renaissance Stage* (London, 1999); Ania Loomba, *Shakespeare, Race, and Colonialism* (Oxford, 2002).

[16] Royster, 'The Chicago Shakespeare Theater's *Rose Rage*', pp. 221, 231; Little, *Shakespeare Jungle Fever*; Mary Floyd-Wilson, *English Ethnicity and Race in Early Modern Drama* (Cambridge, 2003); Sujata Iyengar, *Shades of Difference: Mythologies of Skin Color in Early Modern England* (Philadelphia, 2005).

[17] Chris Fitter, 'Emergent Shakespeare and the politics of protest: *2 Henry VI* in historical contexts', *ELH* 72 (2005), 129–58, pp. 129–30, quoted in Royster, 'The Chicago Shakespeare Theater's *Rose Rage*', p. 224.

[18] Royster, 'The Chicago Shakespeare Theater's *Rose Rage*', pp. 235–7.

addresses a much broader array of 'international digital viewing audiences', of which I myself, as an American, am a member.[19] Thus, in these productions, the semiotics of race and the attendant political and ethical implications must also be considered within this wider field of reception. The terms 'colourblind' and 'colour-conscious' apply not only to the intentions behind non-traditional casting, but also to how those decisions might register to an audience. How attentive a performance is to the implications of cross-racial casting remains necessarily a complex question, outdone only by the even more complex question of how any given audience member might interpret these production choices.[20]

The Hollow Crown's first season, which presented the plays of Shakespeare's second tetralogy, was born out of a national celebration of British culture as part of the 'Cultural Olympiad' of 2012. Critics responded diversely to the first season's overall attitude towards the Britain they were officially intended to celebrate. Although one reviewer describes its concluding episode, *Henry V*, as producing 'a comforting feeling of patriotism for our small island', the scholarly community was by and large disappointed with what it perceived as a jingoistic streamlining of the latter play's complicated and often critical depiction of its title character.[21] The second season, subtitled '*The Wars of the Roses*', built upon the success of the first season by continuing the chronological historical narrative with the plays of Shakespeare's 'first tetralogy'.

Chronology, however, is probably not the only reason for the ordering of these cycles. As mentioned above, the *Henry VI* plays are among the least performed of all Shakespeare's dramatic corpus, especially outside Britain. They are often seen as 'unplayable because unintelligible', and lacking such seeming literary basics as 'a central character' and 'a linear narrative'.[22] Within Britain, these plays have become vehicles for expressing contemporary 'cris[e]s in national identity'.[23] Although the mood of the first season of *The Hollow Crown* is at least nominally celebratory, the second season's perspective on questions of British nationalism is bleaker, in keeping with the cultural crossroads exemplified by the 'Brexit' controversy.

According to former Royal Court Theatre director Dominic Cooke, who took on all three episodes of this cycle as his first foray into directing film or television, this series tells the story of Richard III: 'The question was, how many bad decisions does it take to put a psychopath in power?'[24] But, since the series' big-name star, Benedict Cumberbatch as Richard, does not enter until the second of the three episodes, Margaret is a more consistent anchor of the cycle's narrative arc. Screenwriter Ben Power omits most of the combat scenes in *1 Henry VI*, as well as, somewhat more surprisingly, Cade's Rebellion in *2 Henry VI*. His script instead emphasizes the role played by the Queen and her lover, Somerset – a composite of the characters Somerset and Suffolk in Shakespeare's plays – at this troubled moment in English history. In this context, 'Jewish Nigerian Brit' Sophie Okonedo takes on the role of Margaret on television – a medium, as above, in which audiences are relatively unaccustomed to seeing Black actors in traditionally 'white' roles.

---

19 L. Monique Pittman, 'Colour-conscious casting and multicultural Britain in the BBC *Henry V* (2012): historicizing adaptation in an age of digital placelessness', *Adaptation* 10.2 (2017), 176–91, p. 177.

20 Ayanna Thompson, '(How) should we listen to audiences? Race, reception, and the audience survey', in *The Oxford Handbook of Shakespeare and Performance*, ed. James C. Bulman (Oxford, 2017), pp. 157–69, p. 158.

21 Kirwan, 'The Hollow Crown'; David Livingstone, 'Silenced voices: a reactionary streamlined *Henry V* in *The Hollow Crown*', *Multicultural Shakespeare: Translation, Appropriation, and Performance* 12 (2015), 87–100; Pittman, 'Colour-conscious casting', 176–91; L. Monique Pittman, 'Shakespeare and the Cultural Olympiad: contesting gender and the British nation in the BBC's *The Hollow Crown*', *Borrowers and Lenders* 9.2 (2015), www.borrowers.uga.edu /1580/show%23subtitle3.

22 Stuart Hampton-Reeves and Carol Chillington Rutter, *The Henry VI Plays* (Manchester, 2006), p. 60.

23 Hampton-Reeves and Chillington Rutter, *The Henry VI Plays*, p. 2.

24 'Making of The Hollow Crown', *The Hollow Crown: The Wars of the Roses*, dir. Dominic Cooke, Universal Pictures Home Entertainment, 2016.

Even in the theatre, moreover, the history plays have been sites of greater resistance to non-traditional casting than other Shakespearian drama – especially when it comes to casting their titular monarchs. This 'glass ceiling' was first shattered in 2001, when David Oyelowo successfully took on the role of Henry VI in a 2001 RSC production. Two years later, Adrian Lester played Henry V for the National Theatre. The 2001 RSC *Henry VI* plays were celebrated for their diverse casting, and were successfully revived in 2006 with another Black actor, Chuk Iwuji, in the title role.[25]

As in these examples, the presence of actors of various races and ethnicities in *The Wars of the Roses* is ostensibly the result of colourblind casting. In an interview, Cooke explained his casting of Okonedo as a purely merit-based decision: 'I think Sophie is the best person in this country to play that part, I really do.' But he also made a comment suggesting a motive not entirely blind to colour: 'I don't think that you can do a piece of work that is about who we are as a society and just have white people doing it.'[26] His statement accords with the BBC's most recently published official strategy of diverse hiring practices, with the objective of 'representing and reflecting all the communities of the UK'.[27]

Contemporary as well as historical issues surrounding the representation of gender make a Black Shakespearian queen arguably an even greater site of representational tension than a Black Shakespearian king. Margaret's intratextual otherness as a 'monstrous' French woman at times clashes with Okonedo's function as a Black British woman representing the multicultural Britain of 2016. Although the intersection between questions of race and Margaret's gendered representation in these films produces various, at times contradictory, political frames of reference, those clashes are themselves revealing. In *The Hollow Crown*'s streamlined adaptation of Shakespeare's first tetralogy, Margaret's multidimensional agency – sexual, military, political, maternal and linguistic – is central to the rise and fall of England's most vilified king. Considered from the standpoint of a global audience, moreover, Okonedo's Margaret becomes a figure of both the power and the disempowerment of gendered and racial alterity writ large.

Season two of *The Hollow Crown* begins with a vertiginous bird's-eye view of blue-green water.[28] The shot moves in on the white cliffs of Dover, and a man on horseback takes the viewer leaping over a hedge of red and white roses. This is the messenger bringing bad news from France to the advisors of the new infant King, Henry VI, while the body of his father, Henry V, lies in state. The opening visual reference to the English Channel calls attention to the ongoing Anglo-French conflict and connects it directly to the titular Wars of the Roses. The disorienting camerawork provides a kinesthetic and visceral reminder of how, in his histories, Shakespeare consistently treats Frenchness as otherness: 'quintessentially different with respect to religion, warfare, government, gender, sexuality, and personal ethics'.[29] The ultimate boundary-crosser in this series is Margaret of Anjou, French Princess turned scheming English Queen, whom the chronicle histories blamed for instigating those wars, leading Shakespeare to follow suit.[30]

Meanwhile, the authoritative and familiar voice of Dame Judi Dench recites a pared-down version of Ulysses' famous speech on degree from *Troilus and Cressida*. The speech concludes, 'Take but degree away, untune that string, / And hark what discord follows' (1.3.109–10). The use of Dench's cultural

---

[25] Jami Rogers, 'The Shakespearean glass ceiling: the state of colorblind casting in contemporary British theatre', *Shakespeare Bulletin* 31 (2013), 405–30, pp. 418–24.

[26] Neela Debnath, 'Sophie Okonedo was the "best actress" to play white Shakespeare role in The Hollow Crown', *The Express*, 6 May 2016: www.express.co.uk/showbiz/tv-radio/667894/Sophie-Okonedo-Undercover-The-Hollow-Crown-Benedict-Cumberbatch-Dominic-Cooke.

[27] *Diversity and Inclusion Strategy 2016–20*, 2016: http://downloads.bbc.co.uk/diversity/pdf/diversity-and-inclusion-strategy-2016.pdf.

[28] Descriptions of this production refer to *The Hollow Crown: The Wars of the Roses*, dir. Cooke.

[29] Carole Levin and John Watkins, *Shakespeare's Foreign Worlds: National and Transnational Identities in the Elizabethan Age* (Ithaca, 2012), p. 62.

[30] Lee, 'Reflections of power'.

capital as an 'English heritage' actor gives weight to this interpolated prologue,[31] which reads like 'a message to "respect your betters"'.[32] Although she appears later in episode 3 as the Duchess of York, a character with her own complex relationship to rebellion, here Dench's extradiegetic voice is the voice of the establishment.

In *1 Henry VI*, the primal crime against degree has already taken place: the 1399 deposing of the hereditary monarch, Richard II, by Henry Bolingbroke. The first tetralogy is often seen as Shakespeare upholding a conservative political orthodoxy via the so-called 'Tudor myth'. According to this view, the plays present as divinely sanctioned the defeat of a demonized Richard III and the end of bloodshed through the uniting of York and Lancaster in Henry Tudor's marriage with Elizabeth of York. The Tudor dynasty, therefore, represents the return to divine-right kingship.

If this point of view persisted throughout the series, the final episode should end, as does Shakespeare's *Richard III*, with a speech by the newly crowned Henry VII, forecasting the union of 'the white rose and the red' (5.8.19). Instead, the cycle culminates with another bird's-eye view: this one of a post-apocalyptic Bosworth Field littered with unburied corpses, at the centre of which stands the dispossessed, disheveled, yet almost deified Margaret. How this final shot works with the cycle's opening depends, I suggest, on how much Dench's Duchess of York and Okonedo's Margaret have in common. Phyllis Rackin finds Margaret's voice in *Richard III*, chiming in with other disempowered female voices, to be 'subsumed in its hegemonic discourse' in support of the Tudor myth's 'desired conclusion' – that is, Elizabeth I's reign in Shakespeare's England.[33] But in the year 2016 and beyond, on a potentially global stage, does Okonedo's Margaret, and her representation of 'who we are', fulfil this historical, nation-building role? In this case, who 'we' are and, especially, how 'we' see race very much makes a difference.

'SHE-WOLF OF FRANCE! . . . / O TIGER'S HEART WRAPPED IN A WOMAN'S HIDE!'

In constructing its Margaret-centred narrative, *The Hollow Crown: The Wars of the Roses* strives from the outset to subvert misogynist stereotypes intrinsic to the play it stages, but tends to underplay concomitant stereotypes involving ethnicity, and – at least in its opening episode – largely to ignore the ramifications of casting an actor of colour in this textually contentious role. Shakespearian scholars have long discussed the problem Margaret represents as a woman, queen and foreigner within the masculinist, nationalist genre of the English history play.[34] Her construction as a gendered and ethnic other begins in *1 Henry VI* with her parallels to other foreign, female characters. Three French women – Margaret, Joan la Pucelle and the Countess of Auvergne – 'represent threats to the English protagonists and to the heroic values associated with history as the preserver of masculine fame and glory'.[35] In Shakespeare's post-Reformation 1590s, Protestant English authors increasingly perceived the Catholic French as an enemy race, 'so culturally and linguistically and somatically outlandish as to be outside the bounds of healthy mingling' in marriage.[36] As the only one

---

31 Elizabeth E. Tavares, 'The Hollow Crown's "1 Henry VI": crosscuts, casting, and factional conflict', *In the Glassy Margents*, ed. T. J. Moretti, 17 January 2017 – https://tinyurl.com/y6e4ac30 – citing Andrew Higson, *English Heritage, English Cinema: Costume Drama since 1980* (Oxford, 2003).

32 Peter Kirwan, 'The Hollow Crown: Henry VI Part 1 @ The BBC', U of N Blogs, University of Nottingham, 9 May 2016: http://blogs.nottingham.ac.uk/bardathon/2016/05/09/hollow-crown-henry-vi-part-1-bbc.

33 Phyllis Rackin, 'History into tragedy: the case of *Richard III*', in *Shakespearean Tragedy and Gender*, ed. Shirley Nelson Garner and Madelon G. Sprengnether (Bloomington, 1996), pp. 31–53, p. 37.

34 Beginning with David Bevington, 'The domineering female in *1 Henry VI*', *Shakespeare Studies* 2 (1966), 51–8.

35 Phyllis Rackin, 'Anti-historians: women's roles in Shakespeare's histories', *Theatre Journal* 37 (1985), 329–44, p. 332.

36 Linda Gregerson, 'French marriages and the Protestant nation in Shakespeare's history plays', in *A Companion to Shakespeare's Works*, 4 vols. (Oxford, 2003), vol. 2: *The Histories*, ed. Richard Dutton and Jean E. Howard, pp. 246–62, p. 251.

of the trio to outlast the play and make the journey from France to England, there to marry England's King, Margaret is by far the most significant threat. She exemplifies, for Katherine Schwarz, 'a movement of monstrous female agency from margin to center'.[37] By *3 Henry VI*, she has taken control of both the English court and the Lancastrian army. In between, in *2 Henry VI*, Margaret's move from margin to centre is exemplified by her association with another vilified female character, this time an English one. This is the Lord Protector's wife and Margaret's rival at court, the Duchess Eleanor Cobham, who defies her husband by dabbling in witchcraft and scheming for the throne, ostensibly on his behalf.

In addition to their Frenchness, Margaret and Joan share the characteristics of their military prowess and the sexual wiles they practise on men. As is often noted, Margaret makes her first entrance at the moment Joan is captured by the English and effectively takes over Joan's role: 'as one femme fatale exits to be burnt as a witch, another appears, her double, who practises, as it turns out, even more potent witchcraft'.[38] *The Hollow Crown* uses the Joan–Margaret parallel to quite different ends. Power cuts all scenes depicting Joan as the seducer of men and her claim on the stake to be 'with child' (*1 Henry VI*, 5.6.62). The setting of Joan's capture is relocated from the 'masculine' space of the battlefield to the more enclosed, 'feminine' space of the castle interior. Both women wear white nightgowns that mark their feminine vulnerability. In spite of their physical differences – pale, crop-haired Laura Morgan versus darker-skinned, abundantly tressed Sophie Okonedo – the audience is invited to see them as equals in gendered fragility. Neither, however, is a willing victim. Joan, kneeling before a statue of the Virgin Mary, turns to York with her hands raised – not in surrender, but to reveal freshly bleeding stigmata as she hails York with curses. Similarly, the first part of Okonedo's Margaret to enter the screen's frame is a hand clutching a dagger. Cut are the comical asides that reveal Margaret's wiles as she manipulates Somerset/Suffolk for her own ends.

This is no coy seductress, but, rather, a self-possessed woman genuinely ready to defend herself with violence.

Another misogynist stereotype that the episode subverts is the plays' representation of witchcraft. Joan, who is seen in *1 Henry VI* summoning devils, in Power's script is reinstated as a 'martyr'.[39] Up until her execution, she is seen doing nothing more witchlike than suffering from fainting spells and having visions. An extended on-screen burning sequence graphically displays Joan, head now shorn bald, screaming in agony as her fellow countrymen shriek, weep and pray. We also get reaction shots of the Englishmen watching Joan burn. The villainous Somerset enjoys the show, eating and drinking with gusto. York's gaze is unwavering; his determination to achieve the throne surpasses any compassion he may possess. Later in the episode, the more high-ranking Eleanor is similarly rehabilitated. After laying aside a crystal ball and what appears to be a tiny human skull (calling indirect attention to her childlessness), she takes out a voodoo doll representing King Henry and, after a moment of hesitation, stabs it with a long pin. Her image then blurs as the window behind her comes into focus: Somerset's spy is watching. Subsequent scenes show a barefoot, dishevelled Eleanor in a dirty white shift, facing judgment and humiliating punishment, and calling upon the audience to sympathize with her.

As three victimized women in white,[40] Margaret, Joan and Eleanor in Cooke's *Henry VI Part 1* are far removed from their representation across Shakespeare's first two *Henry VI* plays as 'demonized, ambitious, and warlike' females.[41] In fact, *The Hollow Crown* represents the demonization of

---

[37] Katherine Schwarz, 'Fearful simile: stealing the breech in Shakespeare's chronicle plays', *Shakespeare Quarterly* 49.2 (1998), 140–67, p. 141.

[38] Hampton-Reeves and Chillington Rutter, *The Henry VI Plays*, pp. 75–6.

[39] Kirwan, '*The Hollow Crown: Henry VI Part 1*'.

[40] Tavares, 'The Hollow Crown's "1 Henry VI"'.

[41] Howard and Rackin, *Engendering*, p. 99.

both Joan and Eleanor within these plays itself *as* victimization. Rather than reifying the masculine gaze that views each as a witch or virago, the camera asks the viewer to critique the points of view of an overly ambitious York, a borderline sociopathic Somerset, and a self-serving spy who also represents Somerset's delegated surveillance.

In asking its audience to consider the sameness of these women in their disempowerment on the basis of gender, however, the episode exposes a pitfall of remaining blind to racial difference. In presenting white as a symbol of female innocence, the dressing gown engages the implicitly racialized meanings of the standard Western black/white binary. If we don't see Okonedo's colour, this symbolism threatens to slide into a subtle instance of what Peter Erickson has described, with respect to *Othello*, as a 'white language community' in which 'acceptance is contingent on overlooking or sidestepping … outer blackness'.[42] That is, to see the whiteness of the gown as a positive, while remaining 'blind' to the colour of this Margaret's skin is troublingly close to the Venetian Duke's white supremacist praise of the Moorish General: 'If virtue no delighted beauty lack, / Your son-in-law is far more fair than black' (1.3.289–90).

Exacerbating the dangers of such a partial colourblindness, the early scenes with Margaret in Cooke's *Henry VI Part 1* also obscure another potential element distinguishing Margaret and Joan from Shakespeare's English characters. On the modern stage, Margaret often has a French accent or speaks French: for instance, Peggy Ashcroft in the RSC's *The Wars of the Roses* (1963), Ruth Mitchell in *Henry VI: The Battle for the Throne* (1994) and, as above, Scott Parkinson in *Rose Rage* (2003).[43] In contrast, both Okonedo's Margaret and Morgan's Joan sound British. Moreover, Power's streamlining of the *Henry VI* plays results in the excision of many French scenes and French characters. Unlike Thea Sharrock in the more explicitly French-conscious *Henry V* the previous season, Cooke also casts no French or French-speaking actors.

This paucity of Frenchness in *The Hollow Crown* season 2, in adaptations broadcast the month before

the Brexit referendum, for Anna Blackwell forecasts 'the ominous spectacle of England retreating from Europe'.[44] While Blackwell's claim may be hyperbolic, it nonetheless underscores how apparent nativism can be the flip-side of a well-intentioned disregard of difference. To be 'blind' to Okonedo's skin colour only compounds the problem. A colour-conscious understanding of the actress's presence in *The Hollow Crown*, on the other hand, not only allows for an inclusive interpretation of what it means to be British, but also opens up another avenue for interrogating, rather than substantiating, the play's original constructions of difference.

The reality that a colourblind approach to non-traditional casting 'is never quite free of the specter of racism'[45] becomes more apparent when Okonedo's Margaret arrives in England, where she doesn't wear white for long. As costume designer Nigel Egerton explains, 'in contrast to Henry's neutrality and sort of shapeless garb, she comes in dynamic and sort of red'.[46] His use of the word 'dynamic' reads as a euphemism for Margaret's sexuality, in contrast to her husband's monkish naïveté. Margaret's lover, Somerset, also wears red; the awakening of her sexual power is coded by the change in costume. The association with the red Lancastrian rose, moreover, is not coincidental. In the rose garden scene in *1 Henry VI*, and on several occasions thereafter, Shakespeare has various characters link the 'pale' white rose (2.4.47) with both 'fear' (63) and 'maiden' (47, 74) purity, and the 'sanguine' red rose (4.1.92) with 'blushing' shame (93), anger and bloodshed.

---

[42] Peter Erickson, 'Images of white identity in *Othello*', in *Othello: New Critical Essays*, ed. Philip C. Kolin (New York, 2002), pp. 133–45, p. 139.

[43] Hampton-Reeves and Chillington Rutter, *The Henry VI Plays*, pp. 76, 178.

[44] Anna Blackwell, *Shakespearean Celebrity in the Digital Age: Fan Cultures and Remediation* (Cham, 2018), pp. 172–3.

[45] Thompson, 'Practicing a theory', p. 8.

[46] 'Making of *The Hollow Crown*'.

These associations are also important when it comes to the *Henry VI* plays' historical representations of race. As Floyd-Wilson argues, the humoral physiologies that underlie such descriptions of sanguinity versus faintness of heart are central to emergent English constructions of the superiority of the white complexion, which contemporary Western culture has since so problematically naturalized.[47] While a twenty-first-century audience is not attuned to these humoral meanings, the association of the colour red with sexuality, and the use of this colour to mark the heightened sexuality of a character played by a Black actress, does resonate with contemporary stereotypes of Black female sexual promiscuity, which can be found on both sides of the Atlantic.[48] Such stereotypes become especially noticeable in instances of non-traditional casting in which there is only one non-white cast member.[49] In *The Hollow Crown*, the problem is exacerbated by the distinctly less sexualized portrayals of the two women linked with Margaret but played by white actresses: Eleanor and Joan.

Tensions between *The Hollow Crown*'s acknowledgement of Margaret's textual disempowerment and its perpetuation by cinematic means begin with the character's first appearance in episode 1. When Somerset drags Margaret before her father to bargain for her hand on behalf of King Henry, the camera situates the exchange of daughter for land amidst other mute objects of loot being gathered by English soldiers. However, once the bargain is sealed, Cooke delivers the first of many scenes featuring Margaret in a dark hallway communing secretly with her eventual lover before disappearing behind a closed door. When Somerset initiates a goodbye kiss, ostensibly as a 'loving token to his majesty', she is far from unwilling (*1 Henry VI*, 5.5.137). After the kiss, her parting words are uttered with a restrained but clearly flirtatious edge. A close-up of Margaret's expression as she stands a step above Somerset invites the audience to speculate on her thoughts. Is it this man's body Margaret desires, or being Queen, or both? Or is she a disempowered woman/'girl' simply making do?

The next time we see Margaret in a dark hallway, it will be wordlessly to solve the open question of her degree of agency. For Sandra Logan, the Frenchwoman Margaret in the male-dominated English court of *2 Henry VI* is 'isolated' and 'naïve'; she is 'a pawn of Suffolk, despite her desire for authority'.[50] In contrast, Okonedo's Margaret punctuates her complaints about her husband's lack of kingly power by firmly refusing sex with Somerset/Suffolk in this second hallway scene. After the two jointly plot the downfall of both the Duchess and Duke of Gloucester, and in the aftermath of the third and final hallway assignation, the cries of the Duke as he is murdered in his cell are cross-cut with the cries of Margaret's orgasm as she finally gives Somerset what he's been asking for. In place of Warwick's graphic speech that dwells on the appearance of Gloucester's corpse –

> his face is black and full of blood;
> His eyeballs further out than when he lived,
> Staring full ghastly like a strangled man;
> His hair upreared; his nostrils stretched with
>   struggling;

– all we see of the Duke's earthly remains is a single pale leg through a dungeon doorway (*2 Henry VI*, 3.2.168–71). The camera instead lingers on the climaxing face and clenching hands of Okonedo-as-Margaret. Hers, too, is a 'black' face in a way that can't help but register on the viewer's eye, not least in visual contrast to the whiteness of that dead leg.

Okonedo's Margaret at this point becomes the textbook definition of a *femme fatale*. It is a status

---

[47] Floyd-Wilson, *English Ethnicity and Race in Early Modern Drama*.

[48] Debbie Weekes, 'Get your freak on: how Black girls sexualise identity', *Sex Education* 2.3 (2002), 251–62; C. M. West, 'Mammy, Sapphire, and Jezebel: historical images of Black women and their implications for psychotherapy', *Psychotherapy* 32.3 (1995), 458–66.

[49] Errol Hill, *Shakespeare in Sable: A History of Black Shakespearean Actors* (Amherst, 1984), pp. 162–3; cited in Thompson, 'Practicing a theory', p. 10.

[50] Sandra Logan, *Shakespeare's Foreign Queens: Drama, Politics, and the Enemy Within* (New York, 2018), pp. 213–14.

she will carry through to the end of the episode, in which Power extensively rewrites Shakespeare's plot, making Margaret's impassioned plea to King Henry for the repeal of her lover's banishment successful. In turn, this repeal becomes York's chief pretext to wage his war to gain the crown. The result is not only Somerset's death, but also the King's, the young Prince's, and all the other casualties of the civil wars to follow. Yet the scene in Shakespeare's *Henry VI* plays that most blatantly revels in Margaret's depraved sexuality is one that Cooke and Power displace and drastically revise. That is Margaret's Salome-esque behaviour with her lover's severed head towards the end of *2 Henry VI*, in which 'the public nature of her grief and her fetishizing of the severed body part characterize Margaret as a figure of willful passion, dangerously oblivious to the decorum that should govern the behavior of a king's wife'.[51] At the beginning of episode 2 of *The Hollow Crown: The Wars of the Roses*, Suffolk's beheading in exile by pirates becomes Somerset's slaying in the Battle of St Albans by York's servant, Vernon, who then plays a fairly horrific practical joke on the Queen. Vernon is hiding behind a low wooden barrier when Margaret wanders onto the desolate battlefield, calling her lover's name. When she happens to sit down right in front of Vernon's hiding place, he reaches over her shoulder and drops Somerset's bloody head directly in her lap.

It is a startling moment, but for quite different reasons from in the play. Power cuts lines in which the Queen cradles and fondles what is left of her lover: 'Here may his head lie on my throbbing breast, / But where's the body that I should embrace?' (*2 Henry VI*, 4.4.5–6). An aghast Okonedo, rather, views the head where it has rolled to a stop on the ground. She then kneels down beside it and turns away as tears spill from her eyes. There is nothing erotic in her address: 'Think, [Margaret], on revenge, and cease to weep. / But who can cease to weep and look on this? ... My hope is gone' (4.4.3–4, 55). A turn takes place at this point in *The Hollow Crown*'s representation of Margaret. The audience is invited to sympathize with the Queen's grief and anger and

to condemn Vernon for his adolescent cruelty and voyeurism.

A different sort of turn in Margaret's characterization takes place at this point in Shakespeare's plot, when, to avoid further strife, the King agrees to make the Duke of York his heir. Maternal ire leads Margaret to pronounce: 'I here divorce myself / Both from thy table, Henry, and thy bed' (*3 Henry VI*, 1.1.248–9). She also takes command of her husband's armies. Her actions to restore the patrilineal succession on her son's behalf make her arguably more sympathetic to an early modern audience.[52] However, paradoxically, the demonization of Margaret reaches its pinnacle in the resulting battle when the Queen tortures and kills the Duke of York, a scene that ranks as '"one of the most violent in all Shakespeare's plays"'.[53] Like the affair with Suffolk, this event is largely the playwright's invention.

The paradox persists in *The Hollow Crown*'s version of this scene. Here, again, Cooke and Power raise the stakes on Shakespeare's already vilifying portrayal of Margaret. The scene takes place not on the battleground of Wakefield but in York's own home, where Margaret's forces disrupt a family dinner. Wearing a crown over her black hooded cloak that makes her look incongruously like the evil Queen in Disney's *Snow White*, Margaret sweeps through this domestic interior, sending food and dishes crashing to the floor, and sets a hanging tapestry of the Yorkist white rose ablaze. When she finally confronts a wounded York in the courtyard while his family residence burns behind them, Okonedo is gleeful and especially wicked. Rather than taunting him with a paper crown, she uses a full-blown crown of thorns, which happen to be from a white rose bush. Instead of merely wiping his tears with a cloth drenched in his youngest son's blood, she stuffs it in his mouth, all the while licking her lips in almost sensual

---

[51] Howard and Rackin, *Engendering*, p. 74.
[52] Levine, *Women's Matters*, p. 89.
[53] Levine, *Women's Matters*, pp. 89–90, quoting Emyrs Jones, *The Origins of Shakespeare* (Oxford, 1977), p. 278.

anticipation. She then leans in so close to York's face she could be about to kiss him – except, instead, she thrusts the knife into his heart.

Before his demise, Adrian Dunbar's York delivers a brief speech that highlights the two most oft-quoted one-liners on the Queen's ethnic and gendered alterity:[54] 'She-wolf of France . . . / O tiger's heart wrapped in a woman's hide!' (*3 Henry VI*, 1.4.112, 138). In a script replete with similar epithets, these references to predatory animals present Margaret as an inhuman other by virtue of both her Frenchness and her deviant femininity. Their juxtaposition and foregrounding in Dunbar's delivery of this speech (in the original, they are twenty-six lines apart) put Margaret's foreignness front-and-centre with respect to her perceived inhumanity.

For an early modern English audience, Margaret's unfeminine actions in *3 Henry VI*, all with the goal of defending her son's right to the kingship, place her 'in a contradictory position' within her society, and make her 'a vehicle for exposing the ideological nature of many patriarchal claims'.[55] *The Hollow Crown* presents a somewhat different set of contradictions. With York's slaying, we are asked to sympathize with Margaret, but as an avenging lover, rather than a preserver of the patriarchy. Margaret's last words to York are revised from 'And here's to right our gentle-hearted King' to 'Here's to avenge beloved Somerset' (1.4.177). The concluding close-up shows tears in her eyes. The instability of the viewer's perspective on Margaret in this scene is underscored by Vernon's spectatorship from behind a smouldering wagon, a reprise of his earlier voyeuristic role with Somerset's head. Together, these moments self-consciously expose the constructed and self-contradictory nature of the Queen's gendered and racial representations in both the original play and its adaptation, as the audience must struggle to decide whether she is a hero or a villain.

Not at all coincidentally, this second episode's shift towards a sympathetic Margaret is combined with what appears to be a more colour-conscious use of her character. In the latter half of the series,

the racial otherness of Okonedo's Queen itself becomes a call for the viewer's compassion, to the point that, by the end of *Richard III*, she stands for historical injustices well beyond the scope of four English history plays from the 1590s. Yet this modern sympathy for a marginalized Margaret is initially produced by sacrificing the character's voice and agency. This change is most graphically demonstrated in the aftermath of Margaret's defeat at Tewkesbury, where she takes York's place as the tortured, grieving parent. The play presents the defeated Queen as '[s]wooning, lamenting, begging for death at her captors' hands, but unable to taunt them into doing the deed'.[56] While Cooke and Power's version of this scene does perform what Howard and Rackin describe as the translocation of this 'tigerish hero queen' to a definitively 'feminine subject position', it does so using a different set of signifiers involving Okonedo's race.

When her son is suddenly stabbed in the back by a furious and semi-crazed Richard, Okonedo's Margaret does not swoon. Instead, she delivers the wild, anguished shriek of a mother watching her own son die before her eyes. Following Richard's lead, the soldiers laugh mockingly, even those restraining Margaret on either side. The devastated mother continues to sob and scream while Richard cuts the Prince's throat *at* her: that is, while staring gleefully straight at Margaret. There is something squeamishly self-conscious about this display of visceral maternal grief as a spectacle for mass consumption, in which the episode's audience is also implicated. A brief point of view shot from the most sensitive of the three brothers, the Duke of Clarence, as Margaret weeps over her son's dead body, demonstrates an uncomfortable empathy mingled with responsibility for the Queen's suffering that is simultaneously his, and ours.

---

54 Levine, *Women's Matters*, p. 68.
55 Howard and Rackin, *Engendering*, p. 85.
56 Howard and Rackin, *Engendering*, p. 98.

Margaret's non-verbal utterances become especially important since her speaking lines are almost entirely cut. In addition to calling out her son's nickname, 'Ned!', the only words she speaks are twice to beg for her own death. These changes make Richard's curious question to his brother all the more curious: 'Why should she live to fill the world with words?' (*3 Henry VI*, 5.5.43). Most scholars see this line as auguring Margaret's coming role in *Richard III*.[57] The score that accompanies Cooke's adaptation implies just such a meaning. In the episode to follow, Margaret and her curses have a musical *leitmotif*. It begins with a tremulous, ominous chord, which suggests a brief suspension of mundane reality while supernatural powers reveal their presence. When Richard asks his question as if seeing his own unhappy future, we hear this music for the first time.

In a setting of imbalanced power, this performance of grief, which so heavily relies on non-verbal cues, makes Okonedo's race a key visual signifier. The connotations of a dark-skinned woman dragged away by two armed and grinning white men resonates with unhappily iconic images from subsequent world history, particularly the transatlantic slave trade that was already under way when this play was originally performed. Margaret returns to the screen one more time in this episode. The final scene takes the viewer from the royal court to a dark, dank dungeon where Margaret droops in the background. When a jailer comes by to toss her an unappetizing meal, she rises, revealing wrists shackled by heavy chains to the floor. 'Listen to me', she cries with increasing desperation as her sole addressee departs; 'I am the Queen! I am the QUEEN!'

Her shackled body speaks to the viewer even more than her words. E. Patrick Jonson argues that the proverbial elephant in the room, the fact that 'the Black body has historically been the site of violence and trauma', renders blindness to an actor's race in performance a simultaneous blindness to 'these consequential aspects of bodily harm'.[58] Given the subsequent centuries of slavery and its legacy in the Western world, the implications in the twenty-first century of a Black body in chains cannot be overlooked.

'TO HOLD, AS 'TWERE, THE MIRROR UP TO NATURE . . .'

By *The Hollow Crown*'s final instalment, the deposed Queen is no longer in chains – and her presence alone, regardless of race, no longer 'historically accurate'. Beginning with her opening appearance, at which Rivers marvels, 'I muse why she's at liberty' (*Richard III*, 1.3.303), a small round hand-mirror becomes a recurrent symbol of Margaret's role as 'prophetess', as well as a meditation on the problems of seeing. So often used in Shakespeare's plays to interrogate the power of theatre, mirrors in Cooke's *Richard III* reveal ostensibly sidelined but increasingly present questions surrounding race in this series. In stark contrast to the previous two episodes, in which faces of colour other than Margaret's appear only among unbilled extras, the final episode features numerous darker-skinned actors in speaking parts: most tellingly, Ugandan-born British actor Ivanno Jeremiah as Blunt. In Power's script, Blunt is the soldier who slays Richard's horse – thereby sealing the tyrant's fate, not to mention leading to some of the most famous last words in English literature. In this final episode, racial difference becomes central to engaging Shakespeare's English histories in the ongoing, intertwined projects of constructing a multicultural British nation and interrogating history-making from a transnational perspective.

Margaret first picks up this mirror to hold her enemies spellbound as she utters her infamous curses. In it, each enemy sees her or his reflection, followed by clips from other moments in the show's run. Queen Elizabeth's reflection gives way to flash-forwards of the young Princes heading for their doom. Richard sees, among other things, a flashback of the white rose tapestry in flames from episode 2, and his own fallen form on a muddy battlefield from this episode's foregone conclusion.

Later, when Richard receives the unwelcome news that Buckingham has defected, 'curse music'

---

[57] For instance, Schwarz, 'Stealing the breech', 165.
[58] Thompson, 'Practicing a theory', p. 15, quoting E. Patrick Johnson, *Appropriating Blackness: Performance and the Politics of Authenticity* (Durham, NC, 2003), p. 40.

heralds the reappearance of that same mirror, grasped by a disembodied brown hand. The prop returns again in Richard's dreams, the night before the Battle of Bosworth Field. Margaret appears at his bedside with the mirror, in which he sees the face of the murdered Henry VI. After cursing him one by one, his victims gather together, laughing tauntingly as Margaret holds out the mirror once more. Richard looks for his reflection, even waves his hand before the glass, but, anticipating his pre-battle soliloquy – 'Is there a murderer here? No. Yes, I am' – there is no-one there (5.5.138).

Whether as a supernatural presence, a hallucination, or something in between, Margaret continues to wield that mirror until her final appearance on the battlefield, where it becomes the direct means by which she appears to take Richard down. Richard and Richmond are locked in combat to the death, wrestling in the mud. Richmond is on top, but Richard fights back until he is distracted by a vision of Margaret, who blinds him with the mirror. We see two reflections of Richard as he receives his death blows: the first, while he is still alive; the second, after he is dead.

The most explicit function of the mirror is, as above, to register visually the power of Margaret's curses and her role as an Old Testament-style prophet in what, on some level, functions as a morality play. But the mirror also alludes to the play's perspective on Richard III's physical and moral deformity. Richard is one not 'made to court an amorous looking-glass' (1.1.15). He is also the 'false glass' that reveals and punishes his mother's, and his society's, 'shame' (2.2.53–4). As Elizabeth Tavares notes, Cumberbatch's Richard 'is routinely surrounded by mirrors that wobble and fracture alongside his sense of (and his actual) power . . . [R]efracting his body back to him in these moments of political failure inherently links the two: a broken body so therefore a broken politics'.[59]

Cooke's use of the mirror visually demonstrates the connection often postulated between Richard and Margaret as two villainous rhetorical virtuosos, and emphasizes how both characters inhabit

marginalized bodies subject to an essentializing gaze.[60] While the series' overall sceptical slant on witchcraft suggests a more naturalistic explanation, the possibility that this is really a 'magic' mirror lingers and potentially associates Margaret with another racially problematic American stereotype. That is the 'magical negro': 'a stock character that often appears as a lower class, uneducated Black person who possesses supernatural or magical powers', whose primary function is to save a white person, usually a white man.[61] For L. Monique Pittman, an 'accidental magical negro' previously materializes in *The Hollow Crown* in the form of Paterson Joseph's self-sacrificing Duke of York in Thea Sharrock's *Henry V*.[62] Likewise displaced from American myth and cinema into the realm of televised English nation-building, the dispossessed Queen Margaret's supernatural battlefield assist to the future Henry VII in Cooke's *Richard III* – thereby saving the nation from Richard and ushering in the golden Tudor age – also superficially fits this bill.

That stereotype only works, however, if Margaret's mirror presents a vision compatible with the Tudor myth: if her curses can be allied with the conservative message of the series opener, and a battlefield strewn with the unburied dead represents nothing more than the cost in English lives of failing to adhere to 'degree'. But this is far from the case. The broader symbolic resonances of Margaret's mirror also extend into Shakespeare's second tetralogy and recall the mirror Richard II asks for in that primal deposition scene, 'That it may show me what a face I have, / Since it is bankrupt of his majesty' (*Richard II*,

---

[59] Elizabeth E. Tavares, 'The Hollow Crown's "Richard III": the affective failure of direct address', *In the Glassy Margents*, 2 January 2018: https://glassymargents.com/2018/01/02/the-hollow-crowns-richard-iii-the-affective-failure-of-direct-address.

[60] Rackin, 'History into tragedy', p. 39.

[61] Matthew W. Hughey, 'Cinethetic racism: White redemption and Black stereotypes in "magical negro" films', *Social Problems* 56.3 (2009), 543–57, p. 544.

[62] Pittman, 'Colour-conscious casting', pp. 183–7.

4.1.256–7). Although 'Richard seems with this narcissistic image to be looking at himself', he's actually 'looking at the whole of society'.[63] In Cooke's *Richard III*, Margaret's mirror is likewise held up to Britain as a whole, as well as to a much larger audience.

With this larger audience in mind, the final bird's-eye shot of the episode both deconstructs and transcends the Tudor myth. One reviewer writes, 'The brutality was tantamount to a holocaust . . . Queen Margaret presides over the war dead as their bodies are tipped into huge open graves . . . Sophie Okonedo's warrior queen is transmuted into an angel of despair – at this massacre and all its successors still to come.'[64] In addition to the Holocaust of World War II, culturally pervasive images of which this panorama references with visceral intent, the word 'holocaust', with its connotations of genocide – etymologically, race-murder – also conjures up more recent events. Among them stands the mass slaughter of the Tutsi during the Rwandan Civil War: the massacre represented in the 2004 film *Hotel Rwanda*, in which Okonedo played an acclaimed starring role as an African humanitarian. The actress's

Jewishness must also be acknowledged, although this aspect of her identity doesn't signify visually.

In this moment of contemporary intertextuality not imaginable to Shakespeare, the screen image of Okonedo as Margaret, surrounded by tangled white corpses, links the Battle of Bosworth Field and the dawn of the British nation state under the Tudors with these far darker moments of twentieth-century history. But the profundity of Cooke's Holocaust reference only has real significance if one acknowledges the ever-shifting semantic and semiotic field of race, and how human differences of all types have been constructed and upheld as justifications for the unjustifiable. *Not* to see Okonedo's race is to foreclose many of these important meanings.

---

63 'Director's commentary', *Richard II*, dir. Gregory Doran, performances by David Tennant and Nigel Lindsay. Opus Arte, 2014.

64 Serena Davis, 'A chilling end to The Hollow Crown, series two, review', *The Telegraph*, 21 May 2016: www.telegraph.co.uk/tv/2016/05/21/a-chilling-end-to-the-hollow-crown-series-two-review.

'WHO'S THERE?'
BRITAIN'S TWENTY-FIRST-CENTURY
OBSESSION WITH CELEBRITY
HAMLET (2008–2018)

GEMMA KATE ALLRED[1]

INTRODUCTION: 'WHO'S THERE?' (1.1.1)

Hamlet is an unlikely success story – it is long; to play in full would take over 4 hours and, frankly, until the mass deaths of the final scene, not much happens. As a play obsessed with contradictions, it is perhaps fitting that treatment of *Hamlet* is somewhat polarized: it is either revered or mocked. William Hazlitt claimed that 'Shakespeare has in this play shown more of the magnanimity of genius, than in any other.'[2] Ironically, it is the reverence itself that is often mocked, an idea clearly at play in the 'To be or not to be' sketch of *Shakespeare Live! From the RSC*, a 2016 RSC / BBC Two production marking the 400-year anniversary of Shakespeare's death.[3] Comedian Tim Minchin leads an all-star cast in a sketch based solely on the line 'To be, or not to be; that is the question' (3.1.58). The sketch opens with Paapa Essiedu's recital of the soliloquy, which is then interrupted by Minchin's criticism of Essiedu's delivery: the emphasis should rest heavily on the 'or' he insists, to highlight the choice Hamlet must make. This interruption is followed by others from a series of famous actors, each insisting that the stress ought to lie on a different word. Acting as compere, Minchin questions each actor's credentials, the repeated 'Who are you?' raises questions of identity – related to both the actor and Hamlet – whilst echoing the play's interrogative opening: 'Who's there?' (1.1.1).[4] Any production of *Hamlet* is 'haunted ... by the memories of the famous Hamlets of the past';[5] by parading a series of well-known actors, each with their own take on the

famous line, the sketch acts as a physical embodiment of this ghosting effect, inviting the audience to recall Hamlets they too have seen. In addition to ghosts of Hamlet past, when we watch a production we are also influenced by memories of other iconic roles the actor playing Hamlet has played, and his or her personal life. Asked in this context, 'Who are you?' becomes a loaded question – it is not sufficient for Benedict Cumberbatch to be 'just an actor'; he needs to be identified by both name and famous role.[6] Similarly, David Tennant is identified by reference to his role as a detective in TV drama *Broadchurch* rather than his RSC acting credentials. Despite her long career as a leading Shakespearian actress, Judi Dench is not identified by her work but instead by the Damehood it collectively gained her. Minchin then takes a selfie with Cumberbatch and Harriet Walter

---

[1] I would like to thank (in alphabetical order) Ben Broadribb, Emma Depledge, José A. Pérez Díez, Emma Smith, Tiffany Stern, Nathaniel Taker and Paul Taker for reading and criticizing drafts and earlier versions of this article.
[2] William Hazlitt, *A View of the English Stage, or, A Series of Dramatic Criticisms*, ed. W. Spencer Jackson (London, 1906), p. 12.
[3] *Shakespeare Live! at the RSC*, dir. Gregory Doran (DVD) (2016). Also available at: adorable-bc-pictures, *Hamlet x8 at RSC Live* (online video recording), Vimeo, 1 July 2016, https://vimeo.com/173050475.
[4] *Shakespeare Live!*, dir. Doran, at 1.29.05.
[5] Marvin Carlson, *The Haunted Stage: The Theatre as Memory Machine* (Ann Arbor, 2001), p. 79.
[6] *Shakespeare Live!*, dir. Doran, at 1.29.05; 1.29.08; 1.28.18.

dismisses him as 'a film star' who 'know[s] nothing',[7] a clear reference to Cumberbatch's 2015 portrayal of Hamlet where the audience, attracted by celebrity, were criticized for taking photographs.[8] The intent to ghost Cumberbatch's 2015 Hamlet onto this 2016 sketch is unmistakable.

The inclusion of both Tennant and Cumberbatch in the line-up of Hamlets is very much of the Zeitgeist. In the past decade, there has been a shift towards casting celebrity Hamlets. While famous names have historically taken the role, from Laurence Olivier and John Gielgud to Adrian Lester and Samuel West, these actors have predominantly been stage actors with a grounding in Shakespeare. However, in 2008, Gregory Doran cast Tennant and started a trend whereby actors better known for film and TV work take on Shakespeare's most iconic role.[9] While Tennant had a grounding in Shakespearian acting, having played a number of roles for the Royal Shakespeare Company between 1996 and 2001,[10] by 2008 he was more widely known for his role as The Doctor in *Doctor Who*.[11] In 2009, Jude Law took on the role as part of the *Donmar in the West End* season.[12] An established film actor, it was Law's first Shakespearian role.[13] Cumberbatch and Andrew Scott, well known for their roles in the BBC's *Sherlock*,[14] then took on the role in 2015 and 2017, respectively. They both enjoyed a varied theatre career, but this was their first professional Shakespearian role.[15] Being better known for screen work is not indicative of any lack of suitability or ability to play Shakespearian roles, but their screen-celebrity status does raise questions about the ownership of Shakespearian capital. As Anna Blackwell notes, the casting of Cumberbatch as Hamlet 'evinced an increasing overlap between the value traditionally expected of the "Shakespearean" and the newer sites of cultural capital created through popular, Internet and fan culture'.[16] Questions of audience attraction and reception are brought to the fore. Certainly, Tennant, Law, Cumberbatch and Scott are not the only actors to enjoy cross-over success. One could consider the wider celebrity of Orson Welles, Laurence Olivier and, more recently,

Kenneth Branagh, who, outside of their roles as Shakespearians, have varied film and TV careers. However, where these earlier celebrities differ from Tennant, Law, Cumberbatch and Scott is that their stardom springs from their Shakespearian credentials.[17]

This article considers the impact of celebrity on productions of *Hamlet*. It does so through reference to the Hamlets of Tennant, Law, Cumberbatch and Scott, and aims to analyse how textual choices and staging are influenced by a new target audience.[18] These celebrity Hamlets share a number of similarities. In each case, they generated an inordinate amount of press coverage, not least because of the hysteria surrounding ticket sales. Cumberbatch's production 'sold out in minutes',[19] and tickets for Tennant's *Hamlet* were

---

[7] *Shakespeare Live!*, dir. Doran, at 1.29.50.

[8] See, for example, Jack Malvern, 'Keep your mobiles turned off in interval, Hamlet fans told', *The Times*, 12 August 2015, p. 7.

[9] William Shakespeare, *Hamlet*, dir. Gregory Doran (Stratford-upon-Avon: Courtyard Theatre, 2008).

[10] Including Touchstone, Romeo and Lysander at the Royal Shakespeare Theatre.

[11] *Doctor Who* (television programme) (London: BBC One Television, 2005–10).

[12] William Shakespeare, *Hamlet*, dir. Michael Grandage (London: Wyndham's Theatre, 2009).

[13] Although he had played Giovanni in *'Tis Pity She's a Whore* in 1999, and Faustus in *Doctor Faustus* in 2002.

[14] *Sherlock* (television programme) (London: BBC One Television, 2010–17).

[15] William Shakespeare, *Hamlet*, dir. Lyndsey Turner (London: Barbican, 2015), and William Shakespeare, *Hamlet*, dir. Robert Icke (London: Almeida Theatre, 2017).

[16] Anna Blackwell, *Shakespearean Celebrity in the Digital Age: Fan Cultures and Remediation* (Basingstoke, 2018), p. 98.

[17] For more, see Anna Blackwell's discussion of pre-digital Shakespearian celebrity, in Blackwell, *Shakespearean Celebrity*.

[18] For ease of reference, I will refer to each production by the name of the actor playing Hamlet, i.e. the Tennant *Hamlet* will be shorthand for Doran's 2008 production.

[19] Sarah Crompton, 'Why Benedict Cumberbatch is luckier than Richard Burton', *The Guardian*, 31 July 2015: www.theguardian.com/stage/2015/jul/31/benedict-cumberbatch-richard-burton-hamlet.

being resold for £500 a pair.[20] Celebrity Hamlets bring both new performance and new audiences, who may be carrying negative opinions of Shakespeare based on school experiences and can be deeply impacted by their first positive encounter with Shakespeare. These productions therefore had an opportunity to introduce a disenfranchised audience to the merits of Shakespeare. As Ralph Alan Cohen notes, students complain that Shakespeare is 'too hard ... boring and/or irrelevant'.[21] Increasingly, when considering *Hamlet* in the twenty-first century, the question 'Who's there?' applies as much to the audience as it does to the actor playing the eponymous hero, and the production needs to reflect the new audience that celebrity attracts.

Within these celebrity productions, there was a clear intention to present Shakespeare in a manner that would stimulate and interest that new audience: Michael Grandage wanted to exploit 'Jude's extraordinary ability to communicate with a young audience'.[22] Blurring the line between role and actor, these celebrity productions are self-consciously aware of the position of an actor playing a role. This awareness works on two levels: on the surface, the audience sees the named actor on stage playing Hamlet. The audience is required to suspend disbelief and work collaboratively with the actor to create an abstract imagined world within the confines of the theatre, in which a famous actor ceases to be that actor and becomes Hamlet. However, with *Hamlet* there is a second level of consideration: the play can be viewed through a meta-theatrical lens. Hamlet is acutely aware of the power of drama, using, as he does, a play to 'catch the conscience of the King' (2.6.607). He is obsessed with the roles people play in life: he berates women for painting themselves new faces (3.1.145–7), while his own putting on of an 'antic disposition' (1.5.173) raises questions as to the nature of public versus private personae. These are considerations not limited to Hamlet the character but also to the actor playing the role – all the more so when that actor is a household name. Focusing in particular on notions of identity, this article considers how

celebrity bleeds into the staging of *Hamlet* in these celebrity productions. Furthermore, it considers how these productions are marketed to attract potential new audiences, before finally discussing the critical reception of celebrity productions in the mainstream press.

'WORDS, WORDS, WORDS' (2.2.195): A TEXTUAL ANALYSIS

In editing *Hamlet* for new audiences, there is an element of freedom – the audience are unlikely to arrive with pre-conceived ideas about the text. Moreover, *Hamlet* is fundamentally a series of long set-pieces that, within reason, can be moved around without overly impacting meaning. Notably, 'To be, or not to be' tends to be moved between its Q2 position in Act 3, Scene 1, after the arrival of the players and before the play, and its earlier Q1 position, after Hamlet sees the ghost but before the players arrive. Peter Brook's 2001 *Hamlet* with Adrian Lester moved the soliloquy to Act 4.[23] Similarly, there is the possibility of removing any number of subplots. A family-focused domestic edit could remove Fortinbras and the Norwegian invasion (as in Simon Russell Beale's 2000 *Hamlet* directed by John Caird),[24] and Polonius could be portrayed as a manipulative spymaster (as in Samuel West and Steven Pimlott's 2001 production),[25] or as a bumbling fool depending on whether or not his instruction to spy on Laertes in Act 2, Scene 1, is included and how his

---

[20] Chris Green, 'Hot tickets fetch £500 for a pair', *The Independent*, 6 August 2008, p. 11.

[21] Ralph Alan Cohen, *ShakesFear and How to Cure It: The Complete Handbook for Teaching Shakespeare* (London, 2018), p. 53.

[22] Jonathan Croall, *Performing Hamlet: Actors in the Modern Age* (London, 2018), p. x.

[23] William Shakespeare, *Hamlet*, ed. Abigail Rokison-Woodall (London, 2017), p. xxxv.

[24] William Shakespeare, *Hamlet*, dir. John Caird (London: National Theatre, 2000).

[25] Samuel West, 'Hamlet', in *Performing Shakespeare's Tragedies Today: The Actor's Perspective*, ed. Michael Dobson (Cambridge, 2006), pp. 41–56, p. 50.

interactions with Laertes and Ophelia are edited, in terms both of text and of performance. Perhaps due to their consciousness of new audiences who are unaccustomed to Shakespearian theatre, the celebrity productions made a number of edits to enhance audience understanding.[26] Throughout the productions, there is simplification of diction: often a modern translation is used where word usage has changed, or the word has fallen out of use (for example, all three texts replace Polonius's 'I had not quoted him' (2.1.113) with 'I had not noted him'). Similarly, a number of subject pronouns are replaced with character names or titles – for example, at Act 2, Scene 1, line 1, Polonius states, 'Give him this money' (2.1.1), while 'him' is replaced with 'my son' in the Tennant Hamlet and 'Laertes' in Scott's version. Ideas that are no longer relevant are also excised – none of the productions include Laertes's advice to Ophelia that '[t]he chariest maid is prodigal enough' (1.3.36). The effect of these edits is twofold: deleting text shortens long speeches, and the omission or amendment of archaic ideas or phrasing simplifies the spoken text and eases comprehension. In order to run at a reasonable time, the most expeditious form of editing is deletion of whole scenes or speeches; for example, none of the versions include consideration of danger posed by companies of child actors (2.2.339–63). In reviewing the Law Hamlet, Susannah Clapp, writing for the Observer, notes that Grandage's production is 'quick – the evening runs for about three-and-a-quarter hours – because it's cut. Well cut.'[27] She further notes that the edited text is a 'clearing of the undergrowth', with much of the Player King, Polonius and the soldiers' 'What ho stuff' cut, suggesting that this was a version – as with the other celebrity Hamlet productions – updated and refined to simplify the text.[28]

In the Tennant and Scott Hamlets, Hamlet's boat journey is vastly reduced, either by the insertion of Q1 Scene 14 as in the Scott Hamlet or deletion altogether in the Tennant Hamlet (his escapades by sea are encompassed in one line: 'Rosencrantz and Guildenstern are dead', 5.2.325).[29] In contrast, this subplot is given in its entirety in the

Cumberbatch Hamlet. There are merits to both approaches. The Scott and Tennant versions have a very compressed time frame: the exact time elapsed between Hamlet's exile and return is unclear but seems, in production, fairly swift. Both of these edits are heavily Hamlet-focused, and having Hamlet on stage and talking seems to be a key concern. The Cumberbatch Hamlet is more of an ensemble edit. By including the convoluted pirate plot and allowing reported action through letters, the audience is afforded a sense of time passing and life at Elsinore carrying on. This edit places Ophelia in a prominent position as her madness is given more space within the context of the production and a clearer progression to suicide. The Cumberbatch Hamlet instead deletes the Polonius/Reynaldo subplot – Laertes is not placed under observation. Surveillance is still a key part of Elsinore life, but it is now limited to Hamlet, who is objectively acting out of character. Coupled with the rearrangement of scenes, such that Claudius's actions seem reactive rather than proactive, the overall impression is of a play that is less concerned with politics and power and more with grief and mental health.

Unusually, the textual choices in the Cumberbatch Hamlet became a news story, with Kate Maltby, writing for The Times, criticizing the 'indefensible decision'[30] to move the 'To be, or not to be' soliloquy to the opening of the play. By opening night, the soliloquy had moved to immediately following the fishmonger scene – taking a position found in neither Q1, Q2, nor the Folio. The soliloquy can work in this context – Hamlet has just exclaimed to Polonius that there is

---

[26] Neither the Donmar Theatre, Grandage Company nor the V&A archives hold archive records of the Jude Law production; as such, it has not been possible to analyse the textual choices of this production.

[27] Susannah Clapp, 'Jude Law delivers his soliloquy in an icy rage, but it is Penelope Wilton as Gertrude who makes this a truly memorable Hamlet', The Guardian, 7 June 2009: www.theguardian.com/stage/2009/jun/07/hamlet-wyndhams-jude-law.

[28] Clapp, 'Jude Law'. [29] Shakespeare, Hamlet, dir. Doran.

[30] Kate Maltby, 'What a waste! It's Shakespeare for the kids', The Times, 6 August 2015, p. 3.

nothing 'I will more willingly part withal – except my life, my life, my life' (2.2.217–19), the realization clearly dawning on Hamlet during the repeated 'my life' that suicide is, for him, an option. Left alone, he contemplates suicide but takes strength from the words, seeming to find some element of peace. When he meets Ophelia, he seems genuinely happy to see her and his repeated 'well' (3.1.94) suggests some joy.[31] However, in the context of the production, moving the soliloquy to the opening could be justified, and indeed may be more impactful. The play opens with Hamlet mourning his father, packing away his father's clothes and listening, we assume, to his father's favourite records. To have a soliloquy at this point, in which the protagonist considers life and death, is powerful. This Hamlet is not unreasonably melancholic; he is understandably mourning the death of his father and contemplating what it is to be alive. To have these thoughts at the outset creates a framework within which to place Hamlet's erratic behaviour. By pandering to negative press commentary, this opportunity to explore fully a rational, albeit grieving, Hamlet was lost.

'TO HOLD AS 'TWERE THE MIRROR UP TO NATURE' (3.2.21–22): STAGING CELEBRITY *HAMLET*

It is in staging that celebrity *Hamlet* productions are most influenced by their potential new audiences. The costumes, set and sound are designed to appeal to a young, modern audience. There is an acknowledgement that an audience lured by a celebrity playing Hamlet brings a different set of expectations to, and experience of, the theatre, and that this can influence meaning. Staging decisions need to ensure that meaning is conveyed effectively to an audience that may not have the benefit of a detailed existing understanding of the play.

None of the celebrity productions employs Renaissance dress; as Tennant notes, 'the whole doublet and hose thing is, not insurmountable, but it is a barrier to connecting with a modern-day audience'.[32] The Tennant and Law *Hamlet*s were obviously modern dress, but with no real indicator

as to exactly when the productions were set. The Scott production is specific – the audience is very much led to believe that the production is happening in 2017. The television footage showing Hamlet's father's funeral is in a contemporary style. Indeed, the production notes at the Almeida show that these television reports are reconstructions of actual recent news footage of the current Danish royal family.[33] Scott's *Hamlet* isn't just generic modern, it is today. The Cumberbatch *Hamlet* is harder to pin down: many of the costumes nod towards a 1930s/1940s setting – however, Horatio is dressed throughout as a modern-day hipster with checked shirt and tattoos, and Hamlet too wears a modern-style parka and David Bowie T-shirt. With the action placed in a modern setting, the audience can more readily identify with the characters – it is easier for the audience to find a connection with a character who looks like them. This is important when trying to appeal to a new Shakespearian audience; men in tights and ruffs are indicative of a culture from which they may feel excluded.

However, there is something else at play here. The clothing choices are semiotic, representing externally the internal state of Hamlet's mind. Tennant and Cumberbatch each change into a printed T-shirt (Tennant's red muscle T-shirt became the iconic look of his production). For Tennant, the change into a T-shirt rather than the formal dress of the opening wedding party shows a regression – this is a Hamlet seeking comfort. It is perhaps telling that this T-shirt is not pristine and new like much of the clothing in Elsinore, but rather is faded and well washed. This T-shirt is an old favourite – the one you wear when you feel *out of sorts*, a feeling a young

---

[31] Note all three productions take a Folio reading of 'I humbly thank you, well, well, well'.

[32] Abigail Rokison, 'Interview: David Tennant on *Hamlet*', *Shakespeare* 5.3 (2009), 292–304, p. 302.

[33] Shakespeare, *Hamlet*, dir. Icke (London: Almeida Theatre, 2017). Promptbook, Rehearsal Notes and Production Correspondence file, Almeida Theatre, London (consulted on 15 June 2018).

contemporary audience may recognize. Similarly, Cumberbatch changes into a David Bowie T-shirt for 'The Mousetrap'; again, band T-shirts are a shorthand for modern counter-culture, separating the youth from authority. In the context of a production in which the musical references have been to Nat King Cole, a sudden nod to Bowie is noteworthy. Hamlet is now clearly an outsider at Elsinore, his casual dress at odds with the formal attire of the rest of court. As an artist, Bowie was renowned for his stagecraft. The T-shirt worn by Cumberbatch shows Bowie as Ziggy Stardust – a character that Bowie adopted to perform. This reference would be quickly noted by a modern audience, who would infer that Hamlet, too, is playing a part.[34] Law, in a largely grey-tone production, adds a cardigan over his long-sleeved t-shirt and crouches barefoot in snow for 'To be, or not to be'. Law pulls the cardigan around himself – protection not only against the weather but also the emotion – a movement that would be familiarly comforting to a modern audience and would act as a shortcut to understanding the soliloquy. Even if the nuance of every word is not understood, the meaning behind it is.

The staging of celebrity productions draws on a modern audience's experience both of film and of large-scale West End stage productions. The Tennant and Law *Hamlet*s have similar staging: each employs a predominantly empty stage, and each uses large panels at the rear of the stage to create a sense of changing scene. The panels serve two further purposes: firstly, they turn to allow entrances and exits and provide a sense of both additional rooms and of internal and external spaces. Secondly, the panels are the full height of the theatre and provide a sense of perspective. Next to large panels, the actors can appear smaller, with an increased sense of vulnerability. This is clearly an idea at play in the staging of the Law *Hamlet* – the 'To be, or not to be' soliloquy being performed at the back of the stage against one of the large panels. With an introspective performance, Law does not address the audience, but rather experiences a moment of self-reflection. Crouched in front of

the panel and turned towards it, Law's Hamlet appears vulnerable and exhibits none of the bravado and anger of other scenes. This is not Hamlet's public persona, and, for the audience, the moment feels voyeuristic – we are not part of this scene but eavesdropping on a deeply personal moment. This plays with audience expectation – 'To be, or not to be' is arguably the 'money moment', the speech the audience has paid to see. However, instead of being invited in, the audience is excluded. For an audience whose experience of theatre is more likely to be large-scale West End productions, the expectation would be for the protagonist to be front and centre. However, this staging offers a direct route to meaning. Dwarfed by the panel, Hamlet's position in Elsinore seems equally diminished, not least because this Hamlet has been cast outside into the snow, a slight opening in the panel revealing light and warmth from the interior space, a space from which Hamlet feels excluded. For Grandage, this was a clear directorial decision; he wanted a 'neutral, monumental space [. . . within which] Hamlet seems to be permanently lost'.[35]

In contrast, the Cumberbatch *Hamlet* uses rather than subverts the expectations of West End theatrical productions. This set is large and intricately designed. The audience does not need to rely on the text provided to locate the action; rather, there is an excess of props and scenery, with a focus on showing, as opposed to telling, where the action takes place. This is the expected large-scale

---

34 Indeed, fan commentary on Twitter expressed excitement over the choice of a Bowie T-shirt. An @me2Hannah response is representative – 'Benedict Cumberbatch wears a David Bowie tshirt in his production of Hamlet. I couldn't possibly love this man anymore' (tweet) (@me2hannah, https://twitter.com/me2hannah/status/654856215571202049, 16 October 2015), as is @Samputsimply's response to the NT Live Screening: 'Yoooo ... The @NationalTheatre's production of Hamlet is dope. Benedict Cumberbatch's emotional, Bowie-tee-clad Hamlet is everything' (tweet) (@Samputsimply, https://twitter.com/samputsimply/status/744257577345658881,18 June 2016).
35 Croall, *Performing Hamlet*, p. 105.

production with a sweeping staircase, shining chandeliers and formal family portraits showing, rather than implying, Hamlet's palatial Elsinore. While the images are designed to appeal to an Instagram generation (one can imagine the potential hashtag enthusiasm for aspirational palace living), the intricate details of the Cumberbatch *Hamlet* at times seem to detract from meaning. There is too much for the audience to focus on – while the production retains the political undercurrent of the Fortinbras subplot, much of this is reduced to the presence of maps, globes and military uniforms on stage, and, with the text much cut, the enormity of the threat is underplayed. Relying on an audience to deduce political threat by markers would work if the set were more minimalist; however, these markers are lost within an excess of props. Where this oversized production does work is in the metaphorical destruction of Elsinore. As the production breaks for the interval (at 4.3.75), the large doors open, and the stage is flooded with black debris. The meaning is clear: the exile of Hamlet, and Claudius's plan to have him assassinated, have set in motion a series of events that will lead to a tragic conclusion. Following the interval, Elsinore has been much diminished, with broken and dilapidated furniture and scenery. This Elsinore is no longer aspirational, but instead shrunken and pitiful.

The Scott *Hamlet* employs more filmic devices. The set is extremely realistic, with the stage a credible recreation of idealized modern Scandinavian living. In yet another appeal to a modern Instagram generation, the set takes its cue from the modern predisposition to view a Danish design aesthetic as the epitome of stylish living. The stage is split into two areas with sliding doors and a glass wall separating the two. This hyper-reality is a method more usually exploited in cinema, where the audience accepts a fallacy that what is on screen represents a real, tangible world. This technique is particularly exploited by Baz Luhrmann, who seeks, in his films, to create a '*heightened creative* world' that could exist but is not the real world.[36] Icke applies this technique to theatre, attempting to create an Elsinore that could

be real. This commitment extended to the entrance security cameras used during the production – at the Almeida, during the opening of the play, the actor playing Barnardo is actually outside the theatre when he responds to Francisco's 'Stand and unfold yourself' (1.1.2) and the theatre's existing security camera system is transmitted live to the stage.[37] This heightened reality eases comprehension – the audience does not have to work to create the world of the play, it is presented to them. The production also exploits the multi-track opportunities of film – being able to watch two locations at once through split-screen or layering. By having the rear of the stage visible at several points throughout the production, the action takes place in both areas at once – for example, Act 1, Scene 2, opens with a melancholic Hamlet at the front of the stage, packing his bag and preparing to return to Wittenberg while, at the same time in the rear of the stage, the wedding party takes place. Where this is at its most poignant is when we see Hamlet's visit to Ophelia: in an intimate scene, Ophelia is bathing naked when visited by Hamlet, who is acting aggressively and erratically. When Ophelia reports this visit to Polonius, the audience can benefit from having already seen the action. This acts as a shortcut to understanding – an audience new to Shakespeare may be unused to large swathes of plot being reported rather than seen. Because this scene has been shown as well as reported, the audience has a full understanding of its impact. Shakespeare's reported text uses semiotic markers to note Hamlet's mental condition, and an audience new to Shakespeare may not be aware that Hamlet's shabby dress ('doublet all unbraced' and 'stockings fouled', 2.1.79–80) signifies mental instability. However, the audience *is* clear that Hamlet's actions are unacceptable. As it is this interaction with Hamlet that catalyses Ophelia's descent into madness, it is important that these

---

[36] Toby Malone, 'Behind the red curtain of Verona Beach: Baz Luhrmann's William Shakespeare's Romeo + Juliet', *Shakespeare Survey 65* (Cambridge, 2012), 398–412, p. 398.

[37] Shakespeare, *Hamlet*, dir. Icke: Promptbook, Rehearsal Notes and Production Correspondence file.

meanings are understood. Showing the audience actions to support words, the meaning of which could otherwise be lost, enhances comprehension.

This filmic approach is most noticeable in the final scene where dead characters walk into a party at the rear of the stage, surrendering their watches to the ghost on entry. The surrendering of a watch is symbolic of someone's *time being up* – a metaphor of which the modern audience would be aware. Where this production is clever is that these concepts are introduced from the start – when Hamlet says 'methinks I see my father' (1.2.184), he does: his father is present at the wedding party at the rear of the stage, the party that will become the 'party of the dead' in the final act. Hamlet's first action is putting on his watch – his timer is already running. Further, Polonius foreshadows Laertes's death by giving him a watch on his departure for France, the suggestion being that Laertes's advice to Ophelia has set in train a series of events that will ultimately lead to his death. Obviously, these are details that could be easily missed, but they are filmic in their approach, so an audience accustomed to following convoluted plots in blockbuster movies would be alert to indicators of this kind. Certainly, films such as *The Sixth Sense* and *Fight Club* exploit an audience's ability to notice subconsciously small details that inform meaning.[38] By adapting these filmic devices to the stage, Icke's production appeals more to a modern audience and delivers an up-to-date aesthetic – this is a production that offers relevance to a contemporary audience.

While questions of identity are common to all productions of *Hamlet*, the text lends itself to a consideration of what it is to be human and subject to human emotion. Each of the celebrity productions shows an obsession with identity – in particular, the clash of public and private personae and the need to adopt a role and play a part. This is often not the case in non-celebrity vehicles; Michelle Terry's *Hamlet* at the Globe Theatre places family and domestic relationships at the core, stressing the comfort that young Hamlet received from his father with Colin Hurley's protective ghost offering consolation to Hamlet during the closet scene.[39] David Warner's and Ben Whishaw's *Hamlet*s focus more on the coming-of-age story, looking at Hamlet as an adolescent, and Samuel West's version focuses on political relationships.[40] Where questions of identity centre in these celebrity productions is in the portrayal of Hamlet's madness and the role of the 'The Mousetrap'. These Hamlets are self-consciously acting and playing a role themselves. Law notes of Hamlet that: 'He is an actor. He's a believer in the performances we all put on. It's a wonderful theme – he's an actor talking to us about an actor putting on an act, and being amazed at how he does it.'[41] This meta-theatrical idea, that we see both an actor playing Hamlet, and Hamlet playing a role, highlights notions of celebrity – do we see the actor and his private, off-stage life or do we see the actor and his role of Hamlet? These are notions that Hamlet similarly grapples with – does he reveal his true emotion, his true self, or does he choose to retreat into a role, play a part and assume a feigned 'antic disposition'? Certainly, Law was clear that his Hamlet is not mad, claiming: 'I believe there are elements of hysteria, and to me that's about as close as he gets to true madness' – his Hamlet is angry and puts on an assumed madness to shield his true emotion.[42] Similarly, Cumberbatch is a rational Hamlet – he assumes a role in a calm and collected manner (ahead of Rosencrantz's and Guildenstern's arrival, Cumberbatch's Hamlet waits in his fort, only starting to act erratically when his audience arrives). In contrast, Scott's and Tennant's *Hamlet*s are more conscious of the need to address Hamlet's possible madness, with both finding links between the original text and questions of mental health. Speaking to Andrew Marr, Scott is aware of a modern interest in mental

---

38 *Fight Club*, dir. David Fincher, Fox 2000 Pictures, 1999; and *The Sixth Sense*, dir. M. Night Shyamalan, Hollywood Pictures, 1999.
39 William Shakespeare, *Hamlet*, dir. Federay Holmes and Elle While (London: Shakespeare's Globe Theatre, 2018).
40 Croall, *Performing Hamlet*, pp. 25–8, 90–2, 94–5.
41 Julian Curry, *Shakespeare on Stage: Thirteen Leading Actors on Thirteen Key Roles* (London, 2010), p. 115.
42 Curry, *Shakespeare on Stage*, p. 104.

health and acknowledges that 'you can't ignore this new interest we have in mental health now and just play it as mad, crazy'.[43] He sought instead to portray a man wrought with grief and being deprived the space to acknowledge that grief publicly, and crumbling under the need to maintain a public persona. Tennant, too, expressed unease about portraying Hamlet's madness, claiming that: 'Whether or not he is mad is for the audience or a doctor to decide, it's certainly not for Hamlet to decide. What is madness anyway? Where does madness end and sanity begin? So I just played each scene and tried to make emotional sense within the context of what we were doing.'[44] Essentially, Tennant chose not to play the role of a quintessentially mad person; however, in doing so, and relying solely on the text, he presents the audience with a manic Hamlet as the text itself lacks rationality in regard to Hamlet's actions. As a result, the production in places fails to offer a clear interpretation.

In the Cumberbatch production, Hamlet is infantilized by grief, perhaps trying to relive a childhood in Elsinore with his father. His 'antic disposition' takes a childlike form, with Hamlet dressing as a toy soldier and playing with an oversized toy fort complete with life-sized guards. In addition, much of the action seems to take place in Hamlet's nursery with a doll's house and rocking horse stored under the stairs (as with the fort, these are oversized and could in theory be played with by the adult mourning prince). 'The Mousetrap' and closet scene also take place in this nursery setting. Rather than meeting Hamlet in her space, Gertrude goes to his, with echoes of aristocratic parents paying scheduled visits to children who are kept out of the way of the grown-up business. With Hamlet taking a part in the play, this does smack of a small child pining for attention. However, something else is being explored – this *Hamlet* highlights the roles people have to play and there is an emphasis on acting. Hamlet is play-acting: he searches for his 'antic disposition' in a dressing-up box, assisted by his childhood friend and love, Ophelia. His madness is assumed with a loud song-and-dance performance that takes him

onto a table as an ersatz stage. Cumberbatch's Hamlet is unusually invested in 'The Mousetrap' – taking on the role of Lucianus. In the staging, the audience is not invited to observe Claudius's reaction to the play. The royal family is placed with their backs to the audience – however, we are actively encouraged to watch Hamlet as he assumes another role, that of player. In his role of Lucianus, Hamlet wears a black coat with the word 'King' painted on the back. The effect of this is twofold. It acts as a reminder to the audience that the play is intended to recreate the murder of Hamlet's father by the King, but also it reminds the audience that Hamlet could have been King had Claudius not 'Popped in between th'election and [his] hopes' (5.2.66). Having been himself usurped, the only way Hamlet can be King is through play. Ophelia, too, is obliged to perform – she plays the piano throughout the production, most poignantly when she is pushed to intercept Hamlet; in this context, 'Read on this' (3.1.46) is sheet music and Ophelia is encouraged to play. Ophelia, too, documents much of the action: she is ever present with a camera photographing events, and her abandonment of the camera and her photographs following the flowers scene (4.5) indicates her suicidal thoughts. Without Ophelia, the performances are no longer documented and the edges between reality and play become blurred.

In contrast, with Andrew Scott playing the role at 40, his Hamlet is a mature adult. We lose the reference to Hamlet's being 30, his relationship with Ophelia is clearly sexual, and there are hints of a past relationship with a female Guildenstern. For Scott, Hamlet's madness is subtler – he starts obviously distressed and acts in an increasingly manic manner. For Scott, the taking on of an 'antic disposition' feels less staged than in the other *Hamlets* and closer to genuine madness. Scott's Hamlet feels the pressure of being on

---

[43] Andrew Scott interview with Andrew Marr, *The Andrew Marr Show*, extract shared on The Andrew Marr Show Twitter feed (2.49 p.m. – 26 June 2017), https://twitter.com/marrshow/status/879305630900670464?lang=en.

[44] Rokison, 'Interview: David Tennant', p. 299.

show, and the use of CCTV screens to suggest constant surveillance is a useful device (albeit not unique – a similar device was used in Rory Kinnear's *Hamlet*).[45] Coupling this with constant media coverage, shown by the recreated news report and handheld cameras filming and broadcasting, *inter alia*, the wedding toast (1.2.122–8) and the reactions of the royal family watching 'The Mousetrap', this is an Elsinore where Hamlet is constantly on show, having to play his role as Prince. The records at the Almeida contain additional unused footage for the production. It had originally been intended that Ophelia's madness would play out in what is described as a 'house of detention', with her decline into madness being shown on the CCTV screen.[46] Similarly, the screens were to show footage of a child Hamlet fencing with his father alongside the bout between Hamlet and Laertes. The intention to show 'a mental space as much as a real one'[47] would be a provocative device. Using the screens both for internal thoughts and for portrayals of external public personae would magnify the connection between public and private, and the pressure that brings. It would also depict more clearly that Scott's Hamlet suffers from poor mental health. Moreover, it could have called into question the veracity of everything that we see on screen – including the ghost. It would also have been interesting to see how this idea would have played out with the 'party of the dead' concept.

In celebrity productions, the audience acts as a foil to celebrity – without an audience, the celebrity lacks a form of expression. All the Hamlets acknowledge the presence of the audience by addressing them directly. Law takes a traditional view of the audience as being integral to Hamlet's expression of his thoughts. He directs soliloquies to the audience, treating them as: 'allies within the realms of it being a play [... the soliloquies] are what's going on in his mind, they are conversations he's having with himself [...] in the structure of a play the inside of his mind, if you like, is the audience'.[48] This allows Law's Hamlet to show the audience a vulnerability, in contrast to the anger his Hamlet displays in his public persona. Law's

introspective treatment of the 'To be, or not to be' soliloquy gains greater significance – at this point where Hamlet contemplates suicide, he shuns his imagined allies, creating a greater sense of isolation.

Cumberbatch, too, addresses his soliloquies directly to the audience. However, unlike Law, the soliloquies are not a conversation but a performance – Cumberbatch's Hamlet stands on tables and presents his thoughts; the lighting changes – he has a spotlight – and the rest of the actors on the stage move into slow motion. Cumberbatch's Hamlet needs and demands an audience, treating the modern audience much in the same way as Hamlet does the Danish court – as an observer of the role Hamlet needs to play, albeit with more honesty. Anna Blackwell argues that this placing of Cumberbatch mirrors his depiction of Sherlock Holmes. Presenting his internal thoughts with an 'out-of-time temporality',[49] she notes, is a 'practical transposition that explicated the interior nature of Hamlet's dialogue', a shortcut into comprehension for an audience inexperienced with the theatrical convention of the soliloquy.[50] Tennant's approach is a hybrid – for his soliloquies, he addresses the audience directly. Indeed, in 'To be, or not to be', Tennant stands centre stage and very still, holding his left wrist in his right hand. He looks around the audience, including them in his thoughts without encouraging involvement. It is precisely due to this staging that the audience is placed at the heart of the production. The panels at the rear of the stage are mirrored, constantly reflecting the audience. This production is self-consciously artificial – the audience seeing themselves reflected is acutely aware that the action is staged rather than real. The effect of this is twofold.

45 Croall, *Performing Hamlet*, p. 108.
46 Shakespeare, *Hamlet*, dir. Icke: Promptbook, Rehearsal Notes and Production Correspondence file.
47 Shakespeare, *Hamlet*, dir. Icke: Promptbook, Rehearsal Notes and Production Correspondence file.
48 Curry, *Shakespeare on Stage*, p. 105.
49 Blackwell, *Shakespearean Celebrity*, p.114.
50 Blackwell, *Shakespearean Celebrity*, p.114.

Firstly, the audience acts as an extra player in the production, their omnipresence enhancing the sense that, in this Elsinore, one is always being watched. Secondly, the audience, being constantly reminded that this is a theatrical production, is encouraged to see the actor behind the role, as well as Hamlet the character.

It is the Scott *Hamlet* that uses the audience in the most novel manner. Scott's Hamlet addresses the audience directly, at times leaving the stage and talking directly and intimately to an audience member. He encourages responses, pausing to allow the audience time. This is Hamlet's audience – no other character addresses, or even acknowledges the presence of, an audience. For example, Claudius's confession in Act 3, Scene 3, is directed towards Hamlet, who is present on stage although rehearsal records at the Almeida note that Hamlet's presence is intended to be imagined by Claudius rather than real.[51] This nuance was lost in performance. During 'The Mousetrap', the family joins the audience in the front row, Hamlet's audience becoming complicit in his plan to expose Claudius. In the final scene, as Hamlet dies and asks Horatio to 'tell my story' (5.2.301), Hamlet shows Horatio the audience, and Horatio acknowledges its presence. Hamlet hands his audience over to Horatio; it is this audience that will carry forward Hamlet's story and perpetuate his fame and notoriety – a new audience that Scott, as actor, brought to the theatre.

'I'LL MAKE A GHOST OF HIM THAT LETS ME' (1.4.62): GHOSTING EFFECTS IN CELEBRITY *HAMLETS*

Marvin Carlson argues that 'We are able to "read" new works ... only because we recognise within them elements that have been recycled from other structures of experience that we have experienced earlier'.[52] This is nowhere more evident than in productions of *Hamlet*. Actors' accounts of playing Hamlet invariably reference the illustrious history of *Hamlet* productions and actors who have played the role. This culturally iconic status means that an audience is unable to watch a production of the play without also experiencing its performance history. This play, arguably more than any other, has developed a meaning and an understanding that exceed those imagined by Shakespeare. However, with the new audiences that celebrity Hamlets bring to the theatre, this is problematic. How can an audience that may have no first-hand, direct experience of either Shakespeare or *Hamlet* be influenced by these ghosting effects – or, rather, are other ghosting influences at hand? Certainly, as with these four celebrity productions, it seems impossible to stage a celebrity Hamlet in anything other than a modern twentieth-/twenty-first-century setting. Conversely, recent non-celebrity productions at Shakespeare's Globe have employed a mixture of Renaissance and modern dress (the 2018 Globe Ensemble production with Michelle Terry as Hamlet),[53] and 1940s-inspired costuming (Dominic Dromgoole's 2014 to 2016 *Globe to Globe Hamlet*),[54] demonstrating that there is the potential for non-modern *Hamlets*. Therefore, the extent that this modern-day staging is celebrity-driven, rather than text-driven, merits consideration. Arguably, a celebrity *Hamlet* production is haunted as much by history of performance as it is by the particular actor playing Hamlet and the roles he is famous for portraying.

Moreover, notions of celebrity Hamlets being outside of the norm naturally raises the converse – the idea that there are so-called 'Shakespearian' actors better suited to playing the role. Barbara Hodgdon argues that 'The very term "Shakespearean star" is misleading', claiming that 'with the rise of modernity and mass communication and with the politics of large-scale industrial cultures: the star is a product ... financing a production often depends on a star-property's interest and notice of his casting ... can pre-book

---

[51] Shakespeare, *Hamlet*, dir. Icke: Promptbook, Rehearsal Notes and Production Correspondence file.

[52] Carlson, *Haunted Stage*, p.4.

[53] Shakespeare, *Hamlet*, dir. Holmes and While.

[54] William Shakespeare, *Hamlet*, dir. Dominic Dromgoole and Bill Buckhurst (London: Shakespeare's Globe Theatre, 2014 and 2016).

and sell out a play's run, regardless of the notices'.[55] This is undoubtedly true: it would be naïve to think that the commercial success of celebrity productions is not a key consideration, and that the casting of the celebrity is not a factor in anticipated commercial success. That said, there does seem to be an equally strong commitment to attracting a new audience. All four of the celebrity *Hamlet* productions had well-advertised, affordable ticket schemes – indeed, Law's *Hamlet* employed an 'affordable pricing scheme' with a top-price ticket at just £32.50.[56] Cumberbatch's *Hamlet* was 'the fastest-selling ticket in London theatre history with advance seats selling out in minutes',[57] and with £62.50 tickets being resold on secondary markets at £1,500.[58] As such, there was obviously scope to charge higher prices while still attracting high audience numbers. However, these productions actively sought to attract a new audience, and lower-priced theatre tickets were a key component – a target audience unused to Shakespeare could be repelled by high ticket prices and be unwilling to risk the price of a theatre ticket on an unfamiliar activity. This is an approach adopted by Nicholas Hytner at the National Theatre with the Travelex Tickets.[59] Certainly, Scott was particularly aware of the barriers that expensive tickets could create, making it a condition of transfer to the West End that affordable tickets be made available. He noted that, 'however much we talk in the theatre about bringing young people in, [. . . they] can't pay £75 or £80 or £90 for a ticket'.[60] This scheme was a success, with Scott claiming that 'Something like half of the audience in the West End had never been to the theatre before.'[61]

Affordable ticket schemes cannot operate in isolation. If a target audience is not looking to attend theatre productions, or consider themselves to be excluded in some way, they will still be wary of buying even the affordable tickets designed for them. The tickets must form part of a wider marketing plan. Whereas, traditionally, the critical reviews of opening productions act either to motivate or to demotivate an interested theatre-goer, these celebrity *Hamlet* productions were, for the most part, sold out long before press night. The power of the review to influence attendance is clearly diminished. Michael Billington observed a 'gradual shift towards a PR-led culture . . . a barrage of pre-publicity in every available medium', noting a conflict between critical reviews of productions and pre-production hype.[62] What Billington's observation misses, however, is that, for a celebrity production, the pre-publicity is aimed at a vastly different audience from the traditional critics' readership.

The use of targeted publicity is not a new concept. Carol Chillington Rutter notes that the first Royal Shakespeare Theatre poster was for David Warner's 1965 *Hamlet*. This poster aligned Shakespeare to contemporary, edgy Pop Art-inspired design, offering a Warhol-esque

---

[55] Barbara Hodgdon, 'Shakespearean stars: stagings of desire', in *The Cambridge Companion to Shakespeare and Popular Culture*, ed. Robert Shaughnessy (Cambridge, 2007), pp. 44–66, p. 47.

[56] Theatre Programme for William Shakespeare's *Hamlet*, dir. Michael Grandage (2009).

[57] Daniel O'Brien, 'Benedict Cumberbatch's Hamlet at Barbican sells out in record time', *The Evening Standard*, 11 August 2014: www.standard.co.uk/go/london/theatre/hamlet-at-the-barbican-benedict-cumberbatch-effect-sees-play-become-most-in-demand-theatre-event-9662839.html.

[58] 'Watchdog reveals secondary ticketing "stitch up" as event tickets go on sale before official release', *The Telegraph*, 13 November 2013: www.telegraph.co.uk/news/shopping-and-consumer-news/11993056/Watchdog-reveals-secondary-ticketing-stitch-up-as-event-tickets-go-on-sale-before-official-release.html.

[59] Peter Aspden, 'Travelex chief / theatre sponsor Lloyd Dorfman', *The Financial Times*, 26 September 2014: www.ft.com/content/7f4ace9a-4493-11e4-aboc-00144feabdc0.

[60] Hannah Furness, 'Theatre will be dead in 50 years unless it fixes "disgusting" ticket prices', *The Telegraph*, 14 June 2017: www.telegraph.co.uk/news/2017/06/14/theatre-will-dead-50-years-unless-fixes-disgusting-ticket-prices.

[61] Holly Williams, 'Andrew Scott: "There was no Hamlet rivalry with Benedict Cumberbatch"', *The Guardian*, 17 June 2018: www.theguardian.com/culture/2018/jun/17/andrew-scott-interview-sea-wall-sherlock-hamlet-king-lear-shakespeare.

[62] Michael Billington, 'We will not be muzzled', *The Guardian*, 28 June 2000: www.theguardian.com/culture/2000/jun/28/artsfeatures2.

manipulated double-image of Warner's face in profile and head-on. This offered a young, predominately teen audience a Hamlet 'like them, who gazed *at them* [. . . and] gave 1960s youth culture a Hamlet who stared them down'.[63] This connection between target market and poster image is key. A simple image must serve both to interest and attract the target market and to provide sufficient information to allow that market to act. Reviewing the posters for the celebrity *Hamlet* productions reveals notable trends. For the most part, the posters prominently feature the star: Tennant and Law each stare out of the poster at the viewer, demanding attention.[64] Scott lies in a coffin surrounded by the detritus of a party.[65] Conversely, Cumberbatch does not feature in the poster for his production – instead, a child bearing a passing resemblance to him sits at a table surrounded by other children dressed in what appear to be theatre costumes.[66] The absence of Cumberbatch was noted, with the *Independent* commenting that the fans' first glimpse of Cumberbatch as Hamlet 'might not be what they quite expected'.[67]

However, with the Scott and Cumberbatch posters, there may be something else at play – both of these actors are well known for their roles in *Sherlock* (Scott as Moriarty and Cumberbatch as Sherlock Holmes) and these posters could be interpreted as being subtle references to the TV series.[68] Scott's eyes in the coffin are open and, coupled with a series of opposites listed on the poster ('ghost/devil, acting/madness, be/not be'),[69] the question implicitly asked is 'dead/alive?' *Sherlock* fans had contemplated the same question in respect of Moriarty (the 2016 Christmas special, 'The Abominable Bride', ended with Sherlock concluding that Moriarty was both dead and back).[70] Similarly, season 3 of *Sherlock* (2014), focused on Sherlock's isolated childhood with brother Mycroft, and the extent to which this influenced the adult.[71] Portraying Cumberbatch's Hamlet as a child would not, on reflection, be that unexpected for his core fanbase. The Cumberbatch poster raises further questions: the reader is encouraged to engage with the image in an attempt to unpack its meaning. Children in skeleton costumes

clearly allude to death, but who is the girl with flowers and why are there children dressed as soldiers and fencers? It is a complex image. If you know the play, these images are clearly referencing the plot. However, for a new audience they act as teasers, a hint at what this production will offer. The images invite the reader to work this out – possibly, as Broadway.com notes, the poster acts as 'a puzzle worthy of Sherlock Holmes'.[72]

Similarly, Tennant is pictured in a pastiche of Casper David Friedrich's *Wanderer Above the Sea of Fog*.[73] At first glance, this bears no clear reference to

---

[63] Carol Chillington Rutter, 'Shakespeare's popular face: from the playbill to the poster', in *The Cambridge Companion to Shakespeare and Popular Culture*, ed. Shaughnessy, pp. 248–71, p. 261.

[64] Theatre poster for *Hamlet*, dir. Doran: https://rscprints .org.uk/search?q=hamlet&type=product; and theatre poster for *Hamlet*, dir. Grandage: www.pinterest.com/pin/ 345792077609646806.

[65] Theatre poster for *Hamlet*, dir. Icke: www.slideshare.net /BeaGrist1/mary-stuart-hamlet-poster-late-121016.

[66] Theatre poster for William Shakespeare's *Hamlet*, dir. Lyndsey Turner (2015): www.soniafriedman.com/produc tions/hamlet-barbican.

[67] Neela Debnath, 'Benedict Cumberbatch as Hamlet: poster shows child version of actor as Danish prince', *The Independent*, 3 August 2014: www.independent.co.uk/arts-entertainment/theatre-dance/news/benedict-cumber batch-as-hamlet-new-poster-shows-child-version-of-actor-as-danish-prince-9645096.html.

[68] *Sherlock* (television programme).

[69] Theatre poster for *Hamlet*, dir. Icke.

[70] Ed Power, '*Sherlock*: The Abominable Bride, nine things we learned', *The Telegraph*, 4 January 2016: www .telegraph.co.uk/culture/tvandradio/12073234/sherlock-special-new-years-day-benedict-cumberbatch-abominable-bride-TV.html.

[71] *Sherlock* (television programme); see, in particular, 'The Empty Hearse', Season 3, Episode 1 (1 January 2014).

[72] Imogen Lloyd Webber, 'Odds and ends: poster revealed for Benedict Cumberbatch's Hamlet . . . ', Broadway.com, 1 August 2014: www.broadway.com/buzz/176942/odds-ends-poster-revealed-for-benedict-cumberbatchs-hamlet-made-in-dagenham-casting-more.

[73] Caspar David Friedrich, *Wanderer Above the Sea of Fog* (oil on canvas) (Hamburg: Kunsthalle Hamburg, *c.* 1818). Also at Cody Delistraty, 'The art of wanderlust', *The Paris Review*, 27 August 2018: www.theparisreview.org/blog/2018/08/ 27/the-art-and-politics-of-wanderlust.

Hamlet. However, the target audience, Tennant's fanbase, view the poster through a different lens – that of a Doctor Who fan, or Whovian. For this fanbase, the image of a solitary man at odds with his surroundings acts as a reference to Tennant's role as The Doctor, the last of the Timelords, destined to wander alone through time. The image of Tennant himself wearing an almost identical outfit to the one he wears as The Doctor directly references his role in *Doctor Who*.[74]

There are other notable features. While Shakespeare is mentioned on each of the posters, his name is not given any real prominence. Nor is the celebrity's name – indeed, Scott is not mentioned at all on the poster for his production. This is somewhat at odds with expectations. The closest marketing comparator to celebrity *Hamlet*s would be Shakespeare on film. Emma French notes, in respect of Luhrmann's *Romeo + Juliet*, that making clear references to Shakespeare invokes 'positive connotations that the Shakespeare brand possesses', affording the adaptation an air of authenticity – and certainly Hollywood is not shy of selling its leading men.[75] This absence would suggest that there are other influences at play. The target audience is expected to recognize and respond to the image without textual prompts. These images are pre-publicity, created before the performance with the sole aim of selling tickets – all four posters are clear about when and where the production will take place and how tickets can be purchased. With respect to Shakespeare on film, French observes that posters '"position" a film for its potential audience, in terms of genre, stars, content, [and] tone'.[76] Theatre posters are no different, particularly when, as is the case with these celebrity productions, the star has a well-known on-screen persona. However, by downplaying both playwright and star name, these posters invariably invite the reader to view the actor not as himself, but instead – or simultaneously – as his on-screen alter-ego. Arguably, this actively encourages the target market to engage with the celebrity production not as a purely Shakespearian venture, but rather as an extension of the celebrity's other roles. Carlson would argue that, in performance,

actors 'carry with them memories of their work in previous productions';[77] however, with these posters, the ghosting of the actor's previous roles onto that of Hamlet is actively encouraged from the outset.

The downplaying of Shakespeare on the posters warrants further analysis – it would be easy to say that this is attributable to a simple desire to sell tickets and that, for this new target audience, mentioning Shakespeare would be a disincentive to buy. The exclusion of Shakespeare entirely is problematic. Surely, the aim of attracting a new audience to Shakespeare is exactly that: to invite the new theatre-goer to try other Shakespeare plays. If your aim is simply to bring a new audience to theatre, there are arguably more accessible plays and playwrights. However, as French somewhat flippantly observes in respect of film: 'The most significant goal when creating posters ... is to ensure that audiences buy tickets ... not to accurately reflect the content of the film'.[78] This is clearly at play with these theatre posters – there is very little information as to what the production entails, and the images bear little correlation to the final production as staged. This is not surprising, with respect to the Cumberbatch *Hamlet*, as the poster was released a year in advance of the production, so it would be rather ambitious to expect a clear image at that stage. The blue-lit, T-shirt-clad Scott in his coffin clashes with the clean sophisticated modern Danish aesthetic of the final production – it is hard to imagine that a funeral in Scott's stylish Elsinore would include disposable plates and glasses. It should be noted that, on transfer to the West End, the production poster was

---

74 Image: David Tennant as Doctor Who: www.dailymail.co.uk/tvshowbiz/article-1245927/David-Tennants-plans-break-America-ice-new-TV-hold.html.

75 Emma French, *Selling Shakespeare to Hollywood: The Marketing of Filmed Shakespeare Adaptations from 1989 into the New Millennium* (Hatfield, 2006), p. 107. See: *William Shakespeare's Romeo + Juliet*, dir. Baz Luhrmann (1996).

76 French, *Selling Shakespeare*, p. 27.

77 Carlson, *Haunted Stage*, p. 69.

78 French, *Selling Shakespeare*, p. 48.

redesigned to feature a pensive Scott wearing his fencing jacket with his watch clearly on show – an image much more clearly linked to the final production.[79] Cumberbatch's and Tennant's *Hamlet*s also had a second poster which more closely resembles the actual production. The Cumberbatch production enjoys a continued public presence through National Theatre Live Encore Screenings of the production, which, as of 2019, are regularly scheduled both in the United Kingdom and internationally. The poster for the NT Live screenings is much more closely matched to the production, featuring a still of Cumberbatch in character, staring out of the poster poised to speak.[80] Similarly, on transfer to the Novello Theatre in London, the Tennant *Hamlet*, as with the Scott *Hamlet*, used a redesigned poster featuring a production still of Tennant, wearing a tuxedo and crown at a jaunty angle holding a dagger towards the viewer – an image again much more representative of the final production aesthetic. From a marketing perspective, these second posters perform a different role, aimed as they are at a potentially different target audience. The second-chance audience are those who may not have been attracted by the simple lure of celebrity or alter-ego credentials. These second posters, while again featuring the star front and centre, also place the final production at the core, with a clearer link between poster image and production aesthetic, and invite the viewer to see this *particular* production of *Hamlet*.

Celebrity productions do not happen in a vacuum. The production company does not have exclusive control over a prospective audience and cannot control wider media response. Carlson identifies external ghosting effects, noting that, when a well-known actor takes on a well-known role, 'two repositories of public cultural memory … come into conflict, with potentially powerful dramatic results as they negotiate a new relationship, either a successful new combination or a preservation of a duality'.[81] In a celebrity production of *Hamlet*, these effects are magnified. Not only does *Hamlet* have an iconic status in the cultural memory, the celebrity brings their own iconic status and that of their roles to the production. Carlson's concern is the reception of a production and the extent to which these conflicting cultural

memories impact meaning. However, increasingly, this conflict plays out not in the theatre but in the media. When a celebrity is cast, the very fact of their casting is news. Billington may baulk at the 'barrage of pre-publicity' that surrounds celebrity casting, but it is the media that fuel the interest.[82] In the weeks leading up to a production, there is a flood of newspaper articles. These fall loosely into three categories: a review of *Hamlet*s past (the actors and productions) with consideration of how this new Hamlet will fit into the pantheon;[83] interviews with the director or celebrity;[84] or a report of ticket sales and audience numbers.[85] Media coverage is not limited to pre-publicity: in addition to the traditional reviews, the ongoing production is treated like a news event with, for example, in the case of the Cumberbatch *Hamlet*, paparazzi coverage of Cumberbatch leaving the theatre[86] and accounts of what his mother thought of this performance (not surprisingly she thought her son was 'a bloody good Hamlet').[87] This coverage increases the external ghosting effect, combining the two strands of cultural memory.

---

79 Theatre poster for *Hamlet*, dir. Icke.

80 Cinema poster for William Shakespeare's *Hamlet*, NT Live, dir. Lyndsey Turner (2015): https://bbfc.co.uk/releases/national-theatre-live-hamlet-2015.

81 Carlson, *Haunted Stage*, p. 78.

82 Billington, 'We will not be muzzled'.

83 See, for example, Michael Billington, 'The role to die for', *The Guardian*, 31 July 2008: www.theguardian.com/stage/2008/jul/31/theatre.shakespeare.

84 See, for example, Charles Spencer, 'Jude Law and Michael Grandage discuss Hamlet at Wyndham's Theatre', *The Daily Telegraph*, 26 May 2009: www.telegraph.co.uk/journalists/charles-spencer/5388236/Jude-Law-and-Michael-Grandage-discuss-Hamlet-at-Wyndhams-Theatre.html.

85 See, for example, Jack Malvern, 'Fans camp to see (or not to see) star', *The Times*, 6 August 2015, p. 3.

86 Kate Thomas, 'Triumphant Benedict Cumberbatch leaves the theatre with his arm around wife Sophie Hunter following "electrifying" *Hamlet* debut', *Mail Online*, 6 August 2015: www.dailymail.co.uk/tvshowbiz/article-3186730/Benedict-Cumberbatch-leaves-theatre-Sophie-Hunter-Hamlet-debut.html.

87 Hannah Ellis-Petersen, 'Benedict Cumberbatch is a bloody good Hamlet, says his mum', *The Guardian*, 26 August 2015: www.theguardian.com/culture/2015/aug/26/benedict-cumberbatch-is-a-bloody-good-hamlet-says-his-mum.

The new target audience is educated as to the performance history of *Hamlet*, while the ghosting of both the actor and his previous roles onto the new role of Hamlet is accentuated.

Understandably, celebrity is the focus of the media interest – the story is the celebrity, and without this star touch, the production would be just another opening that might generate a review and a couple of opinion pieces. The media firmly place the celebrity and role at the fore, blurring the line between the actor and the role they play and, by extension, imprinting the ghost of the celebrity's previous role onto Hamlet. The Scott *Hamlet* was screened on BBC Two; the introduction to the production placed Scott's role as Moriarty at the fore, with the announcer introducing the production as 'BBC Two brings you Moriarty as the Prince of Denmark.'[88] Andrew James Hartley noted a similar connection in respect of the Tennant *Hamlet*, arguing that: 'Audiences remember and connect performances, and as if to emphasize the point, the BBC took the extraordinary step of airing [... the production on Boxing Day 2009] between the two parts of Tennant's final performance as the Doctor'.[89] The viewer is encouraged to see Tennant's Hamlet as an extension of his role as The Doctor. This is reflective of the majority of the reviews. There is a sense that it is not the actor who is taking on *Hamlet*, but the character he more famously portrays. With reviews containing comments such as 'Doctor Who Hamlet',[90] 'Alas, poor Dr. Who ... you're okay but not out of this world',[91] 'Moriarty in Elsinore?'[92] and, in respect of Law, 'Oscar-nominated Primrose Hill luvvie',[93] the actors and productions cannot be separated from their perceived low-brow, mass-culture alter-ego. There is an implicit value judgement that these productions are to some extent inferior due to their association with celebrity.

Reviewing Cumberbatch's *Hamlet*, Paul Taylor, despite praising Cumberbatch's 'great gift for portraying the brilliant misfit' and 'natural casting', muses, 'if only he'd done Hamlet before Sherlock'[94] – the implication being that playing mainstream, popular-culture characters somehow diminishes reception of more *serious* roles. Similarly, reviews of Tennant's production observe that '*Hamlet* is the great lake in which elephants and highbrows can swim and lambs and lowborns can paddle', implying that the new audience of 'Doctor Who fans' falls into the latter category.[95] References to the audience are rife in these reviews: from Tennant's *Hamlet* whose audience is 'liberally sprinkled with children',[96] a 'Wyndham's teeming with young people',[97] to Cumberbatch's 'Hamlet for the kids raised on Moulin Rouge ... aimed squarely at those Cumber-fans'.[98] The inclusion of the audience is noteworthy; parallels can be drawn with Paul Prescott's analysis of the role of the Shakespeare's Globe Theatre's audience in the reviews of the theatre's early productions, where the audience 'functioned as culturally incompetent counterpoints to the critic'.[99] This is clearly at play in the commentary on these celebrity productions. For many critics, the young fanbase that the celebrity

---

88 *Hamlet* (London: BBC Two Television, 30 March 2018).

89 Andrew James Hartley, 'Time Lord of infinite space: celebrity casting, Romanticism, and British identity in the RSC's "Doctor Who *Hamlet*"', *Borrowers and Lenders* 4.2 (2009), 1–16, p. 6.

90 Charles Spencer, 'David Tennant: thrills abound in Doctor Who Hamlet', *The Telegraph*, 6 August 2008: www.telegraph.co.uk/culture/theatre/drama/3557930/David-Tennant-thrills-abound-in-Doctor-Who-Hamlet.html.

91 Quentin Letts, 'Alas poor Dr. Who ... you're okay but not out of this world', *Mail Online*, 6 August 2008: www.dailymail.co.uk/tvshowbiz/article-1042018/Alas-poor-Doctor-Who–youre-okay-world.html.

92 Paul Taylor, 'Andrew Scott is a wonderfully moving Hamlet', *The Independent*, 1 March 2017: www.independent.co.uk/arts-entertainment/theatre-dance/reviews/hamlet-almeida-london-review-a7605576.html.

93 'Jude Law: to see or not to see', *The Sunday Times News Review*, 7 June 2009, p. 12.

94 Paul Taylor, 'If only he'd done Hamlet before Sherlock', *The Independent*, 24 August 2015, p. 7.

95 'Who's there? A new Hamlet takes to the stage, Prince Who David Tennant is introducing Shakespeare to new audiences', *The Times*, 6 August 2008, pp. 1–2.

96 Taylor, 'Andrew Scott is a wonderfully moving Hamlet'.

97 Michael Billington, 'Hamlet', *The Guardian*, 4 June 2009: www.theguardian.com/stage/2009/jun/04/review-theatre-hamlet-jude-law.

98 Kate Maltby, 'Hamlet', *The Times*, 7 August 2015, p. 3.

99 Paul Prescott, *Reviewing Shakespeare: Journalism and Performance from the Eighteenth Century to the Present* (Cambridge, 2013), p. 160.

attracts are simply incapable of understanding the play, and Shakespeare is somehow contaminated by its association with popular culture. There is a working assumption that the critics are there as an arbiter of high-brow culture, and that any deviation from the expected or traditional renders a production inferior. The critics take on the protectionist role of defenders of the text, brandishing their expert status. This is evident in the treatment of the unexpected cliff-hanger interval in the Tennant *Hamlet*. In this production, Hamlet overhears Claudius's confession and the interval begins with an unexpected cliff-hanger, as Hamlet stands over Claudius with a knife and declares, 'now might I do it' (3.3.73). Susan Irvine's review is typical: 'Doran pulls off a good gag when he leaves the audience on a cliff-hanger ..., resuming only after the interval to gasps from some of the young audience, who were clearly new to the play'.[100] Irvine mocks the inexperienced audience while making it clear that she, the educated critic, would not fall for such a gag. For all the thinly veiled contempt of the new audiences drawn by the lure of celebrity, the critics seem equally seduced. Unable to see beyond celebrity, the critics too are haunted by both the characters the celebrities make famous, and celebrity itself. They see celebrity as an inherent threat to the purity of Shakespeare and have a negative knee-jerk response. To borrow an analogy from *The Times*, these celebrity productions could, for critics, never be 'caviar to the general', but rather are destined to be 'burger and chips'.[101]

CONCLUSION: 'GOOD NIGHT, SWEET PRINCE' (5.2.312)

Casting a celebrity in the role of Hamlet could easily be dismissed as a gimmick, as a mere ploy to drive ticket sales and ensure commercial success. However, celebrity *Hamlet* productions of the past decade have played an important role in promoting Shakespeare by appealing to a new audience in a way traditional, non-celebrity Shakespearian productions may not. The Tennant, Law, Cumberbatch and Scott *Hamlet*s were unashamedly designed for a new, modern, young audience. The new audience that the celebrity *Hamlet*s brought to the theatre

offered new performance possibilities. The staging of these productions drew heavily on this new audience's lack of knowledge of Shakespeare in performance, exploiting the expressive and aesthetic possibilities of large-scale West End productions, together with familiar filmic references. These *Hamlet*s were exclusively modern, presenting the audiences with an Elsinore to which they could relate. The Danish design aesthetic of the Scott *Hamlet* and the grand, expensive opulence of the Cumberbatch *Hamlet* offered aspirational living – a nod to the Instagram culture of the target audience. A Hamlet in a modern, casual dress allowed the audience to identify readily with the hero, as it is easier for audiences to find a connection with characters who look like them. As Byron put it: 'we love Hamlet as we love ourselves'.[102] Much as David Warner was a Hamlet that 'redefined the role for a generation',[103] with his student gown and Oxbridge scarf 'the very embodiment of a 1960s student',[104] these celebrity Hamlets likewise offer a Hamlet for this generation, one that looks like them, but they do so whilst also welcoming new audiences to the theatre by letting them know Shakespeare is for them too.

The texts were edited to aid comprehension, downplaying politics in favour of Hamlet's personal journey, thus allowing the celebrity to remain the centre of attention. Playing on the nature of celebrity, audiences are encouraged to view the productions through the lens of fandom. There was an explicit acceptance that the audience, drawn by the celebrity, could never completely eradicate the ghosts of the actor or the roles for which he was famous. Blurring the line between role and actor, these celebrity productions exploited the presence of an actor playing a role. There was a duality of reception at work: on the surface, the audience sees the named actor on stage

---

[100] Susan Irvine, 'Hamlet Who?', *The Sunday Telegraph*, 10 August 2008, p. 28.
[101] 'Who's there?', *The Times*.
[102] Cited in Croall, *Performing Hamlet*, p. 6.
[103] Michael Billington cited in Croall, *Performing Hamlet*, p. 28.
[104] Croall, *Performing Hamlet*, p. 26.

playing Hamlet, but underlying this is a previous emotional response to, and relationship with, the actor's earlier roles. As Jonathan Holmes, reviewing the first preview of the Cumberbatch *Hamlet* observed, the staging of the production was: 'weird and deliberately off-putting in places, and if Cumberbatch never fully disappears into the role, it's to use his fame to wrong-foot the audience'.[105] This incisive observation highlights the duality of reception. The audience's existing preconceptions are exploited to aid meaning. The celebrity *Hamlet*s focused heavily on the nature of public versus private personae. Explicitly, the productions focused on Hamlet, the Prince of Denmark, and the pressure of constantly being on show. However, ghosting the celebrity onto the role offers further insight and impacts reception. By drawing parallels between the celebrity actor and Hamlet, the audience is encouraged to draw on their existing understanding of the pressures of fame and to apply that knowledge to the politics of Elsinore, thus aiding understanding. A celebrity needs an audience, and focus on celebrity renders these productions self-consciously artificial. The audience is aware that this is fiction at all times. Moreover, the audience itself acts as a player within these productions. If the celebrities' previous roles are ghosted onto the production, then so too is their fanbase. For the Scott *Hamlet*, the audience played a key role, with Scott not only directing soliloquies to the audience directly, but also walking into the audience addressing individual members. Placing the royal family amongst the audience for 'The Mousetrap' and showing both the cast and audience on the on-stage screens made the audience complicit in Hamlet's plan to trap Claudius. Similarly, mirrored panels in the Tennant *Hamlet* placed the audience constantly on view as an omnipresent observer. The effect of ghosting the audience onto the productions offers another point of recognition for the audience. They understand and are used to their role as an observer of an actor's work, and explicitly drawing their role in the mechanics of the theatre offers security.

Embedded in the critical response was an expectation that any production pandering to a celebrity fanbase would be inherently inferior. Parallels can be drawn with the reception of Baz Luhrmann's *Romeo + Juliet* which was criticized for being a '(mis)appropriation of Shakespeare's play for purposes of parody ... aimed at an irredeemably low-brow audience of clueless teenagers inhabiting an intellectually bankrupt culture'.[106] This notion that the young fanbase that the celebrity attracts is simply incapable of understanding is endemic in the critical reviews, with critics placing themselves as an intellectual counterpoint to the uneducated masses. For the critics, the presence of celebrity and attendant ghosting effects diminished the value of the production. The presence of the audience in the reviews nods to a consideration of these productions as a spectacle in themselves, regardless of the action on stage. However, while the critics generally expressed concern about the apparent dumbing down, and pontificated in their self-appointed role as protectors of the text, the references made by these critics to the actors' low-brow, mass-culture alter-egos added further fuel to the inherent duality of reception. Far from the critics offering an objective view of the productions, they, like the audience, were seduced by the presence of celebrity. It is noted of adaptations of Shakespeare into new media, such as film, that, by its nature, an adaptation is *in addition to*, rather than, *instead of* – the original continues to be relevant in informing our understanding of the adapted text, and the adaptation adds an additional level of understanding to the source.[107] Further, each new adaptation is a new

---

[105] Jonathan Holmes, 'Hamlet first look: "Not what we were expecting from Benedict Cumberbatch – but only he could pull it off"', *Radio Times*, 6 August 2015: www.radiotimes.com/news/2015-08-06/hamlet-first-look-not-what-we-were-expecting-from-benedict-cumberbatch-but-only-he-could-pull-it-off.

[106] Michael Anderegg, 'James Dean meets the Pirate's Daughter: passion and parody in William Shakespeare's Romeo + Juliet and Shakespeare in Love', in *Shakespeare, The Movie, II: Popularizing the Plays of Film, TV, Video, and DVD*, ed. Richard Burt and Lynda E. Boose (London, 2003), pp. 56–71, p. 58.

[107] Julie Sanders, *Adaptation and Appropriation* (London, 2006), p. 32.

work in its own right, to be understood by a different set of expressive possibilities. The celebrity *Hamlet*s self-consciously exploit ideas of ghosting, actively encouraging an audience to use their own existing knowledge of, and relationship with, both the celebrity and the roles he made famous, in order to unlock an understanding of Shakespeare. Indeed, the mere fact of demystifying Shakespeare for this new audience could itself serve to create a greater potential future audience for other Shakespearian theatre, thus further strengthening

Shakespeare's position in our 'cultural memory'.[108] Yes, these celebrity productions were 'Shakespeare for the kids',[109] but with sell-out audiences engaging with Shakespeare, is that really such a bad thing?

---

[108] John Ellis, 'The literary adaptation', *Screen* 23.1 (1982), 3–5, cited in Linda Hutcheon and Siobhan O'Flynn, *A Theory of Adaptation* (London, 2006), p. 122.
[109] Maltby, 'Hamlet', p. 3.

SHAKESPEARE PERFORMANCES
IN ENGLAND, 2019

STEPHEN PURCELL, *London Productions*

A LINE OF KINGS

This year provided the opportunity to see major productions of nearly all of Shakespeare's history plays, most of them in London.[1] My reviewing year started with Joe Hill-Gibbins's cleverly truncated *Richard II* at the Almeida Theatre. The set, by Ultz, was a bare grey vault. As the play started, Simon Russell Beale's Richard, clad in a plain black T-shirt, came downstage, explaining to the audience that 'I have been studying how I may compare / This prison where I live unto the world' (5.5.1–2). The rest of the cast of eight stood behind him, facing the rear wall. 'Here is not a creature but myself' (5.5.4), he assured us; evidently he was in solitary confinement, and these ghostly figures behind him were figments of his imagination. This conceit became clearer as he resolved to generate thoughts that would 'people this little world' (5.5.9), and the cast along the back wall slowly turned around. These were characters 'In humours like the people of this world' (5.5.10): though most of this ensemble of seven would play multiple roles in the 100-minute edit of the play, each actor had a consistent type or 'humour' that spanned their various characters. Thus, for example, Martins Imhangbe (Bagot/Aumerle) and Saskia Reeves (Mowbray / Bushy / Green / Duchess of York) played a range of characters who were loyal to Richard or rebelled against Bolingbroke; Natalie Klamar played both the Lord Marshal and the Bishop of Carlisle, characters who were similarly devoted to a sense of order and propriety. The ensemble remained on stage for the whole play, often in a tight gaggle, pressed against the wall. They tended to move as a unit, in dance-like formations, signalling the alliances and divisions of Richard's people through non-naturalistic and sometimes comical group movements. Beale's Richard seemed to summon the other characters into being: Imhangbe's Bagot and Reeves's Bushy erupted energetically from within the gaggle when called by Richard, while John Mackay's unwilling York had to be forcibly ejected from the pack. Often, as a character came to Richard's mind, the actor playing that role would feature prominently in the scene: Imhangbe and Reeves, for example, delivered the news of Bagot and Bushy's deaths to Richard in 3.2, and Mackay was likewise assigned the speech in which Richard is told of York's betrayal (3.2.190–9).

The text was cut so that separate events unfolded simultaneously. The end of 1.4, in which Richard hears of Gaunt's (Joseph Mydell's) illness, was intercut with the start of 2.1, Gaunt's complaints about the King. Gaunt's 'This England' speech (2.1.31–68) was thus delivered as a direct attack on Richard, who stiffened his back and walked out of Gaunt's line of fire. Leo Bill's Bolingbroke was also physically present (though narratively absent) for all of this, sitting down centre stage with his head lowered in despondency; later, Richard would kneel down

---

[1] *King John* opened in Stratford-upon-Avon towards the end of the year; only *Henry VI Part 1* and *Henry VIII* were unstaged by major theatres this year.

in the same position during Bolingbroke's mustering of support in 2.3 and 3.1. While the edit and the cast's quickfire delivery of the lines created a hurtling pace, this was creepily undercut by the sound of a ticking clock, which underscored much of the action. It all contributed to an unsettling sense that Richard was already living on borrowed time.

The only props used were those on stage from the start: a brassy, slightly flimsy zigzag crown, and a number of black buckets in an upstage corner, labelled with their contents of 'Water', 'Blood' and 'Soil'. The contents of these buckets began to dirty the stage as the plot progressed. Bushy and Bagot were 'executed' as Bolingbroke chucked a bucket of blood over them; the blood continued to slide down the wall, and the bloodstains remained on the actors' costumes, for the rest of the show (Figure 12). In the deposition scene (4.1), Richard grabbed

a bucket of water rather than a mirror in order to 'read' his reflection, and at the point in the scene when he would normally smash the glass, he threw the bucket's contents over the attendant lords, the 'followers in prosperity' (4.1.270) who had deceived him. Richard himself became covered with mud, a visual reminder of his repeated invocation of the ground in 3.2, and of the way in which the events of the play were bringing him 'down to earth'.

By the time the second iteration of the production's opening speech came around, it was clear that we were watching the psychodrama that was unfolding in the 'prison' of Richard's mind. Act 5, Scene 3 had ended in cacophony, the whole cast, bar Richard, drumming on the walls. In this context, 'yet I'll hammer it out' (5.5.5) took on new meaning: the characters who had just been hammering on the walls were, of course, Richard's

12 *Richard II*, 3.1, Almeida Theatre, directed by Joe Hill-Gibbins. Saskia Reeves as Bushy, Martins Imhangbe as Bagot and Leo Bill as Bolingbroke. Photograph by Marc Brenner.

thoughts, drumming at his skull from within. 'Thus play I in one person many people, / And none contented' (5.5.31–2) suggested that all of the play's personages were aspects of his own psyche. For a moment, I half expected the production to end there, the speech bookending the play with Richard in solitary confinement, still alive. Instead, it followed the narrative through to Richard's murder, Richard's sense of imprisonment passing to the sleepless, guilt-ridden and paranoid Bolingbroke.

There was a comparable sensation of confinement in Robert Hastie's *Macbeth*, the first Shakespeare of the Sam Wanamaker Playhouse (SWP) 2018–19 Winter Season. The line that seemed to serve as a keynote for this production was Macbeth's 'I am cabined, cribbed, confined, bound in / To saucy doubts and fears' (3.4.23–4). Hastie and designer Peter McKintosh used sound, space and light to turn the Playhouse into a crucible of claustrophobia. The witches plunged the candlelit theatre into darkness upon Macbeth and Banquo's entrance in 1.3, so that the two thanes, each carrying a flaming torch, paced frantically around the darkened stage, trying to locate the witches. Paul Ready's Macbeth strode into and around the tiring house, flamelight flickering on its black inner walls, creating an eerie display of dynamically jumping shadows. Over the course of the play, he repeatedly retreated into the area enclosed by the tiring house pillars, his twitchy movement all the more striking for its containment within a tiny space. In the scene of Duncan's murder (2.2), the sense of paranoia was intense – the screech, the cries and the knocks came from all around the outer edges of the auditorium, often almost indistinguishable from the regular noises of spectators coughing and the footsteps of offstage actors, making a virtue of the noisiness and creakiness of this small, packed wooden theatre. It was not only Macbeth whom 'every noise appalled' (2.2.56) – audience members were visibly jumpy too. It was almost as if malevolent outside forces were pressing in on us all. This notion was literalized in the apparition scene (4.1), the witches' voices coming from all corners of the darkened playhouse. The apparitions were summoned with an intense drumming from all around the building, so that the room shook with the noise. They were, in fact, invisible; the doors of the tiring house opened one by one, light spilling from within the tiring house onto the dark stage, and sound effects suggesting the pattering of footsteps.

Ready made an intense, jittery Macbeth. There was a strong sense in each of his soliloquies that he was thinking aloud in collaboration with us, running ideas past us, scrutinizing our reactions. His soliloquy in 3.1 was an attempt to persuade us that killing Banquo was justified – he picked a spectator at the front of the pit, trying to impress upon her the injustice of his having jeopardized his peace of mind and prospect of salvation for 'Banquo's issue' (3.1.66), 'To make them kings' (3.1.71); he paused, as if explaining to an uncomprehending student, 'the seed of Banquo, kings!', before giving up in exasperation. He stuttered frequently, a verbal tic that had the effect of making me listen more closely to his choice of words; he often paused as if he were searching for words, or weighing one he had already chosen. This style of delivery made me notice how often the character speaks in euphemisms and convoluted sentences, even when alone, as if desperate to avoid confronting the nature of his desires. This was not a decisive character, nor a particularly strong one; if it was hard to see him as the hardened warrior of the captain's report (1.2.7–41), it was easy to believe he would be underestimated by his fellow thanes. Michelle Terry's Lady Macbeth, by contrast, spoke urgently and decisively. There was a fierce argument between them in 3.2; Macbeth paused as he informed her 'there shall be done . . . ' as if trying to pick the appropriate euphemism, before he chose his words carefully: ' . . . A deed of dreadful note' (3.2.44–5). Furious at being shut out and equivocated with in this way – and by her own husband – Lady Macbeth replied, slowly and with venom, 'What's to be "done"?' (3.2.45), throwing his own word back at him.

Philip Cumbus's Banquo and Kirsty Rider's Fleance had a nicely detailed relationship in this production. Banquo crossly pulled down Fleance's hood in the presence of the King, policing what one sensed was rebellious teenage behaviour. As Fleance left the stage in 2.1, Macbeth muttered something like 'How goes it?', gesturing towards the boy, to which Banquo replied 'All's well' (2.1.18) – the fact of the question itself, and the concerned way in which Macbeth asked it, hinting at past father–son trouble. But their relationship was marked by deep affection, too – 'How goes the night?' (2.1.1) was Banquo's ham-fisted attempt at opening up a chat as Fleance lay on his back looking at the stars. This Banquo had really listened to the witches – he spent a great deal of time scrutinizing his son, trying to work out how he could possibly shape this tearaway into royalty. He clearly struggled with these seditious thoughts, turning away from Fleance for 'Merciful powers, / Restrain in me the cursèd thoughts that nature / Gives way to in repose' (2.1.7–9). Later, as it became clear that they were about to be set upon by three assassins, Banquo selflessly handed his sword to his son, taking on the killers unarmed deliberately, in order to provide his son – and potential father to a line of kings – with a better chance of escaping. Cumbus's Banquo retained his humanity even after death. Throughout the banquet scene, his ghost reached pleadingly towards Macbeth – not a threatening figure, but a bewildered and betrayed friend, reaching out pathetically for a hug, a physical reunion with the brother-in-arms who had betrayed him. It was perhaps this guilt-inducing aspect of the ghost's appearance that so alarmed Macbeth, who ran away and shrank from the ghost's attempts at contact with abject terror. Banquo seemed to realize, with sadness, that Macbeth would not accept his offer of reconciliation, and moved off stage despondently. I am not sure I have ever seen a more thoroughly *motivated* ghost in this scene: this was not just an apparition, but a character with desires like any other.

The year's second major *Richard II* was staged at the SWP later in the same season, the first production of a year-long project in which the Globe would produce nearly all the plays from Shakespeare's two history tetralogies. Adjoa

Andoh and Lynette Linton's *Richard II* assembled a cast and creative team composed entirely of women of colour, the first Shakespearian production on a major UK stage to do so. The company's ancestry, drawn from across the British empire and beyond, was a major feature of the production: attached to the gallery railings in the auditorium were a number of large sepia photographs of what the programme revealed were the mothers, grandmothers and other older female relatives of the cast and the creative team. These pictures were arranged more or less as one would expect portraits of illustrious forebears to be displayed in a royal hall. Indeed, during the performance, the characters frequently nodded or gestured at these images when referring to dead characters from the play's backstory. The company's heritage was reflected in the production itself in various ways: props, costumes and musical instruments represented a rich intercultural mix, and the etiquette and rituals of the imaginary society devised for the show drew from a variety of world cultures, 'from Africa to the West Indies to the Middle East to South Asia and the Far East'.[2] The front of the tiring house was covered with large bamboo poles, the playhouse's gilded decorations just about visible behind them. In another production, this unspecific amalgamation of signifiers and symbols from a wide variety of non-Western cultures might have recalled the aspiration towards acultural universalism typical of directors such as Peter Brook, widely criticized for cultural appropriation and for fetishizing the 'exotic'. Here, though, I think it was doing something rather different. In a play that so frequently reminds us that it is about England and Englishness, the production's interculturalism seemed like a provocation, a reminder that this country's modern cultural heritage is so fundamentally hybrid that all of these superficially 'foreign' elements are English too. Hearing two black women as Mowbray (Indra Ové) and Bolingbroke (Sarah Niles) lamenting their banishment from their native England (1.3.148–67 and 1.3.269–72) may

---

[2] Adjoa Andoh interview, programme.

have been a refreshing and instructive surprise to an audience more used to hearing these lines uttered by white men; in 2019, these speeches also carried unavoidable echoes of the Windrush scandal.

Co-director Adjoa Andoh took the title role. She made a mercurial Richard: restless, impulsive, domineering, but deeply insecure. This was perhaps the most macho interpretation of the role I have seen, full of swaggering, manspreading, and sharp, punchy gestures. Underpinning much of this, though, was a hint that this Richard was a child-king who had never really been allowed to grow up. He could be cruel and intimidating with those who defied him, but he was also in need of continual reassurance and validation. At one point during the quarrel between Mowbray and Bolingbroke, Richard bowed his head towards the Queen (Leila Farzad), inviting her to stroke his hair in an almost motherly way. His costume and make-up emphasized the idea that this was a king who had quite literally gilded himself in order to bolster his fragile authority: an ornate white-and-gold tunic, golden eye shadow, a golden line down his forehead, an elaborate black-and-gold headdress for a crown (Figure 13). He almost looked like part of the playhouse itself, candlelight constantly glinting off the gold on his clothes and skin.

When I saw the production on 26 March, modern political resonances were inescapable. A few days earlier, just the other side of the Thames, hundreds of thousands had marched for a new referendum on Brexit, and now Parliament was preparing controversial indicative votes that looked set to undermine what was left of the government's authority. It felt horribly timely to be watching a play in which multiple characters become exercised as they respond to being called 'traitors'. Gaunt's 'This England' speech seemed especially topical: Dona Croll delivered it with a mournful, pained urgency, and if some of it bordered on the jingoistic, its downbeat climax was more apt to the political moment. The audience began to chuckle grimly as Gaunt lamented that England was now 'bound in with shame, / With inky blots and rotten parchment bonds' (2.1.-63–4), and erupted into an extraordinary groan-

like laugh as he concluded, 'That England that was wont to conquer others / Hath made a shameful conquest of itself' (2.1.65–6). The end of the production tackled English nationalism head-on: the cast draped themselves in white shawls and smeared their faces with white make-up as three red flags were unfurled across the back gallery, and a longer red flag suddenly dropped down the middle of the tiring house from ceiling to floor, creating an image of the white background and red cross of the flag of St George.[3] 'This is England', the production seemed to be saying – this is England in all its diversity, but this is also England in all its dysfunction. The spectacle of these women of colour literally whitening themselves raised some powerful questions. What sort of country validates itself with wars in 'the Holy Land', as Bolingbroke resolves to do in the play's closing moments (5.6.-49–50)? Was this the start of British imperialism? What sort of a country has England become since? Do these women feel pressured to 'whiten' themselves in order to conform to a prevailing sense of national identity?

The Globe's next instalment in its programme of history plays – a trilogy of *Henry IV Parts 1 and 2* and *Henry V* – opened on 10 May. When these plays were programmed, the Globe would have expected the UK to have left the European Union by this date, but as it turned out, of course, the nation was still in limbo. It was nonetheless an apposite moment, in the words of the Globe's Artistic Director Michelle Terry, 'to explore the present and future of our "sceptred isle" through the prism of Shakespeare's history plays'.[4] The plays were retitled *Hotspur*, *Falstaff* and *Harry England*, respectively. Like last year's *Hamlet* and *As You Like It*, they were presented by the Globe Ensemble, a company that featured some of the same actors as the previous ensemble, and, as in

---

[3] The production's poster had also featured an image of Andoh standing in front of the flag of St George. Andoh gave an interview to the *Evening Standard* in which she discussed her feelings about 'what the flag means and who owns it' (21 February 2019).

[4] Season brochure.

13 *Richard II*, 1.1, Sam Wanamaker Playhouse, directed by Adjoa Andoh and Lynette Linton. Ayesha Dharker as Aumerle, Adjoa Andoh as Richard II, and Leila Farzad as Queen. Photograph by Ingrid Pollard.

2018, they were directed in a collaborative style by two directors (Sarah Bedi and Federay Holmes, the latter returning from the 2018 project). The trilogy was, of course, continuing the story directly from *Richard II* in the SWP. One point of continuity was an English King being played by a woman of colour, here Sarah Amankwah's Henry V, and the revised play titles meant that all three title roles (Hotspur, Falstaff and Henry V) were again played, cross-gender, by women. But where the earlier production had been highly conscious of the racial and gender identities of its cast, the *Henry* trilogy cast actors without regard to race, gender or indeed age (much as the Globe Ensemble shows had in 2018). Whether or not this rendered the trilogy 'blind' to the identities of its actors is, of course, another question.

Michelle Terry joined the ten-strong ensemble for only the first play. Her dynamic, highly watchable Hotspur entirely justified the revised title. This Hotspur started louche and ironic, but quickly whipped himself up into a rage that consumed his entire body. Terry is quite a diminutive actor, so there was something appealing in seeing her dominate the stage with an immensely physical performance, repeatedly coiling up like a spring before letting loose like a firework. As so often in the best performances at the Globe, character and actor sometimes blurred into a single stage figure, here a funny, intelligent and impulsive presence. This was illustrated on Press Day by a wonderful moment. Sharing his frustration at the cowardly lord's letter with the audience (2.4.1–34), Terry's Hotspur noticed a father in the yard cradling his young daughter. Going over to them, Hotspur used the child as an illustration of 'this flower safety' (2.4.10). He then shared the next line of the letter with the pair, asking the child for confirmation of his reading: 'Say you so?' (2.4.14). The child nodded, to delighted applause from the audience.

Helen Schlesinger gave a similarly interactive performance as Falstaff. There was more than a touch of Jennifer Saunders's Eddie from *Absolutely Fabulous*: this Falstaff was gushingly posh, carelessly hurrying over his words, constantly running his hands through his long grey hair. He clearly relished his insult competitions with Hal, his face radiating love and admiration as he listened to the prince insult him with such linguistic dexterity. Schlesinger had a tendency to ad-lib, adding several 'okays' and 'actuallys' to the written lines, sometimes repeating a phrase hurriedly for comic emphasis or extemporizing responses while other characters were speaking. The anachronism of this made Falstaff's dialogue sound very much of the present, in contrast with the faraway historical register of the play's blank verse. Like Terry, Schlesinger developed a great rapport with the audience. The catechism towards the end of *Hotspur* (5.1.127–40) worked beautifully, Falstaff gesturing for the audience to answer 'no!' to his questions; when he asked, 'what is that honour?', a single spectator shouted out 'air!', to which Falstaff replied, 'Someone's read it!'. He cast the groundlings as his soldiers in *Hotspur*, pointing at individuals to illustrate 'discarded unjust servingmen, younger sons to younger brothers, revolted tapsters, and ostlers trade-fallen' (4.2.27–8). Schlesinger made nice use of the yard/gallery dynamic here: Falstaff directed virtually all of the speech at the galleries, whom he clearly imagined to be his peers, while waving his hands dismissively at the groundlings. When Hal looked over the yard disdainfully, Falstaff pointed at the spectator/soldier upon whom the Prince's eye had rested, adding 'he's an ostler'. While this was very funny, it was the first stage in a distancing between Falstaff and the yard that would get its payoff in the next play. Falstaff insisted, 'They'll fill a pit as well as better' (4.2.66) – a pun, of course, since they were in the 'pit' of the theatre, but also a chilling indication of his disrespect for human life.

I saw all three plays over just one day, and it must be said that *Part Two*, or *Falstaff*, rather suffered in its 4 p.m. slot. While the programme notes urged spectators to think of it as a stand-alone play, sandwiching it in a late afternoon slot between two much more dynamic plays did not really help audiences to do this. Rather, encouraged by the scheduling to read the three plays as a narrative sequence, the audience on Press Day seemed underwhelmed by the lack of action in *Falstaff*. The slump was visible – the theatre seemed only about half-full, and emptied further as the play progressed. This was a shame, as there were some wonderful moments, not least the scenes between Falstaff and Sophie Russell's Shallow. There was a telling and comical silence after 'O, Sir John, do you remember since we lay all night in the Windmill in Saint George's Field?' (3.2.191–2) – Falstaff clearly didn't. The homophobic and misogynistic laddishness of these two old friends seemed comically obscene when performed by two women – a similar effect to 2018's *Emilia*, in which Russell also played a male role.

There was a very different atmosphere for the final play of the trilogy at 8 p.m., the full auditorium buzzing with excitement. In a sense, two different plays were being performed simultaneously to two different audiences: the much bigger crowd for *Henry V*, or *Harry England*, was an indication that only a minority of the audience would be seeing this as a continuation of the story begun in *Hotspur*. Seeing it immediately after the two earlier plays focused my attention on Henry's arc. In *Hotspur*, Sarah Amankwah's Hal had seemed initially to be precisely the kind of jack-the-lad that everyone said he was, beginning his first soliloquy (1.2.192–214) not with a marked change in tone but with an exuberant whoop. Imagining the future in which 'this loose behaviour I throw off' (1.2.205), he seemed to ask the audience, 'By how much better than my word I am?', before answering, to a warm laugh, 'By *so* much!' (1.2.207–8). This starting point meant that Amankwah's Hal had quite a journey to become the much cooler and more calculating figure of *Harry England*. The Eastcheap characters belonged to the world of the audience, ad-libbing and dressing more anachronistically than their courtly counterparts: Falstaff headed off to war in a modern fur coat and sunglasses, while John Leader's Bardolph wore spectacles and an anorak. Hal wore a modern red leather jacket and woolly cap for his Eastcheap persona, but as he transitioned to become King, he adopted a more historical costume (Figure 14). This sense that he was cutting himself off from the world of the audience came to a climax in his rejection of his old acquaintances at the end of *Falstaff*, which he did from the stage while Falstaff *et al* stood below him, surrounded by spectators in the yard. When it came to the final play, it was thus much harder to like Henry than it might otherwise have been. With Henry IV's dying advice to 'busy giddy minds / With foreign quarrels' (4.3.342-3) and the scheming Prince John's wager that 'ere this year expire, / We bear our civil swords and native fire / As far as France' (5.5.103-5) still fresh in our minds, it was hard to see Henry's actions in

14 *Henry V*, Shakespeare's Globe, Globe Theatre, directed by Sarah Bedi and Federay Holmes. Sarah Amankwah as Henry V. Photograph by Tristram Kenton.

this last play as anything other than ruthless statecraft.

The final instalment of the Globe's Histories project opened at the Sam Wanamaker Playhouse in November: *Henry VI* (comprising an adaptation of Shakespeare's *Henry VI Parts 2 and 3*), and *Richard III*. The productions reunited most of the ensemble from the summer's *Henry* trilogy, and were cast in a similar way, apparently 'blind' to race, gender and age. Where the summer shows had been directed with a light touch, however, these productions – co-directed by Sean Holmes and Ilinca Radulian, and designed by Grace Smart – felt more conceptual in nature. The stage was dominated by a gold-and-red chaise longue representing the throne, and the onstage ensemble spent much of *Henry VI* arranged in a pose around this throne, even when their characters were technically absent from the scene, the shifting configurations of courtiers standing behind the King indicating the evolving power dynamics of his court. The figures standing behind the throne jostled for position, some of them (Suffolk first, later Warwick) planting a proprietorial foot on one end of it. Even if it was sometimes hard to work out exactly who everybody was, the colours of the costumes told their own story: a court initially dominated by the Lancastrian red of Henry's costume was slowly infiltrated by the York family, all in white, and the blue of the unaligned Warwick and Salisbury. This conceit linked the production loosely with the SWP's *Richard II* – the colours, of course, were those of the modern British flag – but more closely with that of the Almeida, with its onstage ensemble moving comically and emblematically as a group.

Over the course of the two plays, England's descent into anarchy was matched by a similar deterioration of the set. During the first of *Henry VI*'s two intervals, the lower half of the tiring house façade was covered over with chipboard, and, as the play progressed, the various factions scrawled partisan graffiti over it. The 'paper crown' was a small pile of earth, Margaret tipping it onto York's head before knocking it off, and then suffocating him in the soil. During the play's second interval, the set was transformed again: the throne was now ripped and damaged, suspended from the ceiling, and beneath it, the pile of earth that Margaret had initiated with the paper crown scene had grown to cover most of the stage. The scenes that followed contained strong echoes of *Richard II* and its symbolism of the soil, the first with its King sitting mournfully upon the ground (*3 Henry VI*, 2.5) and the next with the same character returning from another country 'To greet mine own land with my wishful sight' (*3 Henry VI*, 3.1.14). The production's literalization of these images once again recalled Hill-Gibbins's *Richard II* at the Almeida. The play ended on a tableau of the York family arranged around a ruined throne and chaotic stage, the dead Henry still lying on the earth before them. After they exited, Henry's ghost got up, looked down at his soil-stained hands, and left the stage.

Conflating *Henry VI Parts 2 and 3* at the expense of *Part 1* meant that the first play focused on the parallel stories of Henry and Margaret's relationship, and the rise of the Yorks. Steffan Donnelly's performance as Margaret suggested the character's sharp intelligence: initially bashful, she gained in confidence as she began to realize she could out-think her rivals in the court. Jonathan Broadbent's timid King Henry, meanwhile, was in a permanent state of crisis over whether or not to take action, sitting anxiously through the confrontation over Gloucester's death, for example, clutching the crucifix that hung around his neck. Margaret, of course, remained a central presence in the next play, *Richard III*, and made her first appearance in this play in a costume still stained with mud and blood. She literally carried the baggage of the earlier play, lugging around a large carrier bag filled with bloodstained mementoes of her murdered loved ones, and she threw handfuls of earth at each of the characters on stage in 1.3 for each of her curses. The York family were depicted in both plays as boozy thugs. They gloated loutishly when Henry was cornered into disinheriting Prince Edward (*3 Henry VI*, 1.1); urged by Warwick to 'embrace him' (1.1.203), York (Colin Hurley) patronizingly tapped the King's chest as if he were congratulating an obedient dog. As England descended into full-blown civil war, the two sides came together on stage to change into plimsolls and football shirts – red for the Lancastrians, white for the Yorks. Each character had a squad number, many of them ironically appropriate: YORK 01, for example, hinting at the man's ambition towards primacy, EDWARD 04 and RICHARD 03 foreshadowing later plot developments. The York boys celebrated their ultimate victory over Henry by bellowing 'We Are the Champions' and swigging cans of lager; all three were still in their football shirts, augmenting the sense of laddishness. Clarence and Richard laughingly discussed Edward's sexual intentions towards Lady Grey while she stood listening to them, watchful and stiff.

Sophie Russell's Richard made his first appearance about halfway through *Henry VI*, chasing Somerset offstage with a chainsaw and reappearing with his previously immaculate white suit spattered with blood. The keynote for this Richard was that the character felt he was predestined to 'snarl and bite and play the dog' (*3 Henry VI*, 5.6.77). Russell's body language was distinctly canine, her Richard entering the wooing scene in *Richard III* on all fours, and taking Lady Anne by surprise by lasciviously kissing her leg. The character's teeth were repeatedly emphasized: Richard killed Henry by biting long and deep into his neck, drenching the stage (and another white costume) in blood. When he kissed his infant nephew in the final scene of *Henry VI*, there was a distinctly cannibalistic undertone to it; indeed, the Queen's discomfort at Richard's proximity to her baby was evident. At the start of *Richard III*, the rest of the royal family were attired in clean off-white suits, only Richard still wearing the mud- and blood-stained football shirt of the previous play. Russell played him without any obvious disability, so his sense of being 'rudely stamped' became a reference to this costume rather than to a physical impairment; indeed, the only other character to appear in a similar costume in this play was Margaret, marking both characters as similarly damaged and ostracized. This Richard really loved talking to the audience, making repeated false exits before returning to us to continue a soliloquy; he took great enjoyment in performing for us, too, donning a series of increasingly flamboyant all-white costumes, and archly over-performing his grief at King Edward's death and his humility at Baynard's Castle.

One of the production's boldest choices was in its staging of the murders of Richard's erstwhile allies. This began towards the end of *Henry VI*. As Clarence and Edward brutally killed the struggling Warwick, Richard crooned the classic country break-up song 'For the Good Times':

> Don't look so sad
> I know it's over
> But life goes on
> And this old world will keep on turning.

Richard reprised this song for every subsequent onstage death. As the first murderer began to stab Clarence with a pair of scissors (*Richard III*, 1.4), Richard re-entered to sing it, watching his brother's murder with the glee of an entertainer putting on a great show for the audience. Grey and Rivers were killed in a similar fashion, with a pair of scissors and a plastic bag, respectively, while Richard performed a Mariachi version of the song with a white sombrero and maracas; Hastings was suffocated in a pile of earth, at great length, while Richard warbled the song as a white-wigged Elvis tribute act. Richard entered in white top hat and tails for his final rendition of the song, dancing with Buckingham for a moment before biting into his neck as in *Henry VI*. Ratcliffe served as official executioner in each case, pulling a small floodlight out of his bag and pointing it back towards each of his victims so that they died in a cold, unrelenting light. Each victim spoke their recollection of Margaret's curses *after* they had been killed, meaning these lines took on the quality of posthumous curses themselves, and set up the notion that Richard was filling the world with vengeful ghosts. These ghosts, of course, made their reappearance at the play's climax. When Richard awoke from his dream, everyone he interacted with on his own side took on the appearance of one of his dead, bloodied victims: Ratcliffe appeared as Clarence, Catesby as Lady Anne (John Lightbody and Matti Houghton, respectively, had doubled in these roles). Richard's soldiers, all wearing semi-transparent waterproofs, were similarly ghost-like creatures, their faces all bloodied. In the play's final sequence, they put down their banners as one, turning on the desperate King and spraying him with blood while the band played a reprise of 'For the Good Times'. As Richard gasped, dying, the ghosts bundled up the plastic sheet on the floor with him still inside it.

All of the Globe's plays this year featured what might be called 'gender-blind' and 'race-blind' casting, but gender and race were far from invisible. *Richard II* had, of course, invited its audience to notice the politics of staging a play about English history with an all-women-of-colour cast, and while *Macbeth*, the *Henry* trilogy, *Henry VI* and *Richard III* were less explicit in this respect, similar resonances could be found across all of these productions. The sexism of the plays' language leapt out whenever it was spoken to, or by, female actors playing men: when Northumberland chided Hotspur for breaking into 'this woman's mood' (*1 Henry IV*, 1.3.235), for example, or when Richard drily observed, 'Why, this it is when men are ruled by women' (*Richard III*, 1.1.62). The audience laughter as Richard marvelled at Anne's ability to find him 'a marv'lous proper man' (1.2.241) emphasized, for me, the sense that both *Henry VI* and *Richard III* were exploring the performance of masculinity, with their braying, beer-swigging lads, their football shirts and their repeated scenes of sexual harassment. When Margaret, played by a male actor, chastised Suffolk, played by a woman, with 'Fie, coward woman and soft-hearted wretch!' (*2 Henry VI*, 3.2.311), it produced a sort of Brechtian effect, jolting the audience out of gendered norms and assumptions. Nina Bowers's Suffolk was a cocksure alpha male, but he straddled Margaret in a distinctly feminine fashion during their final embrace, creating a wonderfully genderless romance between the characters. Macduff was the only substantial role in *Macbeth* to be cast cross-gender, and though Anna-Maria Nabirye played him as aggressively masculine, her female identity kept coming to the fore when Macduff's grief was so heavily gendered by the dialogue in 4.3. Her identity as a black woman produced a doubly alienating effect in the same scene, with the dialogue's repeated linking of blackness with evil. In this way, the casting drew attention to the racism and sexism inherent in the play's imagery.

MISCHIEF IN THE WOODS

The Globe staged three main-house productions of Shakespearian comedies over their summer season: *The Merry Wives of Windsor*, *A Midsummer Night's Dream* and a revival of last year's *As You Like It* (reviewed in last year's article). The first of these to open was Elle While's *Merry Wives*, which featured some alumni of last year's Globe Ensemble, but the production was directed in a very different style from those more open and flexible productions. It was much more controlled, with highly choreographed sequences of movement and a more specific historical setting (provincial England in the 1930s). The set design, by Charlie Cridlan, was more dominant than has generally been the case since the start of Michelle Terry's artistic directorship at the Globe, with set dressing on the tiring house and stage extensions jutting into the yard. Two empty door frames, the same size as those of the actual tiring house doors, were moved around the stage to sketch in various boundaries between interior and outdoor spaces in Windsor. The acting style was broad, leaning heavily into the comedy of humours genre and defining most of the characters with a single exaggerated tic: Dickon Tyrell's Shallow, for example, was constantly getting worked up and needing pills or smelling salts to stave off a heart attack, while Richard Katz's Dr Caius recalled the 1980s sitcom *'Allo 'Allo* with his risqué mispronunciations. Every innuendo was exploited to maximum effect, and physical comedy was used fairly heavily. Pearce Quigley was not a typical Falstaff, tall and slim (aside from a padded beer-belly), drily deadpan and slightly mournful. His text was augmented throughout with a number of extra-textual interpolations, explaining difficult words, lapsing into fragments of song lyrics, or creating new puns:

FALSTAFF. I will ensconce me behind the . . . elbow?
MRS FORD. Arras.
FALSTAFF. I don't know me arras from me elbow.

(Based on 3.3.83–4)

The merry wives of the title were perhaps the most adept in the cast at interacting with the audience; Sarah Finigan's Mistress Page asked 'How shall I be revenged on him?' (2.1.62–3) of a nearby groundling, pausing insistently for an answer until the spectator shrugged and replied she did not know. When, later in the scene, Falstaff's duplicity came to light and Bryony Hannah's Mistress Ford asked the same spectator the same question, Mistress Page gestured dismissively at her and said 'She doesn't know.' This playful back-and-forth encouraged a sense of conversation between stage and yard, to the point that when Mistress Ford asked 'How might we disguise him?' in a later scene (4.2.61), one groundling helpfully shouted out, 'A woman!'. An essay in the programme on the politics of the 1930s led me to anticipate that the production might explore such themes as the rise of fascism, social mobility and the Great Depression, but I am not sure that it addressed these in any serious way. There were some nods to the shifting social dynamics of race in the period – Fenton (Zach Wyatt) was played as a black American, and Mistress Quickly (Anita Reynolds) as a Jamaican immigrant – and, of course, the plot allowed the central characters to become figures of female emancipation. But the production seemed content to eschew a more challenging exploration of these issues in favour of energetic, crowd-pleasing comedy.

There were three major productions of *A Midsummer Night's Dream* in London this summer, all of them opening within a month of each other. Their proximity to each other invited direct comparisons, and indeed there were numerous connections between the three. The first was Nicholas Hytner's production at the Bridge Theatre, a follow-up of sorts to the same creative team's 2018 production of *Julius Caesar*. Like that production, this one reconfigured the Bridge as a semi-immersive space, arranging galleries on four sides around a central pit area of standing spectators and multiple platform stages that were raised and lowered as necessary. The production's pre-show sequence sketched in a world something like that of *The Handmaid's Tale*: Gwendoline Christie's Hippolyta was standing inside a large rectangular glass cabinet, on display as a trophy, perhaps as part of Theseus's victory parade. Around her, a stony-faced choir of dark-suited men, and women in smocks and headscarves, sang fierce hymns. Oliver Chris's Theseus was clearly a fascist autocrat, wearing a dark suit and a lightning-shaped lapel badge; in the play's first scene, all the other men wore the same, while Hermia (Isis Hainsworth) was

dressed in a shapeless grey smock and headscarf. In this context, it was easy to believe that two powerful men would conspire to condemn a disobedient young woman to death. Theseus was nastily ironic over this first scene, revelling in his power over the women; Hippolyta was cool in her replies to him, evidently being careful not to provoke his anger, but a few lines into his confrontation with Hermia, she leaned forward in her box, staring at Hermia with a half-smile on her face. Hermia, transfixed, went over to her, and as Hippolyta's breath fleetingly clouded the glass, the younger woman seemed inspired with a new confidence, returning to Theseus to entreat his pardon as she defied his authority. 'I know not by what power I am made bold', she said (1.1.59), but it was fairly clear: this Hippolyta was magic.

The transition into the forest at the start of Act 2 opened with a montage of four bedrooms across the space, each one showing a different night-time scene: Hippolyta sitting up in bed, Theseus struggling to sleep, Lysander packing for his escape and awaking Hermia, and Helena waking Demetrius. As David Moorst's Philostrate approached Hippolyta, she ripped off his suit in a single flourish to reveal him as Puck – a punky, tattooed figure with a ripped T-shirt and embroidered jeans, glittery and subversive. The fairies dangled acrobatically from white bedsheets in the style of aerial silks, climbing on and around the bedframes. When the dialogue introduced Oberon and Titania, Theseus and Hippolyta's nightwear was torn away to reveal the luscious green costumes of the King and Queen of the Fairies (Figure 15). This strongly implied that what happened in the wood was the shared dream of Theseus, Hippolyta and perhaps the four young lovers – the set of the wood was made from their beds and bedsheets, so in a sense we never really left those four bedrooms. As the play went on, several of the lovers' woodland squabbles played out as tussles on the beds, emphasizing the sexual undercurrents. Oberon and Titania, of course, signified as the dream alter-egos of Theseus and Hippolyta, but if this is a fairly standard doubling, it was upended here by giving most of Oberon's role to

15 *A Midsummer Night's Dream*, 2.1, Bridge Theatre, directed by Nicholas Hytner. David Moorst as Puck and Gwendoline Christie as Titania. Photograph by Manuel Harlan. Manuel Harlan / Arenapal.

Titania, and vice versa, so that it was Titania playing a trick on Oberon rather than the other way around.

It could be argued that having Oberon rather than Titania fall in love with Bottom had the effect of queering the play. Oberon seemed suddenly vulnerable upon waking up and falling in love with Bottom; Hammed Animashaun's appealing and enthusiastic Bottom took this unsolicited attention in his stride, and seemed perfectly happy to allow himself to be seduced. The first half climaxed with Oberon and Bottom being wheeled around in their bed in a carnivalesque procession, followed by members of the audience. But while this was all rather charming, I was slightly troubled by the implications. Reversed in this way, Titania's trick was to render Oberon ridiculous by awakening his homoerotic desires – he straddled Bottom in

3.1, nibbling erotically on his donkey-ear to hoots of laughter from the audience. It thus seemed uncharacteristically homophobic for Titania and Puck, cast here as figures of sexual liberation, to refer to this liaison as 'monstrous' and 'hateful' (3.2.6, 378; 4.1.48, 62). Puck and Titania continued to make sexually subversive mischief during the lovers' quarrel; at one point, Puck applied the love potion to Lysander and Demetrius, so that the two men kissed passionately before Puck removed the spell and they returned, disoriented, to their argument. Titania joined in too, pulling the same trick on Helena and Hermia during the eminently queerable 'double cherry' speech (3.2.196–220). These moments hinted nicely at the latent homoerotic attraction between the same-sex couples, and at Titania's celebration of female sexuality, but both went unremarked-upon after they had happened, rendering them as self-contained and unthreatening as a dream.

The ambiguous sexual politics of the production were best illustrated by the way it ended. When Theseus returned to the stage in his own guise in 4.1, he was still an unreformed character, his bragging about his hounds full of the same sort of passive aggression as the play's first scene. The hunting rifle in his hands as he woke the runaways was ominous, a reminder of the life-or-death stakes he had set up earlier in the play. But after Demetrius's speech explaining the transfer of his affections to Helena, Hippolyta called Theseus's name and glanced up at the suspended double bed upon which Bottom was still sleeping. Fragments of lines from Oberon's liaison with Bottom sounded, as Theseus stared at Hippolyta – evidently this was a moment of magical agency for her, effecting a similar change to the one she had inspired in Hermia in Act 1. Troubled by these echoes of what seemed to have been *his* dream, Theseus relented. The Theseus of Act 5 was a reformed man, newly converted to empathy and the imagination and full of ideas about art. It was not clear exactly to what extent his whole kingdom had been revolutionized overnight, but it seemed to have been – there was not a headscarf in sight, and everyone seemed relaxed and happy. The austere choral music was replaced with pop songs: the mechanicals' bergomask was to Dizzee Rascal's 'Bonkers', and the show was rounded off with a burst of disco, Beyoncé's 'Love on Top' sounding out as two gigantic inflatable moons were bounced around the auditorium, the cast jollying the groundlings into dancing. On some level, the production was clearly a celebration of diverse sexualities – at one point towards the end, a gigantic rainbow flag was passed over the groundlings' heads. The suggestion was that a night of uninhibited gay sex had relaxed Oberon/Theseus's authoritarian tendencies and made him a better, more generous person. This felt to me a little double-edged – Oberon/Theseus and the lovers all returned to their heterosexual relationships after their dabblings with queerness in the woods, and, beyond a few fleeting moments of

awkward eye-contact, there was little space for same-sex desire upon their return to 'normality' in Act 5. Despite its obvious queering of the play, then, it could also be argued that the production paradoxically rendered it even more heteronormative than usual, presenting same-sex desire merely as a carnivalesque inversion.

At the Globe, Sean Holmes's production of the play aimed at a similar sense of carnival. At the start, a huge cardboard box marked 'fragile' was delivered onto the stage and Victoria Elliott's Hippolyta, bound and gagged with parcel tape, kicked her way out of it. Theseus (Peter Bourke) was a tin-pot dictator in a bright pink military uniform that was slightly too big for him, his huge cap and knickerbockers emphasizing his scrawny frame and stooping posture. This Theseus was something of a Pantalone, ridiculous and impotent; while the take was superficially similar to that of the Bridge production, with both Theseuses dictators and both Hippolytas their captives, here the silliness of the scenario undercut any sense of menace. The *commedia dell'arte* flavour continued with the presentation of the lovers, all four of them in deconstructed black-and-white Pierrot costumes with gigantic half-ruffs sweeping over their shoulders. When the scene moved to the forest, four massive multi-coloured hanging garlands dropped from the tiring house roof, reading as carnivalesque 'trees'. The fairies wore bizarre outfits that looked like something from children's television: lots of colours and ribbons, and strange conical hats with large cartoon eyes attached to them. Oberon (Bourke again) appeared in a ludicrously excessive costume – entirely gold, with massive circular embroidered panels behind his head and in front of his legs. It was so over-the-top that his line 'I am invisible' (2.1.186) got a big laugh of incredulity. The mechanicals, meanwhile, did a fair bit of audience interaction and ad-libbing: Quince (Nadine Higgin) treated the whole auditorium as present for the casting session in 1.2, calling the actors one-by-one up from the yard (another echo of the Bridge production). A genuine member of the audience was recruited to play Starveling, ushered up to the stage by Jacoba

Williams's Snout, who functioned as his onstage director/chaperone for much of what followed. Jocelyn Jee Esien's Bottom was an exuberant comic improviser, adding madly to the text; the character elaborated on his reference to a 'French-crown-colour beard' (1.2.88), for example, by spewing out a fast-paced stream of all the French he could think of ('voulez-vous coucher avec moi? . . . ménage a trois . . . Je t'aime . . . ').

One of the production's most interesting aspects was its use of race-conscious casting. Like Hytner's production, Holmes's associated power with whiteness. At the Bridge, Hytner had cast white actors as Theseus/Oberon and Egeus, actors with darker skin tones as Lysander and Demetrius, and black actors as all the male mechanicals, visualizing the hierarchy of the male characters in the play in explicitly racialized terms. In the Globe's production, Egeus, Hermia and Lysander were played by black actors, the mechanicals mostly by women of colour, and Theseus/Oberon, Hippolyta/Titania and Demetrius were white. There were hints that internalized racism might have been behind Egeus's preference for Demetrius, and that Lysander took on some of these racist attitudes himself while under the influence of the spell. Key lines about race really popped out here: when Lysander (Ekow Quartey) compared the black Hermia (Faith Omole) with the mixed-race Helena (Amanda Wilkin) by insisting 'Who will not change a raven for a dove?' (2.2.120), there were howls of outrage and disapproval from the audience (who were, it should be noted, a more obviously racially diverse crowd than their counterparts at the Bridge). He did not do much to redeem himself later when he called Hermia 'you Ethiope!' (3.2.258), prompting a similar audience response.

Like Hytner's production, Holmes's ended in a celebratory riot of audience participation. A piece of scenery was wheeled on from the discovery space for 'Pyramus and Thisbe', the audience member playing Starveling pedalling a bike to generate the electricity for the lamp which was affixed to his head. Quince delivered the plot summary like a rapper, into a mic, whipping up the audience to applause and cheering. Four of the mechanicals formed a human chain to play the lion during the dumb show, singing 'The Lion Sleeps Tonight' and encouraging the audience to join in; instead of the bergomask, the mechanicals sang 'Caravan of Love', spectators clapping and singing along in the yard. There was a vague attempt to address the unequal power relationship hinted at in the first scene: Hippolyta entered 5.1 in a gigantic frilly wedding dress, knocking back champagne as if she were enduring the wedding against her will. But there was no real sense of *coercion* – she seemed assertive and in control. She and Bottom began to kiss passionately at the end of 'Pyramus and Thisbe', and when Theseus said 'Lovers, to bed' (5.1.357), his new wife and her lover took it as their cue to run off stage together. Left alone on stage, Theseus's promise to keep celebrating for another fortnight thus sounded rather as though he were trying to put a brave face on it.

Dominic Hill's *A Midsummer Night's Dream* at Regent's Park Open Air Theatre provided a much darker counterpoint to these more jubilant productions. It opened on the scene of some sort of dinner party – a large, messy table strewn with balloons. Hermia, Lysander, Demetrius and Helena were all guests, and a movement sequence suggested the romantic dynamics between the quartet. Kieran Hill's Theseus was an alpha male: mid-thirties, tall and muscular, physically dominating those around him. He invaded Hippolyta's (Amber James's) personal space over their opening exchange, leaning in towards her with sexual aggression; she, by contrast, was cool and aloof. Egeus (Gareth Snook) interrupted the party, and Theseus immediately took his side: he was, once again, the kind of man who likes to be able to control a woman's sexuality. When Hermia (Gabrielle Brooks) started to push back against patriarchal authority, Theseus snapped back at her in anger, shouting and thumping the table. He decided impulsively to give Demetrius and Egeus 'some private *schooling*', patronizingly emphasizing the last of these words – perhaps he thought he was going to teach them both a lesson about how to dominate women more effectively. But these three were not the only examples of toxic masculinity in this scene. When Michael Elcock's Lysander publicly revealed Helena's (Remy Beasley's) relationship with Demetrius (Pierro Niel-Mee), it was clearly humiliating for her, and she reached out begging him to stop. He ploughed on regardless of her feelings.

The forest in this production was by far the scariest of the three this year, a space that was consistently underscored by drones, hoots, bird and insect cries. The fairies skulked around the sides of the stage, quietly observing the humans; they were huge, dark, spiky creatures, most of them with stilts attached to their arms and legs so that they prowled across the stage like gigantic spiders. They wore broken-down versions of evening suits, suggesting that they somehow embodied the undercurrents of the raucous dinner party that had opened the show. Indeed, the wood was a space of cruel and dangerous sexuality. As Helena urged Demetrius to 'spurn me, strike me' (2.1.205), she took his hands to make him literally inflict these blows upon her; when he threatened to do her 'mischief in the woods' (2.1.237), he positioned himself between her legs. The fairies made eerie popping noises into the stage-side microphones when Lysander awoke under the charm of the love spell, and he took on some of their physicality, leaning forward hungrily as Helena backed away. The quarrel between the four lovers in 3.2 was highly physical, farcical in places, but the lurking fairies, creepy noises and threats of sexual violence from the earlier scenes all gave it a strong undertone of menace, and climaxed in a moment when Lysander very nearly strangled Hermia, stopped only by an intervention from Helena. Susan Wokoma's sweet-natured Bottom was also ill at ease in the forest, waking Titania (Amber James) with a nervous rendition of The Spice Girls' '2 Become 1'. She laughed bashfully at the fairy Queen's advances, but was clearly not at all comfortable. She panicked at the appearance of Titania's fairies, repeatedly shrieking 'What *is* that?', but calmed down as she realized they meant her no harm. By 4.1, she had relaxed

a little in Titania's company, riding a mattress down the set's steps like a toboggan, but from her squirms and starts it was clear that she was still on edge.

Oberon and Titania doubled with Theseus and Hippolyta, and, as in the other versions, there was a suggestion that the supernatural storyline was playing out the tensions inherent in the mortals' relationship. There were certainly flashes of the controlling and possessive Theseus in Oberon: he was stroppy even with the audience, insisting 'As I *can* take it with another herb' (2.1.184) and 'I am invisible' (2.1.186) as if petulantly anticipating our disbelief in his magical prowess. The changeling boy was represented by a toddler-sized puppet, operated by the fairies, and the puppet's physical presence on stage helped to map the arc of Oberon and Titania's relationship throughout the play. Titania seemed to give the boy to Oberon when he asked for it in 2.1, only to cast a spell and reveal the blanket in his arms to be empty, as the child reappeared a safe distance away. Later, as the lovestruck Titania processed off stage with Bottom and the fairies (Figure 16), the final image before the interval was of the boy left up on the bower, forgotten. Oberon was carrying the child as he came in to observe the sleeping Titania and Bottom in 4.1, his line 'Seest thou this sweet sight?' (4.1.45) referring not to the lovers but to the newly relinquished baby. When Titania awoke to see Puck holding the baby, she screamed and hurled herself at Oberon; but it transpired that Oberon meant to share the child, and, at the end of the scene, she directed the line 'Come, my lord' (4.1.98) not at Oberon but at the boy, who toddled over to her and took her hand. She turned to Oberon to continue the speech, and as they were reunited, their two bodies intertwined with the child's, who crawled up Titania's back.

The final scenes of the play, however, suggested a rather less harmonious ending. Left alone on stage at the end of 4.1, the lovers were all isolated figures, shell-shocked and disoriented; Hermia did not take Lysander's hand as they followed to the palace. Theseus appeared unchanged by the experiences of his magical alter-ego, nastily enjoying his ability

16 *A Midsummer Night's Dream*, 3.1, Regent's Park Open Air Theatre, directed by Dominic Hill. Susan Wokoma as Bottom, Amber James as Titania, and the company. Photograph by Jane Hobson.

to overbear Egeus's will (4.1.178). He remained impulsive and sulky even after his own wedding: having heard how terrible 'Pyramus and Thisbe' was, he nevertheless decided 'I will hear that play!' (5.1.81), and as all the other newlyweds objected, he angrily insisted 'I will hear it!' Theseus and the boys went on to bully the amateur actors, interrupting loudly with nasty humour designed to humiliate. There was little sense, then, that the toxic patriarchy of the first scene had been mitigated or healed by the events in the forest. Perhaps for this reason, the final reappearance of the fairies was not, as in the other two productions this year, celebratory and carnivalesque, but rather slow, melancholy and haunting. The whole cast entered, some of them to dance with the fairies, others carrying illuminated balloons on sticks. These lights were extinguished as Puck's epilogue ended, plunging us into darkness.

The most hopeful Shakespearian production I saw this year was Public Acts' *As You Like It*, a collaboration between the National Theatre, the Queen's Theatre Hornchurch, and eight London community organizations representing a number of different disadvantaged or vulnerable groups. Directed by Douglas Rintoul, it featured 5 professional actors alongside a community cast of well over 100 performers, including several in substantial featured roles. This was Public Acts' second project of this sort, following *Pericles* at the National Theatre last year, but where that production had been staged at the heart of the capital, this one took place in suburban East London. It was also the European premiere of Shaina Taub and Laurie Woolery's musical adaptation of Shakespeare's play, which had been created for a similar community project in New York in 2017. The original songs were derived loosely from Shakespearian lines, while the spoken dialogue was drawn directly from the original text.

The adaptation focused heavily on the theme of social life as a form of role-playing. It opened with Jaques (Beth Hinton-Lever) sitting alone in spotlight, singing a solo: 'All the world's a stage, / And everybody's in the show; / Nobody's a pro'. This Jaques was a writer, scribbling away in her notebook as she struggled to compose a story. The implication was that the play *was* her story, and that it illustrated her central metaphor, showing its central characters go through a series of gendered 'acts'. Orlando's (Linford Johnson's) first song was a pugnacious number about the performance of masculinity, warning his brother that 'I'm becoming the man I'm supposed to be.' Rosalind's (Ebony Jonelle's) introductory song picked up on the same phrase, as she commanded herself to 'just play the girl that you're supposed to be ... dress up like a puppet and put on another show'. Orlando's attachment to unrealistic notions of romance was evidently what kept Rosalind from revealing her true identity to him; the song that replaced his poem at the start of 3.2 was a love song full of sexist clichés that rapidly degenerated into an absurd parody of boyband pop. Rosalind's project as Ganymede thus became an explicit attempt to teach Orlando not to idealize the object of his affections. In the song 'Imagine I'm Your Lover', she rejected his cheesy lines and offers of roses, pointing out 'I'm not a baby to be nursed.' Their next song together, 'When I'm Your Wife', replaced the lines beginning 'I will be more jealous of thee than a Barbary cock-pigeon over his hen' (4.1.141–2), and really made me consider the scene anew. What had always appeared to me to be a parodic exchange became a moment of heartfelt self-exposure in which Rosalind admitted to her flaws. Revealing her deep-seated insecurities, Rosalind concluded by asking 'Could you still love me / For what's left of my life / When I'm your wife?'. Having laid herself bare like this, it was plain to see how much it stung her when Orlando failed to reply, saying simply that he was going to leave her for two hours to attend the Duke. *As You Like It*'s central love plot can sometimes feel a little shapeless, narratively speaking, but the reinvention of this moment allowed it to climax with a real sense of crisis.

The Forest of Arden was a space of fellowship and equality. Many of the scenes featuring the Duke's court-in-exile featured the full community chorus singing and dancing together. 'Under the Greenwood Tree' had new lyrics, inviting its hearers to 'Come and live with me / If you want to be free', and observing – in a nod to the civil rights movement – that 'I will not be free / Until we all are free.' As Orlando and Adam were welcomed into the Duke's party and the stage cleared, a single cast member, Mequannt Assefa, stayed behind to welcome Adam with a song that I learned had been written by Assefa himself, a recent immigrant to the UK, during rehearsals. Arden was visibly a space of inclusivity, a disability-positive and racially diverse community (Figure 17). It was sexually diverse, too, the roles of Silvius and Audrey being re-gendered as Sylvia (Malunga Yese) and Andy (Harleigh Stenning) so that two of the play's eventual marriages were between same-sex couples. The re-gendering of Sylvia in particular changed the nature of the joke in the Phoebe/Ganymede plot, so that it was no longer predicated on the homophobic notion that a lesbian crush is inherently comic; instead, the production implied that Phoebe (Malini Murphy) was in denial about her sexuality, which made her eventual marriage to Sylvia not an enforced partnership but a happy acknowledgement of her true sexuality.

The production's ending brought all these themes together. Rosalind got a new soliloquy-song just before her wedding, expressing her anxieties about who she would be after dropping her Ganymede act. Wracked with doubts, she then heard the people of Arden singing, and from this she drew the strength she needed. From this point onwards, the show was astonishingly moving. In an ending that Shakespeare kept off stage, Duke Frederick (Curtis Young) barged in with his minions to object to the weddings, but was embraced without acrimony or judgement by his estranged brother and daughter as the chorus sang out a reminder of the philosophy of Arden: 'Under the greenwood tree / You shall see no enemy.' After a joyful burst of gospel-inspired song and an eruption of dhol drumming, the production returned to the melancholy note on which it had started. Jaques reprised her opening song, finishing

17 *As You Like It*, Public Acts, Queen's Theatre Hornchurch, directed by Douglas Rintoul. Beth Hinton-Lever as Jaques, and the company. Photograph by Camilla Greenwell.

the metaphor, as elderly versions of the characters disappeared into darkness. Promising that 'We leave a ghostlight for the ones who'll start again when we are gone', she then left her own centre-stage spot to a 6-year-old girl wearing a version of her own costume. The child was listed in the programme as 'Young Jaques', but seemed to me to represent the next generation of humanity, whom Jaques hopes will 'live to see a better version of the play'. The little girl sang a final chorus of 'All the world's a stage' in an exposed, wavering voice, and the entire audience was on their feet in seconds.

I cannot think of a production upon which I would rather end my five-year tenure as *Shakespeare Survey* theatre reviewer. The year 2019 was a grim one on the level of national and inter-national politics, and this unabashed celebration of

inclusivity and diversity by members of some of London's most marginalized communities was exactly what I needed to see. What could have felt quite sentimental in another performance somehow just seemed brimming with hope and kindness here; this production was keenly alert to social inequal-ities, and hopeful that we can do better in the future. The times may be darkening, but the hours I have spent over the last few years watching Shakespearian performance have left me optimistic about the role that culture can play in keeping the light burning. Casting practices that were unusual enough to be worth remarking upon when I started reviewing – 'gender-blind' and disability-positive casting, for example – are now widespread. I put the first of these terms in quotation marks because, as I have argued, actors' visible gender and racial identities are often central to a production's politics, allowing a show to subvert some of the problematic attitudes expressed in the early modern text. Shakespearian productions now are frequently re-gendering characters in order to challenge patriarchal and hetero-normative plots. Audiences seem alert to these issues, and indeed to the resonances between Shakespeare's plays and current affairs more broadly, and productions seem increasingly willing to trust their audiences to make these connections. It struck me that the social diversity of the audiences at the Globe and the Queen's Theatre Hornchurch had a direct impact on the politics of the productions staged there, and that other theatres would do well to reflect on what they can do to broaden their audiences. There is a great deal of work ahead of us; may we live to see a better version of the play.

PROLOGUE

Friday 13th December, 2019. By a cruel and unusual coincidence, the deadline for filing this piece fell hours after a UK General Election in which the turkeys voted emphatically for Christmas. Amid the louring clouds, a small silver lining: it will be at least five years before the Prime Minister returns to his unfinished biography of William Shakespeare. It is not a pleasant thought, but I would rather he was finishing the book, even if (like his biography of Churchill) it is bound to be an exercise in regurgitation, vanity and self-projection. The relevance of the General Election result to this column – and especially those that follow it in the years ahead – lies in the direction of travel it implies for the UK and its cultural life. The new government will likely double down on the culture wars to distract from the continuing erosion of public services and the immiseration of large parts of the population. Leftie-bashing is back in vogue and this will be felt keenly by theatre-makers. Arts education will continue to be a privilege and not a right, a gift reserved largely for the privately educated, with severe implications for actor training and the pipeline of talent. Government funding for the theatre will continue to decrease, and theatre-makers will have to look to private sponsorship and collaborations with, for example, China to plug the gap. This money will come with strings attached. Progressive casting, gender quotas, black actors playing 'white' kings – all will be sneeringly lampooned in the right-wing press. Pressure will be applied to artistic directors to avoid 'controversy'. Johnson is fond of quoting and misquoting Shakespeare. On a recent campaign visit to the fishing town of Grimsby, he announced his arrival with the words 'Cry haddock, and let loose the cod of war.' He is invested in Shakespeare, and his iteration of the Conservative Party, while it prefers long boozy Wagnerian matinees, will also fight for its white nationalist version of Shakespeare. The borders of 'This England' just shrank, and sooner or later this will have repercussions for the Shakespearian stage.

SHAKESPEARE'S ROSE THEATRE, YORK

July 2019. Sunnier times. I covered the first ever season of Shakespeare's Rose Theatre in *Shakespeare Survey 72* and readers can find a full description of the theatre and the visitor experience there (for a quick sense of the playing-space, see Figure 18 below, the pre-set for *Henry V*). In 2019, the fourteen-sided polygonal auditorium popped up for a ten-week season in both York and the grounds of Blenheim Castle, Oxfordshire (revivals of last year's York productions played at Blenheim). Again, the York season consisted of four different shows performed by two sub-companies of actors.

First up, *Twelfth Night* directed by Joyce Branagh (yes, his sister) in a world she described as 'The Great Gatsby meets P. G. Wodehouse with a touch of Some Like It Hot'. This was a Jazz-Age, broad, clear and sunny production largely untroubled by any hint of emotional turmoil or complexity – more Blandings Castle than Gatsby's mansion. The set was simply dressed in a red and gold motif with a period band positioned downstage right. The word 'Illyria' flared in a neon art deco font above the centre stage (so unavoidably that the sea captain was baffled that Viola needed to enquire as to her whereabouts). The opening minutes set the tone of uncomplicated engagement. The groundlings were encouraged to flutter blue hankies to create the 'waves' for the storm; the shipwreck itself was narrated in an original song performed by a lounge singer.

Through this chirpy world skittered a succession of attractive, well-defined characters. Clare

18 The interior of Shakespeare's Rose Theatre, York. Pre-set for *Henry V*, directed by Gemma Fairlie. Photograph by Paul Prescott.

Corbett's Feste was a Chaplinesque vagabond, blond tresses beneath bowler hat, who nicked and drained the dregs of a groundling's pint in 1.3, but delightfully magicked a fresh beer for the punter in 2.3. Cassie Vallance's Fabian – present throughout as one of the conspirators – a toothy, gurning chambermaid, a little hard of understanding. A Sir Andrew (Alex Phelps) for whom the arms were the chief medium of expression, trigger ready to run through a repertoire of moves, including such flagrant anachronisms as the Floss and the Dab. A conventionally bibulous, smoking-jacketed Sir Toby from Fine Time Fontayne in the role that he was surely born (or stage-named) to play.

These revellers were in firm control of the tone of the production, aware as they were throughout of the audience and its inferred need for midsummer escapism. In the piss-up of 2.3, 'Shall we make the welkin dance?' was addressed to us; the snatch of 'Three merry men be we' (2.3.76) inclusively adjusted to 'Six hundred merry men are we.' The single line 'O' the twelfth day of December' grew into a full-throated 'Twelve Days of Christmas', with Sir Toby reminding us 'You know this bit!' just before the caterwauling 'Five Gold Rings' chorus prompted Malvolio's entrance and the complaint of untimely behaviour. '*We* did keep time', Toby riposted, gesturing sweepingly around the auditorium.

Oddly enough, Malvolio (Claire Storey) was one of the few characters who was apparently not aware of – and playing to – the audience. The performance was not without crowd-pleasing flourishes: in 3.4, he (the role was played as male) entered with an absurdly blow-dried bouffant and, on 'greatness thrust upon them', whipped off his plus-fours (in the style of Bucks Fizz at Eurovision) to reveal mustardy undergarments. But, elsewhere, this was a restrained, self-contained performance, a Reverse Donald Sinden, if you will. Because the role wasn't played by (and directed as if for) a star, the effect was not to unbalance the production. For much of the Box Tree scene, the conspirators scurried around the pit, the only time I've ever seen Malvolio *down*-staged.

The central love quartet was solid, but perhaps suffered from the production's lack of depth. Representative was the staging of 'Come Away Death': for the most part, there was little intimacy or proximity between Cesario and Orsino during the scene, but on 'I am all the daughters ... ' (tearfully, stilly delivered, underscored by cello and violin), Orsino went to kiss her. A potentially poignant/erotic moment immediately reverted to farce: she screamed and he retreated, obscuring his erection with a handy cushion. This was typical of a show in which there was no firm or sustained attempt to span the emotional spectrum, no great sense of loss or love or lust. Declan Wilson's Antonio was possibly the only performance to attempt a 'real' person with genuine feelings, but this attempt was fatally upstaged by the delightful cameo of the incompetent copper who arrested the wrong person twice before finally laying hands on Antonio.

We learned in the curtain call that this useless bobby was informally known as 'PC Hamlet', for indeed the role was played by David Oakes, star of Damian Cruden's production of *Hamlet*. Oakes's Hamlet offered something of a throwback: charming, conventionally handsome, socially at ease, self-possessed, the matinee idol of Elsinore. While this production's Ghost tore his passion to tatters (I suppose there is quite a lot for him to be upset about), Hamlet's reactions to the tale were very muted, regarding the wailing corpse with what could be interpreted as 'aristocratic' detachment. The subdued key and low affect of the performance were sustained throughout: the antic disposition consisted of a small costume adjustment, five buttons undone on the still-sable doublet – very little else. He certainly, in Guildenstern's words, '[kept] aloof', though here it was not with 'a crafty madness'. In the great central soliloquy, it was

revealing that the passage from 'Am I a coward' to 'what an ass am I' was cut, thus tastefully avoiding the psychic meltdown (and the challenge it poses to an actor). Again, on 'What a piece of work is a man', intense self-scrutiny was avoided as Oakes descended into the pit and jokily illustrated the speech with the enforced assistance of a groundling ('Turn round, face the audience'). In short, this Hamlet was not crazy, cruel or quirky and there were fewer notes to be sounded on his recorder. Vocally, Oakes is gifted with a resonant, precise and powerful voice – I just wish it had been given more of an orchestral and emotional workout (though I might, of course, simply have caught an anomalously under-powered performance).

More widely, Cruden's production made many smart and interesting choices, a large proportion of which related to Serena Manteghi's Ophelia. At the end of 1.3, on Polonius's 'come your ways', he snapped his fingers towards a door, but she exited, strong-willed, in the opposite direction. Polonius then nodded to Reynaldo to follow her. Taking her cue from the surveillance culture around her, Ophelia then turned into a serial eavesdropper. She overheard Hamlet taking the ghost's word for a thousand pound; even the last third of Claudius's 'My offence is rank' was addressed directly to her – 'Help, angel [singular]!' he pleaded to her. Richard Standing's lubricious Claudius needed her forgiveness. When Polonius read Hamlet's love poem and got to the line about Ophelia's 'white bosom', Claudius sent a dirty, man-of-the-world laugh up towards Ophelia on the balcony. After the Nunnery scene, he hugged her in a way that was very uncomfortable. Later, this libidinal aggression would bite back: when he addressed her as 'pretty lady', she shuddered, was sick in her mouth, then adeptly placed him in a headlock. Her subsequent dialogue with her brother was striking: he insisted on describing her madness while she, severely frustrated, tried to use her lines as a kind of code to clarify how their father died (and that it was Claudius, rather than Hamlet, who was really responsible). His failure to catch on to this riddling was the final straw for her.

The production was costumed in a narrow palette of black, white and grey. (Most puzzlingly, Gertrude wore black for the arrival of Rosencrantz and Guildenstern, then later switched back to the white of 1.2, as if the semiotic burden of each were not a pressing issue at Elsinore.) 'The Mousetrap' brought some colour. It also featured an intriguingly eccentric, over-sized performance from the Player King, who began with a physical theatre routine which included tumbles, a Robot Dance (as popularized by the footballer Peter Crouch) and lewdly percussive taps of his own codpiece, but which then got 'serious' with Hecuba, scaling the performance right down (cf. those 'Pyramus and Thisbe's where Thisbe's lamentation cuts through the preceding bombast). Original, too, was the sequence during the dialogue 'If once a widow . . .', when the whole onstage audience, with the exception of the King and Queen, took slow paces towards the action on the inner stage, variously concerned, hostile and incredulous to find themselves watching something so near the royal knuckle.

Gemma Fairlie's *Henry V* began with a five-person chorus in contemporary street clothes in front of an enormous flag of St George. This was a modern dress production with two key exceptions. Maggie Bain's Henry began in medieval gear, then travelled sartorially through subsequent ages, first into a Napoleonic-era frock coat, then into World War II uniform, and finally into modern war combats. Uncle Exeter offered a different kind of anachronism, stuck for much of the action in Sandhurst khaki, perhaps representing that Little Englander mentality that is always re-fighting the Second World War. By contrast, the French were defined by their leisure wear. All were members of the TCV (the Tennis Club du Versailles), and loafed around in creamy Lacoste (though suspicion should perhaps have fallen on Alice, kitted out in perfidious Slazenger – perhaps a signal of her incipient Anglophilia?). The language lesson was wittily staged as an actual tennis match between Alice and Kate, with Kate's mother spectating. The rallies were gentle but they both – *à la* the

professionals – accompanied each return shot with primal squeaks and grunts.

Fairlie also acted as choreographer and there were some impressive examples of combat ballet at Harfleur, involving red ladders and Henry athletically crawling and scaling these ladders as they were lifted and rotated by four squaddies. Music was as important as movement throughout this production. After the scaling of ladders, the reluctant cockney recruits geed themselves up with shouts of 'Eng-er-land' and a rendition of 'Back Home'. The second half began with the weary troops singing 'Swing Low, Sweet Chariot' in a round, hymn-like. Henry's Harfleur speech was underscored by a quite magical arrangement of the theme of the 'Last Call'. Here, Eamonn O'Dwyer's music – scored for accordion, bass clarinet and percussion – was almost distractingly beautiful.

Maggie Bain's Henry offered an energetic, sharply defined and business-like performance. There were times – especially in 'Upon the King' – when more might have been done to vary the delivery, but there was a clarity and directness that worked for at least one audience member: when Bain stepped into the audience pit during the Crispian Day speech, a groundling initiated a handshake with the King, apparently spontaneously seeking a little touch of Harry in the afternoon. Later, the same man pumped his fist in the air when Hal said he loved France so much he would not part with a village of it. It was heartening to note that this apparently extrovert jingoist also couldn't wait to applaud the moment when (female) Harry kissed (black) Kate. (This was a year in which the 'actual' Prince Harry's mixed-race wife Meghan Markle was subjected to a fair amount of gutter-press xenophobia.)

For Hal's triumphant return to London, the audience was handed a mixture of flags to wave, mostly Union Jacks and George's crosses, but also – in smaller quantities – EU flags. We were instructed to wave these during the Epilogue. The coup here: a baby 'child' was brought on – a crappy little Henry VI – and the swaddling was unfurled to reveal yet another bloodied flag, on which revelation, the cheerleading onstage flag-wavers abruptly stopped and the chastened audience instantly followed suit.

Phillip Franks's fine production of *The Tempest* offered a kind of delayed riposte to the ultra-high-tech, motion-capturing, bells and whistles of the Intel–RSC production of 2017. Where that show had sought to realize the play's imagery and topography in a series of spectacular, computer-generated and rather literal illusions, Franks had neither the budget nor the inclination to rely, as he put it, on 'tricksy technology'. He therefore found inspiration in the Steampunk aesthetic, one which exposes rather than conceals labour and the mechanical, its thrown-togetherness an apt visual correlative for the play's action, characters and generic promiscuity.

More than most productions of this play, one was conscious of a densely populated spirit world on the island. A chorus of six Steampunky spirits worked hard throughout, engineering visions, masques and mayhem, while also channelling and intensifying onstage feeling: Ariel's memory of the 'cloven pine' put all the spirits (and the empathetic sleeping Miranda) into horizontal spasms. Prospero's valediction to 'ye elves!' had an unusual poignancy when these spirits had been omnipresent throughout. Leander Deeny's Ariel was more simply dressed in black Chinese pyjamas and white-face paint. Manic and mercurial, he worked the shipwreck report like a music hall comedian and there was great relish in his account of how he'd made Neptune's 'bold waves tremble, / YEAH! [Not 'yea'] his dread trident shake' (1.2.205–6). Deeny captured the arc and variety of the character beautifully: when he reported that Gonzalo's tears ran 'down his beard like . . . '. He paused slightly. 'Like' what? Searching for an environmental analogy for something he was on the species border of understanding, he found it: 'like . . . like winter's drops, / From eaves of reeds' (5.1.15–6).

Although the production wasn't especially interested in a colonial reading of the play, its racial dynamics were intriguing, if inconsistent. Caliban was played by a black actor (Raphael Bushay) with startlingly blue contact lenses and a left-arm appendage that resembled a lobster's claw. I wasn't sure how to read this. Perhaps the claw, rather than suggesting a 'fish-like' being, was something he was forced to wear to denote 'monster'? ('There would this monster make a man' (2.2.29–30), says Trinculo of England, punningly reminding us that white Western definitions of 'man' have always relied on a monstrous other against which that privileged manhood is 'made'.) Less complicatedly, Gonzala (Flo Wilson) was played with a broad West Indian accent; the spirits hissed Sebastian's rebuke to Alonso about losing his daughter 'to an African', but tended to side with Gonzala's counsels and even applauded her vision of exceeding the golden age.

As Prospero, Sam Callis was not obviously bookish. With his earth-toned, patch-worked trousers and waistcoat, leather wristbands, ponytail and Steampunk staff (a harpoon with taped-on wheels and celestial models), he more resembled a vigorous, sometimes angry, tribal lord from, for example, *Game of Thrones*. (He was also a worldly and worried dad: his imperative 'No tongue!' (4.1.59) to Ferdinand and Miranda before the masque was a prohibition on French kissing.) In the final minutes, he ordered Caliban back to his upstage cell, only for Caliban to turn at the last moment, hurtle back down stage and exit through the audience. Only Antonia, Prospero and Ariel remained. Antonia went to exit, and Prospero chased her in a clear attempt to force a hug, a gesture she met by slapping him in the face. During evening performances, Prospero's Epilogue was lit by a single spotlight – the nymphs had departed, and this felt like a very bare and small island indeed.

When I saw these shows, the pit was half full and there were scores of empty seats. It came as no great surprise, then, that a few weeks after the season ended, the company behind the project announced that the second season of Shakespeare's Rose would also be its last. This is a great shame. In two short years, the theatre had hosted eight productions and employed dozens of actors and other theatre-workers; the quality of productions and ensembles could bear comfortable comparison with those at Shakespeare's Globe or the RSC.

BRISTOL AND LEEDS

Elizabeth Freestone's *Henry V* had been one of the highlights of last year's regional Shakespeare. I found her *Much Ado about Nothing* to be less consistently successful and thought-provoking, but there was still much to admire, not least the in-the-round setting of the Bristol Tobacco Factory that provided many more opportunities for 'noting' than a proscenium production. It started with a battlefield dumbshow in which one soldier ran away from combat and was consequently demoted for her cowardice. In her place, a second soldier was promoted for his bravery. This is how we were introduced to Don John and Claudio, respectively. This lent an interesting Iago–Cassio dynamic to Don John's revenge plot but also raised the question (which does not apply to Iago) of why anyone would trust the word of someone who had so abjectly displayed their untrustworthiness on the battlefield. 'Would Don John and the Prince lie?' – well, certainly the former, yes. (Also: in a world in which women are free to join the army, Beatrice's 'Oh God, that I were a man' rang less true.)

The setting was ostensibly Mediterranean (the men smeared themselves with sun cream in the gulling scene), but the dominant atmosphere was of a middle-class English summer: disco balls, bunting, barbecues. (Did the seagull sound effects at the interval imply a distinctly Bristolian setting?) The party was a fancy dress on the theme of the superhero. Hero herself came as Wonder Woman, Beatrice as Banana Man (not only leading, but also feeding, those apes into hell?). Dorothea Myer-Bennett's Beatrice was younger than is now usual – arch, knowing, 'self-endeared' to her husky timbre, especially in its disyllabic delivery of 'no-oo'. She was especially good when, hungover, mascara-stained and clutching a medicinal 7-Up, she bid Benedick come to dinner. Geoffrey Lumb's Benedick was, for most of the performance, consciously lightweight, a good-looking if aimless man who had learned, possibly in adolescence, that he could get away with a lot simply by grinning at the end of every speech. He found new depths as the action darkened, but never entirely lost his goofiness: his shoes squeaked awkwardly in the split-second before he said, 'I do love nothing in the world so well as you.' I hadn't seen either of these actors before and they certainly did not carry the accrued associations that 'star' actors often bring to these roles – all of which was refreshing and reinforced the equitable, ensemble-based atmosphere of this show.

This ensemble was at its finest in the effectively paced and directed sequence of action around the aborted wedding and its aftermath. The nuptial scene was simply established with fairy lights, colourful floor cushions and a beautiful trio, sung as the guests entered. The pain of the scene was most strikingly realized in Alice Barclay's 'Ursula' (the name is misleading; she was really a female version of Antonio, re-imagined as Don Leonato's wife and present throughout the action). She it was who slapped Don Pedro when he called her daughter a 'common stale'; and it was to her maternal grief and anger that Leonato addressed the line, 'If you go on thus, you will kill yourself' (5.1.1). The challenge to Claudio in 5.1 came, therefore, not from the usual pair of old duffers but from a middle-aged husband-and-wife team galvanized by injustice. The final moments of the show sustained its general approach of fresh inquiry. Benedick had earlier tried to kiss Beatrice after 'Serve God, love me, and mend' (5.2.90), but she'd swerved away from this; the line that often mandates a kiss in the final scene ('Peace, I will stop your mouth' (5.4.97)) was cut; Beatrice reserved, as it were, her kiss for her cousin Hero on the moment her innocence was publicly established. And when Claudio tried to joke to Benedick about cudgelling him out of a single life (etc.), Beatrice, suddenly furious, squared up to him with an extra-textual 'seriously?'. All had ended, but not entirely well.

Amy Leach's sprightly *Hamlet* played during the major renovation of the West Yorkshire (now Leeds) Playhouse in a temporary warehouse space with a shallow but wide end-on stage. A series of security beam lights suggested a perimeter fence to a military complex or a prison yard, while beneath the elevated stage was a dropped area with lilies and funeral flowers, an unweeded garden, frozen in mourning. Although not an especially large venue, there would be very few moments of intimacy with the audience, and actors very rarely used the downstage ramp to address us directly; the effect was more akin to observing the contents of an aquarium. The company consisted of nine professional actors (five women, four men), supplemented by a handful of non-professionals drawn from the theatre's youth programmes.

The most notable feature of the adaptation was its interest in showing, not telling. Elsinore is full of dumbshows even before the Players arrive, but this production added more – some suggested by the script, others less so. In an opening prologue, we saw Horatio and Hamlet's fencing practice at Wittenberg interrupted by the arrival of a letter: Hamlet's father is dead, and Hamlet was helped into a black mourning costume for her return to Denmark. Cut then to the court at King Hamlet's funeral. Ophelia and Hamlet briefly escaped for a quick snog, and Hamlet gave Ophelia one of the letters she will later return. In 1.2, Hamlet left the scene early and, following the interchange between Claudius, Laertes and Polonius, she returned in college gear and backpack: she was on her way back to Wittenberg and to life. The commitment to showing not telling logically meant that scenes that are merely narrated in the text were here staged: we saw the dumbshow of Hamlet's lunacy as described by Ophelia (NB: 'you need not tell us Ophelia, we saw it all ... ') – Ophelia, in flimsy shift and headphones, was reading Hamlet's letters when Hamlet bounded on, as if directly from the encounter with the Ghost, with knife drawn; Hamlet (wo)manhandles Ophelia; Polonius enters, scans the letters and whisks her daughter away. Like most thoughtful modern productions, an effort was made to beef up Ophelia's part, and here she was forced to read out loud Hamlet's embarrassing 'Doubt not' letter-poem. In the most sinister interpolation (which also helpfully obviated the need for a chunk of text in Act IV), we saw Laertes don blue medical gloves to envenom the blade tip while Claudius looked on approvingly in a villainous burgundy turtleneck.

This was, then, a pacey, often imaginative modern-dress production with a Q1 lick to it: 'Seems madam, nay it is. I know not seems' was all we heard of Hamlet's first major speech. The Q1-ness extended to the occasional modern paraphrase and word substitution, not all of which felt fully intentional or reasoned. Much of this was standard adaptive fare ('Might not *allow* the winds of heaven ... '; 'From whose *boundary* no traveller returns ... '; 'Grounds more *relevant* than this ... '; and so on). The 'whole of Denmark' (rather than its 'ear') had been rankly abused. Fortinbras was cut until right at the very end, so the 'army of great charge' in Act 4 was the Danish army and 'led by a bloated and corrupted king' (i.e. Claudius). But other choices struck my ear (or 'whole') as clumsy or inconsistent (e.g. 'Though you can manipulate me, you can't play on me'). There was also a tendency to drop stresses, so 'longéd long to redeliver' became 'longed long to redeliver', and 'incestuous, murderous, damnéd Dane' became ' ... damned Dane'.

Tessa Parr's Hamlet was always watchable, and her relationship with Simona Bitmate's Ophelia was intensely delineated and poignant. But the performance sometimes felt too rushed and unmodulated, very rarely affording the space in which something shifted in the head and the heart of the character. Pivoting points and epiphanies were glided over. Perched over the praying Claudius, Hamlet's line 'That would be scanned' is most obviously played as a self-interruption and a crucial turning point in the speech; here, it was delivered with the same pace and tone as the lines before and after it. Similarly, reflecting on Yorick's skull, no air was afforded to the idea of the 'base uses' to which we all must return; the skull was simply returned and we were on to the Next Bit. New story beats and twists were added, not least when Gertrude told Hamlet in the closet scene that 'I swear by Heaven I never knew of this most horrid murder', but Hamlet failed to register the denial and simply ploughed on with the guilt-tripping the regular script demands. (The production doubled down on Gertrude's innocence by including the Horatio–Gertrude vignette scene of Q1.) Perhaps the general paciness of the evening precluded too much inflection, but I would love to see what Parr would do with the role in a more modulated and psychologically nuanced production.

THE ROYAL SHAKESPEARE COMPANY

The year witnessed two important developments at the RSC, one on stage and one off. Off stage, the Company finally bowed to increasing public pressure and abandoned its financial relationship with the oil company BP (the National Theatre also stopped taking money from Shell). For years, BP had subsidized the RSC's £5 ticket policy for 16- to 25-year-olds; some of those young people sent an expertly crafted open letter to the Company, pointing out 'We are the audiences of the future and we will not support theatre that accepts sponsorship from a company that is continuing to extract fossil fuels while our earth burns.' Progress was also apparent on stage. The three shows in the main-house summer season were performed by a 50–50 gender-balanced ensemble that, according to Gregory Doran, the artistic director, reflected 'the ethnic, geographical and cultural diversity of Britain today'.

***

Simon Godwin's production of *Timon of Athens* played in the Swan Theatre over the 2018–19 winter season, a chilly anti-masque to the crowd-warming *A Christmas Carol* which ran concurrently in the Royal Shakespeare Theatre next door. This *Timon* was most notable for its reimagining of the play's gender dynamics: not only the title role, but also Alcibiades, Apemantus, Lucius and Flaminius were all played by and as women. The pre-show featured preparations for a banquet – Greekish music from the gallery, Turkish delights bestowed on audience members by Timon's trio of obsequious servants – and for much of the first half we were in an abstract version of somewhere in contemporary Europe, or at least that part of it

occupied by the 1 per cent and its parasitic dependents and precariat workforce. Suitably enough, the (expensive) costumes shimmered in front of a metallic backcloth that, under Tim Lutkin's skilful lighting, glowed gold and silver. Classy free-loaders guzzled and simpered, while Apemantus and Flavius lurked like spectres at the feast – she from the sceptical left, as it were, in a Smiths 'Meat is Murder' T-shirt, he from a more buttoned-up position of conservative fiscal responsibility (though paternalistically kind enough to slip each of Timon's servants a €500 note on their dismissal).

Much of the contemporary relevance was evocative rather than specific, with the important exception of the attempted coup led by Alcibiades, the 'defender of the wretched of the earth' as she was described by Timon in an interpolated line that seemed to reference Franz Fanon's seminal book of that name. Played by Debbie Korley as a latter-day Angela Davis, her virtue was first signalled by her quietly returning one of the golden party bags distributed to guests at the conclusion of the opening banquet (at which she cut an incongruous figure anyway). After the interval, she led a mob of revolutionaries bearing placards with slogans such as 'Down with Usury' and (more awkwardly) 'Banish Your Dotage'. Many of these protesters wore the yellow high-visibility vests worn in France throughout 2018–19 by the so-called 'gilets jaunes', so conflating the anti-austerity protests seen in Greece and across Europe in the 2010s with exactly contemporary ones in France. In Shakespeare and Middleton's text, it is Timon's martial experience that gives him leverage with Alcibiades and his followers (14.94), but in this production it was less than clear why this Timon was so beloved of the common people, or how she could in any way save Athens from Alcibiades and the Yellow Vests.

At the centre of the production was Kathryn Hunter's Timon. Hunter is one of the most distinctive and original actors of her generation, with an uncanny combination of fragility and fierceness. It is perhaps a backhanded compliment to say that, in the first half, she never quite convinced me of the character's stupidity, nor of the relatedly unreflective pleasure she derived from her generosity. Although she became briefly emotional on the line 'we were born to do benefits', the moment when she pledged the dowry for Lucilius was unmarked, her philanthropy apparently without a wellspring of psychological need, nor providing any obvious dopamine hit. I would have welcomed a greater sense of the handouts as so many slippery band-aids over some unhealable psychic wound.

Hunter was more at home in the misanthropic knockabout of the second half. This took place in an urban wasteland of rubble, braziers and soiled duvets. Timon was discovered under a white sheet, groaning as her alarm clock went off. Haggard and earth-bound, the unwanted love-child of Mother Courage and the Gravedigger, she had much more fun both with her visitors and with the audience (Figure 19). We'd already been invited to think of

this Timon as a kind of corporate Christ, a sacrificial victim of the global financial crisis – in the banquet scene, she had sprayed her guests with blood (rather than tried to feed them with rocks); at the end of the production, she was carried off on three wooden planks which formed an improvised crucifix, only to be resurrected, as it were, and reintroduced into a final tableau with Alcibiades and the protesters that demanded, implausibly, to be read as a *pietà*. But for a majority of the second half, the feel was more Beckettian than Christian (if that's not an entirely false dichotomy). There was a fair amount of clowning. On 'all erections' (14.164), she cheekily pointed out an audience member on the front row. When visited by the Painter and the Poet, she forced them to drink what looked like urine and to eat the 'root' –

19 *Timon of Athens*, The Swan Theatre, directed by Simon Godwin. Kathryn Hunter as Timon, Debbie Korley (third from right) as Alcibiades, and the company. Photograph by Simon Annand.

here, a worm-like creature in a jam jar, the sort of gross-out challenge beloved of *I'm a Celebrity ... Get Me Out of Here!*

Hunter was never less than compelling and always intelligent, but the effectiveness of some of her physical choices is perhaps a matter of taste. In the great tirade of Scene 12, her arms executed a series of angular gestures from 'decline to your confounding contraries' (12.20) to 'drown themselves in riot' (28). This was semi-abstract expressionism, suggestive both of a deranged priestess sawing the air and of a hieroglyph guiding a plane to land.

***

The summer season opened with Kimberley Sykes's *As You Like It*. As with all RSC productions under review here, I saw this show twice, once in previews (flat, over-long – frankly, a slog), and again in the middle of its Stratford run (better, brighter, tighter). More than most productions of this play, it was over-dependent on a virtuoso central performance from Lucy Phelps as Rosalind; elsewhere, the quality of characterization was uneven. This, in turn, had much to do with an unevenly applied concept and an under-realized sense of the psychic and sexual possibilities of Arden.

Duke Frederick's court was one of tacky authoritarianism, with well-drilled flag-waving flunkies cheering on Charles the Wrestler in a bout that took place on a large disc of Astroturf. On banishment, Phelps's Rosalind screamed and, in her anger, peeled back the Astroturf, revealing the theatre's bare boards, thus clearing away the artificial, and making space for the richer potential of artifice. The transition to Arden might have been subtitled 'Metatheatre 101' (Figure 20). The house lights came up, costume rails were pushed on, and we were suddenly 'backstage'. On the tannoy, a Deputy Stage Manager cued the actor playing Jaques: 'Miss Stanton to the stage. All the world's a stage, please, all the world's a stage.' The band played snatches of Mozartian overtures and all was pre-show bustle, with Antony Byrne, changing costumes from Duke Frederick to Duke Senior, as the focus.

The moment provided a welcome injection of energy, and its implications were clear enough (Arden, like the theatre, is a site of transformation, of lies that become truths, etc.). When Rosalind, perched on the gantry that spanned the upper stage, surveyed the house-lighted auditorium, and pronounced 'Well, this is the forest of Arden', I guess it was intended to be heard as 'Ooo, I'm in a theatre, I can do anything now.' But the concept was very erratically sustained over the next two hours. Exhibit A: the lighting states. The house lights stayed up for a long time after the transition, only beginning to dim during Orlando and Adam's exchange about hunger. The lights came up again for 'Blow, blow, thou winter wind' but *not* for 'All the world's a stage' shortly before that. This continued. It felt like the lighting board had been hacked by Puck. Other questions nagged: if 'Arden' is the 'theatre', why did Frederick's followers take soup from a realistic cooking pot and ladle it, steaming, into canteen mugs? If imagination – ours, the actors' – is sovereign, why not 'pretend' to eat and drink? If the costume rails signify something important, why did they only reappear once, in 3.3., to tart up Audrey and create the character of Sir Olivia Martext? If theatre is inherently about imagination, why spend a ton of money on a distractingly enormous puppet of Hymen? Much vexation in 'if'.

Fortunately, there was Lucy Phelps. This was a metatheatrical performance, but in a more subtle sense of the term than that offered in the Big Transition. Phelps seemed to understand that she was in a sometimes sluggish, conceptually erratic production, and therefore did everything she could to provide drive, energy and detail to her scenes. Here was a Rosalind even cleverer than the script she'd been dealt: on 'this poor world is almost six thousand years old', Phelps gave a lightning shrug, as if to say 'I know the world is actually 5.4 million years old, but I have to say what's in the text.' There was also a whiff of in-house satire about the way she tried to scan Orlando's poetic line 'Her worth being mounted on the wind', beating out the rhythm on her chest and pretending to find

20 *As You Like It,* Royal Shakespeare Theatre, directed by Kimberley Sykes. The transition to Arden. Photograph by Topher McGrillis.

it wanting because it did not conform to the iambic fundamentalist 'heartbeat' of RSC schools workshops. There was silliness – when she first met Orlando, she ran through a repertoire of accents (Mancunian, Irish, French) to see if any would fadge; but there was also stillness – after hurtling through the symptoms a lovesick man should display, she slowed right down and brought an unusual intensity to 'But in good sooth, are you he that hangs the verses on the trees ... ?' (3.2.375–6). 'Time travels in divers paces with divers persons' (3.2.299–300), and Phelps's Rosalind was capable of ambling and trotting – but she mostly galloped, and for that I was grateful.

Sandy Grierson's Touchstone provided the other performance that will last in the memory. A lanky, intense figure in tartan drainpipes and a sequined vest under a crusty dressing gown, one last scalp-spanning hair hanging on for dear life, Grierson could do slapstick, madcap and sinister. He propelled one of the production's more notable

sequences – those featuring Audrey, played by the deaf actor Charlotte Arrowsmith. 'When a man's verses cannot be understood' became his somewhat irritable response to her deafness and his own inability to sign; he fetched William, who was fluent in British Sign Language (BSL), to act as interpreter, but then grew jealous of the two. He held William's hands behind his back so that he could no longer communicate with Audrey ('abandon the society of this woman'), a choice that made this Touchstone more malicious than most, especially as William clearly had an affinity with Audrey that the interloping and aggressive courtier did not.

***

In the Prologue to *Supposes,* one of Shakespeare's sources for *The Taming of the Shrew,* Gascoigne defined a 'suppose' as 'but a mistaking or imagination of one thing for another'. Justin Audibert's production asked us to make a rather big suppose: imagine that early modern England was a matriarchy in which all the positions of power were held by women, and in which men were commoditized chattels. (Oddly, the women still wore corsets and heels and other uncomfortable patriarchal encumbrances.) In this topsy-turvy world, Baptista (who already sounded quite feminine) was a wealthy matriarch with two sons, one preening and obedient, the other moody and morose. (On the brothers' first entrance, Moody, chewing a chicken leg, is attempting to cut off Obedient's bum-length hair.) Their suitors are all women of varying economic status and temperament, including a fiery out-of-towner, Petruchia. The Christopher Sly frame was cut, so there was no transition into this counter-factual, which played out on Stephen Brimson-Lewis's beautiful set – an Elizabethan manor house, oak panelling, ravishing floorboards of blues, russet and copper, a cyclorama of clouded sky like oil on vellum – the latest of the RSC's periodic attempts to create the National Trust experience in the comfort of their own theatre.

What ensued was not only the vehicle for this lavish design and extraordinary period costumes, but also for a string of fine performances, none better than Claire Price's Petruchia, which had much in common with Lucy Phelps's Rosalind: both were up-tempo, mercurial but precise, production-driving turns. Sporting an enormous, flame-coloured wig (picture Elizabeth I upon receiving an electric shock), Price was boisterous, space-taking and delightfully uncomplicated – unlike some recent male Petruchios, she didn't attempt to psychologize the character by way of an apology for his behaviour: the announcement that 'Antonia, my mother, is deceased' was accompanied by a split-second nose-rub of emotion, but really there was no hinterland here. This Petruchia simply needed money and also happened to fancy Kate – on their first meeting, he made a slow entry along the upper balcony, he below, playing the harpsichord; when she copped her first proper look at him, she turned to the audience, blowing out her cheeks in comic sexual approval.

By contrast, it wasn't always clear what was going on in the mind of Joseph Arkley's Katherine (even

harder to work out why the production had retained that name: Bianca had become Bianco, and all the other names were re-gendered; so why not Christopher Miola? My dainty Kit, Kit of Kit Hall, 'Come, kiss me Kit!', etc., etc.?). As most press reviews concluded, Arkley's performance was weirdly subdued, more sullen than shrewish per se. The problem is obvious: when a man raises his voice and threatens to strike a woman (as the text demands 'Kate' does), it is very hard to repress fully an instinctual fear for the woman concerned. We can't 'suppose' away everything we know about male violence and female victimhood. (In this respect, this production reminded me of Jude Kelly's 'photo-negative' Othello starring Patrick Stewart as a white Othello: the inversion can be thought-provoking but those thoughts pull you out of investment in the drama, as the proposition – it's hard to be the only white man in an all-black world, or a subjected male in a matriarchy – doesn't really seem worth worrying about, given its counter-factuality.) I did admire Arkley's performance, though, especially the way he subtly, silently charted his growing fascination with Petruchia in the aftermath of their first meeting. When she pronounced to Baptista that 'I chose him for myself', he tuned into her brave new world of brazenly alternative facts, fully realizing what an attractive weirdo she was. From that point, he could not take his eyes from her, and on 'Give me thy hand', he instinctively leapt from the harpsichord stool and gave it. I suppose that will have to do for consent.

Sophie Stanton's Gremia enjoyed herself tremendously (Figure 21). The running gag of her hovering around as if on castors was probably funnier if you hadn't seen Mark Rylance do exactly the same as Olivia in the Globe's celebrated Twelfth Night, but other aspects of the characterization were more original. This Gremia was not especially bright and had a habit of running out of conversational rope: the proffered schoolmaster was 'Well read in poetry . . . / [pause – thinks: what other genres are there? Nope.] . . . And other books' (1.2.168); when presenting 'Cambia' in the flesh, she introduced her as 'cunning in Greek, Latin . . . [pause – thinks:

21 *The Taming of the Shrew*, Royal Shakespeare Theatre, directed by Justin Audibert. Joseph Arkley as Kate, Claire Price as Petruchia.
Photograph by Ikin Yum.

what other languages do I know? Nope.] . . . and *other* languages' (2.1.80). She also had a repeated gag about trying to remove her sword and repeatedly failing, until the moment in Act 4 when it came out clean as a whistle and she exclaimed 'Oh my God!' in amazement. Elsewhere, the talent ranged from the luxury casting of Amanda Harris as Baptista, to Amelia Donkor (Hortensia) and Laura Elsworthy (Trania), very good young actors, excellent both in this and in *As You Like It*.

***

235

It has become a commonplace to describe *Measure for Measure* as Shakespeare's #MeToo play, and many productions in the last few years have sought to explore the parallels. Gregory Doran steered clear of any obvious contemporary resonance by placing his production in Vienna at the turn of the twentieth century. *Fin-de-siècle* Vienna is not a new setting for this play. Jonathan Miller (whose death was mourned this year) did the same in 1975, directly inspired by the evocative photos of August Sander, and Trevor Nunn did likewise for the RSC in 1991. Both were interested in the perils of sexual repression, and in Vienna as the cradle of psychoanalysis. The programme for Doran's production featured an excellent note on the cultural and psychological ferment that was Vienna in 1900, but most of the evocative analogies sketched in the note did not obviously materialize in the production. I was expecting Claudio as Egon Schiele, Juliet as the artist's mistress; Lucio as a satirist in the mould of Karl Krauss; even – as Nunn had done – the Duke as a Freud figure. But, while Stephen Brimson Lewis's design had distinctly Austrian touches – the striking projections included a shimmering Klimtian wood for Mariana's moated grange, and an imposing *Hauptbahnhof* interior for the Duke's return in Act 5 – the production wasn't over-schematically anchored in the place, and was perhaps more Ruritanian than Viennese per se. Nevertheless, this was the most satisfying and consistent of the year's main-house productions, thanks to well-paced direction, beautiful but unobtrusive designs, and, above all, a high-calibre cast; here, the benefits of being the last production in the season and absorbing all the experience of the ensemble were very evident. There were no great revelations or innovations – except, perhaps, for the effect of having two excellent female actors in the roles of the Provost (Amanda Harris) and Escalus (Claire Price).

The show began at a ducal soirée, three couples waltzing beneath the double-headed eagle of the Austro-Hungarian empire. In the fashion of Ravel's *La Valse*, the music and the dancers sped up into a nightmarish gallop, or so it appeared to the on-looking Duke (Antony Byrne), who was a needy ball of nerves throughout the opening scene. Later, liberated by the disguise, Byrne's Duke explored a wide spectrum of moods. He could be quietly playful, as when defending the Duke's reputation to the slanderous Lucio: 'You are deceived [little smile, almost corpses]: 'Tis not possible. / He was not inclined *that* way'; comic, too, was the elongated wail with which he remonstrated 'Owwwwww, death's a great disguiser!' In anger, his voice would coarsen and rasp. Indeed, temperamental parallels were drawn between the three leads, each of whom had explosive moments of anger and self-disgust.

Up stage were placed six movable mirrors, a signal that the production was interested in reflections, alter-egos and doppelgangers. Sandy Grierson's blond-wigged Angelo was clearly meant to mirror Lucy Phelps's Isabella. Grierson's Angelo was more accustomed than most to the company of women: in the law court of 2.1, he was accompanied by not only a female Provost and Escalus, but also two female notaries. (David Ajao's Pompey was excellent in this scene, revelling in derailing the case against his client Froth with an exuberant Columbo-style case for the defence. Price's worldly, indulgent Escalus conceded Pompey a laugh on 'if the law would allow it' – she couldn't quite hide her affection for this streetwise survivor.) This largely female work environment diluted the power of Isabella's entry into his world, but it did underscore Angelo's need for secrecy; only in soliloquy could he painfully accept that 'blood, thou art blood', peeling his trousers down to reveal a spiked cilice digging into his bloodied thigh. No doubt he pressed hard on this when in company – his dirty, if devout, little secret.

The Angelo–Isabella encounters of Act 2 were sensitively delineated. In 2.2, Angelo grew increasingly dazed by the brilliance of her compassion. At the end of the scene, she encouraged everyone to their knees in prayer; although he fell to his knees a few yards up stage of her, he was unable to pray, but could only stare at her with appalled fascination. (This voyeuristic dynamic was exactly echoed in 3.1, when the Duke would discover Isabella praying after her encounter with Claudio, and took a hard look at her before announcing his presence with the creepy line conflating her inner and outer beauty: 'the hand that have made you fair hath made you good'.) In 2.4, Phelps and Grierson allowed the dialogue to develop quietly and stealthily, each really hearing the intellectual and spiritual challenge of the other. On 'What would you do?', she took a long pause to really consider the enormity of the question. They later found unexpected affinities – they both agreed on the frailty of women, and her relief that they were finally speaking the same language, as it were, emboldened him to take her hands in his. Only

on 'fix thy consent to my sharp appetite' did he grab her from behind and place his hand on her crotch, which paralysed her with fear and shock (Figure 22).

The denouement was mapped via a series of genuflections. Played out in front of a larger-than-usual crowd of onlookers, Mariana knelt for Angelo's life and implored Isabella to join her. Isabella approached her, and for a split second it seemed as if she was trying to raise Mariana off her knees. Instead, she joined her. Minutes later, Angelo, having responded furiously to the accusations at first, now wearily signalled his guilt by kneeling and begging for capital punishment.

22 *Measure for Measure*, Royal Shakespeare Theatre, directed by Gregory Doran. Sandy Grierson as Angelo, Lucy Phelps as Isabella. Photograph by Helen Maybanks.

Finally, Joseph Arkley's Lucio, an angular and unpleasant dandy, was forced to kneel for clemency, but not before he had daintily prepared the ground with a perfumed handkerchief. The Duke's first attempt at a proposal ('He is my brother too') prompted Isabella to turn with disgusted confusion from the reunion hug with Claudio. 'But fitter time for that ... '. The final proposal was cheered by the onlooking crowd which then conveniently exited, as did the named characters, leaving the Duke and Isabella alone. As she had been with Angelo, Phelps's Isabella was once again frozen, this time in anger and uncertainty. And then a sob broke from her before a quick blackout.

***

Of the RSC's seven productions of *King John* since 1970, all but two were directed by a woman. By contrast, all seven of the last *King Lears* were directed by men. What's going on? The subtext seems to be: 'We need to do *King John* once a decade or so, but it's niche and weird, so we'll stick it in a small venue. Oh, and we also need to hire more women directors. Here you are [*presenting pristine Penguin edition to young female director*]. Good luck!' As was the case with her immediate predecessor (Maria Aberg), this was Eleanor Rhode's first production for the RSC (indeed, appeared to be her first professional Shakespeare show anywhere). *King John* is a curate's – or maybe a cardinal's – egg of a play for modern audiences, and it does seem unusual (and perhaps unfair) that female directors have been disproportionately charged with making sense of it, while many of their male colleagues have been granted more straightforward debuts with which to build their reputations.

The most striking design element consisted of a vast upstage tapestry. It seemed to commemorate a series of battles combining rebels with automatic weapons pitched against archers and cannons; dominating its centre, a young King (although clearly female) staring out with the melancholy fixity of a medieval Greta Thunberg. If the tapestry promised a polychronic approach, most of the other design elements were anchored in the late 1950s – early 1960s. The 'men' of Angiers, rather

than being represented by *Hubert upon the walls*, were actually three female secretarial types who sashayed their way on to the balcony, adjusted their period spectacles, and did not seem unduly perturbed by the double siege. The subsequent 'excursions' were played as a boxing match between the red of England and the blue of France (for which spectacle the stalls audience was provided with over-sized and colour-coded foam hands; the ladies of Angiers munched popcorn). This larky treatment extended to a number of musical dance sequences (Austria's first entrance at head of an Austin [Austrian?] Powers boy band; the English arrival in France, everyone in shades, strutting to a pastiche of the bass line from The Stranglers' 'Peaches'). The wedding scene featured more dancing and descended into an entertaining food fight, after which France's 'I am perplexed and know not what to say' was warmly received. At the top of the scene, large golden balloons spelled out 'JUST MARRIED'; by the end – and after some strategic punctures applied by a scissor-wielding Constance – they spelled 'JUST DIE'. Thus, she enacted a private revenge on the 'golden letters' of this 'wicked day' (cf. 3.1.83–5).

In terms of tone and period setting, then, much of the first half of the production felt like an homage to *One Man, Two Guvnors* (*One King, Two Coronations?*). The second half then inverted Marx's dictum – in this production, history indeed repeated itself, but the first time as farce, the second as tragedy. John's first entry, worse for wear, was to the breakfast table where she fixed herself a restorative Bloody Mary; three hours later, she's coughing up blood in a tin bath, the arc of the performance bookended by those acts of ingestion and ejection. The message, I guess, was that there are plenty of things in life that start in a game-like, playful fashion but end in anger, factionalism, self-hatred and death. Fair enough. But is that what *King John* is about? (Does anybody know what *King John* is about?)

I sometimes felt like I was watching a less effective version – a shadow of a shadow? – of Swedish director Maria Aberg's 2012 RSC production (also in the Swan), but one which lacked Aberg's non-native interest in English myth-making, and the emotive anchor that that production found in the love affair *manqué* between Alex Waldemann's John and Pippa Nixon's Bastard. *The Stage* described Rhodes's production as 'bombastic, stylish and stylised' and gave it four stars; they might have awarded it fewer and for the same reasons. There were many fine performances. Charlotte Randle's Constance was not afraid of that character's less appealing traits (e.g. body fascism) but movingly pivoted the show in the direction of tragedy with her hair-tearing lament for her lost son, no mean feat given that this was the first scene (about 1 hour 30 minutes into the production) that we were meant to take seriously. And I especially enjoyed Brian Martin's Dauphin and Katherine Pearce's Pandulph (both RSC debut performances).

EPILOGUE

I am loathe to draw too many conclusions about the state of Shakespearian theatre in England based on the relatively small sample of shows described above. I am also conscious of having had to miss many interesting-sounding productions (including Lucy Ellinson as Macbeth at the Manchester Royal Exchange, *A Midsummer Night's Dream* at the Tobacco Factory, and touring productions of *Richard III* by Headlong and *Much Ado about Nothing* by Northern Broadsides). But this was clearly a year in which it became almost normative for women to play lead male roles: Petruchio, Timon of Athens and King John at Stratford; Henry V and Malvolio in York; Hamlet in Leeds; and Macbeth in Manchester. Impossible to tell whether this is the new normal or a high-water mark.

The Oxford 'Word of the Year' for 2018 was 'toxic'. For 2019 it was, not unrelatedly, 'climate emergency' (even though that's technically two words). I would expect the climate crisis to be more directly reflected in productions next year, in ways that both celebrate the natural world and force us to imagine the strain on human relations posed by a massive ecological collapse (Rufus Norris's *Macbeth* at the National Theatre attempted to do this in 2018, for which it received a kicking from conservative critics: 'Humankind cannot bear very much reality').

Finally, and for the record: the best Shakespeare production I saw in 2019 was the first ever Faroese-language production of *Hamlet* in Tórshavn, the capital of the Faroe Islands. There is a world elsewhere.

PROFESSIONAL SHAKESPEARE PRODUCTIONS IN THE BRITISH ISLES, JANUARY–DECEMBER 2018

JAMES SHAW

Most of the productions listed are by professional companies, but some amateur productions are included. The information is taken from *Touchstone* (www.touchstone.bham.ac.uk), a Shakespeare resource maintained by the Shakespeare Institute Library. *Touchstone* includes a monthly list of current and forthcoming UK Shakespeare productions from listings information. The websites provided for theatre companies were accurate at the time of going to press.

ALL'S WELL THAT ENDS WELL

Shakespeare's Globe. Sam Wanamaker Playhouse, London, 11 January–3 March.
www.shakespearesglobe.com
Director: Caroline Byrne

ANTONY AND CLEOPATRA

Royal Shakespeare Company. Royal Shakespeare Theatre, Stratford-upon-Avon, 11 March–7 September 2017; Barbican Centre, London, 30 November 2017–20 January. Broadcast to cinemas 24 May.
www.rsc.org.uk
Director: Iqbal Khan
Cleopatra: Josette Simon
Mark Antony: Antony Byrne
Part of the Shakespeare's Rome season.

National Theatre. Olivier Theatre, London, 11 September–19 January 2019.
www.nationaltheatre.org.uk
Director: Simon Godwin
Cleopatra: Sophie Okonedo
Antony: Ralph Fiennes

AS YOU LIKE IT

Shakespeare's Globe. Globe Theatre, London, 2 May–26 August.
www.shakespearesglobe.com
Director: Federay Holmes and Elle While
Rosalind: Jack Laskey

Fourways. Pipers Corner School, Great Kingshill, High Wycombe, 17–26 May.
www.fourways.org.uk
Director: Barney Powell
Open-air production.

Shakespeare in the Squares. Leinster Square, 20 June and tour to various London squares.
www.shakespeareinthesquares.co.uk
Regents Park Open Air Theatre, Regent's Park, London, 6–28 July.
https://openairtheatre.com
Director: Max Webster

Adaptation

Ganymede
Typecast Productions. Paradise in Augustines, Edinburgh, 3–25 August.
Playwright: Jamie Gould
LGBT themes.

THE COMEDY OF ERRORS

Cambridge Shakespeare Festival. St John's College Gardens, Cambridge, 30 July–18 August.
www.cambridgeshakespeare.com

Royal Shakespeare Company. Swan Theatre, Stratford-upon-Avon, 19 October–2 November and UK tour.
www.rsc.org.uk

Director: Alex Thorpe
Adaptation for 7- to 13-year-olds.

CYMBELINE

Cambridge Shakespeare Festival. Robinson College Gardens, Cambridge, 9–28 July.
www.cambridgeshakespeare.com

HAMLET

Royal Shakespeare Company. Salford, Lowry, 31 January–3 February and tour. Revival of 2016 production.
www.rsc.org.uk
Director: Simon Godwin
Hamlet: Paapa Essiedu

University of Bolton. Octagon Theatre, Bolton, 15 February–10 March.
www.octagon.co.uk
Director: David Thacker

Shakespeare's Globe. Globe Theatre, London, 25 April–26 August.
www.shakespearesglobe.com
Director: Elle While and Federay Holmes
Hamlet: Michelle Terry
The inaugural production of Michelle Terry's term as Globe artistic director.

Three Inch Fools. Coggeshall Grange Barn, National Trust, Colchester, 3 June and tour to 19 August.
www.threeinchfools.com

Another Way Theatre Company. Minack Theatre, Penzance, 4–8 June.

Adaptation

Hamlet (An Experience)
Brite Theater (Reykjavik). Dukebox Theatre, Brighton, 5–19 May; Prague Fringe, Prague, 31 May–2 June; The Rose Playhouse, London, 12–13 October and UK tour.
http://britetheater.weebly.com
Director: Kolbrún Björt Sigfúsdóttir
Hamlet: Emily Carding
Solo performance. Scripts handed to audience members to invite volunteers for various characters.

Hamnet
Dead Centre. Tramway, Glasgow, 19 May; Southbank Centre, London, 26–28 May; Warwick Arts Centre, Coventry, 20–22 November.

www.deadcentre.org
Director: Bush Moukarzel and Ben Kidd
Solo performance cast with 11-year-old actor.

Hamlet – Horatio's Tale
Maverick Theatre. Assembly Rooms, Edinburgh, 3–26 August.
www.maverick-theatre.org
Director and Adaptor: Nick Hennegen
Solo performance from Horatio's perspective.

Super Hamlet 64
Edward/Edalia Day Theatre Company. OFS Studio, Oxford, 13 September.
Playwright: Edward Day

HENRY IV, PART I

Carnon Downs Drama Group. Minack Theatre, Penzance, 19–21 April.
www.carnondownsdrama.org.uk
Director: John Frankland

HENRY V

Shakespeare at the Tobacco Factory. Bath Theatre Royal, Ustinov Studio, Bath, 21 June–21 July; Tobacco Factory, Bristol, 12 September–6 October and UK tour.
http://stf-theatre.org.uk
Director: Elizabeth Freestone

The Petersfield Shakespeare Festival. Bedales School, Steep, Petersfield, 18–24 July.
www.petersfieldshakespearefestival.co.uk

Adaptation

Greyhounds
Time & Again Theatre Company. theSpace on the Mile, Space 2, Edinburgh, 3–18 August. Festival Fringe.
https://timeandagaintheatre.com
Director: Jacqueline Wheble
A blend of Shakespeare and stories of wartime Britain during World War II.

JULIUS CAESAR

Royal Shakespeare Company. Royal Shakespeare Theatre, Stratford-upon-Avon, 3 March–9 September 2017; Barbican Centre, London, 24 November 2017–20 January.
www.rsc.org.uk

Director: Angus Jackson
Part of Shakespeare's Rome season.

London Theatre Company. Bridge Theatre, London, 20 January–15 April and on tour. Broadcast to cinemas 24 November.
https://bridgetheatre.co.uk
Director: Nicholas Hytner
Julius Caesar: David Calder
Brutus: Ben Wishaw
Mark Antony: David Morrissey
Promenade production. First Shakespeare production at the Bridge Theatre.

Spada Productions. Courtyard Theatre, London, 5 March–1 April.
Director: William Vercelli

Nova Theatre Company. OFS Studio, Oxford, 3–5 May. All-female cast.

KING JOHN

American Performing Arts International. theSpace @ Niddry Street, Lower Theatre, Edinburgh, 9–11 August. 90-minute version with the cast seated amongst the audience.

KING LEAR

Royal Shakespeare Company. Royal Shakespeare Theatre, Stratford-upon-Avon, 23 May–9 June. Revival of 2016 production.
www.rsc.org.uk
Director: Gregory Doran
Lear: Antony Sher

Chichester Festival Theatre. Duke of York's, London, 26 July–3 November. Transfer from Chichester Festival Theatre 2017.
www.cft.org.uk
Director: Jonathan Munby
Lear: Ian McKellen
McKellen first played Lear for the RSC in 2007.

Adaptation

King Lear Retold
Greenwich Theatre, London, 5–6 February.
Adaptor and performer: Debs Newbold
Solo storytelling in modern language.

Lear
Southbank Centre, London, 20 May. First performed at Kilkenny Arts Festival 2014.

www.johnscottdance.com
Performer: John Scott
Solo dance adaptation.

The Delusion of Home
Our Theatre. Summerhall, Techcube 0, Edinburgh, 1–26 August. Festival Fringe.
Taiwanese drama connecting Lear with rural life in Taiwan.

Trump Lear
Pleasance Theatre, Edinburgh, 1–27 August. Edinburgh festival.
Political satire.

King Lear (Alone)
PQA venues @ Riddles Court, PQA Two, Edinburgh, 12–15 August. Festival Fringe.
Playwright and performer: Frank Bramwell
One-man show.

A Bunch of Amateurs
Priory Theatre, Kenilworth, 5–15 September.
Playwright: Ian Hislop and Nick Newman
Director: Karen Shayler
An ageing Hollywood star plays Lear with a local amateur dramatics company.

LOVE'S LABOUR'S LOST

Unfolds Theatre. Rose Playhouse, Bankside, London, 27 February–24 March.
www.unfoldstheatre.co.uk
Director: Marnie Nash

Guildford Shakespeare Company. University of Law, Guildford, Surrey, 13–28 July.
www.guildford-shakespeare-company.co.uk
Director: Tom Littler

Folksy Theatre Company. Queens Park Arena, Glasgow, 16 July and tour 1 September.

Shakespeare's Globe. Sam Wanamaker Playhouse, London, 23 August–15 September.
www.shakespearesglobe.com
Director: Nick Bagnall

MACBETH

Out of Chaos Theatre Company. The Playground, London, 20 January and tour to 10 March.
www.out-of-chaos.co.uk

Unfolds Theatre. Rose Playhouse, London, 30 January–24 February.
www.unfoldstheatre.co.uk
Director: Alex Pearson

Icarus Theatre Collective. Millennium Forum Theatre, Killarny, Ireland, 31 January–1 February and tour to April.
www.icarustheatre.co.uk
Director: Max Lewendel

Bits and Bobs Theatre Company. The Shakespeare Institute, Stratford-upon-Avon, 14–17 February.

Shakespeare at the Tobacco Factory. Tobacco Factory, Bristol, 27 February–7 April.
https://stf-theatre.org.uk
Director: Adele Thomas

The National Production Company. Gordon Craig Theatre, Stevenage, 1–3 March; The Old Rep Theatre, Birmingham, 10–14 April.

National Theatre. Olivier Theatre, London, 6 March–23 June and UK tour. Broadcast to cinemas 10 May.
www.nationaltheatre.org.uk
Director: Rufus Norris
Macbeth: Rory Kinnear
Lady Macbeth: Anne-Marie Duff

Royal Shakespeare Company. Royal Shakespeare Theatre, Stratford-upon-Avon, 13 March–18 September; Barbican, London 23 October–18 January 2019 and UK tour. Broadcast to cinemas 11 April.
www.rsc.org.uk
Director: Polly Findlay
Lady Macbeth: Niamh Cusack
Macbeth: Christopher Eccleston

Factory Theatre. Electricity Showrooms (Downstairs), London, 8 April; Great Northern Railway Tavern, London, 19 April.
www.factorytheatre.co.uk
Director: Alex Hassell

Lunchbox Theatrical Productions. Shakespeare's Rose Theatre, York, 4 July–31 August.
www.lunchbox-productions.com
Director: Damian Cruden
Billed as staged using the first pop-up Elizabethan theatre in Europe.

Cambridge Shakespeare Festival. Trinity College Gardens, Cambridge, 30 July–18 August.
www.cambridgeshakespeare.com

Merely Theatre. Arts Centre, Aberystwyth, 16 August; Open House Festival, Bangor, 18 August and UK tour to 25 October.
https://merelytheatre.co.uk
Director: Abigail Anderson

Shakespeare's Globe. Sam Wanamaker Playhouse, London, 7 November–2 February 2019.
www.shakespearesglobe.com
Director: Robert Hastie
Lady Macbeth: Michelle Terry
Macbeth: Paul Ready
Duncan and the Porter doubled.

National Youth Theatre. Garrick Theatre, London. 23 November–7 December.
www.nyt.org.uk
Director: Natasha Nixon
Gender-reversed roles for Macbeth and Duncan.

Adaptation

That Scottish Play
Commedia of Errors Theatre Company. Lyric Theatre, Belfast, 23–26 January.
https://commediaoferrors.co.uk
Director: Benjamin Gould
Comic version.

Mark Bruce Company. Merlin Theatre, Frome, 25–27 January; Theatre Royal, Winchester, 31 January–1 February; Wilton's Music Hall, London, 23 February–17 March and UK tour.
www.markbrucecompany.com
Choreographer: Mark Bruce
Dance adaptation.

FRED Theatre. The Bear Pit Theatre, Stratford-upon-Avon, 5 and 7 February; The Cockpit Theatre, London, 20 February.
www.fred-theatre.co.uk
Version for schools.

The Paper Cinema's Macbeth
Paper Cinema. BAC (Battersea Arts Centre), London, 20 March–4 April and 9–27 October.
www.thepapercinema.com
Silent film with puppetry and live score.

Macbeth: A Tale of Sound and Fury
6FootStories Theatre Company. Greenwich Theatre, London, 17 April and tour.
www.6footstories.co.uk
Director: Jake Hassam
Performed by three storytellers.

Flabbergast Theatre Company. Wilton's Music Hall, London, 18 June–2 July.
Performed after one week of rehearsals.

About Lady White Fox with Nine Tales
YVUA Arts, Korea. Assembly George Square Studios, Three, Edinburgh, 2–27 August.

Is This a Dagger? The Story of Macbeth
Scottish Storytelling Centre, The Netherbow Theatre at Fringe, Edinburgh, 22–26 August.
Adaptor and performer: Andy Cannon

othellomacbeth
HOME and Lyric Hammersmith. HOME Theatre, Manchester, 14–29 September; and at the Lyric Hammersmith Theatre, London, 5 October–3 November.
https://homemcr.org
Director: Jude Christian
Conflated adaptation of *Othello* and *Macbeth*.

The Macbeths
Citizens Theatre. Dundee Repertory Theatre, Dundee, 3–4 October and tour to 27 October.
www.citz.co.uk
Playwrights: Alexander Raptotasios and Manolis Tsiipos
Director: Dominic Hill
Condensed version concentrating on the central characters.

Macbeth – Director's Cut
Volcano Theatre Company. Waterside Arts Centre, Sale, 9–10 October and tour to 14 November. First performed in 1999.
www.volcanotheatre.co.uk
Director: Paul Davies
Not suitable for children.

Queer Lady M – Work in Progress
1623 Theatre Company. Attenborough Arts Centre, Leicester, 8 December.
www.1623theatre.co.uk
A workshop performance in advance of a 2019 tour.

MEASURE FOR MEASURE

RoughCast Theatre Company. Old Kings Head, Brockdish, 12 March and tour to 31 March.

www.roughcast.co.uk
Director: Paul Baker

Changeling Theatre. Open air UK tour July–August.
http://changeling-theatre.com
Director: Robert Forknall

Donmar Warehouse. Donmar, London, 28 September–1 December.
www.donmarwarehouse.com
Director: Josie Rourke
Isabella: Hayley Atwell
Angelo: Jack Lowden
An abridged version, followed, post-interval, by a shorter version with Angelo/Isabella roles reversed.

Adaptation

Measure for Measure (LGBT Version)
All or Nothing Repertory Theatre Company. Courtyard Theatre, London, 19 June–7 July.
'Remember the Clause' Season. Angelo implements Section 28.

Opera

Royal Opera House, London, 25 March–10 April.
www.roh.org.uk
Composer: Giuseppe Verdi
Director: Phyllida Lloyd

THE MERCHANT OF VENICE

Shakespeare's Globe. Globe Theatre, London, 14–16 May, 8 September and UK tour.
www.shakespearesglobe.com
Director: Brendan O'Hea
Shylock: Sarah Finigan

Stamford Shakespeare Company. Rutland Open Air Theatre, Tolethorpe Hall, Stamford, Lincolnshire, 12 June–4 August.
http://stamfordshakespeare.co.uk

Bowler Crab Productions. Mermaid Inn, Rye, 13–14 June and tour to 28 July.
www.bowler-crab.com

Illyria Theatre Company. Trebah Amphitheatre, Falmouth, 22 June and tour to 16 September.
Cambridge Shakespeare Festival. Downing College Gardens, Cambridge, 9–28 July.
www.cambridgeshakespeare.com

PROFESSIONAL SHAKESPEARE PRODUCTIONS

Bury Theatre Workshop. Abbey Gardens, Bury St Edmunds, 31 July–4 August.
www.burytheatreworkshop.org.uk
Director: Tim Lodge

Bedouin Shakespeare Company. Silvano Toti Globe Theatre, Rome, 10–14 October; Duke of York's Theatre, London, 22 October.
www.bedouinshakespeare.com
Director: Chris Pickles
Shylock: Clare Bloomer

Adaptation

Shit-Faced Shakespeare – The Merchant of Venice
Leicester Square Theatre, London, 18 April–2 June.

Gratiano
Grist to the Mill Productions Ltd. Assembly Rooms, Drawing Room, Edinburgh, 8–22 August. Festival Fringe. Sequel from Gratiano's perspective.

THE MERRY WIVES OF WINDSOR

Stamford Shakespeare Company. Rutland Open Air Theatre, Tolethorpe Hall, Stamford, Lincolnshire, 10 July–1 September.
http://stamfordshakespeare.co.uk

Royal Shakespeare Company. Royal Shakespeare Theatre, Stratford-upon-Avon, 4 August–22 September; Barbican Theatre, London, 7 December–5 January 2019; and UK tour. Broadcast to cinemas 12 September.
www.rsc.org.uk
Director: Fiona Laird
Falstaff: David Troughton

Opera

Falstaff
Garsington Opera Chorus. Wormsley Estate, High Wycombe, 16 June–22 July.
www.garsingtonopera.org
Composer: Giuseppe Verdi
Director: Bruno Ravella

Falstaff
Royal Opera House, London, 7–21 July.
www.roh.org.uk
Composer: Giuseppe Verdi
Director: Robert Carsen

Falstaff
Opera Bohemia. St Cuthbert's Church, Main Sanctuary, Edinburgh, 24 August.
www.operabohemia.co.uk
Composer: Giuseppe Verdi
Director: Adrian Osmond

A MIDSUMMER NIGHT'S DREAM

Tread the Boards Theatre Company. The Attic Theatre, Stratford-upon-Avon, 29 March–22 April.
www.treadtheboardstheatre.com

Daniel Taylor Productions. Epstein Theatre, Liverpool, 12–21 April.
Director: Daniel Taylor

Filter Theatre Company. Lyric Theatre Hammersmith, London, 13–14 April and tour to 9 June.
http://filtertheatre.com
Director: Sean Holmes

Watermill Theatre Company. Watermill, Newbury, 10 May–16 June.
www.watermill.org.uk
Director: Paul Hart
Bottom: Victoria Blunt

Lazarus Theatre Company. Greenwich Theatre, London, 15–26 May.
www.lazarustheatrecompany.com
Director: Ricky Dukes

Three Inch Fools. Eastbury Manor House, National Trust, Essex, 1 June and tour to 15 August.
www.threeinchfools.com

Chapterhouse Theatre Company. Henry Moore Studios & Gardens, Perry Green, Much Hadham, 8 June and tour to 29 August.
www.chapterhouse.org

Quantum Theatre. Hannah's at Seale-Hayne, Newton Abbot, 16 June and tour to 4 August.
www.quantumtheatre.co.uk
For school audiences.

The Faction. Wilton's Music Hall, London, 26–30 June.
www.thefaction.org.uk
Director: Mark Leipacher

Lunchbox Theatrical Productions. Shakespeare's Rose Theatre, York, 5 July–2 September.
www.lunchbox-productions.com
Director: Juliet Forster

Cambridge Shakespeare Festival. King's College Gardens, Cambridge, 9–28 July.
www.cambridgeshakespeare.com

Shakespeare in the Garden (Open Bar Theatre Company). The Pilot, Greenwich, 31 July–1 August and tour to 15 September.

Theatre Tropicana, Weston-super-Mare, 1–4 August.
Director: Blair Ruddick

Sheffield Theatres. Crucible Theatre, Sheffield, 28 September–20 October.
www.sheffieldtheatres.co.uk
Director: Robert Hastie

Adaptation

LVM. Waterloo East Theatre, London, 28–29 July.
Director: Leo Sene
A Midsummer Night's Droll
The Owle Schreame. Edinburgh Festival Fringe, theSpace on the Mile, Edinburgh, 4–26 August and tour.
https://owleschrea.me
Director: Brice Stratford
Billed as a production of the seventeenth-century adaptation *The Merry Conceited Humors of Bottom the Weaver*.

Ballet

Ballet Theatre UK. Middlesbrough Theatre, Middlesbrough, 9 February and tour to 21 March.
www.ballettheatreuk.com
Composer: Felix Mendelssohn

A Dream within A Midsummer Night's Dream
Ballet Black. Eden Court, Inverness, 4 June and tour to 19 November.
http://balletblack.co.uk
Choreographer: Arthur Pita

Opera

English National Opera. London Coliseum, London, 1–15 March.
www.eno.org
Director: Robert Carson
Composer: Benjamin Britten

MUCH ADO ABOUT NOTHING

Shakespeare's Globe. Globe Theatre, London, 24 February–20 March.

www.shakespearesglobe.com
Director: Michael Oakley

Wigan Little Theatre Company. Little Theatre, Wigan, 11–21 April.
www.wiganlittletheatre.co.uk
Director: Caroline McCann

Antic Face. Rose Theatre, Kingston, 18 April–6 May.
www.anticface.com
Director: Simon Dormandy
Beatrice: Mel Geldroyc

Everyman Playhouse, Liverpool, 28 April–10 July.
www.everymanplayhouse.com
Director: Gemma Bodinetz

Middlesbrough Little Theatre Company. Middlesbrough Theatre, Middlesbrough, 2–5 May.
www.middlesbroughtheatre.co.uk
Director: Rob Clilverd

Rain or Shine Theatre Company. Wolvesey Gardens, Winchester, 2 June and tour to 30 August.
www.rainorshine.co.uk

Iris Theatre Company. St Paul's Church, London, 22 June–22 July.
http://iristheatre.com
Director: Amy Draper

Storyhouse. Grosvenor Park Open Air Theatre, Chester, 6 July–25 August.
www.storyhouse.com
Director: Bill Buckhurst

OVO Theatre Company. Roman Theatre of Verulamium, St Alban's, 11–21 July; Minack Theatre, Penzance, 27–31 August.
www.ovotheatre.org.uk
Director: Adam Nichols and Janet Podd

Open Bar Theatre Company. Plough Inn, Ealing, 12–13 July and tour of pub gardens to 31 July.

Bard in the Botanics. Botanic Gardens, Glasgow, 13–28 July.
www.bardinthebotanics.co.uk
Director: Jennifer Dick

Merely Theatre. Arts Centre, Aberystwyth, 16 August and tour to 25 October.
https://merelytheatre.co.uk
Director: Abigail Anderson

Antic Disposition. Gray's Inn Hall, London, 17 August–1 September and UK tour.

PROFESSIONAL SHAKESPEARE PRODUCTIONS

www.anticdisposition.co.uk
Directors: Ben Horslen and John Risebero

OTHELLO

Unicorn Theatre, London, 8 February–3 March.
www.unicorntheatre.com
Director: Ian Nicholson
Adaptor: Ignace Cornelissen
For 8- to 12-year-olds.

Liverpool Everyman, Liverpool, 2 May–10 July.
www.everymanplayhouse.com
Director: Gemma Bodinetz
Othello: Golda Rosheuvel
Gender reversal of the title role.

Shakespeare's Globe. Globe Theatre, London, 20 July–
13 October.
www.shakespearesglobe.com
Director: Claire Van Kampen
Othello: André Holland
Iago: Mark Rylance

English Touring Theatre (in association with Oxford
Playhouse and the Tobacco Factory). The Playhouse,
Oxford, 18–22 September and tour to 20–24 November.
www.ett.org.uk
Director: Richard Twyman

Adaptation

othellomacbeth
HOME and Lyric Hammersmith. HOME Theatre,
Manchester, 14–29 September; and at the Lyric
Hammersmith Theatre, London, 5 October–3 November.
https://homemcr.org
Director: Jude Christian
Conflated adapation of *Othello* and *Macbeth*.

PERICLES

Cheek by Jowl. Barbican, London, 9–21 April and international tour.
www.cheekbyjowl.com
Director: Declan Donnellan
In French.

Cambridge Shakespeare Festival. Robinson College
Gardens, Cambridge, 30 July–25 August.
www.cambridgeshakespeare.com

National Theatre. Olivier Theatre, London, 26–28 August.
www.nationaltheatre.org.uk
Director: Emily Lim
Pericles: Ashley Zhangazha
A company of over 200 including only 6 professional
actors.

RICHARD II

Anərkē Shakespeare. Rose Studio, Rose Theatre
Kingston, London, 24 March; and at the Rose
Playhouse, London, 13–18 August 2019.

The Tragedy of King Richard the Second
Almeida Theatre, London, 10 December–
2 February 2019.
https://almeida.co.uk
Director: Joe Hill-Gibbins
Richard II: Simon Russell Beale
100-minute version with cast of 8.

RICHARD III

Perth Theatre and Perth Youth Theatre. Perth Theatre,
Scotland, 22–31 March.
Director: Lu Kemp

Tread the Boards Theatre Company. The Attic Theatre,
Stratford-upon-Avon, 29 March–2 April.
www.treadtheboardstheatre.com

Chiltern Shakespeare Company. Hall Barn,
Beaconsfield, Buckinghamshire, 13–23 June.
www.chiltern-shakespeare.co.uk

Lunchbox Theatrical Productions. Shakespeare's Rose
Theatre, York, 9 July–1 September.
www.lunchbox-productions.com
Director: Lindsay Posner

Adaptation

Richard III (A One-Woman Show)
Brite Theater. Citizens Studio, Glasgow, 10–14 April.
https://britetheater.weebly.com
Director: Kolbrun Bjort Sigfusdittir

ROMEO AND JULIET

Shakespeare Up Close. Orange Tree Theatre,
2–13 February.
Director: Gemma Fairlie
For schools.

Guildford Shakespeare Company. Holy Trinity Church, Guildford, Surrey, 3–24 February.
www.guildford-shakespeare-company.co.uk
Director: Charlotte Conquest

FRED Theatre. The Bear Pit Theatre, Stratford-upon-Avon, 6–9 February; The Cockpit Theatre, London, 21 February.
www.fred-theatre.co.uk
90-minute version for schools.

Daniel Taylor Productions. Epstein Theatre, Liverpool, 11–21 April.
Director: Daniel Taylor

Bits and Bobs Theatre Company. The Willows Theatre at Stratford-upon-Avon College, Stratford-upon-Avon, 2–5 May.

Royal Shakespeare Company. Royal Shakespeare Theatre, Stratford-upon-Avon, 17 May–21 September; Barbican Theatre, London, 2 November–19 January 2019; and UK tour. Broadcast to cinemas worldwide, 18 July.
www.rsc.org.uk
Director: Erica Whyman
Mercutio: Charlotte Josephine
Friar Laurence: Andrew French

The HandleBards. Pound Arts, Corsham, 30 May and tour to 6 September.
www.handlebards.com
All-female cast of four.

Controlled Chaos Theatre Company. Waterloo East Theatre, London, 25 June–8 July.

Girl Gang Manchester. Hope Mills Theatre, Ancoats, Manchester, 26–30 June.
www.girlgangmcr.com
Director: Kayleigh Hawkins
All-female cast.

Lunchbox Theatrical Productions. Shakespeare's Rose Theatre, York, 5 July–2 September.
www.lunchbox-productions.com
Director: Lindsay Posner

Fluellen Theatre Company. Grand Theatre, Swansea, 2–4 October and tour to 18 October.
www.fluellentheatre.co.uk

Adaptation

Juliet and Romeo: A Guide to Long Life and Happy Marriage
Lost Dog Theatre at Battersea Arts Centre, London, 15–24 February.

Director: Ben Duke
In their middle age, Romeo and Juliet's marriage hits difficulties.

Romeo and Juliet – Mods v Rockers
Oddsocks Theatre Company. The Church Green, Much Wenlock, 7 June and tour to 24 August.
Comic version.

The Rubbish Shakespeare Company. Liverpool Central Library, 23 June and tour to 27 August.
www.rubbishshakespearecompany.com
Comic version.

Romea and Julian
Purple Ostrich Productions Company. Bread and Roses, London, 6–10 November.
Director: Kerry Fitzgerald and Joe Miller
Gender-swapped version.

Re-defining Juliet
The Pit, Barbican Centre, London, 29–30 November.
Director: Robin Norton Hale
Cast of three share the role of Juliet.

Ballet

Russian State Ballet and Opera House. Theatre Severn, Shrewsbury, 15 October 2017 and tour to Theatre Royal, Norwich, 4 April.
Composer: Prokofiev

Moscow City Ballet. Theatre Royal, Nottingham, 7–8 February.
Composer: Prokofiev

Birmingham Royal Ballet. Sadler's Wells, London, 12–13 June; Birmingham Hippodrome, Birmingham, 26–30 June.

Opera

I *Capuleti e i Montecchi*
Opera Holloway. The Woolstore, Codford, 31 August and tour to 30 September.
www.operaholloway.co.uk
Composer: Vincenzo Bellini
Director: Fiona Williams

THE TAMING OF THE SHREW

Actors from the London Stage. The Cockpit Theatre, London, 7–8 May.
Shared directorial responsibility.

PROFESSIONAL SHAKESPEARE PRODUCTIONS

Shakespeare's Globe. Globe Theatre, London, 14–16 May and on tour.
www.shakespearesglobe.com
Director: Brendan O'Hea
Voter's Choice tour, with the audience voting for one of four possible Shakespeare plays.

Cambridge Shakespeare Festival. St John's College Gardens, Cambridge, 9–28 July.
www.cambridgeshakespeare.com

The Petersfield Shakespeare Festival. Bedales School, Steep, Petersfield, 25–29 July.

Shake-Scene Shakespeare Theatre Company. Tristan Bates Theatre (TBT), London, 8–13 October.
www.shake-sceneshakespeare.co.uk
Prepared using cue script technique.

Adaptation

Kiss Me Kate
Opera North. Leeds, Grand, 23–26 May and UK tour.
www.kissmekatethemusical.co.uk
Directors: Jo Davies and Ed Goggin

THE TEMPEST

Controlled Chaos UK Theatre Company. Studio Theatre, London, 13 February–3 March.
Director: Dylan Lincoln
All-female cast.

The Lord Chamberlain's Men. Brighton Festival, Brighton Open Air Theatre, Brighton, 24–26 May and tour to 31 August.
www.tlcm.co.uk
All-male cast.

Oddsocks Productions. Lichfield Garrick Theatre, Lichfield, 1 June and tour to 25 August.
www.oddsocks.co.uk
Comic version.

Iris Theatre Company. St Paul's Church, London, 20 June–28 July.
http://iristheatre.com
Director: Daniel Winder

Storyhouse. Grosvenor Park Open Air Theatre, Chester, 27 July–26 August.
www.storyhouse.com
Director: Alex Clifton

Adaptation

Return to the Forbidden Planet
Ovation Theatres Company. Upstairs at the Gatehouse, London, 12 May–17 June.
www.ovationtheatres.com
Director: John Plews

Return to the Forbidden Planet
Eastbourne Theatres Company. Devonshire Park Theatre, Eastbourne, 9 August–1 September.
Director: Chris Jordan

Opera

Eboracum Baroque – The Tempest
Glastonbury Abbey, Glastonbury, 21 July.
Composer: Henry Purcell

TIMON OF ATHENS

Royal Shakespeare Company. Swan Theatre, Stratford-upon-Avon, 7 December–22 February 2019.
www.rsc.org.uk
Director: Simon Godwin
Lady Timon: Kathryn Hunter
Apemantus: Nia Gwynne

TITUS ANDRONICUS

Royal Shakespeare Company. Royal Shakespeare Theatre, Stratford-upon-Avon, 23 June–2 September 2017; Barbican Centre, London, 7 December 2017–19 January.
www.rsc.org.uk
Director: Blanche McIntyre
Titus: David Troughton

Exadus Theatre Company. Paradise in the Vault, the Annexe, Edinburgh, 13–18 August. Festival Fringe.

TROILUS AND CRESSIDA

Royal Shakespeare Company. Royal Shakespeare Theatre, Stratford-upon-Avon, 12 October–12 November. Broadcast to cinemas worldwide on 14 November.
www.rsc.org.uk
Director: Gregory Doran
Music: Evelyn Glennie
Billed as having the first RSC 50/50 gender-balanced cast.

TWELFTH NIGHT

Royal Shakespeare Company. Royal Shakespeare Theatre, Stratford-upon-Avon, 2 November 2017–24 February.
www.rsc.org.uk
Director: Christopher Luscombe
Malvolio: Adrian Edmondson
Viola: Dinita Gohil

The London Theatre, London, 14–18 February.
www.thelondontheatre.com
Director: Harry Denford
All-female cast.

Shakespeare's Globe. Globe Theatre, London, 14–16 May and UK tour.
www.shakespearesglobe.com
Director: Brendan O'Hea
Voter's Choice tour, with the audience voting for one of four Shakespeare plays to be performed.

The HandleBards. JAGS Sports Club, London, 24 May and tour to 4–5 September.
www.handlebards.com
All-male cast of four.

Cambridge Shakespeare Festival. King's College Gardens, Cambridge, 30 July–25 August.
www.cambridgeshakespeare.com

Watermill Theatre. Wilton's Music Hall, London, 12–22 September.
www.watermill.org.uk
Director: Paul Hart

Royal Lyceum Theatre Edinburgh and the Bristol Old Vic. Royal Lyceum Theatre, Edinburgh, 18 September–6 October; and at the Bristol Old Vic, 17 October–17 November.
Director: Wils Wilson

Creation Theatre Company. The Electric Theatre, Guildford, 5–8 December.

Adaptation

Toby Belch is Unwell
The Theatre, Chipping Norton, 29 March.
An actor reflects on his life and playing the role of Toby Belch.

Young Vic, London, 8 October–17 November.
www.youngvic.org

Director: Kwame Kwei-Armah and Oskar Eustis
Music and lyrics: Shaina Taub
Revival of a musical adaptation first performed in New York Central Park by Public Theater in 2016. Included a community chorus of sixty from Southwark and Lambeth.

THE TWO NOBLE KINSMEN

Shakespeare's Globe. Globe Theatre, London, 30 May–30 June.
www.shakespearesglobe.com
Director: Barrie Rutter
The director's first Shakespeare production since leaving Northern Broadsides.

THE WINTER'S TALE

National Theatre. Dorfman Theatre, National Theatre, London, 6–21 February.
www.nationaltheatre.org.uk
Director: Ruth Johnson
Abbreviated version for young audiences.

The Festival Players. Kington and Dormston Village Hall, Dormston, 19 May and tour to 28 August.
www.thefestivalplayers.co.uk
All-male cast.

Shakespeare's Globe. Globe Theatre, London, 22 June–14 October. Broadcast to cinemas worldwide, 4 October.
www.shakespearesglobe.com
Director: Blanche McIntyre
New Wimbledon Theatre, London, 13–17 November.

Ballet

The Royal Ballet Company. Royal Opera House, London, 13 February–21 March.
www.roh.org.uk
Choreography: Christopher Wheeldon

POEMS AND APOCRYPHA

Venus and Adonis

Act V Theatre Company. Alma Tavern Theatre, Bristol, 3–7 April.
www.act-v.com

PROFESSIONAL SHAKESPEARE PRODUCTIONS

Opera

The Rape of Lucretia. The Arcola Theatre, London,
24 July–4 August.
www.arcolatheatre.com
Composer: Benjamin Britten

MISCELLANEOUS (IN ALPHABETICAL ORDER)

Comedy Store Players. Globe Theatre, London,
19 October.
An evening of comedy ending with an improvised
Shakespeare play.

The Complete Works of William Shakespeare
(Abridged)
The National Production Company. New Wimbledon
Theatre, London, 2–5 May and tour to 24–28 July.

Dark Lady of the Sonnets (Opera)
Pegasus Opera Company. St Paul's Church (The Actors
Church), London, 28 February–4 March.
Based on the play by Bernard Shaw. Part of a double bill
of one-act operas.

The Dramatic Exploits of Edmund Kean
Georgian Theatre, Richmond, North Yorkshire,
4 March.
www.edmundkean.co.uk
Playwright and performer: Ian Hughes

Emilia
Shakespeare's Globe. Globe Theatre, London,
15 August–1 September.
www.shakespearesglobe.com
Playwright: Morgan Lloyd Malcolm
Director: Nicole Charles

The Knights of the Rose
Arts Theatre, London, 29 June–26 August.
Playwright: Jennifer Marsden
A medieval tale combining Marlowe, Shakespeare and
Chaucer, mixed with classic rock music.

*Ministers of Grace: The Unauthorised Shakespearean
Parody of Ghostbusters*
REDuck ProDucktions. theSpace on the Mile, Space 3,
Edinburgh, 6–10 August. Festival Fringe.
Whom wilt thou call?

Queen Margaret
Royal Exchange Theatre. Manchester, 14 September–
6 October.
www.royalexchange.co.uk
Playwright: Jeanie O'Hare
Director: Elizabeth Freestone
The Wars of the Roses from the perspective of
Margaret.

Shakespeare in Love
Theatre Royal, Bath, 11–13 October and tour.
Director: Phillip Breen
Revival of the film adaptation, first performed in
2014.

She Wolf
Voodoo Rooms, French Quarter, Edinburgh,
4–26 August.
Playwright: Gillian English
Solo show about Queen Margaret.

*The Touches of Sweet Harmony: Shakespeare's
Songs*
OVO Theatre. Maltings Arts Theatre, St Albans,
23–24 March.
Album launch for a collection of songs with original folk
settings.

*Will or Eight Lost Years of Young William
Shakespeare's Life*
The Rose Playhouse, London, 27 March–21 April.
www.rosetheatre.org.uk
Playwright and director: Victoria Baumgartner
Biographical drama about young Shakespeare.

Your Bard
Joanne Hartstone and Nicholas Collett Productions.
Assembly Hall, Baillie Room, Edinburgh, 2–27 August.
Biographical drama.

THE YEAR'S CONTRIBUTIONS
TO SHAKESPEARE STUDIES

I. CRITICAL STUDIES
REVIEWED BY CHARLOTTE SCOTT

PROSTHESIS AND POWER

After nearly ten years as critical studies reviewer for *Shakespeare Survey*, I am looking fondly on my over-burdened and groaning table of books for the last time. To kick off my co-mixture of joy and lamentation, I begin with Genevieve Love's *Early Modern Theatre and the Figure of Disability*. Here Love approaches the figure of disability, less as an embodiment of physical capacity than as a trope, a rhetorical figure, through which the theatre comes to express its primary function as both prosthesis and representation. The figure of her title is not then the body of the actor or character, the human subject or experience of being dis-abled, but the language through which the theatre experiences itself as a representation of something else. Love makes no claims to examine disability as a condition or experience, but rather focuses on the mobile networks of metaphor through which the body of both actor and character is described. For Love, disability is a language, not a condition, and is therefore set up through a series of semantic relations that define the actor's relationship to the stage as well as to character. Focusing on how this language 'works', Love attends to how 'disability representations' 'are a means of pointing back to mimetic challenges and opportunities, showing off the challenges on

which the theatre is founded'. These challenges are twofold: one is representational, and the other textual. Beginning with the representational, Love explores theatrical authority in the movement or oscillation between actor and character, between 'excess and disappearance' and the 'range of demands on the theatrical body', which can become symbolic as well as discursive. Cripple, a character from the anonymous *The Fair Maid of the Exchange*, becomes a developed site for the exploration of this metaphoric relationship between 'prosthetic disabled embodiment and theatrical personation'. Extending this argument into the questions of textual identities, Love attends to the language of 'lameness' as it comes to describe the relationship between performance and print. Focusing on Marston's address to *The Malcontent* in 1604, Love observes the text as a misshapen and evacuated site of meaning, bereft of the bodies – and even the author – who can give the words 'shape'. Within these terms, the performance–text relationship becomes a surrogate host for the dynamic between what is there and what is imagined. Textual instabilities, variants and conflations become variable memes for the discourses of disability that the book explores. Working through the terms of movement, transit, prosthesis as process, standing in for as representation, Love

examines how 'prosthetic disabled characters parade the being of theatrical persons, and animate
dramatic textual forms'. Moving through *The Fair
Maid of the Exchange* and Cripple's 'locomotive
verbs', to another anonymous play, *A Larum for
London*, Love focuses on Stump, and his multiva-
lent role as analogy and critique of likeness, spatial
and temporal, as well as the intersections between
theatre and print, past and present, excess and lack.
The second half of the book focuses on *Doctor
Faustus* and *Richard III* and provides some terrific
explorations of theatrical prosthesis and the separ-
ability of actor and character, body and form.
Considering the dismembered body of Faustus
becomes analogous to the 'mangled and torn'
Faustus of the divergent texts. The text as
a deformed body comes to stand as a powerful
index to attitudes to early modern editing: 'The
figure of the disabled body ... reveals the furtive
dependence of textual studies on the theatrical
medium, allowing a site of collaboration – rather
than opposition, rivalry or impasse – between page
and stage'. Continuing the focus on 'locomotive
verbs' in *Richard III*, Love examines the 'busy
dynamism' of Richard's incessant 'bustling' and
its inextricable 'alliance of disability and theatricality'. Considering the figure both within and without the playworlds, Love establishes the complex
language of disability as a set of semantic relations
that determine the actor's relationship to the theatre as well as the character to the role. There are
some terrific readings of the plays, which open up
the virtuosity of mobile terms and locomotive
verbs. The rich language of oscillation and movement is analysed alongside the prosthetic and the
metatheatric to produce a compelling and thoughtful account of theatre's relationship to itself, both as
misshapen text and prosthetic performance.

From the prosthetic to the political, we move to
Shakespeare's London 1613 in which David Bergeron
provides not so much a year in the life of William
Shakespeare as a truly wonderful exploration of the
reign of James VI and the lead-up to his accession
to the English throne. The year 1613 is pivotal for
Bergeron because it marks a decisive point in
James's personal and political life, and forms

a wholly evocative nexus for the exploration of
the relationship between Tudor and Stuart politics.
The book focuses on the now iconic images of
Holbein and Blackfriars Gatehouse as a visual aid
to the narrative arc of a story which seeks to position a much more nuanced, imbricated and
dynamic relationship between court and city, theatre and politics and, crucially, Elizabeth and James.
Standing, as it were, on the pinnacle of 1613, as
a year in which more drama was published and
performed than in any year before, Bergeron
looks backwards to James's life as child to an absent
mother, under house arrest in Scotland, and the
political allies and networks he developed as an
ambitious young man, keen to seize monarchical
responsibility. Bergeron paints a compelling portrait of the formative relationships that James developed during this period, in order to support his
latent claim to the English throne, as well as protect
his religious and political positions in an increasingly fraught environment. The focus on Esme
Stuart and Lennox is fascinating and reveals the
workings of James's networks and allies through
the dense political landscape of a divided country.
There are glimpses into James's life that provide
brilliantly evocative links to Shakespeare's plays,
not least of all *Macbeth* and the attempted murder
of the King by Gowrie, who, with his brother, had
lured the King away from hunting and into
a remote and locked part of their castle. James
cried out, escaped and dined out, it seems, on the
story of his attempted murder, which no-one
believed. But the most significant events to dominate the life and times of James are the death of
Prince Henry and the marriage of Princess
Elizabeth. Indeed, the co-mixture of loss and
birth, grief and celebration, funerals and marriages
supports the book's exploration of the dominant
forces that shaped not only James's reign in
England, but the theatrical relationships between
court and city in which civic pageants and masques
came to reflect London's developing sense of itself
as the country's capital. The death of Prince Henry
is a central motif for the book since it provides
a framework for the exploration of private feeling
in a public context and the theatrical apparatus

through which loss, hope, destruction and renewal become representative structures with which James embeds his reign in the public consciousness. There are some wonderful moments on Shakespeare – telling allusions to the proximity of marriage and funerals in *Hamlet*, death and marriage in *The Winter's Tale* (although here I think Bergeron is very restrained on the exhumation of Mary in relation to the later play's fascination with bringing dead women back from their respective graves), *Henry V* and the martial hope of the young Prince Henry, and the many plays of the late 1590s that are preoccupied with questions of rule – but Shakespeare is woven into the book with a light touch. Often speculative, imaginative and allusive, the links to Shakespeare sit as only one element of a much more intricate and larger narrative about the relationship between court and city. Much more detail is invested in pageants and masques and the ornate and hybrid worlds of civic entertainment. There are many powerful motifs throughout the book – translation (in reference to the moving of Mary's corpse) and transformation are particularly key to the ways in which art and royal life become intertwined through a culture of celebration and commemoration, as Bergeron suggests: 'If statues can be transformed, why not lives, ideas, countries?'. Whilst the imaginative leaps here are sometimes quite large, the book is rich with scholarly material and I learned a huge amount from it. It was deeply rewarding to read a book that looks, as it were, at the other side of the Tudor reign and draws deep on the relationship between Elizabeth and James, as well as the financial, religious and political networks that supported their alliance, long before Elizabeth's death in 1603. While the historical detail is often dense, Bergeron has a light touch and the book deserves a wide readership. There is much here that even scholars of the period will not be familiar with, and compelling and nuanced accounts of James's life and the fascinating world of Stuart politics that predates James's accession to the English throne. Invested in securing a relationship between court and civil life, Bergeron's focus on the symbolic positioning of the Blackfriars and Holbein

Gatehouses establishes the imaginative view from which London comes alive to support the kinetic development of ceremony, celebration and commemoration through some of the major monarchical events of 1612 and 1613. Beginning and ending with the Accession Day Tilt, Bergeron takes us into the spring of 1614, where he imagines Lennox, now having worked with James for nearly thirty years, preparing for the tilt, and recalling Shakespeare's Phoenix and the Turtle: 'Two distincts, division none'. Distinction and division are central to Bergeron's book in the exploration of dynasties, marriages, deaths, births and an overarching sense of power that 'moved ceaselessly along the axis from Holbein Gatehouse to Blackfriars, from Whitehall to Guildhall in Shakespeare's London'.

The book is full of wonderful material and glimpses into formative events within the civic life of London: not least of all, Henry Wotton's exceptionally sanguine response to the Globe's burning in 1613, where he noted that spectators ignored the smoke as 'their eyes were more attentive to the show'; and the exhumation and reburial of Mary in the dark watches of an autumn night. The details through which Bergeron records James's anodyne letter to Elizabeth pleading for his mother's life to be spared, and his later request to have Mary's body moved to Westminster, draw a powerful portrait of James's self-fashioning as the 'motherless son' who attempts to rewrite his destiny towards the English throne.

Yasmin Arshad's Cleopatra is also a figurehead who not only attempts to rewrite her destiny but is almost obsessively rewritten by others. In *Imagining Cleopatra: Performing Gender and Power in Early Modern England*, Arshad addresses 'this most controversial of history's queens' and discovers, not wholly unsurprisingly, that there 'was a strong interest in the Egyptian queen and her story in the sixteenth century, well before Shakespeare wrote his play, and views towards her were deeply conflicted and multi-faceted'. Arshad's other central claim is that Shakespeare's Cleopatra is only one version of 'a continuum, a cornucopia, of Cleopatras', which 'turn Shakespeare's version into a work that is part of a dialogue, rather than an isolated monolith'. Approaching the cornucopia of Cleopatras in this way, Arshad also discovers that representations of the Egyptian Queen become windows into how art, history and politics responded to 'race, female sovereignty and classical antiquity'. Investigating the various and varied representations of Cleopatra, Arshad's book explores how the image and story of Cleopatra were mobilized across a range of instances, materials, dramas and moments, to reveal the contexts and agendas behind her representations. Central to this investigation is a focus on material culture and the 'intersections' between 'portraiture, performance and politics in the period'. The desire to 'de-centre' Shakespeare, as well as explore a variety of Cleopatras, supports the majority of the book's attention to Samuel Daniel's *Tragedie of Cleopatra* and Arshad's claim that the anonymous portrait of a young Jacobean woman, depicted as Cleopatra, is of Lady Anne Clifford. The portrait, alongside a staging of Daniel's play at University College London, prompts Arshad to examine the theatrical relationships between Daniel and Shakespeare, and to survey the shifting representations of the Queen as an index to political and cultural responses to gender, race and power. Within this investigation, Cleopatra is variously represented as monstrous, unruly, drunken and lascivious, and she is often condemned by association with other such representations of women in power. Tracing a classical narrative in which Cleopatra is wrested from a Greek to a Roman history, Arshad also uncovers a shifting focus, moving from her as lustful destroyer to 'pale-skinned courtly love heroine'. Skirting over a vast range of European representations of Cleopatra, Arshad presents a predominantly Westernized response to the motifs of suicide, sexuality and power that became so imbricated in artistic images of the Queen. Tracing this story through the plays of Mary Sidney, Samuel Daniel and Shakespeare, Arshad explores the various 'statements' that these plays make in relation to 'topical political uses of classical history'. Among these statements are reflections on female sovereignty, closet drama, maternity and eroticism.

TRAVELLING HOPEFULLY

There is much in *Travel and Travail: Early Modern Women, English Drama and the Wider World* that would have benefitted Arshad's thesis – not least of all a fascinating chapter on the travel writings of Lady Anne Clifford, as well as a very historically nuanced account of Black Madonna narratives, and the multiple identities of Pocahontas. Situating women in the shadows, and at the centre, of geographical, social, symbolic and economic networks between east and west, this edited collection presents a new methodological approach to the understanding of both women and travel. The collection is divided into two parts, roughly representing historical and literary approaches to the subject. The sixteen contributors set out to explore the narratives of early modern women travelling between England, North America and the Islamic world, to establish the contexts and representations of how 'a wide range of girls and women engaged in extensive movement within and beyond the British Isles'. Using various representations of women's travel, including drama, the collection aims to contest the widely held view that Elizabethan restrictions on foreign travel impacted on women's movement in the period. Reviewing the terms of 'travel' beyond the concept of voluntary endeavour, the essays seek to expand the semantics of women's mobility and agency, as well as the genre of 'travel writing' in relation to the contribution of women. Within this frame, travel becomes an intersectional term through which race, religion, gender, ethnicity, sexuality and class can be explored. Equally varied is the way in which the term can work as a metaphor, a material site, physical activity or cultural experience. The aim of the collection is to 'build a vocabulary, a canon, and a comparative apparatus for discussing writing by women ... when travel took on new meanings associated with tourism, science, and exile'. Many of the usual suspects are here, notably *Othello* and the Sherley brothers, but what really comes alive in many of these essays are the multiple ways in which women – as symbols, bodies, sites and selves – come to represent a vast network for the analysis of cultural response. There are some brilliant essays on the creation of icons – Ruben Espinosa's discussion of the black image of the Virgin Mary in the Holy House of Loreto, as discussed by Montaigne, and the ways in which the icon becomes a transactional opportunity for the exploration of foreign femininity; Elisa Oh's essay on the native American traveller and Mrs Rolfe, embodied as the figure of Pocahontas who becomes a mobile image for the exchange and representation of colonial propaganda. Unsurprisingly, perhaps, most of these women belong to an aristocratic culture that enables the transit of women – as consort, in the case of Lady Sherley – to define a socially acceptable version of the journeying woman. Similarly, the focus on material culture – Loreto's Black Madonna and the Carmelite relic worn by Lady Sherley – demonstrates the extensive and often mysterious ways in which women could cultivate and procure a sense of self across a wide range of interlinking histories, which in many, if not most, cases, defied the traditional 'east'–'west' divide. Dyani Johns Taff provides a wonderful essay on the sea as metaphor, stage space, and no space, and the ways in which sea travel becomes a powerful motif for transition and fragility, while Suzanne Tartamella examines the Book of Ruth in relation not only to *As You Like It*, but to the 'role of female travellers in effecting cultural exchange'. Across and throughout the collection, the contributors draw on a wide range of materials – from conduct books, travel writings, visual and material cultures, diaries, letters, drama, prose and paintings – to explore how women were represented as moveable, and the domestic and cultural categories they both imported and exported across geographical contours. The collection does not make any grand claims to be representative or definitive but it puts in place a powerful opportunity for the exploration of gender in transit, and the important ways in which we can observe cultural and geographical boundaries as both porous and formative in the evolution of early modern identities.

Taking a different route, but nevertheless focused on the 'global scope' of early modern drama, Claire Jowitt and David McInnis's collection *Travel and Drama in Early Modern England : The Journeying Play* prioritizes the relationship between travel and theatre in the period, through a more specific engagement with dramaturgy. Asserting the comprehensive aim of opening up the discourse on early modern travel, the collection seeks to include a variety of different approaches to and definitions of travel, including the imaginative and the authoritative, the experienced and the suggestive. Opening up the notion of travel writing to include the imaginative and the imagined, the collection expands the conventional range of contexts to collapse the boundaries between fiction and non-fiction. Beginning with the premise that 'the twin fields of theatre and travel in early modern England were changing at the fastest pace *ever* in the history of either domain', the collection sets out to establish a critical vocabulary for the understanding of place and movement, of 'voyage drama' and of the historical networks through which travellers and journeys were made visible. Some of the essays here are concerned with specific geographies and travellers – John Smith, Thomas Stukeley and the Sherley brothers – while others seek to trace journeying metaphors through an analysis of the pilgrimage or spiritual journey. Julie Sanders considers the genre of the journeying play, and Edward Dering's attempts at voyage drama and the representation of moving from place to place, both in abstract but also in the construction of imaginative associations and affiliations. The status of the voyage drama or travel play is also explored through the intersections between traveller and playwright, and the manifest ways in which 'actual travellers' chose to represent their experiences in drama. The hinterlands between the 'frivolous and feigned' and the 'serious, true or good' become a generative space for the exploration of how travel drama emerged in the public imagination. Referring to a 'nation of armchair travellers', Jowitt and McInnis assert that travel dramas 'became the most popular and easily accessible sources of information about this newly envisaged world'. The cross-overs between theatre and travelling extend beyond the imaginative scope of both to harness, in McInnis's chapter, the representation and experience of pleasure and satisfaction. Organized chronologically, the collection begins with a focus on the journeying plays of the 1570s and ends with Jowitt's chapter on Davenant and his abiding interest in voyage drama. Hakluyt's collection, *The Principle Navigations*, takes a prominent role in the book and becomes a focus for the ways in which 'travel (and the colonial, imperial, and mercantile opportunities it engenders) was beginning to be decisive in shaping the English nation's fortunes and identity'. Throughout the collection, the terms of travel are capacious and move through the local and domestic to the global and geopolitical to consider the generative dynamic between imagination and meditation. Steve Mentz's essay on 'oceanic hybridity' extends the vocabulary of the collection to explore the maritime world as a cultural contact zone. How those within and without the playworlds responded to travelling is also of interest to some of the contributors, and Andrew Gordon's essay on forms of movement opens up the discourse to consider the regimes of value through which travel represented itself. Considering the critical legacies of 'encounters' as well as 'cosmopolitanism', the collection marks a major contribution to the development of a critical discourse that looks beyond individual locations, journeys or travellers to the networks of images, ideas, actions and media through which travel mobilized across genre and performance conditions to chart an evolving and changing awareness of the theatrical relationship between movement and imagination.

In *Shakespeare and Post Colonial Theory*, Jyotsna Singh continues the focus on travel, not only in the pursuit of wider global and international discourses of race, identity, and colonial and postcolonial representations, but also as a metaphor for the movement that the book makes in its peripatetic exploration of the intersections between history, representation and reflection. Beginning with a brief assessment of the cultural legacy of European colonialism, postcolonial perspectives and their critical role as proleptic historical function, especially within the contexts of early modern English expansionism, Singh makes a powerful argument for the apprehension of alterity, difference and inequity in tracing Shakespeare's interactions with native cultures, local knowledges and east–west geopolitics. The book's project is to follow 'a trajectory of "travelling" Shakespeares through intersecting itineraries of exploration and discovery in the early modern period as well as in contemporary appropriations within diverse multicultural, native and global settings'. To this end, Singh's book is divided into three sections. The first section approaches early modern London and Shakespeare's worlds through a historicist analysis of travel narratives, and their traces of 'England's global colonizing imaginary' as well as discerning the impacts and representations of commercial and cultural expansion. Here the focus is largely on *Othello*, *The Merchant of Venice* and *The Tempest*. The second section charts responses to Shakespeare and provides a particular focus on critical works from the 1960s onwards, including Said's *Orientalism*, and the formation of postcolonial theories. The final part considers 'afterlives' – mostly productions on screen and stage, including Iqbal Khan's *Othello* and *Much Ado About Nothing* (2015), and Tim Supple's *A Midsummer Night's Dream* (2004) – as well as adaptations, including the work of Sulayman Al-Bassam, and moving finally to consider the 'intercultural Shakespeare in contemporary, multiracial, multi ethnic Britain'. Singh's work continues to raise fundamental questions about the annexing of postcolonial approaches to Shakespeare on conventional curriculums, and the importance of embedding multiple approaches, both historicist and contemporary, to the representation of race and identity in Shakespeare studies.

Travelling forth to Laurence Publicover's *Dramatic Geography, Romance, Intertheatricality, and Cultural Encounter in Early Modern Mediterranean Drama*, we continue this year's focus on mobility, space and the geographical imagination. Publicover's project is to situate the locations of many early modern plays within the context of romance, and the generic sympathies that it generates across travel narratives. Alongside the imaginative and interpretative networks that romance produces, Publicover develops a methodology he calls 'intertheatricality' to examine the relationships between geographical spaces across the plays, rather than as historically distinct places. Considering the traces of locations as they move between reference, allusion and imaginative responses, the book seeks to assert that 'fictional locations of early modern plays are consistently structured through generic forces'. Bringing the generic structures of romance into conversation with the allusive contexts of the playworlds, Publicover argues for a networked system of thought within the early modern theatre in which imagination, allusion, location and theatrical space collude to create a distinct sense of 'dramatic geography'. Publicover begins his argument with a call for time travel as he 'imagines [himself] back into the world of those playgoers' and discovers a metaphorical greenhouse in which the windows are 'a boundary that admitted ideas that were then concentrated and re-visited'. Understanding the production of theatre as a dynamic exchange of ideas, Publicover goes on to explore the interrelationships between plays through their invocation of place. Surveying plays concerned with the Mediterranean, Publicover traces the dynamic exchange of space that represents 'cultural contact: geographically and ethnographically they construct whirlpools, either spinning characters between lands (thus evoking the Latin root of *Mediterranean*) or assembling characters of differing cultural backgrounds on an island or within a port-city'. Thus spinning and assembling in our metaphorical greenhouse, we move between the geographical imaginations of Marlowe, Kyd, Heywood, Beaumont and Shakespeare, as well as the works of anonymous playwrights, including little-known plays such as *Clyomon and Clamydes* and *Guy of Warwick*, to highlight how romance supports a dynamic exchange between the inner worlds of psyche and the outer worlds of environment. Considering a range of early modern texts, including the ever popular Sherley brothers, Richard Knolles and Boccaccio, Publicover attends

to the rich world of global exchange as it is imagined on the early modern London stage.

THIS ENGLAND

In *Shakespeare's Englishes: Against Englishness*, Margaret Tudeau-Clayton seeks to situate the comedies and histories of the 1590s 'in relation to the discursive struggle within post-Reformation England over the "property" of (the) English'. Taking up the vernacular in relation to ideas of authenticity, honesty and plainness, the book repositions Shakespeare's exploration of national identity as one which is in conflict with the 'exclusionary ideology of this cultural re-formation'. In resisting the centre that such ideologies produce, Tudeau-Clayton argues for a 'mobile and inclusive mix' of terms and bodies which promotes belonging not through a homogeneous cultural centre, but through the depiction of England as 'a nation of mutual strangers'. Hospitality, charity and a pre-modern sense of community come to shape many of the arguments here, in which Shakespeare's Englishes emerge as diversions, wanderings and dynamics that find their authority not in uniformity, but in a wider and more discursive 'gallimaufry'. The material is very dense, and sometimes it is not always clear as to which side of the debate about language and cultural authority Shakespeare is on: Tudeau-Clayton moves between setting up an early modern context of the 'King's English' and Shakespeare's disruption of that centre, through an analysis of what constitutes the 'true born', 'native' or 'normative centre' of vernacular identity. There are so many strands to the argument here, which make it so capacious that it veers into a veritable cornucopia, on the one hand, and an amblongus pie on the other. But perhaps that's the point. Tracing the various and variant ways in which Shakespeare creates new ethical and semantic networks through the 'mobile and inclusive mix' of 'strangers', the book pursues a central argument in which the Christianized languages of hospitality, charity, wandering, reformation and law reproduce a more secular focus on the interactions between human and linguistic markers of mobility. Central to this discussion is an exploration of the carnivalesque, festivity and release in *The Merry Wives*, *Henry IV*, *The Merchant of Venice*, *Twelfth Night*, *The Comedy of Errors* and *Love's Labour's Lost*. Beginning with an exploration of the exclusionary nature of the 'King's English', Tudeau-Clayton seeks to animate the many and divergent ways in which language disrupts the centre – from drunkenness to malapropisms, foreign languages, banishment, exclusion, deconstruction, pun and moving words about the place. Shakespeare's Englishes emerge not so much as an imagined community, but as a verbal play on the status of representation itself, and the value – both culturally and linguistically – of the sign as native hue. In the broad and brilliant range of the book, Tudeau-Clayton examines the language of strangeness, the nomadic, the errant and the contingent as Shakespeare's playworlds set up the multiple conditions of both belonging and exclusion: language is, of course, central to this, but so, too, are the imaginative geographies through which difference is explored. The recurrent theme of the 'mutual stranger' supports a powerful readjustment of the playworld's terms of inclusion, so that the often-cited argument for 'plainness' as the recursive centre of English vernacular becomes displaced to consider geographical as well as cultural difference. Within these terms, 'communities' are often diverse spaces of belonging, in which characters may travel – settle, even – but rarely with a sense of deviating from a centre: rather, from another periphery. *Sir Thomas More* runs as a thread throughout the book for its exploration of hospitality, charity, enmity and exclusion, as well as a resonant focus on the terms of 'mistaking' as they are mobilized in *The Comedy of Errors* as well as *Twelfth Night*: 'These mistakings are, moreover, specifically linked to the case of the stranger in the (hostile) city and, though there may be no overt lesson, there is, . . ., a call to recognise and welcome as citizens and 'brethren' (Abbot) those viewed as strangers, a view which, from the perspective of the shaping biblical plot, is exposed as a category mistake'. The 'category mistake' is an important element of the book since it seeks to dismantle the

'centripetal drive of cultural reformation ideology' through a focus on straying. *Shakespeare's Englishes* is very dense and there is a huge amount of material here, not only archival contexts and paratexts but also a great deal of assimilated work that Tudeau-Clayton began to explore, with Willy Maley, in *This England, That Shakespeare* (2010). The interest in nationhood extends beyond the boundaries of regional difference to something much more widely invested in language use and the complex and often opaque histories that semantic networks both produce and reinvent. The deeper stories that are told here belong to shared communities of thought as well as expression, and resonate across boundaries that are at once distinctly human and profoundly abstract.

The emphasis on the reformation continues in *Ruin and Reformation in Spenser, Shakespeare and Marvell* in which Stewart Mottram explores the relationship between the past and the future as it becomes symbolized in the remains of the dissolved monasteries. Attending to the different ways in which the ruin was preserved in the cultural imagination, Mottram analyses its 'unruly potential' to provide a 'window on the past' and a 'prospective mirror on the future'. Building on this approach, the ruin becomes a mobile figure for the analysis of the 'past as prologue', and an exploration of the historical process that is both contingent and recursive. Central to Mottram's argument is an awareness of the spectre of dissolution and the ruin as a continual reminder not only of what has happened, but of what might happen again. The attention here to the possible and plausible becomes a key part of the critical analysis of history, religion and culture, and the intersections between writing, recording and representing. Ideas of nationhood, belonging and identification come to reside in the imaging of an Englishness that is attendant on both political community and church history, and Mottram steers the focus to a 'grammar of English Protestantism' and 'faith in fiction'. Mottram's aim is not to provide an analysis of sectarian sympathies in any of these writers but to invest in the ruin as a record of 'particular moments of reformation', and therefore at the thresholds between culture and religious identity. Beginning with Spenser and the language of the plough, Mottram explores the relationships between agrarian complaint and the neglect of communities. Tracing the remains of monastic culture through Spenser's works, Mottram explores representations of and attitudes to violence and ruination. Situating Shakespeare's *Cymbeline* within the context of anxieties about Catholic threats to Europe, Mottram considers domestic and local images of insurrection and the circumstances of rebellion and intolerance that give way to a cycle of fear and destruction. Mottram's argument, which seeks to unpack the interrelations between heritage, destruction, legacy and tradition, focuses on the monastic ruin as a central image in the restructuring of English identity as well as the representations of possible and different religious futures. Seeking to destabilize the terms of peace and unity so often explored in the play, Mottram uncovers the multiple ghosts of rebellion that the play accommodates, and the conflicted models of heroism that it draws on in its representation of invasions. Revisiting the terms of Essex's uprising and the potential and different outcomes that it might have hoped to achieve, Mottram reconsiders the representations of violence, hubris and potential sites of invasion in *Cymbeline* in pursuit of an argument for religious toleration and the 'topicality of treason'. Drawing widely on the work of Spenser, Marvell and, to a lesser extent, Shakespeare and Denham, Mottram provides a clear, thoughtful and intelligent account of the meditative, creative, reflective and cultural opportunities that the monastic ruin offers for the analysis of 'authorial introspection on the complex and conflicted processes of protestant identity formation that defined England's century-long experience of reformation'.

CLOSER TO HOME

In *Shakespeare's Domestic Tragedies, Violence in the Early Modern Home*, Emma Whipday examines the relationship between violence in the home and its representation on stage. Considering the representation of the domestic through neighbours,

interiors, privacy and household chores, Whipday focuses on the space of the home and the representation of household bonds as either 'fatal' or nurturing. Rooted in contemporary chronicles and texts that record domestic violence, Whipday's book seeks to unpack the emergence of a new and formative genre in the representation of the domestic space and to position the home at the centre of early modern theatre. Collapsing the boundaries between 'cheap print' and historical or legal accounts, Whipday reappraises the genre of domestic tragedy to include a wide variety of plays concerned with familial relationships and interior spaces. Whipday's intention, to 'trace ideas of home' in 'early modern popular culture', claims a new angle on the subject by investing in the historicized contexts of non-elite literature. Moving between salacious accounts of homicide, violence and abuse, Whipday explores the various ways in which the home was represented as a place of violation in the early modern imagination, and how this fed into, created or reflected a dominant appetite for domestic plays on the stage. There is a huge and fascinating body of work on the domestic in this period, including the seminal contributions of Natasha Korda, Lena Orlin and Frances Dolan, as well as the more theoretically inflected models which seek to explore the codes of hospitality and charity. What Whipday seems to bring to this conversation is a reappraisal of genre and an emphasis on the interconnectedness of plays that stage 'violent homes'. Crossing traditional generic divisions with the insertion of *The Taming of the Shrew* into the tragic context, Whipday brings together *Hamlet*, *Othello*, *Macbeth* and, to a lesser extent, *King Lear* under the auspice of 'home'. As an intersectional space, the domestic becomes a nexus for the exploration of the theatrical relationships between tragedy and household. In many ways, of course, all of Shakespeare's plays include a home in which, or from which, the characters set out their playworlds, and conceptualizing the 'home' in the early modern imagination, as well as in the plays, provides some of the biggest challenges that Whipday's argument faces. Understanding the home as a material structure involving legal rights, privacy and ownership, and as a symbolic space, in which certain expectations, ceremonies and power dynamics are expressed, becomes the most contested aspect of the book. Unpicking the interrelationships between house and home, family and household, responsibilities and rights becomes a necessary adjunct to Whipday's argument and supports her pursuit of the 'domestic' as a space that levels many of the more layered – and often paradoxical – considerations of home and autonomy. One of the most interesting elements of the book is the exploration of the power relations on which 'homes' are built – whether between host and guest, master and servant, children and father or husband and wife, the set of conditions that the home provides determines a range of symbolic and material experiences, as well as expectations. Central to Whipday's thesis is a revision of generic categories and a reassertion of the importance of understanding domestic tragedy as an important contribution to the developing range of early modern drama. Unpicking the traditional binaries between comedy and tragedy, including subject matter, style and significance, Whipday demonstrates the intersectional space that domestic drama occupies between tragedy and comedy. Yet, rather than colonize this hinterland through the terms of tragi-comedy, the book shows that domestic tragedy occupied a specific moral and political space all of its own. The moral space of tragedy has often been supported by Thomas Heywood's much-cited anecdote of the female audience member who confesses her part in household murder on the basis of what she sees in the play *Friar Francis*. The reflective opportunities that drama affords for moral revelation and social justice come to rest in the domestic setting, as one of both political and local significance. Whipday pays special attention to the drama's self-reflective attempts to record its relationship to contemporary contexts, not only in the allusions to 'actual' murders – whether recorded in ballads, news or broadsides – but also in the meta-theatrical infrastructures of inductions, epilogues, choruses and narrative descriptions. Whipday's thesis is that domestic tragedy, although

not named as such, emerges as a new genre in this period, and is distinct in its treatment and reflection of the domestic space and enabling of the mixing of both the quotidian and the elite; and that Shakespeare 'borrows' from this tradition whilst retaining the defining elitism of high tragedy. Her three central plays are *Othello*, *Hamlet* and *Macbeth*, although she also draws on *King Lear* and *The Taming of the Shrew*, for the ways in which they share a 'domestic specificity' that is unique in its portrayal of 'household disorder that threatens the state'. The relationship between Shakespearian tragedy and domestic tragedy isn't always clear: on the one hand, Shakespeare 'borrows', and on another he 'appropriates and transforms the genre'. Whipday recognizes that drama is dominated by familial or domestic dynamics and this is not in itself sufficiently selective to support generic boundaries, but, at the same time, the prevailing impulse towards the quotidian or ordinary in domestic drama is not relevant to Shakespeare's tragedies of high state. What seems to matter most is the descriptive detail of the domestic spaces and the ways in which they draw on different or alternative considerations of the personal, intimate or psychological struggles of the home. Within these terms, a consideration of the fly scene in *Titus Andronicus* would have been fascinating, especially within the context of Middleton's authorship and Whipday's wider exploration of the trafficking of genre across the drama of this period. But Whipday's focus remains largely on the generic relationships between popular and performance culture and how, by reading the plays through the wider discursive networks of the spatial, psychological and material iterations of the home, we can discover a culture in search of its own representation, as well as its communities. The real strengths of the book lie not in the specific arguments for Shakespeare's use of genre but in the focus on the home and the multiple ways in which Whipday engages critical responses to gender and space, whilst retaining an adroit grip on contemporary material. There's a huge amount of material here that confronts many dearly held binaries of the critical tradition and, in that, challenges us to rethink the relationships between theatre and culture in very productive ways.

CONTAGION

Eric Langley's *Shakespeare's Contagious Sympathies* stands out as an exceptional contribution to the field this year. Considering the terms and functions of sympathy, compassion and tenderness, Langley sets out to examine the dynamic and dialogic function of what it is to touch and be touched by human feeling. Approaching the mind and body both in symbiosis and as distinct in their vulnerabilities, Langley interrogates the multiple networks and connections through which compassion and contagion link the body to both its environment and its community. At the centre of the discussion is a focus on communication, both in its abstract function as a marker of human kinship but also as a biological – pathological, even – set of interrelationships on which transmission and flow depend. Drawing on medical, philosophical, literary and conduct texts, Langley sets out to examine the ambivalent ways in which compassion and contagion interact with each other in the social domain; 'To contact may be to contract. To converse may be to convert. To be informed may be to be deformed.' Contagion, conversation, conversion and compassion become inexorably linked through the necessary activity that each requires and the threat and opportunities that they give rise to. Teasing out the survival functions of mercy but not pity, reciprocity but not receptivity, Langley offers an abundant and utterly engaging analysis of the state of compassion: 'Compassion comes to constitute a network, a community of communication, establishing an interchange with pity as its pathways.' But pity is a dangerous thing, as the Stoics warn: 'to waile with them', is to open oneself up to affliction. Langley's approach combines theory – psychoanalytical, medical, critical and linguistic – with historicism and brings an intellectual rigour to the copious and often divergent contemporary attitudes to feeling. As Langley notes, the vocabulary employed for empathy can also be employed for

infection, and it is this kinetic dynamic that informs the argument of the book. The overarching narrative, as Langley sees it, is that the period witnesses, and produces, a story of 'faith under fire', and this fire is driven by 'a loss of faith in the sympathetic structures which bind the Renaissance subject into its compassionate universe'. Following the blurred lines between physiological and psychological interactions, Langley explores the processes of transmission in which the friendly can let in the poisonous. Questioning how we show compassion 'in a world of contagion', the book evaluates the relationship between the microcosm and the macrocosm through the dynamic force of the human body. Correspondence – in how communication takes place as well as similitude – informs the approach to the book's three parts, which seek to expose the dynamics, from the cosmic to the domestic, involved in influential exchange. Beginning with a detailed focus on *Troilus and Cressida*, Langley examines Shakespeare's vocabulary of disease and interdependency. Considering the philosophical implications of communal identity, Langley interrogates the wars within and without the self to exist 'being singular plural'. Moving from sympathy to antipathy, the book considers the pharmaceutical metaphor of the bittersweet, and the inherent capacities it holds to kill and/or cure. Drawing on a number of plays, including *The Winter's Tale*, *Titus*, *King Lear*, *Coriolanus* and *All's Well*, this section considers 'the "slippery turns" of unstable antithesis' and the terrifying but productive proximities between terror and comfort. The following chapter focuses exclusively on *Othello*, where Iago becomes a Harold Shipman figure who preys upon the 'victim-patient' with his 'contagiously sympathetic attentions'. Part 3 moves to the vocabulary of tenderness and examines the 'extended subject' through the figure of stretching towards another, as well as putting oneself out to tender, to retract and to maintain. Here the focus is on *The Tempest* and *Venus and Adonis*, and the cost of compassion. The penultimate chapter considers those characters who avoid or reject infectious others and the drive to isolation and self-protection, archetyped by figures such as Coriolanus and, to a lesser extent, Prince Hal. Hamlet is an interesting case in point, too, for he becomes something of a tragic victim of the contagion/compassion dialectic since he is forced into isolation as a marker of a 'period whose faith in subjective sympathetic interactivity has been so infectiously tested'. Langley covers a staggering range of diverse materials, which he lucidly synthesizes to travel between Galen, Montaigne and Descartes, Butler and Kristeva, Derrida and Bacon, among many other early modern and contemporary writers. There's a multitude of compelling references to contemporary attitudes to cosmology, infection and pollution. The image of the parasite and corporeal sympathy become powerful testimonies to the multiple networks through which compassion travels and the dynamic between the host and hostility, as so brilliantly set out by Derrida. There is a wonderful richness and diversity of material here, including poignant and personal anonymous letters, as well as medical treatises and philosophical discourse. The emphasis on the corporeal as well as the cognitive, the spatial as well as the psychological, allows Langley to range fluently across the often atomized fields of science and art, the personal and the polemic: extending his reach to almost anything that moves, the book provides a very brilliant study of 'communicative exchange' and the perils and potentials of the 'tenderized subject' who, much to the author's regret, recedes increasingly from view over the course of the study to reveal a responsive subject more invested in immunity than community.

Many of the seeds (or perhaps germs) of Langley's arguments are also at work in *Contagion and the Shakespearean Stage*, ed. Darryl Chalk and Mary Floyd-Wilson. In this also very thought-provoking and intelligent book, the various essays seek to establish a wider discourse for the analysis of contagion as a prescient metaphor for, as well as experience of, the early modern theatre. The theatre as a site of both infection and affection becomes the central focus for the essays that examine contagion as a metaphor for the interactions between spectator and playworld, as well as character and actor. Like Langley, many of the contributors here

are interested in the mimetic opportunities that theatre provides for imitation and investment, and the essays by Jennifer Panek and Jennifer Feather, respectively, explore the sympathetic networks available to the audience in *More Dissemblers Besides Women*, and the failure of fellow feeling in *Titus Andronicus*. Here, the imagination becomes the primary site of transmission as affect makes itself known through the 'fraught operation of pity'. Feather does not distinguish between pity and mercy in the nuanced and stoically inflected ways that Langley does – but, rather, she examines the relationship between violence and sympathy, defence and invasion. The focus on the theatre provides a specific thread in the dual processes of imitation and counterfeiting, and the extents to which contagion can take effect across the boundaries of both bodies and space. Bringing together 'various kinds of contagious operations', the collection establishes 'the variety of things or conditions, material or immaterial, thought able to pass between individuals, or to cause action at a distance'. Informed by the history of disease transmission as well as attitudes to theatre-going, the collection is divided into three sections, which foster various different approaches. Beginning with sensation, and the susceptible body, essays on *The Comedy of Errors*, *Troilus and Cressida*, *The Witch of Edmonton* and *Julius Caesar* examine smell, touch, taste and breath through a dual focus on both the instigator and the recipient. Here, the 'socially contagious processes of human collectivity' are examined, and the often gendered way in which words, more than kisses, 'constitute a dangerous source of contagion'. The second section on abjection tends towards space, and the various cultural fantasies of self-replication. Exploring sex and invasion in *The Changeling* and *Othello*, Emily Weissbourd addresses the body of the woman as a socially functioning site of contamination where the male gaze can scrutinize the female body for its potential vulnerability to 'foreign infection'. In the final section, the essays turn to the assemblage, and the contexts and capacities in which ideas, images or narratives can replicate and survive, adapt and reproduce. Clifford Werier's essay explores gene replication and meme theory in relation to the oppositional forces in *Coriolanus*, in which one set of attitudes or conditions must subsume, or adapt to overcome, the other. As he explains, however, the power of the meme lies in its adaptability rather than eradication. J. F. Bernard's essay on *Hamlet* takes the conversation into the direction of publicity and how theatre acts as a point and place of advertisement and evolution through the idea of the viral. Exploring the theatrical possibilities of publicity and narrative dissemination, Bernard considers the cultural vocabularies of contagion though the idea of storytelling and how 'popular theatre mimics the contagion process by constantly seeking to infect new carriers with its stories'. The invasive power of the story becomes a potent model for the play's excavation of the power of metatheatricality that pervades the playworld, making spectators and actors of almost every character. The final essays focus on environments, rather than individuals, and analyse the networks and assemblages through which contagion is made possible. Understanding the plague – for example, in J. Charles Estabillo's essay on *The Alchemist* or Rebecca Totaro's essay on *Romeo and Juliet* – allows us to see the threat of disease as 'a backdrop, a discourse that informs the play but which Jonson [in the case of *The Alchemist*] transforms into a dramatic system that speaks primarily to related but distinct social issues'. In Totaro's reading of *Romeo and Juliet*, such a dramatic system authorizes the tragedy, rather than the individuals. *Contagion on the Shakespearean Stage* provides a clever, engaging and accomplished way in to the complex and erudite subject of contagion in the period, while Langley takes the argument much further and in much more detail; but, together, both books provide a formidable contribution to the field, and a rich and stimulating discussion of the reciprocal networks of social formation.

ENDINGS

To conclude this year's illustrious contributions to the field of Shakespeare studies, and my time in reviewing them, I turn to John S. Garrison's *Shakespeare and the Afterlife*, which is the most recent book to come out of the Oxford Shakespeare Topics series. At first glance, I thought the book was going to be about Shakespeare's afterlives and the many and varied ways in which his work lives on, and I felt a little weary: happily, the rather oblique term 'afterlife' refers much more specifically to the presence of ghosts, the occult and the undiscovered country from which no traveller (or so we are led to believe) returns. Because, of course, many travellers do come back in Shakespeare's plays, and it is with this fascinatingly macabre subject that the book is concerned. Considering 'figurations of life after death', Garrison finds that Shakespeare is much preoccupied with the subject of heaven and hell, and the afterlife is 'very much on the minds of Shakespeare's characters and speakers'. Reading across allusions, imaginings, prefigurations, spectres and dreams, Garrison illuminates the many vibrant and often touching ways in which characters imagine death and experience life in their playworlds. Considering the divergent strands of belief that the plays offer and multiple opportunities that death provides for the interrogation of life, the book provides a very compelling, erudite, thoughtful and nuanced exploration of individual and social meaning, and the 'powerful hold that loss and reunion have on our private emotions and collective consciousness'. Attending to 'remains', transitions, traces, spectres and objects, *Shakespeare and the Afterlife* builds connections between texts as it approaches the question of death, focusing both on individual characters' concerns and on the wider impact of those concerns within the playworlds. Beginning with suicide and memory, expectation and fear, in a range of plays, Chapter 1 concludes with an analysis of *Measure for Measure*. Each chapter moves its focus across a number of plays, and, over the course of the book, these include *The Tempest, Measure for Measure, Twelfth Night, Julius Caesar, Richard III, Macbeth, Antony and Cleopatra, Titus Andronicus, Timon of Athens, Hamlet* and the *Sonnets*. The sections are brief but the subjects are huge, and the approach surveys the philosophical, religious, psychoanalytical, anthropological and political. The readership of the

Oxford Shakespeare Topics series is broad and Garrison has a suitably light touch, but even within that he manages to offer a variety of approaches that consider the beliefs of the reader and audience member as well as the characters. Concluding with the *Sonnets*, Garrison considers the ambiguous legacies of 'eternal lines', and the 'shadowy realm of death' that flickers in every beginning and 'bears it out even to the end of doom'. Despite the often gloomy prospects of death, much that this book celebrates is about life, and, more so, love.

WORKS REVIEWED

Akhimie, Patricia, and Bernadette Andrea, eds., *Travel and Travail: Early Modern Women, English Drama and the Wider World* (Lincoln and London, 2019)

Arshad, Yasmin, *Imagining Cleopatra: Performing Gender and Power in Early Modern England* (London, 2019)

Bergeron, David, *Shakespeare's London 1613* (Manchester, 2018)

Chalk, Darryl, and Mary Floyd-Wilson, eds., *Contagion and the Shakespearean Stage* (Basingstoke, 2019)

Garrison, John S., *Shakespeare and the Afterlife* (Oxford, 2019)

Jowitt, Claire, and David McInnis, *Travel and Drama in Early Modern England: The Journeying Play* (Cambridge, 2019)

Langley, Eric, *Shakespeare's Contagious Sympathies* (Oxford, 2019)

Love, Genevieve, *Early Modern Theatre and the Figure of Disability* (London, 2019)

Mottram, Stewart, *Ruin and Reformation in Spenser, Shakespeare and Marvell* (Oxford, 2019)

Publicover, Laurence, *Dramatic Geography, Romance, Intertheatricality, and Cultural Encounter in Early Modern Mediterranean Drama* (Oxford, 2017)

Singh, Jyotsna, *Shakespeare and Post Colonial Theory* (London, 2019)

Tudeau-Clayton, Margaret, *Shakespeare's Englishes: Against Englishness* (Cambridge, 2020)

Whipday, Emma, *Shakespeare's Domestic Tragedies: Violence in the Early Modern Home* (Cambridge, 2019) *reviewed by* RUSSELL JACKSON

The title of Thomas Cartelli's *Reenacting Shakespeare in the Shakespeare Aftermath: The Intermedial Turn and Turn to Embodiment* calls for some clarification, which is provided in due course. Cartelli addresses the question of exactly what it is in which our 'faith' must be 'awaked' for Shakespeare's plays 'to engage their receivers/audiences with the kind of "nervous novelty" they presumably brought to the Elizabethan stage when Shakespeare himself took old matter and remixed it into new theatrical blends' (17). Is 'contaminated representation' – a term borrowed from the work of Rebecca Schneider – the answer?[1] This is where, in the current state of 'excess' and 'exhaustion', 'Reenactments' come in. These are productions making use of one media or several to 'interrupt and redirect, in unprecedented ways, the transmission of the play from point to point over time'. The 'aftermath' is construed 'less as a specifically demarcated zone or moment of time or history than as a discursive and performative space and condition of awareness theoretically shared by the makers, if not the receivers, of the performances or experiences on offer that all things Shakespearean are present and available for redoing and reenactment *differently*' (12–13, emphasis in original). We are a long way from such simple labels, serviceable in their time, as Ruby Cohn's 'Shakespeare offshoots'.[2] (Cartelli's definition, which cannot be said to leap off the page, is easier to follow once one has typed it out.) Some of the usual suspects, such as Heiner Müller, The Wooster Group, Peter Greenaway and Ivo van Hove, are rounded up, and a few more are added: Jawad al-Asadi (*Forget Hamlet*), Annie Dorsen (*A Piece of Work*) and Péter Lichter and Bori Máté (*The Rub*). The choices prioritize work that may perhaps be classed as interventions as much as reenactments, where the confluence of different media trumps simple shifting from one medium to another. In the 60 minutes of *The Rub*, for example, 'an often laconic voice' runs, and occasionally

re-runs, Hamlet's lines 'while thousands of vividly painted or deliberately traumatized film frames scroll past, many of them rubbed with dirt and sand to make them seem older and more damaged than when they were harvested' (282). In the case of the Wooster Group's work alongside the RSC in the 2012 production of *Troilus and Cressida*, Cartelli examines the consequences of what turned out to be more a collision than a collaboration between divergent cultures. The RSC's prioritizing of intelligibility clashed with the American ensemble's operation 'at what could be construed as the rough edges of the theatrical cutting edge' by 'tasking' audiences with 'unexplained (and often inexplicable) collidings of material drawn from disparate sources of high and popular culture' (63). The chapter headings, like the book's title, tend to offer terms that promise the definition of terms, and consequent scrutiny through definition: thus, *A Piece of Work* and *The Rub* figure as examples of 'disassembly, meaning and montage' (255). The inclusion of Greenaway's film in this alternative canon of innovation, and Cartelli's characteristically sophisticated and persuasive analysis of it, suggest that its time has come, and that it has found, perhaps belatedly, its true context. Even for those readers who prefer not to spend time at those 'rough edges' of the cutting edge, this is a rewardingly provocative and persuasive study of works that inevitably inform arguments about the definition of theatrical and interpretive practice.

The Oxford Handbook of Shakespeare and Dance, edited by Lynsey McCullough and Brandon Shaw, takes the reader from the significance and practices of dance on stage in the playwright's time, to such familiar pieces as the *Midsummer Night's Dream* ballets created by Ashton and Balanchine, John

[1] Rebecca Schneider, *Performing Remains: Art and War in Times of Theatrical Reenactment* (London and New York, 2011), p. 52.
[2] Ruby Cohn, *Modern Shakespeare Offshoots* (Princeton, 1976).

Cranko's *Taming of the Shrew*, and Kenneth MacMillan's *Romeo and Juliet*, and on to works in which 'dance theatre' and 'physical theatre' revisit the plays in a more challenging idiom. The first section 'Shakespeare *and* dance' (emphasis in original) begins with Emily Winebrook's '"The Heaven's true figure" or an "Introit to all kind of lewdness"?', in which she elucidates the 'competing conceptions of dance in Shakespeare's England' and examines the ways in which the playwright 'uses in-text references to invoke the rich diversity of associations his audiences had with the art of Terpsichore' (21). Subsequent essays document the social (and moral) connotations of dancing; incidental dances in and after plays; 'masquing practice' in court and on stage; and such specifics as the explication of 'passy-measures pavin' and Sir Toby Belch's advocacy of making water 'in a cinquepace' (*Twelfth Night*, 5.1.197, 1.3.125). A bridge between the first ten chapters in this part of the volume is provided by Evelyn O'Malley's 'Dancing with the archive: early dance for Shakespearean adaptation', an account of the practical artistic application of such knowledge in a practice-as-research piece, 'envisioned as a conversation between *The Winter's Tale* and [Ben Jonson's] *Oberon*', originally staged at the Northcott Theatre, Exeter, in May 2012. The fourteen chapters of Part Two, 'Shakespeare *as* Dance', describe and analyse works in idioms ranging from 'classical' ballet to 'synetic theatre and physical Shakespeare'. The relationship between Shakespearian text and the (mostly) silent eloquence of dance emerges as one of productive creative tension rather than contradiction. Not only is it received wisdom that in classical ballet there is no direct way of saying 'she is my mother-in-law', twentieth-century experimental dance (as Susan Jones explains in her chapter on 'Shakespeare, modernism, and dance') 'frequently focused on formal abstraction, rather than the transmission of narrative, plot and character'. Consequently, 'the reception of Shakespeare in certain modernist one-act works of pure dance, where the "essence" of the play is presented without recourse to text, rather than in film or opera, poses the specific question of how to treat the play when words are altogether absent' (287).

The varied definitions of the 'essence' of the source texts in question and the means of conveying it are represented in Jones's illuminating analyses of Robert Helpmann's *Hamlet* (1942), José Limón's *The Moor's Pavane* (1949), and *Barren Sceptre* by Limón and Pauline Koner (1960). The three harlots in Kenneth MacMillan's *Romeo and Juliet* provide a memorably sassy response to the testosterone-happy trio of young noblemen, and flout the attacks (with broom in hand) of the righteously indignant townswomen. In '"Hildings and harlots": Kenneth MacMillan's *Romeo and Juliet*', Lynsey McCulloch shows how the choreographer uses the harlots to extend the ballet's engagement with sexuality, and add, in the simply expressed grief of one of them at Mercutio's death, a counterpart to the elaborate lamentations of Lady Capulet over Tybalt, with which MacMillan (and Prokofiev) end the ballet's first part. (In Frederick Ashton's version, which has been overshadowed by MacMillan's, the street life of Verona is harlot-free, and the response to this part of the score is lively and charming – but in comparison seems limply festive.) To narrative ballets of this kind, it is especially appropriate to apply a term adopted by Lincoln Kerstein in *Movement and Metaphor: Four Centuries of Ballet* (1970): the source text is the dance's 'pretext', not in the sense of being some kind of excuse, but as providing a rationale and inspiration. There is also a strong element of commentary on the 'pretext' in such works – a view of the play that revisits and responds in a transformative manner: Cranko's *Taming of the Shrew* (1969) is not so much a translation of the play into dance terms as a revision of it. In his final scene, the newfound tenderness between Katherine and Petruchio is expressed touchingly when she places her hands beneath his and rests her cheek on them. Iris Bührle ('Shakespeare ballets in Germany, from Jean-Georges Noverre to John Neumeier') observes that Cranko portrays the couple as 'strong, authentic characters who genuinely fall in love during the course of the ballet', while his use of the *commedia* conventions reveals 'potential meanings of the text that can go unnoticed, such as the possibility of interpreting the main couple's behaviour as highly theatrical' (373).

Creating 'authentic' and psychologically intelligible characters remains a priority in these works from the middle of the twentieth century, while others have tended towards deconstruction and a more radical interrogation of the text. In this part of the *Handbook*, the nature of the performances described makes the writer's task difficult, and precludes concise description in this review. The contributors all rise to the challenge, although sometimes the vocabulary appropriate to situating and describing a piece may seem forbidding to an inexpert reader. For example, Kathrina Farrugia-Kriel writes that South African choreographer and dancer Dada Masilo's *The Bitter End of Rosemary* (2011) 'embraces the collision and convergence of multiple dimensions of "otherness"', and 'in its transmodern dimension ... elicits pluralistic possibilities that eliminate any overriding artistic monopolies and hierarchies' (492). It is hard to see, though, how else Farrugia-Kriel could account for the complexities of this re-visioning of Ophelia in terms of the maker's situation as a woman of colour in postcolonial and post-Apartheid society. Other postmodern performances, less challenging to cultural and political assumptions and conditions, are more immediately accessible, but no less radical in terms of their art form. The narratives of the source plays were articulated by a combination of spoken word and dance in John Faranesh-Bocca's *Pericles Redux* (2008) and Crystal Pite's *The Tempest Replica* (2009), examples of the 'physical theatre' practices that can be traced back to Artaud and Grotowski. The relationships between text and movement and dance and mime were explored in both, and, as Linda McJannett relates, reviewers of *Pericles Redux* were 'moved primarily by the physical aspects of the performance', and one 'lauded Pite's ability to take "a sacred cultural text like The Tempest" and "to make the words have flesh"' (561). This *Handbook* is skilfully organized, informative and persuasive in its historical essays, and challenging and stimulating throughout – a welcome and overdue contribution to the study of Shakespearian adaptation, hitherto dominated by spoken theatre, film and television.

In '*Hamlet' and World Cinema*, Mark Thornton Burnett explores 'adaptations ... outside of the UK/US axis'. Moving between a 'range of periods from the 1930s to the present day', they demonstrate 'the play's manoeuvrability – its capacity for commenting on local situations and ideologies that run along asymmetrical lines' (2). This wide-ranging and acutely argued study draws attention to the ways 'a western canonical Hamlet is constantly flipped, augmented and re-envisioned' (16). Not only does it introduce the reader to many films that are likely to be unfamiliar (and often difficult to come by), but it also sheds new light on some well-known, indeed canonical, versions. For example, *The Bad Sleep Well*, Akira Kurosawa's modern-dress thriller, is compared with the period drama *Castle of Flames*, by Katô Tai. Both were released in 1960, and both are discussed in terms of what the chapter's section title identifies as 'protesting Japan', the reaction against the compromises with corruption that attended the post-war social and political settlement in the country. 'China rising', the second section of the chapter on Hamlet in China and Japan, complements the discussion of Kurosawa's and Tai's films with an examination of *The Banquet* and *Prince of the Himalayas* (both 2006): whereas both *Castle of Flames* and *Prince of the Himalayas* 'espouse notions of collectivity and human alliance', *The Bad Sleep Well* and *The Banquet* 'contemplate ideas of singleness and individual will, debating the degree of power to which the solitary avenger has access'(146).

Neil Forsyth's *Shakespeare the Illusionist* is a study of (as its subtitle indicates) 'Magic, dreams and the supernatural on film'. From the earliest uses of *trucage* to render ghosts and magic effects in the silent era to such recent works as Julie Taymor's *Tempest*, Forsyth encompasses a wide range of films, both mainstream and avant-garde. A guiding principle (not in itself a theme) emerges: the need to establish what the film-makers' intentions may have been, and the context in which they were working, as a prerequisite of analysis. This makes for an open-minded and generous book that can accommodate differences of response on the part of the reader while suggesting interpretations that will

stimulate a new look at familiar films. This sometimes arises in the case of details, as in the reference
to the fairies' dancing in Reinhardt and Dieterle's
1935 *Midsummer Night's Dream* as 'Busby Berkeley
routines' (77). Although this seems inadequate as a
summary description of Bronislava Nijinska's
choreography, it does suggest further reflection
on the relationship between the mixture of modern
dance and ballet in the sequences and the familiar
styles and resources of musicals from Warner Bros.
Reading across the book's chapters to the account
of Peter Greenaway's *Prospero's Books* prompts
reflections on its kinship with the 1935 *Dream*, in
which one never knows on a first viewing exactly
what kind of spectacle will come next. The *bricolage*
of Greenaway's 'performance of the retelling of the
story', by '[r]eversing the troublesome priority for a
filmmaker of Shakespeare's texts to the images he
derives from them, makes Prospero's books into
collections of images in his imagination, and so the
source of the texts being written' (59). This is
Shakespeare as 'a magician' in the sense of being
posthumously endowed with the filmmaker's
resources – one in the fantasy tradition associated
with Georges Méliès, rather than the 'realism'
(itself, of course, illusory) derived from the
Lumière brothers. Forsyth traces the screen's treat-
ments of Shakespearian ghosts and apparitions, not
so much to evaluate them technically as being more
or less 'convincing', as to elucidate the nature of
that conviction. An example of the conflict that
may arise between a director's aesthetic instincts
and the requirements of the moment is the presentation of the ghost in Franco Zeffirelli's *Hamlet*,
where 'even the night outside on the castle battle-
ments is oddly bright' and staging and photography, identifying the spectre's position and identity
with clarity, obey 'an important consideration for
Zeffirelli, that the audience be given little trouble'
(108). This parenthetical comment, which goes to
the heart of the director's aesthetic, is representative of the incidental insights that enliven Forsyth's
enjoyable and informative writing.

As a member of its advisory board, I have to
recuse myself from reviewing in detail *Shakespeare
on Screen: 'King Lear'*, the latest in the series of

collections of essays edited by Sarah Hatchuel and
Nathalie Vienne-Guerrin. But it is appropriate to
note here the range and depth of the contributions,
which encompass both familiar screen adaptations
(such as those of Brook and Kurosawa) and many
that have received relatively little critical attention
or have had only limited currency. An example is
The King Is Alive (directed by Kristian Levring),
which has probably enjoyed greater attention (and
favour) among students of Shakespeare and film
than in the wider public since its release in 2000.
Essays by Lois Leven and Peter Kapitaniak discuss
the play's presence in the Canadian television series
Slings and Arrows (2003–6) and the made-for-tele-
vision film *The King of Texas* (2002). Both are well
established as '*Lear* spinoffs', but it is probably fair
to say, as Diana Henderson points out, that David
Lean's *Hobson's Choice* (1954) is 'at the comic end of
the spectrum', and has been 'under-acknowledged
by Shakespeareans' (126). Rachael Nicholas analyses live broadcasts of the play, arguing that the
screen-director's choices work to limit the cinema
audience's access and support, or modify the interpretive choices and emphases of the stage directors
and actors.

Developments over the past ten years in both the
live streaming and recording of theatrical performance – distinct but overlapping activities – are
placed in their historical and technical context in
John Wyver's 'critical history' *Screening the Royal
Shakespeare Company*. Wyver's involvement in
such projects as producer and director, and his
meticulous historical research, inform this study
of the company's engagements with film and television. Wyver elucidates the sometimes tortuous
dealings of the Stratford theatre with television and
film companies, both before and since the establishment of the RSC. This reveals the relationship
between revenue-earning potential, the assertion
of 'prestige' and achievement of recognition, and
the incidental but problematic archival significance
of films and videos. At the same time, Wyver gives
a detailed account of the technical specifics of the
process as it has evolved in the second decade of the
century. As well as evidence of the value of broadcasts to the theatre, historical perspective shows

how its media partners have benefitted: 'The BBC, for example, has collaborated on screen versions of RSC productions of Shakespeare at key moments of challenge to the corporation's legitimacy.' In 1955, the broadcast of part of *The Merry Wives of Windsor* supported the BBC's response and 'reminded the nation of [its] values just after the launch of the commercial network ITV' (4). As well as such substantial and 'complete' recordings from earlier decades as the 1964 *Wars of the Roses*, videotaped on the stage of the theatre, and the television versions of Trevor Nunn's *Macbeth* (broadcast 1979) and *Othello* (1990), Wyver tracks down important 'screen traces' that surface in arts and news programmes, documentaries and other broadcast contexts. He describes that Holy Grail of Shakespeare performance studies, the long-lost Japanese telerecording by NHK of Peter Brook's 1970 *Dream*. This can now be reported as found (though not generally accessible) in an off-air copy in private hands, though other 'traces' of the production 'may circulate as a network of fragments and relics, and further shards may come to light' (99). The account of the archaeological efforts Brook's production has occasioned, and the necessarily tantalizing description of viewing the (effectively pirated) copy of the NHK broadcast, form one of the book's highlights. *Screening the Royal Shakespeare Company* will appeal directly to viewers of recent RSC productions on DVD and in broadcasts, and researchers working on material in the company's archive. But there are implications beyond those bearing directly on the Stratford-based company in the discussions of the ephemerality of the video archive, the adjustments made to staging and acting for broadcast, and the commercial aspects of the various productions.

Visual interpretation of a different kind is the subject of *Shakespeare as Seen: Image, Performance and Society*, which has its origins in Stuart Sillars's decision to bring together 'articles published and lectures given in other places and earlier times'. In the course of preparing them, he has taken the opportunity to 'make them into a more coherent whole and to bind them together by exploring avenues they left untraveled' (16). The result is a collection of eight studies in the interplay between stage performance, literary interpretation and graphic rendering, mainly during the eighteenth and nineteenth centuries. These are rich in detail, as well as suggestive of important developments in print and theatrical culture of the kind outlined in more general chapters on the ways in which performance reading figures in the illustrators' work. In the final pages of a chapter on 'rhythms of action and feeling in illustrations to the Roman plays', Sellars reproduces prints by George Cruikshank and J. L. Marks that satirize, respectively, King George III's opposition to reform and Robert Walpole responding to agitation for the repeal of the Corn Laws. He points to the use here of 'a degree of explicit anachronism in visual treatment' opening 'the possibility of positive anachrony that has become, since the mid-twentieth century, one of the basic principles of Shakespearean production' (170), Elsewhere, he identifies nuances of characterization in frontispieces to editions of *Othello* that show changing attitudes to the play and to the racial identity of the hero, and 'text, image and temper' in *King Lear*. One of the most interesting aspects of the editions examined by Sellars is the role played by illustrations that constitute a running commentary on the plays, in which the single image, often reproduced from a well-known painting, as preface to the play is supplemented or replaced in popular editions by the 'through illustration form' (152). In the case of two late versions of the Cowden Clarkes' often-reissued *Shakespeare* (1838–40 and 1856–60), the 'multiple imaging' allows a 'wholly different relationship between image, word and reader'. By responding to the nature of the 'unfolding text', these may offer 'a more complete analogy to the theatrical currency of the play, either when read or in performance', than texts provided with one governing image (115). The illustrators' contributions, from being merely decorative, become interpretive acts, and Sellars provides important guidance to the ways in which they could be understood by readers versed in the genre.

Interpretations of film, theatre and in literary criticism are studied in *Shakespeare Between the World Wars: The Anglo-American Sphere*. Robert

Sawyer examines the linkage between the 'turbulence of the times' and Shakespearian undertakings on both sides of the ocean, and his accounts of criticism in the United Kingdom and the establishment of Shakespearian institutions in the United State are persuasive. His examples of performance include Paul Robeson's performances as Othello, Orson Welles's 'Voodoo' *Macbeth* and 'fascist' *Julius Caesar*, and Komisarjevsky's Stratford-upon-Avon production of *Macbeth*. However important these may be, though, do they give a sufficiently full picture of what was being done with Shakespeare in the period? In the final chapter, 'Transnational Shakespeare, then and now', Sawyer identifies Max Reinhardt and William Dieterle's 1935 *Midsummer Night's Dream*, the 1936 MGM *Romeo and Juliet* and Paul Czinner's 1935 *As You Like It* as 'transnational', on account of the participation of émigré artists in their production teams and (in the case of *As You Like It*) leading actors. The point is arguable, although, given the already international nature (and staffing) of production companies on both sides of the Atlantic, the new label may lack force. At what point did (or does) immigrant talent become assimilated into the essentially 'transcultural' culture of the film industry? This is not so much a reproach to the author as a suggestion that at some points his book raises more questions than it can answer.

Regrettably, the book's production standards leave much to be desired, with only one black-and-white illustration (of Picasso's *Guernica*) and nothing to represent the look of the film or stage productions discussed. There are also many minor errors, some of which are simple misprints that should have been caught by an editor or in proof. These include 'F.E. Caroline Spurgeon', 'vaiorum' for 'Variorum', the addition of '*The*' to *Seven Types of Ambiguity*, 'new Critical tenants' for 'tenets', and 'Henry Granville Barker.' There are also moments when an editor might have helped Sawyer resist the lure of the extended metaphor. We are told that 'it is easy to sense in [I. A.] Richards's writings a longing to find some calm in the turbulent, current cultural political climate, a safe harbor in a world recently rocked by rough waves across transatlantic oceans, tidal shifts which even Arnold could not have anticipated even as he viewed the deceptively calm surface of the pebbly beach at Dover' (39). The point about Richards's desire to find stability in the notion of a 'standard reading' of poetry has already been made effectively enough, and invoking Matthew Arnold's poem does nothing to reinforce the point. William Wordsworth makes a ghostly guest appearance when it is asserted that, in embracing the new technologies of sound recording and broadcasting, Welles and Robeson were at a point when 'for the first time in history, an authorial voice detached from its body could be reproduced again and again, over and over, not only expanding the notion of agency, but also invoking new odes of immortality' (179).

An aspect of American culture in the 1930s absent from Sawyer's account is the all-pervasive influence of radio. 'I don't understand a word they're saying, but I think it's wonderful' was the response of a man-in-the-street interviewed about the CBS Radio *Shakespeare Cycle* in 1937: this early vox-pop ends the chapter on the series in Michael P. Jensen's splendidly researched account of the competition for prestige between the rival networks, NBC and CBS. *The Battle of the Bard: Shakespeare on U.S. Radio in 1937* appears in the series 'Recreational Shakespeare', and is appropriately engaging and entertaining, as well as shedding light on a relatively neglected medium for Shakespearian performance. NBC took the risk of entrusting their series, *Streamlined Shakespeare*, to the brilliant but wayward John Barrymore, leading a virtual repertory company, while CBS opted for eight plays, cast with different principal actors each week and with a distinctively Hollywood flavour. Listeners were offered such rarities as Humphrey Bogart's Hotspur, Edward G. Robinson's Petruchio and Burgess Meredith's Hamlet, and Rosalind Russell was paired with Leslie Howard as Beatrice and Benedick. Guest appearances by film and theatre celebrities were not unusual in the prestige slots in the networks' programming, adding lustre to sponsors as well as kudos for the broadcasters. Among the examples Jensen uncovers is the appearance of Charles Laughton 'as a guest of Rudy Valee's *Royal Gelatin Hour* on NBC ... on May 3, 1937'. The actor 'extolled the virtues of Shakespeare, talked about the historic Old Vic Theatre, and overacted excerpts from three plays, including two by Shakespeare' (16). These were *Macbeth* and *Measure for Measure*, the latter perhaps a surprising choice for the airwaves, probably included because Laughton had recently appeared as Angelo at the Old Vic. Wherever they can be found, Jensen gives detailed accounts of the scripts and audience responses to the programmer, and sets them in the context of the evolution of the medium in the 1930s.[3]

Of the two additions to the New Arden *Shakespeare's Theatre* series, one focuses on an individual who was a major force in the 'mainstream' British theatre, the other on a company whose work continues to be representative of an approach to Shakespeare of a very different kind. The career of Sir Peter Hall was notable for a recurrent paradox, in that radicalism co-existed with the establishment of institutions, first in Stratford-upon-Avon, then on the South Bank of the Thames. In *Shakespeare in the Theatre: Peter Hall*, Stuart Hampton-Reeves identifies the use of nostalgia in Hall's early, pre-RSC, productions as not being a 'retreat from modernity' but rather 'a strategy for rethinking Shakespeare's role in post-war Britain', and 'simultaneously claiming Shakespeare and the past as a way of also claiming Shakespeare in the present' (16). The 'contemporary theme' of his 1958 *Twelfth Night* might not have been 'immediately apparent', but, Hampton-Reeves suggests, the play's 'concerns with reconciliation and harmony' were 'developed into a brilliantly realized theatrical fantasy in which both peace and regret were intensely felt ... a striking riposte to the critical and political developments of the day' (24–5). The difference between Hall's work before and after the establishment of the RSC is identified as the replacement of a 'sense of decline from an idealized past with an equally compelling sense of the absence of a future' (50). Anxiety about the threat of nuclear Armageddon, especially strong in the mid-1950s and 1960s, was a factor in the cultivation of 'an audience with an ingrained sense of

anti-authoritarianism' and 'hungry for works which overturned the past and created something new with an immediate sense of the modern'. This was happening, paradoxically, even as Hall himself was 'busy building the RSC as a new cultural authority' (50–1).

Similar paradoxes recur in Hampton-Reeves's account, notably in the case of Hall's directorship on the South Bank, encapsulated in the chapter heading 'Authority in crisis at the National Theatre'. The comparison between the new NT regime and the radicalism of the early years of the RSC is exemplified in the contrast between the *Hamlet* productions of 1965 and 1975, with David Warner and Albert Finney as student prince and angry older man, respectively. 'Nothing about the [1975] production suggested youth', and this was 'a middle-aged man's Hamlet, confronting mortality and decay not with the reflective melancholy of an undergraduate, but with the frustrated rage of a theatrical mid-life crisis' (98). My own memory of the 1965 production – my first *Hamlet* – is that it conveyed not so much a sense of 'generational apathy' as thwarted indignation at the corruption of a formidable establishment, which is not altogether the same thing. Nevertheless, Hampton-Reeves's interpretation of Hall's mindset in relation to the temper of the times is convincing, even though allowance has to be made for the difference between the enthusiasm aroused by the earlier production and the general agreement that the later one was not nearly as exciting. The accounts of individual productions gain from Hampton-Reeves's proposal of a through line of paradoxes in the director's artistic and managerial career, providing an illuminating background to such relative failures as the 1975 *Tempest*, as well as undisputed

---

[3] Jensen makes a fair bid for the footnote-of-the-year award (should some enlightened sponsor back it) when, after discussing the possibility that an excerpt from *Romeo and Juliet* was broadcast in an episode of the Marx Brothers' *Flywheel, Shyster and Flywheel* comedy show on NBC in February 1933, he reaches the admirable conclusion that 'this minor point in my history hardly seems worth a trip to the Library of Congress, so I will leave it to others to settle'.

successes like the 1978 *Antony and Cleopatra*, in which Judi Dench came as close as anyone could hope to qualifying for that dangerous adjective 'definitive'. Her costumes, jewellery and make-up created a 'mixture of the plain and the exotic, the controlled and uncontrollable', which was 'a brilliant foundation' for her 'extraordinary performance' (120). Credit here is, of course, due to the designer Alison Chitty, as well as to Hall's own vision of the play and the actor's response to it. Hampton-Reeves suggests an additional 'temptation' for the historian, in which 'echoes of Hall's institutional position' can be found in the production: 'Hall was neither the ever-changing Cleopatra using all her wiles to stay in the game nor a great man trading off past glories as Antony was, viewing the empire he had set up from the outside with jealousy and despair – but he was, like both, a survivor capable of surpassing his critics' expectations' (121). Even if the temptation should be resisted, it is worth entertaining for a while. It supports the narrative line of this detailed and thorough account of the Shakespearian elements of one of the defining theatrical careers of British theatre from the 1950s to the present century. Hall's personal journey also exemplifies some of the tensions between stable institutions and radical creativity that have characterized Shakespearian production. A degree of conservatism, as in his ideas on the speaking of verse and the (temporary) embracing in the mid-1970s of 'Free Shakespeare', has sometimes proved, in yet another paradox, a form of radicalism.

Radicalism of a different kind is represented by Cheek by Jowl, whose productions have been a source of energy and pleasure for audiences and actors since 1981. Declan Donnellan (director) and Nick Ormerod (designer) have evolved an approach that sometimes involves extensive cutting and redaction – as exemplified in the 2007 *Cymbeline* discussed in rewarding detail by Peter Kirwan – and is always centred on a clarity derived from meticulous engagement with the text. Donnellan's approach, which he describes in *The Actor and the Target* (revised edition, 2005), with its emphasis on the actor's body within the performance space, achieves a richness, indeed plenitude, even in the absence of elaborate scenery and properties. In *The Duchess of Malfi* (1995–6) and *Macbeth* (2009–11), Kirwan observes, the simplicity of the design and 'the careful management of the space between actors' bodies both emphasized the importance of those bodies and used the space between to create powerful dynamics of movement and proximity that shaped Cheek by Jowl's storytelling'. The company does not so much 'strip away' as 'start with a blank canvas and build up' (46, 47). Donnellan's approach (shared by Ormerod as designer) is not easily summarized, but Kirwan is able to provide some key elements succinctly. The idea of 'targets' is their 'most significant governing principle' and they 'insist on the identification of the external object of the actor's action'. The space between the actors 'may be unpopulated, but never empty' (71). The aim in the preparation of the playing text and in rehearsal is one of 'helping actors find the life in a given moment and simultaneously liberating them from the constraints of theatrical naturalism'. This practice 'focuses on getting to the stakes and freeing the actors to discover something genuinely alive' (43). Given the great number of productions between 1981 and the time of writing (2019), Kirwan is obliged to be strategic in his selection of case studies, and they are linked to specific aspects of the company's approach. Rather than attempt a summary of Donnellan's writing, he provides a series of studies of interpretations from across the decades exemplifying key concepts, with the emphasis on continuities and developments, rather than on 'landmark' productions. Although some (notably *As You Like It* in 1991–2) have been identified as such, this approach is true to the spirit of a team whose work is in constant (re)development.

Directing Shakespeare in America: Historical Perspectives complements Charles Ney's earlier collection of interviews, *Directing Shakespeare in America: Current Practices* (2016). As well as an overview of the changing status and varying job description of directors from the 1870s to the present day, in the new book Ney provides an important account of the institutional contexts. The focus here is on artistic policy, the establishment, growth and (in a few cases) decline of notable companies across the United States (from sea to shining sea) and the kind of production they have fostered. A notable instance of a company unsure of its intentions is described in a chapter on the American Shakespeare Festival Theatre (ASF) in Stratford, Connecicut. From its inception, the ASF project suffered from being initiated in 1950 by a veteran producer, Lawrence Langner, 'rather than ... an artistic director with a distinct vision of the theatre' (84). The first season was in 1955, and over subsequent years its stage was continually redesigned, with the playing space moving closer to the audience, and 'signifying artistic dissatisfaction with the architectural space that persisted over several artistic directors' reign' (84). The name changed as well: originally the American Shakespeare Festival Theatre and Academy, it became the American Shakespeare Festival Theatre in 1963 and, from 1972 to its closure in 1981, the American Shakespeare Theatre. Ney examines the pressures under which its directors and administrators worked – not least a 'micromanaging board that employed a Broadway business model instead of a non-profit regional theatre one', preventing the development of 'an enduring artistic vision'. By 1967, the theatre had yet to find a distinctive identity, and (as Bernard Beckermann wrote) 'though productions [were] often tasteful and occasionally stirring, they [did] not create unforgettable images' or 'give fresh voice to Shakespeare's enduring eloquence' (95). Michael Kahn, appointed as artistic director in 1969, was 'influenced by Brecht, Jan Kott and Julian Beck' and was a bold choice, being 'a conceptual director' who 'tackled Shakespeare with a revisionist view of the plays' (95). Like other theatres with 'summer festival' origins, not least the Stratford-upon-Avon theatre in the 1950s, the theatre in Stratford, Connecticut had to strike a balance between the conservative tastes of many of its audiences (and their desire to see stars on its stage) with a sincere desire to innovate. It also suffered from proximity to New York City, which offered both the allure of Broadway and the riskier excitements of Off-Broadway and Off-Off-Broadway, not to mention the growing Joseph Papp empire with its summer seasons in Central Park. Ney points out that, 'despite all its problems and instability, the ASF's twenty-seven seasons significantly impacted the work of artistic directors, directors, other practitioners and audiences' (112), Like his account of the ASF, Ney's historical perspective on the other Shakespeare theatres is even-handed, respecting sincere artistic ambitions and alert to the social and commercial factors that sometimes (but not invariably) hindered their fulfilment.

Directors are among the thirty 'theatre makers' whose short essays make up *Shakespeare in Action: 30 Theatre Makers on Their Practice*, edited by Jaq Bessell. Designed to be of interest to other practitioners and actors in training, the collection offers insights into a range of methodologies in accounts grounded in experience. The rehearsal techniques described share the goal of freeing the actor's emotional imagination and engagement with the dramatic situation. As the director Polly Findlay puts it, with reference to the practice of 'paraphrasing' as a way into speeches of Rosalind, the experience is not merely one of translation: 'If you can help the actor fight for the thoughts in the same way that the character is always fighting for their thoughts, then something interesting about their personality is always thrown up in the course of that exercise' (129). Both Mike Alfreds and Gregory Doran outline approaches that foster the actor's ownership of the text. In Doran's tablework, actors read round the table, with nobody ever allowed to speak his or her own lines, which 'makes you attend to the language in a completely different way' (122). Hamlet may have thought he had 'worked out what the part was all about', but now he hears Ophelia 'reading his lines and putting them into her own words'. Among other exercises that make similar demands on attention to the text, Alfreds insists on the importance of dealing with the differences between rhetorically organized language, especially in long speeches, and the habits of everyday talk: 'actors have to relearn a skill that's more or less atrophied through desuetude: how to sustain long speeches and complex thoughts' (96). As well as being what its blurb describes as a 'toolkit' for actors, *Shakespeare in Action* is effectively a snapshot of present-day practice, and as such it will be valuable to the theatre historians of the future.

The first part of *Shakespeare: Actors and Audiences*, edited by Fiona Banks, consists of essays addressing actor/audience relationships from a historical and theoretical perspective; the second part, 'Actors and audiences: in their own words', homes in on specific productions, viewed from both stage and auditorium, and complements the first in addressing from first-hand experience the ways in which performances are effectively constructed by collaboration between the two constituencies. This is especially striking in the account by the actor Mathew Romain of the 'Globe-to-Globe' *Hamlet* that toured the world between 2014 and 2016: 'The audience's response changed the nature of the performance. The extent to which the play was a comedy, tragedy, melodrama etc. varied from country to country, region to region' (146), Whereas, in a performance of *Hamlet* in Britain or Europe, laughter at some 'wrong' points might be taken as a sign of a production's failure to connect, elsewhere it suggested a different kind of appreciation, and the recognition that even genre might be a variable concept is an important factor in discussions of 'global' Shakespeare. Susan Bennett, in 'Audiences: the architecture of engagement' notes that, since Shakespeare's Globe on the Bankside 'first invited audiences into its space, the reference point of the stage–audience relationship in proscenium-arch theatres seems to have become much less important as an imagined default position'. This suggests that the 'Globe Theatre' experience itself, considered in terms of what audiences are used to, has changed over time, as performance 'saturates twenty-first-century life, staged in a multitude of venues other than theatre buildings' (78). Other contributors to *Shakespeare: Actors and Audiences* illustrate the contention that, in Stephen Purcell's words, 'notions of "the audience" are constructed by Shakespearean plays in performance' (18) and the effect of Shakespearian characters who 'seem to be aware of their own fictional status', another connection that reinforces the sense of performance achieved by collaborative creation

between stage and spectator that is analysed by Jeremy Lopez in '"Do it, England", the actor and the audience in *Hamlet*' (59).

There has been no shortage lately of books in which actors describe their work on a role and the life of a production. *Performing Shakespeare's Women Playing Dead* is an outstanding and fresh addition to the list. Paige Martin Reynolds describes the 'interventionist work' of her book as 'threefold: ... an ethical intervention in the conventions of casting and critical response, an interdisciplinary and personal intervention in the theoretical dialogue about theatrical practice and a feminist intervention in the history of how we talk about women in Shakespeare' (14). Awareness of the significance as well as practicalities of her roles when viewed from the triple perspectives as actor, scholar and teacher gives a special strength to the account of her experiences in rehearsal and on stage. She starts from the ways in which events in her personal life – injuries, funerals, motherhood, finishing a dissertation – have not so much impinged on her theatre work as informed it. An argument of the book is that '"playing dead" is, in fact a defining condition of portraying female characters in Shakespeare'. After having 'performed death by murder and by suicide, both onstage and off', Regan 'marked the first time [she] had begun dying onstage, had finished dying offstage and had been brought back onstage for inspection' (41). In her vivid accounts of the actor's experience – such as having her face covered when Regan is brought back on – Reynolds investigates what may seem the trivial aspects of performance in terms of immediate physical sensations, their psychological effect on her, and the reflections they suggest about the play and its women: 'The covering of the sisters' faces [in the final scene] functions not only as defacement but also effacement' (60). This goes beyond such apparently simple elements of the actor's preparation as analysing what, for example, Gertrude or Lady Capulet do and do not say, to the perception that 'Shakespeare's investment in monumental women (alive or dead) and the various fractures they suffer is enough to sharply remind the female actor of her own restraint.'

Having begun her chapter on Gertrude with the story of the two occasions on which she had broken bones, once at a school track meet and again on a rollercoaster ride at Disneyworld, by this point Reynolds has earned the wry conclusion that 'In this way, some theatrical "big breaks" [as a leading role] can be more precarious than a foot fractured in the name of fun' (110). Writing from her own experience of anorexia, Reynolds observes that 'emaciated textually, critically and, as it turns out, emotionally', Lady Capulet is the only female character in the book 'who does not die by the time the play ends; rather, she is dying from the time it begins' (136), The wit, realism and critical acumen of *Performing Shakespeare's Women Playing Dead* (the absence of a comma after 'Women' is significant) recommend it as a (re)reading of the plays to audiences, actors and directors – especially, I would suggest, to the men among them.

WORKS REVIEWED

Banks, Fiona, *Shakespeare: Actors and Audiences* (London, 2019)

Bessell, Jaq, ed., *Shakespeare in Action: 30 Theatre Makers on Their Practice* (London, 2019)

Bladen, Victoria, Sarah Hatchuel and Nathalie Vienne-Guerrin, eds., *Shakespeare on Screen: 'King Lear'* (Cambridge, 2019)

Burnett, Mark Thornton, *'Hamlet' and World Cinema* (Cambridge, 2019)

Cartelli, Thomas, *Reenacting Shakespeare in the Shakespeare Aftermath: The Intermedial Turn and Turn to Embodiment* (New York, 2019)

Forsyth, Neil, *Shakespeare the Illusionist: Magic, Dreams and the Supernatural on Film* (Athens, OH, 2019)

Hampton-Reeves, Stuart, *Shakespeare in the Theatre: Peter Hall* (London, 2019)

Jensen, Michael P., *The Battle of the Bard: Shakespeare on U.S. Radio in 1937* (Leeds, 2018)

Kirwan, Peter, *Shakespeare in the Theatre: Cheek by Jowl* (London, 2019)

McCullough, Lynsey, and Brandon Shaw, eds., *The Oxford Handbook of Shakespeare and Dance* (Oxford, 2019)

Ney, Charles, ed., *Directing Shakespeare in America: Historical Perspectives* (London, 2019)

Reynolds, Paige Martin, ed., *Performing Shakespeare's Women Playing Dead* (London, 2019)

Sawyer, Robert, *Shakespeare Between the World Wars: The Anglo-American Sphere* (New York, 2019)

Sillars, Stuart, *Shakespeare as Seen: Image, Performance and Society* (Cambridge, 2019)

Wyver, John, *Screening the Royal Shakespeare Theatre: A Critical History* (London, 2019)

3. EDITIONS AND TEXTUAL STUDIES
reviewed by PETER KIRWAN

Following a number of years which have seen major new *Complete Works* volumes or brand-new series of editions, 2018–19 was a quieter year for Shakespeare editions, with one new Arden, a rare Variorum, and a large number of second and third issues of pre-existing editions with minor updates. Collectively – and in concert with a number of excellent books aimed at newcomers to textual studies – they represent an effort to update and revise knowledge, with a focus on entry points into interpreting the Shakespearian text and understanding the afterlives of plays and poems.

NEW EDITIONS

The penultimate entry in the third series of the Arden Shakespeare is *All's Well That Ends Well*, with Helen Wilcox editing the text and providing notes, and Suzanne Gossett taking responsibility for introduction and commentary. The Textual Appendix outlines the complexities of editing *All's Well*, a play which presents an unusual number of textual difficulties despite its single early witness in the Folio. Wilcox and Gossett, as has now become standard in all textual essays, pay dutiful attention to Paul Werstine's cautions about autograph manuscripts and foul papers, revising the standard twentieth-century line that the play was set from Shakespeare's 'working autograph manuscript' (335). Taking account of the work of the *New Oxford Shakespeare*, the editors adopt as their working hypothesis the notion that the play was set from a scribal transcript at an indeterminate remove from a holograph left in a relatively raw state. They point to the ghost character of Violenta, the unusual stage directions and the variety in character names as evidence for the 'authorial' nature of the underlying copy (342–4), while suggesting that the efficiency of the compositorial setting – which has relatively few significant issues in the use of space, albeit

evidence of attempts to save or fill space can be found throughout – implies the relative tidiness of a scribal manuscript (347). There is an interesting note pondering whether documents within the play, such as the ballad and letters, were separate from the scribal manuscript (348), which would align with a separate point drawn from Tiffany Stern's work that Helen's 'etc' when describing the contents of the letter in an unmetrical line (5.3.311) suggests that she rereads the letter out loud at this point (340).

The edition acknowledges, without intervening in, the recent debate about Middleton's potential authorship of parts of the play, surveying the arguments of Laurie Maguire and Emma Smith in favour, Brian Vickers and Marcus Dahl against, and the *New Oxford Shakespeare* (*NOS*) in developing the case that Middleton adapted the play for a revival (359–68). Other than remarking that the play 'stands on its merits, quite regardless of how "many hands" took part in its authorship' (368), in a bid to ensure that discussion of collaboration doesn't become one of reduced quality, the editors themselves remain agnostic. They selectively mention the possibility of Middleton's presence in the textual commentary, implying a greater confidence in Gary Taylor's claims for Middleton's authorship of the virginity debate of 1.1.110–63 than in John Nance's for the King's speech in 2.3.117–44. The editors also briefly address the question of how Middleton's additions might have been added to Shakespeare's, noting that there is no obvious difficulty in the setting of the texts at these points (348), which might suggest that the scribal manuscript consolidated the adaptations made for performance in the indoor theatres after 1609 and the Middleton additions that *NOS* dates to 1616–22.

The text is clearly presented and annotated throughout. The commentary is profuse, with very few pithy glosses and a commitment to tying individual words and phrases back to the larger networks of associations that connect them. It makes for a rich, literary commentary that some-times pays less attention to textual history. For instance, the Folio's most famous crux, 'make rope's in such a scarre', is here rendered 'may rope's in such a snare' (4.2.38), following P. A. Daniel's conjecture in the previous Arden edition. While the commentary justifies this read-ing, there is no discussion of the 'alternative con-jectures' (89) for which the introduction refers the reader to the commentary. The many letters are rendered clearly in italics, and the edition is espe-cially useful in distinguishing the Brothers Dumaine, using the speech prefixes LORD E. and LORD G., and providing a very helpful separate appendix to unpack the textual confusion around these two characters, suggesting that 'G' is older and wise, while 'E' is younger and closer to Bertram (371); this appendix alone should be required reading for directors of the play.

The introduction takes a thematic approach, integrating discussion of the play's afterlives in per-formance and criticism into the main body of the introduction rather than separating them into dis-crete sections. Many of the sections take a particular character as the focal point for consid-eration of a broader issue: Paroles is central to a section entitled 'The name and not the thing' (75–84) which treats the play's equivocations and lies; Helen is discussed in a section on 'The world of women' (31–44); and 'Masters and men' (61–75) traces Bertram's interactions with authority and male friends. The approach is effective, giving all the main figures a turn without defaulting to rote character criticism. The emphasis from the start of the introduction is on leaving debate open and not attempting to resolve the play's issues, and the integration of character, performance, criticism and theme develops the editors' thesis that this is a fascinatingly complex play.

The opening sections of the introduction con-cern genre, sources, plot, date and authorship. The term 'problem play' has, the editors argued, created nothing but confusion (4), and the play's primary mode is instead protean, switching from fairytale to romantic comedy to a prodigal narrative that cul-minates in something closer to tragicomedy (5–6).

This is an important point, downplaying the importance or utility of categorization in favour of something closer to a Derridean notion of parti-cipating in genre, utilizing the conventions of dif-ferent modes of comedy to explore a series of key issues, including female agency, aristocratic privi-lege and more. In particular, the editors argue that the play is constantly concerned with rank (11), foregrounding the disparity in status between Helen and Bertram that is itself a change from the sources. As well as emphasizing class, the play is also 'as much concerned with the passing of the impo-tent older generation as with the young people' (10), suggesting Shakespeare was experimenting with the formal and generic conventions of his source and developing more deeply interwoven thematic interests in truth and falsehood, duty and responsibility. In addition, the shift from the long-standing assumption that *All's Well* preceded *Measure for Measure* – an understandable assumption based on the presence of the bed-trick in both, which is found in *All's Well*'s source but not *Measure*'s – helps draw attention to its similarities to the late plays, in both its 'miraculous' events and its exploration of difficulties following marriage (16). Wilcox and Gossett agree with a date of 1605–6, though note that it may not have been staged until after the long theatre closure in 1608 (21).

The thematic sections are consistently insightful, drawing repeated attention to structures within the play that shape and are shaped by the actions of characters. The section on 'Family Structures', which points out that all members of the older generation are single or widowed, and all of the younger generation have lost a parent, puts pres-sure on Bertram, reading his role in the play as to free himself of his mother and establish a lineage, in the face of doubts that he can do this (25). The play 'stands apart from other Shakespearean comedies in its strong images of female solidarity' (33), espe-cially in the households of the Countess and the Widow, but the family structures of the play need to be reconfigured in order to satisfy everyone (31), especially as Bertram's reluctance to be in a relationship with Helen seems partly to stem from a fear of incest. The editors prefer the name 'Helen' to 'Helena', noting that this is the name consistently used in stage directions apart from the first, and dwelling on the name allows the editors to pursue the similarities to the Helena of *A Midsummer Night's Dream* – both Bertram and Demetrius love their Helens under a form of compulsion (36). Throughout the introduction, the editors trace the shifting critical fortunes of Helen and Bertram, noting how Helen's use of the bed-trick led to her being judged as 'less than chaste in her actions' (51) and the play itself being rarely staged for 200 years. Readings of Bertram, meanwhile, have written him off as childish, whiny, immature or prodigal, and yet he discharges honourable service in war and discards Paroles as Hal discards Falstaff (73). The ambiguities and ambivalences surrounding the central lovers, as outlined by Gossett and Wilcox, make a persuasive case for the play's dramatic interest.

The play's subjunctivity, emphasized by the recurrent use of 'if' (98), is, for this important new edition, central to *All's Well*'s problems and potential. A concluding section points to the varying readings and performance of the final scene, which raise questions about how much has been learned, about the certainty of future happiness, and about what is represented by the final decisions. It's a play that ironizes its own title, hoping for a happy ending while repeatedly making that ending conditional or partial. The excellent section on keywords demonstrates the play's dependence on religiously inflected concepts such as grace and sanctity (100) and on the language of bonds, bands and knots (101), concepts and words that offer surety that is undermined by the equivocation and lies of Paroles and the ease with which bonds are broken. It's a rich reading of the play that should do much to encourage renewed attention to it.

The other significant new edition this year is David George's *Coriolanus*, billed as a 'New Variorum' edition. George credits a team of research assistants including Thomas Clayton (who oversaw the early collation and setting up of the Folio text), Niels Herold (author of a short section on music and sound effects), Megan-Marie Johnson (Plan of Work,

collations and commentary) and Ashley Spriggs (Plan of Work and textual notes). The edition's history is long and complex and, despite its acknowledgement of the input of the New Variorum Shakespeare (NVS) General Editors and the Modern Language Association, the edition has been independently published outwith the auspices of the series. While a great deal of labour has clearly gone into the edition, the limitations of the publisher (Accurance) have had a serious impact on the presentation of the edition – rather than text, textual notes and commentary appearing on the same page, as with official New Variorum editions, the three are instead published as three sequential sections, severely diminishing the edition's utility and convenience.

The text itself is straightforward, preserving the spelling and typographical layout of the Folio with no inaccuracies that I have spotted (with the exception of the Act titles, rendered as italics of the same font and size as the rest of the text, rather than representing their large and separated appearance in the Folio). The edition inserts Rowe's 1709 *dramatis personae* for the play at the start. The textual notes collate seventy-one editions, up to and including Peter Holland's 2013 Arden 3 edition (skipping Jonathan Bate and Eric Rasmussen's 2007 RSC edition and the *New Oxford Shakespeare*, the latter presumably published too recently for this edition). While the work here follows the conventions of the NVS series, there are omissions which suggest that collation of Holland's edition, at least, was unsatisfactorily completed – for example, against F's 'o're-beate' (TLN 2789), the edition records the emendations 'o're-bear' (Rowe) and 'o'er-bear it', attributing the latter to Richard Grant White; Holland, however, reads 'o'er-bear't' (following White). Holland's added stage direction at TLN 686 is also not collated in the unadopted conjectures. The notes are more complete up to and including Lee Bliss's 2000 New Cambridge edition.

It is perhaps inevitable that a project of the size and scale of a print Variorum edition feels a little dated on arrival. The effective end-date for this edition is 2009, with only a handful of critical references from after that year; the stage history ends in 2007 with Gregory Doran's RSC production. It is the role of the Variorum to chronicle historical trends rather than current thinking, though the inclusion in the 'Themes and significance' section of almost six pages of psychoanalytical criticism seems unbalanced compared to only two paragraphs on 'male bonding' (i.e. queer readings) and no section on women beyond the discussions of individual characters. The belatedness of the edition also means that it hasn't had time to take into account some important resources on the play's reception, not least Robert Ormsby's excellent 2014 monograph on the play's stage history. Frustratingly, then, while the edition has much in it that is useful, the material has already been overtaken by current thinking on *Coriolanus*.

The commentary is thorough. As per Variorum convention, it predominantly quotes directly from critics in the form of a list, though the editorial voice emerges at times when summarizing earlier editorial choices or discussing sources (especially in commentary on the *dramatis personae*, which concentrates on the source material). There is pleasing variety throughout the commentary, both in the chronological range of critics cited, and in the integration of performance history with critical views. One of the first entries in the commentary offers an extended discussion of the difficulties and constraints facing modern directors in determining the size of the crowd and the evidence of whether or not Rome has grain (1.138). The editor chips in throughout to gloss early references (1.188) or to disagree with recent critics, as when he notes that Holland's recall of Shakespeare's use of 'vent' in *The Tempest* refers to 'low characters, and Martius is unlikely to have used "vent" this way' (1.189). Where a moment engages with a long textual or performance tradition, such as Aufidius standing on Martius' body, George breaks the discussion into shorter paragraphs which list the critical quotations separately; otherwise, the selections are kept as pithy as possible throughout. The commentary represents a useful distillation of the critical tradition, especially as it pertains to individual lines.

The second volume contains longer summaries of the criticism of the play, broken into sections on textual issues, sources, criticism and performance. Philip Brockbank's 1976 Arden 2 edition is an important reference point for the textual scholarship, with George often deferring to Brockbank's summaries but regularly cross-checking with Holland and the work of Charlton Hinman, Paul Werstine and Peter Blayney, especially in relation to the Folio copy. George's own contributions include the note that the variations in white space around SDs would merit further discussion (2.52) and his suggestion, in a section on the reliability of the printer, that the copy was probably fifteen years old by 1623 'and had suffered some wear' (2.58), which he suggests is what led to a lost line at TLN 3228–30. The long summary of positions on date of composition concludes that the play couldn't have been performed earlier than April 1608, but that the use of Chapman's *Iliad* suggests composition was finished later in the year (2.68). The Sources section includes lengthy transcripts of the pertinent extracts in Plutarch and Livy, along with extensive summaries of the critical commentary both on Shakespeare's generic use of sources, on specific minor sources and on the sources for individual characters; this is one of the fullest sections of the edition, and its thoroughness (combined with the presence of the Plutarch and Livy sources) will be of especial use to scholars.

In the lengthy survey of Criticism, the most frustrating section is the opening 'General assessments' (2.172–91), which is effectively a survey of impressions that lack the necessary broader contextualization. The survey gains focus with a series of sections on the generic categorization of the play, pitting arguments for the play as tragedy against others that see it as Roman play, historical play, tragedy/comedy, political play or satire. The thematic sections are, as already noted, a mixed collection; indeed, the first is an oddly defined 'Multiple themes'. Quite what qualifies as a 'theme' is not completely clear, but it is interesting to see that one of the largest sections deals with 'Dismemberment and wounds', anticipating more recent work on embodiment. Surprisingly, the most fascinating section concerns individual characters. Even Adrian and

Nicanor, the spies of 4.3, get three short paragraphs to themselves; the 'Common people' get seven pages, and Coriolanus himself unsurprisingly takes the lion's share (2.240–71). While the character-based approach has its limitations, here it offers one of the more useful organizing principles for bringing together a narrative of critical history, with the sections on the three women standing in for the lack of a thematic discussion of gendered relations. The performance history that follows (2.293–332) is historical and judicious in its choice of evocative extracts that capture something of the flavour of each production. The assault on Corioles and the women's welcome into Rome get more extended discussion for their staging requirements and potential, and a subsequent section detailing eighty-five promptbooks and the history of cuts to each scene will be invaluable to dramaturges. While the edition's functionality for use by other editors is damaged by the inconvenient layout and by the lag in the edition's attention to recent work and performance, elements such as the compilation of sources and the list of promptbooks will be a helpful resource for scholars working in those areas.

The Arden Performance Editions are supplemented this year by Katherine Steele Brokaw's *Macbeth*. This is a fine edition that exemplifies the aims of the series, offering a spacious, large-print text on verso pages and copious notes on pronunciation, metre and sense on the facing recto. Brokaw has a practitioner's eye for the information that will be useful to those acting from the text, leading to an efficient and uncluttered recto page that leaves plenty of space for notes while highlighting you/thou usage, clarifying stressed syllables and keeping glosses pithy. For larger contextual issues such as historical figures, readers are redirected to the introduction.

Brokaw's introduction dispenses quickly with the contextual issues, noting that 'some scholars' believe Middleton revised passages throughout the play in addition to writing the Hecate scenes (22), and covering the major differences between the sources and the play, providing the backstory of

Lady Macbeth's (Gruoch's) son Lulach and noting the choice to make Banquo innocent of Duncan's murder. Brokaw is especially interested in the play's brevity and constant references to time (26), and points out the compressed timescale of the first half that slows down in the fourth act. An interesting section on *Macbeth*'s plot inconsistencies is a little strained – for instance, Brokaw argues that Lennox is an enemy of Macbeth in 3.6 but seems to be an ally in 4.1 when he brings news of Macduff's flight, but this seems to assume very simple characterization (the obvious reading that Lennox is continuing to serve Macbeth while expressing private doubts to a friend is not mentioned). But this and the other inconsistencies largely serve to flag things that might inflect the choices of a production.

The strength of the introduction is its detailed work on the presentation of the text and the nuances of language. The Arden edition is unusually sparing in its use of exclamation marks, and Brokaw provides a number of examples of potential alternative punctuation choices that readers and directors could use (28–9). A long discussion of the variations on iambic lines concentrates on short lines, anapests and unstressed endings, and a separate discussion considers the 'rhythmic uncanniness' of the witches (42) as they vacillate between trochaic and iambic rhyme. They are especially irregular when they meet Macbeth in 1.3, adding to the uncanniness of that scene. Brokaw gives an overview of the decision to refer to the Witches as 'weïrd' or 'weyward', and draws on Ayanna Thompson's work to suggest that the racially inflected otherness of the Witches offers the potential for both racist and anti-racist interpretations of the play (44–5). While the series format does not allow space for as full discussion as might be desirable, Brokaw's introduction offers useful tools for unpacking the options and performative effects of the text.

A frustrating presentational feature of the Arden Performance Editions becomes apparent in Brokaw's edition. Several line references in the introduction do not match those in the main text (examples can be found on 27, 42 and 51). Trying to find the correct lines is then made more difficult by the series' choice regarding the navigational line references at the top of the verso page. Where normal Arden convention logically uses the first line on the page, the Arden Performance Editions bizarrely use the last line on the page that is divisible by 5. To take an extreme example, p. 268 contains the following text: 5.5.49–53, 5.6.1–10 and 5.7.1; the navigational reference number, however, is 5.6.10. The combination of the errors and the awkward navigational aid make using the introduction in conjunction with the text very cumbersome, and hopefully future editions will revert to normal Arden conventions.

As a final curio, Methuen have published the playtext of Josie Rourke's 2018 production of *Measure for Measure* at the Donmar Warehouse. That production presented a slimmed-down version of the play twice: once in period dress in the first half, and then repeated in modern dress in the second half with the roles of Angelo and Isabella reversed, so the corrupt Deputy became a woman. The playtext pedantically replicates the planned performance text exactly, meaning the purchaser gets the same trimmed version of *Measure for Measure* twice in a single book, with names and pronouns of four characters reversed in the second half. Rourke's introduction draws attention to the ways in which the change flips or reveals the sexuality of the Duke, who ends the second half of the play asking Angelo to marry him. An accompanying essay by Emma Smith reads the play in the light of Shakespeare's other comedies, arguing that it is a deliberately unromantic comedy which still pursues certain of the structures of romantic comedy. By the end of the play, Smith argues, the Duke is the only character on stage who seems to think he is still participating in a traditional romance.

REVISED EDITIONS

Among the many revised editions of the last year, *Hamlet* is the play that benefits most, with Heather Hirschfeld contributing an entirely new introduction to Philip Edwards's 1985 New Cambridge Edition. The text, as with most New Cambridge updates, remains substantially unchanged, with the occasional short gloss added, abbreviated or removed, and Edwards's own textual analysis is preserved as an appendix to the edition.

Hirschfeld's introduction foregrounds the play's genre, outlining the conventions of revenge tragedy in a way that emphasizes just how conventional *Hamlet* is (2). She spends time considering Shakespeare's transformation of the source materials, considering the interplay of Shakespeare's added cosmic frame – including the Ghost – and the development of philosophical scepticism through Hamlet's riddling and wit. What distinguishes Hamlet, for Hirschfeld, is Hamlet's own conflicted and resistant attitude to his revenger role (6), which, she argues, would have rendered the play unusual in its own moment. Theatre, she argues, 'serves as a rich analogue for this kind of existential confusion' (7), and in exploring the ambivalence to prescribed roles, the play repeatedly highlights the disjunction between seeing and hearing. Hirschfeld's chronological summary of historical critical responses to the play traces the ambivalence to it in the eighteenth century, before Hamlet himself became a model of emotional and intellectual sensitivity in the nineteenth, to the point where 'Hamletism' became an acknowledged approach to life (22). The sheer volume of material makes a pithy summary difficult, but Hirschfeld captures the major trends of the twentieth and twenty-first century in a brief essay that reads like a history of twentieth-century literary criticism itself, devoting time to psychoanalysis and moving on to historicism and New Historicism, political and feminist readings, and (with special attention to Margreta de Grazia) approaches that have moved away from character to consider plot and history.

Hirschfeld's brief section on the text introduces the theory underlying Edwards's textual work, which assumed Q2 was set from an early authorial copy, Q1 from memorial reconstruction, and F from a revision of 'foul papers' (15). Hirschfeld notes the shifting attitudes to Q1 that have increasingly treated it as an earlier or abridged version, rather than a memorial reconstruction, and points readers towards other studies for a more substantial discussion of current textual theory. Her scene-by-scene analysis is incisive and literate, and will be of especial use to newcomers to the play, paying attention to the broader implied world of the play, especially its climate of surveillance (39). The section is full of useful observations, such as Ophelia's death being 'the real version of Hamlet's imagined one' (48), and Laertes representing unadulterated vengeance in contrast to Hamlet's ambivalent motivations. The concluding section on performance history is a largely descriptive history that covers a great deal of ground, integrating major films (Olivier, Kozintsev, Branagh) with the discussion of stage traditions, addressing global productions (with particular emphasis on Germany) and concluding by listing a range of more recent adaptations and trends.

The three other revised New Cambridge Shakespeares are much more lightly augmented, all adding seventeen pages to their predecessors. Ann Thompson takes responsibility for updating her own 1984 *Taming of the Shrew* (last updated in 2003). She generously points to the five excellent new editions that have come out in the thirty-five years since she first edited the play, all edited by women (42), and points out the value in *The Taming of a Shrew* having been made more available (including as an appendix to Barbara Hodgdon's Arden 3 edition), even if the jury is still out on the text's relationship to *The Shrew*. The majority of the new material is given over to the stage tradition, which has increasingly seen female directors exploring the play, often with single-sex casts that have restored gender issues to the play's stage history (48). Thompson's sensitive analysis is mostly focused on UK productions, but captures the ways in which *Shrew* has been made to speak to a range of cultures and political issues. A couple of brief pages on new critical approaches finds most value in work that recontextualizes *Shrew* in relation to early modern gender assumptions, and in approaches that have considered the play through alternative cultural frameworks.

Claire McEachern contributes new material to Andrew Gurr's 1984 *Richard II*. Perhaps unsurprisingly for this play, her focus is on the influence of New Historicism on criticism in the last decades of the twentieth century, arguing that historicist enquiry was concerned with various types of identification, including questions of relative sympathies for Richard or Bolingbroke (51). Of particular importance were the insights of Paul Hammer and Jonathan Bate in 2008, which challenged whether the Essex Rising of 1601 had been intended, complicating some of the assumptions about the play's perceived conservative/subversive potential (53–4). Beyond this, McEachern gives an efficient and invigorating summary of the varied thematic issues that have exercised critics. The section on performance since 1984 is regrettably UK-focused, with only a single non-UK performance mentioned, but captures some of the most important trends, including the destabilization of norms around gender and sexuality, especially in performances by Fiona Shaw, Mark Rylance and Jonathan Slinger.

Finally, Travis D. Williams provides the updates to F. H. Mares's 1998 *Much Ado about Nothing*. This is a less successful revision, partly owing to Williams's frustrating tendency to prioritize subjective comparative evaluation of the 'success' of productions, and partly because the discussion is structured haphazardly and unevenly, meaning that important thematic insights about (for instance) the racial politics of casting in Joss Whedon's film, or the fortunes of Dogberry, pop up unexpectedly amid more rote overviews of particular companies or traditions. A brief survey of recent criticism, finally, concentrates on uncertainty, rank and the recuperation of Hero as 'a real and influential voice within her society' (62).

Robert Miola's updated edition of his 2011 Norton Critical *Hamlet* substitutes Benedict Cumberbatch for Jude Law on the volume's cover, a transposition of one for the other that reflects the changes throughout the edition, which replace rather than supplement. The value of the Norton Critical Editions is in the selection of critical materials that accompany the text, and the most disappointing choice is to make swingeing cuts to its 'Criticism' section. Nothing is added (the most recent piece is still from Tony Howard's 2007 *Women as Hamlet*), but essays by Harry Levin, Elaine Showalter, Kenneth Rothwell and Margreta de Grazia are all removed. This has the effect of leaving the Criticism section entirely male-authored, and of reducing the number of entries post-1922 from six to two. The 'Afterlives' section, meanwhile, cuts an extract from John Updike's *Gertrude and Claudius* (2000) to make way for the entirety of Margaret Atwood's 'Gertrude talks back' (1992) – a valuable inclusion, but contributing to the effect of the 2019 edition's inclusions skewing earlier than the 2011 edition's. There is also a surprising shift away from film, with the 'Actors' gallery' section cutting contributions by John Gielgud, Laurence Olivier, Kenneth Branagh and Jude Law, and replacing them with notes from Ralph Alan Cohen on a 2007 production of Q1, and an interview with David Tennant.

Miola's introduction is lightly updated, and here the changes seem better to reflect shifts in critical priorities. The most substantial update expands a section on 'Global imaginings', adding new subsections on *Hamlet*'s fortunes in China and India, and lengthening the discussion of African *Hamlet*s. The textual discussion incorporates the work of the *New Oxford Shakespeare* and the third *Norton Shakespeare*, as well as mentioning new thinking on Q1 *Hamlet* perhaps being an earlier version of the play. Interestingly, the edition alters the hesitant choice of 2011 to go with 'solid flesh' to a similarly hesitant choice of 'sallied' in 2019 (1.2.129). The edition's discussion of afterlives is updated as far as Gillian Flynn's (apparently) forthcoming novelization of *Hamlet*, as well as the recent surge of response texts focusing on Ophelia.

Peter Hulme and William H. Sherman have had a lot longer to revise their 2004 Norton Critical Edition of *The Tempest*, and the changes are more extensive. Their preface, only a little over five pages long, remains substantially unaltered, other than removing references to films of the play (as with Miola, a slightly puzzling deprioritization of screen adaptations). There are small changes to the text and textual notes, but the text introduces some odd inconsistencies around the lineation of short lines. In 5.1, 'That doth not wish you joy. / Be it so. Amen.' (216) is rendered as a single line in both the 2004 and 2019 editions, but 'When no man was his own. / Give me your hands' (213–14) is now rendered as two; and 'We first put out to sea. / Sir, all this service / Have I done since I went / My tricksy spirit' (226–9) treats as four short lines what the 2004 edition treated as two split verse lines, with no explanation for the change.

Eight articles are removed from the Criticism section; tastes will vary, but I mourn the loss of Leah Marcus's 'The blue-eyed witch' and Barbara Mowat's piece on 'Prospero, Agrippa, and hocus pocus'. The new inclusions by Octave Mannoni, Coppélia Kahn, Julia Reinhard Lupton, John Gillies (replacing an earlier piece of his own) and Michael Neill are worthy selections, and Sherman's own piece on sleep and transformation in *The Tempest* from 2009 enters, displacing co-editor Hulme's older piece on 'Prospero and Caliban'. There is a substantial new contribution by the two editors on 'Performances and productions' (293–303), which concentrates on twentieth-century stage and screen adaptations, beginning with Percy MacKaye's community masque *Caliban by the Yellow Sands*, performed by 1,500 participants; the editors include a generous excerpt from this unusual piece. Professional stage productions take up a surprisingly small amount of this chapter, limited to those by Giorgio Strehler, Peter Brook and Jonathan Miller, but this is in keeping with an edition that feels refreshingly committed to a wider range of performance traditions, tracing ballet, classical music and film (including Julie Taymor's major adaptation), and adding two poems to an already lengthy anthology of poetic responses to the play that offers a unique teaching resource.

TEXTUAL STUDIES

A major contribution to textual scholarship on Shakespeare's poetry is Jane Kingsley-Smith's important book *The Afterlife of Shakespeare's Sonnets*, which offers a deft interweaving of textual studies and reception history. This is the first monograph to deal with the critical, editorial and creative afterlives of the Sonnets, arguing that the failure to do so 'has led to a number of erroneous assumptions' (4). The aim here is to provide for the Sonnets the same kind of historical reassessment that the dramatic canon has enjoyed in recent years, concentrating on a series of editorial and critical moments that challenge the inevitability of the received editorial tradition. Importantly, this involves treating the Sonnets as individual poems rather than deferring to the sequence, which allows Kingsley-Smith to remind readers of facts that may seem anomalous, such as the disappearance of Sonnet 18 from the canon for a century, or the recovery of Sonnet 130 in the early twentieth century (7). The first three chapters are those most pertinent to this review, with their sustained interest in (respectively) the 1609 Quarto, John Benson's *Poems*, and the period of their editorial treatment as spurious throughout the eighteenth century. Later chapters consider the Sonnets' re-readings in the nineteenth and twentieth centuries, concentrating more on critical and creative responses.

Chapter 1 argues that 'both the printed forms in which the *Sonnets* first appeared did more to alienate readers than to inspire their admiration' (13). This surprising argument suggests that 'the cultural prestige of the poet was achieved at the expense of the Sonnets' (13), offering a re-reading of the history that sees the fortunes of the 'genuine' work and the poet in tension with one another. Kingsley-Smith provides a careful re-reading of *The Passionate Pilgrim* and the 1609 quarto of *Shakespeare's Sonnets*, and offers the intriguing suggestion that William Jaggard marketed the former 'so as to allow for the possibility of its being Shakespeare's third narrative poem' (19). The title page of the first edition is unusually blank, containing no categorizing information about the formal properties of its contents, and Kingsley-Smith shows through comparative example some of the unusual features of the collection compared with either a miscellany, a sonnet sequence or an epyllion. The 1609 Quarto, conversely, 'seems designed to eliminate any possible confusion about what it is' (34), but is unusually ambiguous in its epigraph, the effect of which 'was to distance the volume from Shakespeare' (36). The absence of plot, or even distinct addressees, distinguishes the collection further from the narrative poems – much more heavily excerpted in commonplace books and miscellanies – and may partly account for its apparent lack of reprinting compared to *The Passionate Pilgrim*, whose title at least alludes to some of the conventions of the narrative poem. Kingsley-Smith gives a list of all the allusions to and reprintings of the Sonnets that she can find between 1598 and 1622, coming up with only ten (40–1), and notes how little evidence this affords of their early manuscript circulation or of contemporary response. The exceptions that prove the role are Sonnets 116 and 128, which prompted creative responses among the Pembroke circle (including Mary Wroth in some important original work) that Kingsley-Smith suggests speaks to their discrete private circulation, rather than to visibility among a broader public.

The provocations that Kingsley-Smith offers invite careful rethinkings of assumptions about the extent of the Sonnets' circulation and the various interventions that helped them reach wider audiences. She argues that it was only through 'a fundamental dismantling of the Quarto sequence, and a more Cavalier approach to individual lyrics' (53) that they found a substantial audience beyond the elite. Chapter 2 covers the period 1623–1708, the period of their 'apocryphal' status, during which meaningful engagement with limited numbers of the poems shaped their legacy. Sonnets 2 and 106 are singled out here for their inclusion in altered form in several manuscripts, and Kingsley-Smith reads these altered forms in the light of Caroline seduction poetry (62). This is the tradition into which John Benson's 1640 *Poems* slots, implicitly presenting the poems as if they were previously unpublished manuscript lyrics, and he reworks them into a Caroline form, including individual poem titles that offer interpretive thresholds (70). Kingsley-Smith considers the responses of other seventeenth-century writers, such as John Suckling and John Milton, to the poems; the recent discovery of what may well be Milton's annotations to a copy of the First Folio comes too late for Kingsley-Smith to take into account here, but she persuasively traces allusions and concerns in Milton that resonate with the Sonnets and with other Shakespeare attributions. Finally, she considers the circulation of the Sonnets under Royalist auspices, from booksellers to allusions, which may suggest partisan agendas at play in the Sonnets' reception.

Chapter 3, focused on the eighteenth century, again challenges key narratives. While Edmund Malone's editing of the Sonnets had a lasting impact on the inclusion of the sequence in *Complete Works* volumes, Kingsley-Smith argues that he 'arguably did lasting damage to how the Sonnets would be read as individual lyrics' (98). The point here is important – that the editorial manoeuvres that pivot critical reception towards what is now accepted also come with losses. To this end, she traces the publishing ventures of Bernard Lintott and Charles Gildon between 1709 and 1711, arguing that the greater care Gildon took with his annotation and presentation of Benson's *Poems* helped perpetuate these versions over Lintott's unannotated, unintroduced publication of the 1609 sequence (104). Kingsley-Smith also helpfully pays attention to the significant *absences* of the Sonnets, not only from the majority of eighteenth-century Shakespeare editions but also from anthologies and quotation books (109) and from broader literary allusion – though, even here, Kingsley-Smith's work on Samuel Richardson and Thomas Edwards suggests that they were not quite so absent from discourse as is sometimes suggested. She concludes with Malone's pivotal engagement with the Sonnets, including their extensive annotation and glossing for the first time, but also their attachment to Shakespearian biography.

The rest of the book focuses more on interpreters of the Sonnets, though their later print tradition remains part of the narrative. Keats's

reappraisal 'ushers in a new, more receptive age' (135), which includes the excerption and anthologization of several individual poems and more overt celebration and creative response by the major poets of the nineteenth and twentieth centuries. In printing terms, the nineteenth century saw an explosion of books of the Sonnets, with 150 editions of the poems and the inclusion of the Sonnets in an increasing number of editions of the *Works* (154), making them available to a much wider variety of readers. Several of these collections posed resistance to the idea that the Sonnets were autobiographical – or even entirely Shakespeare's – and continued to print the poems in sequences other than that of 1609, even as that sequence began developing a general dominance. Important inclusions here are *The Golden Treasury* of 1861, which reintroduced Sonnet 18 to canonicity (with the title 'To his love'), and the introduction of certain sonnets to lesson books that began the tradition of their involvement in pedagogy. All of this underpins the twentieth-century critical traditions that increasingly centralized the Sonnets in discussions of sexuality, gender and race, which Kingsley-Smith traces in eloquent detail as she brings the book up to the present day. The achievement of Kingsley-Smith's important book is in its attention to the implications of local decisions in the context of their historical moment, positioning the development of the Sonnets' critical reception as contingent, and sometimes arbitrary.

A pair of articles offer some important provocations for reading texts this year, including Erika Boeckeler's work on Q1 *Hamlet*. After an opening assertion that scholars have 'ignored' Margreta de Grazia and Peter Stallybrass's suggestion that we attend to 'the semantic fields prompted by spelling variation' – which seems to rather downplay the huge body of work in recent years on typography and orthography, especially in Shakespeare – Erika Boeckeler offers a readerly approach to Q1 *Hamlet* that finds value in considering, for example, the rendering of 'To be, or not to be, I there's the point' in the context of a speech about the 'I' of the self. The essay focuses on how spellings within Q1 allow for the grouping of thematically connected words, arguing that the anagrammatic 'power/powre', for instance, allows the act of pouring to be read as an exercise in power (63), or that the resemblance between 'foule' and 'foule' emphasizes semantic connection (67). Boeckeler uses her insights here to make a broader plea for attention to the visual as well as verbal quality of punning, as part of interpreting the literary word as graphic text (78).

Matt Vadnais, meanwhile, intervenes in the ongoing debate about minimal/performance and maximal/authorial texts, suggesting that the distinctions become self-reinforcing and need further evaluation. His suggestion is to move from a consideration of the number of lines to a consideration of speeches and speech order, giving 'a more specific and practical picture of how a scene or play text may have actually taxed the capabilities of players and companies' (659). His argument – focused on *Henry V, Hamlet, The Merry Wives of Windsor* and *Romeo and Juliet* – is that the variant texts have striking similarities in their distribution of speeches, and in the relative prevalence of speech patterns that were intended to ease the difficulty of performance according to cued parts. Vadnais's premise is that the number of speeches – and thus the number of cues an actor had to learn – was limited in order to spread the burden for actors in any given scene, and that both the longer and shorter versions of these four plays appear to bear this principle in mind. He then turns his attention to the patterns of cutting in extant theatrical manuscripts, arguing that, 'overwhelmingly', cuts made tend to preserve cues (671). The most important provocation of his conclusion is that, rather than long versions being cut for performance, the shorter versions of the plays preceded the longer versions, which were revised and expanded, but still with performance in mind.

I conclude this year's survey with brief mention of three excellent books that do not focus on Shakespeare, but which offer important resources which will be useful to scholars working on Shakespeare's print lives and afterlives. Sarah Werner's *Studying Early Printed Books, 1450–1800: A Practical Guide* is destined to be set reading for advanced undergraduate and graduate students encountering book history for the first time, and will be invaluable to everyone working with early books. Her aim is simple: 'to show you how to think about the connections between the material form of a book … and how that book conveys its meaning and how it is used by readers' (5). It includes a detailed overview of the processes of making a book, including casting off, setting by forme, printing, folding and so on, offering a clear explanation of the processes and their consequences. Following the overview, she then breaks down the processes even further, offering lengthy discussions of paper, type, format, printing, corrections and changes, illustrations and binding, accompanied by her own invaluable diagrams. As a practical guide, it then offers useful advice for how to reference early books and take notes, and gives lists of questions that newcomers to the discipline might want to ask of books they encounter. As a practical handbook it is peerless, and a copy should be at every editor's side.

Werner concludes with a call to 'Go find the stories that these books tell us. And share them' (151), and Tamara Atkin's *Reading Drama in Tudor England* does just that. With its chronological range, focusing on drama up to 1576, it's a welcome addition to the growing body of work on the materiality of early modern dramatic texts that establishes the pre-history of many of the conventions discussed in relation to Shakespeare's print presence. She argues that this was the period that developed a series of strategies for presenting printed drama, and especially that the theatrical framing of early playbooks was designed to enhance a *readerly* experience, rather than reflecting performance. As such, Atkin provides important re-readings of phenomena such as cast lists (as opposed to doubling lists), which Atkin argues are designed to help readers navigating the conventions of a text imagined as drama, rather than as an imagined resource for future production. Her concluding chapter, concentrating on 'Reading early printed drama', is the book's highlight, looking at the full range of signs of use by early readers, rather than focusing on privileged or known users, concentrating especially on bindings and marks made by readers. Atkin's systematic work – which includes a full tabulation of all ninety-two known playbooks printed up to 1576 – is an important and timely contribution that reorients the history of reading playbooks to earlier than is often accounted for.

Finally, Dennis Duncan and Adam Smyth's collection *Book Parts* is one of the most beautiful books to cross my desk in years. Dedicated to all the people who have helped physically to make the book, it takes the form of twenty-two short chapters, each one devoted to a different component of a book, from 'Tables of contents' to 'Dust jackets' to 'Page numbers' to 'Footnotes'. Each chapter is introduced by a title page that playfully illustrates its own content (for instance, Jenny Davidson's chapter on footnotes gives the chapter title, then puts the author's name in a footnote). The chapters primarily give histories of the development of the 'book part' they discuss, and/or offer guidance on how to read and interpret their use. The most Shakespeare-inflected chapter is Tiffany Stern's on stage directions, which argues that the form settled somewhat by the 1590s, including in its odd English–Latin medley, and that the term itself emerged from Pope and Theobald's editorial disputes. The First Folio is used for illustration in Meaghan Brown's chapter on addresses to the reader, Whitney Trettien's on title pages, and Luisa Cale's on frontispieces, but all of the chapters provide useful thinking points for reconsidering the presentation of information on the page. And in Helen Smith's chapter on 'Acknowledgements and dedications', the book contains the year's funniest piece of literary criticism, without sacrificing an iota of insight.

WORKS REVIEWED

Atkin, Tamara, *Reading Drama in Tudor England* (London, 2018)

Boeckeler, Erika Mary, 'The *Hamlet* First Quarto (1603) & the play of typography', *Early Theatre* 21.1 (2018), 59–86

Brokaw, Katherine Steele, ed., *Macbeth*, Arden Performance Editions (London, 2019)

Duncan, Dennis, and Adam Smyth, eds, *Book Parts* (Oxford, 2019)

Edwards, Philip, ed., *Hamlet, Prince of Denmark*, 3rd edn, with new introduction by Heather Hirschfeld, New Cambridge Shakespeare (Cambridge, 2019)

George, David, ed., *Coriolanus*, 2 vols. (n.p., 2019)

Gossett, Suzanne, and Helen Wilcox, eds, *All's Well That Ends Well*, Arden Shakespeare (London, 2019)

Gurr, Andrew, ed., *King Richard II*, 3rd edn, with updated introduction by Claire McEachern, New Cambridge Shakespeare (Cambridge, 2019)

Hulme, Peter, and William H. Sherman, eds., *The Tempest*, 2nd edn, Norton Critical Editions (New York, 2019)

Kingsley-Smith, Jane, *The Afterlife of Shakespeare's Sonnets* (Cambridge, 2019)

Mares, F. H., ed., *Much Ado about Nothing*, 3rd edn, with updated introduction by Travis D. Williams, New Cambridge Shakespeare (Cambridge, 2018)

Miola, Robert, ed., *Hamlet*, 2nd edn, Norton Critical Editions (New York, 2019)

Rourke, Josie, ed., *Measure for Measure* (London, 2018)

Thompson, Ann, ed., *The Taming of the Shrew*, 3rd edn, New Cambridge Shakespeare (Cambridge, 2017)

Vadnais, Matt, 'The distribution and ordering of speeches and Shakespearean revision', *Shakespeare Bulletin* 36.4 (2018), 657–86.

Werner, Sarah, *Studying Early Printed Books, 1450–1800: A Practical Guide* (Wiley Blackwell, 2019)

ABSTRACTS OF ARTICLES
IN *SHAKESPEARE SURVEY 73*

KAREN NEWMAN

Continental Shakespeare
'Continental Shakespeare' considers the evidence of Shakespeare on the Continent, including the 1622 advertisement of the First Folio in a supplemental listing of *English* books to a *Latin* catalogue for the *German* book fair at Frankfort-on-the-Main, to argue that even before there were modern nation-states, Shakespeare was already transnational.

NANDINI DAS

The Stranger at the Door: Belonging in Shakespeare's Ephesus
The stranger was everywhere in early modern England. Part of a larger project about sixteenth- and seventeenth-century English perceptions of identity, human mobility and belonging, this article shows how *The Comedy of Errors* unfolds against the backdrop of the city of London's own troubled relationship with 'strangers'.

ALICE LEONARD

City Origins, Lost Identities and Print Errors in *The Comedy of Errors*
This article is concerned with printing error in the First Folio of *The Comedy of Errors*. It examines the effect of these errors on the reader, and argues for a revision of their silent correction in modern editions. In so doing, it highlights a seventeenth- and early-eighteenth-century history of reading that tried, and often failed, to correct them.

HARRY R. MCCARTHY

The Circulation of Youthful Energy on the Early Modern London Stage: Migration, Intertheatricality and 'Growing Common Players'
This article traces the careers of thirty-two early modern actors, recorded as having begun as boy players, who transferred from one acting company to the other at least once, considering how the arrival of star players such as Nathan Field and Stephen Hammerton might have affected a company's repertory.

CHI-FANG SOPHIA LI

In Conversation with Shakespeare in Jacobean London: Social Insanity and Its Taming Schools in *1&2 Honest Whore*
This article places Dekker and Middleton's *1&2 Honest Whore* and contemporary plague pamphlets in conversation with Shakespeare's work of 1604–5. It reveals a Shakespeare silent about social dispossession in Jacobean London.

LARS ENGLE

Hearing Voices: Signal versus Urban Noise in *Coriolanus* and Augustine's *Confessions*
Discussing *Coriolanus* alongside Augustine's *Confessions*, this article argues that, in both works, the protagonist searches for a true and worthwhile voice amid urban

noise. Treating the signal–noise ratio as something both protagonists anticipate and describe, it invites readers to respect Coriolanus' search by comparing it to Augustine's eminently respectable one.

MIRIAM LEUNG CHE LAU **Caesar and Lear in Hong Kong: Appropriating Shakespeare to Express the Inexpressible**
This article discusses the emergence of a distinctive Hong Kong Shakespeare and a newfound Hong Kong identity in Hardy Tsoi's *Julius Caesar* (2012) and *Shamshuipo Lear* (2015), in which Tsoi merely appropriates Shakespeare to illustrate the socio-political problems of Hong Kong.

NEIL RHODES **Before We Sleep: *Macbeth* and the Curtain Lecture**
Macbeth is unusual in its representation of marital intimacy and in its central dynamic of a husband and wife working together in partnership. This article argues that this intimacy is realized in the imaginary private space of the curtained bed, and through the speech form known as the curtain lecture.

CHARLOTTE SCOTT **'The Story Shall be Changed': Antique Fables and Agency in *A Midsummer Night's Dream***
This article explores the role of the story – allusion, paradigm, precedent and narrative structure – as an agent of change in Shakespeare's *A Midsummer Night's Dream*. With a particular focus on women, this article analyses the pivotal role that storytelling plays in Shakespeare's construction of both opportunity and imagination.

NICHOLAS LUKE **A Lawful Magic: New Worlds of Precedent in *Mabo* and *The Winter's Tale***
This article examines the unsettling ways in which historical 'redemption' is rendered in *The Winter's Tale* and Australia's landmark legal decision on Indigenous property rights (*Mabo*). It explores how creative and shame-filled forms of remembrance can interrupt the tragic law that condemns us to repeat the horrors of the past.

MICHAEL CORDNER **'Cabined, Cribbed, Confined': Advice to Actors and the Priorities of Shakespearian Scholarship**
Over the last few decades advice books on how to handle Shakespearian verse have proliferated. But much of the advice they offer is misleading. This article explores some of their most striking errors, but also highlights the radical challenge they represent to the default priorities of Shakespearian scholarship.

PETER J. SMITH **'What Country, Friends, Is This?': Tim Supple's *Twelfth Night* Revisited**
This article revisits Tim Supple's film version of *Twelfth Night* (2003) fifteen years after it was made in the light of some recent (2018) correspondence with its director. It shows how Supple's multicultural version anticipates contemporary crises over asylum, immigration and refugees.

JENNIE M. VOTAVA **Through a Glass Darkly: Sophie Okonedo's Margaret as Racial Other in *The Hollow Crown: The Wars of the Roses***
This article presents a case for the importance of seeing race in the non-traditional casting of Shakespeare's English histories, as exemplified by the presence of Nigerian-British actress Sophie Okonedo as Margaret of Anjou in the BBC's *The Hollow Crown: The Wars of the Roses*.

GEMMA KATE ALLRED

'Who's There?': Britain's Twenty-First-Century Obsession with Celebrity *Hamlet* (2008–2018)

This article considers the impact of celebrity on productions of *Hamlet*. It does so through reference to the Hamlets of David Tennant (2008), Jude Law (2009), Benedict Cumberbatch (2015) and Andrew Scott (2017), and aims to analyse how textual choices, staging and marketing are influenced by a new target audience.

INDEX

Abbas, Ackbar, 99
Aberg, Maria, 238–9
Acheson, Katherine, 40–1n.77
Adams, Roger D., 155n.60
Adams, Thomas, 111n.23
Adelman, Janet, 89n.15
Adorno, Theodor, 1, 143
Agamben, Giorgio, 67n.19
Ajao, David, 236
Akhimie, Patricia, 255–6, 265
Al-Bassam, Sulayman, 257
Alexander, Michael, 149n.22
Alfreds, Mike, 274
Alleine, Joseph, 115
Alleyn, Edward, 48
Allred, Gemma Kate, 184–202
Amankwah, Sarah, 208, 210Illus.14, 210
Anderegg, Michael, 201n.106
Anderson, Abigail, 243, 246
Andoh, Adjoa, 206–7, 208Illus.13
Andrea, Bernadette, 255–6, 265
Andrews, Richard, 44
Animashaun, Hammed, 215
Annand, Simon, 231Illus.19
Apuleius, 127
Archer, Ian, 11n.7
Archer, John Michael, 12n.12
Arendt, Hannah, 120
Ariosto, Ludovico, 74–5, 76
Aristotle, 159
Arkley, Joseph, 234, 235Illus.21, 238
Arrowsmith, Charlotte, 233
Arshad, Yasmin, 254–5, 265
al-Asadi, Jawad, 266
Ashcroft, Peggy, 177
Ashton, Frederick, 266, 267
Aspden, Peter, 195n.59
Assefa, Mequannt, 220
Astington, John H., 48n.37, 121n.14
Atkin, Tamara, 287–8
Atkins, Eileen, 146, 147, 156
Attridge, Derek, 149n.23
Attwell, Hugh, 45, 52Illus.10
Atwell, Hayley, 244
Atwood, Margaret, 284

Audibert, Justin, 233–5, 235Illus.21
Augustine of Hippo, St., 79–92
Aydelotte, Laura, 124n.28

Babham, Christopher, 43
Bachelard, Gaston, 110n.19, 117n.52
Bacon, Francis, Baron Verulam and
        Viscount St Albans, 5, 17n.31,
        263
Bagnall, Nick, 242
Bain, Maggie, 226
Baker, Paul, 244
Bal, Mieke, 119n.2,3
Balanchine, George, 266
Bamford, Karen, 112n.27
Banham, Martin, 47n.27
Banks, Fiona, 275, 276
Bannerman, Andrew, 162, 164, 165
Barber, C. L., 69n.20
Barclay, Alice, 228
Barker, Roberta, 56n.64
Barksted, William, 45–6, 51Illus.9,
        52Illus.10, 58
Barnard, John, 5n.23
Barrymore, John, 271
Al-Bassam, Sulayman, 257
Bate, Jonathan, 107n.2, 165n.24, 283
Bates, Catherine, 126n.36
Batsaki, Yota, 121n.16
Baumgartner, Victoria, 251
Baxter, Richard, 46, 53Illus.11
Beale, Simon Russell, 186, 203, 247
Beasley, Remy, 218
Beaumont, Francis, 43–4, 45–7, 48, 49, 50,
        56n.65, 57, 59, 258
Beck, Julian, 274
Beckermann, Bernard, 274
Beckwith, Sarah, 134, 140
Becon, Thomas, 116
Bednarz, James P., 54
Beeston, Christopher, 46, 51Illus.9,
        52Illus.10
Bellini, Vincenzo, 248
Bellow, Saul, 79, 80, 90
Benedict, David, 162

Benfield, Robert, 46, 52Illus.10
Benjamin, Walter, 1, 129, 134, 135, 139
Bennett, Andrew, 166
Bennett, Susan, 275
Benson, John, 285–6
Bentley, Eric, 127n.37
Bentley, G. E., 43n.3, 44,
        46n.16,17,18,21,22,23,
        47n.25,26,27,28,29,
        48n.31,32,33,34,36,38,
        49n.39,40,41,42,43,44, 50n.46
Bergeron, David, 253–4, 265
Bernadette, Andrea, 15n.29
Bernard, J. F., 264
Berners, John Bourchier, Lord, 124n.28
Berry, Cicely, 146, 147
Berry, Herbert, 48n.33
Bessell, Jaq, 274–5, 276
Betteridge, Thomas, 12–13n.13
Bevington, David, 13n.15, 58n.72,
        175n.34
Bhabha, Homi, 100n.54, 105
Bill, John, 2–6, 9
Bill, Leo, 203–4, 204Illus.12
Billington, Michael, 162, 166, 195,
        198n.83, 198, 199n.97,
        200n.103
Bird, Theophilus, 46, 53Illus.11
Bitmate, Simona, 229
Blackburn, Richard, 134, 137
Blackwell, Anna, 177, 185n.17, 185, 193
Bladen, Victoria, 276
Blagrave, William, 43
Bland, D. S., 109n.11
Blayney, John, 46, 52Illus.10, 53Illus.11
Blayney, Peter, 2, 3, 280
Bliss, Lee, 279
Block, Giles, 152–6, 157, 159, 160
Bloomer, Clare, 245
Blount, Edward, 9
Blount, Ivanno, 181
Blunt, Victoria, 245
Bly, Mary, 46n.16
Boas, F. S., 74n.29
Boccaccio, Giovanni, 258

Bodinetz, Gemma, 246
Bodley, Sir Thomas, 5, 9
Boeckeler, Erika Mary, 286–7, 288
Bogart, Humphrey, 271
Bonian, Richard, 1
Boose, Lynda E., 201n.106
Bosman, Anston, 6n.37, 6–7, 7n.41,
    8n.51,52, 8, 9n.55,58
Boston, Jane, 154n.49,50,
Boswell, Eleanore, 54n.54
Bourke, Peter, 216
Bourne, Claire, 22n.7, 25n.24, 29n.28
Bowers, Fredson, 23n.8, 63n.3
Bowers, Nina, 213
Bowie, David, 189
Boyle, Nicola, 46n.18
Bramwell, Frank, 242
Branagh, Joyce, 223–5
Branagh, Kenneth, 185, 284
Brandon, James R., 96, 100
Brandt, Geeraardt, 8
Brathwait, Richard, 108n.9, 112, 114, 116
Braunmuller, A. R., 107–8, 108n.9,
    116n.50, 116
Brecht, Bertolt, 97, 104, 139, 274
Breen, Phillip, 251
Brennan, Gerard, 129n.2, 130n.6, 130,
    131, 132, 135, 136–7, 138,
    141n.74, 141–2
Brenner, Marc, 204Illus.12
Brimson-Lewis, Stephen, 234
Brindley, Susan, 95n.23
Britten, Benjamin, 246, 251
Broadbent, Jonathan, 211
Brockbank, Philip, 280
Brokaw, Katherine Steele, 281–2, 288
Brome, Richard, 49
Brook, Peter, 165n.24, 186, 206, 269, 270,
    284
Brooke, Nicholas, 21–2
Brooke, Ralph, 21n.2,3,4
Brooks, Douglas A., 40–1n.77
Brooks, Gabrielle, 217
Brown, Meaghan, 288
Brown, Peter, 86
Browne, Robert, 9
Bruce, Mark, 243
Bruster, Douglas, 1n.4, 6
Buckhurst, Bill, 194n.54, 246
Buckler, Edward, 115
Bührle, Iris, 267
Bullinger, Heinrich, 116n.48
Bulman, James C., 173n.20
Burbage, Cuthbert, 54
Burbage, Richard, 49, 54, 58n.71
Burghley, William Cecil, 1st Baron, 16–17
Burness, Edwina, 116n.50
Burnett, Mark Thornton, 23n.8, 166n.31,
    268, 276
Burrow, Colin, 125n.29
Burt, Nicholas, 46, 53Illus.11

Burt, Richard, 201n.106
Burton, Robert, 58n.71
Buruma, Ian, 95
Bushay, Raphael, 227
Butler, Judith, 263
Butler, Martin, 16, 47n.29, 60n.84
Byrne, Antony, 232, 236, 240
Byrne, Caroline, 240
Byron, George Gordon, 6th Baron, 200

Caird, John, 186
Calder, David, 242
Cale, Luisa, 288
Callaghan, Dympna, 172n.15
Callis, Sam, 227
Calvin, John, 91, 113
Cannon, Andy, 244
Capell, Edward, 32, 34, 37
Carding, Emily, 241
Carey, David, 154n.49
Carlell, Lodowick, 46, 49
Carlson, Marvin, 58, 184n.5, 194, 197, 198
Carson, Robert, 245, 246
Cartelli, Thomas, 266, 276
Cartwright, Kent, 14n.18
Cartwright, William Jr., 46, 53Illus.11
Cary, Giles, 47, 52Illus.10
Cato the Younger, 91
Catterall, Douglas, 11n.8
Cavell, Stanley, 121n.14, 134, 143
Cecil, Robert, 1st Earl of Salisbury, 19
Cecil, William, 1st Baron Burghley, 16–17
Cellan-Jones, James, 41
Chalk, Darryl, 263–4, 265
Chambers, E. K., 115n.41
Champion, Larry S., 64n.7,14,
Chan, Bernice Kwok-wai, 96, 97n.36, 101
Chan, Joanna, 94n.17
Chan, Kin-hao, 100n.56
Chan, Shelby Kar-yan, 104n.79, 106
Chapman, George, 47, 49, 56n.65, 61–2,
    280
Charles II, King of England, Scotland and
    Ireland, 30, 115–16
Charles, Nicole, 251
Chaucer, Geoffrey, 119n.5, 120n.8
Chen, Chapman, 105n.89
Chenovik, Clarissa, 154n.54
Chitty, Alison, 273
Chow Yung-ping, 94n.17
Choy, Howard Yuen-Fung, 95
Chris, Oliver, 214
Christian, Jude, 244, 247
Christie, Gwendoline, 214, 215Illus.15
Christodoulidis, Emilios, 131n.17
Cicero, 159
Clapp, Susannah, 187
Clark, Hugh, 47, 53Illus.11
Clark, Sandra, 107n.2
Clark, W. G., 109n.12,13
Clavell, John, 46, 48, 49

Clayton, Thomas, 279
Cleaver, Robert, 112n.26, 115
Cleopatra, Queen of Egypt, 254–5
Clifford, Lady Anne, 40, 255
Clifton, Alex, 249
Clilverd, Rob, 246
Clubb, Louise George, 9n.58
Cobb, Christopher J., 139n.63, 141
Coghill, Nevill, 138
Cohen, Ralph Alan, 2n.6, 186, 284
Cohn, Albert, 7n.42, 8
Cohn, Ruby, 266
Collett, Nicholas, 251
Comensoli, Viviana, 64
Condell, Henry, 54
Conquest, Charlotte, 248
Conybeare, Catherine, 85
Cook, Nicholas, 157n.72,73
Cook, Rena, 154n.49,50
Cooke, Dominic, 170–83, 174n.28
Corbett, Clare, 223–4
Cordner, Michael, 145–60
Cornelissen, Ignace, 247
Cotton, Clement, 113n.34
Cowden Clarke, Mary and Charles, 270
Cox, John D., 2n.8
Cranko, John, 266, 267
Creaser, John, 58
Cridlan, Charlie, 213
Croall, Jonathan, 186n.22, 189n.35,
    191n.40, 193n.45,
    200n.102,103,104
Croll, Donna, 207
Crompton, Sarah, 185n.19
Cromwell, Thomas, 1st Earl of Essex,
    75–6
Crouch, Humphrey, 58n.71
Cruden, Damian, 225–6, 243
Cruikshank, George, 270
Csenger, Karen, 109n.12
Cumberbatch, Benedict, 173, 182, 184–5,
    187–8, 189–90, 191, 192, 193,
    195, 196, 197, 198, 199, 200,
    201, 283
Cumbus, Philip, 205–6
Curry, Julian, 191n.41,42, 193n.48
Curthoys, Ann, 132
Cusack, Niamh, 243
Czinner, Paul, 271

Daalder, Joost, 64, 65n.16
Dahl, Marcus, 277
Daltry, Roger, 41
Daniel, P.A., 278
Daniel, Samuel, 255
Darnley, Lyn, 145–6
Das, Nandini, 10–20
Dasent, J. R., 14n.22, 15n.24
Davenant, William, 257
Davenport, Robert, 47, 48
Davidson, Jenny, 288

INDEX

Davies, Jo, 249
Davies, Paul, 244
Davis, Natalie Zemon, 121n.13
Davis, Pamela J., 155n.60
Davis, Serena, 183n.64
Davison, Francis, 16–17, 17n.31
Dawson, Daryl, 129, 136, 137,
    141n.75
Day, Edward, 241
Dean, David, 14n.19
Deane, William, 129n.1, 130n.9, 130,
    136, 138
Debnath, Neela, 174n.26, 196n.67
Dee, John, 40
Deeny, Leander, 227
de Grazia, Margreta, 23n.8, 36, 282, 284,
    286
Dehaisnes, C., 31n.44
Dekker, Thomas, 39–40, 41, 47, 63–78,
    263
de Melo, Wolfgang, 10n.2
Dench, Judi, 174–5, 184, 272–3
Denford, Harry, 250
Denham, John, 260
Dent, R. W., 117n.51
Dering, Edward, 256
Derrida, Jacques, 263
Descartes, René, 263
Devereux, Robert, 2nd Earl of Essex,
    17n.31, 260, 283
D'Ewes, Simonds, 14n.19,20,21
Dharker, Ayesha, 208Illus.13
Dick, Jennifer, 246
Dieterle, William, 269, 271
Dillon, Janette, 120n.12
Dionne, Craig, 165n.27
Dobson, Michael, 2n.13, 165, 186n.25
Dolan, Frances, 260
Donkor, Amelia, 235
Donne, John, 112, 116n.49, 168
Donnellan, Declan, 154, 247, 273
Donnelly, Steffan, 211
Doran, Gregory, 183n.63, 230, 236–8,
    237Illus.22, 242, 249, 274,
    279–80
    Hamlet with David Tennant, 184n.4,6,
    185n.7, 185–6, 187, 188–9, 191,
    192, 193–4, 196–7, 198, 199,
    200, 201
Dormandy, Simon, 246
Dorsen, Annie, 266
Dowd, Michelle, 12n.12
Drábek, Pavel, 6–7
Draper, Amy, 246
Dromgoole, Dominic, 194
Drummond, William, 42
Duff, Anne-Marie, 243
Duke, Ben, 248
Dukes, Ricky, 245
Dunbar, Adrian, 180
Duncan, Dennis, 288

Dutton, Richard, 46n.18, 122n.21,
    124n.27, 175n.36
Dyke, Jeremiah, 112–13, 118

Eblan, Ernie, 157n.74
Eccles, Mark, 44, 45n.15, 47n.26,
    49n.41,43
Eccleston, Christopher, 243
Ecclestone, William, 47, 52Illus.10
Edgecombe, David, 50
Edmondson, Adrian, 250
Edmondson, Paul, 164
Edwards, Philip, 288
Edwards, Thomas, 286
Egerton, Nigel, 177
Ejiofor, Chiwetel, 161n.4, 163, 164
Elam, Keir, 121n.14
Elcock, Michael, 218
Eliot, George, 90
Elizabeth, Princess (*later* Queen of
    Bohemia), 253
Elizabeth I, Queen of England, 15, 16–17,
    254
Ellinson, Lucy, 239
Elliott, Victoria, 216
Ellis, Elizabeth, 155n.60
Ellis, John, 202n.108
Ellis-Petersen, Hannah, 198n.87
Elsworthy, Laura, 235
Engle, Lars, 79–92
English, Gillian, 251
Erasmus, Desiderius, 111, 116, 117–18
Erickson, Peter, 177
Erne, Lukas, 8n.47, 41n.79
Esien, Jocelyn Jee, 217
Espinosa, Ruben, 15n.25, 256
Essex, Robert Devereux, 2nd Earl of,
    17n.31, 260, 283
Essiedu, Paapa, 184, 241
Estabillo, J. Charles, 264
Estienne, Henri, 3
Estill, Laura, 32
Ettenhuber, Katrin, 112n.31
Euripides, 124
Eustis, Oskar, 250
Evans, G. Blakemore, 30n.31,33,34,35,37,
    30–2, 31n.39,44, 33n.50, 34,
    37n.68
Evans, Henry, 54

Fairlie, Gemma, 223, 224Illus.18, 226–7,
    247
Fanon, Frantz, 95, 230
Faranesh-Bocca, John, 268
Farmer, Alan B., 47n.29
Farmer, Lindsay, 131n.17
Farrugia-Kriel, Kathrina, 268
Farzad, Leila, 207, 208Illus.13
Feather, Jennifer, 263
Fellini, Federico, 98n.43
Fenn, Ezekiel, 47, 53Illus.11

Fenton, Sir Geoffrey, 72n.25
Fernie, Ewan, 139, 140n.72
Fernyhough, Charles, 80
Field, Nathan, 47, 48, 49, 52Illus.10, 54,
    55–9, 61–2
Fiennes, Ralph, 89n.15, 240
Finch, Henry, 19–20
Findlay, Polly, 243, 274
Finigan, Sarah, 213, 244
Finney, Albert, 272
Finney, Gavin, 166
Finney, Gretchen, 154n.52
Fish, Stanley, 89n.15
Fitter, Chris, 172n.17
Fitzpatrick, Peter, 130
Fleay, F. G., 64n.14
Flemming, Willi, 7n.41
Fletcher, John, 43–4, 45–7, 48, 49, 50,
    56n.65, 59, 61, 72n.24
Flood, John L., 3n.19,20,21, 5n.30,
Florio, John, 91n.18
Floyd-Wilson, Mary, 172, 178, 263–4, 265
Flynn, Gillian, 284
Foakes, R. A., 23n.12, 23, 25n.20, 63n.2
Fong, Gilbert, 105
Fontayne, Fine Time, 224
Ford, John, 46, 48, 49, 263
Forknall, Robert, 244
Forman, Simon, 115
Forster, Juliet, 245
Forsyth, Neil, 276
Foucault, Michel, 95
Fouquet, Nicolas, 9
Foxe, John, 75–6
Frankland, John, 241
Franks, Phillip, 227
Fraser, G. S., 149n.23
Fraunce, Abraham, 159n.80
Freeman, Arthur, 15n.26,27
Freestone, Elizabeth, 228, 241, 251
French, Andrew, 248–8
French, Emma, 197
Frescobaldi family, 74–6
Friedrich, Caspar David, 196–7
Fuller, Nicholas, 14
Fulwell, Ulpian, 12
Fung, Michael, 100–6
Furness, Hannah, 195n.60

Gair, W. Reavely, 48n.35, 49n.45
Galen, 263
Gardner, Helen, 109n.11
Garner, Shirley Nelson, 175n.33
Garrison, John S., 264–5
Gascoigne, George, 233
Gatens, Moira, 144n.85,86
Gaudron, Mary, 129n.1, 130n.9, 130, 136,
    138
Gavin, Adrienne E., 48n.31
Gelder, Ken, 134–5
Gellert, Roger, 153n.45

George III, King of Great Britain, 270
George, David, 279–81, 288
Gesua, Rachel, 163, 164
Gibson, Rex, 95
Giedroyc, Mel, 246
Gielgud, John, 185, 284
Gildon, Charles, 286
Giles, Thomas, 49
Gillespie, Stuart, 116n.50
Gillies, John, 96n.32,33,34, 284
Glapthorne, Henry, 47
Glennie, Evelyn, 249
Godwin, Simon, 230–2, 231Illus.19, 240,
    241, 249
Goggin, Ed, 249
Gohil, Dinita, 250
Golding, Arthur, 122, 126n.34,35
Goldthwaite, R., 75n.36
Goodwin, Philip, 115
Goose, Nigel, 11n.5, 13n.17
Gordon, Andrew, 257
Gossett, Suzanne, 277–9, 288
Gouge, William, 108
Gould, Benjamin, 243
Gould, Jamie, 240
Gowrie, John Ruthven, 3rd Earl of, 253
Grandage, Michael: *Hamlet* with Jude
    Law, 185n.12, 185, 186,
    187n.26, 188, 189, 191, 193,
    195, 196, 198n.84, 199
Grant, Neva, 102n.70, 103n.75
Green, Chris, 186n.20
Greenaway, Peter, 266, 269
Greenblatt, Stephen, 44, 107n.1, 113n.35
Greene, Robert, 75, 124n.28
Greenhalgh, Susanne, 166
Greenwell, Camilla, 221Illus.17
Greg, W. W., 2–3, 6, 9, 15n.28,
    29n.30
Gregerson, Linda, 175n.36
Grierson, Sandy, 233, 236, 237Illus.22,
    237
Griffin, Eric, 15n.25
Griffith, Eva, 46n.18, 47n.26
Gross, Kenneth, 55, 83, 88, 89n.15
Gurr, Andrew, 45n.15, 46n.18,23, 47n.29,
    49n.43,44, 110n.17,18, 288
Guy, John, 16n.30
Gwynne, Nia, 249

Habenicht, Rudolph E., 117n.54
Habib, Imtiaz, 11n.5
Hainsworth, Isis, 214
Hakluyt, Richard, 257
Halasz, Alexandra, 1n.4
Hale, Robin Norton, 248
Hall, Edward, 171
Hall, Kim F., 172n.15
Hall, Peter, 145, 155n.57, 155, 272–3
Hamling, Tara, 110n.15, 111
Hammer, Paul, 283

Hammerton, Stephen, 43–62,
    53Illus.11
Hampton-Reeves, Stuart, 173n.22,23,
    176n.38, 177n.43, 272–3, 276
Hanmer, Thomas, 34
Hannah, Bryony, 213–14
Harbage, Alfred, 50
Hardy, Barbara, 121
Harington, Sir John, 75
Harlan, Manuel, 215Illus.15
Harris, Amanda, 235, 236
Harris, Jonathan Gil, 110n.18
Harris, Michael, 3n.19
Harry, Prince, Duke of Sussex, 226
Hart, Paul, 245, 250
Hartley, Andrew James, 93n.9, 155n.57,
    199
Hassam, Jake, 244
Hassell, Alex, 243
Hastie, Robert, 205–6, 243, 246
Hatchuel, Sarah, 269, 276
Haughton, William, 14n.20
Hawkins, Kayleigh, 248
Hayles, N. Katherine, 81n.6
Hazlitt, William, 64–4, 184
Hedbäck, Ann-Mari, 31n.43
Heim, Otto, 96
Helgerson, Richard, 2, 172n.14
Helpmann, Robert, 267
Heminges, John, 49, 54
Hemingway, Samuel B., 123n.24
Henderson, Diana, 269
Henke, Robert, 8n.45,46,51, 44n.8
Hennegen, Nick, 241
Henning, Standish, 38n.69
Henry, Prince of Wales, 253–4
Henry VIII, King of England, 75, 76
Henslowe, Philip, 9, 63n.2
Herbert, George, 110, 154
Herold, Niels, 279
Hewitt, Gwen, 155n.61
Heywood, Thomas, 21n.5,21, 46, 47, 48,
    51–2, 72n.26, 112, 116n.45,46,
    117, 258, 261
Hibbard, G. R., 55n.58
Hickeringill, Edmund, 113n.33
Higgin, Nadine, 216
Higson, Andrew, 175n.31
Hill, Dominic, 217–19, 219Illus.16, 244
Hill, Errol, 178n.49
Hill, Kieran, 217
Hill-Gibbins, Joe, 203–5, 204Illus.12, 211,
    247
Hindle, Maurice, 162–3, 164
Hinds, Andy, 147–8, 150, 151
Hinman, Charlton, 280
Hinton-Lever, Beth, 219–20, 221Illus.17
Hirschfeld, Heather, 282–3, 288
Hislop, Ian, 242
Ho, Richard, 94n.17
Hobson, Jane, 219Illus.16

Hodgdon, Barbara, 171n.3, 194–5, 283
Hoffmeister, Gerhart, 7n.42
Holland, André, 247
Holland, Peter, 7n.38, 80n.3, 83n.10, 83,
    89n.15, 120, 124, 161, 279, 280
Holm, Ian, 150
Holmes, Federay, 191n.39, 194n.53,
    207–8, 240, 241
Holmes, Jonathan, 201
Holmes, Sean, 210–13, 216–17, 245
Hopper, Thomas Warren, 107n.3
Horslen, Ben, 246
Hoskins, W. G., 108, 110–11
Houghton, Matti, 212
Houlbrooke, Ralph A., 111n.25
Howard, Jean E., 64n.11, 172n.14,
    175n.36, 176n.41, 179n.51,
    180n.55,56
Howard, Leslie, 271
Howard, Tony, 284
Hoy, Cyrus, 64n.14,15, 64
Huang, Alexa, 93, 95, 96, 101
Hughes, Charles, 7–8n.44
Hughes, Ian, 251
Hughey, Matthew W., 182n.61
Hui, Sam, 105–6
Hulme, Peter, 284, 288
Hulme, T. E., 109n.12
Hulse, Lynn, 48n.31
Hunter, Kathryn, 41, 230–2, 231Illus.19,
    249
Hunter, Kelly, 148–52, 156, 157, 159, 160
Hurley, Colin, 191, 211
Hutcheon, Linda, 101, 202n.108
Hutchinson, Lucy, 25–6
Hutson, Lorna, 16n.30, 122, 124
Huydekooper van Maarseveen, Johan, 9
Huygens, Constantijn, 9
Hytner, Nicholas, 43n.1, 195, 214–16,
    215Illus.15, 242

Icke, Robert: *Hamlet* with Andrew Scott,
    185, 187, 188, 190–3, 194, 195,
    196, 197–8, 199, 200, 201
Imhangbe, Martins, 203, 204Illus.12
Ingham, Mike, 100n.51
Irvine, Susan, 200
Iwuji, Chuk, 174
Iyengar, Sujata, 172

Jackson, Angus, 241–2
Jackson, Ken, 64
Jackson, Russell, 266–76
Jacobs, Jane, 134–5
Jaggard, William, 3n.17,3,21, 285
James VI and I, King of Scotland and
    England, 5, 6, 72, 107, 253–4
James, Amber, 217, 218, 219Illus.16
Jauss, Hans Robert, 2n.6
Jenkinson, Anthony, 15
Jensen, Michael P., 271–2, 276

Jhutti, Ronny, 163
Johnson, Boris, 223
Johnson, Linford, 220
Johnson, Megan-Marie, 279
Johnson, Nora, 55n.58, 56
Johnson, Ruth, 250
Johnson, Samuel, 34, 37, 109
Jonelle, Ebony, 220
Jones, James, 47, 52Illus.10
Jones, Susan, 267
Jones-Davies, M. T., 63n.4
Jonson, Ben, 42, 45–7, 48, 49, 50, 52, 53,
    54, 55–6, 64, 264, 267
Jonson, E. Patrick, 181
Jordan, Chris, 249
Jordan, Thomas, 47–8, 53Illus.11
Joseph, Paterson, 182
Josephine, Charlotte, 248–8
Jowett, John, 22, 36, 74n.28
Jowitt, Claire, 12–13n.13, 256–7, 265
Juvenal, 111n.23

Kahn, Coppélia, 284
Kahn, Michael, 274
Kapadia, Parmita, 165n.27
Kapitaniak, Peter, 269
Karpf, Anne, 158
Kastan, David Scott, 1, 2n.8, 2, 121n.13
Kathman, David, 44, 46n.18,22,
    47n.27,30, 48n.32,34,38,
    49n.40,41,44, 50n.46, 54, 55
Katritzky, M. A., 6–7, 8n.46,53,
    9n.56,57, 9
Katz, Richard, 213
Kazamia, Andrew, 163
Keats, John, 125, 286
Kelliher, Hilton, 57n.69
Kelly, Jude, 234
Kemp, Lu, 247
Kennedy, Dennis, 93
Kenton, Tristram, 210Illus.14
Kermode, Lloyd, 12–13
Kerrigan, John, 121n.14, 125n.29,31
Kerry, Fitzgerald, 248
Kerstein, Lincoln, 267
Kesson, Andy, 44
Khan, Iqbal, 240, 257
Kidd, Ben, 241
Kidnie, Margaret Jane, 25n.24, 41n.79
Killigrew, Thomas, 30n.32, 43, 47, 59–60
King, Kimball, 72n.27
King, Ros, 149n.22
Kingsley-Smith, Jane, 284–6, 288
Kinnear, Rory, 193, 243
Kinney, Arthur F., 32n.47, 107n.1,3,
Kirwan, Peter, 171n.6, 173n.21, 175n.32,
    176n.39, 273, 276, 277–88
Kitchen, Michael, 41
Kittredge, George Lyman, 37
Klamar, Natalie, 203
Klein, Alyssa, 170n.1, 171n.9

Knolles, Richard, 258
Knutson, Roslyn L., 44, 54–5
Kolin, Philip C., 177n.42
Komisarjevsky, Theodore, 271
Koner, Pauline, 267
Korda, Natasha, 12n.12, 110n.18, 260
Korley, Debbie, 230, 231Illus.19
Koselleck, Reinhart, 132
Kott, Jan, 274
Kreps, Barbara, 64n.11
Kristeva, Julia, 263
Kurosawa, Akira, 268, 269
Kuzner, James, 135
Kwei-Armah, Kwame, 250
Kwong, Kevin, 105n.91,92
Kyd, Thomas, 258

Lai, Jane, 100n.53
Laird, Fiona, 245
Lamb, Edel, 55
Lamb, Mary Ellen, 112n.27
Langley, Eric, 262–3, 264, 265
Langner, Lawrence, 274
La Salle, Mick, 161
Laskey, Jack, 240
Lau, Miriam Leung Che, 93–106, 96n.29
Laughton, Charles, 271–2
Lavagnino, John, 63n.3
Law, Jude, 185, 186, 187n.26, 188, 189,
    191, 193, 195, 196, 198n.84,
    199, 283, 284
Lawson, Leigh, 145–6, 147, 151, 155
Leach, Amy, 228–30
Lean, David, 269
Lee, Adele, 95, 102
Lee Chee-keng, 93n.9
Lee, Heung-sing, 97n.36
Lee, Patricia-Ann, 171n.3, 174n.30
Lee, Richard, 111
Leggatt, Alexander, 55n.58
Lei, Beatrice Bi-qi, 93n.3, 94
Leipacher, Mark, 245
Lennox, Esmé Stuart, 1st Duke of, 253,
    254
Leo, Russ, 8, 9n.61
Leonard, Alice, 21–42
Leonard, Kendra Preston, 165, 169
Lesser, Zachary, 1n.4, 1–2, 9
Lester, Adrian, 174, 185, 186
Letts, Quentin, 199n.91
Leven, Lois, 269
Levin, Carole, 174n.29
Levin, Harry, 284
Levine, Laura, 123n.25
Levine, Nina, 12n.10, 171n.3, 179n.52,53,
    180n.54
Levring, Kristian, 269
Lewendel, Max, 243
Lewis, Stephen Brimson, 236
Li, Chi-Fang Sophia, 63–78
Li, Joseph, 98n.41

Li, Ruru, 96n.32,33,34
Lichter, Péter, 266
Lightbody, John, 212
Lim, Emily, 247
Limon, Jerzy, 6–7
Limón, José, 267
Lincoln, Dylan, 249
Linton, Lynette, 206–7, 208Illus.13
Lintott, Bernard, 286
Little, Arthur L. Jr., 170, 172
Littler, Tom, 242
Liu, Oi-ling, 100n.56
Liu, Si-yuan, 93n.8
Liu Ching-chih, 105
Livy, 280
Lloyd, Genevieve, 144n.85,86
Lloyd, Phyllida, 243
Lodge, Tim, 245
Loewenstein, Joseph, 2
Loftis, Sonya Freeman, 148n.13
Logan, Sandra, 178
Loomba, Ania, 172n.15
Lopez, Jeremy, 45, 275
Louis XIV, King of France, 8, 9
Love, Genevieve, 252, 265
Lowden, Jack, 244
Luhrmann, Baz, 190, 197, 201
Luke, Nicholas, 129–44
Lumb, Geoffrey, 228
Lupton, Julia Reinhard, 284
Luscombe, Christopher, 250
Luther, Martin, 91
Lutkin, Tim, 230
Luu, Lien Bich, 11n.5, 13n.17

Maas, P., 19n.34
Mabo, Eddie, 129–44
McCann, Caroline, 246
McCarthy, Harry R., 43–62
McCluskey, Peter Matthew, 12n.10
McCoy, Richard, 16
McCullough, Lynsey, 266–8, 276
MacDonald, Glynn, 152
McDade, Sandy, 162
McDonald, Peter D., 1n.3
McDonald, Russ, 117n.52, 156
McEachern, Claire, 172n.14, 283, 288
McGrillis, Topher, 233Illus.20
Machin, Lewis, 58
McHugh, Michael, 138n.60
McInnis, David, 256–7, 265
McIntyre, Blanche, 249, 250
McJannett, Linda, 268
Mack, Peter, 149n.24
Mackay, John, 203
MacKaye, Percy, 284
McKellen, Ian, 107n.2, 145, 242
McKenzie, D. F., 1
McKernan, Bethan, 171n.7,8
McKerrow, R. B., 2, 25, 29
McKintosh, Peter, 205

McLeod, Randall, 23n.8
MacLarnon, Ann, 155n.61
MacMillan, Kenneth, 267
Maguire, Laurie, 121n.17, 277
Maitre, Doreen, 127
Malcolm, Morgan Lloyd, 251
Maley, Willy, 259
Malone, Edmond, 27, 28Illus.4, 29Illus.5,
    32, 34, 37, 286
Malone, Toby, 190n.36
Maloney, Michael, 161n.4, 168
Maltby, Kate, 187, 199n.98, 202n.109
Malvern, Jack, 185n.8, 198n.85
Mandelbrote, Giles, 3n.19
Manheim, Michael, 64n.7,14
Mannery, Samuel, 48, 53Illus.11
Mannoni, Octave, 284
Manteghi, Serena, 225
Mao Ze-dong, 95
Marcus, Leah S., 2, 23n.8, 171n.3,
    171, 284
Mares, F. H., 288
Margalit, Avishai, 95
Markle, Meghan, Duchess of Sussex, 226
Marks, J. L., 270
Marlowe, Christopher, 13, 15, 48, 253,
    258
Marmion, Shakerley, 48
Marotti, Arthur, 32
Marr, Andrew, 192n.43
Marrapodi, Michele, 64n.8
Marsden, Jennifer, 251
Marshall, Cynthia, 89n.15
Marston, John, 56n.65, 58, 64, 159, 252
Martin, Brian, 239
Marvell, Andrew, 260
Marx Brothers, 272n.3
Mary, Queen of Scots, 254
Masilo, Dada, 268
Mason, Anthony, 138n.60
Mason, Pamela, 107n.2
Massai, Sonia, 22n.6, 25n.24, 34n.54, 37
Massinger, Philip, 46, 48, 49
Masten, Jeffrey, 2
Matchett, William, 139n.63
Máté, Bori, 266
Mateer, David, 48n.37
Maybanks, Helen, 237Illus.22
Mayer, Jean-Christophe, 25n.24, 32n.48
Melchiori, Giorgio, 46n.16, 58n.74
Méliès, Georges, 269
Melo, João Vicente, 13n.17
Mendelssohn, Felix, 246
Mentz, Steve, 257
Menzer, Paul, 148
Meredith, Burgess, 271
Merritt, Stephanie, 164
Middleton, Thomas, 49, 64, 72–4, 159,
    230, 261, 263, 277, 281
Miller, Joe, 248
Miller, Jonathan, 236, 284

Milton, John, 82, 286
Minami, Ryuta, 93n.1, 96n.32,33,34
Minchin, Tim, 184–5
Miola, Robert, 41n.78, 104, 283–4, 288
Mitchell, Jessie, 132
Mitchell, Ruth, 177
Modenessi, Alfredo Michel, 162, 164
Money, John, 121n.18
Monk, Sir Anthony, 115–16
Montaigne, Michel Eyquem de, 91, 256,
    263
Moore, Francis, 14
Moorst, David, 214, 215Illus.15
More, Sir Thomas, 259
Moretti, T. J., 175n.31
Morgan, Laura, 176, 177
Morgann, Maurice, 2
Morrissey, David, 242
Moryson, Fynes, 7–8, 9
Motha, Stewart, 130n.15, 131n.16,
    142n.80
Mottram, Stewart, 259–60, 265
Moukarzel, Bush, 241
Mowat, Barbara A., 119n.5, 120n.8, 284
Muir, Kenneth, 138n.61
Mukherji, Subha, 121n.16
Mulcaster, Richard, 56–7, 57n.68, 154
Müller, Heiner, 266
Munby, Jonathan, 242
Munro, Lucy, 45n.15, 46n.16,21,
    47n.24,28, 48n.31,33,35,36,
    49n.39,42,43,45, 50n.46,
    56n.65, 60n.84, 61n.93, 62n.95
Murphy, Andrew R., 23n.8
Murphy, Malini, 220
Mydell, Joseph, 203
Myer-Bennett, Dorothea, 228
Myers, Robin, 3n.19

Nabbes, Thomas, 46, 47, 48
Nabirye, Anna-Maria, 213
Nagra, Parminder, 161n.4, 163
Nance, John, 277
Nash, Marnie, 242
Neill, Michael, 284
Neville, Sarah, 38n.73
Newbold, Debs, 242
Newman, Karen, 1–9
Newman, Nick, 242
Ney, Charles, 273–4, 276
Nicholas, Rachael, 269
Nichols, Adam, 246
Nicholson, Eric, 8n.45,46,51, 44n.8
Nicholson, Ian, 247
Nicoli, Vincenzo, 167
Nicoll, Allardyce, 54n.54
Niel-Mee, Pierro, 218
Nijinska, Bronislava, 269
Niles, Sarah, 206–7
Nixon, Natasha, 243
Nixon, Pippa, 239

Noble, Adrian, 145
Norris, Rufus, 239, 243
Norton, Bonham, 6
Norton, John, 5, 6
Nungezer, Edwin, 46n.17
Nunn, Trevor, 161–2, 163, 164, 166, 168,
    169, 236, 270
Nuttall, Anthony, 120, 121n.16, 124

Oakes, David, 225
Oakley, Michael, 246
O'Brien, Daniel, 195n.57
O'Dwyer, Eamonn, 226
O'Flynn, Siobhan, 202n.108
Oh, Elisa, 256
O'Hare, Jeanie, 251
O'Hea, Brendan, 244, 249, 250
Okonedo, Sophie, 170–83, 240
Oldenburg, Scott, 12n.10
Olivier, Laurence, 185, 283, 284
O'Malley, Evelyn, 267
Omole, Faith, 217
Ooi, Vicki, 100
Oppitz-Trotman, George, 6–7
Orgel, Stephen, 40–1n.77, 142
Orkin, Martin, 116n.50
Orlin, Lena Cowen, 107n.3, 111n.20, 260
Orman, Steve, 56n.65, 58
Ormerod, Nick, 273
Ormsby, Robert, 280
Osmond, Adrian, 245
Ostler, William, 48, 51Illus.9, 54, 59, 62
Ové, Indra, 206–7
Ovid, 109, 119n.5, 124–5, 126
Oyelowo, David, 174

Page, John, 48, 53Illus.11
Painter, William, 115
Palfrey, Simon, 133, 139
Palgrave, Francis Turner, 286
Panek, Jennifer, 263
Panja, Shormishtha, 93n.8, 94n.15,
    95n.19,20
Pao, Angela C., 172n.12
Parker, Martin, 116
Parker, Patricia, 41n.80
Parkinson, Scott, 171, 177
Parr, Tessa, 229–30
Parsons, Elinor, 165
Patterson, R. F., 42n.82
Paul, St, 10–12, 19, 20, 134
Pavy, Salomon, 48, 51Illus.9, 52–3
Pearce, Edward, 48
Pearce, Katherine, 239
Pearson, Alex, 243
Penn, William, 48, 52Illus.10, 53Illus.11
Percy, William, 48, 52–3
Perkins, Richard, 48, 50, 51Illus.9,
    52Illus.10, 53Illus.11
Perng, Ching-Hsi, 93n.3
Perry, William, 47

Pettegree, Andrew, 11
Phelps, Alex, 224
Phelps, Lucy, 232–3, 234, 236, 237Illus.22, 237, 238
Philip, Ian, 5n.23
Phillip, Arthur, 129
Phillips, Augustine, 46
Philo, John-Mark, 115n.40
Pickles, Chris, 245
Pimlott, Steven, 186
Pirandello, Luigi, 127
Pita, Arthur, 246
Pitcher, John, 139
Pite, Crystal, 268
Pittman, L. Monique, 173n.19,21, 182
Plautus, 10, 11–12, 17–19, 20, 24–5, 25n.20
Plews, John, 249
Plutarch, 119n.5, 280
Pocahontas, 256
Podd, Janet, 246
Pollard, A. W., 2
Pollard, Thomas, 48, 52Illus.10
Pope, Alexander, 32, 34, 36, 37, 38, 39Illus.8
Portelli, Alessandro, 158
Posner, Lindsay, 247, 248
Potter, Lois, 41, 64n.14
Powell, Barney, 240
Power, Ben, 173, 176, 177, 178–9, 180
Power, Ed, 196n.70
Prater, John, 26–7, 28Illus.4, 29Illus.5
Prescott, Paul, 199, 203–22, 223–39
Price, Claire, 167, 234, 235Illus.21, 236
Price, John, 115–16
Prokofiev, Sergei, 248
Publicover, Laurence, 257–8, 265
Purcell, Henry, 249
Purcell, Stephen, 203–22, 275
Puttenham, George, 122
Pye, Tom, 166

Qin, Cai, 94n.17
Quartey, Ekow, 217
Quigley, Pearce, 213

Rackin, Phyllis, 172n.14, 175n.35, 175, 176n.41, 179n.51, 180n.55,56, 182n.60
Radulian, Ilinca, 210–13
Raleigh, Sir Walter, 14, 17, 20
Randle, Charlotte, 239
Randolph, Thomas, 60–1
Raptotasios, Alexander, 244
Rasmussen, Eric, 13n.15, 107n.2
Ravella, Bruno, 245
Rawlins, Thomas, 47–8
Ray, John, 111
Reade, Emmanuel, 49, 52Illus.10
Reade, Timothy, 49, 53Illus.11
Ready, Paul, 205, 243

Redgrave, Michael, 156
Rees, Graham, 5, 6n.31,33,34, 6, 9n.59, 9
Rees, Joan, 120n.6
Reeves, Saskia, 203, 204Illus.12
Reinhardt, Max, 269, 271
Reynolds, Anita, 214
Reynolds, Paige Martin, 275–6
Rhode, Eleanor, 238–9
Rhodes, Neil, 107–18
Rhodes, W. E., 75n.33
Rice, John, 49, 52Illus.10
Richardson, Catherine, 44n.4, 45n.14, 48n.36, 110n.15, 111
Richardson, Ralph, 157
Richardson, Samuel, 286
Ricoeur, Paul, 120
Rider, Kirsty, 205–6
Rintoul, Douglas, 219–21, 221Illus.17
Risebero, John, 246
Roberts, Sasha, 110n.18
Robeson, Paul, 271
Robinson, Edward G., 271
Robinson, James, 49
Robinson, Richard, 49, 52Illus.10, 56n.64
Rogers, Jami, 174n.25
Rojas, Mercedes, 158
Rokison-Woodall, Abigail, 147n.10, 186n.23, 192n.44
Rolfe, Rebecca (Pocahontas), 256
Romain, Mathew, 275
Rosheuvel, Golda, 247
Rostand, Edmond, 146
Rothwell, Kenneth, 284
Rourke, Josie, 244, 282, 288
Rouse, W. H., 122n.23
Rowe, Nicholas, 21, 32, 34–6, 37, 41, 108–9, 279
Rowley, William, 47, 263
Royle, Nicholas, 166
Royster, Francesca T., 171, 172n.18, 172
Ruddick, Blair, 246
Ruiter, David, 15n.25
Ruo-cheng, Ying, 94n.17
Rushdie, Salman, 164, 166
Russell, Rosalind, 271
Russell, Sophie, 209–10, 212
Rutherford, Jonathan, 105n.88
Rutter, Barrie, 250
Rutter, Carol Chillington, 107n.1, 173n.22,23, 176n.38, 177n.43, 195–6
Rylance, Mark, 152n.38, 247, 283
Rylands, George, 155n.57

Sackville, Thomas, 9
Said, Edward, 103–4, 106, 257
Saintsbury, George, 74n.30
Salkeld, Duncan, 15n.29
Salmon, Vivian, 116n.50
Samuel, Raphael, 157–8
Sander, August, 236

Sanders, Julie, 98, 101, 201n.107, 256
Sapori, A., 75n.36
Sarah, Bedi, 207–8
Sawhney, Nitin, 165
Sawyer, Robert, 270–1, 276
Scales, Prunella, 151
Schehr, Lawrence R., 80n.2
Schlesinger, Helen, 209
Schneider, Rebecca, 61, 266
Schramm, Jan-Melissa, 121n.16
Schwarz, Katherine, 176, 181n.57
Scot, Reginald, 119n.5
Scott, Andrew, 185, 187, 188, 190–3, 194, 195, 196, 197–8, 199, 200, 201
Scott, Charlotte, 119–28, 252–65
Scott, Grant F., 125n.31
Scott, John, 242
Scott, Sarah, 64
Seaton, Ethel, 159n.80
Segal, Erich, 25n.20
Selwood, Jacob, 11, 13n.17
Sene, Leo, 246
Seneca the Younger, 109, 124
Serres, Michel, 79–80, 81
Sforza, Ludovico, 72
Shakespeare, William
  acting career, 54
  editions
    Arden 2
      Coriolanus, 280
    Arden 3
      All's Well That Ends Well, 277–9
      Coriolanus, 279
      The Taming of the Shrew, 283
    Arden Performance
      Macbeth, 281–2
    Capell, 34
    Douai Manuscript (MS 787), 31–2
    Folio, 2–9, 47, 48, 49, 288
      All's Well That Ends Well, 278
      Coriolanus, 279
      Hamlet, 53–4, 282–3
      Macbeth, 110
    Hanmer, 34
    Johnson, 34
    Johnson-Steevens, 34, 37
    Johnson-Steevens-Reed, 34
    Kittredge, 37
    Malone, 34
    New Cambridge revisions
      Hamlet, 282–3
      Much Ado About Nothing, 283
      Richard II, 283
      The Taming of the Shrew, 283
    New Oxford, 37n.62, 277
      The Comedy of Errors, 38
      Hamlet, 284
    New Variorum
      Coriolanus, 279–81
    Norton
      Hamlet, 284

INDEX

Macbeth, 107n.1
Norton Critical
   Hamlet, 283–4
   The Tempest, 284
Nursery Promptbooks
   The Comedy of Errors, 30–1, 32
Oxford
   The Comedy of Errors, 38
Pope, 34, 39Illus.8
quarto
   Hamlet, 229, 282–3, 284,
     286–7
   Sonnets, 285
   Troilus and Cressida, 1
Riverside
   The Comedy of Errors, 37
Rourke
   Measure For Measure playtext, 282
Rowe, 34–6, 108–9, 279
Smock Alley promptbook
   The Comedy of Errors, 32–4
     33Illus.6, 35Illus.7
Theobald, 34, 36–7
Variorum
   The Comedy of Errors, 38
Warburton, 34
plays
   All's Well That Ends Well, 240, 262,
     277–9
   Antony and Cleopatra, 240, 254–5,
     264, 272–3
   As You Like It, 164, 185n.9, 213,
     219–21, 232–3, 233Illus.20, 240,
     256, 271, 273, 274
   The Comedy of Errors, 10–20, 21–42,
     71n.22, 164, 240–1, 259, 263
   Coriolanus, 79–92, 114, 262–4,
     279–81
   Cymbeline, 241, 260
   Hamlet, 1, 8, 49, 53–4, 55, 62, 65–7,
     74, 97, 121, 131–2, 184–202,
     225–6, 228–30, 239, 241, 254,
     260, 261, 263, 264, 268, 271,
     272, 274, 275, 276, 282–4,
     286–7
   Henry IV, 259
   1 Henry IV, 207–9, 212–13, 241,
     262–3, 271
   2 Henry IV, 207–10, 212–13
   Henry V, 173, 174, 207–9, 210,
     212–13, 223, 224Illus.18, 226–7,
     239, 241, 254, 287
   Henry VI, 210–12
   Julius Caesar, 94, 97–9, 100, 152,
     153–4, 159, 241–2, 263, 264,
     271
   King John, 203n.1, 238–9, 242
   King Lear, 74, 94n.17, 94, 97, 102–6,
     242, 260, 261, 262, 269, 270,
     275, 276
   Love's Labour's Lost, 242, 259

Macbeth, 74, 94n.17, 107–18, 205–6,
   212–13, 239, 242–4, 253, 260,
   261, 264, 270, 271–2, 273,
   281–2
Measure For Measure, 64–5, 67, 68, 72,
   74n.28, 74, 76, 77, 94n.17, 159,
   236–8, 244, 264, 271–2, 278,
   282
The Merchant of Venice, 71n.23, 93,
   94n.17, 94, 244–5, 257, 259
The Merry Wives of Windsor, 213–14,
   245, 259, 270, 287
A Midsummer Night's Dream, 30, 66,
   94n.17, 119–28, 145–6, 165,
   213, 214–19, 239, 245, 257, 266,
   270, 271
Much Ado About Nothing, 94n.17, 94,
   228, 239, 246, 257, 271, 283
Othello, 49, 74, 94n.17, 94, 121, 153,
   177, 234, 247–7, 255, 257, 260,
   261, 262, 263, 270, 271
Pericles, 247
Richard II, 182–3, 203–5, 206–7, 211,
   212–13, 247, 283
Richard III, 120–1, 153n.45, 181, 210,
   212–13, 239, 247, 253, 264
Romeo and Juliet, 65–6, 67–9, 70, 71,
   94n.17, 94, 123, 164, 185n.9,
   247–8, 264, 271, 272n.3, 276,
   287
Sir Thomas More, 19
The Taming of the Shrew, 65, 68–72,
   78, 94n.17, 233–5, 235Illus.21,
   239, 248, 260, 261, 266, 271,
   283
The Tempest, 151–2, 156, 164, 227,
   249, 257, 262, 264, 272, 284
Timon of Athens, 230–2, 231Illus.19,
   239, 249, 264
Titus Andronicus, 1, 8, 74, 121,
   125n.33, 249, 261, 262, 263, 264
Troilus and Cressida, 1, 83, 150, 174–5,
   249, 262, 263, 266
Twelfth Night, 94n.17, 94, 97, 161–9,
   223–5, 239, 250–50, 259, 264,
   267, 272
The Two Noble Kinsmen, 250
The Winter's Tale, 121, 129–44, 250,
   254, 262, 267
poems
   The Passionate Pilgrim, 285
   'The Phoenix and the Turtle', 254
   The Rape of Lucrece, 251
   Sonnets, 264, 265, 284–6
     (2), 285
     (18), 285, 286
     (106), 285
     (116), 285
     (128), 285
     (130), 285
   Venus and Adonis, 250, 262

adaptations
   of *As You Like It*
     As You Like It (film, Czinner), 271
     As You Like It (musical adaptation,
       Taub and Woolery), 219–21
     Ganymede (LGBT themes, Gould),
       240
   of *The Comedy of Errors*
     The Comedy of Errors (for 7- to 13-
       year-olds, Thorpe), 240–1
   of *Coriolanus*
     Coriolanus (film, Fiennes), 89n.15
   of *Hamlet*
     The Bad Sleep Well (film,
       Kurosawa), 268
     The Banquet (film, Chinese), 268
     The Bitter End of Rosemary (ballet,
       Masilo), 268
     Castle of Flames (film, Tai), 268
     Der bestrafte Brudermord
       (seventeenth-century German,
       anon), 8
     Gertrude and Claudius (novel,
       Updike), 284
     Gertrude Talks Back (short story,
       Atwood), 284
     Hamlet (ballet, Helpmann), 267
     Hamlet (Faroese-language
       production), 239
     Hamlet (film, Branagh), 283
     Hamlet (film, Kozintsev), 283
     Hamlet (film, Olivier), 283
     Hamlet (film, Zeffirelli), 269
     Hamlet (An Experience) (solo
       performance by Carding, dir.
       Sigfúsdóttir), 241
     Hamlet – Horatio's Tale (solo
       performance, Hennegen), 241
     Hamlet: Sword of Vengeance (Ho),
       94n.17, 97
     Hamnet (solo performance, 11-
       year-old actor, dir. Moukarzel),
       241
     Prince of the Himalayas (film,
       Chinese), 268
     Shakespeare Live! From the RSC
       (RSC/BBC Two, Doran),
       184–5
     Super Hamlet 64 (Day), 241
   of *1 Henry IV*
     Hotspur (Globe Ensemble), 207–9
   of *2 Henry IV*
     Falstaff (Globe Ensemble), 207–10
   of *Henry V*
     Greyhounds (blended with stories
       from World War II, dir.
       Wheble), 241
     Harry England (Globe Ensemble),
       207–9, 210
     The Hollow Crown (BBC TV,
       2012), 173, 182

Shakespeare, William (cont.)
  of *Henry VI*
    Henry VI (dir. Holmes and
      Radulian), 210–13
    *The Hollow Crown: The Wars of the
      Roses* (BBC TV, 2016), 170–83
    Rose Rage (Edward Hall), 171
  of *King Lear*
    A Bunch of Amateurs (Hislop and
      Newman), 242
    The Delusion of Home (Taiwanese
      drama), 242
    Hobson's Choice (film, Lean), 269
    The King Is Alive (film, Levring),
      269
    King Lear (film, Brook), 269
    King Lear (Alone) (one-man show,
      Bramwell), 242
    King Lear Retold (storytelling in
      modern language, Newbold),
      242
    The King of Texas (TV film), 269
    Lear (solo dance adaptation, Scott),
      242
    Ran (film, Kurosawa), 269
    Shamshuipo Lear (Tsoi and Fung),
      97, 100–6
    Slings and Arrows (Canadian TV
      series), 269
    Trump Lear (political satire), 242
  of *Macbeth*
    *About Lady White Fox with Nine
      Tales* (Korean version), 244
    Barren Sceptre (ballet, Limón and
      Koner), 267
    *Is This a Dagger? The Story of
      Macbeth* (Cannon), 244
    Macbeth (dance adaptation, Bruce),
      243
    Macbeth (opera, Verdi), 243
    Macbeth (TV film, Nunn), 270
    Macbeth: A Tale of Sound and Fury
      (three storytellers, dir. Hassam),
      244
    Macbeth – Director's Cut (not
      suitable for children; dir.
      Davies), 244
    The Macbeths (condensed,
      Raptotasios and Tsilipos), 244
    othellomacbeth (conflated adapation
      of Othello and Macbeth, dir.
      Christian), 244
    The Paper Cinema's Macbeth (silent
      film, puppetry, live scores), 243
    Queer Lady M – Work in Progress
      (workshop performance), 244
    That Scottish Play (comic version,
      Gould), 243
  of *Measure for Measure*
    Measure for Measure (LGBT
      version), 244

  of *The Merchant of Venice*
    The Merchant of Venice (Cantonese
      translation), 94
    Gratiano (sequel from Gratiano's
      perspective), 245
    *Shit-Faced Shakespeare – The
      Merchant of Venice*, 245
    *Shylock, or The Merchant of
      Venice Preserved* (burlesque,
      Talfourd), 93
  of *The Merry Wives of Windsor*
    Falstaff (opera, Verdi), 245
    *The Merry Wives of
      Windsor* (TV broadcast, 1955),
      270
  of *A Midsummer Night's Dream*
    *A Dream within A Midsummer
      Night's Dream* (ballet, Pita), 246
    *The Merry Conceited Humors of
      Bottom the Weaver* (Cox; dir.
      Sene), 246
    A Midsummer Night's Dream
      (ballet, Ashton), 266
    A Midsummer Night's Dream
      (ballet, Balanchine), 266
    A Midsummer Night's Dream
      (ballet, Mendelssohn), 246
    A Midsummer Night's Dream (film,
      Reinhardt/Dieterle), 269, 271
    A Midsummer Night's Dream
      (NHK TV recording of Brook
      production, 1970), 270
    A Midsummer Night's Dream
      (opera, Britten), 246
    A Midsummer Night's Droll (dir.
      Stratford), 246
  of *Much Ado About Nothing*
    Much Ado About Nothing (film,
      Whedon), 283
  of *Othello*
    The Moor's Pavane (ballet, Limón),
      267
    Othello (for 8–12-year-olds,
      Cornelissen), 247
    Othello (TV film, Nunn), 270
    othellomacbeth (conflated adapation
      of Othello and Macbeth, dir.
      Christian), 247
  of *Pericles*
    Périclès (in French, dir. Donnellan),
      247
    Pericles Redux (ballet, Faranesh-
      Bocca), 268
  of *The Rape of Lucrece*
    The Rape of Lucretia (opera, Britten),
      251
  of *Richard III*
    The Hollow Crown (BBC TV, 2016),
      175, 180, 181–3, 183n.64
    Richard III (one-woman show, dir.
      Sigfúsdóttir), 247

  of *Romeo and Juliet*
    I Capuleti e i Montecchi (opera,
      Bellini), 248
    *Juliet and Romeo: A Guide to Long Life
      and Happy Marriage* (dir. Duke),
      248
    Re-defining Juliet (dir. Hale), 248
    Romea and Julian (gender swapped
      version), 248
    Romeo and Juliet (ballet, Prokofiev),
      248
    Romeo and Juliet (ballet, Prokofiev,
      Ashton), 267
    Romeo and Juliet (ballet, Prokofiev,
      MacMillan), 267
    Romeo and Juliet (comic version), 248
    Romeo and Juliet (film, MGM, 1936),
      271
    Romeo and Juliet – Mods v Rockers
      (comic version), 248
    William Shakespeare's Romeo + Juliet
      (film, Luhrmann), 197, 201
  of *The Taming of the Shrew*
    Kiss Me Kate (musical), 249
    The Taming of the Shrew (ballet,
      Cranko), 266, 267
  of *The Tempest*
    Caliban by the Yellow Sands
      (community masque,
      MacKaye), 284
    Eboracum Baroque – The Tempest
      (Purcell), 249
    Prospero's Books (film, Greenaway),
      269
    Return to the Forbidden Planet (dir.
      Jordan), 249
    Return to the Forbidden Planet (dir.
      Plews), 249
    The Tempest (film, Taymor), 268, 284
    The Tempest Replica (ballet, Pite),
      268
  of *Twelfth Night*
    Toby Belch is Unwell, 250
    Twelfth Night (Channel 4 TV film,
      Supple), 161–9
    Twelfth Night (film, Nunn), 161–2,
      163, 164, 166, 168, 169
    Twelfth Night (musical adaptation,
      Taub), 250
    '21st Century Bard: The Making of
      Twelfth Night' (TV
      documentary, Supple), 161n.4,
      161, 162n.7, 163n.13,14, 163,
      165n.26, 166n.30,32,34,35,
      167n.37,38
  of *The Winter's Tale*
    The Winter's Tale (ballet, Wheeldon),
      250
  miscellaneous, 251–1
    CBS Shakespeare Cycle (radio
      broadcasts, 1937), 271–2

INDEX

The Complete Works of William Shakespeare (abridged), 251
The Dark Lady of the Sonnets (opera), 251
The Dramatic Exploits of Edmund Kean (Hughes), 251
Emilia (Malcolm), 251
The Knights of the Rose (Marsden), 251
Ministers of Grace: the Unauthorised Shakespearean Parody of Ghostbusters, 251
Queen Margaret (O'Hare), 251
Romantic Shakespeare (dir. Tsoi), 97
Shakespeare in Love (film adaptation, dir. Breen), 251
Shakespeare Live! From the RSC (RSC/BBC Two, Doran), 184–5
She Wolf (Gillian English), 251
Streamlined Shakespeare (radio broadcasts, NBC, 1937), 271–2
The Touches of Sweet Harmony: Shakespeare's Songs (album launch), 251
The Wars of the Roses (BBC TV, 1964), 270
Will or Eight Lost Years of Young William Shakespeare's Life (Baumgartner), 251
Your Bard (biographical drama), 251
Shank, John, 43, 46, 48
Shannon, Claude, 81
Shapiro, James, 107n.1
Shapiro, Michael, 52n.50
Sharrock, Thea, 171n.6, 177, 182
Shattuck, Charles, 32
Shaughnessy, Robert, 166, 196n.63
Shaw, Brandon, 266–8, 276
Shaw, David J., 5n.28
Shaw, Fiona, 283
Shaw, James, 240–51
Shayler, Karen, 242
Sheppard, Philippa, 161
Sher, Antony, 146, 147, 242
Sherley, Teresia, 256
Sherley brothers, Thomas, Anthony and Robert, 255, 256, 258
Sherman, William H., 40–1n.77, 284, 288
Shih Wing-ching, 106n.95
Shirley, James, 43, 46, 47, 48, 49, 59, 60, 61
Shmygol, Maria, 8n.47
Showalter, Elaine, 284
Sidney, Mary, Countess of Pembroke, 255
Sidney, Philip, 8, 122–3, 124
Siebenkees, Johann Christian, 8
Sigfúsdóttir, Kolbrún Björt, 241, 247
Sillars, Stuart, 270, 276
Simon, Josette, 240
Singh, Jyotsna, 257, 265
Slinger, Jonathan, 283
Sloan, LaRue Love, 112n.27

Smallwood, Robert, 162, 163, 164
Smart, Grace, 210
Smith, Bruce R., 7n.38, 80, 82n.7, 82
Smith, Emma, 12n.12, 25, 29, 30n.32, 31, 277, 282
Smith, Haig, 13n.17
Smith, Helen, 288
Smith, Captain John, 256
Smith, Kathleen Kalpin, 112n.27
Smith, Peter J., 161–9
Smith, William, 76n.39
Smyth, Adam, 288
Snawsel, Robert, 112n.26
Snook, Gareth, 217
Soriano, Jianne, 99n.48
Soto-Morettini, Donna, 155n.58
Speed, John, 112
Spencer, Charles, 164, 198n.84, 199n.90
Spenser, Edmund, 260
Sprengnether, Madelon G., 175n.33
Spriggs, Ashley, 279
Stallybrass, Peter, 23n.8, 286
Standing, Richard, 225
Stanivukovic, Goran, 12–13n.13
Stanton, Sarah, 7n.38
Stanton, Sophie, 234–5
Stapylton, Robert, 111n.23, 114–15n.38
Steevens, George, 34, 37
Steggle, Matthew, 48n.35, 53n.52
Stenning, Harleigh, 220
Stern, Tiffany, 8n.48, 31, 277, 288
Stewart, Alan, 12–13n.13, 18n.32, 115n.43
Stewart, Patrick, 234
Storey, Claire, 224–5
Strada, Famiano, 114
Stratford, Brice, 246
Straznicky, Marta, 1n.4, 2
Strehler, Giorgio, 284
Strype, J., 14n.23
Stuart, Esmé, 1st Duke of Lennox, 253, 254
Stubbs, Imogen, 168
Stukeley, Thomas, 256
Sturgess, Keith, 55n.58
Suarez, Michael F., 1n.3
Suckling, John, 43, 47, 59, 60, 61, 286
Sumimoto, Noriko, 26n.26
Supple, Tim, 161–9, 257
Swinburn, Algernon Charles, 64–4
Sykes, Kimberley, 232–3, 233Illus.20
Syme, Holger Schott, 54n.56, 55n.58

Tablian, Vic, 163
Taff, Dyani Johns, 256
Tai, Katô, 268
Tait, James, 75n.33
Talfourd, Thomas, 93
Tam Kwok-kan, 94n.12, 94–5
Tanner, Tony, 114
Tarlinskaja, Marina, 156n.62
Tartamella, Suzanne, 256

Taub, Shaina, 219, 250
Tavares, Elizabeth E., 175n.31, 176n.40, 182
Taverner, Richard, 117–18
Taylor, Barry, 5n.28
Taylor, Daniel, 245, 248
Taylor, Gary, 22n.6, 36n.58, 38n.73, 63n.3, 74n.28, 277
Taylor, John, 58n.71
Taylor, Joseph, 44n.4, 49, 52Illus.10
Taylor, Paul, 199n.92,96, 199
Taymor, Julie, 268, 284
Tennant, David, 184, 185–6, 187, 188–9, 191, 192, 193–4, 196–7, 198, 199n.90,95, 199, 200, 201, 284
Terry, Michelle, 191, 194, 205, 207, 209, 213, 241, 243
Thacker, David, 241
Theobald, Lewis, 26, 27Illus.3, 27, 34, 36–7
Thomas, Adele, 243
Thomas, Kate, 198n.86
Thompson, Ann, 283, 288
Thompson, Ayanna, 171n.5, 172, 173n.20, 177n.45, 181n.58, 281
Thompson, Craig R., 111n.25
Thompson, James Westfall, 3n.19,22
Thomson, Leslie, 110n.16,17
Tilley, Morris Palmer, 117n.51
Tilney, Edmund, 111, 112
Tobin, J. J. M., 37n.68
Toot, T. F., 75n.33
Totaro, Rebecca, 264
Trettien, Whitney, 288
Tribe, Keith, 132n.20
Trigg, William, 49, 53Illus.11
Trivedi, Poonam, 93, 96n.32, 33,34
Troughton, David, 167, 245, 249
Trump, Donald J., 163–4
Trussell, Alvery, 49, 51Illus.9
Tsipos, Manolis, 244
Tso, Anna Wing-bo, 96n.29
Tsoi, Hardy, 96–106
Tu Wei-ming, 94
Tudeau-Clayton, Margaret, 19n.34, 258–9, 265
Turing, Alan, 81
Turner, Henry S., 45n.9
Turner, Lyndsey: *Hamlet* with Benedict Cumberbatch, 184–5, 185n.15, 187–8, 189–90, 191, 192, 193, 195, 196, 197, 198, 199, 200, 201
Twyman, Richard, 247
Twyning, John, 64
Tynan, Kathleen, 157n.74
Tynan, Kenneth, 157n.74
Tyrell, Dickon, 213

INDEX

Udall, Nicholas, 117
Ultz, 203
Underwood, John, 50, 51Illus.9, 54, 55, 59, 62
Ure, Peter, 64n.14, 64
Usher, Simon, 159

Vadnais, Matt, 287, 288
Valee, Rudy, 271–2
Vallance, Cassie, 224
Valls-Russell, Janice, 165n.24,25
Vance, Eugene, 85n.12
van Hove, Ivo, 266
Van Kampen, Claire, 247
Varla, Zubin, 164
Veitch, Scott, 130n.15, 131n.17
Vercelli, William, 242
Verdi, Giuseppe, 243, 245
Vickers, Brian, 277
Vienne-Guerrin, Nathalie, 269, 276
Vincent, Augustine, 21n.4
Virgil, 119
Vives, Juan Luis, 111
Vondel, Joost van den, 9
von Neumann, John, 81
Votava, Jennie M., 170–83

Wakely, Maria, 5, 6n.31,33,34, 6, 9n.59, 9
Waldemann, Alex, 239
Walker, Greg, 12–13n.13
Wallace, Charles William, 45
Walley, Harold Reinoehl, 71n.23
Walley, Henry, 1
Walpole, Robert, 270
Walter, Harriet, 184–5
Walters, Ewart James, 167
Wapull, George, 12
Warburton, William, 34
Warner, David, 191, 195–6, 200, 272
Warren, Michael, 41
Watford, Glen, 94n.17
Watkins, John, 174n.29
Watson, Irene, 130n.8, 130, 134, 142
Watson, Robert N., 83n.10, 88n.14
Wayne, Valerie, 111n.24
Webster, John, 48, 49, 50, 159, 273
Webster, Max, 240
Weekes, Debbie, 178n.48

Weiner, Norbert, 81
Weis, René, 108n.7
Weissbourd, Emily, 263
Welles, Orson, 185, 271
Wells, Stanley, 7n.38, 169
Werier, Clifford, 263–4
Werner, Sarah, 147n.10, 287, 288
Werstine, Paul, 23n.9, 31, 32, 277, 280
Wesley, John, 158n.79, 159n.81
West, Anthony James, 26n.25
West, C. M., 178n.48
West, Samuel, 185, 186, 191
West, Timothy, 151
West, William N., 6–7, 8n.52, 44–5
Whateley, William, 112n.26
Wheble, Jacqueline, 241
Whedon, Joss, 283
Wheeldon, Christopher, 250
While, Elle, 191n.39, 194n.53, 213–14, 240, 241
Whipday, Emma, 108, 260–2, 265
Whishaw, Ben, 191, 242
White, Richard Grant, 279
Whiting, John, 150
Whitworth, Charles, 38, 41
Whyman, Erica, 248–8
Wickham, Glynne, 57n.68
Wiggins, Martin, 44n.4, 45n.14, 48n.36
Wilcox, Helen, 110n.14, 277–9, 288
Wild, Claire, 163
Wilkin, Amanda, 217
Willett, John, 104n.81
Williams, Andy, 162
Williams, Fiona, 248
Williams, George Walton, 23n.8
Williams, Gordon, 114n.37
Williams, Holly, 195n.61
Williams, Jacoba, 216–17
Williams, Margaret Ellen, 47n.28
Williams, Simon, 6–7, 7n.42,43, 8n.45
Williams, Travis D., 283, 288
Willis, Jerome, 146
Wills, Garry, 82n.9
Wilson, Arthur, 46, 48, 49
Wilson, August, 172
Wilson, Declan, 225
Wilson, F. P., 3, 6, 109n.11
Wilson, Flo, 227
Wilson, John Harold, 71n.23

Wilson, Rawdon, 119, 121n.15,18
Wilson, Richard, 124, 125
Wilson, Robert, 12–13, 14n.20, 17
Wilson, Wils, 250
Winder, Daniel, 249
Winebrook, Emily, 267
Winkworth, Alison L., 155n.60
Wintle, Sarah, 108n.7
Wokoma, Susan, 218, 219Illus.16
Wolin, Richard, 129n.4, 134n.33, 135n.39, 143n.82,83
Wong, Dorothy, 94n.12, 13,14
Wong Hung, 100
Wood, Christopher, 171
Woolery, Laurie, 219
Woolley, Sir John, 19
Wooster Group, 266
Working, Lauren, 13n.17
Wotton, Henry, 8, 254
Wray, Ramona, 23n.8, 166n.31
Wright, Adam, 105n.90
Wright, George T., 151, 156
Wright, James, 43–4, 56, 59
Wright, Nicholas, 43n.1, 43
Wright, W. A., 109n.12,13
Wroth, Mary, 285
Wyatt, Zach, 214
Wyver, John, 269–70, 276

Xu, Hua-long, 105n.87

Yang, Chih-chiao Joseph, 102n.69
Yang, Daniel S. P., 94, 100
Yese, Malunga, 220
Yong Li-lan, 93n.9
Young, Curtis, 220
Yum, Ikin, 235Illus.21
Yungblut, Laura Hunt, 11n.5
Yunupingu, Galarrwuy, 143–4

Zeffirelli, Franco, 269
Zhangazha, Ashley, 247
Zhou Enlai, 97
Zi, Su, 97n.37, 103n.73,74
Zipes, Jack, 125n.32
Žižek, Slavoj, 140
Zucker, Adam, 47n.29
Zucker, Carole, 146n.8